WOMAN UNDER MONASTICISM.

WOMAN UNDER MONASTICISM

CHAPTERS ON

SAINT-LORE AND CONVENT LIFE

BETWEEN A.D. 500 AND A.D. 1500

BY

LINA ECKENSTEIN.

'Quia vita omnium spiritualium hominum sine litteris mors est.'

ACTA MURENSES.

NEW YORK

RUSSELL & RUSSELL · INC

1963

FIRST PUBLISHED IN 1896

REISSUED, 1963, BY RUSSELL & RUSSELL, INC.

L. C. CATALOG CARD NO: 63—11028

PRINTED IN THE UNITED STATES OF AMERICA

TO

MY FRIENDS

KARL AND MARIA SHARPE PEARSON.

PREFACE.

THE restlessness, peculiar to periods of transition, is a characteristic of the present age. Long-accepted standards are
being questioned and hitherto unchallenged rules of conduct
submitted to searching criticism. History shows us that our
present social system is only a phase in human development, and
we turn to a study of the past, confident that a clearer insight into
the social standards and habits of life prevalent in past ages will
aid us in a better estimation of the relative importance of those
factors of change we find around us to-day.

Monasticism during the ten centuries between A.D. 500 and
A.D. 1500 exhibits phases of vital significance for the mental and
moral growth of Western Europe. However much both the aims
and the tone of life of the members of the different religious orders
varied, monasticism generally favoured tendencies which were
among the most peaceful and progressive of the Middle Ages.
For women especially the convent fostered some of the best sides
of intellectual, moral and emotional life. Besides this it was for
several centuries a determining factor in regard to women's
economic status.

The woman-saint and the nun are however figures the importance of which has hitherto been little regarded. The woman-saint
has met with scant treatment beyond that of the eulogistic but too
often uncritical writer of devotional works ; the lady abbess and
the literary nun have engrossed the attention of few biographers.
The partisan recriminations of the Reformation period are still
widely prevalent. The saint is thrust aside as a representative of

gross superstition, and the nun is looked upon as a slothful and hysterical, if not as a dissolute character. She is still thought of as those who broke with the Catholic Church chose to depict her.

The fact that these women appeared in a totally different light to their contemporaries is generally overlooked; that the monk and the nun enjoyed the esteem and regard of the general public throughout a term bordering on a thousand years is frequently forgotten. Even at the time of the Reformation, when religious contentions were at their height, the nun who was expelled from her home appeared deserving of pity rather than of reproach to her more enlightened contemporaries. As part of an institution that had outlived its purpose she was perhaps bound to pass away. But the work she had done and the aims for which she had striven contributed their share in formulating the new standards of life. The attitude of mind which had been harboured and cultivated in the cloister, must be reckoned among the most civilizing influences which have helped to develop mental and moral strength in Western Europe.

The social value of cloistered life in itself may be disputed. To the Protestant of the 16th century a profession which involved estrangement from family ties appeared altogether harmful. Moreover monasteries and religious houses were bound up in the reformer's mind with the supremacy of Rome from which he was striving hard to shake himself free. Wherever the breach with Rome was effected the old settlements were dissolved and their inmates were thrust back into civic life. To men this meant much, but it meant less to them than to women. In losing the possibility of religious profession at the beginning of the 16th century, women lost the last chance that remained to them of an activity outside the home circle. The subjection of women to a round of domestic duties became more complete when nunneries were dissolved, and marriage for generations afterwards was women's only recognised vocation.

But even in some of these same Protestant countries where nunneries were summarily dissolved, the resulting complete subjection of women has in modern times been felt to have outlived its purpose. How far this subjection was a needful stage of growth which has helped to develop a higher standard of willing purity and faithfulness need not now be discussed. In certain countries, however, where the monastic system with all the privileges it conferred on women was swept away, we now find a strong public opinion against the restriction of women's activity to the domestic circle, and these countries were among the first to, break down the artificial barriers imposed on woman's influence and grant her some share in the intellectual and political life of the community.

The right to self-development and social responsibility which the woman of to-day so persistently asks for, is in many ways analogous to the right which the convent secured to womankind a thousand years ago. The woman of to-day, who realises that the home circle as at present constituted affords insufficient scope for her energies, had a precursor in the nun who sought a field of activity in the convent. For the nun also hesitated, it may be from motives which fail to appeal to us, to undertake the customary duties and accept the ordinary joys of life. This hesitation may be attributed to perversion of instinct, it can hardly in the case of the nun be attributed to weakness of character, for she chose a path in life which was neither smooth nor easy, and in this path she accomplished great things, many of which have still living value.

It is with a view to the better appreciation of the influence and activity of women connected with the Christian religion that the following chapters have been written. They contain an enquiry into the cult of women-saints, and some account of the general position of woman under monasticism. These subjects however are so wide and the material at the disposal of the student is so abundant that the analysis is confined to English and German women.

At the outset an enquiry into the position of women among the Germans of pre-Christian times appeared necessary, for early hagiology and the lives of women who embraced the religious profession after Christianity was first introduced, recall in various particulars the influence of woman and her association with the supernatural during heathen times. The legends of many saints contain a large element of heathen folk-tradition, together in some cases with a small, scarcely perceptible element of historical fact. In order therefore to establish the true importance of the Christian women, whose labour benefited their contemporaries, and who in recognition of their services were raised to saintship, the nature of early women-saints in general had to be carefully considered.

In the chapters that follow, the spread of monasticism is dealt with in so far as it was due to the influence of women, and some of the more representative phases of convent life are described. Our enquiry dealing with monasticism only as affecting women, the

larger side of a great subject has necessarily been ignored. There
is a growing consciousness now-a-days of the debt of gratitude
which mankind as a whole owes to the monastic and religious
orders, but the history of these orders remains for the most part
unwritten. At some periods of monasticism the life of men and
that of women flow evenly side by side and can be dealt with
separately, at others their work so unites and intermingles that it
seems impossible to discuss the one apart from the other. Regarding some developments the share taken by women, important
enough in itself, seemed to me hardly capable of being rated at its
just value unless taken in conjunction with that of men. These
developments are therefore touched upon briefly or passed over
altogether, especially those in which the devotional needs of the
women are interesting chiefly in the effect which they had in
stimulating the literary productiveness of men. Other phases are
passed over because they were the outcome of a course of development, the analysis of which lies beyond the scope of this work.
This applies generally to various continental movements which are
throughout treated briefly, and especially to convent life in the
Netherlands, and to the later history of mysticism. The history
of the beguines in the North of France and the Netherlands is full
of interesting particulars, marked by the inclusion in the *Acta
Sanctorum* of women like Marie of Oignies (✝ c. 1213), Lutgardis of
Tongern (✝ 1246) and Christine of Truyen (✝ 1224), whose fame
rests on states of spiritual ecstasy, favoured and encouraged by the
Dominican friars. So again the women in Southern Germany,
who cultivated like religious moods and expressed their feelings in
writing, were largely influenced by the Dominicans, apart from
whom it seemed impossible to treat them. In England the
analysis of writings such as the 'Revelations' of Juliana of
Norwich and of Margery Kempe necessitates a full enquiry into
the influence and popularity of Richard Rolle (✝ 1349) and Walter
Hylton (✝ 1395).

During the later Middle Ages the study of the influences at
work in the convent is further complicated by the development of
religious associations outside it. Pre-eminent among these stands
the school of Deventer which gave the impulse to the production
of a devotional literature, the purity and refinement of which has
given it world-wide reputation. These associations were founded
by men not by women, and though the desire to influence nuns
largely moulded the men who wrote for and preached to them,

still the share taken by women in such movements is entirely subordinate.

It is needless to multiply instances of the chapters on convent life which are here omitted; in those which I place before the reader it has been my aim not so much to give a consecutive history of monasticism as it affected women, as to show how numerous are the directions in which this history can be pursued. Having regard to the nature of the subject I have addressed myself in the first place to the student, who in the references given will, I trust, find corroboration of my views. In quoting from early writings I have referred to the accounts printed in the *Acta Sanctorum Bollandorum* and to the edition of Latin writings published under the auspices of Migne in the 'Patrologiae Cursus Completus,' except in those few cases where a more recent edition of the work referred to offered special advantages, and regarding the date of these writings I have been chiefly guided by A. Potthast, *Wegweiser durch die Geschichtswerke des europäischen Mittelalters*, 1862. In accordance with a division which has been adopted by some histories of art and seems to me to have much in its favour, I have taken Early Christian times to extend to the close of the 10th century; I have spoken of the period between 1000 and 1250 as the Earlier, and of that between 1250 and 1500 as the Later Middle Ages. The spelling of proper names in a work which extends over many centuries has difficulties of its own. While observing a certain uniformity during each period, I have as far as possible adhered to the contemporary local form of each name.

While addressing myself largely to the student, I have kept along lines which I trust may make the subject attractive to the general reader, in whose interest I have translated all the passages quoted. There is a growing consciousness now-a-days that for stability in social progress we need among other things a wider scope for women's activity. This scope as I hope to show was to some extent formerly secured to women by the monastic system. Perhaps some of those who are interested in the educational movements of to-day may care to recall the history and arrangements of institutions, which favoured the intellectual development of women in the past.

I cannot conclude these prefatory remarks without a word of thanks to those who have aided me by criticism and revision. Besides the two friends to whom I have dedicated this book, I have to cordially thank Mrs R. W. Cracroft for the labour she has

spent on the literary revision of my work in manuscript. To
Dr H. F. Heath of Bedford College I am indebted for many
suggestions on points of philology, and to Robert J. Parker, Esq.
of Lincoln's Inn for advice on some points of law and of general
arrangement. Conscious as I am of the many defects in my work,
I cannot but be grateful to the Syndics of the University Press,
for the assistance they have rendered me in its publication, and I
trust that these defects may not deter readers from following me
into somewhat unfrequented paths, wherein at any rate I have not
stinted such powers of labour as are mine.

LINA ECKENSTEIN.

December, 1895.

CONTENTS.

CHAPTER IV.

ANGLO-SAXON NUNS IN CONNECTION WITH BONIFACE.

CHAPTER V.

CONVENTS IN SAXON LANDS BETWEEN A.D. 800—1000.

CHAPTER VI.

THE MONASTIC REVIVAL OF THE MIDDLE AGES.

CHAPTER VII.

ART INDUSTRIES IN THE NUNNERY.

CHAPTER VIII.

PROPHECY AND PHILANTHROPY.

CHAPTER IX.

EARLY MYSTIC LITERATURE.

CHAPTER X.

SOME ASPECTS OF THE CONVENT IN ENGLAND DURING THE LATER MIDDLE AGES.

CHAPTER XI.

MONASTIC REFORM PREVIOUS TO THE REFORMATION.

CHAPTER XII.

THE DISSOLUTION.

ERRATA.

Page 23, note 1, date of St Ida in A. SS. Boll. should be *Sept.* 4 instead of *June* 20.
,, 26, line 7, read *tilth* instead of *silk*.
,, 162, ,, 21, read *Martianus* instead of *Marianus*.
,, 190, ,, 32, read 1240 as the date of Jacobus di Vitriaco's death.
,, 241, ,,   8, read *Bergen* instead of *Berg*.

CHAPTER I.

'Die mit dem goldenen Schuh und dem Geiger ist auch eine Muttergottes.'
Bavarian Saying.

§ 1. The Borderland of Heathendom and Christianity.

IN order to gain an insight into the causes of the rapid
development of monasticism among the German races, it is
necessary to enquire into the social arrangements of the period
which witnessed the introduction of Christianity, and into those survivals of the previous period of social development which German
Christianity absorbed. Among peoples of German race monastic
life generally, and especially monastic life which gave scope for
independent activity among women, had a development of its own.
Women of the newly-converted yet still barbarian race readily
gathered together and dwelt in religious settlements founded on
their own initiative and ruled independently of men. A reason
for this must be sought in the drift of contemporary life, which
we shall thus have to discuss at some length.

During the period of declining heathendom—for how long,
measuring time by centuries, it is not yet possible to say—the
drift of society had been towards curtailing woman's liberty of
movement and interfering with her freedom of action. When the
Germans crossed the threshold of history the characteristics of the
father-age were already in the ascendant; the social era, when the
growing desire for certainty of fatherhood caused individual women
and their offspring to be brought into the possession of individual
men, had already begun. The influence of women was more and
more restricted owing to their domestic subjection. But traditions
of a time when it had been otherwise still lingered.

Students of primitive history are recognising, for peoples of
German race among others, the existence of an early period of
development, when women played a greater part in both social

and tribal life.   Folk-lore, philology, and surviving customs
yield overwhelming evidence in support of the few historic data
which point to the period, conveniently called the mother-age,
when women held positions of authority inside the tribal group
and directly exercised influence on the doings of the tribe[1].

This period, the mother-age, is generally looked upon as an
advance from an earlier stage of savagery, and considered to be contemporaneous with the beginnings of settled tribal life.   It brought
with it the practice of tilth and agriculture, and led to the domesti-
cation of some of the smaller animals and the invention of weaving
and spinning, achievements with which it is recognised that women
must be credited.

In matters of polity and sex it established the paramount
importance of the woman ; it is she who regulates the home, who
notes the changes of the seasons, who stores the results of experience, and treasures up the intellectual wealth of the community
in sayings which have come down to us in the form of quaint
maxims and old-world saws.   As for family arrangements, it
was inside the tribal group and at the tribal festival that sex unions
were contracted ;   and this festival, traditions of which survive in
many parts of Europe to this day, and which was in its earliest
forms a period of unrestrained license for the women as well as the
men, was presided over by the tribal mothers, an arrangement
which in various particulars affords an explanation of many ideas
associated with women in later times.

The father-age succeeding to the mother-age in time altogether
revolutionised the relations of the sexes ; transient sex unions,
formerly the rule, were gradually eliminated by capture and re-
tention of wives from outside the tribal group.   The change marks
a distinct step in social advance.   When men as heads of families
succeeded to much of the influence women had held in the tribe,
barbarous tendencies, such as blood sacrifice, were checked and a
higher moral standard was attained.   But this was done at the cost
of her prerogative to the woman ; and her social influence to some
extent passed from her.

It must be granted that the character of the mother-age in
some of its bearings is hypothetical, but we can infer many of the
social arrangements of the period from surviving customs and

[1] The literature on this subject is daily accumulating.   Among older authorities are
Bachofen, *Das Mutterrecht*, 1861; Zmigrodski, *Die Mutter bei den Völkern des
arischen Stammes*, 1886;   Pearson, K., *Ethic of Free Thought*, 1888.

usages, and its organisation from the part woman played in tradition and saga, and, as we shall see later, from folk-traditions preserved in the legends of the saints. And further, unless we admit that the social arrangements of the earlier period differed from those of the later, we are at a loss to account for the veneration in which woman was held and for the influence exerted by her as we confront her on the threshold of written history. When once we grasp the essentials of these earlier arrangements, we hold the clue to the existence of types of character and tendencies which otherwise appear anomalous.

For at the time when contact with Christianity brought with it the possibility of monastic settlements, the love of domestic life had not penetrated so deeply, nor were its conditions so uniformly favourable, but that many women were ready to break away from it. Reminiscences of an independence belonging to them in the past, coupled with the desire for leadership, made many women loth to conform to life inside the family as wives and mothers under conditions formulated by men. Tendencies surviving from the earlier period, and still unsubdued, made the advantages of married life weigh light in the balance against a loss of liberty. To conceive the force of these tendencies is to gain an insight into the elements which the convent forthwith absorbs.

In the world outside the convent commanding figures of womankind become fewer with outgoing heathendom, and the part played by women becomes of less and less importance. There is less room left for the Gannas of history or for the Kriemhilds of saga, for powerful natures such as the Visigoth princess Brunihild, queen of the Franks, or Drahomir of Brandenburg, queen in Bohemia, who gratify their passion for influence with a recklessness which strikes terror into the breasts of their contemporaries. As the old chronicler of St Denis remarks, women who are bent on evil do worse evil than men. But in the convent the influence of womankind lasted longer. Spirited nuns and independent-minded abbesses turn to account the possibilities open to them in a way which commands respect and repeatedly secures superstitious reverence in the outside world. The influence and the powers exerted by these women, as we shall see further on, are altogether remarkable, especially during early Christian times. But we also come across frequent instances of lawlessness among the women who band together in the convent,—a lawlessness to which the arrangements of the earlier age likewise supply a clue. For that very love of independence, which led to beneficial results where it was coupled with self-control and consciousness of greater responsibility, tended in the direction of vagrancy and dissoluteness when it was accompanied by distaste for every kind of restraint.

In this connection we must say a few words on the varying status of loose women, since the estimation in which these women were held and the attitude assumed towards them affected monasticism in various particulars. It is true that during early Christian times little heed was taken of them and few objections were raised to their influence, but later distinct efforts were made by various religious orders to prevent women from drifting into a class which, whatever may have been its condition in past times, was felt to be steadily and surely deteriorating.

The distinction of women into so-called respectable and disreputable classes dates from before the introduction of Christianity. It arose as the father-age gained on the mother-age, when appropriated women were more and more absorbed into domesticity, while those women outside, who either resented or escaped subjection, found their position surrounded by increasing difficulties, and aspersion more and more cast on their independence. By accepting the distinction, the teachers of Christianity certainly helped to make it more definite ; but for centuries the existence of loose women, so far from being condemned, was hardly discountenanced by them. The revenues which ecclesiastical courts and royal households derived from taxes levied on these women as a class yield proof of this[1]. Certainly efforts were made to set limits to their practices and the disorderly tendencies which in the nature of things became connected with them and with those with whom they habitually consorted. But this was done not so much to restrain them as to protect women of the other class from being confounded with them. Down to the time of the Reformation, the idea that the existence of loose women as a class should be discountenanced does not present itself, for they were a recognised feature of court life and of town life everywhere. Marshalled into bands, they accompanied the king and the army on their most distant expeditions, and stepped to the fore wherever there was question of merrymaking or entertainment. Indeed there is reason to believe, improbable though it may seem at first sight, that women of loose life, as we come across them in the Middle Ages, are successors to a class which had been powerful in the past. They are not altogether depraved and

[1] Kriegk, G. L., *Deutsches Bürgerthum im Mittelalter*, 1868, ch. 12–15.

despised characters such as legislation founded on tenets of Roman Law chose to stamp them. For law and custom are often at variance regarding the rights and privileges belonging to them. These rights and privileges they retained in various particulars till the time of the Reformation, which indeed marks a turning point in the attitude taken by society towards women generally.

Different ages have different standards of purity and faithfulness. The loose or unattached women of the past are of many kinds and many types; to apply the term prostitute to them raises a false idea of their position as compared with that of women in other walks of life. If we would deal with them as a class at all, it is only this they have in common,—that they are indifferent to the ties of family, and that the men who associate with them are not by so doing held to incur any responsibility towards them or towards their offspring.

If we bear in mind the part these women have played and the modifications which their status has undergone, it will be seen that the subject is one which nearly affects monasticism. For the convent accepted the dislike women felt to domestic subjection and countenanced them in their refusal to undertake the duties of married life. It offered an escape from the tyranny of the family, but it did so on condition of such a sacrifice of personal independence, as in the outside world more and more involved the loss of good repute. On the face of it, a greater contrast than that between the loose woman and the nun is hard to conceive; and yet they have this in common, that they are both the outcome of the refusal among womankind to accept married relations on the basis of the sub-jection imposed by the father-age.

In other respects too the earlier heathen period was not without influence on the incoming Christian faith, and helped to determine its conceptions with regard to women. In actual life the sacerdotal privileges, which tribal mothers had appropriated to themselves at the time of the introduction of Christianity, were retained by the priestess; while in the realm of the ideal the reverence in which tribal mothers had been held still lived on in the worship of the tribal mother-divinity. It is under this twofold aspect, as priestess and as tribal mother-goddess, that the power of women was brought face to face with Christianity; the priestess and the mother-goddess were the well-defined types of heathen womanhood with which the early Church was called upon to deal.

We will show later on how the ideal conception prevailed, and how the heathen mother-goddess often assumed the garb of a Christian woman-saint, and as a Christian woman-saint was left to exist unmolested. Not so the heathen priestess and prophetess. From the first introduction of Christianity the holding of sacerdotal powers by women was resented both within and without the Church, and opprobrium was cast on the women who claimed to mediate between the human and the divine.

At the time of the advent of Christianity the Gannas and Veledas of the Roman period are still a living reality ; they are the 'wise women' who every now and then leave their retreat and appear on the stage of history. A prophetess in gorgeous apparel makes her entry into Verdun in the year 547, drawing crowds about her and foretelling the future. She is in no way intimidated by the exorcisms of prelates, and presently leaves to betake herself to the court of the Frankish queen Fredegund. Again in 577 we find the Frankish king Guntchramm in consultation with a woman soothsayer, and other cases of the kind are on record[1].

In the ninth century the Church more effectually exercised her influence in the case of the woman Thiota, who coming from Switzerland inflamed the minds of the folk in Mainz; for she was accused of profanity and publicly scourged[2]. But for all the attacks of the Church, the folk persisted in clinging to its priestesses and in believing them gifted with special powers. Grimm shows how the Christian accusers of soothsaying women made them into odious witches[3]; Wuttke and Weinhold, both well-known students of folk-lore, consider that witches were originally heathen priestesses[4]. The intrinsic meaning of the word *hexe*, the German designation for witch, points to some one who originally belonged to a group living in a particular manner, but whose practices made her obnoxious to those who had apprehended the higher moral standard of a later social period. But the Church failed to stamp even the witch as wholly despicable; for in popular estimation she always retained some of the attributes of the priestess, the wise woman, the *bona domina*, the 'white witch' of tradition ; so that the doctrine that the soothsaying woman is necessarily the associate of evil was never altogether accepted.

[1] Gregorius Tur., *Hist. Eccles.* 5, ch. 14, 16, 19.
[2] Grimm, J., *Deutsche Mythologie*, 1875, p. 78.   [3] Ibid. p. 881 ff.
[4] Wuttke, *Deutscher Volksaberglaube*, 1869, p. 141 ; Weinhold, K., *Deutsche Frauen*, 1882, vol. 1, p. 73.

Even now-a-days incidents happen occasionally in remote districts which show how the people still readily seek the help of women in matters of wisdom, of leechcraft, and of prescience. It was only under the influence of a scare that people, who were accustomed to consult the wise woman in good faith, could be brought to abhor her as a witch. It was only during the later Middle Ages that the undisputed and indisputable connection of some 'wise women' with licentious customs gave their traducers a weapon of which they were not slow to avail themselves, and which enabled them to rouse fanaticism of the worst kind against these women.

The practices and popularity of witchcraft were in truth the latest survivals of the mother-age. The woman, who devised love-charms and brewed manifold remedies for impotence and for allaying the pangs of childbirth, who pretended to control the weather and claimed the power to turn the milk of a whole village blue, carried on traditions of a very primitive period. And her powers, as we shall see, always had a close parallel in those attributed to women-saints. For example St Gertrud of Nivelles has left a highly prized relic to womankind in the form of a cloak which is still hung about those who are desirous of becoming mothers[1]; and the hair of a saint, Mechthild, is still hung outside the church at Töss in Switzerland to avert the thunderstorm[2]; and again St Gunthild of Biberbach and others are still appealed to that they may avert the cattle plague[3]. What difference, it may be asked, is there between the powers attributed to these saints and the powers with which witches are usually credited? They are the obverse and reverse of woman's connection with the supernatural, which in the one case is interpreted by the sober mind of reverence, and in the other is dreaded under the perturbing influence of a fear encouraged, if not originated, by Christian fanatics.

In the Christian Church the profession of the nun was accepted as holy, but an impassable gulf separated her from the priestess. During early Christian times we come across the injunction that women shall not serve at the altar[4], and that lady abbesses shall not take upon themselves religious duties reserved to men by the Church. When we think of women gathered together in a religious

---

[1] Rochholz, E. L., *Drei Gaugöttinnen*, 1870, p. 191.

[2] Menzel, *Christliche Symbolik*, 1854, article 'Haar.'

[3] *A. SS. Boll.*, St Gunthildis, Sept. 12.

[4] Bouquet, *Recueil Hist.*, vol. 5, p. 690. Capitulare incerti anni, nr 6, 'ut mulieres ad altare non ingrediantur.'

establishment and dependent on the priest outside for the performing of divine worship, their desire to manage things for themselves does not appear unnatural, encouraged as it would be by traditions of sacerdotal rights belonging to them in the past. And it is worthy of notice that as late as the 13th century, Brother Berthold, an influential preacher of south Germany, speaks ardently against women who would officiate at divine service and urges the mischief that may result from such a course.

Turning to the question of how far these obvious survivals from a heathen age are determined by time and place, we find broad lines of difference between the heathen survivals of the various branches of the German race, and considerable diversity in the character of their early Christianity and their early women-saints. This diversity is attributable to the fact that the heathen beliefs of these various peoples were not the same at the time of their first contact with Christianity, and that they did not accept it under like circumstances.

For while those branches of the race who moved in the vanguard of the great migration, the Vandals, the Burgundians and the Goths, readily embraced Christianity, it was Christianity in its Arian form. Arianism, which elsewhere had been branded as heresy and well-nigh stamped out, suddenly revived among the Germans; all the branches of the race who came into direct contact with peoples of civilized Latinity readily embraced it. Now one of the distinguishing features of Arian belief was its hatred of monasticism[1]. The Arian convert hunted the monk from his seclusion and thrust him back to the duties of civic life. It is not then among Germans who adopted Arian Christianity that the beginnings of convent life must be sought. Indeed as Germans these peoples soon passed away from the theatre of history; they intermarried and fell in with the habits of the people among whom they settled, and forfeited their German language and their German traditions.

It was otherwise with the Franks who entered Gaul at the close of the fourth century, and with the Anglo-Saxons who took possession of Britain. The essentially warlike character of these peoples was marked by their worship of deities such as Wodan, a worship before which the earlier worship of mother-divinities was giving way. Women had already been brought into subjection, but they had a latent desire for independence, and among the Franks and Anglo-

[1] Montalembert, *Monks of the West*, I, p. 359.

Saxons women of the newly converted race eagerly snatched at the possibilities opened out by convent life, and in their ranks history chronicles some of the earliest and most remarkable developments of monasticism.   But the Franks and the Anglo-Saxons, in leaving behind the land of their origin, had left behind those hallowed sites on which primitive worship so essentially depends.   It is in vain that we seek among them for a direct connection between heathen mother-divinity and Christian woman-saint ; their mother-divinities did not live on in connection with the Church.   It is true that the inclination to hold women in reverence remained, and found expression in the readiness with which they revered women as saints.   The women-saints of the Anglo-Saxons and the Franks are numerous, and are nearly all known to have been interested in convent foundations.   But the legends, which in course of time have crystallised round them, and the miracles attributed to them, though containing certain elements of heathen folk-tradition, are colourless and pale compared with the traditions which have been preserved by saint legend abroad.   It is in Germany proper, where the same race has been in possession of the same sites for countless generations, that the primitive character of heathen traditions is most pronounced and has most directly determined and influenced the cult and the legends of women-saints.

Besides the reminiscences of the early period which have survived in saint legend, traditions and customs of the same period have lived on in the worship of the Virgin Mary.   The worship of the Virgin Mary was but slightly developed in Romanised Gaul and Keltic Britain, but from the beginning of the sixth century it is a marked feature in the popular creed in those countries where the German element prevailed.

As Mrs Jameson says in her book on the legends of the Madonna : ' It is curious to observe, as the worship of the Virgin mother expanded and gathered in itself the relics of many an ancient faith, how the new and the old elements, some of them apparently most heterogeneous, became amalgamated and were combined into the earlier forms of art...[1].'

Indeed the prominence given to the Virgin is out of all proportion to the meagre mention of her in the gospels.   During the early Christian period she was largely worshipped as a patron saint in France, England and Germany, and her fame continued steadily increasing with the centuries till its climax was reached in the

[1] Jameson, *Legends of the Madonna,* 1857, Introd. xix.

Middle Ages, which witnessed the greatest concessions made by the Church to the demands of popular faith.

According to Rhys[1] many churches dedicated to Mary were built on spots where tradition speaks of the discovery of a wooden image, probably a heathen statue which was connected with her.

In the seventh century Pope Sergius (687–701) expressly ordered that the festivals of the Virgin Mary were to take place on heathen holy days in order that heathen celebrations might become associated with her[2]. The festivals of the Virgin to this day are associated with pilgrimages, the taste for which to the Frenchman of the Middle Ages appeared peculiarly German. The chronicler Froissart, writing about 1390, remarks 'for the Germans are fond of performing pilgrimages and it is one of their customs[3].'

Mary then, under her own name, or under the vaguer appellation of *Our Lady* (Unser liebe frau, Notre Dame, de heilige maagd), assimilated surviving traditions of the heathen faith which were largely reminiscences of the mother-age ; so that Mary became the heiress of mother-divinities, and her worship was associated with cave, and tree, and fountain, and hill-top, all sites of the primitive cult.

'Often,' says Menzel[4], 'a wonder-working picture of the Madonna is found hung on a tree or inside a tree ; hence numerous appellations like "Our dear Lady of the Oak," "Our dear Lady of the Linden-tree," etc. Often at the foot of the tree, upon which such a picture is hung, a fountain flows to which miraculous power is ascribed.'

In the Tyrol we hear of pictures which have been discovered floating in a fountain or which were borne to the bank by a river[5].

As proof of the Virgin Mary's connection with festivals, we find her name associated in Belgium with many pageants held on the first of May. Throughout German lands the Assumption of the Virgin comes at the harvest festival, and furnishes an occasion for some pilgrimage or fair which preserves many peculiar and perplexing traits of an earlier civilization.

The harvest festival is coupled in some parts of Germany with

---

[1] Rhys, J., *Lectures on the origin and growth of religion as illustrated by Celtic Heathendom*, 1888, p. 162.

[2] Frantz, C., *Versuch einer Geschichte des Marien und Annencultus*, 1854, p. 54 ff.

[3] Froissart, *Chronicle*, c. 162, in English translation ; also Oberle, K. A., *Ueberreste germ. Heidentums im Christentum*, 1883, p. 153.

[4] Menzel, *Christ. Symbolik*, 1854, article 'Baum.'

[5] Oberle, K. A., *Ueberreste germ. Heidentums im Christentum*, 1883, p. 144.

customs that are of extreme antiquity. In Bavaria the festival sometimes goes by the name of the 'day of sacred herbs,' *kräuterweihtag*; near Würzburg it is called the 'day of sacred roots,' *würzelweihtag*, or 'day of bunch-gathering,' *büschelfrauentag*[1]. In the Tyrol the 15th of August is the great day of the Virgin, *grosse frauentag*, when a collection of herbs for medicinal purposes is made. A number of days, *frauentage*, come in July and August and are now connected with the Virgin, on which herbs are collected and offered as sacred bunches either on the altar of Our Lady in church and chapel, or on hill-tops which throughout Germany are the sites of ancient woman-worship[2]. This collecting and offering of herbs points to a stage even more primitive than that represented by offerings of grain at the harvest festival.

In a few instances the worship of Mary is directly coupled with that of some heathen divinity. In Antwerp to this day an ancient idol of peculiar appearance is preserved, which women, who are desirous of becoming mothers, decorate with flowers at certain times of the year. Its heathen appellation is lost, but above it now stands a figure of the Virgin[3].

Again we find the name of Mary joined to that of the heathen goddess Sif. In the Eiffel district, extending between the rivers Rhine, Meuse and Mosel, a church stands dedicated to Mariasif, the name of Mary being coupled with that of Sif, a woman-divinity of the German heathen pantheon, whom Grimm characterizes as a giver of rain[4]. The name Mariahilf, a similar combination, is frequently found in south Germany, the name of Mary as we hope to show further down being joined to that of a goddess who has survived in the Christian saint Hilp[5].

These examples will suffice to show the close connection between the conceptions of heathendom and popular Christianity, and how the cloak of heathen association has fallen on the shoulders of the saints of the Christian Church. The authorities at Rome saw no occasion to take exception to its doing so. Pope Gregorius II. (590–604) in a letter addressed to Melitus of Canterbury expressly

---

[1] Menzel, *Christl. Symbolik*, 1854, article 'Himmelfahrt.'

[2] Ibid., article 'Frauenberg'; also Oberle, K. A., *Ueberreste germ. Heidentums im Christentum*, 1883, p. 38.

[3] Rochholz, *Drei Gaugöttinnen*, 1870, p. 81, calls it Walburg; Reinsberg-Düringsfeld, *Traditions et légendes de la Belgique*, 1870, p. 286, calls it Fro or Frigg.

[4] Simrock, K., *Handbuch der deutschen Mythologie*, 1887, p. 379; also Grimm, J., *Deutsche Mythologie*, 1875, p. 257.

[5] Comp. below, p. 35.

urged that the days of heathen festival should receive solemnity through dedication to some holy martyr[1]. The Christian saint whose name was substituted for that of some heathen divinity readily assimilated associations of the early period. Scriptural characters and Christian teachers were given the emblems of older divinities and assumed their characteristics. But the varying nature of the same saint in different countries has hardly received due attention. St Peter of the early British Church was very different from St Peter who in Bavaria walked the earth like clumsy good-natured Thor, or from St Peter who in Rome took the place of Mars as protector of the city. Similarly the legends currently told of the same saint in different countries exhibit markedly different traits.

For the transition from heathendom to Christianity was the work not of years but of centuries; the claims made by religion changed, but the underlying conceptions for a long time remained unaltered. Customs which had once taken a divine sanction continued to be viewed under a religious aspect, though they were often at variance with the newly-introduced faith. The craving for local divinities in itself was heathen; in course of time the cult of the saints altogether re-moulded the Christianity of Christ. But the Church of Rome, far from opposing the multitude of those through whom the folk sought intercession with the Godhead, opened her arms wide to all.

At the outset it lay with the local dignitary to recognise or reject the names which the folk held in veneration. Religious settlements and Church centres regulated days and seasons according to the calendar of the chief festivals of the year, as accepted by the Church at Rome; but the local dignitary was at liberty to add further names to the list at his discretion. For centuries there was no need of canonisation to elevate an individual to the rank of saint; the inscribing of his name on a local calendar was sufficient. Local calendars went on indefinitely swelling the list of saintly names till the Papal See felt called upon to interfere[2]. Since the year 1153 the right to declare a person a saint has lain altogether with the authorities at Rome[3].

Considering the circumstances under which the peoples of

---

[1] Bede, *Ecclesiastical History*, 1, ch. 30.

[2] On English calendars, Piper, F., *Kalendarien und Martyrologien der Angelsachsen*, 1862; Stanton, R., *Menology of England and Wales*, 1887.

[3] Stadler und Heim, *Vollständiges Heiligenlexicon*, 1858–62, vol. 2, Einleitung.

German race first came into contact with Christianity, it is well to recall the fact that a busy Church life had grown up in many of the cities north of the Alps, which were centres of the Roman system of administration previous to the upheaval and migration of German heathen tribes, which began in the fourth century. Legend has preserved stories of the apostles and their disciples wandering northwards and founding early bishoprics along the Rhine, in Gaul and in Britain[1]. The massacres of Christians in the reign of Diocletian cannot be altogether fabulous; but after the year 313, when Constantine at Rome officially accepted the new faith, until the German invasion, the position of Christianity was well secured.

A certain development of monastic life had accompanied its spread. In western Gaul we hear of Martin of Tours (†400) who, after years of military service and religious persecution, settled near Poitiers and drew about him many who joined him in a round of devotion and work. The monastic, or rather cœnobite, settlement of his time consisted of a number of wattled cells or huts, surrounded by a trench or a wall of earth. The distinction between the earlier word, *coenobium*, and the later word, *monasterium*, as used in western Europe, lies in this, that the *coenobium* designates the assembled worshippers alone, while the monastery presupposes the possession of a definite site of land[2]. In this sense the word monastery is as fitly applied to settlements ruled by women as to those ruled by men, especially during the early period when these settlements frequently include members of both sexes. St Martin of Tours is also credited with having founded congregations of religious women[3], but I have found nothing definite concerning them.

Our knowledge of the Christian life of the British is very limited; presumably the religious settlement was a school both of theology and of learning, and no line of distinction divided the settlements of priests from those of monks. From Gildas, a British writer, who at the time of the Anglo-Saxon invasion (c. 560) wrote a stern invective against the irreligious ways of his countrymen, we gather that women lived under the direction of priests, but it is not clear whether they were vowed to continence[4]. But as far

---

[1] For France, Guettée, *Histoire de l'Église de France*, 1847-55, vol. I, p. 1; for England, Bright, W., *Early English Church History*, 1878, pp. 1 ff.; for Germany, Friedrich, *Kirchengeschichte*, 1867, vol. I, pp. 86 ff.

[2] Ducange, *Glossarium*: 'coenobium.'

[3] Dupuy, A., *Histoire de S. Martin*, 1852, p. 176. [4] Gildas, *Epistle*, c. 66.

as I am aware, there is no evidence forthcoming that before the Saxon invasion women lived in separate religious establishments, the rule of which was in the hands of one of their own sex[1].

The convent is of later date. During the early centuries of established Christianity the woman who takes the vow of continence secures the protection of the Church but does not necessarily leave her home-surroundings.

Thus Ambrosius, archbishop of Milan († 397), one of the most influential supporters of early Christianity, greatly inflamed women's zeal for a celibate life. But in the writings of Ambrosius, which treat of virginity, there is no suggestion that the widow or the maiden who vows continence shall seek seclusion or solitude[2]. Women vowed to continence moved about freely, secure through their connection with the Church from distasteful unions which their relatives might otherwise force upon them. Their only distinctive mark was the use of a veil.

Similarly we find Hilarius († 369), bishop of Poitiers, addressing a letter to his daughter Abra on the beauties of the unmarried state. In this he assures her, that if she be strong enough to renounce an earthly bridegroom, together with gay and splendid apparel, a priceless pearl shall fall to her share[3]. But in this letter also there is no suggestion that the woman who embraces religion should dwell apart from her family. It is well to bear this in mind, for after the acceptance of Christianity by the peoples of German race, we occasionally hear of women who, though vowed to religion, move about freely among their fellows; but Church councils and synods began to urge more and more emphatically that this was productive of evil, and that a woman who had taken the religious vow must be a member of a convent.

To sum up ;—the peoples of German race, at the time of their contact with Christianity, were in a state of social development which directly affected the form in which they accepted the new faith and the institutions to which such acceptance gave rise. Some branches of the race, deserting the land of their birth,

---

[1] In Ireland we hear of nunneries founded by St Bridget in the fifth century, the chief of which was at Kildare; also that this saint crossed the Irish Sea and founded nunneries at Glastonbury in England and at Abernethy in Scotland. The accounts of the work of Bridget are numerous, but have not been subjected to criticism. Comp. *A. SS. Boll.*, St Brigida, Feb. 1, and Lanigan, *Eccles. History of Ireland*, 1829, 1, pp. 377 ff.

[2] Ambrosius, *Opera* (edit. Migne, *Patrol. Cursus Comp.* vol. 16), *De virginibus*, p. 187; (vol. 17) *Ad virginem devotam*, p. 579.

[3] Hilarius, *Opera* (edit. Migne, vol. 10), *Ad Abram*, p. 547.

came into contact with peoples of Latin origin, and embraced Christianity under a form which excluded monasticism, and soon lost their identity as Germans. Others, as the Franks and Anglo-Saxons, giving up the worship of their heathen gods, accepted orthodox Christianity, and favoured the mode of life of those who followed peaceful pursuits in the monastery, pursuits which their wives especially were eager to embrace. Again, those peoples who remained in possession of their earlier homes largely preserved usages dating from a primitive period of tribal organization, usages which affected the position of their women and determined the character of their women-saints. It is to Germany proper that we must go for the woman-priestess who lives on longest as the witch, and for the loose women who most markedly retain special rights and privileges. And it is also in Germany proper that we find the woman-saint who is direct successor to the tribal mother-goddess.

§ 2.   The Tribal Goddess as a Christian Saint.

Before considering the beginnings of convent life as the work of women whose existence rests on a firm historic basis, we must enquire into the nature of women-saints. From the earliest times of established Christianity the lives of men and women who were credited with special holiness have formed a favourite theme of religious narratives, which were intended to keep their memory green and to impress the devout with thoughts of their saintliness.

The Acts of the Saints, the comprehensive collection of which is now in course of publication under the auspices of the Bollandists, form a most important branch of literature. They include some of the most valuable material for a history of the first ten centuries of our era, and give a most instructive insight into the drift of Christianity in different epochs. The aims, experiences and sufferings of Christian heroes and heroines inspired the student and fired the imagination of the poet. Prose narrative told of their lives, poems were written in their praise, and hymns were composed to be sung at the celebration of their office. The godly gained confidence from the perusal of such compositions, and the people hearing them read or sung were impressed in favour of Christian doctrine.

The number of men and women whom posterity has glorified as saints is legion. Besides the characters of the accepted and the apocryphal gospels, there are the numerous early converts to

Christianity who suffered for their faith, and all those who during
early Christian times turned their energies to practising and preaching the tenets of the new religion, and to whose memory a loving
recollection paid the tribute of superstitious reverence.   Their
successors in the work of Christianity accepted them as patron
saints and added their names to the list of those to whose memory
special days were dedicated.   Many of them are individuals whose
activity in the cause of Christianity is well authenticated.   Friends
have enlarged on their work, contemporary history refers to their
existence, and often they have themselves left writings, which give
an insight into their lives.   They are the early and true saints of
history, on whose shoulders in some cases the cloak of heathen
association has fallen, but without interfering with their great and
lasting worth.

But besides those who were canonised for their enthusiasm in
the cause of early Christianity, the Acts of the Saints mention a
number of men and women who enjoy local reverence, but of
whose actual existence during Christian times evidence is wanting.
Among them are a certain number of women with whom the
present chapter purposes to deal, women who are locally worshipped as saints, and whose claims to holiness are generally
recognised, but whose existence during Christian times is hypothetical.   Their legends contain a small, in some cases a scarcely
sensible, basis of historic fact, and their cult preserves traits which
are pre-Christian, often anti-Christian, in character.

The traveller Blunt, during a stay in Italy in the beginning of
this century, was struck with the many points which modern saints
and ancient gods have in common.   He gives a description of the
festival of St Agatha at Catania, of which he was an eye-witness,
and which to this day, as I have been told, continues little changed.
The festival, as Blunt describes it, opened with a horse-race, which
he knew from Ovid was one of the spectacles of the festival of the
goddess Ceres; and further he witnessed a mummery and the
carrying about of huge torches, both of which he also knew formed
part of the old pagan festival.   But more remarkable than this was
a great procession which began in the evening and lasted into the
night; hundreds of citizens crowded to draw through the town
a ponderous car, on which were placed the image of the saint
and her relics, which the priests exhibited to the ringing of bells.
Among these relics were the veil of Agatha, to which is ascribed
the power of staying the eruption of Mount Aetna, and the breasts

of the saint, which were torn off during her martyrdom[1]. Catania, Blunt knew, had always been famous for the worship of Ceres, and the ringing of bells and a veil were marked features of her festivals, the greater and the lesser Eleusinia. Menzel tells us that huge breasts were carried about on the occasion[2]. Further, Blunt heard that two festivals took place yearly in Catania in honour of Agatha; one early in the spring, the other in the autumn, exactly corresponding to the time when the greater and lesser Eleusinia were celebrated. Even the name Agatha seemed but a taking over into the new religion of a name sacred to the old. Ceres was popularly addressed as *Bona Dea,* and the name Agatha, which does not occur as a proper name during ancient times, seemed but a translation of the Latin epithet into Greek.

The legend of Agatha as contained in the *Acta Sanctorum* places her existence in the third century and gives full details concerning her parentage, her trials and her martyrdom; but I have not been able to ascertain when it was written. Agatha is the chief saint of the district all about Catania, and we are told that her fame penetrated at an early date into Italy and Greece[3].

It is of course impossible actually to disprove the existence of a Christian maiden Agatha in Catania in the third century. Some may incline to the view that such a maiden did exist, and that a strange likeness between her experiences and name on the one hand, and the cult of and epithet applied to Ceres on the other, led to the popular worship of her instead of the ancient goddess. The question of her existence as a Christian maiden during Christian times can only be answered by a balance of probabilities. Our opinion of the truth or falsehood of the traditions concerning her rests on inference, and the conclusion at which we arrive upon the evidence must largely depend on the attitude of mind in which we approach the subject.

The late Professor Robertson Smith has insisted that myths are latter-day inventions which profess to explain surviving peculiarities of ritual. If this be so, we hold in the Eleusinia a clue to the incidents of the Agatha legend. The story for example of her veil, which remained untouched by the flames when she was burnt, may be a popular myth which tries to account for the presence of the veil at

---

[1] Blunt, J. J., *Vestiges of Ancient Manners in Italy and Sicily,* 1823, pp. 56 ff.

[2] Menzel, W., *Christl. Symbolik,* 1854, article 'Brust,' makes this statement. I do not see where he takes it from.

[3] *A. SS. Boll.,* St Agatha, Feb. 5.

the festival. The incident of the breasts torn off during martyrdom was invented to account for the presence of these strange symbols.

Instances of this kind could be indefinitely multiplied. Let the reader, who wishes to pursue the subject on classic soil, examine the name, the legend and the emblem of St Agnes, virgin martyr of Rome, who is reputed to have lived in the third century and whose cult is well established in the fourth; let him enquire into the name, legend and associations of St Rosalia of Palermo, invoked as a protectress from the plague, of whom no mention occurs till four centuries after her reputed existence[1].

I have chosen Agatha as a starting point for the present enquiry, because there is much evidence to hand of the prevalence of mother-deities in pre-Christian Sicily, and because the examination of German saint-legend and saint-worship leads to analogous results. In Germany too the mother divinity of heathendom seems to survive in the virgin saint; and in Germany virgin saints, in attributes, cult and name, exhibit peculiarities which it seems impossible to explain save on the hypothesis that traditions of the heathen past survive in them. So much is associated with them which is pre-Christian, even anti-Christian in character, that it seems legitimate to speak of them as pseudo-saints.

I own it is not always possible to distinguish between the historical saint and the pseudo-saint. Sometimes data are wanting to disprove the statements made by the legend-writer about time and place; sometimes information is not forthcoming about local traditions and customs, which might make a suggestive trait in saint-legend stand out in its full meaning. In some cases also, owing to a coincidence of name, fictitious associations have become attached to a real personage. But these cases I believe are comparatively few. As a general rule it holds good that a historical saint will be readily associated with miraculous powers, but not with profane and anti-Christian usages. Where the latter occur it is probable that no evidence will be forthcoming of the saint's actual existence during Christian times. If she represents a person who ever existed at all, such a person must have lived in a far-distant heathen past, at a time which had nothing in common with Christian teaching and with Christian tenets.

There is this further peculiarity about the woman pseudo-saint of Germany, that she is especially the saint of the peasantry; so that we rarely hear more of her than perhaps her name till centuries

---

[1] *A. SS. Boll.*, St Agnes, Jan. 21; St Rosalia, Sept. 4.

after her reputed existence.   Early writers of history and biography
have failed to chronicle her doings.   Indeed we do not hear of her
at all till we hear of her cult as one of long standing or of great
importance.

It is only when the worship of such saints, who in the eyes of
the common folk are the chief glory of their respective districts,
attracts the attention of the Church, that the legend-writer sets to
work to write their legends.   He begins by ascribing to the holder
of a venerated name human parentage and human experiences, he
collects and he blends the local traditions associated with the saint
on a would be historical background, and makes a story which
frequently offers a curious mixture of the Christian and the profane.
Usually he places the saint's existence in the earliest period of
Christianity; sometimes at a time when Christianity was unknown
in the neighbourhood where she is the object of reverence.

Moreover all these saints are patronesses of women in their
times of special trial.   Their cult generally centres round a cave, a
fountain of peculiar power, a tree, or some other site of primitive
woman-worship.   Frequently they are connected with some peculiar
local custom which supplies the clue to incidents introduced by the
legend-writer.   And even when the clue is wanting, it is sometimes
possible to understand one legend by reading it in the light of
another.   Obscure as the parallels are in some cases, in others
they are strikingly clear.

The recognised holiness of the woman pseudo-saint is in no
way determined by the limit of bishopric and diocese; she is
worshipped within geographical limits, but within limits which have
not been marked out by the Church.   It was mentioned above that
separate districts of Germany, or rather tribes occupying such districts, clung to a belief in protective mother-goddesses (Gaumütter).
Possibly, where the name of a pseudo-saint is found localised in
contiguous districts, this may afford a clue to the migration of tribes.

The *Acta Sanctorum* give information concerning a large number
of pseudo-saints, but this information to be read in its true light
needs to be supplemented by further details of local veneration and
cult.   Such details are found in older books of devotion, and in
modern books on mythology and folk-lore.   Modern religious
writers, who treat of these saints, are in the habit of leaving out or
of slurring over all details which suggest profanity.   Compared
with older legends, modern accounts of the saints are limp and
colourless, and share the weak sentimentality, which during the

last few centuries has come to pervade the conceptions of Catholic Christianity as represented in pictorial art.

The names of a number of women whom the people hold in veneration have escaped the attention of the compilers of the *Acta Sanctorum*, or else they have been purposely passed over because their possessors were held unworthy of the rank of saint. But the stories locally told of them are worth attention, and the more so because they throw an additional light on the stories of recognised saints.

The larger number of recognised pseudo-saints are found in the districts into which Christianity spread as a religion of peace, or in remoter districts where the power of the Church was less immediately felt. They are found most often north of the Danube and east of the Rhine, especially in the lake districts of Bavaria and Switzerland, in the marshy wilds of the Low Countries, and in the remote forest regions of the Ardennes, the Black Forest, the Spessart or the Vosges. Where Christianity was established as the result of political subjection, as for example among the Saxons, the woman pseudo-saint is hardly found at all. Perhaps the heathenism of the Saxons differed from the heathenism of other German folk ; perhaps, like the Anglo-Saxons in England, the Saxons were conquerors of the land they inhabited and by moving out of their old homes had lost their local associations and their primitive cult. But, however this may be, it is not where Christianity advanced at the point of the lance, but in the districts where its spread was due to detached efforts of missionaries, that the woman pseudo-saint is most frequently met with.

Wandering away into forest wilds, where scattered clearings lay like islets in an ocean, the missionary sought a retreat remote from the interference of government, remote also from the interference of the episcopate, where he could realise his hope of living a worthier life. Naturally his success largely depended on his securing the goodwill of the people in whose neighbourhood he settled. He was obliged to adapt himself to their mode of thought if he would win favour for his faith, and to realise their views if he wished to modify them in the direction of his own. To bridge over the abyss which separated his standard of life from theirs, he was bound to defer whenever he could to their sentiments and to their conceptions of holiness.

How far these holy men ignored, how far they countenanced, the worship of local divinities, necessarily remains an open question.

Rightly or wrongly popular tradition readily coupled the names of these early Christians with those of its favourite women-saints.

Thus Willibrord, the Anglo-Saxon missionary who settled abroad in the eighth century, is said to have taken up and translated relics of the woman-saint Cunera and to have recognised her claim to veneration ; her cult is localised in various places near Utrecht. The life of Willibrord († 739), written by Alcuin († 804), contains no mention of Cunera, for the information we have concerning Willibrord's interest in her is to be found in the account of her life written centuries later[1]. This account offers such a picturesque medley of chronological impossibilities that the commentators of the *Acta Sanctorum* have entirely recast it.

The gist of the legend as told in the beginning of the 14th century is as follows[2]. Cunera was among the virgin companions of St Ursula, and the date of her murder, near Cöln, is given as 387, or as 449. Before the murder Cunera was borne away from Cöln by King Radbod of Friesland, who covered her with his cloak, an ancient symbolic form of appropriation. Arrived at Renen he entrusted her with the keys of his kingdom, which incensed his wedded wife to such an extent that she caused Cunera to be strangled and the body hidden away. But the site where the saint lay was miraculously pointed out, and the wicked queen went mad and destroyed herself. In vain we ask why a king of the Frisians, who persistently clung to their heathendom, should be interested in a Christian virgin and carry her off to preside over his household, and in vain we look for the assertion or for the proof that Cunera was a Christian at all. The *Acta Sanctorum* reject the connection between Cunera and St Ursula of Cöln, but the writer Kist, who considers her to have been a real Christian individual, argues in favour of it. In the 12th century we find a certain Adelheid swearing to the rightfulness of her cause on the relics of St Cunera at Renen[3].

Similarly the story goes that Agilfrid, abbot of the monastery of St Bavon in Flanders, afterwards bishop of Liège (765—787), about the year 754 acquired the relics of the woman-saint Pharaildis and brought them to Ghent[4]. When the Northmen ravaged Flanders in 846 the bones of Pharaildis were among those carried

---

[1] *A. SS. Boll.*, St Cunera, June 12.

[2] Kist, N. C., in *Kerkhistorisch Archiv*, Amsterdam, 1858, vol. 2, p. 20.

[3] *Vita St Meinwerci*, bishop of Paderborn (1009–39), written about 1155 (Potthast), c. 37.

[4] Hautcœur, *Actes de Ste Pharailde*, 1882, Introduction, p. xc.

away to St Omer by the Christians as their most valued possession, and in 939 they were brought back to Ghent[1].

The legend of Pharaildis gives no clue to the Christian interest in her, nor to the veneration of her, which is localised at Ghent, Hamm, Steenockerzeel, and Loo. We hear that she was married against her inclination, that she cured her husband who was a huntsman of a wound, and that after his death she dwelt in solitude to an advanced age, and that occasionally she wrought miracles. Further, in popular belief, she crossed the water dryshod, she chased away geese from the corn, and she struck the ground and the holy fountain at Bruay welled up for the benefit of the harvesters— incidents which are not peculiar to her legend. The festival of Pharaildis is kept on different dates at Ghent, Cambray, Maastricht and Breda. At Ghent it is associated with a celebrated fair, the occasion for great rejoicings among the populace. At the church of Steenockerzeel stones of conical shape are kept which are carried round the altar on her festival[2], in the same way as stones are kept elsewhere and considered by some writers to be symbols of an ancient phallic cult. The legend explains the presence of these stones by telling how the saint one day was surreptitiously giving loaves to the poor, when her act would have been discovered but that by intercession the loaves were transformed into stones. This incident, the transformation of gifts secretly given to the poor, is introduced into the legends of other women-saints, but only in this case have I found it mentioned that the transformed food was preserved. We shall have occasion to return to Pharaildis, whose legend and cult offer nothing to support the view that she was an early Christian.

There are numerous instances of a like connection between holy missionary and woman pseudo-saint. A fair example is yielded by Leodgar (St Léger) bishop of Autun († 678), a well-defined historical personality[3], whom tradition makes into a near relative of Odilia, a saint widely venerated, but whose reputed foundation of the monastery on the Hohenburg modern criticism utterly discards[4].

But it is not only Christian missionaries who are associated with these women-saints. Quite a number of saints have been brought into connection with the house of the Karlings, and

[1] *A. SS. Boll.*, Gloria posthuma St Bavonis, Oct. 1, p. 261.

[2] Wauters, A., *Histoire des environs de Bruxelles*, 1852, vol. 3, pp. 111, 123 ff.

[3] *A. SS. Boll.*, Vita St Leodgarii, Oct. 2.

[4] Roth, K. L., 'St Odilienberg' in *Alsatia*, 1856, pp. 91 ff.

frequently Karl the Great himself figures in the stories told of them. I do not presume to decide whether the legendary accounts of these women are pure invention; some historic truth may be embodied in the stories told of them. But judging by the material at hand we are justified in disputing the existence of St Ida, who is said to have been the wife of Pippin of Landen and ancestress of the Karlings on the sole authority of the life of St Gertrud, her daughter. This work was long held to be contemporary, but its earliest date is now admitted to be the 11th century[1]. It is less easy to cast discredit on the existence of the saints Amalberga, the one a virgin saint, the other a widow, whom hagiologists find great difficulty in distinguishing. Pharaildis, mentioned above, and the saints Ermelindis, Reinildis and Gudila, are said to be Amalberga's daughters, but together with other saints of Hainault and Brabant they are very obviously pseudo-saints. The idea of bringing Karl the Great into some relation with them may have arisen from a twofold desire to justify traditions concerning them and to magnify the Emperor's importance.

In this connection it seems worth while to quote the passage in which Grimm[2] describes the characteristic traits of the German goddess in his German Mythology, and to consider how these traits are more or less pronounced in the women we have called pseudo-saints.

'It seems well,' he says, in the opening of his chapter on goddesses, 'to treat of goddesses collectively as well as individually, since a common conception underlies them all, which will thus stand out the more clearly. They are conceived essentially as divine mothers, *travelling about* and *visiting mortals*, from whom mankind learn the ways and arts of housekeeping and tilth: *spinning*, *weaving, guarding the hearth, sowing* and *reaping*' (the italics are his).

The tendency of the goddess to wander from place to place is reflected in many women pseudo-saints who are represented in their legends as inhabiting at various periods of their lives different parts of the district in which they are the object of veneration. Verena of northern Switzerland dwelt first at Solothurn, where a cave, which was her dwelling-place, is now

---

[1] Bonnell, H. E., *Anfänge des karolingischen Hauses*, 1866, pp. 51, 149 etc. It is noticeable that another woman-saint Ida (*A. SS. Boll.*, St Ida, June 20) figures as ancestral mother of the Liudolfings, who became kings in Saxony and emperors of Germany, comp. Waitz, *Jahrbücher des deutschen Reichs unter Heinrich I.* 1863, Nachtrag I.

[2] Grimm, J., *Deutsche Mythologie*, 1875, p. 207.

transformed into a chapel. Later she took boat to the place where the Aar, Reuss and Limmat meet, where she dwelt in solitude, and her memory is preserved at a spot called the cell of Verena (Verenazell). Later still she went to dwell at Zurzach, a place which was celebrated for a fair, called Verena's fair, of which more anon. All these places are on or near the river Aar, at no inconsiderable distance from each other. The legend, as told by Stadler, takes them all into account, explaining how Verena came to be connected with each [1].

Similarly the legend of the saint Odilia [2], referred to above in connection with the Hohenburg, explains how the saint comes to be worshipped on both sides of the Rhine, a cruel father having driven her away from home. On the eastern side of the river there is a hill of St Odilia, Odilienberg, where there is a fountain which for its healing powers is visited twice a year and the site of which is guarded by a hermit. At Scherweiler there is also a site hallowed to her worship, and local tradition explains that she stayed there as a child; according to another version she was discovered floating in a wooden chest on the water [3]. Finally she is said to have settled on the Hohenburg west of the Rhine and to have founded a monastery. The critic Roth has written an admirable article on Odilia and the monastery of Hohenburg. He shows that the monastery was ancient and that at first it was dedicated to Christ and St Peter, though afterwards their names were supplanted by that of St Odilia [4]. Here, as on the other side of the Rhine, the folk celebrate her festival by pilgrimages to a fountain which has miraculous healing power, and by giving reverence to a sacred stone, on which Odilia is said to have knelt so long in prayer for the soul of her wicked father, that her knees wore holes in it [5].

We hear that other saints travelled about and stayed now at one place, now at another. St Notburg visited different parts of the Neckar district [6], Godeleva of Ghistelles [7] passed some time of her life in the marshy district between Ostend and Bruges.

---

[1] Stadler und Heim, *Vollständiges Heiligenlexicon*, 1858–82.

[2] *Lebensgeschichte der heil. Othilia.* Freiburg, 1852.

[3] *Alsatia*, 1858–60, p. 268, contains local stories.

[4] Roth, K. L., 'St Odilienberg' in *Alsatia*, 1856, p. 95.

[5] Menzel, *Christliche Symbolik*, article 'Knieen.'

[6] Du Bois de Beauchesne, *Madame Ste Notburg*, 1888, pp. 85, 197 etc. Stadler und Heim, *Vollständiges Heiligenlexicon*, and *A. SS. Boll.* so far, omit her.

[7] Lefebure, F. A., *Ste Godeleine et son culte*, 1888. *A. SS. Boll.*, St Godelewa, July 6.

This Godeleva is addressed in her litany as the saint of marriage ; she was buried, we are told, in a cave, which was held holy as late as the present century.   The pond, into which she was thrown after death, for which act no reason is given, obtained, and still retains, miraculous healing powers[1].   Her legend in other respects offers the usual traits.   She is Godeleva in some parts of the country ; in others she is Godeleina, and her life according to Potthast was written in the 11th century by Drago, a monk of Ghistelles.

It is a curious trait in German saint-legend that the saint is often spoken of as coming from afar—from across the sea, from Britain, from Ireland, even from the Orkney Isles.   It is thus with Ursula of Cöln, Christiane of Dendermonde (Termonde), Lucie of Sampigny and many others.   The idea had taken root at a very early date that St Walburg, whose cult is widespread, was identical with a sister of the missionaries, Wilibald and Wunebald, who went from England to Germany under the auspices of the prelate Boniface in the eighth century.   We shall return to her further on[2].   It is sufficient here to point out that there is little likeness between the sober-minded women-missionaries of Boniface's circle and the woman-saint who is localised under such different aspects, sometimes as a saint whose bones exude oil of miraculous power, sometimes as a valkyrie who anoints warriors for battle, sometimes as a witch who on the first of May leads forth her train to nightly riot on hill tops[3].

Again the love of home industry, which Grimm claims for mother goddesses, is reflected in the legends of many saints, to whose real existence every clue is wanting.   This holds good especially of spinning and of weaving.   Lufthildis, whose date and whose very name are uncertain, is represented as dwelling on a hill-top near a village and marking the limits of her district by means of her spindle, which is preserved and can be seen to this day in the chapel of Luftelberg, the hill which is connected with her[4].   Lucie of Sampigny, to whose shrine women who are sterile make a pilgrimage in order to sit on the stone consecrated to her[5] ; Walburg, referred to above ; Germana, whose cult appears at Bar-sur-Aube[6] ; and one of the numerous localised saints

---

[1] *Wonderlyk Leven.*   Cortryk 1800, anon., pp. 42, 45 etc.

[2] Comp. below, ch. 4, § 2.

[3] Rochholz, L., *Drei Gaugöttinnen*, 1870, pp. 26, 80 etc.

[4] Simrock, K., *Handbuch der deutschen Mythologie*, p. 389.

[5] Clouet, *Histoire de Verdun*, p. 180 ; *A. SS. Boll.*, St Lucie, Sept. 9.

[6] *A. SS. Boll.*, St Germana, Oct. 1 ; Husenbeth, F. C., *Emblems of the Saints*, 1882.

Gertrud[1], are all connected with the distaff. In the church of Frauenkirchen, which stands near the site of the celebrated old abbey of Lach, St Genovefa of Brabant, whose legend is most picturesque and who is in some degree akin to Geneviève of Paris, is believed to be sitting behind the altar from which the buzz of her spinning-wheel is audible[2].

Again the protective interest in silk and agriculture, which Grimm claims for the German goddess, comes out in connection with the pseudo-saint. The harvest festival, so often associated with the Virgin Mary, is frequently also associated with the name of a pseudo-saint. Thus we find these saints represented with ears of corn, as Mary too has been represented[3]. The emblem of the three ears of corn was probably accepted owing to Roman influence. Verena of Zurzach, Notburg of Rottenburg, and Walburg, are all pictured holding a bunch of corn in one hand. Through the intercession of Walburg full barns are secured, while Notburg or Nuppurg of Rottenburg, one of the chief saints of Bavaria, to whose shrine many pilgrimages are made, holds a reaping hook as well as a bunch of corn, and throughout the Tyrol is looked upon as patron saint of the peasantry[4].

At Meerbeck in Brabant corn is blessed before it is sown under the auspices of the saint Berlindis, who protects tree planting. She is a saint of many associations and we shall hear more of her later[5]. In some parts of Brabant seed sown at the time of the new moon in the month of June is protected by the saint Alena. We know little of Alena except that her arm was torn off in expiation of an unknown trespass and is kept as a relic in the church of Voorst, and that the archduchess Maria Anna of Spain sent for this relic in 1685 in the hope of securing a son by means of the saint's intercession[6]. To the shrine of Lufthildis corn is also brought as an offering to be distributed among the poor, while St Gertrud in Belgium protects bean and pea sowing[7].

---

[1] Rochholz, L., *Drei Gaugöttinnen*, p. 164.

[2] Zacher, J., *St Genovefa Pfalzgräfin*, 1860, p. 55.

[3] Menzel, *Christliche Symbolik*, article ' Aehre,' refers to *Notre Dame de trois épis* in Elsass.

[4] Stadler und Heim, *Vollständiges Heiligenlexicon*, St Nothburga, nr 2.

[5] Wauters, A., *Histoire des environs de Bruxelles*, 1, p. 302 ; Corémans, *L'année de l'ancienne Belgique*, 1844, p. 76.

[6] *A. SS. Boll.*, St Alena, June 19; Menzel, W., *Christliche Symbolik*, 1854, article ' Arm.' Corémans, *L'année de l'ancienne Belgique*, 1844, June 19.

[7] Corémans, *L'année etc.*, p. 77.

Further traits in saint worship, which suggest woman's connection with the beginnings of settled civilization, are found in the pseudo-saint's frequent association with cattle and dairy produce.

Peasants, men and women, may be seen to this day touching in reverence the udder of the cow which a rudely cut relief in wood represents by the side of the saint Berlindis at Meerbeck[1]. Gunthild, the patron saint of Biberbach in Würtemburg[2], is represented holding in her hand a milk-jug, the contents of which were inexhaustible during her lifetime. The connection of saints with butter-making is frequent. St Radiane, otherwise called Radegund, is chiefly worshipped at Wellenburg near Augsburg, and her intercession secures milk and butter in plenty to her worshippers. She was torn in pieces by wolves[3].

Judging by her cult and her legends the pseudo-saint practises and protects in endless ways the early arts of settled agriculture and civilization. She herds cattle, she guards flocks of sheep, she weaves and she spins, and she is careful of the dairy. In her representations she is associated with 'emblems' which point to these various interests, and we find her holding corn, a reaping-hook, or a spindle. Domestic animals are pictured by her side, most frequently sheep, geese, cows and dogs. The cat appears rarely[4], perhaps because it was associated with the evil side of woman's power. The besom too, the ancient symbol of woman's authority, is rarely, if ever[5], put into the saint's hands, perhaps for a similar reason.

One other peculiarity remains to be mentioned, which also has its counterpart in the witches' medicinal and curative power. The pseudo-saint's relics (after death) exude oil which is used for medicinal purposes. This peculiarity is noticed of the bones of the saints Walburg[6], Rolendis[7], and Edigna[8], but it is also noticed in connection with the relics of historical saints.

But over and above these traits in the character of the pseudo-saint, legend often points to a heathen custom in connection with

---

[1] Reinsberg-Düringsfeld, *Traditions et légendes de la Belgique*, 1870, vol. 1, p. 99.

[2] *A. SS. Boll.*, St Gunthildis, Sept. 22.

[3] *Imagines SS. Augustanorum*, 1601 ; also Stadler and Heim, *Vollständiges Heiligen-lexicon*, St Radegundis, nr 3.

[4] Pharaildis has been depicted with one, *A. SS. Boll.*, St Pharaildis, Jan. 4 ; also Verena, comp. below.

[5] Husenbeth, F. C., *Emblems of the Saints*, 1870, mentions one instance.

[6] Rochholz, *Drei Gaugöttinnen*, 1870, p. 7.

[7] Stadler und Heim, *Vollständiges Heiligenlexicon* ; *A. SS. Boll.*, St Rolendis, May 13.

[8] *A. SS. Boll.*, St Edigna, Feb. 26.

her of which we have definite information. Tacitus tells how the image of the German goddess Nerthus was carried about on festive occasions in a chariot drawn by cows. The pseudo-saint either during her lifetime or after her death was often similarly conveyed. Sometimes the animals put themselves to her chariot of their own accord, frequently they stopped of their own accord at the particular spot which the saint wished to be her last resting-place. Legend tells us of such incidents in connection also with historical saints, both men and women, and we hear further that the relics of saints sometimes and quite suddenly became so heavy that it was impossible to move them, a sure sign that it was safest not to try.

So far the parallels between mother-goddess and woman pseudo-saint recall the practices of the heathen past, without actually offending against the tenor of Christianity. But the pseudo-saint has other associations of which this cannot be said, associations which are utterly perplexing, unless we go back for their explanation to the ancient tribal usages when the meeting of the tribe was the occasion for settling matters social and sexual. These associations introduce us to an aspect of the cult of the saints which brings primitive usages into an even clearer light, and shows how religious associations continued independently of a change of religion.

§ 3.   Further Peculiarities of this Type of Saint.

The Church, as mentioned above, had put every facility in the way of transforming heathen festivals into its own festal days. The heathen festival in many ways carried on the traditions of the tribal festival; the tribal festival was connected with the cult of tribal goddesses. If we bear in mind the many points mother-goddess, witch, and woman pseudo-saint have in common, the association of the pseudo-saint with practices of a profane character no longer appears wonderful. Both in the turn saint legend takes, and in the character of festivities associated with the saint's name, we discern the survival of ideas which properly belong to differently constituted family and social arrangements, the true meaning of which is all but lost.

On looking through the legends of many women-saints, it is surprising how often we find evil practices and heathen traditions associated with them, practices and traditions which the legend writer naturally is often at a loss to explain in a manner acceptable to Christianity. Thus the father of St Christiane of Dendermonde is said to have set up a temple where girls did service to Venus[1]; doing service to Venus being the usual way of describing licentious pursuits.

In the metrical life of Bilihild, patron saint of Würzburg and Mainz, a description is introduced of the marriage festival as it was celebrated by the Franks in the Main district about the year 600, as this account would have it. Dances took place and unions were contracted for the commencing year. The Christian woman Bilihild was present at the festival, though we are of course told that she found it little to her taste and determined to abolish it[2]. The legend of Bilihild has very primitive traits and is wanting in historical foundation and probability; and it is at least curious that her name should be coupled with a festival which Christian religion and morality must have condemned.

Again it is curious to find how often these women-saints die a violent death, not for conscience sake, nor indeed for any obvious reason at all. Radiane of Wellenburg, as mentioned above, was torn to pieces by wolves[3]; Wolfsindis of Reisbach, according to one account, was tied to wild oxen who tore her to pieces, according to another version of her story she was tied to a horse's tail[4]. St Regina of Alise, in the bishopric of Autun, is sometimes represented surrounded by flames, sometimes in a steaming caldron[5] which recalls the caldron of regeneration of Keltic mythology.

Frequently the saints are said to have been murdered like Cunera of Renen[6], and St Sura otherwise Soteris or Zuwarda of Dordrecht[7]; sometimes their heads are cut off as in the case of Germana worshipped at Beaufort in Champagne[8]; sometimes like Godeleva they are strangled, and sometimes burnt; but Christianity is not the reason assigned for their painful deaths. For even the legend writer does not go so far as to bring in martyrdom at a period and in districts where suffering for the Christian faith is altogether out of the question.

---

[1] *A. SS. Boll.*, St Christiane, July 26.

[2] Rochholz, L., *Drei Gaugöttinnen*, p. 37.

[3] Stadler und Heim, *Vollständiges Heiligenlexicon*, 1858–82, St Radegundis, nr 3.

[4] Ibid., Appendix, p. 998, footnote.

[5] Stadler und Heim, *Vollständiges Heiligenlexicon*, 1858, St Regina, nr 4.

[6] Kist, N. C., 'Reenensche Kuneralegende' in *Kerkhistorisch Archiv*, Amsterdam, 1858, vol. 2, p. 5.

[7] Stadler und Heim, *Vollständiges Heiligenlexicon*, 1858, St Sura.

[8] *A. SS. Boll.*, St Germana, Oct. 1.

Panzer tells us about a group of three women-saints, to whom we shall presently return. He says in some churches masses are read for their souls and prayers offered for their salvation. Though reverenced by the people in many districts of Germany, they are as often said to have been hostile to Christianity as favourably disposed towards it[1].

We find immoral practices and violence ascribed to some of the English women-saints by Capgrave in the 15th century. He says of Inthware or Iuthware, who perhaps belongs to Brittany, that she was accused of being a harlot and put to death. Similarly he says of Osman or Oswen that she was accused of being a witch, but when brought before a bishop she consented to be baptized[2]. Stanton notifies of Iuthware that her translation was celebrated at Shirbourne[3]. Winifred too, who is worshipped in Shropshire, had her head cut off and it rolled right down the hill to a spot where a fountain sprang up, near St Winifred's well. The head however was miraculously replaced, Winifred revived and lived to the end of her days as a nun[4]. The want of information about these women makes it impossible to judge how far their existence is purely legendary ; certainly their stories are largely coloured by heathen traditions. The names Iuthware and Oswen are probably not Germanic ; and the fact of Winifred's living on the confines of Wales makes it probable that she is a Keltic rather than a Germanic saint.

In connection with the festivals of some women pseudo-saints we find celebrations of a decidedly uproarious character taking place at a comparatively recent time. The feast of St Pharaildis, called locally Fru Verelde, used to be the chief holiday at Ghent, and was the occasion for much festivity and merrymaking[5]. At Lüttich (Liège) stood a chapel dedicated to St Balbine, who is said to have been venerated far and wide in the 14th century. On her day, the first of May, there was a festival called Babilone at which dancing was kept up till late at night[6]. The festival of St Godeleva kept at Longuefort maintained even in the 18th century a character which led to a violent dispute between the

---

[1] Panzer, F., *Beitrag zur deutschen Mythologie*, 1848, pp. 5 ff., 272 ff.

[2] Capgrave, *Catalogus SS. Angliae*, 1516.

[3] Stanton, R., *Menology of England and Wales*, 1887.

[4] Capgrave, *Catalogus SS. Angliae*, 1516. Comp. Surius, *Vitae SS.* 1617.

[5] Hautcœur, *Actes de Ste Pharailde*, 1882, Introd. cxxviiii.

[6] Reinsberg-Düringsfeld, *Traditions et légendes de la Belgique*, 1870, vol. 1, p. 288.

populace and the Church dignitaries, who were determined to put it down[1]. Coincident with the festival known as the day of St Berlindis, a saint frequently referred to as a protectress of the peasantry, there is a festival called the Drunken Vespers, in which as early as the 16th century the archbishop forbade his clergy to take part[2].

But by far the most striking and the most conclusive instances of the pseudo-saint's association with heathen survivals are afforded by St Verena of Switzerland and St Afra of Augsburg, whose worship and history we must examine more closely.

Verena's association with various rites has already been referred to; she is represented sometimes with ears of corn, sometimes accompanied by a cat, and sometimes, which is even more suggestive, she is brought into connection with a brothel. The procession of St Verena's day from Zurzach to a chapel dedicated to St Maurice passed an old linden tree which, so the legend goes, marked the spot where the saint used to dwell. Hard by was a house for lepers and a house of ill fame, where on the same day the district bailiff (landvogt) opened the fair. He was obliged by old custom to pass this tree, at which a loose woman stood awaiting him, and to dance round the tree with her and give her money[3].

The legend of St Verena written between 1005 and 1032[4] does not explain these associations. We are told of a woman who came from the east with the Theban legion, which is generally supposed to have been massacred in 287. She is said to have made her home now in one district now in another, and one modern writer goes so far as to suggest that she was zealous in converting the Allemans to Christianity before the coming of Irish missionaries.

According to folk-custom in districts between the Aar and the Rhine, girls who have secured husbands sacrifice their little maiden caps to Verena. At Zurzach married couples make pilgrimages to the Verenastift in order to secure offspring. Several dukes of the Allemans and their wives made such pilgrimages in the 9th and 10th centuries. It would lead too far to enumerate the many directions in which Verena is associated with heathendom. Her day, which comes at the harvest festival, was a time of un-

---

[1] Lefebure, *Ste Godeleine et son culte*, p. 209.

[2] Wauters, A., *Histoire des environs de Bruxelles*, 1852, vol. I, p. 304.

[3] Rochholz, *Drei Gaugöttinnen*, 1870, p. 154.

[4] Potthast, *Wegweiser durch die Geschichtswerke des europ. Mittelalters*, 1862; Rochholz, *loc. cit.*, p. 108, prints an early poetic version of the story in the vernacular.

restrained license in Zurzach, a fact on which the *Acta Sanctorum* cast no doubt.

Rochholz considers Verena to be a tribal mother of heathendom; Simrock in his mythology considers her to be identical with the goddess Fru Frene, in whom he sees a kind of German Venus[1]. Grimm tells how the version of the Tannhäuser saga, current in Switzerland, substitutes the name Frau Frene for that of Frau Venus[2]. The hero Tannhäuser, according to mediæval legend, wavers between a baser and a higher interpretation of love; the acceptance of the name Frene as representative of sensuousness shows the associations currently preserved in connection with this so-called saint.

A similar association occurs in Belgium, where a saint Vreken (*Sint Vreke*), otherwise Vrouw Vreke, in mediæval legend is the representative of sensual as opposed to spiritual love. Corémans describes how in the version of the saga of the faithful Eckhardt (*Van het trouwen Eckhout*) current in Belgium, the hero wavers between spiritual love of Our Lady and sensual love of Vreke. Among the folk Vrouw Vreke is a powerful personage, for the story goes that the Kabauters, evil spirits who dwell on the Kabauterberg, are in her service. In the book *Reta de Limbourg*, which was re-written in the 17th century, the Kabauterberg becomes a Venusberg, and Vreke is no longer a great witch (*eene grote heks*) but a goddess with all the alluring charms of Venus[3]. Grimm includes a Fru Freke among his German goddesses[4]. She retains her old importance among the folk as a protective saint and presides over tree-planting[5].

Like the saints Verena and Vreke, St Afra of Augsburg is associated with licentiousness; Wessely expressly calls her the patron saint of hetairism[6]. Her legend explains the connection in a peculiar manner; as told by Berno, abbot of Reichenau (✝1048), it is most picturesque. We hear how Afra and her mother came from Cyprus, an island which mediæval, following the classical writers, associated with the cult of Venus, and how she settled at Augsburg and kept a house of ill fame with

---

[1] Simrock, K., *Handbuch der deutschen Mythologie*, 1887, p. 393.

[2] Grimm, J., *Deutsche Mythologie*, 1875, p. 254, footnote.

[3] Corémans, *L'année de l'ancienne Belgique*, pp. 61, 113, 158.

[4] Grimm, J., *Deutsche Mythologie*, 1875, p. 252.

[5] Corémans, *L'année de l'ancienne Belgique*, p. 76; Stadler und Heim, *Vollständiges Heiligenlexicon*, and the *A. SS. Boll.* pass her over.

[6] Wessely, J. G., *Iconographie Gottes und der Heiligen*, 1874.

three companions. Here they entertained certain Church dignitaries (otherwise unknown to history) who persuaded the women to embrace Christianity and give up their evil practices. They became virtuous, and when persecutions against Christians were instituted they all suffered martyrdom; Afra was placed on a small island and burnt at the stake[1]. The legend writer on the basis of the previous statement places the existence of these women in the early part of the fourth century during the reign of Diocletian. Curiously enough the legend of Afra is led up to by a description of the worship of the heathen goddess Zisa, a description to which Grimm attaches great importance[2]. This goddess was worshipped at or near Augsburg. Velserus[3], who in the 16th century compiled a chronicle of Augsburg, gives us a mass of information about traditions connected with her and her worship, as he also does about St Afra. There is in his mind of course no shadow of a suspicion of any connection between them. But he informs us that the Zizenberg, or hill of Zisa, and the Affenwald which he interprets as Afrawald or wood of Afra, are one and the same place.

Berno also wrote a life of Ulrich (St Udalricus), bishop of Augsburg (†973), who boldly defended the town at the time of the invasion of the Hungarians. In this life the bishop has a miraculous vision of St Afra, who takes him on a pilgrimage by night and points out the site where he afterwards founded a monastery, known to later ages as the monastery of St Ulrich and St Afra. The worship of Afra is referred to by the poet Fortunatus as early as the sixth century; the story of the saint's martyrdom is older than that of her conversion. The historian Rettberg is puzzled why so much stress should be laid on her evil ways[4]; but the historian Friedrich, regardless of perplexing associations, sees the beginnings of convent life for women in Augsburg in the fact of Afra and her companions dwelling together between their conversion and martyrdom[5].

There are other traits in saint legend which point to the customs and arrangements of a more primitive period, and tempt

---

[1] *A. SS. Boll.*, St Afra, Aug. 5.

[2] Grimm, J., *Deutsche Mythologie*, 1875, p. 242.

[3] Velserus, *Antiqua monumenta, Chronica der Stadt Augsp.* 1595; pp. 4, 14, 17, 32, 88.

[4] Rettberg, F. W., *Kirchengeschichte*, 1846, vol. 1, p. 147.

[5] Friedrich, *Kirchengeschichte*, 1867, vol. 1, p. 413.

the student to fit together pieces of the past and the present which appear meaningless if taken separately.

It seems probable that in early times the term mother was applied to a number of women of a definite group by all the children of the group, and that the word had not the specialized meaning of one who had actually borne the children who termed her mother.

The story of a number of children all being born at once by one woman is possibly due to a confused tradition dating from this period. In local saga, both in Germany and elsewhere, there are stories in which a woman suddenly finds herself in the possession of a number of offspring, and often with direful consequences to herself, because of the anger of her husband. The same incident has found its way into saint legend. Thus Notburg, patron saint of Sulz, had at a birth a number of children, variously quoted as nine, twelve and thirty-six. Stadler says that she is represented at Sulz holding eight children in her arms, a ninth one lying dead at her feet[1]. Lacking water to christen these children, she produced from the hard rock a fountain which even to the present day is believed to retain the power to cure disease.

A similar story is told of Achachildis, popularly known as Atzin, who is held in veneration at Wendelstein near Schwabach. She bore her husband five children at once and then took a vow of continence. Her legend has never been written, but she enjoys a great reputation for holiness, and a series of pictures represent various incidents in her life[2].

Images of women sheltering children, usually beneath their cloaks, are frequently found abroad built into the outer wall of the church, the place where Christian teachers felt justified in placing heathen images[3]. Students of pictorial art will here recall the image of St Ursula at Cöln sheltering 11,000 virgins under her cloak.

Again there are other emblems in saint worship which cannot be easily accounted for, such for instance as the holy combs of Verena and Pharaildis, which remind one of the comb with which the witch Lorelei sat combing her hair, or, on classic soil, of the comb of the Venus Calvata; or the holy slippers of St Radiane, which

---

[1] Stadler und Heim, *Vollständiges Heiligenlexicon*, 1858, St Notburg, nr 1. *A. SS. Boll.*, St Notburga, Jan. 26.

[2] Stadler und Heim, *Vollständiges Heiligenlexicon*, 1858, Appendix, St Achachildis.

[3] Birlinger, A., *Schwäbische Sagen*, vol. 2, p. 341.

are preserved to this day in the church of Wellenburg and which, as Stadler informs us, had been re-soled within his time[1]. Slippers and shoes are ancient symbols of appropriation, and as such figure in folk-lore and at weddings in many countries to this day. The golden slipper was likewise a feature at the witches' festival, in which the youthful fiddler also figured[2]. Both the golden slipper and the youthful fiddler form important features in the legend of the saint Ontkommer or Wilgefortis. The images and legend of this saint are so peculiar that they claim a detailed account.

It is evident from what has been said that the legends and cult of many women pseudo-saints have traits in common; indeed the acts ascribed to different saints are often exactly similar. The stories of Notburg of Rottenburg, of Radiane of Wellenburg, and of Gunthild of Biberbach, as Stadler remarks, are precisely alike; yet it is never suggested that these saints should be treated as one; each of them has her place in the *Acta Sanctorum* and is looked upon as distinct from the others.

There is, however, a set of women-saints whose images and legends have features so distinctive that hagiologists treat of them collectively as one, though they are held in veneration in districts widely remote from each other, and under very dissimilar names.

The saint, who is venerated in the Low Countries as Ont-kommer or Wilgefortis, is usually considered identical with the saint Kümmerniss of Bavaria and the Tyrol; with the saint Livrade, Liberata or Liberatrix venerated in some districts of France as early as the 9th century when Usuard, writing in the monastery of St Germain-des-Près, mentions her; with Gehulff of Mainz; with Hilp of the Hülfensberg at Eichsfelde; and with others called variously Regenfled, Regenfrith, Eutropia, etc.[3] The name Maria-hilf, which is very common in south Germany, is probably a combination of the name of the Virgin Mother with that of St Hilp or St Gehulff.

The legends of this saint, or rather of this assembly of saints, are characterized by Cuper in the *Acta Sanctorum* as an endless labyrinth[4]. Whatever origin be ascribed to them, when once we examine them closely we find explanation impossible on the hypothesis

---

[1] Stadler und Heim, *Vollständiges Heiligenlexicon*, 1858, St Radegundis, nr 3.
[2] Grimm, J., *Deutsche Mythologie*, 1875, p. 896.
[3] Stadler und Heim, *Vollständiges Heiligenlexicon*, 1858, St Kumernissa.
[4] *A. SS. Boll.*, St Liberata, July 20.

that they relate to a single Christian woman living during Christian times.

A considerable amount of information on this group of saints has lately been collected by Sloet, who deals also with their iconography[1]. The peculiarity of the images of Ontkommer or Kümmerniss consists in this, that she is represented as crucified, and that the lower part of her face is covered by a beard, and her body in some instances by long shaggy fur. Her legend explains the presence of the beard and fur by telling us that it grew to protect the maiden from the persecutions of a lover or the incestuous love of her father; such love is frequently mentioned in the legends of women pseudo-saints.

The fact that Ontkommer or Kümmerniss is represented as crucified might be explained on the hypothesis that the common folk could not at first grasp the idea of a god and looked upon Christ as a woman, inventing the legend of the woman's persecution and miraculous protection in order to account for the presence of the beard. But other accessories of the representations of Ontkommer or Kümmerniss lead us to suppose that her martyrdom, like that of other saints, has a different origin and that she is heiress to a tribal goddess of the past[2].

In many of her representations Ontkommer or Kümmerniss is seen hanging on the cross with only one golden slipper on, but sometimes she wears two slippers, and a young man is sitting below the cross playing the fiddle. Legend accounts for the presence of this young man in the following manner. He came and sat at the foot of the image and was playing on his fiddle, when the crucified saint suddenly awoke to life, drew off a slipper and flung it to him. He took it away with him, but he was accused of having stolen it and condemned to death. His accusers however agreed to his request to come with him into the presence of the holy image, to which he appealed. Again the crucified saint awoke to life and drew off her second slipper and flung it to the fiddler, whose innocence was thereby vindicated and he was set free. Where shall we go for a clue to this curious and complicated legend? Grimm tells us that a young fiddler was present at a festival

---

[1] Sloet, *De heilige Ontkommer of Wilgeforthis*, 1884.

[2] I cannot account for the presence of the beard; St Paula, venerated at Avila in Spain, is also represented with one (Stadler und Heim). Macrobius (*Sat.* bk 3, c. 8) tells us that the Venus Barbata was represented in Cyprus in the form of a man with a beard and wearing female clothing, which shows that goddesses of this type were venerated during heathen times.

of the witches, and that he played at the dance in which he was not allowed to take part. Grimm also tells us that one of the witches on this occasion wore only one golden slipper[1]. The association of Kümmerniss with a golden slipper is deep-rooted, especially in Bavaria, for the saying goes there that 'She with the golden slipper and with the youthful fiddler is also a mother of God[2].'

Many years ago Menzel wrote[3]: 'Much I believe concerning this saint is derived from heathen conceptions.' Stories embodying heathen traditions are preserved in connection with this saint in districts abroad that lie far apart.

Thus the image of her which is preserved in North Holland is said to have come floating down the river, like the images of the Virgin referred to above. At Regensburg in Bavaria an image is preserved which is said to have been cast into the water at Neufarn. It was carried down by the river and thrown on the bank, and the bishop fetched it to Regensburg on a car drawn by oxen. In the Tyrol the image of the saint is sometimes hung in the chief bed-room of the house in order to secure a fruitful marriage, but often too it is hung in chapel and cloister in order to protect the dead. Images of the saint are preserved and venerated in a great number of churches in Bavaria and the Tyrol, but the ideas popularly associated with them have raised feelings in the Church against their cult. We hear that a Franciscan friar in the beginning of this century destroyed one of the images, and that the bishop of Augsburg in 1833 attempted in one instance to do away with the image and the veneration of the saint, but refrained from carrying out his intention, being afraid of the anger of the people[4].

It has been mentioned above that associations of a twofold character survive in connection with Verena and Vreke, who are to this day popularly reckoned as saints, but who are introduced in mediæval romance as representatives of earthly love as contrasted with spiritual. Associations of a twofold character have also been attached to the term Kümmerniss. For in the Tyrol Kümmerniss is venerated as a saint, but the word Kümmerniss in ordinary parlance is applied to immoral women[5].

---

[1] Grimm, J., *Deutsche Mythol.* 1875, p. 896.
[2] Sloet, *De heilige Ontkommer of Wilgeforthis*, 1884, p. 36.
[3] Menzel, W., *Christl. Symbolik*, 1854, article 'Bart.'
[4] Sloet, *De heilige Ontkommer of Wilgeforthis*, 1884, pp. 31, 33, 36, 42 etc.
[5] Ibid. p. 32.

Other heathen survivals are found attached to the Ontkommer-Kümmerniss group of saints. At Luzern the festival of the saint was connected with so much riotous merrymaking and licentiousness that it was forbidden in 1799 and again in 1801. The story is told of the saint under the name Liberata that she was one of a number of children whom her mother had at a birth[1].

Sloet, on the authority of the philologist Kern, considers that the various names by which the saint is known in different districts are appellatives and have the same underlying meaning of one who is helpful in trouble. According to him this forms the connecting link between the names Ontkommer, Kümmerniss, Wilgefortis, Gehulff, Eutropia, etc., of which the form Ontkommer, philologically speaking, most clearly connotes the saint's character, and on this ground is declared to be the original form. The saint is worshipped at Steenberg in Holland under the name Ontkommer, and Sloet is of opinion that Holland is the cradle of the worship of the whole group of saints[2]. But considering what we know of other women-saints it seems more probable that the saints who have been collected into this group are the outcome of a period of social evolution, which in various districts led to the establishment of tribal goddesses, who by a later development assumed the garb of Christian women-saints.

The cult of women-saints under one more aspect remains to be chronicled. Numerous traditions are preserved concerning the cult of holy women in triads, who are locally held in great veneration and variously spoken of as three sisters, three ladies, three Marys, three nuns, or three women-saints.

The three holy women have a parallel in the three Fates of classic mythology and in the three Norns of Norse saga, and like them they probably date from a heathen period. Throughout Germany they frequently appear in folk-lore and saga, besides being venerated in many instances as three women-saints of the Church.

In stories now current these three women are conceived sometimes as sisters protecting the people, sometimes as ladies guarding treasures, and sometimes as a group of three nuns living together

---

[1] Stadler und Heim, *Vollständiges Heiligenlexicon*, 1858, St Liberata, footnote, p. 807.

[2] Sloet, *De heilige Ontkommer of Wilgeforthis*, 1884, pp. 5, 50 etc. Ellis, H., *Original Letters*, series III, vol. 3, p. 194, quotes the following sentence from Michael Woddes, *Dialogues*, 1554: '...if a wife were weary of her husband she offered Otes at Poules (St Paul's) at London to St Uncumber,' a proof that the veneration of Ontkommer had found its way into England.

and founding chapels and oratories, and this too in places where history knows nothing of the existence of any religious settlement of women.

Panzer has collected a mass of information on the cult of the triad as saints in southern Germany[1]; Corémans says that the veneration of the Three Sisters (*dry-susters*) is widespread in Belgium[2], but the Church has sanctioned this popular cult in comparatively few instances.

The story is locally current that these three women were favourably disposed to the people and bequeathed to them what is now communal property. Simrock considers that this property included sites which were held sacred through association with a heathen cult[3]. 'In heathen times,' he says, 'a sacred grove was hallowed to the sister fates which after the establishment of Christianity continued to be the property of the commune. The remembrance of these helpful women who were the old benefactresses of the place remained, even their association with holiness continued.' By these means in course of time the cult of the three goddesses was transformed into that of Christian saints.

Besides bequeathing their property to the people it was thought that these three women-saints protected their agricultural and domestic interests, especially as affecting women. In Schlehdorf in Lower Bavaria pilgrimages by night were made to the shrine of the triad to avert the cattle plague ; the shrine stood on a hill which used to be surrounded by water, and at one time was the site of a celebrated fair and the place chosen for keeping the harvest festival[4]. At Brusthem in Belgium there were three wells into which women who sought the aid of these holy women cast three things, linen-thread, a needle and some corn[5]. Again in Schildturn in Upper Bavaria an image of the three women-saints is preserved in the church which bears an inscription to the effect that through the intercession of these saints offspring are secured and that they are helpful at childbirth[6]. In the same church a wooden cradle is kept which women who wished to become mothers used to set

[1] Panzer, F., *Beitrag zur deutschen Mythologie,* 1848, pp. 5 ff., 272 ff.
[2] Corémans, *L'année de l'ancienne Belgique,* 1844, p. 149.
[3] Simrock, K., *Handbuch der deutschen Myth.,* 1887, p. 344.
[4] Panzer, F., *Beitrag zur deutschen Myth.,* 1848, p. 23.
[5] Corémans, *L'année de l'ancienne Belgique,* 1844, p. 148.
[6] Panzer, F., *Beitrag zur deutschen Myth.,* 1848, pp. 69 ff.

rocking. A second cradle which is plated is kept in the sacristy, and has been substituted for one of real silver[1].

In some districts one of these three saints is credited with special power over the others either for good or for evil. The story goes that one of the sisters was coloured black or else black and white[2].

In many places where the triad is worshipped the names of the individual sisters are lost, while in districts far apart from one another, as the Tyrol, Elsass, Bavaria, their names have considerable likeness. The forms generally accepted, but liable to fluctuation, are St Einbeth, St Warbeth and St Wilbeth[3]. The Church in some instances seems to have hesitated about accepting these names, it may be from the underlying meaning of the suffix *beth* which Grimm interprets as holy site, *ara, fanum*, but Mannhardt connects it with the word to pray (beten)[4]. Certainly the heathen element is strong when we get traditions of the presence of these women at weddings and at burials, and stories of how they went to war, riding on horses, and achieved even more than the men[5]. Where their claim to Christian reverence is admitted by the Church, the stories told about them have a very different ring.

According to the legend which has been incorporated into the *Acta Sanctorum*, St Einbetta, St Verbetta, and St Villbetta were Christian maidens who undertook the pilgrimage to Rome with St Ursula, with whose legend they are thus brought into connection. The three sisters stayed behind at Strasburg and so escaped the massacre of the 11000 virgins[6].

The tendency to group women-saints into triads is very general. Kunigund, Mechtund and Wibrandis are women-saints who belong to the portion of Baden in the diocese of Constance[7]. The locus of their cult is in separate villages, but they are venerated as a triad in connection with a holy well and lie buried together under an ancient oak[8]. We hear also of pilgrimages being made to the image of three holy sisters preserved at Auw on the Kyll in the valley of the Mosel. They are represented as sitting side by side on the back

---

[1] Cradles are frequently kept in churches in Bavaria, and form, I am told, part of the furniture which was formerly used at the celebration of the Nativity play at Christmas (Weihnachtskrippenspiel).

[2] Panzer, F., *Beitrag zur deutschen Myth.*, 1848, p. 273.

[3] Simrock, K., *Handbuch der deutschen Myth.*, 1887, pp. 344, 349, gives lists of their names.

[4] Grimm, *Wörterbuch*, 'Bett'; Mannhardt, W., *Germanische Mythen*, 1858, p. 644.

[5] Panzer, F., *Beitrag zur deutschen Mythol.*, 1848, p. 180.

[6] *A. SS. Boll.*, St Einbetta, Sept. 16.

[7] *A. SS. Boll.*, St Kunegundis, June 16.

[8] Panzer, *Beitrag zur deutschen Myth.*, 1848, p. 379.

of an ass(?), one of them having a cloth tied over her eyes. The three sisters in this case are known as Irmina, Adela and Chlotildis, and it is said they were the daughters or sisters of King Dagobert[1]. Irmina and Adela are historical; they founded nunneries in the diocese of Trier.

In another instance the sisters are called Pellmerge, Schwellmerge and Krischmerge, *merg* being a popular form of the name Mary which is preserved in many place-names[2].

I have been able to discover little reference to local veneration of saints in a triad in England. But there is a story that a swineherd in Mercia had a vision in a wood of three women who, as he believed, were the three Marys, and who pointed out to him the spot where he was to found a religious settlement, which was afterwards known as Evesham.

A curious side-light is thrown on the veneration of the three women-saints abroad by recalling the images and inscriptions about Mothers and Matrons, which are preserved on altars fashioned long before the introduction of Christianity under heathen influence.

These altars have been found in outlying parts of the Roman Empire, especially in the districts contiguous to the ancient boundary line which divided Roman territory from Germania Magna. They bear inscriptions in Latin to the effect that they are dedicated to Mothers and Matrons, and sometimes it is added that they have been set up at the command of these divine Mothers themselves. The words *imperio ipsarum*, 'by their own command,' are added to the formula of dedication, and as it seems that they never occur on altars set up and dedicated to specified Roman or Gallo-Roman divinities, they yield an interesting proof of the wide-spread character of the worship of tribal goddesses[3].

At one time it was supposed that these altars were of Keltic origin, but some of the tribes mentioned in their inscriptions have been identified with place-names in Germany. Altars found in outlying parts of the Empire primarily served for the use of the soldiery, for sacrifice at the altar of the gods was a needful preliminary to Roman military undertakings. The view has been

---

[1] Menck-Dittmarsch, *Des Moselthals Sagen*, 1840, pp. 178, 258.

[2] Grimm, *Wörterbuch*, ' Marge.'

[3] Lersch, *Centralmuseum rheinl. Inschriften*, vol. 1, p. 23; also *Jahrbücher des Vereins von Altertumsfreunden im Rheinlande*, Bonn: J. 1852, Freudenberg, ' Darstellungen der Matres oder Matronae'; J. 1853, ' Neue Matronensteine'; J. 1857, Eick, ' Matronensteine'; J. 1858, Becker, ' Beiträge' etc.

advanced that, as the altars dedicated to pagan divinities served for the devotions of the Roman and Gallo-Roman troops, it is possible that these other altars dedicated to Mothers served for the devotions of the German heathen soldiery, who were drafted from districts beyond the Rhine, and at an early date made part of the Roman legions.

The parallels between the mothers of the stones and the three women-saints are certainly remarkable.

Where a representation, generally in rude relief, occurs on the altar stones, the Mothers are represented in a group of three, holding as emblems of their power fruit, flowers, and the spindle. These recall the emblems both of the heathen goddess of mythology and of the pseudo-saint. Moreover one of the Mothers of the altars is invariably distinguished by some peculiarity, generally by a want of the head-dress or head-gear worn by the two others, perhaps indicative of her greater importance. This has its parallel in the peculiar power with which one member of the saint triad is popularly credited.

The erection of the altars belongs to a time before the introduction of Christianity ; our information about the three women-saints dates back earlier than the 12th century in a few cases only ; it chiefly depends on stories locally current which have been gleaned within the last hundred years. If the hypothesis of the mother-age preceding the father-age holds good, if the divine Mothers imaged on the stones are witnesses to a wide-spread worship of female deities during the period of established Roman rule, these tales told of the triad carry us back nearly twenty centuries. The power ascribed to tribal goddesses in a distant heathen past survived in the power ascribed to Christian women-saints; the deep-rooted belief in protective women-divinities enduring with undying persistence in spite of changes of religion.

In conclusion, a few words may be acceptable on the names of pseudo-saints, which I believe to be largely epithetic or appellative. Grimm holds that the names of the German goddesses were originally appellatives. In a few cases the name of the goddess actually becomes the name of a saint. Mythology and hagiology both lay claim to a Vrene and a Vreke; but from the nature of things these cases are rare. The conception of the protective divinity is ancient; her name in a philological sense is comparatively new.

With few exceptions the names are German; sometimes in contiguous districts variations of the same name are preserved. The saint Lufthildis is sometimes Linthildis[1]; Rolendis is sometimes Dollendis[2]; Ida, Itta, Iduberga, Gisleberga are saints of Brabant and Flanders, whom hagiologists have taken great trouble to keep separate. In some cases the name of a real and that of a fictitious person may have become confounded. The names are all cognate with the word *itis*, an ancient term applied to the woman who exercised sacred functions.

The attempt to connect the group Ontkommer-Wilgefortis by the underlying meaning of the several names has been mentioned. It has also been mentioned that this saint is sometimes spoken of as a mother of God. Similarly St Geneviève of Paris is worshipped as Notre-Dame-la-petite, and again the saint Cunera of Reenen is popularly known as Knertje, which signifies little lady[3].

On every side the student is tempted to stray from the straightforward road of fact into the winding paths of speculation. The frequent association abroad of female deities with hill tops suggests a possible explanation why the word *berg*, which means remoteness and height, so often forms part of the name of the woman pseudosaint, and of women's names generally. For the beginnings of tilth and agriculture are now sought not in the swampy lowlands, but on the heights where a clearance brought sunlight and fruitfulness. Hill tops to this day are connected with holy rites. Is it possible that the word *berg*, designating hill top, should have become an appellative for woman because the settlements on the hills were specially connected with her?

Philology hitherto has been content to trace to a common origin words cognate in different languages, and on the conceptions attaching to these words, to build up theories about the state of civilization of various peoples at a period previous to their dispersion from a common home. But the study of local beliefs and superstitions in western Europe tends more and more to prove that usages pointing to a very primitive mode of life and to a very primitive state of civilization are indissolubly connected with certain sites; and that the beginnings of what we usually term civilization, far from being imported, have largely developed on native soil.

Thus, at the very outset of our enquiry into saint-worship and the convent life of the past, we have found ourselves confronted by a class of women-saints who must be looked upon as survivals from

---

[1] Stadler und Heim, *Vollständiges Heiligenlexicon*, 1858, St Lufthildis.
[2] Ibid. St Rolendis.
[3] *A. SS. Boll.*, St Cunera, June 12.

heathen times, and who are in no way connected with the beginnings of Christianity and of convent life ; their reputation rests on their connection with some hallowed site of the heathen period and the persistence of popular faith in them. But the feeling underlying the attribution of holiness to them, the desire for localized saints, yields the clue to the ready raising to saintship of those women who in England, in France, and in Germany, showed appreciation of the possibilities offered to them by Christianity, and founded religious settlements. In some cases superstitions of a heathen nature which are of value to the hagiologist, if not to the historian, cling to these women also, but fortunately a considerable amount of trustworthy material is extant about their lives. These women during the earliest period were zealous in the cause of Christianity, and it is to them that our enquiry now turns.

CHAPTER II.

CONVENTS AMONG THE FRANKS, A.D. 550—650.

'Sicut enim apis diversa genera florum congregabat, unde mella conficiat, sic illa ab his quos invitabat spirituales studebat carpere flosculos, unde boni operis fructum tam sibi quam suis sequacibus exhiberet.'

The nun Baudonivia on St Radegund (Vita, c. 13).

§ 1. At the Frankish Invasion[1].

THE great interest of early monastic life among the Franks lies in the conversion of this hardy and ferocious people to Christianity just at the moment of their emergence from a state of barbarism. Fierce, warlike and progressive, the Franks were brought face to face with cultured Latinity. The clerical student who claimed direct descent from the Gallo-Roman rhetorician, and the bishop who was in possession of the municipal government of the town, found themselves confronted by shaggy-haired, impetuous men from forest wilds. At the outset an all but immeasurable distance separated the social and intellectual development of the Gallo-Roman from that of these strangers. Compared with the cultivated man of letters and with the veteran, grown grey in imperial service, the German invader was little more than a savage; nevertheless he succeeded in holding his own. At first his standards of life and conduct gave way before those of the Gallo-Romans. The lives of early Frankish princes, as their contemporary, the historian Gregory of Tours, depicts them, are marked by ceaseless quarrels and feuds, by numberless instances of murder, perjury and violence. The bonds of union among them were forcibly relaxed, as often happens in those periods of history when restraint and responsibility are broken through by a sudden and overwhelming inrush of new ideas. A prey to intemperance and greed, the descendants of the

---

[1] Fustel de Coulanges, *L'invasion germanique*, 1891; Gérard, P. A. F., *Histoire des Francs d'Austrasie*, 1864; Ozanam, *Civilisation chrétienne chez les Francs*, 1855.

great Merovech dwindled away.   But other men of the same race, stronger than they in mind and less prone to enervating luxury, pressed in from behind.   And after the temporary mental and moral collapse which followed upon the occupation of Gaul by the Franks, the race rose to new and increased vigour.   New standards of conduct were evolved and new conceptions of excellence arose, through the mingling of Latin and German elements.   For the great Roman civilization, a subject of wonder and admiration to all ages, was in many of its developments realized, appropriated, and assimilated by the converted Germans.   Three hundred years after their appearance in Gaul, the Franks were masters of the cultivated western world ; they had grasped the essentials of a common nationality and had spread abroad a system of uniform government.

The Franks at first showed a marked deficiency in the virtues which pagan Rome had established, and to which Christianity had given a widened and spiritualized meaning.   Temperance, habitual self-control and the absorption of self in the consciousness of a greater, formed no part of this people's character.   These virtues, together with peaceableness and a certain simplicity of taste, laid the groundwork of the monasticism which preceded the invasion. Persons who were vowed to religion were averse to war, because it disturbed study and industry, and they shrank from luxury of life, because it interrupted routine by exciting their appetites.   An even tenor of life was the golden mean they set before themselves, and in some degree they had realized it in Roman Gaul before the barbarian invasion.

The Frank at first felt little tempted in the direction of monastic life.   His fierce and warlike tendencies, love of personal predominance and glory, and impatience of every kind of restraint, were directly opposed to the uniform round of devotion and work to which the religious devotee conformed.

The attitude of Frankish men towards monasticism was at best passive ; on the other hand convent life from the first found sympathy among Frankish women.   Princesses of pure German blood and of undisputed German origin left the royal farms, which were the court residences of the period, and repaired to the religious houses, to devote themselves to religion and to the learning of cultured Latinity.   Not one of the princes of the royal Frankish race entered a convent of his own accord, but their wives, widows, and daughters readily joined houses of religion.

Meekness and devotion, self-denial and subservience are not the most prominent features in the character of these women. The wives and daughters of men to whom Macaulay attributes all vices and no virtues, are of a temper which largely savours of the world. What distinguishes them is quick determination and clear-sighted appreciation of the possibilities opened out to them by the religious life. Fortunately the information which we have concerning them is not confined to the works of interested eulogists. Accounts of women whom posterity estimated as saints lay stress on those sides of their character which are in accord with virtues inculcated by the Church. But we have other accounts besides these about women who had taken the vows of religion, but whose behaviour called forth violent denunciations from their contemporaries. And over and above these, passages in profane literature are extant which curiously illustrate the worldly tone and temper of many women who had adopted religion as a profession.

These women were driven to resort to convents chiefly as the result of their contact with a great civilization, which threw open unknown and tempting possibilities to men, but raised many difficulties in the way of women.

The resources of the districts acquired by the Franks were immeasurably greater than those of the lands they had left. Wealth and intemperance readily join hands. The plurality of recognised and unrecognised wives in which the Frankish princes indulged resulted in great family difficulties. The royal farms and the ancient cities, where these petty kings resided, were the scenes of continual broils and squabbles in which royal wives and widows took the leading parts. From the chequered existence which this state of things implies, convent life alone afforded a permanent refuge. Sometimes a princess left home from a sense of the indignities she was made to suffer; sometimes a reverse of fortune caused her to accept, willingly or unwillingly, the dignified retirement of the cloister.

During the centuries preceding the Frankish conquest the development of religious and monastic life in Gaul had been considerable, for the Church had practically appropriated what was left of the Roman system of organization, and since this system had been chiefly municipal, the municipal bodies were largely composed of bishops and clerks.

The monastic life of men in Gaul had a number of independent centres in the western provinces, due to the enthusiastic zeal of St Martin of Tours († 400), to whom reference has been made.

In the beginning of the 6th century a settlement of nuns was founded in the south, where monasteries already existed, perhaps as the result of direct contact with the east. A rule of life was drafted for this convent shortly after its foundation.

Caesarius, bishop of Arles (501–573), had persuaded his sister Caesaria to leave Marseilles, where she dwelt in a convent associated with the name of Cassian. His plan was that she should join him at Arles, and preside over the women who had gathered there to live and work under his guidance.

Caesarius now marked out a scheme of life for his sister and those women whom she was prepared to direct. He arranged it, as he says himself, according to the teachings of the fathers of the Church and, after repeated modifications, he embodied it in a set of rules, which have come down to us[1]. Great clearness and directness, a high moral tone, and much sensible advice are contained in these precepts of Caesarius. 'Since the Lord,' he says, addressing himself to the women, 'has willed to inspire us and help us to found a monastery for you, in order that you may abide in this monastery, we have culled spiritual and holy injunctions for you from the ancient fathers; with God's help may you be sheltered, and dwelling in the cells of your monastery, seeking in earnest prayer the presence of the Son of God, may you say in faith, "we have found him whom we sought." Thus may you be of the number of holy virgins devoted to God, who wait with tapers alight and a calm conscience, calling upon the Lord.—Since you are aware that I have worked towards establishing this monastery for you, let me be one of you through the intercession of your prayer.'

Caesarius goes on to stipulate that those who join the community, whether they be maidens or widows, shall enter the house once for all and renounce all claims to outside property. Several paragraphs of the rule are devoted to settling questions of property, a proof of its importance in the mind of Caesarius. There were to be in the house only those who of their own accord accepted the routine and were prepared to live on terms of strictest equality without property or servants of their own.

Children under the age of six or seven were not to be received

---

[1] *A. SS. Boll.*, St Caesaria, Jan. 12, *Regula*, pp. 730–737; also *A. SS. Boll.*, St Caesarius episcopus, Aug. 27.

at all, 'nor shall daughters of noble parentage or lowly-born girls be taken in readily to be brought up and educated.'

This latter injunction shows how the religious at this period wished to keep the advantages to be derived from artistic and intellectual training in their own community. They had no desire for the spread of education, which forms so characteristic a feature of the religious establishments of a later date.

After their safe housing the instruction of the nuns at Arles was the most important matter dealt with in the 'rule.' Considerable time and thought were devoted to the practice of chants and to choir-singing, for the art of music was considered especially fitted to celebrate God. In an appendix to the rule of Caesarius the system of singing is described as similar to that adopted in the cœnobite settlement at Lerins[1]. Apparently following Keltic usage, the chant was taken up in turn by relays of the professed, who kept it up night and day all the year round in perpetual praise of the Divinity. At this period melody and pitch were the subjects of close study and much discussion. The great debt owed by the art of music to the enthusiasm of these early singers is often overlooked.

The women who joined the community at Arles also learned reading and writing ('omnes litteras· discant'). These arts were practised in classes, while domestic occupations, such as cooking, were performed in turns. Weaving, probably that of church hangings, was among the arts practised, and the women also spun wool and wove it into material with which they made garments for their own use.

There are further injunctions about tending the infirm, and stern advice about the hatefulness of quarrels. Intercourse with the outside world is restricted, but is not altogether cut off.

'Dinners and entertainments,' says the rule, 'shall not be provided for churchmen, laymen and friends, but women from other religious houses may be received and entertained.'

In the year 506 Caesarius, the author of this rule, was present at the synod of Agde at which it was decreed that no nun however good in character should receive the veil, that is be permanently bound by a vow, before her fortieth year[2]. This decree, taken together with the rule, proves the sober and serious spirit of

---

[1] *A. SS. Boll.*, St Caesaria, Jan. 12, *Regula*, c. 66.

[2] Guettée, *Histoire de l'Église de France*, 1847, vol. 2, 46; Labbé, *Sacr. Conc. Collectio*, Conc. Agathense, canon nr 19.

these early settlements and the purpose which their founder set before him.

The teaching of Caesarius generally reflects the spirit of cautious reserve characteristic of the rule instituted by the great St Benedict of Nursia for the monks he had assembled together on Monte Casino in Central Italy. His efforts like those of Caesarius were directed to the creation of conditions favourable to the devoutly disposed, not to the leavening of the outside world by the spread of Christian doctrine.

It was part of the plan of Caesarius to secure independence to the communities he had founded; for in his capacity as bishop he addressed a letter to Pope Hormisda († 523) in which he asked the Pope's protection for his monasteries, one of which was for men and one for women, against possible interference from outside. He also begged that the Pope would confirm the grants of property which had already been made to these establishments. In his reply to this letter the Pope declared that the power of the bishop in regard to these settlements should be limited to visitation[1].

It must be borne in mind that Arles and the southern parts of Gaul were overrun by the Goths, who inclined to Arianism and opposed the Church of Rome. Fear of this heresy induced the prelates of the Church to favour Frankish rule. After the alliance of the Frankish kings with the Church the religious establishments in the land remained undisturbed, and numerous new monasteries were founded.

It is evident from what we know of the nuns at Arles, and of other bands of women whom the Church took under her protection, that they readily accepted life on the conditions proffered and were content to be controlled and protected by men. It is only when the untamed German element with its craving for self-assertion came in, that difficulties between the bishops and heads of nunneries arose, that women of barbarian origin like Radegund, Chrodield, and others, appealed to the authority of ruling princes against the bishop, and asserted an independence not always in accordance with the usual conceptions of Christian virtue and tolerance.

---

[1] Guettée, *Histoire de l'Église de France*, 1847, vol. 2, p. 109.

§ 2. St Radegund and the Nunnery at Poitiers.

Certain settlements for women in northern France claim to have existed from a very early period, chiefly on the ground of their association with Geneviève, patron saint of Paris, and with Chrothild (Clothilde, † 545), wife of the first Christian king of the Franks. The legend of St Geneviève must be received with caution[1]; while bands of women certainly dwelt at Paris and elsewhere previously to the Frankish invasion, under the protection of the Church, it is doubtful whether they owed their existence to Geneviève.

A fictitious glamour of sanctity has been cast by legendary lore around the name and the doings of Queen Chrothild, because her union with King Clovis, advocated by the Gallo-Roman Church party, led to his conversion to Christianity[2]. In the pages of Gregory's history the real Chrothild stands out imperious, revengeful and unscrupulous. It is quite credible that she did service for a time as deaconess (diacona) at the church of Tours, and that she founded a religious house for women at the royal farm Les Andelys near Rouen, but we can hardly believe that the life she lived there was that of a devout nun.

Radegund of Poitiers and Ingetrud of Tours are the first Frankish women who are known to have founded and ruled over nunneries in France. Their activity belongs to the latter half of the 6th century, which is a date somewhat later than that of the official acceptance of Christianity, and one at which the overlordship of the Franks was already well established throughout France. The settlements they founded lay in close proximity to cities which were strongholds of Church government. Poitiers had become an important religious centre through the influence of St Hilary, and Tours, to which the shrine of St Martin attracted many travellers, was of such importance that it has been called the centre of religion and culture in France at this period.

The historian Gregory, afterwards bishop of Tours, to whom we are largely indebted for our knowledge of this period, was personally acquainted with the women at Tours and at Poitiers. He probably owed his appointment to the bishopric of Tours in 573 to the favour he had found with Radegund[3]. He has treated

---

[1] Keller, Ch., *Étude critique sur le texte de la vie de Ste Geneviève*, 1881; also *A. SS. Boll.*, St Genovefa, Jan. 3.

[2] Darboy, Mgr, *Sainte Clothilde*, 1865; also *A. SS. Boll.*, St Chrothildis, June 3.

[3] Giesebrecht, W., *Fränkische Geschichte des Gregorius*, 1851, Einleitung xviii.

of her in his history and has written an account of her burial at
which he officiated[1], whilst a chapter of his book on the *Glory of
Martyrs* praises the fragment of the Holy Cross[2], which had
been sent to Radegund from Constantinople and from which the
nunnery at Poitiers took its name.

Besides this information two drafts of the life of Radegund
are extant, the one written by her devoted friend and admirer
the Latin poet Fortunatus, afterwards bishop of Poitiers, the
other by the nun Baudonivia, Radegund's pupil and an inmate
of her nunnery[3]. Fortunatus has moreover celebrated his intercourse with Radegund in a number of verses, which throw great
light on their interesting personal relations[4].

A letter is also extant written by Radegund herself and preserved by Gregory in which she addresses a number of bishops on
the objects of her nunnery. She begs the prelates of the Church
to protect her institution after her death and, if need be, assist
those who are carrying on life there in her spirit against hindrance from without and opposition from within. The letter is
in the usual wordy style of the Latin of that day.

'Freed from the claims of a worldly life, with divine help and
holy grace, I,' she says, 'have willingly chosen the life of religion
at the direction of Christ; turning my thoughts and powers
towards helping others, the Lord assisting me that my good
intentions towards them may be turned to their weal. With the
assistance of gifts granted me by the noble lord and king Clothacar,
I have founded a monastery (monasterium) for maidens (puellae);
after founding it I made it a grant of all that royal liberality had
bestowed on me; moreover to the band assembled by me with Christ's
help, I have given the rule according to which the holy Caesaria
lived, and which the holy president (antistes) Caesarius of Arles
wisely compiled from the teachings of the holy fathers. With
the consent of the noble bishop of this district and others, and
at the desire of our congregation, I have accepted as abbess my
sister, dame Agnes, whom from youth upwards I have loved and
educated as a daughter; and next to God's will I have conformed

---

[1] Gregorius Tur., *De Gloria Confessorum*, ch. 106 (in Migne, *Patrol. Cursus Completus*, vol. 71).

[2] Gregorius Tur., *De Gloria Martyrum*, ch. 5 (in Migne, *Patrol. Cursus Compl.*,
vol. 71).

[3] *A. SS. Boll.*, St Radegundis, Aug. 13 (contains both these accounts).

[4] Fortunatus, *Opera poetica*, edit. Nisard, 1887.

to her authority. I myself, together with my sisters, have followed the apostolic example and have granted away by charter all our worldly possessions, in fearful remembrance of Ananias and Sapphira, retaining nought of our own. But since the events and duration of human life are uncertain, since also the world is drawing to its close (mundo in finem currente), many serving their own rather than the divine will, I myself, impelled by the love of God, submit to you this letter, which contains my request, begging you to carry it out in the name of Christ[1].'

Radegund was one of an unconquered German race. Her father was Hermafried, leader of the Thuringians, her mother a grandniece of the great Gothic king, Theodoric. She was captured as a child together with her brother in the forest wilds of Thüringen during one of the raids made into that district by the Frankish kings Theuderic (Thierry) of Metz, and Clothacar (Clothair) of Soissons. Clothacar appropriated the children as part of his share of the booty and sent Radegund to a 'villa' in the neighbourhood of Aties, in what became later the province of Picardie, where she was brought up and educated. 'Besides occupations usual to those of her sex,' her biographer says, 'she had a knowledge of letters' (litteris est erudita). From Aties she vainly tried to make her escape, and at the age of about twelve was taken to the royal farm near Soissons and there married to Clothacar[2]. In the list of King Clothacar's seven recognised wives Radegund stands fifth[3].

From the first Radegund was averse to this union. She was wedded to an earthly bridegroom but not therefore divided from the heavenly one[4]. Her behaviour towards her husband as described by her biographers can hardly be called becoming to her station as queen. She was so devoted to charitable work, we are told, that she often kept the king waiting at meals, a source of great annoyance to him, and under some pretext she frequently left him at night. If a man of learning came to the court she would devote herself to him, entirely neglecting her duty to the king[5]. Quarrels between the couple were frequent, and the king declared that he was married to a nun rather than to a queen[6]. The murder of her younger brother finally turned the

---

[1] Gregorius Tur., *Hist. Franc.* bk 9, ch. 42.
[2] Gregorius Tur., *Hist. Franc.* bk 3, ch. 7; Fortunatus, *Vita*, ch. 2–4.
[3] Giesebrecht, W., *Fränkische Geschichte des Gregorius*, 1851, appendix.
[4] Fortunatus, *Vita*, ch. 3.   [5] Ibid., ch. 10.   [6] Ibid., ch. 5.

balance of the queen's feelings against the king. With fearless determination she broke down all barriers. She was not lacking in personal courage, and had once calmly confronted a popular uproar caused by her having set fire to a sacred grove[1]. Now, regardless of consequences, she left the court and went to Noyon, where she sought the protection of Bishop Medardus († 545), who was influential among the many powerful prelates of his day[2]. But the bishop hesitated, his position was evidently not so assured that he could, by acceding to the queen's request, risk drawing on himself the king's anger[3]. However Radegund's stern admonition prevailed : 'If you refuse to consecrate me,' she cried, 'a lamb will be lost to the flock[4].' Medardus so far consented as to consecrate her a deaconess, a term applied at the time to those who, without belonging to any special order, were under the protection of the Church.

In the oratory of St Jumer Radegund now offered up the embroidered clothes and jewelry she was wearing, her robe (indumentum), her precious stones (gemma), and her girdle weighty with gold. Both her biographers[5] lay stress on this act of self-denial, which was the more noteworthy as love of gorgeous apparel and jewelry was characteristic of early Frankish royalty. Kings and queens were content to live in rural dwellings which were little more than barns; life in cities was altogether uncongenial to them, but they made up for this by a display of sumptuous clothes as a mark of their rank. Already during her life with the king Radegund is described as longing for a hair-cloth garment as a sign of unworldliness. She now definitely adopted the raiment of a nun, a dress made of undyed wool.

She subsequently wandered westwards from Noyon and came into the district between Tours and Poitiers, where she settled for some time at a 'villa' her husband had given her called Sais[6]. She entered into friendly relations with the recluse Jean of Chînon (Johannes Monasteriensis[7]), a native of Brittany, who with many

---

[1] Baudonivia, *Vita*, ch. 2.

[2] *A. SS. Boll.*, St Medardus, June 8.

[3] Commentators are much exercised by this summary breaking of the marriage tie; some urge that Radegund's union had not been blessed by the Church. In the *A. SS.* it is argued that the Gallic bishop Medardus in pronouncing her divorce acted in ignorance of certain canons of the Church.

[4] Fortunatus, *Vita*, c. 10.

[5] Ibid., ch. 11; Baudonivia, *Vita*, ch. 6.

[6] Ibid., *Vita*, ch. 12.

[7] Stadler und Heim, *Vollständiges Heiligenlexicon*, Johannes, nr 52; Gregorius Tur., *De Gloria Confessorum*, ch. 23.

other recluses like himself enjoyed the reputation of great holiness. Jean of Chînon is represented as strengthening Radegund in her resolution to devote herself to religion, and it is probable that he helped her with practical advice.

Radegund now devoted herself to the relief of distress of every kind, her practical turn of mind leading her to offer help in physical as well as in mental cases. Her biographer tells us how—like a new Martha, with a love of active life—she shrank from no disease, not even from leprosy[1].

When she saw how many men and women sought her relief the wish to provide permanently for them arose. She owned property outside Poitiers which she devoted to founding a settlement for women; in all probability she also had a house for men near it[2]. Various references to the settlement show that it extended over a considerable area. Like other country residences or ' villae,' it was surrounded by walls and had the look of a fortress, although situated in a peaceful district. As many as two hundred nuns lived here at the time of Radegund's death[3]. When the house was ready to receive its inmates, they entered it in a procession starting from Poitiers. We hear that by this time the doings of Radegund ' had so far increased her reputation that crowds collected on the roofs to see them pass.'

King Clothacar, however, did not calmly submit to being deserted by his wife; he determined to go to Poitiers with his son to find her and to take her back. But the queen, firm in her resolve, declared she would sooner die than return to her husband. She notified this resolution to Bishop Germanus of Paris, who besought the king not to go to Poitiers. His entreaties were successful. Clothacar left his wife unmolested, and seems to have come to some kind of agreement with her. In her letter to the bishops, Radegund speaks of him as the noble lord, King Clothacar, not as her husband.

Radegund did not herself preside over the women in her nunnery. With their consent the youthful Agnes, the pupil of Radegund, but by no means her intellectual equal, was appointed abbess. Difficulties very soon occurred between Radegund and the bishop of Poitiers, who was probably jealous of her attracting

---

[1] Fortunatus, *Vita*, ch. 26.

[2] Lucchi, *Vie de Venantius Fortunatus*, ch. 85 (in Fortunatus, *Opera poetica*, edit. Nisard, 1887).

[3] Gregorius Tur., *De Gloria Confessorum*, ch. 106.

religious women from himself. Radegund is said to have gone to Arles in order to learn about the life of the women gathered together there. Against the accuracy of this statement it is urged[1] that a written copy of the rule, together with an eloquent exhortation to religious perfection and virtue, was forwarded from Arles by the Abbess Caesaria († c. 560), the second of that name.

The rule was established in Poitiers in 559. In the previous year King Clothacar, Radegund's husband, through the death of his brothers and their sons, had become sole king of France[2]. His monarchy thus included the whole of what is now called France, the contiguous districts of Burgundy and Thüringen, and the lands which had been taken from the Goths in Italy and Spain. This great kingdom remained united for a few years only. In 561 Clothacar died and his realm was divided by his four sons, with whose reigns a tempestuous period begins in the history of the Franks. During more than forty years the rivalry and jealousy of the monarchs, aggravated by the mutual hatred of the queens Brunihild and Fredegund, overwhelmed the country with plots, counterplots, and unceasing warfare.

An eloquent appeal to the kings was called forth from the historian Gregory by the contemplation of this state of things. It is contained in the preface to the fifth book of his history. Calling upon them to desist from the complications of civil war, he thus addresses them :

'What are you bent on ? What do you ask for ? Have you not all in plenty ? There is luxury in your homes ; in your storehouses wine, corn, and oil abound ; gold and silver are heaped up in your treasuries. One thing only you lack ; while you have not peace, you have not the grace of God. Why must the one snatch things from the other ? Why must the one covet the other's goods ? '

Living at Poitiers Radegund was close to the scene of these turmoils. The cities of Tours and Poitiers had fallen to the share of Charibert. When he died in 562 his kingdom was divided between his three brothers by cities rather than by districts. Tours and Poitiers fell to Sigebert of Rheims, who was comparatively peace-loving among these brothers. But his brother Chilperic of Soissons, dissatisfied with his own share, invaded Touraine and Poitou and forced Poitiers to submit to him. He was subsequently

---

[1] Fortunatus, *Opera poetica*, edit. Nisard, 1887, note III, 3, p. 214.

[2] Gérard, P. A. F., *Histoire des Francs d'Austrasie*, 1864, vol. 1, p. 272.

made to give way to Sigebert, but this did not bring their feuds to an end. In 575 Sigebert was raised on the shield and proclaimed king of Neustria (the western part of France), but on being lifted down from the shield he was forthwith assassinated. New complications resulted and new factions were formed. In the interest of her son, Brunihild, the powerful widow of Sigebert, pursued with inveterate hatred Chilperic and his wife, the renowned Fredegund, for she looked upon Fredegund as the assassin of Sigebert her husband and of Galesuith her sister.

Radegund had close relations with these impetuous, headstrong and combative persons. King Sigebert was throughout well disposed towards her.

'In order to show his love and affection for her,' says Gregory[1], 'he sent a deputation of ecclesiastics to the Emperor Justinus II and his wife Sophia at Constantinople.' The Franks entertained friendly relations with the imperial court, and the surviving members of Radegund's family had found a refuge there. In due course gifts were sent to Radegund,—a fragment of the Holy Cross set in gold and jewels, together with other relics of apostles and martyrs. These relics arrived at Tours some time between 566 and 573[2]. It was Radegund's wish that they should be fetched from Tours to her nunnery by a procession headed by the bishop of Poitiers. But Bishop Maroveus, who was always ready to thwart the queen, forthwith left for his country seat when he heard of her request[3]. Radegund, much incensed, applied in her difficulty to King Sigebert, and Eufronius, bishop of Tours, was ordered to conduct the translation.

Radegund's adoption of the religious profession in no way diminished her intercourse with the outside world or the influence she had had as queen. We find her described as living on terms of friendship with Queen Brunihild 'whom she loved dearly.' Even Queen Fredegund, Brunihild's rival and enemy, seems to have had some kind of intimacy with her. Fortunatus in one of his poems suggests that Fredegund had begged Radegund to offer prayers for the prosperity of her husband Chilperic.

It seems that Radegund's word was generally esteemed, for in a family feud when a certain Gundovald claimed to be the son of Clothacar and aspired to the succession, we find him coupling

---

[1] Gregorius Tur., *Hist. Franc.* bk 9, ch. 40.

[2] Fortunatus, *Opera poetica*, edit. Nisard, 1887, note II, 1, p. 76.

[3] Gregorius Tur., *Hist. Franc.* bk 8, ch. 40.

the name of Radegund with that of Ingetrud in asseveration of his statements.

'If you would have the truth of what I declare proven,' Gundovald exclaimed, 'go and enquire of Radegund of Poitiers and of Ingetrud of Tours; they will tell you that what I maintain is the truth[1].'

In an age of endless entanglements, Radegund evidently did her best to mediate between contending parties. 'She was always favourable to peace and interested in the weal of the realm whatever changes befell,' writes the nun Baudonivia[2]. 'She esteemed the kings and prayed for their welfare, and taught us nuns always to pray for their safety. If she heard that they had fallen out she felt troubled: and she appealed in writing, sometimes to one, sometimes to another, in order that they should not fight and war together, but keep peaceful, so that the country might rest securely. Similarly she exhorted the leaders to help the great princes with sensible advice, in order that the common people and the lands under their rule might prosper.'

What is here said of her peace-loving disposition is corroborated by traits in her character mentioned by Gregory and Fortunatus. The friendly intercourse between Radegund and Fortunatus necessitates a few remarks on the life and doings of this latter-day Roman poet before he came to Poitiers and entered the Church.

For years Fortunatus had lived the life of a fashionable man of letters at Ravenna, but about the year 568 the occupation of that city by the Langobards forced him to leave Italy. He wandered north from court to court, from city to city, staying sometimes with a barbarian prince, sometimes with a Church-prelate, who, one and the other, were equally ready to entertain the cultivated southerner. In return for the hospitality so liberally bestowed on him he celebrated his personal relations to his benefactors in complimentary verses. He has good wishes for prelates on the occasion of their appointment, flattering words for kings, and pleasant greetings for friends. In some of his poems he gives interesting descriptions of the districts through which he has travelled, his account of a part of the Rhine valley being specially graphic[3]. He glorifies the saints of the Church in terms formerly used for celebrating classic divinities, and addresses Bishop Me-

---

[1] Gregorius Tur., *Hist. Franc.* bk 7, ch. 36.
[2] Baudonivia, *Vita*, c. 11.
[3] Fortunatus, *Opera poetica*, edit. Nisard, 1887, bk 10, nr 9.

dardus of Noyon as the possessor of Olympus[1]. He even brings in Venus to celebrate a royal wedding, and lets her utter praises of the queen Brunihild[2].

Besides these poetical writings Fortunatus has left prose accounts of several of his contemporaries. An easy-going man of pleasant disposition, he combined in a curious way the traditions of cultured Latinity with the theological bent peculiar to the Christian literature of the day. His poems, though somewhat wanting in ideas, show a ready power of versification and a great facility in putting things politely and pleasantly. He wrote some hymns for church celebration which became widely known. The one beginning 'Pange, lingua, gloriosi' was adopted into the Roman Liturgy for the adoration of the Cross on Good Friday, and it was repeatedly modified and re-written during the Middle Ages. Another hymn written by him is the celebrated 'Vexilla regis prodeunt,' the words of which are comparatively poor, but the tune, the authorship of which is unknown, has secured it world-wide fame[3].

The relic of the Holy Cross kept at Poitiers may have inspired Fortunatus with the idea of composing these hymns; in a flattering epistle, written obviously at Radegund's request, he thanks Justinus and Sophia of Constantinople for the splendour of their gift to her[4].

Fortunatus had come to Tours on a pilgrimage to the shrine of St Martin, to whose intercession he attributed the restoration of his eyesight. Passing through Poitiers he made the acquaintance of Radegund, who at once acquired a great influence over him.

'Radegund wished me to stay, so I stayed,' he writes from Poitiers to some friends[5], and he enlarges on the superiority, intellectual and otherwise, of the queen, whose plain clothing and simple mode of life greatly impressed him. Naming Eustachia, Fabiola, Melania, and all the other holy women he can think of, he describes how she surpasses them all. 'She exemplifies whatever is praiseworthy in them,' he says; 'I come across deeds in her such as I only read about before. Her spirit is clothed with flesh that has been overcome, and which while yet abiding in her body holds all things cheap as dross. Dwelling on earth, she has entered heaven, and freed from the shackles of sense, seeks companionship in the

---

[1] Fortunatus, *Opera poetica*, edit. Nisard, bk 2, nr 16.

[2] Ibid., bk 6, nr 1.

[3] Mone, F. J., *Lateinische Hymnen des Mittelalters*, 1853-5, vol. 1, 101; Fortunatus, *Opera poetica*, edit. Nisard, note, p. 76.

[4] Fortunatus, *Opera poetica*, Appendix, nr 2.   [5] Ibid., bk 8, nr 1.

realms above. All pious teaching is food to her; whether taught by Gregory or Basil, by bold Athanasius or gentle Hilary (two who were companions in the light of one cause); whether thundered by Ambrose or flashed forth by Jerome; whether poured forth by Augustine in unceasing flow, by gentle Sedulius or subtle Orosius. It is as though the rule of Caesarius had been written for her. She feeds herself with food such as this and refuses to take meat unless her mind be first satisfied. I will not say more of what by God's witness is manifest. Let everyone who can send her poems by religious writers; they will be esteemed as great gifts though the books be small. For he who gives holy writings to her may hold himself as giving to the accepted temples (templa) of God.'

Judging from this passage, Nisard, the modern editor of Fortunatus, thinks it probable that Radegund was acquainted with Greek as well as with Latin[1], a statement which one cannot endorse.

The queen was much interested in the poet's writings. 'For many years,' he writes in one poem, 'I have been here composing verses at your order; accept these in which I address you in the terms you merit[2].'

Radegund too wrote verses under Fortunatus' guidance. 'You have sent me great verses on small tablets,' he writes. 'You succeed in giving back honey to dead wax; on festal days you prepare grand entertainments, but I hunger more for your words than for your food. The little poems you send are full of pleasing earnestness; you charm our thoughts by these words[3].'

Among the poems of Fortunatus are found two which modern criticism no longer hesitates in attributing to Radegund. They are epistles in verse written in the form of elegies, and were sent by the queen to some of her relatives at Constantinople. Judging by internal evidence a third poem, telling the story of Galesuith, Queen Brunihild's sister, who was murdered shortly after her marriage to King Chilperic, was composed by her also; though Nisard claims for her not the form of the poem but only its inspiration[4]. 'The cry,' he says, 'which sounds through these lines, is the cry of a woman. Not of a German woman only, who has in her the expression of tender and fiery passion, but a suggestion of the strength of a woman of all countries and for all time.' The lament in this poem is intoned by several women in turn. Whoever may

[1] Fortunatus, *Opera poetica*, note 9, p. 213.

[2] Ibid., Appendix, nr 16.   [3] Ibid., nr 31.

[4] Nisard, Ch., *Des poesies de Radegonde attribuées jusqu'ici à Fortunat*, 1889, p. 5.

have composed it, the depth of feeling which it displays is certainly most remarkable.

One of these poems written by Radegund is addressed to her cousin Hermalafred, who had fled from Thüringen when Radegund was captured, and who had afterwards taken service in the imperial army of Justinian[1]. Hermalafred was endeared to Radegund by the recollections of her childhood, and in vivid remembrance of events which had made her a captive she begins her letter[2] in the following strain :

'Sad is condition of war! Jealous is fate of human things! How proud kingdoms are shattered by a sudden fall! Those long-prosperous heights (culmina) lie fallen, destroyed by fire in the great onset. Flickering tongues of flame lapped round the dwelling which before rose in royal splendour. Grey ashes cover the glittering roof which rose on high shining with burnished metal. Its rulers are captive in the enemy's power, its chosen bands have fallen to lowly estate. The crowd of comely servants all dwelling together were smitten to the dust in one day; the brilliant circle, the multitude of powerful dependents, no grave contains them, they lack the honours of death. More brilliant than the fire shone the gold of her hair, that of my father's sister, who lay felled to the ground, white as milk. Alas, for the corpses unburied that cover the battle-field, a whole people collected together in one burial place. Not Troy alone bewails her destruction, the land of Thüringen has experienced a like carnage. Here a matron in fetters is dragged away by her streaming hair, unable to bid a sad farewell to her household gods. The captive is not allowed to press his lips to the threshold, nor turn his face towards what he will never more behold. Bare feet in their tread trample in the blood of a husband, the loving sister passes over her brother's corpse. The child still hangs on its mother's lips though snatched from her embrace; in funeral wail no tear is shed. Less sad is the fate of the child who loses its life, the gasping mother has lost even the power of tears. Barbarian though I am, I could not surpass the weeping though my tears flowed for ever. Each had his sorrow, I had it all, my private grief was also the public grief. Fate was kind to those whom the enemy cut down; I alone survive to weep over the many. But not only do I sorrow for my dead relatives, those too I deplore whom life has preserved. Often my

---

[1] Fortunatus, *Opera poetica*, edit. Nisard, 1887, note III, 2, 3, etc., p. 284.

[2] Ibid., 'De Excidio Thoringiae,' Appendix, nr 1.

tear-stained face is at variance with my eyes; my murmurs are silenced, but my grief is astir. I look and long for the winds to bring me a message, from none of them comes there a sign. Hard fate has snatched from my embrace the kinsman by whose loving presence I once was cheered. Ah, though so far away, does not my solicitude pursue thee? has the bitterness of misfortune taken away thy sweet love? Recall what from thy earliest age upwards, O Hermalafred, I, Radegund, was ever to thee. How much thou didst love me when I was but an infant; O son of my father's brother, O most beloved among those of my kin! Thou didst supply for me the place of my dead father, of my esteemed mother, of a sister and of a brother. Held by thy gentle hand, hanging on thy sweet kisses, as a child I was soothed by thy tender speech. Scarce a time there was when the hour did not bring thee, now ages go by and I hear not a word from thee! I wrestle with the wild anguish that is hidden in my bosom; oh, that I could call thee back, friend, whenever or wherever it might be. If father, or mother, or royal office has hitherto held thee, though thou didst hasten now to me, thy coming is late. Perhaps 'tis a sign of fate that I shall soon miss thee altogether, dearest, for unrequited affection cannot long continue. I used to be anxious when one house did not shelter us; when thou wast absent, I thought thee gone for ever. Now the east holds thee as the west holds me; the ocean's waters restrain me, and thou art kept away from me by the sea reddened by the beams of the sun (unda rubri). The earth's expanse stretches between those who are dear to each other, a world divides those whom no distance separated before.'

She goes on to speculate where her cousin may be, and she says if she were not held by her monastery she would go to him; storm and wind and the thought of shipwreck would be nothing to her. The fear of incriminating her, she says, was the cause of the death of her murdered brother. Would that she had died instead of him! She beseeches Hermalafred to send news of himself and of his sisters, and ends her letter with these words: 'May Christ grant my prayer, may this letter reach those beloved ones, so that a letter indited with sweet messages may come to me in return! May the sufferings wrought by languishing hope be alleviated by the swift advent of sure tidings!'

This poem expresses great and lasting affection for her race. But her relatives were a source of continued grief to the queen. She received no reply to her letter to Hermalafred, and later she heard of his death. She received this news from his nephew Artachis, who sent her at the same time a present of silk, and Radegund then wrote another letter[1] which is addressed to Artachis and is even sadder in tone. In it she deplores the death of Hermalafred, and asks the boy Artachis to let her have frequent news of himself sent to her monastery.

It is pleasant to turn from the sad side of Radegund's life which these poems exhibit to her friendly intercourse with Fortunatus, which was no doubt a source of great comfort to her during the last years of her life. With the exception of short intervals for journeys, the Latin poet lived entirely at Poitiers, where he adopted the religious profession, and dwelt in constant communication with Radegund and the abbess Agnes, in whose society he learned to forget the land of his birth. The numerous poems and verses which he has addressed to these ladies throw a strong light on his attitude towards them and their great affection for him.

Radegund was wont to decorate the altar of her church with a profusion of flowers[2]. Again and again the poet sends her flowers, accompanying his gift with a few lines. With a basket of violets he sends the following[3]:

' If the time of year had given me white lilies, or had offered me roses laden with perfume, I had culled them as usual in the open or in the ground of my small garden, and had sent them, small gifts to great ladies. But since I am short of the first and wanting in the second, he who offers violets must in love be held to bring roses. Among the odorous herbs which I send, these purple violets have a nobleness of their own. They shine tinted with purple which is regal, and unite in their petals both perfume and beauty. What they represent may you both exemplify, that by association a transient gift may gain lasting worth.'

The interchange of gifts between the poet and the ladies was mutual, the nuns of Ste Croix lacked not the good things of this world and were generous in giving. Fortunatus thanks them for gifts of milk, prunes, eggs, and tempting dishes[4]. On one occasion they send him a meal of several courses, vegetables and meat, almost too much for one servant to carry, and he describes his greedy (gulosus) enjoyment of it in graphic terms[5].

---

[1] Fortunatus, *Opera poetica*, Appendix, nr 3.   [2] Ibid., bk 8, nr 8.
[3] Ibid., bk 8, nr 6.   [4] Ibid., bk 11, nr 10.
[5] Ibid., bk 11, nr 9.

Are we to take the lines literally which tell us that when they entertained him at dinner the table was scarcely visible for the roses with which it was strewn, and that the foliage and flowers spread about made the room into a bower of greenery[1]?

Sometimes a fit of indigestion was the result of the too liberal enjoyment of what his friends so freely provided[2]. The poet was evidently fond of the pleasures of the table, and accentuates the material rather than the spiritual side of things. Once addressing Agnes he tells her that she shines in the blending of two things, she provides refreshment for the poet's mind and excellent food for his body[3].

But the 6th century poet is generally somewhat plain-spoken on delicate topics. In a poem addressed to Radegund and Agnes he openly defends himself against the imputation that the tone of his relations to them is other than is signified by the terms mother and sister by which he is wont to address them[4]. Still these platonic relations do not preclude the use of expressions which border on the amorous, for he tells them that they each possess one half of him[5], and he calls Radegund the light of his eyes[6].

'My dear mother, my sweet sister,' he writes, 'what shall I say, left alone in the absence of the love of my heart[7]?...' And again[8], 'May a good night enfold my mother and my sister; this brings them the good wishes of a son and a brother. May the choir of angels visit your hearts and hold sweet converse with your thoughts. The time of night forces me to be brief in my greetings; I am sending only six lines of verse for you both!'

The vocabulary used to denote the different kinds of human affection contains, no doubt, many terms common to all, and if the poems of Fortunatus sometimes suggest the lover, it must be remembered that as poems of friendship they are among the earliest of their kind. They are throughout elegant, graceful, and characterized by a playful tenderness which a translator must despair of rendering.

Radegund died in the year 587, and her death was a terrible loss to the inmates of her settlement. Gregory, bishop of Tours, who officiated at the burial, gives a detailed description of it, telling

---

[1] Fortunatus, *Opera poetica*, bk 11, nr 11.   [2] Ibid., bk 11, nr 22.
[3] Ibid., bk 11, nr 8.   [4] Ibid., bk 11, nr 6.
[5] Ibid., Appendix, nr 21.   [6] Ibid., bk 11, nr 2.
[7] Ibid., bk 11, nr 7.   [8] Ibid., Appendix, nr 15.

how some two hundred women crowded round the bier, bewailing her death in such words as these[1]:

'To whom, mother, hast thou left us orphans? To whom then shall we turn in our distress? We left our parents, our relatives and our homes, and we followed thee. What have we before us now, but tears unceasing, and grief that never can end? Verily, this monastery is to us more than the greatness of village and city.... The earth is now darkened to us, this place has been straitened since we no longer behold thy countenance. Woe unto us who are left by our holy mother! Happy those who left this world whilst thou wast still alive...!'

The nun Baudonivia says that she cannot speak of the death of Radegund without sobs choking her. Her account was written some time after Radegund's death during the rule of the abbess Didimia to whom it is dedicated; Didimia probably succeeded Leubover, who witnessed the serious outbreak of the nuns at Poitiers. This outbreak throws an interesting light on the temper of professed religious women at this period, and illustrates how needful it was that a religious establishment should be ruled by a woman of character and determination at a time when the monastic system was only in its infancy.

§ 3. The Revolt of the Nuns at Poitiers[2]. Convent Life in the North.

The revolt of the nuns at Poitiers, which happened within a few years of the death of Radegund, shows more than anything else the imperious and the unbridled passions that were to be found at this period in a nunnery. Evidently the adoption of the religious profession did not deter women from openly rebelling against the authority of the ministers of the Church, and from carrying out their purpose by force of arms. The outbreak at Poitiers, of which Gregory has given a description, shows what proud, vindictive, and unrelenting characters the Frankish convent of the 6th century harboured.

Already during Radegund's lifetime difficulties had arisen. King Chilperic had placed his daughter Basina in the nunnery, and after a time he asked that she should leave to be married. Radegund refused and her authority prevailed, but we shall find

---

[1] Gregorius Tur., *De Gloria Confessorum*, ch. 106.
[2] Gregorius Tur., *Hist. Franc.*, bk 9, chs. 39—44; bk 10, chs. 15—17, 20.

this Basina taking an active part in the rebellion.   Other incidents
show how difficult it was for Radegund even to uphold discipline.
A nun escaped through a window by aid of a rope and, taking
refuge in the basilica of St Hilary, made accusations which
Gregory, who was summoned to enquire into the matter, declared
to be unfounded.   The fugitive repented and was permitted to
return to the nunnery; she was hoisted up by means of ropes so
that she might enter by the way she had gone out.   She asked to
be confined in a cell apart from the community, and there she
remained in seclusion till the news of the rebellion encouraged her
to again break loose.

Agnes the abbess appointed by Radegund died in 589.   The
convent chose a certain Leubover to succeed her, but this appointment roused the ire of Chrodield, another inmate of the nunnery.

Chrodield held herself to be the daughter of King Charibert,
and relying on her near connection with royalty persuaded forty
nuns to take an oath that they would help her to remove the hated
Leubover and would appoint her, Chrodield, as abbess in her stead.
Led by Chrodield who had been joined by her cousin Basina, the
daughter of Chilperic mentioned above, the whole party left the
nunnery.   'I am going to my royal relatives,' Chrodield said,
'to inform them of the contumely we have experienced.   Not as
daughters of kings are we treated but as though we were lowly
born[1].'

Leaving Poitiers the women came to Tours where Chrodield
applied for assistance to the bishop and historian Gregory.   In
vain he admonished her, promising to speak to Bishop Maroveus
of Poitiers in her behalf, and urging her to abide by his decision, as
the penalty might be excommunication.

The feeling of indignation in the women must have been
strong, since nothing he could say dissuaded them from their
purpose.   'Nothing shall prevent us from appealing to the kings,'
said Chrodield, 'to them we are nearly related.'

The women had come on foot from Poitiers to Tours, regardless
of hardships.   They had had no food and arrived at a time of year
when the roads were deep in mud.   Gregory at last persuaded them
to postpone their departure for the court till the summer.

Then Chrodield, leaving the nuns under the care of Basina,
continued her journey to her uncle, King Guntchram of Orléans,

---

[1] Gregorius Tur., *Hist. Franc.*, bk 9, ch. 39.

who at the time was residing at Chalôns-sur-Saône. She was well received by him and came back to Tours there to await the convocation of bishops who were to enquire into the rights of her case. But she found on her return that many of her followers had disbanded, and some had married. The arrival too of the bishops was delayed, so that she felt it expedient to return with her followers to Poitiers where they took possession of the basilica of St Hilary.

They now prepared for open hostility. 'We are queens,' they said, 'and we shall not return to the monastery unless the abbess is deposed.'

At this juncture they were joined by other dissatisfied spirits, 'murderers, adulterers, law-breakers and other wrong-doers,' as Gregory puts it[1]. The nun too who had previously escaped and been taken back, now broke loose from her cell and returned to the basilica of Hilary.

The bishop of Bordeaux and his suffragan bishops of Angoulême, Perigueux, and Poitiers, now assembled by order of the king (Guntchram), and called upon the women to come into the monastery, and on their refusal the prelates entered the basilica of St Hilary in a body urging them to obey. The women refused, and the ban of excommunication was pronounced, upon which they and their followers attacked the prelates. In great fear the bishops and clergy made off helter-skelter, not even pausing to bid each other farewell. One deacon was so terrified that in his eagerness to get away he did not even ride down to the ford, but plunged with his horse straight into the river.

King Childebert (✝ 596), the son and successor of King Sigebert, now ordered Count Macco to put an end to the rebellion by force of arms, while Gondegisel, bishop of Bordeaux, sent a circular letter to his brethren, describing the indignity to which he had been exposed. Chrodield's chance of success was evidently dwindling, when she determined to carry her point by a bold assault, the account of which may fitly stand in the words of Gregory[2].

'The vexations,' he says, 'which sown by the devil had sprung up in the monastery at Poitiers, daily increased in troublesomeness. For Chrodield, having collected about her, as mentioned above, a band of murderers, wrong-doers, law-breakers, and vagrants of all kinds, dwelt in open revolt and ordered her followers to break into the nunnery at night and forcibly to bear off the abbess. But

[1] Gregorius Tur., *Hist. Franc.*, bk 9, ch. 41.   [2] Ibid., bk 10, ch. 15.

the abbess, on hearing the noise of their approach, asked to be carried in front of the shrine of the Holy Cross, for she was suffering from a gouty foot, and thought that the Holy Cross would serve her as a protection in danger. The armed bands rushed in, ran about the monastery by the light of a torch in search of the abbess, and entering the oratory found her extended on the ground in front of the shrine of the Holy Cross. Then one of them, more audacious than the rest, while about to commit the impious deed of cutting her down with his sword, was stabbed by another, through the intercession I believe of Divine Providence. He fell in his own blood and did not carry out the intention he had impiously formed. Meanwhile the prioress Justina, together with other sisters, spread the altar-cover, which lay before the cross, over the abbess, and extinguished the altar candles. But those who rushed in with bared swords and lances tore her clothes, almost lacerated the hands of the nuns, and carried off the prioress whom they mistook for the abbess in the darkness, and, with her cloak dragged off and her hair coming down, they would have given her into custody at the basilica of St Hilary. But as they drew near the church, and the sky grew somewhat lighter, they saw she was not the abbess and told her to go back to the monastery. Coming back themselves they secured the real abbess, dragged her away, and placed her in custody near the basilica of St Hilary in a place where Basina was living, and placed a watch over her by the door that no one should come to her rescue. Then in the dark of night they returned to the monastery and not being able to find a light, set fire to a barrel which they took from the larder and which had been painted with tar and was now dry. By the light of the bonfire they kindled, they plundered the monastery of all its contents, leaving nothing but what they could not carry off. This happened seven days before Easter.'

The bishop of Poitiers made one more attempt to interfere. He sent to Chrodield and asked her to set the abbess free on pain of his refusing to celebrate the Easter festival. ‘If you do not release her,’ he said, ‘I shall bring her help with the assembled citizens.’ But Chrodield emboldened by her success said to her followers: ‘If anyone dare come to her rescue, slay her.’

She seems now to have been in possession of the monastery; still we find defection among her party. Basina, who throughout had shown a changeable disposition, repented and went to the imprisoned Leubover, who received her with open arms. The bishops, mindful of the treatment they had received, still refused to assemble in Poitiers while the state of affairs continued. But Count Macco with his armed bands made an attack on the women and their followers, causing 'some to be beaten down, others struck down by spears, and those who made most strenuous opposition to be cut down by the sword.'

Chrodield came forth from the nunnery holding on high the relic of the Cross; 'Do not, I charge you, use force of arms against me,' she cried, 'I am a queen, daughter to one king and cousin to another. Do not attack me, a time may come when I will take my revenge.' But no one took any notice of her. Her followers were dragged from the monastery and severely chastised. The bishops assembled and instituted a long enquiry into the grievances of Chrodield, and the accusations brought against Leubover by her. They seem to have been unfounded or insignificant. Leubover justified herself and returned to the monastery. Chrodield and Basina left Poitiers and went to the court of King Childebert.

At the next Church convocation the king tendered a request that these women should be freed from the ban of excommunication. Basina asked forgiveness and was allowed to return to the monastery. But the proud Chrodield declared that she would not set foot there while the abbess Leubover remained in authority. She maintained her independence and went to live in a 'villa' which the king had granted her, and from that time she passes from the stage of history.

The revolt of the nuns at Poitiers, which for two years defied the efforts of churchmen and laymen, is the more noteworthy in that it does not stand alone. Within a year we find a similar outbreak threatening the nunnery at Tours where a certain Berthegund, similarly disappointed of becoming abbess, collected malefactors and others about her and resorted to violent measures. The circumstances, which are also described by Gregory, differ in some respects from those of the insurrection at Ste Croix[1].

Ingetrud, the mother of Berthegund, had founded a nunnery at Tours close to the church of St Martin, and she urged her daughter, who was married, to come and live with her. When Berthegund did so, her husband appealed to Gregory, who threatened her with excommunication if she persisted in her resolve. She returned to her husband, but subsequently left him

---

[1] Gregorius Tur., *Hist. Franc.*, bk 9, ch. 33; bk 10, ch. 12.

again and sent for advice to her brother who was bishop of
Bordeaux. He decreed that she need not live with her husband if
she preferred convent life. But when this bishop of Bordeaux died,
his sister Berthegund and her mother Ingetrud quarrelled as to the
inheritance of his property, and Ingetrud, much incensed against
her daughter, determined at least to keep from Berthegund her own
possessions at the nunnery and succession to her position there.
She therefore appointed a niece of hers to succeed her as abbess
after her death. When she died the convent of nuns looked upon
this appointment as an infringement of their rights, but Gregory
persuaded them to keep quiet and abide by the decision of their
late abbess. Berthegund however would not agree to it. Against
the advice of the bishop she appealed to the authority of King
Childebert, who admitted her claim to the property. 'Furnished
with his letter she came to the monastery and carried off all the
moveable property, leaving nothing but its bare walls,' Gregory
says. Afterwards she settled at Poitiers, where she spoke evil
of her cousin the abbess of Tours, and altogether 'she did so much
evil it were difficult to tell of it all.'

From the consideration of these events in central France we
turn to the religious foundations for women in the northern districts.
With the beginning of the 7th century a change which directly
influenced convent life becomes apparent in the relations between
the Frankish rulers and the representatives of Christianity. Influential posts at court were more and more frequently occupied by
prelates of the Church, and kings and queens acted more directly
as patrons of churches and monasteries. Hitherto the centres of
religious influence had been in southern and central France, where
the Gallo-Frankish population and influence predominated, and
where monasteries flourished close to cities which had been strongholds of the Roman system of administration. New religious
settlements now grew up north of the rivers Seine and Marne,
where the pure Frankish element prevailed and where Christianity regained its foothold owing to the patronage of ruling
princes.

Whatever had survived of Latin culture and civilisation in these
districts had disappeared before the influence of the heathen invaders;
the men whose work it was to re-evangelise these districts found few
traces of Christianity. Vedast (St Vaast, † 540), who was sent by
bishop Remigius (St Rémy) of Rheims († 532) into the marshy districts of Flanders, found no Christians at Arras about the year 500,

and only the ruins of one ancient church, which he rebuilt[1].   The
author of the life of Vedast gives the ravages made in these districts
by the Huns as the reason for the disappearance of Latin culture
and of Christianity.   But the author of the life of Eleutherius,
bishop of Tournai († 531), holds that the Christians had fled from
these districts to escape from the inroads of the heathen Franks[2].

It was chiefly by the foundation of monasteries in these districts
that Christianity gained ground during the 7th century. 'Through
the establishment of monasteries,' says Gérard[3], 'the new social
order gained a foothold in the old Salic lands.'   Among the names
of those who took an active part in this movement stand the
following : Wandregisil (St Vandrille, † 665) founder of the abbey
of Fontenelle; Waneng († c. 688) founder of Fécamp; Filibert
(† 684) founder of Jumièges; Eligius bishop of Noyon († 658) and
Audoenus (St Ouen, † 683) archbishop of Rouen.   These men
were in direct contact with the court and were much patronised
by the ruling princes, especially by the holy queen Balthild.
Early and reliable accounts concerning most of them are extant[4].

With regard to political events the 7th century is the most
obscure period of Frankish history, for the history of Gregory of
Tours comes to an end in 591.   Feuds and quarrels as violent as
those he depicts continued, and important constitutional changes
took place as their result.   The vast dominions brought under
Frankish rule showed signs of definitely crystallising into Austrasia
which included the purely Frankish districts of the north, and
Burgundy and Neustria where Gallo-Frankish elements were
prevalent.

The latter half of the life of the famous Queen Brunihild[5] takes
its colouring from the rivalry between these kingdoms ; during fifty
years she was one of the chief actors in the drama of Frankish
history.   At one time she ruled conjointly with her son Childebert,
and then as regent for her grandsons, over whom she domineered
greatly.   In the year 613, when she was over eighty years old, she
was put to a cruel death by the nobles of Austrasia.

The judgments passed on this queen are curiously contradictory.
Pope Gregory († 604) writes to her praising her great zeal in

---

[1] *A. SS. Boll.*, St Vedastus, Feb. 6.

[2] *A. SS. Boll.*, St Eleutherius, Feb. 20, *Vita* I, ch. 3 (Potthast, Wegweiser: '*Vita auctore anonymo sed antiquo*').

[3] Gérard, P. A. F., *Histoire des Francs d'Austrasie*, 1864, vol. I, p. 384.

[4] Comp. throughout *A. SS. Boll.*, St Wandregisilus, July 22; St Waningus, Jan. 9, etc.

[5] Drapeyron, L., *La reine Brunehilde*, 1867.

the cause of religion, and thanks her for the protection she has afforded to Augustine on his passage through France, which he considers a means to the conversion of England[1]. On the other hand the author of the life of St Columban[2], whom she expelled from Burgundy, calls her a very Jezebel[3]; and the author of the life of Desiderius, who was murdered in 608, goes so far as to accuse her of incestuous practices because of her marriage with her husband's nephew[4]. Indirect evidence is in favour of the conclusion that Queen Brunihild disliked monasticism; she was by birth of course a princess of the Gothic dynasty of Spain who had accepted Christianity in its Arian form.

During the reign of Brunihild's nephew Clothacar II († 628), under whose rule the different provinces were for a time united, a comprehensive and most interesting edict was issued, which affords an insight into the efforts made to give stability to the relations between princes and the representatives of religion. In this edict, under heading 18, we are told that 'no maidens, holy widows or religious persons who are vowed to God, whether they stay at home or live in monasteries, shall be enticed away, or appropriated, or taken in marriage by making use of a special royal permit (praeceptum). And if anyone surreptitiously gets hold of a permit, it shall have no force. And should anyone by violent or other means carry off any such woman and take her to wife, let him be put to death. And if he be married in church and the woman who is appropriated, or who is on the point of being appropriated, seems to be a consenting party, they shall be separated, sent into exile, and their possessions given to their natural heirs[5].'

From these injunctions it can be gathered that the re-adjustment of social and moral relations was still in progress; women who were vowed to a religious life did not necessarily dwell in a religious settlement, and even if they did so they were not necessarily safe from being captured and thrown into subjection. Clothacar II had three wives at the same time and concubines innumerable; plurality of wives was indeed a prerogative of these Frankish kings.

---

[1] Gregorius, Papa, *Epistolae*, liber 9, epist. 109 (in Migne, *Patrol. Cursus Compl.* vol. 77).

[2] St Columban who went abroad and died in 615 should be kept distinct from St Columba who died in 597, sometimes also called Columban. Both of them wrote rules for monks (cf. *Dictionary of Nat. Biography*).

[3] Bouquet, *Recueil Hist.*, vol. 3, p. 478.   [4] *A. SS. Boll.*, St Desiderius, May 23.

[5] Guettée, *Histoire de l' Église de France*, vol. 1, p. 317.

Monastic life in northern France at this period was also in process of development. It has been mentioned how Radegund adopted the rule of life framed and put into writing by Caesarius at Arles. The rule contemporaneously instituted by Benedict at Nursia in central Italy spread further and further northwards, and was advocated by prelates of the Romish Church. It served as the model on which to reform the life of existing settlements[1].

During the first few centuries religious houses and communities had been founded here and there independently of each other, the mode of life and the routine observed depending in each case directly on the founder. Many and great were the attempts made by the advocates of convent life to formulate the type of an ideal existence outside the pale of social duties and family relations, in which piety, work and benevolence should be blended in just proportions. The questions how far the prelates of the Church should claim authority over the monastery, and what the respective positions of abbot or abbess and bishop should be, led to much discussion.

During the period under consideration the rules drafted by different leaders of monastic thought were not looked upon as mutually exclusive. We are told in the life of Filibert († 684), written by a contemporary[2], that he made selections from 'the graces of St Basil, the rule of Macarius, the decrees of Benedict and the holy institutions of Columban.' Eligius, bishop of Noyon, says in a charter which he drafted for the monastery founded by him at Solemny that the inmates of the settlement shall follow the rules of St Benedict and of St Columban[3].

Towards the close of the 6th century Columban came from Ireland into France and northern Italy and founded a number of religious settlements. What rule of life the inmates of these houses followed is not quite clear, probably that drafted by Columban. The convents in Elsass, Switzerland and Germany, which considered that they owed their foundation to Irish monks, were numerous and later became obnoxious to the Church in many ways. For in after years, when the feud arose between the Romish and the Irish Churches and the latter insisted on her independence, the houses founded by Irishmen also claimed freedom

---

[1] Opinions differ as to the original form of the rule of St Benedict. Comp. Benedictus, *Opera*, pp. 204 ff. (in Migne, *Patrologiae Cursus Complet.*, vol. 66).

[2] *A. SS. Boll.*, St Filibertus, Aug. 20.

[3] Roth, P., *Geschichte des Beneficialwesens*, 1850 Appendix, gives the Charter.

and remained separate from those which accepted the rule of St Benedict.

The property granted to religious foundations in northern France went on increasing throughout the 7th century. The amount of land settled on churches and monasteries by princes of the Merovech dynasty was so great that on Roth's computation two-thirds of the soil of France was at one time in the hands of the representatives of religion[1]. Under the will of Dagobert, who first became king of Austrasia in 628 and afterwards of the whole of France, large tracts were given away. Through the gifts of this king the abbey of St Denis became the richest in France, and his great liberality on the one hand towards the Church, on the other towards the poor and pilgrims, is emphasized by his biographer. His son Chlodwig II, king of Neustria and Burgundy, followed in his footsteps. He was a prince of feeble intellect and his reign is remarkable for the power increasingly usurped by the house-mayor, who grasped more and more at the substance of royal authority while dispensing with its show.

Chlodwig II was married to Balthild, who is esteemed a saint on the strength of the monastery she founded and of the gifts she made to the Church. There are two accounts of her works; the second is probably a re-written amplification of the first, which was drafted within a short period of her death[2]. As these accounts were written from the religious standpoint, they give scant information on the political activity and influence of the queen, which were considerable. They dwell chiefly on her gifts, and concern the latter part of her life when she was in constant communication with her nunnery.

Balthild was of Anglo-Saxon origin, and her personality and activity form the connecting link between the women of France and England. It is supposed that she was descended from one of the noble families of Wessex, and she favoured all those religious settlements which were in direct connection with princesses of the Anglo-Saxon race.

She had been captured on the north coast of France and had been brought to Paris as a slave by the house-mayor Erchinoald, who would have married her, but she escaped and hid herself. Her beauty and attractions are described as remarkable, and she found favour in the eyes of King Chlodwig II who made her his

---

[1] Roth, P., *Geschichte des Beneficialwesens*, 1850, p. 249.
[2] *A. SS. Boll.*, St Bathildis, Jan. 26 (contains both accounts).

wife. The excesses of this king were so great that he became
imbecile. Balthild with Erchinoald's help governed the kingdom
during the remainder of her husband's life and after his death in
the interest of her little sons. From a political point of view
she is described as 'administering the affairs of the kingdom
masculine wise and with great strength of mind.' She was especially energetic in opposing slavery and forbade the sale of
Christians in any part of France. No doubt this was due to her
own sad experience. She also abolished the poll-tax, which had
been instituted by the Romans. The Frankish kings had carried
it on and depended on it for part of their income. Its abolition
is referred to as a most important and beneficial change[1].

During the lifetime of Chlodwig and for some years after his
death the rule of Balthild seems to have been comparatively peaceful. The house-mayor Erchinoald died in 658 and was succeeded
by Ebruin, a man whose unbounded personal ambition again
plunged the realm into endless quarrels. In his own interest
Ebruin advocated the appointment of a separate king to the
province Austrasia, and the second of Balthild's little sons was
sent there with the house-mayor Wulfoald. But the rivalry between the two kingdoms soon added another dramatic chapter to
the pages of Frankish history. At one time we find Ebruin ruling
supreme and condemning his rival Leodgar, bishop of Autun,
to seclusion in the monastery of Luxeuil. An insurrection broke
out and Ebruin himself was tonsured and cast into Luxeuil.
But his chief antagonist Leodgar was murdered. Ebruin was then
set free and again became house-mayor to one of the shadow
kings, *rois fainéants*, the unworthy successors of the great Merovech.
His career throughout reflected the tumultuous temper of the age;
he was finally assassinated in the year 680.

Queen Balthild had retired from political life long before this.
She left the court in consequence of an insurrection in Paris which
led to the assassination of Bishop Sigoberrand, and went to live at
a palace near the convent of Chelles, which she had founded and
which she frequently visited. In the account of her life we read
of her doing many pious deeds[2]. 'A fond mother, she loved the
nuns like her own daughters and obeyed as her mother the holy
abbess whom she had herself appointed ; and in every respect she
did her duty not like a mistress but like a faithful servant. Also

---

[1] Roth, P., *Geschichte des Beneficialwesens*, 1850, p. 86.
[2] *A. SS. Boll.*, St Bathildis, Jan. 26; *Vita* II., ch. 14.

with the humility of a strong mind she served as an example; she did service herself as cook to the nuns, she looked after cleanliness, —and, what can I say more,—the purest of pearls, with her own hands she removed filth's impurities....'

At various times of her life Balthild had been in friendly intercourse with many of the chief prelates and religious dignitaries of the day. She had taken a special interest in Eligius, bishop of Noyon, who was a Frank by birth and the friend and adviser of King Dagobert.

We hear how Eligius took a special interest in monastic life; how at Paris he collected together three hundred women, some of whom were slaves, others of noble origin; how he placed them under the guidance of one Aurea; and how at Noyon also he gathered together many women[1].

On receiving the news that Eligius was dying, Balthild hurried with her sons to Noyon, but they came too late to see him. So great was her love for him, that she would have borne away his body to Chelles, her favourite settlement, but her wish was miraculously frustrated. The writer of the life of Eligius tells that the holy man's body became so heavy that it was impossible to move it.

When Eligius appointed Aurea as president of his convent at Paris she was living in a settlement at Pavilly which had been founded by Filibert, an ecclesiastic also associated with Queen Balthild. On one occasion she sent him as an offering her royal girdle, which is described as a mass of gold and jewels[2]. It was on land granted to him by Balthild and her sons that Filibert founded Jumièges, where he collected together as many as nine hundred monks. At his foundation at Pavilly over three hundred women lived together under the abbess Ansterbert[3].

It is recorded that Ansterbert and her mother Framehild were among the women of northern France who came under the influence of Irish teachers. The same is said of Fara († 657)[4], the reputed founder of a house at Brie, which was known as Faremoutiers, another settlement indebted to Queen Balthild's munificence. Similarly Agilbert and Theodohild[5] († c. 660) are supposed to have been taught by Irish teachers who had collected women about them at Jouarre on the Marne. This house at Jouarre

[1] *A. SS. Boll.*, ibid., St Aurea, Oct. 4.
[2] Ibid., St Filibertus, Aug. 20, *Vita*, ch. 5.   [3] Ibid., St Austreberta, Feb. 10.
[4] Regnault, *Vie de Ste Fare*, 1626.   [5] *A. SS. Boll.*, St Teclechildis, Oct. 10.

attained a high standard of excellence in regard to education, for we are informed that Balthild summoned Berthild[1] from here, a woman renowned for her learning, and appointed her abbess over the house at Chelles.

Yet another ecclesiastic must be mentioned in connection with Balthild, viz. Waneng, a Frank by birth. He was counsellor for some time to the queen who gave the cantle of Normandy, the so-called Pays de Caux, into his charge. He again founded a settlement for religious women at Fécamp which was presided over by Hildemarque.

The foundation and growth of so many religious settlements within so short a period and situated in a comparatively small district shows that the taste for monastic life was rapidly developing among the Franks.

'At this period in the provinces of Gaul,' says a contemporary writer, 'large communities of monks and of virgins were formed, not only in cultivated districts, in villages, cities and strongholds, but also in uncultivated solitudes, for the purpose of living together according to the rule of the holy fathers Benedict and Columban[2].'

This statement is taken from the life of Salaberg, a well written composition which conveys the impression of truthfulness. Salaberg had brought up her daughter Anstrud for the religious life. Her husband had joined the monastery at Luxeuil and she and other women were about to settle near it when the rumour of impending warfare drove them north towards Laon where they dwelt on the Mons Clavatus. This event belongs to the period of Queen Balthild's regency. It was while Anstrud was abbess at Laon that the settlement was attacked and barely escaped destruction in one of the wars waged by the house-mayor Ebruin. This event is described in a contemporary life of Anstrud[3].

It is interesting to find a connection growing up at this period between the religious houses of northern France and the women of Anglo-Saxon England. We learn from the reliable information supplied by Bede that Englishwomen frequently went abroad and sometimes settled entirely in Frankish convents. We shall return to this subject later in connection with the princesses of Kent and East Anglia, some of whom went to France and there became abbesses. The house at Brie was ruled successively by Saethrith

---

[1] *A. SS. Boll.*, St Bertilia, Jan. 3.
[2] Ibid., St Salaberga, Sept. 22, *Vita*, ch. 8.
[3] Ibid., St Austrudis, Oct. 17.

(St Syre), and Aethelburg (St Aubierge), daughters of kings of East Anglia, and Earcongotha, a daughter of the king of Kent. About the same time Hereswith, a princess of Northumbria, came to reside at Chelles[1].

We do not know how far the immigration of these women was due to Balthild's connection with the land of her origin, nor do we hear whether she found solace in the society of her countrywomen during the last years of her life. Her death is conjectured to have taken place in 680.

With it closes the period which has given the relatively largest number of women-saints to France, for all the women who by founding nunneries worked in the interests of religion have a place in the assembly of the saints. They were held as benefactors in the districts which witnessed their efforts, and the day of their death was inscribed in the local calendar. They have never been officially canonised, but they all figure in the Roman Martyrology, and the accounts which tell of their doings have been incorporated in the Acts of the Saints.

---

[1] Bede, *Hist. Eccles.*, bk 3, ch. 8; bk 4, ch. 23. Comp. below, ch. 3, § 1.

CHAPTER III.

CONVENTS AMONG THE ANGLO-SAXONS, A.D. 630–730.

'Ecce catervim glomerant ad bella phalanges
Justitiae comites et virtutum agmina sancta.'
Ealdhelm, *De laude Virginum.*

§ 1. Early Houses in Kent.

THE early history of the convent life of women in Anglo-Saxon England is chiefly an account of foundations.   Information on the establishment of religious settlements founded and presided over by women is plentiful, but well-nigh a century went by before women who had adopted religion as a profession gave any insight into their lives and characters through writings of their own.   The women who founded monasteries in Anglo-Saxon England have generally been raised to the rank of saint.

'In the large number of convents as well as in the names of female saints among the Anglo-Saxons,' says Lappenberg[1], 'we may recognise the same spirit which attracted the notice of the Roman army among the ancient Germans, and was manifested in the esteem and honour of women generally, and in the special influence exercised by the priestess.'

A great proportion of the women who founded religious houses were members of ruling families.   From the first it was usual for a princess to receive a grant of land from her husband on the occasion of her marriage, and this land together with what she inherited from her father she could dispose of at will.   She often devoted this property to founding a religious house where she established her daughters, and to which she retired either during her husband's lifetime or after his death.   The great honour paid by Christianity to the celibate life and the wide field

---

[1] *History of the Anglo-Saxons*, transl. Thorpe, 1845, vol. 2, p. 247.

of action opened to a princess in a religious house were strong
inducements to the sisters and daughters of kings to take the veil.

We have trustworthy information about many of the Anglo-
Saxon women who founded and presided over religious settlements and whom posterity reverenced as saints ; for their work
has been described by writers who either knew them, or gained
their information from those who did.   But there are other women
whose names only are mentioned in charters, or correspondence, or
in the Anglo-Saxon Chronicle.   Historians however welcome such
references as chronological evidence and as proofs of these
women's real existence; without them they would have nothing
to rely upon but accounts dating from a later period and often
consisting of little more than a series of incidents strung together
in order to explain the miracles with which the saints' relics were
locally credited.   There is a certain similarity between these later
accounts and those we have of pseudo-saints, but they differ from
those of an earlier date, for the writers of the 8th and 9th
centuries were not actuated like those of a later period by the
desire to give a miraculous rendering of fact.   Bede († 735) stands
pre-eminent among the earlier writers, and our admiration for
him increases as we discover his immense superiority to other
early historians.

Most of the women who were honoured as saints in England
belong to the first hundred years after the acceptance of
Christianity in these islands.   A few other women have been
revered as saints who lived in the 10th century and came under
the influence of the monastic revival which is associated with the
name of Dunstan († 988).   But no woman living during Anglo-
Norman times has been thus honoured, for the desire to raise
women to saintship was essentially Anglo-Saxon and was strongest
in the times which immediately followed the acceptance of Christianity.

It was more than two hundred years after the Anglo-Saxons
first set foot on British shores that they accepted Christianity.
The struggles between them and the inhabitants of the island had
ended in the recognised supremacy of the invaders, and bands of
heathen Germans, settling at first near the shore, for the sake of
the open country, had gradually made their way up the fruitful
valleys and into adjoining districts till they covered the land with
a network of settlements.   After the restlessness of invasion and
warfare the Anglo-Saxons settled down to domestic life and

agriculture, for compared with the British they were eminently tillers of the soil. Under their régime the cities built by the Romans and the British fastnesses alike fell into decay. The Anglo-Saxons dwelt in villages, and the British either lived there in subservience to them or else retired into districts of their own which were difficult of access.

The re-introduction of Christianity into these islands is associated with the name of Pope Gregory. Zealous and resolute in his efforts to strengthen the papal power by sending forth missionaries who were devoted to him, he watched his opportunity to gain a foothold for the faith in Kent.

Tradition connects the first step in this direction with the name of a Frankish princess, and Bede in his Church History tells how the marriage of Berhta, daughter of King Charibert of Paris (561–567), to King Aethelberht of Kent (586–616) brought an ecclesiastic to Canterbury who took possession of the ancient British church of St Martin : this event was speedily followed by the arrival of other ecclesiastics from Rome, who travelled across France under the leadership of Augustine.

At the time of Augustine's arrival the position of Kent was threatened by the growing supremacy of Northumbria. Through the activity both of Aethelfrith (✝617) and of Eadwin his successor, the land extending from the Humber to the Firth of Forth had been united under one rule; Northumbria was taking the lead among the petty kingdoms which had been formed in different parts of the island. The king of Kent strengthened his independent position by accepting the faith which had proved propitious to the Franks and by entering into alliance with his neighbours across the Channel; and it was no doubt with a view to encouraging peaceful relations with the north that Aethelburg the daughter of Aethelberht and Berhta was given in marriage to King Eadwin of Northumbria during the reign of her brother Eadbald (616–640).

Again the marriage of a Christian princess was made an occasion for extending the faith ; an ecclesiastic as usual followed in her train. Paulinus, the Roman chaplain who came north with Aethelburg, after various incidents picturesquely set forth by Bede, overcame King Eadwin's reluctance to embrace Christianity and prevailed upon him to be baptized at York with other members of his household on Easter day in the year 627. The event was followed by an influx of Christians into that city, for British Christianity had receded before the heathen Angles, but it still had strongholds in the north and was on the alert to regain lost ground. The city of York, during Roman rule, had been of great importance in affairs of administration. The Roman Eboracum nearly died out to arise anew as Anglian Eoforwic. King Eadwin recognised Paulinus as bishop and a stone church was begun on part of the ground now occupied by the Minster[1].

Bede loves to dwell on the story of this conversion, which was endeared to all devout churchmen by many associations. Eanflaed, the child of Eadwin and Aethelburg, whose baptism was its immediate cause, was afterwards a staunch supporter of Roman versus British Church tendencies. She was the patron of Wilfrith, in his time the most zealous advocate of the supremacy of Rome.

Among the members of Eadwin's household who were baptized on the same Easter day in 627 was Hild, a girl of fourteen, who afterwards became abbess of Whitby. She was grand-niece to Eadwin through her father Hereric, who had been treacherously made away with; her mother Beorhtswith and her sister Hereswith were among the early converts to Christianity. Hereswith afterwards married a king of the Angles, and at a later period was living in the Frankish settlement of Chelles (Cala), where her sister Hild at one time thought of joining her. Nothing is known of the life of Hild between the ages of fourteen and thirty-four, but evidently she had not dwelt in obscure retirement, for the Scottish prelate Aidan in 647, knowing that she was living in the midlands, begged her to return to the north. It is a noteworthy circumstance if, in an age when marriage was the rule, she remained single without taking the veil, but she may have been associated with some religious settlement[2].

It was only a few years after the acceptance of Christianity at York that the days of King Eadwin's reign, 'when a woman with her babe might walk scatheless from sea to sea,' came to an abrupt close. Eadwin was slain in 633 at the battle of Hatfield, a victim to the jealousy of the British king Caedwalla, who combined with the heathen king Penda of Mercia against him.

---

[1] Raine, *Historians of the Church of York.* Rolls series, vol. 1, Preface, p. xxiii.

[2] It is probable such settlements existed. Dugdale, *Monasticon*, vol. 3, p. 302, holds a religious foundation to have existed in Tinmouth founded 617–33, but in Bede, *Life of Cuthbert*, transl. Stevenson, T., 1887, ch. 3, it is referred to as a monastery formerly of men, now of ' virgins.'

Queen Aethelburg with her children and Paulinus fled from York to the coast and went by sea to Kent, where they were welcomed by her brother King Eadbald and by Archbishop Honorius.

At the beginning of his reign Eadbald of Kent had been in conflict with the Church owing to his marriage with his father's relict, a heathen wife whom Aethelberht had taken to himself after the death of Berhta. It is characteristic of the position held at first by Christian prelates in England that they depended entirely on the ruling prince for their position. Paulinus fled from York at the death of Eadwin, and Eadbald's adherence to heathen customs temporarily drove the Kentish prelate abroad. The king of Kent had, however, found it well to repudiate his heathen wife and to take a Christian princess of the Franks in her stead. This act restored him to the goodwill of his prelate, who returned to English shores.

Eadbald had settled a piece of land at Folkestone on his daughter Eanswith, and there about the year 630 she founded what is held to be the first religious settlement for women in Anglo-Saxon England[1]. The fact of this foundation is undisputed, but all we know of Eanswith's life is in the account given of her by Capgrave, an Augustinian monk who lived in the 15th century[2]. He tells us how she went to live at Folkestone and how a king of Northumbria wished to marry her, but as the king was a heathen, she made their union conditional on his prevailing upon his gods to manifest their power by miraculously lengthening a beam. In this he failed and consequently departed. There follows a description how Eanswith made a stream to flow 'againste the hylle,' from Smelton, a mile distant from Folkestone, possibly by means of a well-levelled water conduit. Capgrave also describes how she enforced the payment of tithes.

Eanswith's settlement was in existence at the close of the century, when it was destroyed or deserted during the viking invasion. A charter of King Athelstane dated 927 gives the land where ' stood the monastery and abbey of holy virgins and where also St Eanswith lies buried' to Christ Church, Canterbury, the

---

[1] Dugdale, *Monasticon*, ' Folkestone,' vol. 1, p. 451.

[2] Hardy, Th. D., *Descriptive Catalogue of Materials*, 1862, vol. 1, p. 226 : ' the life of Eanswith cannot be traced to any earlier authority than John of Tinmouth († c. 1380) whose account Capgrave († 1484) embodied in his collection of saints' lives.' The work of Capgrave, *Catalogus SS. Angliae*, was printed in 1516; the *Kalendre of the newe Legende of Englande*, printed 1516 (Pynson), from which expressions are quoted in the text, is an abridged translation of it into English.

house having been destroyed by the 'Pagans[1].' Capgrave says that its site was swallowed by the sea, perhaps in one of the landslips common to the coast; the holy woman's relics were then transferred to the church of St Peter. A church at Folkestone is dedicated conjointly to St Mary and St Eanswith, and a church at Brensett in Kent is dedicated solely to her[2].

Queen Aethelburg coming from the north also settled in Kent at a place called Liming[3]. Bede knows nothing of her after her departure from the north, and we have to depend on Canterbury traditions for information concerning her and the religious house she founded. Gocelin, a monk of Flanders who came into Kent in the 11th century, describes Queen Aethelburg as 'building and up-raising this temple at Liming, and obtaining the first name there and a remarkable burial-place in the north porch against the south wall of the church covered with an arch[4].' Modern research has shown that the buildings at Liming were so arranged as to contain a convent of monks as well as of nuns. The church is of Roman masonry and may have been built out of the fragments of a villa, such as the Anglo-Saxons frequently adapted to purposes of their own, or it may have been a Roman basilica restored.

Queen Aethelburg, foundress of Liming, is not usually reckoned a saint; she has no day[5] and collections of saints' lives generally omit her. The identity of name between her and Aethelburg († c. 676), abbess of Barking at a somewhat later date, has caused some confusion between them[6]. Gocelin mentions that both Queen Aethelburg and 'St Eadburga' were buried at Liming[7]. A well lying to the east of the church at Liming is to this day called St Ethelburga's well, and she is commonly held to be identical with Queen Aethelburg[8].

At a somewhat later date another religious settlement for women was founded at Sheppey in Kent by Queen Sexburg, the wife of Earconberht of Kent (640–664), the successor of Eadbald.

---

[1] Dugdale, *Monasticon*, 'Folkestone,' vol. 1, p. 451, nr 2.

[2] Smith and Wace, *Dictionary of Christian Biography*, 1880, 'Eanswitha'; also *A. SS. Boll.*, St Eanswida, Aug. 31.

[3] Dugdale, *Monasticon*, 'Liming,' vol. 1, p. 452.

[4] Jenkins, R. C., in *Gentleman's Magazine*, 1862, August, p. 196 quotes this statement; I do not see where he takes it from.

[5] Stanton, R., *Menology of England and Wales*, 1887, p. 144.

[6] Hardy, Th. D., *Descriptive Catalogue of Materials*, 1862, vol. 1, p. 475.

[7] Gocelinus, *Vita St Wereburgae*, c. 1 (in Migne, *Patrol. Cursus Compl.*, vol. 155).

[8] Bright, W., *Early English Church History*, 1878, p. 130 footnote.

We know little of the circumstances of the foundation[1]. Sexburg was a princess of East Anglia, where Christianity had been accepted owing to the influence of King Eadwin of Northumbria[2] and where direct relations with France had been established.

'For at that time,' says Bede, writing of these districts[3], 'there being not yet many monasteries built in the region of the Angles, many were wont, for the sake of the monastic mode of life, to go from Britain to the monasteries of the Franks and of Gaul; they also sent their daughters to the same to be instructed and to be wedded to the heavenly spouse, chiefly in the monasteries of Brie (Faremoutiers), Chelles, and Andelys.'

Two princesses of Anglia, Saethrith and Aethelburg, who were sisters or half-sisters to Sexburg, remained abroad and became in succession abbesses of Brie as mentioned above. Sexburg's daughter Earcongotha also went there, and was promoted to the rank of abbess. Both Bede and the Anglo-Saxon Chronicle speak in praise of her. For her other daughter Eormenhild, who was married to Wulfhere, king of Mercia, Queen Sexburg of Kent founded the house at Sheppey; she herself went to live at Ely in her sister Aethelthrith's convent.

The statement of Bede that women at this time went abroad for their education is borne out by the traditional records of Mildthrith, first abbess of a religious settlement in Thanet which rose to considerable importance[4]. A huge mass of legend supplements the few historical facts we know of Mildthrith, whose influence, judging from the numerous references to her and her widespread cult, was greater than that of any other English woman-saint. Several days in the Calendar are consecrated to her, and the site where her relics had been deposited was made a subject of controversy in the 11th century. As late as 1882 we find that some of her relics were brought from Deventer in Holland to Thanet, and that Pope Leo XIII granted a plenary indulgence on the occasion[5]. Churches in London, Oxford, Canterbury and other

---

[1] Dugdale, *Monasticon*, 'Sheppey,' vol. 2, p. 49.

[2] Bright, W., *Early English Church History*, 1878, p. 123.

[3] Bede, *Hist. Eccles.*, bk 3, ch. 8, transl. Gidley, 1870.

[4] Dugdale, *Monasticon*, 'Thanet,' vol. 1, p. 447; Hardy, Th. D., *Descriptive Catalogue of Materials*, 1862, on lives of St Mildred, vol. 1, p. 376; *A. SS. Boll.*, St Mildreda, July 13.

[5] Stanton, R., *Menology of England and Wales*, 1887, July 13.

places are dedicated to St Mildred[1], and Capgrave, William of Malmesbury and others give details of her story, which runs as follows:

Her mother Eormenburg, sometimes called Domneva, was married to Merewald, prince of Hacanos, a district in Herefordshire. King Ecgberht (664–673) of Kent gave her some land in Thanet as a blood-fine for the murder of her two young brothers, and on it she founded a monastery. She asked for as much land as her tame deer could run over in one course, and received over ten thousand acres of the best land in Kent[2].

Besides Mildthrith Eormenburg had two daughters, Mildburg and Mildgith, and a boy, the holy child Merwin, who was translated to heaven in his youth. Mildburg presided over a religious house at Wenlock in Shropshire, and her legend contains picturesque traits but little trustworthy information[3]. We know even less of the other daughter Mildgith. It is doubtful whether she lived in Kent or in the north, but she is considered a saint[4]. An ancient record says that 'St Mildgith lies in Northumbria where her miraculous powers were often exhibited and still are,' but it does not point out at what place[5].

According to her legend, Mildthrith, by far the best known of the sisters, was sent abroad to Chelles for her education, where the abbess Wilcoma wished her to marry her kinsman, and on the girl's refusal cast her into a burning furnace from which she came forth unharmed. The girl sent her mother a psalter she had written together with a lock of her hair. She made her escape and arrived in England, landing at Ebbsfleet. 'As she descended from the ship to the land and set her feet on a certain square stone the print of her feet remained on it, most life-like, she not thinking anything; God so accomplishing the glory of his handmaid. And more than that; the dust that was scrapen off thence being drunk did cure sundry diseases[6].' It appears that a stone to which a superstitious reverence was attached was walled into the Church of St Mildred in Thanet.

---

[1] Smith and Wace, *Dictionary of Christian Biography*, article 'Mildred' by Bishop Stubbs.

[2] Dugdale, *Monasticon*, 'Thanet,' vol. 1, p. 447.

[3] *A. SS. Boll.*, St Milburga, Feb. 23.

[4] Ibid., St Mildwida, Jan. 17.

[5] Stanton, R., *Menology of England and Wales*, Jan. 17.

[6] 'Lives of Women Saints' (written about 1610) p. 64, edited by Horstman for the Early Engl. Text Soc., London, 1887.

Other incidents told of her influence are not without their humorous side. One day a bell-ringer, forgetful of his duties, had dropped asleep, when Mildthrith appeared to him and gave him a blow on the ear, saying, ' Understand, fellow, that this is an oratory to pray in, not a dormitory to sleep in,' and so vanished.

Thus writes the author of her legend. The fact remains that Mildthrith was presiding over a settlement in Kent towards the close of the 7th century. For in a charter of privileges granted between 696 and 716 by King Wihtred and Queen Werburg to the churches and monasteries of Kent granting them security against interference, her name is among those of the five lady abbesses who place their signatures to the document[1]. These names stand after those of the archbishop of Canterbury and the bishop of Rochester and are as follows ; ' Mildritha, Aetheldritha, Aette, Wilnotha and Hereswytha.' The settlements mentioned in the body of the charter[2] as being subject to them are Upminstre (or Minstre) in Thanet, afterwards known as St Mildred's, Southminstre, a colony of Minstre, Folkestone, Liming and Sheppey, the foundation of which has been described.

Thus at the close of the 7th century there existed in the province of Kent alone five religious settlements governed by abbesses who added this title to their signatures, or who, judging from the place given to them, ranked in dignity below the bishops but above the presbyters (presbyteri), whose names follow theirs in the list. From the wording of the charter we see that men who accepted the tonsure and women who received the veil were at this time classed together. Those who set their signatures to the charter agreed that neither abbot nor abbess should be appointed without the consent of a prelate.

The charter is the more valuable as it establishes the existence of the Kentish convents and their connection with each other at a period when we have only fragmentary information about the religious houses in the south. We must turn to the north for fuller information as to the foundation and growth of religious settlements presided over by women during the early Christian period.

---

[1] Haddon and Stubbs, *Councils and Ecclesiastical Documents*, 1869, vol. 3, p. 240.

[2] ' Upmynstre, Suthmynstre, Folcanstan, Limming, Sceppeis.'

§ 2.   The Monastery at Whitby[1].

A temporary collapse of the Christian faith had followed the death of King Eadwin of Northumbria, but the restoration of King Oswald, who was not so strong as his predecessor in administrative power but whose religious fervour was greater, had given it a new impulse and a new direction.

Oswald had passed some time of his life in Iona or Hii, the great Scottish religious settlement and the stronghold of British Christianity in the Hebrides.   Here he had made friends with the ecclesiastic Aidan, who became his staunch supporter.   Soon after his accession Oswald summoned a monk from Iona 'to minister the word of the faith to himself and to his people,' and when it was found that the monk made no progress, Aidan was moved to go among the Angles himself.   In preference to York he chose the island Lindisfarne for his headquarters, but he spent much of his time with Oswald, helping him to set the practice and teaching of religion on a firmer footing.

It was during this part of Aidan's career that he consecrated Heiu[2], according to Bede 'the first woman who took the vow and the habit of a nun in the province of Northumbria.'   Heiu presided over a congregation of women at Hartlepool in Durham, from which she removed to Calcaria of the Romans, which is perhaps identical with Healaugh near Tadcaster, where apparently Heiu's name is retained.   Further details of her career are wanting.

Aidan's labours were interrupted for a time.   Again the fierce and impetuous King Penda of Mercia invaded Northumbria, and again the Christian Angles fled before the midland heathens. King Oswald fell in battle (642) and Aidan retired to his rocky island, from which he watched the fires kindled all over the country first by the raids of Penda, and afterwards by civil strife between the two provinces of Northumbria, Deira and Bernicia. This arose through the rival claims to the throne of Oswiu, Oswald's brother, and Oswin, who was King Eadwin's relative.

An understanding was at length effected between them by which Oswiu accepted Bernicia, while Oswin took possession of Deira, and Aidan, who found a patron in Oswin, returned to his work.

---

[1] Dugdale, *Monasticon*, 'Whitby,' vol. 1, p. 405.

[2] Bede, *Eccl. Hist.*, bk 4, ch. 23 transl. Gidley, 1870. Dugdale, *Monasticon*, 'Hartlepool,' vol. 6, p. 1618, places the foundation about the year 640.

He now persuaded Hild[1], who was waiting in Anglia for an opportunity to cross over to France, where she purposed joining her sister, to give up this plan and to return to the north to share in the work in which he was engaged. Hild came and settled down to a monastic life with a few companions on the river Wear. A year later, when Heiu retired to Calcaria, Hild became abbess at Hartlepool. She settled there only a few years before the close of Aidan's career. He died in 651 shortly after his patron Oswin, whose murder remains the great stain on the life of his rival Oswiu.

A 12th century monk, an inmate of the monastery of St Beeves in Cumberland, has written a life of St Bega, the patron saint of his monastery, whom he identifies on the one hand with the abbess Heiu, consecrated by Aidan, and on the other with Begu, a nun who had a vision of Hild's death at the monastery of Hackness in the year 680. His narrative is further embellished with local traditions about a woman Bega, who came from Ireland and received as a gift from the Lady Egermont the extensive parish and promontory of St Beeves, which to this day bear her name[2].

There has been much speculation concerning this holy woman Bega, but it is probable that the writer of her life combined myths which seem to be Keltic with accounts of two historical persons whom Bede keeps quite distinct. There is no reason to doubt Bede's statements in this matter or in others concerning affairs in the north, for he expressly affirms that he 'was able to gain information not from one author only but from the faithful assertion of innumerable witnesses who were in a position to know and remember these things; besides those things,' he adds, 'which I could ascertain myself.' He passed his whole life studying and writing in the monasteries of SS. Peter and Paul, two settlements spoken of as one, near the mouth of the river Wear, close to where Hild had first settled. He went there during the lifetime of Bennet Biscop († 690), the contemporary of Hild and a shining representative of the culture the Anglo-Saxons attained in the 7th century.

Hild settled at Hartlepool about the year 647. Eight years later Oswiu finally routed the army of Penda, whose attacks had been for so many years like a battering ram to the greatness of Northumbria. And in fulfilment of a vow he had made that the

---

[1] Bede, *Eccl. Hist.* bk 3, chs. 24–25 ; bk 4, chs. 23–24.

[2] *A. SS. Boll.*, St Bega, Sept. 6; Tomlinson, G. C., *Life and Miracles of St Bega*, 1839.

Christian religion should profit if God granted him victory, he gave Hild the charge of his daughter Aelflaed 'who had scarcely completed the age of onė year, to be consecrated to God in perpetual virginity, besides bestowing on the Church twelve estates.' Extensive property came with the child into the care of Hild, perhaps including the site of Streaneshalch[1], which is better known as Whitby, a name given to it at a later date by the Danes. Bede says that Hild here undertook to construct and arrange a monastery.

Bede thus expresses himself on the subject of Hild's life and influence during the term of over thirty years which she spent first as abbess of Hartlepool and then as abbess of Whitby[2]:

'Moreover, Hild, the handmaid of Christ, having been appointed to govern that monastery (at Hartlepool), presently took care to order it in the regular way of life, in all respects, according as she could gain information from learned men. For Bishop Aidan, also, and all the religious men who knew her, were wont to visit her constantly, to love her devotedly, and to instruct her diligently, on account of her innate wisdom, and her delight in the service of God.

'When, then, she had presided over this monastery for some years, being very intent on establishing the regular discipline, according as she could learn it from learned men, it happened that she undertook also to construct and arrange a monastery in the place which is called Streanshalch; and this work being enjoined on her, she was not remiss in accomplishing it. For she established this also in the same discipline of regular life in which she established the former monastery ; and, indeed, taught there also the strict observance of justice, piety, and chastity, and of the other virtues, but mostly of peace and charity, so that, after the example of the primitive Church, there was therein no one rich, no one poor; all things were common to all, since nothing seemed to be the private property of any one. Moreover, her prudence was so great that not only did ordinary persons, but even sometimes kings and princes, seek and receive counsel of her in their necessities. She made those who were under her direction give so much time to the reading of the Divine Scriptures, and exercise themselves so much in works of righteousness, that very many, it appeared, could readily be found there,

---

[1] *Carthularium abbathiae de Whiteby*, publ. Surtees Soc., 1879.

[2] Bede, *Eccles. History*, bk 4, ch. 23, translat. Gidley, 1870, with additions and alterations.

who could worthily enter upon the ecclesiastical grade, that is
the service of the altar.'

In point of fact five men who had studied in Hild's monastery
were promoted to the episcopate. Foremost among them is John,
bishop of Hexham (687–705) and afterwards of York († 721), the
famous St John of Beverley, a canonised saint of the Church, of
whose doings Bede has left an account. In this[1] we hear of the
existence of another monastery for women at Watton (Vetadun)
not far from Whitby, where Bishop John went to visit the abbess
Heriburg, who was living there with her 'daughter in the flesh,'
Cwenburg, whom she designed to make abbess in her stead.
We hear no more about Watton till centuries later, but Bede's
remark is interesting as showing how natural he felt it to be that
the rule of a settlement should pass from mother to daughter.

Cwenburg was suffering from a swollen arm which John tells us
was very serious, 'since she had been bled on the fourth day of the
moon,' 'when both the light of the moon and the tide of the ocean
were on their increase. And what can I do for the girl if she is
at death's door?' he exclaims. However his combined prayers and
remedies, which were so often efficacious, helped to restore her.

Aetla, another of Hild's scholarly disciples, held the see of
Dorchester, though perhaps only temporarily during the absence
of Aegilberht. A third, Bosa, was archbishop of York between
678 and 686; Bede speaks of him as a monk of Whitby, a man
of great holiness and humility. Oftfor, another of Hild's monks,
went from Whitby to Canterbury, to study 'a more perfect'
system of discipline under Archbishop Theodore († 690), and
subsequently became bishop of Worcester.

The career of these men shows that the system of discipline
and education under Hild at Whitby compared favourably with
that of other settlements. At the outset she had followed the
usages of the Scottish Church, with which she was familiar through
her intercourse with Aidan, but when the claims for an independent
British Church were defeated at Whitby, she accepted the change
and adopted the Roman usage.

The antagonism which had existed from the first appearance
of Augustine in England between Roman Christianity and British
Christianity as upheld by the Scottish and Welsh clergy took the
form of open disagreement in Northumbria. On one side was
the craving for ritual, for refinement and for union with Rome;

[1] Bede, *Eccles. History*, bk 5, ch. 3.

on the other insistence by the Scottish clergy on their right to independence.

Aidan had been succeeded at Lindisfarne by Finnan, owing to whose influence discussion was checked for the time being. But after his death (661) the latent antagonism came to a head over the practical difficulty due to the different dates at which King Oswiu and Queen Eanflaed kept Easter. Thus the way was cleared for the Whitby synod (664), a 'gathering of all orders of the Church system,' at which the respective claims of Roman and of British Christianity were discussed.

The British interest was represented among others by Colman, Finnan's successor at Lindisfarne, who temporarily held the see at York, and by Aegilberht, bishop of Dorchester. The opposite side was taken by the protégé of Queen Eanflaed, Wilfrith, abbot of Ripon, whose ardour in the cause of Rome had been greatly augmented by going abroad with Bennet Biscop about the year 653. Besides these and other prelates, King Oswiu and his son and co-regent Ealhfrith were present at the synod. The abbess Hild was also there, but she took no part in the discussion.

The questions raised were not of doctrine but of practice. The computation of Easter, the form of the tonsure, matters not of belief but of apparently trivial externals, were the points round which the discussion turned. Owing chiefly to Wilfrith's influence the decision was in favour of Rome, and a strong rebuff was given for a time to the claim for an independent British Church in the north.

The choice of Whitby as the site of the synod marks the importance which this settlement had attained within ten years of its foundation. Those who have stood on the height of the cliff overlooking the North Sea and have let their gaze wander over the winding river course and the strand below can realize the lordly situation of the settlement which occupies such a distinguished place among the great houses and nurseries of culture at Hexham, Wearmouth, Jarrow, Ripon and York.

The property which the monastery held in overlordship extended along the coast for many miles, and the settlement itself consisted of a large group of buildings; for there are references to the dwellings for the men, for the women, and to an outlying house for the sick. These dwellings were gathered round the ancient British Church of St Peter, which was situated under the shelter of the brow of the cliff where King Eadwin lay buried, and which continued to be the burial-place of the Northumbrian kings. Isolated chapels and churches with separate bands of religious votaries belonging to them lay in other parts of the monastic property, and were subject to the abbess of Whitby. We hear of a minor monastery at Easington (Osingadun)[1] during the rule of Aelflaed, Hild's successor, and at Hackness (Hacanos) on the limit of the monastic property, thirteen miles south of Whitby, a monastery of some importance had been founded by Hild[2]. Bands of men and of women dwelt here under the government of Frigith, and it was here that the nun Begu had a vision of Hild on the night of her death, when she saw her borne aloft by attendant angels[3].

The name of Hild and the monastery at Whitby are further endeared to posterity through their connection with Caedmon, the most celebrated of the vernacular poets of Northumbria and the reputed author of the Anglo-Saxon metrical paraphrases of the Old Testament[4]. It was his great reputation as a singer that made Hild seek Caedmon and persuade him to join her community. Here the practice of reading Holy Scripture made him familiar with the stories of Hebrew literature in their grand and simple setting, and he drank of the waters of that well to which so many centuries of creative and representative art have gone for inspiration.

Caedmon's power of song had been noticed outside the monastery.

'And all concluded that a celestial gift had been granted him by the Lord. And they interpreted to him a certain passage of sacred history or doctrine, and ordered him to turn it if he could into poetical rhythm. And he, having undertaken it, departed, and returning in the morning brought back what he was ordered to do, composed in most excellent verse. Whereupon presently the abbess, embracing heartily the grace of God in the man, directed him to leave the secular habit, and to take the monastic vow; and having together with all her people received him into the monastery associated him with the company of the brethren, and ordered him to be instructed in the whole course of sacred history. And he converted into most sweet song whatever he could learn from hearing, by thinking it over by himself, and,

---

[1] Bede, *Life of St Cuthbert*, ch. 10; Dugdale, *Monasticon*, vol. 1, p. 233, mentions Easington only as a manor of Durham.

[2] Dugdale, *Monasticon*, 'Hackness,' vol. 3, p. 633.

[3] Bede, *Eccles. History*, bk 4, ch. 23.

[4] *Dictionary of Nat. Biography*, article 'Caedmon' by Henry Bradley.

as though a clean animal, by ruminating; and by making it resound more sweetly, made his teachers in turn his hearers[1].'

These passages are curious as showing that a singer of national strains was persuaded to adapt his art to the purposes of religion. The development of Church music is usually held to have been distinct from that of folk-music, but in exceptional cases such as this, there seems to have been a relation between the two.

Excavations recently made on several of the sites of ancient northern monasteries have laid bare curious and interesting remains which add touches of reality to what is known about the houses of the north during this early period[2]. In a field called Cross Close at Hartlepool near Durham skeletons of men and women were found, and a number of monumental stones of peculiar shape, some with runic inscriptions of women's names. Some of these names are among those of the abbesses inscribed in the so-called 'Book of Life of Durham,' a manuscript written in gold and silver lettering in the early part of the 9th century[3]. Again, an ancient tombstone of peculiar design was found at Healaugh; and at Hackness several memorial crosses are preserved, one of which bears the inscription of the name Aethelburg, who no doubt is the abbess of that name with whom Aelflaed, Hild's successor at Whitby, in 705 travelled to the death-bed of King Ealdfrith[4].

Finally on the Whitby coast on the south side of the abbey a huge kitchen-midden was discovered. A short slope here leads to the edge of the cliff, and excavations on this slope and at its foot, which was once washed by the tide, have revealed the facts that the denizens of the original monastery were wont to throw the refuse of their kitchen over the cliff, and that the lighter material remained on the upper ledges, the heavier rolling to the bottom.

Among the lighter deposits were found bones of birds, oyster, whelk and periwinkle shells, and two combs, one of which bears a runic inscription. Among the heavier deposits were bones of oxen, a few of sheep, and a large number of the bones and tusks of wild swine, besides several iron pot-hooks and other implements; a bone spindle and a divided ink-horn are among the objects specified. An inscribed leaden bulla found among the

---

[1] Bede, *Eccles. History*, bk 4, ch. 24, transl. Gidley, 1870.

[2] Haigh, D. H., 'On the monasteries of St Heiu and St Hild,' *Yorksh. Archaeolog. Journal*, vol. 3, p. 370. I do not know on what authority Haigh designates Heiu as saint.

[3] Gray, de Birch, *Fasti Monastici Aevi Saxonici*, 1872, p. 15.

[4] Comp. below, p. 106.

refuse is declared by experts to be earlier than the 8th century; it is therefore proof that these remains were deposited during the earlier period of the existence of Hild's monastery, possibly during her lifetime.

Hild died after an illness of several years on November 17, 680. Would that there were more data whereby to estimate her personality! The few traits of her character that have been preserved, her eagerness to acquire knowledge, her success in imparting it to others, her recognition of the need of unity in the Church, the interest she took in one who could repeat the stories of the new faith in strains which made them intelligible to the people, are indicative of a strong personality and of an understanding which appreciated the needs of her time.

Various myths, of which Bede knows nothing, have been attached to her name in course of time. According to a popular legend she transformed the snakes of the district into the ammonites familiar to visitors to those parts. And it is said that at certain times of the day her form can be seen flitting across the abbey ruins[1].

At her death the rule of the settlement passed to Aelflaed, the princess who had been given into her care as a child. After King Oswiu's death in 670 Queen Eanflaed joined her daughter in the monastery. The princess and abbess Aelflaed proved herself worthy of the influence under which she had grown up, and we shall find her among the persons of importance who took up a decided attitude in regard to the disturbances which broke out through the action of Bishop Wilfrith. The beginnings of these difficulties belong to the lifetime of Hild : we do not know that she took any interest in the matter, but judging from indirect evidence we should say that she shared in the feeling which condemned the prelate's anti-national and ultra-Roman tendencies.

§ 3. Ely and the influence of Bishop Wilfrith.

The further history of the monastery of Whitby and the history of the foundation of Ely are closely connected with the prelate Wilfrith, and for this reason his actions and attitude claim our attention. In him we recognise a direct advocate of the principle that a queen could if she chose leave her husband and retire to a religious settlement, and that such a course would secure her the favour of the Church.

[1] Charlton, L., *History of Whitby*, 1779, p. 33.

It has been said of him that he was the most important man in Northumbria for forty years after the Whitby synod[1]. He owed his education to Queen Eanflaed, whose attention he had attracted when quite a youth, and who had sent him into Kent to complete his education; there he imbibed strong Roman sympathies. He lived for some years in France and Italy in the society of Bennet Biscop, and he was already held in high esteem at the time of the Whitby synod, which he attended in the character of abbot of the monastery at Ripon, a house he had founded with the help of Ealhfrith.

When Colman and his adherents beat a rapid retreat to the north in consequence of the decision of the synod, Wilfrith became bishop of York, an appointment which meant ecclesiastical supremacy over the whole vast province of Northumbria. His intellectual brilliancy gained him many admirers, but an innate restlessness of disposition and a wilful determination to support the power of Rome to the national detriment launched him into repeated difficulties with temporal and spiritual rulers. He was at the height of prosperity and popularity when Ecgfrith succeeded Oswiu in 670 after the death of Ealhfrith. Wilfrith had hitherto been on good terms with Ecgfrith, but a breach in their relations soon occurred, partly owing to the conduct of Ecgfrith's wife, Aethelthrith, whom Wilfrith supported against the king.

Aethelthrith, known to a later age as Etheldred or Awdrey, was the daughter of King Anna of the East Angles (635–645), whose province, including the present shires of Norfolk and Suffolk, was removed from direct intercourse with others by the almost impassable reaches of the fens. Anglia has not left any annals of her own, and we have to depend for the names and dates of her kings on the slight information which other provinces have preserved.

Written legends generally consider Anna as the father also of Sexburg, the foundress of Sheppey, and of Aethelburg and Saethrith, two princesses who had settled in France, as well as of Wihtburg, a woman-saint of whom very little is known, and who was associated with a religious foundation at East Dereham in Norfolk[2]. We further learn from legend that King Anna was married to Hereswith, sister of Hild of Whitby, and Aethelthrith is spoken of as niece

---

[1] Raine, *Historians of the Church of York*, Rolls series, vol. 1, Preface p. xxvii. This volume contains reprints of several accounts of the life of Wilfrith, including the one by Eddi.

[2] *A. SS. Boll.*, St Withburga, March 17; Dugdale, *Monasticon*, 'East Dereham,' vol. 2, p. 176.

to the great abbess Hild. But this connection is discredited by a statement in Bede which suggests that Hild's sister Hereswith was married not to King Anna but to his successor King Aethelhere (654–664). It is difficult to decide to which of the kings of the East Angles Hereswith was married, but Anna was certainly not her husband[1].

The princess Aethelthrith at the time of her marriage with the king of Northumbria was the widow of Tunberht prince of the South-Gyrvi, or fen-country men. Anglia stood at this time in a relation of dependence to Northumbria, and in 664, four years before the Whitby synod, Aethelthrith a woman of over thirty was married to Ecgfrith a boy of fifteen, the heir-apparent to the throne of Northumbria. The marriage was no doubt arranged for political reasons.

The consequences which followed render these facts worthy of notice. For Aethelthrith on her arrival in the north at once conceived a great admiration for the prelate Wilfrith, while she treated her husband with contumely. She bestowed on Wilfrith the extensive property at Hexham which she had received from her husband, and on which Wilfrith built the church which was spoken of in his days as the most wonderful building on this side of the Alps[2]. Judging from what Wilfrith himself told him about the queen's attitude Bede says 'the king knew that she loved no man more than Wilfrith.'

The events that followed bear out this statement, for after living about ten years with the king, Aethelthrith left him and repaired to the monastery of Coldingham (Coludesburg) in Berwickshire, which had been founded and was ruled over by Aebbe, sister, or perhaps half-sister, of the kings Oswald and Oswiu[3]. King Ecgfrith may or may not have agreed to this step. Eddi, the friend and biographer of Wilfrith, maintains a judicious silence on the relations of the king and queen, while Bede represents[4] that Aethelthrith had always had an aversion to the married state and describes how he had been told by Wilfrith himself that Ecgfrith

---

[1] Haigh, D. H., 'On the monasteries of St Heiu and St Hild,' *Yorkshire Archaeol. Journal*, vol. 3, p. 352, decides in favour of Aethelric.

[2] Bright, W., *Early English Church History*, 1878, p. 235.

[3] Dugdale, *Monasticon*, 'Coldingham,' vol. 6, p. 149. The promontory of St Abb's Head retains her name. She is believed to have founded another religious settlement at a place in Durham on the river Derwent called Ebbchester, and the village church there is dedicated to her (*Dict. of Nat. Biog.*).

[4] Bede, *Eccles. History*, bk 4, ch. 19.

promised much land and money to the prelate if he persuaded the queen to allow him conjugal rights.

At Coldingham Wilfrith gave Aethelthrith the veil ; this act involved her breaking all marital ties. But she cannot have deemed her position secure, for she presently left Coldingham, which was within her husband's territory, and went to Ely, the island in the fens which her first husband Tunberht had bestowed on her.

Under the date 673 stand in the Anglo-Saxon Chronicle these words : 'And Aetheldryth began the monastery at Ely.' It was situated on a hill prominent above the flatness of the surrounding fen-land, which at that time consisted of a wilderness of marsh and water. Men and women readily flocked thither to live under the guidance of the queen. We hear that she received material aid from her cousin King Ealdwulf of Anglia, that Hunna acted as her chaplain, and that Bishop Wilfrith stayed with her on his passage from Northumbria to Rome. Thomas of Ely (fl. c. 1174) has embellished the account of Aethelthrith's flight and journey south by introducing into the story various picturesque incidents, which Bede does not mention. She, with her companions Sewenna and Sewara[1], was saved from her pursuers by water rising round a rock on which they had taken refuge, and she was sheltered by an ash-tree which grew in one night out of her pilgrim's staff and which can still be seen at a place called Etheldredstowe[2]. As Aethelthrith of Ely is a favourite saint of English legend it is interesting to find water and the tree miraculously associated with her.

Shortly after Aethelthrith's departure Ecgfrith summoned Theodore, archbishop of Canterbury, to the north to divide the diocese of York into three separate districts. Wilfrith resented these proceedings as an infringement of his rights, but as he was unable to influence the king he determined to seek the intervention of the Pope and set out for Rome. His absence extended over several years.

It was at this time, Bede tells us, that Aethelthrith 'having built a monastery at Ely began both by example and by admonition of heavenly life to be a virgin mother of very many virgins[3].' The particulars he gives of her life show that she had renounced the splendours which constituted so essential a feature of royalty and had willingly devoted herself to humility and self-denial. She wore no linen, only wool, rarely used a warm bath, save on the

[1] *A. SS. Boll.*, St Etheldreda June 23, Thomas of Ely, *Vita* ch. 41.
[2] Bright, W., *Early English Church History*, 1878, p. 252 footnote.
[3] Bede, *Eccles. History*, bk 4, ch. 19.

eve of great festivals, and assisted at the washing of others. When she fell ill of a tumour in her throat, she told the physician Cynefrith, who lanced it, that she looked upon it as a chastisement for her love of wearing necklaces in her youth. And on her death-bed she desired to be buried in a wooden coffin in the nun's ordinary cemetery.

The fame of Aethelthrith spread rapidly. She was looked upon as a virgin, and her name with the epithet virgin was inscribed at an early date in both the Anglo-Saxon and Roman Calendars, and to this day it is to be found in the Book of Common Prayer. Later writers of her legend say that she lived with Ecgfrith 'not as a wyfe but as a lady,' and add as a fitting pendant to this story that she maintained similar relations with her first husband Tunberht[1]. She died in the year 679, having presided over her monastery only six or seven years, but during that time it had gained marked importance. Many women had come to live there with her, and among them her sister Sexburg, widow of the king of Kent, who had founded the monastery at Sheppey and now succeeded Aethelthrith as abbess of Ely.

The chief event of Sexburg's rule at Ely was the exhumation of the bones of Aethelthrith in 695, which were transferred to a stone coffin of antique workmanship which had been opportunely, or miraculously as contemporaries thought, discovered at the old Roman colony of Grantchester near Cambridge[2]. This translation took place on the 17th of October, a day on which the relics were again transferred in 1106, and which is the date of the important fair of Ely[3].

In a supplement to the History of Ely by Bentham, Essex gives an account of the ruins of the conventual church begun by Aethelthrith[4]. Judging from his investigations the church consisted of two parts, the nave and the choir, the windows of the nave outside being ornamented with pillars and arches, and the choir being arched with stone. Traces were still left of the apartments of the abbess from which she could enter the church in a private manner, and of a building opposite of equal dimensions which served as a dormitory for the nuns. At a little distance the remains of another large building were discovered, one room

---

[1] *Kalendre of the newe Legende of Englande*, printed 1516 (Pynson) fol. 39 b.
[2] Bede, *Eccles. History*, bk 4, ch. 19.
[3] *Dictionary of National Biography*, 'Etheldreda, Saint.'
[4] Bentham, *History of Ely*, 1817, p. 9.

of which, near the entrance to the settlement, was a parlour for the reception of strangers, and the apartment over it a dormitory for the men.

We know little more than the name of the next abbess of Ely. She was Sexburg's daughter Eormenhild, wife of King Wulfhere of Mercia, who had hitherto dwelt in the monastery of Sheppey. Eormenhild in her turn was succeeded by her daughter, the celebrated St Werburg of Chester, who was never married. Various stories are preserved about Werburg's influence, but without reference to her work at Ely. We are indebted to Gocelin for the oldest account of her[1]. He tells us that her uncle King Aethelraed of Mercia entrusted her with the care of all the monasteries in his kingdom, that she had founded religious houses at Trentham and at Hanbury, besides turning a palace at Wedon-le-Street into a monastery[2]. He speaks of her as a person of great cheerfulness and benevolence, and of a peaceful and happy disposition. Several accounts of her are extant in manuscripts of different dates, and as late as the 15th century her life was made the subject of a most graceful metrical epic by the poet Henri Bradshaw († 1513)[3].

We are told that Werburg died at Trentham and that the society of that place wished to keep her body, but the nuns of Hanbury carried it off by force and enshrined it at Hanbury where the day of her deposition was kept[4]. During the viking invasion in 875 the body for the sake of safety was conveyed to Chester, of which town St Werburg then became patron saint. This incident gave rise at a later date to the story that the saint had founded the monastery and the chief church at Chester on land given to her by her father. Livien mentions that nine churches in England are dedicated to St Werburg, who appears to have been a person of considerable importance[5].

Once more we must return to the north and to the work of Bishop Wilfrith, as he came into contact with various other religious women. When he returned to England after an absence of several

---

[1] Gocelinus, *Vita St Wereburgae* (in Migne, *Patrol. Cursus Compl.* vol. 155).

[2] Stanton, R., *Menology of England and Wales*, 1887, p. 49, calls it Weedon in Northamptonshire; Dugdale, *Monasticon*, 'Wedon,' vol. 6, p. 1051, doubts its existence.

[3] *Life of St Werburgh*, 1521, reprinted for the Early Engl. Text Soc., 1887.

[4] Stanton, R., *Menology of England and Wales*, 1887, p. 49.

[5] Livien, E., 'On early religious houses in Staffordshire,' *Journal of the British Archaeolog. Assoc.*, vol. 29, p. 329. (The widespread cult of St Werburg may be due to there having been several saints of this name; comp. Stanton, R., *Menology.*)

years Aethelthrith was dead, but King Ecgfrith's hatred of him had not abated. Insulted in his person and nation he caused Wilfrith to be thrown into prison, offering to give him back part of his bishopric and other gifts if he would submit to royal authority and disclaim the genuineness of the document brought from Rome[1]. Queen Eormenburg, whom Ecgfrith had taken to wife in place of Aethelthrith, further embittered the king against the unlucky prelate. She appropriated the reliquary Wilfrith had brought from Rome and wore it as an ornament. For nine months the prelate was kept imprisoned, and the story how he regained his liberty brings us back to Aebbe, abbess at Coldingham, who had formerly sheltered Aethelthrith[2].

According to the account of Eddi, Wilfrith's biographer, the king and queen of Northumbria were staying at Coldingham when the queen was suddenly taken ill. 'At night she was seized like the wife of Pilate by a devil, and worn out by many ills, hardly expected to see the day alive.' The abbess Aebbe went to King Ecgfrith and represented to him that the reason of this seizure was their treatment of Wilfrith.

'And now, my son,' she said, 'do according to the bidding of your mother; loosen his bonds and send back to him by a trusty messenger the holy relics which the queen took from him and like the ark of God carried about with her to her harm. It were best you should have him as your bishop, but if you refuse, set him free and let him go with his followers from your kingdom wherever he list. Then by my faith you will live and your queen will not die; but if you refuse by God's witness you will not remain unpunished.'

Aebbe carried her point and Wilfrith was set free. He went into Mercia which was at war with Northumbria, but he was not suffered to stay there, for Queen Ostrith, the sister of King Ecgfrith, shared her brother's hatred of him. Forced to fly from Mercia he went into Wessex, but King Centwin's wife prevented him from staying there. It is curious to note the hatred with which these married women pursued him while lady abbesses were his friends. At last he found protection among the south Saxons, who fifteen years before had nearly killed him, but their king Aethelwalch († 686) had lately been converted to Christianity and gave him a friendly reception. Wilfrith is represented as joining

---

[1] Eddi, *Vita*, c. 34 (in Raine, *Historians of the Church of York*, Rolls series).

[2] Bright, W., *Early English Church History*, 1878, p. 300, casts discredit on this story, which is told by Eddi, *Vita*, c. 38.

his civilizing influences to those of the Irish monks who had settled on the coast. An interesting episode of his sojourn here was his intercourse with Caedwalla, afterwards king of Wessex (685–688), who at the time was living as an outlaw in the forests of Sussex[1].

We get further glimpses of Aebbe and the settlement at Coldingham. She entertained a great admiration for the holy man Cuthberht († 687), one of the most attractive figures among the evangelizing prelates of the north, of whom Bede has left an account.

Cuthberht was brought both by birth and education under Scottish influences. He was prior at Melrose before the Whitby synod, but after it came to Lindisfarne where his gentleness of temper and sweetness of disposition won over many to accept Roman usages. Overcome by the longing for solitude and contemplation which was so characteristic of many early Christian prelates, he dwelt as a recluse on the desert island of Farne from 676 to 685. There are many accounts of his life and of his wanderings[2].

At the time when Cuthberht's fame was spreading, Aebbe of Coldingham 'sent to this man of God, begging him to come and condescend to edify both herself and the inmates of her monastery by the grace of his exhortation. Cuthberht accordingly went thither and tarrying for some days he expounded the ways of justice to all; these he not only preached, but to the same extent he practised[3].'

It is recorded that during his stay at Coldingham Cuthberht went at night to pray on the deserted beach, and the seals came out of the water and clustered around him.

The first instance mentioned by Bede of a lapse of monastic discipline was at Coldingham where disorders occurred during Aebbe's rule[4]. An Irish monk who was on a visit to the monastery had a vision of its destruction by fire, and when questioned about it by the abbess interpreted it as an impending retribution for the tenor of life of those assembled there.

'For even the dwellings,' he said, 'which were built for praying and reading are now converted into places of revelling, drinking, conversation and other forbidden doings; the virgins who are vowed to God, laying aside all respect for their profession, whenever

[1] Bright, W., *Early English Church History*, 1878, pp. 301 ff.
[2] Hardy, Th. D., *Descriptive Catalogue of Materials*, 1862, vol. 1, pp. 297 ff.
[3] Bede, *Life of St Cuthbert*, ch. 10.
[4] Bede, *Eccles. History*, bk 4, ch. 25.

they have leisure spend all their time in weaving fine garments
with which they adorn themselves like brides, to the detriment of
their condition, and to secure the friendship of men outside.'

Through Aebbe's efforts things somewhat improved, but after
her death, the date of which is uncertain, the monastery really was
destroyed by fire[1]. The story is told that Cuthberht at Lindisfarne
forbade women to cross the threshold of his conventual church on
account of the life of the nuns at Coldingham[2], but another version
of his doings considers that his attitude was due to an episode with
a Scottish king's daughter which turned him against the sex[3].

Cuthberht was also the friend of Aelflaed, abbess of Whitby,
who entertained unbounded reverence for him. On one occasion[4]
she had fallen ill and, as she herself told the monk Herefrid,
suffered so from cramp that she could hardly creep along. 'I
would,' she said, 'I had something belonging to my dear Cuthberht, for I believe and trust in the Lord that I should soon
be restored to health.'

In compliance with her wish the holy man sent her a linen
girdle, which she wore for a time and which entirely cured her.
Later a nun by the help of the same girdle was relieved of a head-
ache, but after that the girdle of miraculous power miraculously
disappeared. The reason given for this disappearance illustrates
naïvely enough how divine power was considered to be justified in
making itself manifest with a reservation. 'If this girdle had remained present,' Bede argues, 'the sick would always flock to it ; and
whilst some one of these might not be worthy to be healed, its
efficacy to cure might have been denied, whereas their own unworthiness was perhaps to blame. Therefore, as was said above,
Heaven so dealt its benevolence, that, after the faith of believers
had been confirmed, then immediately the opportunity for de-
traction was entirely withdrawn from the malice of the un-
righteous.'

Contemporary witnesses bear testimony to the wisdom and
prudence of the abbess Aelflaed of Whitby, for Bede says in the
life of Cuthberht that 'she increased the lustre of her royal lineage

---

[1] The Anglo-Saxon Chronicle gives 679 as the date of the fire; Eddi's account
represents Aebbe as alive in 681. Perhaps she died in 680 ; comp. Smith and Wace,
Dictionary of Christian Biography, 1877, Ebba, nr 1 ; also Bright, W., *Early English
Church History*, 1878, p. 300, footnote.

[2] Bright, W., ibid., p. 255, footnote.

[3] Hardy, Th. D., *Descriptive Catalogue of Materials*, 1862, vol. 1, p. 312.

[4] Bede, *Life of St Cuthbert*, ch. 23.

with the higher nobility of a more exalted virginity'; whilst Eddi speaks of her as 'the most virtuous virgin who is actually a king's daughter,' and in another passage characterizes her as 'ever the comforter and best counsellor of the whole province.'

We find her in Cuthberht's society on more than one occasion. Once he met her at the monastery of 'Osingadune' (Easington) where he went to dedicate the church, and while sitting by her at table he had a prophetic vision of the death of one of her servants[1].

The abbess Aelflaed directly appealed to this prophetic insight of Cuthberht's when troubled in her mind about her brother King Ecgfrith, whose expedition against the Picts filled her with apprehension[2]. In the words of Bede: 'At another time, the same most reverend virgin and mother of Christ's virgins, Aelflaed, sent to the man of God, adjuring him in the name of the Lord that she might be allowed to see him, to converse on some pressing affairs. Cuthberht accordingly went on board ship, accompanied by some of the brethren, and came to the island which from its situation opposite to the river Coquet receives its name, and is celebrated for its community of monks; there it was that the aforesaid abbess had requested him to meet her. When she was satisfied with his replies to her many enquiries, on a sudden, while he was yet speaking, she fell at his feet and adjured him by the sacred and venerable Name of the Heavenly King and His angels, to tell her how long Ecgfrith, her brother, should live and rule over the kingdom of the Angles; "For I know," she said, "that you abound in the spirit of prophecy, and that you can tell me this, if you will." But he, trembling at her adjuration, and yet not wishing openly to reveal the secret which she asked for, replied, "It is marvellous that you, a woman wise and well-instructed in the Holy Scriptures, should speak of the term of human life as if it were long, seeing that the Psalmist says, 'Our years shall be considered as a spider[3],' and that Solomon warns us that, 'If a man live many years and have rejoiced in them all, he must remember the darksome time and the many days, which, when they shall come, the things passed shall be accused of vanity[4].' How much more then ought he, to whom only one year of life remains, to be considered as having lived a short time, when death shall stand at his gates?"

[1] Bede, *Life of St Cuthbert*, ch. 34.   [2] Ibid., ch. 24.

[3] Psalm lxxxix. 10 (The Vulgate here follows the LXX.; it would be interesting to know what sense they or indeed Bede gave to the passage).

[4] Eccles. xi. 8.

'The abbess, on hearing this, lamented the dreadful prophecy with floods of tears, and having wiped her face, with feminine boldness she adjured him by the majesty of the sovereignty of God to tell her who would be the heir of the kingdom, since Ecgfrith had neither sons nor brothers. Cuthberht was silent for a short time, then he replied, "Say not that he is without heirs, for he shall have a successor whom you may embrace with sisterly affection as you do Ecgfrith himself." But she continued: "Tell me, I beseech you, where he is now." And he said, "You see this mighty and wide ocean, how it abounds with many islands. It is easy for God from one of these to provide a ruler for the kingdom of the Angles." Then she understood that he spoke of Ealdfrith (Aldfrid) who was said to be the son of Ecgfrith's father, and who at that time lived in exile, in the islands of the Scots, for the sake of studying letters.'

This meeting, if we credit the historian, took place in 684, and Aelflaed's forebodings were realized. Ecgfrith lost his life, and part of his kingdom was taken by the Picts. In consequence of his defeat the settlement Whithern, set up as a religious outpost in the territory south of the Firth of Forth, was destroyed. Trumwin who had been entrusted with it was forced to fly. He and his friends sought refuge at Whitby where he remained and had much intercourse with Cuthberht and Aelflaed. Bede says that the abbess found 'great assistance in governing and also comfort for her own life' in Trumwin[1].

Northumbria had now passed the zenith of her greatness as a political power, for the territory in the north which was lost through Ecgfrith's defeat was not regained, while in the south the province of Mercia began to shake off the Northumbrian yoke. King Ecgfrith had been succeeded by his half-brother Ealdfrith († 705) and owing to his attitude Wilfrith's exile came to an end. Theodore, archbishop of Canterbury, wrote a letter in his behalf to Ealdfrith and also one to Aelflaed of Whitby begging her to be at peace with him[2]. The prelate left Sussex for the north, where he remained for five years in undisturbed possession of his see[3]. But again the old quarrels revived, and Wilfrith in consequence of a council assembled by order of Ealdfrith at Eastrefield was robbed of his episcopal dignity and reduced to his abbacy at Ripon. He again insisted that the king and bishops should submit to the Pope, and at the age of well-nigh seventy he under-

---

[1] Bede, *Eccles. Hist.*, bk 4, ch. 26.   [2] Eddi, *Vita*, c. 43.
[3] Bright, W., *Early English History*, 1878, p. 448, from 686–691.

took another journey to Rome. But it was in vain he sent envoys to the king on his return. Ealdfrith was determined not to relent, but afterwards approaching death intimidated him. Feeling his end draw nigh he sent for Aelflaed of Whitby, who with the abbess Aethelburg (probably of Hackness) came to where he lay ill at Driffield in the East Riding. Aelflaed received the king's dying words, and at a council of prelates subsequently assembled on the river Nidd bore testimony that he had spoken in favour of making peace. Wilfrith regained part of his influence but remained in retirement at his monastery.

Aelflaed outlived him and her friend Cuthberht who died in 687. It is probable that she assisted at the translation of Cuthberht's body in 698, for in the inventory of the church at Durham one of the linen cloths or outer envelopes of his body, which was taken from it in 1104, is described as 'a linen cloth of double texture which had enveloped the body of St Cuthbert in his grave; Elfled the abbess had wrapped him up in it[1].'

Aelflaed is the last abbess of Whitby known by name. Her death is supposed to have taken place in 713. Her monastery, like so many houses in the north, which had grown to prosperity with the rising power of Northumbria, sank into insignificance with the decadence of that power. This decline was partly due to political reasons, but the dislike which the later kings of Northumbria felt towards monasteries may have had something to do with it. For as we shall see later on the example Queen Aethelthrith had set was probably followed by two other Northumbrian queens, Cyneburg, the wife of Ealhfrith, and Cuthburg, wife of Ealdfrith († 705), who returned to their own countries and there founded monasteries.

§ 4. Houses in Mercia and in the South.

From the north we turn to Mercia and Wessex, the central and south-western provinces of England. Mercia had clung longest to her heathen beliefs, for Christianity was not accepted there till after the defeat of Penda in 655 when Northumbria gained supremacy. Penda, king of Mercia, remained faithful to his gods to the end himself, but his children adopted the new faith. His son Peada had already been baptized in Northumbria by Finnan who

[1] Haigh, D. H., 'On the monasteries of St Heiu and St Hild,' *Yorksh. Archaeol. Journal*, vol. 3, p. 375.

sent four ecclesiastics back with him to evangelise the Midlands, and Wulfhere (c. 658–675) Peada's brother and successor was married to the Christian princess Eormenhild of Kent, for whom Queen Sexburg had made the religious foundation at Sheppey. Peada had founded a religious settlement at Burh or Medehampstead which is better known as Peterborough, a name bestowed on it after its restoration in 970. The charter of the foundation of Burh is dated 664, and besides the signatures of Wulfhere and other princes and thanes it bears those of Wulfhere's sisters Cyneburg and Cyneswith[1].

Cyneburg and Cyneswith were esteemed as saints on the strength of their religious foundations at Castor, a village some miles distant from Peterborough; the name Cyneburg is held by the local historian to survive in the appellations of Lady Connyburrow Walk and Coneygreve Close[2]. Cyneburg had been married to Ealhfrith, who was for some time co-regent of Northumbria, but little is known of him after his presence at the synod of Whitby in 664. The charter of the Medehampstead foundation above referred to establishes beyond a doubt that Cyneburg had left her husband to found and preside over her monastery; for she is designated as 'formerly a queen who had resigned her sway to preside over a monastery of maidens[3].' Her legend, which is not older than John of Tinmouth[4], enlarges on this fact, and like Aethelthrith of Ely, Cyneburg together with her sister Cyneswith has found a place in the Calendar as a virgin saint[5].

The legend which tells of Cyneburh and Cyneswith also refers to St Tibba or Tilba, their kinswoman, who dwelt at Ryhall not far from Castor. The same day was kept in commemoration of all these three saints at Peterborough, to which place their bodies were transferred at an early date. For the Anglo-Saxon Chronicle (972) says of Aelfsi, abbot of Peterborough: 'And he took up St Kyneburg and St Kyneswith who lay at Castor, and St Tibba who lay at Ryhall, and brought them to Burh, and offered them all to St Peter in one day.' Camden[6] speaks of Tibba as a 'saint of inferior

---

[1] Dugdale, *Monasticon*, 'Peterborough,' vol. 1, p. 377, nr 2, prints the charter.

[2] Gough, R., *Parochial History of Castor*, 1819, p. 99.

[3] 'Cum beatissimis sororibus meis Kyneburga et Kyneswida, quarum prior regina mutavit imperium in Christi ancillarum praesidens monasterio...etc.'

[4] Hardy, Th. D., *Descriptive Catalogue of Materials*, 1862, vol. 1, p. 370.

[5] *A. SS. Boll.*, St Kineburga et St Kineswitha, virgines, March 6, argue the existence of a third sister.

[6] Camden, *Britannia*, edit. 1789, vol. 2, pp. 219, 223.

order, who was worshipped as another Diana by fowlers, a patroness
of hawking,' and adds information which shows that she was popularly connected with heathen survivals.

Mercia was the birthplace of many picturesque legends about
the conversion of members of the ruling family and about their
religious foundations. When once Christianity was accepted the
activity which kings, queens and prelates displayed in its favour was
great, but the historical information we have about them is meagre.

Thus Repton (Repandune) in Derbyshire, a monastery for
women, had gained considerable importance when the noble youth
Guthlac repaired thither in 694 to devote himself to learning under
the abbess Aelfthrith[1]. Nothing is known about the beginnings
of the house, and if the abbess Aelfthrith founded it she has not
on this account been accepted as a saint like the founders of other
houses. This omission may however be due to the difficulties
which arose between Aelfthrith and the prelates of Mercia. We do
not know their nature, but in 705 a council of Mercian clergy assembled to consider the re-admission of Aelfthrith to Church privileges[2]. A letter is also extant from Bishop Waldhere of London
to Archbishop Brihtwald of Canterbury in which he mentions that
a reconciliation has taken place[3].

The noble youth Guthlac who came to study at Repton afterwards became famous, and many accounts of his life have been
written[4]. The earliest version, drafted by his friend Felix, supplies
some interesting details of the life at Repton and the studies there[5].

We are told that Guthlac's progress was wonderful. 'When
he had been there two years he had learnt the psalms, the canticles,
the hymns and prayers after the ecclesiastical order,' but he met
with disapproval in the monastery by refusing to drink wine. The
accounts which he read of the solitary life of the older monks filled
him with a longing for solitude, and he left Repton and wandered
about till he found the place of his heart's desire at Crowland in
the fen country, where he determined to settle. He had received
the tonsure at Repton and returned there on a visit before finally
settling at Crowland. He did not break his connection with Repton,

---

[1] Dugdale, *Monasticon*, 'Repton,' vol. 6, p. 429; the abbesses he mentions should
stand in this order : Alfritha, Edburga.

[2] Haddon and Stubbs, *Councils and Eccles. Documents*, 1869, vol. 3, p. 273.

[3] Ibid., vol. 3, p. 274.

[4] Birch, W. de Gray, *Memorials of St Guthlac of Crowland*, 1881.

[5] *A. SS. Boll.*, St Guthlac, April 11 ; Felix, *Vita*, c. 12.

for we hear that the abbess Ecgburh who succeeded Aelfthrith sent him as a gift a coffin made of wood and lead, together with a linen winding-sheet, and asked who should be warden of the place after him, as though she regarded Crowland as a dependency of Repton[1].

The abbess Ecgburg was the daughter of King Ealdwulf of East Anglia († 714)[2], and an eloquent letter which is quoted later in my account of Boniface's correspondents was probably written by her[3].

In connection with Guthlac's solitary life we hear of a woman Pega, who had also chosen a retreat in the fen country, at a place afterwards known as Peykirk, which is now situated on a peninsula formed by the uplands of Northamptonshire and connected with the mound on which Guthlac dwelt by a ridge of gravel, but which at that time formed an island[4]. One version of Guthlac's life tells how 'he had a sister called Pega whom he would not see in this life, to the intent that they might the rather meet in the life to come'; and another manuscript life says that the Evil One appeared to the saint in the form of Pega. Mr W. de Birch Gray who has reprinted these accounts notices that the tone in which Florence of Worcester speaks of Pega suggests that to him at least she appeared more famous than Guthlac[5].

Different accounts of Guthlac agree that at his death his companions at once departed to fetch Pega. In the celebrated series of drawings of the 12th century, which set forth the story of St Guthlac, the holy woman Pega is depicted twice[6]. In one picture she steps into the boat, in which the companion of Guthlac has come to fetch her, and in the other she is represented as supporting the saint, who is enveloped in his shroud.

The connection between Guthlac and Pega is at least curious, and the authority she at once assumed is noteworthy. 'For three days' space with sacred hymns of praise she commended the holy

---

[1] Felix, *Vita*, c. 33.

[2] Ibid., 'Egburgh abbatissa, Aldulfi regis filia'; Smith and Wace, *Dictionary of Christian Biography*, 1877, call her 'Eadburga (nr 3)'; two abbesses Ecgburh occur in the Durham list of abbesses, comp. Gray, W. de Birch, *Fasti Monastici Aevi Saxonici*, 1872, p. 70.

[3] Comp. below, ch. 4, § 1.

[4] Holdich, B., *History of Crowland Abbey*, 1816, p. 2.

[5] Gray, W. de Birch, *Memorials of St Guthlac of Crowland*, 1881, Introd. p. l, footnote.

[6] Brit. Mus. MS. Harleian Roll, Y 6, reproduced Gray, W. de Birch, *Memorials of St Guthlac of Crowland*, 1881, pp. 14, 16 etc.

man to God,' says the Anglo-Saxon prose version of his life[1]. And further, 'After his death when he had been buried twelve months God put it into the heart of the servant of the Lord that she should remove the brother's body to another tomb. She assembled thither many of the servants of God and mass-priests, and others of the ecclesiastical order.... She wound the holy corpse, with praises of Christ's honour, in the other sheet which Ecgbriht the anchoress formerly sent him when alive for that same service.'

The Acts of the Saints give an account of St Pega or Pegia and tell us that she went to Rome where she died[2]. Her reputation for holiness, as far as it is preserved, is based chiefly on her connection with Guthlac, but these accounts leave room for much that must necessarily remain conjecture.

Other women-saints who were reputed to have lived about this period, and who were brought into connection with the rulers of Mercia, claim a passing attention, although their legends written at a much later date supply the only information we have about them. Thus there is St Osith[3] of Colchester, whose legend written in the 13th century is full of hopeless anachronisms. The house of Augustinian canons at Chich[4] in the 12th century was dedicated conjointly to the saints Peter and Paul and to the woman-saint Osith ; a canon of this house, Albericus Veerus, probably wrote her legend. Perhaps St Osith of Aylesbury is identical with her[5].

Our information is equally untrustworthy concerning St Frideswith, patron saint of Oxford, for it dates no further back than the 12th century[6]. The chief interest in her legend is that its author establishes a connection between incidents in the life of Frideswith, and the dread which the kings of England had of entering Oxford ; a dread which as early as 1264 is referred to as an 'old superstition[7].'

All these women are credited in their legends with founding monasteries and gaining local influence, and excepting in the case of St Tibba, I have come across no coupling of their names with profane cults. Other women-saints who may perhaps be classed with

---

[1] Goodwin, C. W., *The Anglo-Saxon version of the life of St Guthlac*, 1848, p. 93.

[2] *A. SS. Boll.*, St Pega sive Pegia, Jan. 8.   [3] *A. SS. Boll.*, St Ositha, Oct. 7.

[4] Dugdale, *Monasticon*, ' Chich Priory,' vol. 6, p. 308.

[5] Hardy, Th. D., *Descriptive Catalogue of Materials*, vol. 1, pp. 524 ff.

[6] *A. SS. Boll.*, St Frideswida, Oct. 19; Dugdale, *Monasticon*, 'Christ Church,' vol. 2, p. 134.

[7] *Dictionary of National Biography*, Frideswide.

them, though little survives except their names, are St Osburg of Coventry[1], St Modwen of Strenhall in Staffordshire and Burton-on-Trent[2], and St Everhild of Everingham in Yorkshire[3].

Other names which occur in local calendars will be found in the *Menology* of Stanton, who has compiled a very complete list of men- and women-saints in England and Wales from a number of local calendars.

In contrast to the uncertainty which hangs about the settlements under woman's rule in the Midlands and around their founders, two houses founded in the south of England during the 7th century stand out in clear prominence. Barking in Essex, and Wimbourne in Dorsetshire, attained a considerable degree of culture, and the information which has been preserved concerning them is ample and trustworthy.

Bede has devoted several chapters of his history to stories connected with Barking[4]. It owed its foundation to Earconwald sometime bishop of London (675–693) who, after founding a settlement at Chertsey in Surrey under the rule of an abbot, in 666 made a home for his sister Aethelburg at Barking[5] where 'he established her excellently in the regular discipline.' Aethelburg appears to have been an energetic person, and has been raised to the rank of saint[6]. Her settlement included men as well as women, and young children seem to have been entrusted to her care for their education.

Bede says that 'having taken the rule of the monastery she showed herself worthy of her brother the bishop in all respects, both by living rightly herself, and by the pious and prudent course she took to rule those who were subject to her; this was proved by celestial miracles.'

A number of these miracles are described by him with considerable power. Between 664 and 684, a great pestilence, the

---

[1] Stanton, R., *Menology of England and Wales*, 1887, p. 137 : 'we have no records of Osburg till 1410.'

[2] Ibid., p. 310 : 'there is much obscurity in the history of St Modwenna. It seems that she must be distinguished from one or perhaps two other Irish saints...' Also Livien, E., 'On early religious houses in Staffordshire' in *Journal of the British Archaeol. Association*, vol. 29, p. 333; Hardy, Th. D., *Descriptive Catalogue of Materials*, pp. 94 ff.

[3] Stanton, R., *Menology of England and Wales*, 1887, p. 328.

[4] Bede, *Eccles. Hist.*, bk 4, chs. 7–10.

[5] Dugdale, *Monasticon*, 'Barking,' vol. 1, p. 436.

[6] *A. SS. Boll.*, St Ethelburga, Oct. 11; Stanton, R., *Menology of England and Wales*, p. 485.

earliest on record in Christian times, visited England and carried
off many of the inmates of Barking.   First a boy of three years
fell ill and in dying called by name the nun Eadgith, who presently
died.   Another nun called Torctgith[1] also had a vision of impending death.   'One night at the beginning of dawn, having
gone forth from the chamber in which she abode, she saw plainly
as it were a human body, which was brighter than the sun, carried
up on high, wrapped in fine linen, and lifted apparently from the
house in which the sisters were usually placed to die.   And when
she looked more intently to see by what means the apparition
of a glorious body which she beheld was raised on high, she saw
that it was lifted up into the upper regions as it were by cords
brighter than gold, until being introduced into the opening heavens
it could no longer be seen by her.'

This imagery foretold the death of Abbess Aethelburg, who
was carried off by the pestilence.   She was succeeded at Barking
by Hildelith, whom Boniface refers to as a very estimable person
and who has also found a place among the saints[2].   Capgrave
speaks of her having been educated in France, whence she came
to Barking at the desire of Bishop Earconwald to help in establishing the foreign system of discipline.

It was for the abbess Hildelith and her companions at Barking
that the scholar Ealdhelm († 709) wrote his great treatise on
Virginity, a long and elaborate composition which sets before
these women the beauties of the virgin life with a mass of illustration taken from religious and classical literature.   From the point
of view of women's religious life, it is worth while to describe this
treatise at some length, for it shows what a high degree of culture
had been attained at Barking towards the close of the seventh
century.

Ealdhelm, born of noble parentage about the year 640, is
the representative in southern England of the classical revival
which was about this time engrafted on Christian teaching.   He
studied first at Malmesbury under the learned Scot Maidulf and
then at Canterbury where Archbishop Theodore and Abbot Hadrian
were attracting many students, and where he perfected his Latin
and musical studies and acquired in some measure the rare and
much esteemed knowledge of Greek.   'A wonder of erudition in
liberal as well as in ecclesiastical writings,' Bede calls him[3].   From

---

[1] Stanton, R., *Menology*, calls her Theorigitha but says, p. 36, that she has no day.
[2] *A. SS. Boll.*, St Hildelitha, March 24.   [3] Bede, *Eccles. Hist.*, bk 5, ch. 18.

Canterbury he returned to Malmesbury, which owing to his influence attained a fame which it kept till the Middle Ages. In 705
when Wessex was divided into two bishoprics, Ealdhelm was
made bishop of the see of Sherbourne.

The interest Ealdhelm took in women was so great that posterity
pictured him as continually in their society[1]. Besides his great
treatise, passages in his other works bear witness to this interest.
In a letter addressed to Sigegith[2], he gave advice about the
baptism of a nun who had been received into her community
while still a heathen ; to another nun whose name is not mentioned
he sent a letter together with several poems[3]. He composed verses
in praise of a church which Bugga, a daughter of King Centwin
(670–685), had built[4]. And besides the prose treatise on virginity
addressed to the sisterhood of Barking, he wrote a long poem in
heroic hexameters on the same subject called the 'Praise of Virgins';
it has a preface addressed to the abbess Maxima, and is followed by
a poem on the 'Eight chief Sins,' likewise intended for the perusal
of nuns[5].

Ealdhelm opens his prose work on virginity[6] with thanks to
the women of Barking for the writings they have sent to him.
Hildelith, Justina, Cuthburg, Osburg, Ealdgith, Scholastica, Hid-
burg, Burngith, Eulalia and Tecla are addressed by name. He
praises them as gymnosophists, as scholars and as fighters in the
arena of discipline (c. 2). Like unto bees, he says (c. 4), they collect
everywhere material for study.

Sometimes, he says, you study the Prophets, sometimes the
Books of the Law, 'now skilfully tracking the fourfold wording of
the gospel story, expounded in the mystic commentaries of the
Catholic fathers, and spiritually bared to the kernel, and disposed
fitly according to the four-square pattern of ecclesiastical usage,
namely according to the letter, allegory, tropology and anagogy[7];
now carefully searching into the writers of history and into the

---

[1] Capgrave, T., *Catalogus SS. Angliae*, 1516, fol. 10, b.

[2] *Monumenta Moguntina*, edit. Jaffé, Epist. nr 2, written between 675 and 705;
Giles (Aldhelm, *Opera Omnia*, 1844, p. 90) calls her Osgith, a name which occurs several
times in the Durham 'Liber Vitae.'

[3] Aldhelm, *Opera*, edit. Giles, 1844, p. 103.   [4] Ibid., p. 115, *De Basilica*, etc.

[5] Ibid., p. 135, *De Laudibus Virginum* (it is not known over which house Maxima
presided); p. 203, *De octo Principalibus Vitiis.*

[6] Ibid., p. 1, *De Laudibus Virginitatis* (chapter references in the text are to this
edition).

[7] Mediaeval exegesis interpreted in these four ways, comp. Cassian Erem., *De Spiritu
Sc.*, c. 8.

collections of chronographers, who have handed down the changing events of the past in wording that impresses the mind. Sometimes you carefully examine the rules of grammarians, the laws of accentuation measured by tone and time, fixed in poetic feet by marks of punctuation, that is divided into parts of verse consisting of two and a half and three and a half feet, and changed in endless varieties of metre.'

Ealdhelm then enlarges on the beauties of the virgin's life, and dwells especially on the charms of peaceful companionship which it secures. Again in their dwelling and working together the women are likened to bees.

The charms of the virgin's life are then set forth in language redundant of imagery, verbose and grandiloquent in the extreme. We are told of the temptations which those who have adopted a religious life must guard against (c. 11). There are eight sins as to which they are especially warned; the chief of these is pride. Women are then directed as to the books they should make a special subject of study, and are recommended to peruse the works of Cassian (who in the 5th century wrote the 'Duties of Monastic Life') and the 'Moralities' of Gregory the Great (which contain reflections suggested by the book of Job), and they are advised to study the Psalms to avoid unhappiness (c. 14). With the love of contrast peculiar to early writers, Ealdhelm shows how the women who serve God and those who do not are different in their bearing and outward appearance, and enlarges on the relative value of different estates (c. 17): virginity is of gold, chastity is of silver; marriage (jugalitas) is of brass; and again: virginity is wealth, chastity is sufficiency, marriage is poverty, etc.

He then displays the wide range of his learning by adducing many writers in support of his views (c. 20–40), in passages which are elaborate and instructive but wearisome through their reiterations. He enumerates all the women famous for their religious lives. The Virgin Mary comes first and she is followed by many women-saints of Italy and the East, on whom there is in some cases much, in others little, comment. In this list we in vain look for the names of religious women living on this side of the Alps. Helen the mother of Constantine (c. 48) is referred to, but her British origin is not mentioned and the idea of it had probably not arisen in Ealdhelm's time.

The writer again turns to those who are devoted to religion, and in passages which are full of interest as a study of the times complains of the personal appearance of the clergy and of those women who have chosen religion as a profession. These passages are among the most instructive in regard to women and clearly show how completely life in a nunnery at the beginning of the 8th century differed from what it was later on.

'It shames me,' he says, 'to speak of the bold impudence of conceit and the fine insolence of stupidity which are found both among nuns (sanctimoniales) who abide under the rule of a settlement, and among the men of the Church who live as clergy under the rule of the Pontiff. These act contrary to canonical decrees and to the rule of regular life, for with many-coloured vestments[1] and with elegant adornments the body is set off and the external form decked out limb by limb. The appearance of the other sex agrees with it; a vest of fine linen of a violet colour is worn, above it a scarlet tunic with a hood, sleeves striped with silk and trimmed with red fur; the locks on the forehead and the temples are curled with a crisping iron, the dark head-veil is given up for white and coloured head-dresses which, with bows of ribbon sewn on, reach down to the ground; the nails, like those of a falcon or sparrow-hawk, are pared to resemble talons'…. This state of things Ealdhelm strongly condemns. But he adds the remark that he is addressing no one in particular, evidently to avoid any umbrage his women friends might take at these remarks. His reference to luxurious clothing does not stand alone. The description Bede gives of the women at Coldingham has been quoted, and Boniface in a letter[2] to Cuthberht of Canterbury speaks of 'the adornment of clothes, trimmed with wide edging of purple,' which, he says, is deteriorating the young men in the monasteries, and foretells the coming of Antichrist. Sumptuous clothes as vestments during religious service remained in use, but in all other respects they were condemned as prejudicial to the welfare of those who were vowed to religion.

Ealdhelm's work on virginity closes with an affectionate greeting to his women friends in which he addresses them finally as 'Flowers of the Church, sisters of monastic life, scholarly pupils, pearls of Christ, jewels of Paradise, and sharers of the eternal home.'

His work was greatly prized and widely read both by his own

---

[1] I take 'crustu' to go with 'crusta,' comp. Ducange.
[2] *Monumenta Moguntina*, edit. Jaffé, Epist. nr 70.

and by later generations. It is extant in several copies of the 8th century[1], and maintained its reputation throughout the Middle Ages. William of Malmesbury († 1141) in his account of Ealdhelm specifies the work on virginity as one 'than which nothing can be more pleasing[2].' It still held its own when printing was introduced, for it was published at Deventer in Holland in 1512, and has since been reprinted for devotional purposes[3].

Among those on whom the book made a profound impression was Cuthburg, sister of King Ina of Wessex (688–725). She was at one time an inmate of the Barking settlement and was probably one of those to whom the work was addressed.

Cuthburg was held as a saint for founding a settlement at Wimbourne in Dorset[4], where the cult of her sister Cwenburg was associated with hers. Cuthburg as mentioned above was said to have left her husband Ealdfrith of Northumbria († 705) from religious motives. Her being held in veneration as a virgin saint may be due to her name being coupled with that of a virgin sister[5]. Missals printed at Rouen in 1515, and at Paris in 1519 and 1529, have an office prescribed for Cuthburg as a virgin[6]. The statement that she was the mother of Osred, afterwards king of Northumbria (706–717), is perhaps unfounded.

There is no doubt as to Ealdhelm's friendly relations both with Cuthburg and her husband. He dedicated his enigmas to Ealdfrith under the title 'Adcircius[7],' and in a letter dated 705 he declares that liberty of election is granted to all congregations under his government including that called 'Wimburnia,' over which Cuthburg, the king's sister, presides[8]. A manuscript of the 14th century, preserved in the nunnery of Romsey, contains a collection of saints' lives, and gives a full account of a conversation Cuthburg had with her husband previous to their separation[9]. It further relates how she placed the basilica of her settlement under the protection of the Mother of God, and was herself buried in it. She died some time between 720 and 730, probably nearer the earlier

---

[1] Dugdale, *Monasticon*, 'Sherbourne,' vol. 1, p. 331, footnote K.

[2] Will. of Malmesbury, *History*, c. 31.   [3] *Dict. of Nat. Biography*, 'Aldhelm.'

[4] Dugdale, *Monasticon*, 'Wimbourne,' vol. 2, p. 88.

[5] *A. SS. Boll.*, St Cuthberga, Aug. 31.

[6] Dugdale, *Monasticon*, 'Wimbourne,' vol. 2, p. 88.

[7] *Opera* edit. Giles, 1844, p. 216; *Dict. of Nat. Biog.*, 'Aldfrith,' he is sometimes called Alfred.

[8] Dugdale, *Monasticon*, 'Wimbourne,' vol. 2, p. 89, nr 2.

[9] *Brit. Mus. MSS. Lansdowne*, 436 f., 38 b.

date, for several abbesses are said to have ruled between her and
Tetta. The name of Tetta has been brought into connection with
a place named Tetbury, but we know nothing definite concerning a
monastery there[1]. As abbess of Wimbourne she was the teacher
of Lioba, called also Leobgith, who went abroad at the desire of
Boniface as we shall see further on.

In the life of Lioba we get a description of the settlement of
Wimbourne[2], which may be somewhat coloured to show the result
of Tetta's strict and beneficent rule, but which deserves attention
as yielding a fair example of the arrangements which in the eyes
of its author appeared desirable for a monastery of women. The
author, Rudolf of Fulda, was a monk who wrote between 800
and 850, and who compiled his work from notices which Magno
(✝ c. 838) had collected from women pupils of Lioba[3].

'There were two settlements at Wimbourne, formerly erected
by the kings of the country, surrounded by strong and lofty
walls and endowed with ample revenues. Of these one was
designed for men, the other for women; but neither, for such
was the rule of their foundation, was ever entered by any member
of the other sex. No woman had permission to come among the
congregation of the men, no man to enter into the dwellings of
the women, with the exception of the priests who entered to celebrate mass and withdrew at once when service was over. If a
woman, desirous of quitting the world, asked to be admitted to
the sisterhood (collegium), she joined it on condition that she
should not leave it unless a reasonable cause or a special occasion
took her out with the leave of the abbess. The abbess herself,
when she gave orders in affairs of the settlement or tendered
advice, spoke through a window and there gave her decision....'

Wimbourne stands last in the list of well authenticated monastic
foundations made by women during the early Anglo-Saxon period;
of such foundations more than twenty have been mentioned in the
course of this chapter. Others no doubt existed at this time,
but we only hear of them at a later date. We find among them
some of the centres most influential in enabling the Anglo-Saxons
to attain a high degree of culture within a hundred years of their
conversion to Christianity.

[1] Dugdale, *Monasticon*, 'Tetbury,' vol. 6, p. 1619.

[2] *A. SS. Boll.*, St Lioba, Sept. 28, c. 2.

[3] Arndt, W., Introd. to translation into German (in Pertz, *Geschichtsschreiber der
deutschen Vorzeit*, Jahrhundert 8, Band 2), p. xix.

CHAPTER IV.

ANGLO-SAXON NUNS IN CONNECTION WITH BONIFACE.

'Et ut dicitur, quid dulcius est, quam habeas illum, cum quo omnia possis loqui ut tecum?' *Eangith to Boniface.*

§ 1. The Women corresponding with Boniface.

IN the course of the 6th and 7th centuries a number of men left England and settled abroad among the heathen Germans, partly from a wish to gain new converts to the faith, partly because a change of affairs at home made them long for a different field of labour.   Through the influx of the heathen Anglo-Saxons, the British Christians had been deprived of their influence, and when Christianity was restored it was under the auspices of princes who were favourably inclined towards Rome.   Men who objected to the Roman sway sought independence among the heathens abroad in preference to dependence on strangers at home, and it is owing to their efforts that Christianity was introduced into the valleys leading up from the Rhine, into the lake districts of Bavaria, and into Switzerland.

A century later the Church had so far extended the limits of her power that it was felt desirable at Rome that these Christian settlers should be brought into subjection.   For the tenets which they held and the traditions which had been handed down to them differed in many ways from what Rome could countenance. They were liberal in tolerating heathen practices, and ignorant of matters of ritual and creed which were insisted on in the Church of Rome.   The bishops, who were self-appointed, were won over by the promise of recognising the title to which they laid claim, but the difficulty remained of weaning them from their objectionable practices.   Efforts were accordingly made to reconvert the converted districts and to bring some amount of pressure to bear on the clergy.

The representative of this movement in South Germany was Boniface, otherwise called Wynfred, on whom posterity has bestowed the title Apostle of Germany, in recognition of his services in the twofold character of missionary and reformer. He was a native of Wessex, and his mission abroad has an interest in connection with our subject because of the friendly relations he entertained with many inmates of women's houses in England, and because he invited women as well as men to leave England and assist him in the work which he had undertaken.

Boniface had grown up as an inmate of the settlement of Nutshalling near Winchester and first went abroad in 716, but proceeded no further than Utrecht. Conjecture has been busy over the difficulties which took him away, and the disappointments which brought him back. Utrecht was an old Roman colony which had been captured from the Franks by Adgisl, king of the Frisians, who gave a friendly reception there to Bishop Wilfrith in 678. But King Radbod, his successor, was hostile to the Franks and to Christianity, and it was only in deference to the powerful Frankish house-mayor Pippin that he countenanced the settling of Willibrord, a pupil of Wilfrith, with eleven companions in 692. However, owing to Radbod's enmity the position of these monks was such that they were obliged to leave, and it is possible that Boniface when he went to Utrecht was disappointed in not finding them there.

Two years later Boniface went on a pilgrimage to Rome, where the idea of bringing his energies to assist in the extension of Papal influence originated. The Pope furnished him with a letter[1] in which he is directed to reclaim the faithless, and armed with this he travelled in the districts of the Main. But as soon as the news of the death of Radbod the Frisian († 719) reached him he went to Utrecht, where Willibrord had returned. We do not know what afterwards prompted him to resume his work in Germany, but perhaps the proposal of Willibrord that he should settle with him altogether awakened Boniface to the fact that he was not working for the Pope as he proposed. His reception at Rome, where he again went in 722, and the declaration of faith he handed in, are

---

[1] Epist. nr 12. The only edition of the letters of Boniface which attempts chronological order is that of Jaffé, Ph., *Monumenta Moguntina*, 1866, the numeration of which I have followed. Additional remarks on the dates of some of the letters are contained in Hahn, H., *Bonifaz und Lull, ihre angelsächsischen Correspondenten*, 1883.

in favour of this view. But Gregory II who was aware of the abilities of Boniface forgave him, and on the strength of his declaration provided him with further letters. One of these was addressed to the Christians of Germany, to the representative clergy and to the Thüringians, and another to the house-mayor, Karl Martel, who had succeeded Pippin ; both letters commanded that the authority of Boniface was to be everywhere recognised.

From this time for a period of over thirty years Boniface devoted his energies to extending, organizing and systematizing the power of Rome in Germany. His character appears in different lights varying with the standpoint from which he is regarded. Judging from his letters he is alternately swayed by doggedness of purpose, want of confidence in himself, dependence on friends, and jealous insistence on his own authority. He has a curious way of representing himself as persecuted when in fact he is the persecutor, but his power of rousing enthusiasm for his work and for his personality is enormous.

His biographer Wilibald describes this power as already peculiar to him during his stay at Nutshalling, where many men sought him to profit by his knowledge, 'while those who on account of their fragile sex could not do so, and those who were not allowed to stay away from their settlements, moved by the spirit of divine love, sought eagerly for an account of him[1]....'

The interest Boniface had aroused at home accompanied him on his travels. He remained in friendly communication with many persons in England, to whom he wrote and who wrote to him. Among the friends and correspondents whose letters are preserved are churchmen, princes, abbesses, clerics of various degrees, and nuns. From the point of view of this book the letters addressed to women are of special interest, since they bring us into personal contact so to speak with the abbesses and inmates of English convents, and we hear for the first time what they personally have to tell us of themselves.

Among Boniface's early friends and correspondents was Eadburg[2], abbess of the monastery in Thanet. She was a woman of great abilities, zealous in the pursuit of knowledge, and her influence secured several royal charters for her settlement. She had probably

---

[1] Willibaldus presb., *Vita Bonifacii*, edit. Jaffé, Ph., *Monumenta Moguntina*, 1866, pp. 422–506, c. 2.

[2] Whether Eadburg of Thanet is identical with St Eadburga buried at Liming (comp. p. 84), is uncertain.

succeeded Mildthrith, but at what date is not known. Her letters
to Boniface unfortunately have not been preserved, but the letters
he wrote to her are full of interesting matter. The earliest of
these was written between 718 and 719; in it Boniface does not
yet address her as abbess[1].

In this letter Boniface in compliance with a wish Eadburg had
expressed, describes a vision of the future life which a monk living
at Mildburg's monastery at Wenlock had seen during a state of
suspended animation. Boniface had first heard of this vision from
the abbess Hildelith of Barking, and he writes a graphic and eloquent account of it, parts of which are put into the mouth of the
monk himself. The account gives curious glimpses of that imagery
of the future life which early Christians dwelt upon and elaborated
more and more. Nuns at this time as well as later took a special
interest in the subject.

First the monk is carried aloft through flames which enwrap
the world. He sees many souls for the possession of which angels
and devils are fighting. Impersonations of his sins confront and
accost him, but his virtues arise also and enter into conflict with
the sins. The virtues are supported by angels and the fight ends to
the monk's advantage. He also sees fiery waters flowing towards
hell: and souls like black birds which hover over waters from
whence proceed the wails of the damned. He sees Paradise,
and a river of pitch over which a bridge leads to Jerusalem, and
souls are trying to cross it. Among others suffering torments he
catches sight of King Ceolred of Mercia. At last the angels cast
the monk down from the height and he re-awakens to life.

Such descriptions of a future life multiply as one nears the
Middle Ages. By the side of the one which Boniface sent to
Eadburg should be read another by him, a fragmentary one, which
supplements it[2]. The sufferers in hell mentioned in this are Cuthburg, Ceolla and Wiala (of whom nothing is known), an unnamed
abbot and Aethelbald, king of Mercia († 756).

The description of the after life given by Boniface agrees in
various ways with one contained in the works of Bede. According
to this account there was a man in Northumbria named Drycthelm,
who died, came to life again, and described what he had seen of
the world to come.

The other letters which Boniface addressed to Eadburg are of

---

[1] Epist. nr 10.   [2] Epist. nr 112.

later date and were written when he had settled abroad and was devoting his energies to converting the Hessians and Thüringians. At this time he asked her to send him through the priest Eoban the letters of the apostle Peter, which she was to write for him in gold characters. 'Often,' he says, 'gifts of books and vestments, the proofs of your affection, have been to me a consolation in misfortune. So I pray that you will continue as you have begun, and write for me in gold characters the epistles of my master, the holy apostle Peter, to the honour and reverence of holy writ before mortal eyes while I am preaching, and because I desire always to have before me the words of him who led me on my mission....' He ends his letter by again hoping that she will accede to his request so 'that her words may shine in gold to the glory of the Father in heaven[1].'

The art of writing in gold on parchment was unknown to Scottish artists and had been introduced into England from Italy. Bishop Wilfrith owned the four gospels 'written in purest gold on purple-coloured parchment,' and a few of the purple gospels with gold writing of this period have been preserved. The fact that women practised the art is evident from the letter of Boniface. Eadburg must have had a reputation for writing, for Lul, one of Boniface's companions, sent her among other gifts a silver style (*graphium argenteum*) such as was used at the time for writing on wax tablets[2].

Boniface received frequent gifts from friends in England. Eoban, who carried his letter asking Eadburg for the Epistles of St Peter, was the bearer of a letter to an Abbot Duddo in which Boniface reminding him of their old friendship asked for a copy of the Epistles of St Paul[3]. Again Boniface wrote asking Abbot Huetberht of Wearmouth for the minor works (*opuscula*) of Bede[4], and Lul, who was with him, wrote to Dealwin to forward the minor works of Ealdhelm, bishop of Sherbourne, those in verse and those in prose[5].

Judging from the correspondence the effective work of Boniface resulted in the execution of only a small part of his great schemes. His original plan was repeatedly modified. There is extant a letter from the Pope which shows that he hoped for the conversion of the heathen Saxons and Thüringians[6], and the idea was so far

---

[1] Epist. nr 32, written 735 (Jaffé); after 732 (Hahn).
[2] Epist. nr 75. [3] Epist. nr 31. [4] Epist. nr 62.
[5] Epist. nr 76. [6] Epist. nr 22, written 722 (Jaffé).

embraced by Boniface that he wrote a letter to the bishops, priests, abbots and abbesses in England asking them to pray that the Saxons might accept the faith of Christ[1]. But the plan for their conversion was eventually abandoned.

At this period belief in the efficacy of prayer was unbounded, and praying for the living was as much part of the work of the professed as praying for the dead. Settlements apparently combined for the purpose of mutually supporting each other by prayer. A letter is extant in the correspondence of Boniface in which the abbot of Glastonbury, several abbesses and other abbots agree to pray at certain hours for each other's settlements[2].

In his times of trouble and tribulation Boniface wrote to all his friends asking for prayers. 'We were troubled on every side,' he wrote to the abbess Eadburg, quoting Scripture[3], 'without were fightings, within were fears.' She was to pray for him that the pagans might be snatched from their idolatrous customs and unbelievers brought back to the Catholic mother Church.

Eadburg had liberally responded to his request for gifts. 'Beloved sister,' he wrote[4], 'with gifts of holy books you have comforted the exile in Germany with spiritual light! For in this dark remoteness among German peoples man must come to the distress of death had he not the word of God as a lamp unto his feet and as a light unto his paths[5]. Fully trusting in your love I beseech that you pray for me, for I am shaken by my shortcomings, that take hold of me as though I were tossed by a tempest on a dangerous sea.' This consciousness of his shortcomings was not wholly due to the failure of his plans, for Boniface at one period of his life was much troubled by questions of theology. The simile of being tempest-tossed is often used by him. In a letter addressed to an unnamed nun he describes his position in language similar to that in which he addresses Eadburg. This nun also is urged to pray for him in a letter full of biblical quotations[6].

Among the letters to Boniface there are several from nuns and abbesses asking for his advice. Political difficulties and the changed attitude of the ruling princes of Northumbria and Mercia towards convents brought such hardships to those who had adopted the religious profession that many of them wished to leave their homes, and availed themselves of the possibility of doing so which was afforded by the plan of going on pilgrimage to Rome.

---

[1] Epist. nr 39. [2] Epist. nr 46. [3] Epist. nr 72, 2 Cor. vii. 5.
[4] Epist. nr 73. [5] Comp. Ps. cxix. 105. [6] Epist. nr 87.

The wish to behold the Eternal City had given a new direction to the love of wandering, so strong a trait in human nature. The motives for visiting Rome have been different in different periods of history. To the convert in the 8th and 9th centuries Rome appeared as the fountain-head of Christianity, the residence of Christ's representative on earth, and the storehouse of famous deeds and priceless relics. Architectural remains dating from the period of Roman rule were numerous throughout Europe and helped to fill the imagination of those dwelling north of the Alps with wonder at the possible sights and treasures which a visit to Rome itself might disclose. Prelates and monks undertook the journey to establish personal relations with the Pope and to acquire books and relics for their settlements, but the taste for travelling spread, and laymen and wayfarers of all kinds joined the bands of religious pilgrims. Even kings and queens, with a sudden change of feeling which the Church magnified into a portentous conversion, renounced the splendour of their surroundings and donned the pilgrim's garb in the hope of beholding the Eternal City in its glory.

Among the letters which are preserved in the correspondence of Boniface there is one from Aelflaed, abbess of Whitby, in which she writes to the abbess Adolana (probably Adela) of Pfälzel (Palatiolum) on the Mosel near Trier, recommending to her care a young abbess who is on her way to Rome. This letter shows that Aelflaed was well versed in writing Latin. The name of the abbess in whose behalf the letter was penned is not known, but she may be identical with Wethburg, who lived and died at Rome[1].

'To the holy and worshipful abbess Adolana, a greeting in the Lord of eternal salvation.

'Since we have heard of your holiness from those who have come from your parts, and from widespread report, in the first place I pray for your warm affection, for the Lord has said: This is my command, that ye love one another[2].

'Further we make humble request that your holy and fervent words may commend us worthily to God Almighty, should it not be irksome to you to offer devotion in return for ours; for James the Apostle has taught and said: Pray for one another, that ye may be saved.

---

[1] Epist. nr 8; written between 709 and 712 (Hahn). Boniface is known to have travelled in the district of the Mosel; there is no other reason why this letter should be included in the correspondence.

[2] John xv. 12.

'Further to your great holiness and usual charity we humbly and earnestly commend this maiden vowed to God, a pious abbess, our dear and faithful daughter, who since the days of her youth, from love of Christ and for the honour of the apostles Peter and Paul, has been desirous of going to their holy threshold, but who has been kept back by us until now because we needed her and in order that the souls entrusted to her might profit. And we pray that with charity and true kindness she may be received into your goodwill, as well as those who are travelling with her, in order that the desired journey with God's help and your willing charity may at last be accomplished. Therefore again and again we beseech that she may be helped on her way with recommendations from you to the holy city Rome, by the help of the holy and signbearing leader (signifer) of the apostles Peter; and if you are present we hope and trust she may find with you whatever advice she requires for the journey. May divine grace watch over your holiness when you pray for us.'

The desire to go southward was strengthened among religious women by the increasing difficulties of their position at home. Monastic privileges were no longer respected by the kings of Mercia and Northumbria, and the Church lacked the power of directly interfering in behalf of monks and nuns. There is in the correspondence a letter which Boniface wrote in his own name and in that of his foreign bishops to Aethelbald, king of Mercia (716–756); he sharply rebukes him for his immoral practices and urges on him the desirability of taking a lawful wife. He accuses the king of indulging his wicked propensities even in monasteries and with nuns and maidens who were vowed to God; following the example of Tacitus, he praises the pure morals of the heathen Germans. The passages which bear on the subject are worthy of perusal, for they show how uncertain was the position of monasteries and how keenly Boniface realized the difficulties of nuns. He tells the king 'that loose women, whether they be vowed to religion or not, conceive inferior children through their wickedness and frequently do away with them.' The privileges of religious houses, he says, were respected till the reign of King Osred (706–17) of Northumbria, and of King Ceolred (709–16) of Mercia, but 'these two kings have shown their evil disposition and have sinned in a criminal way against the teaching of the gospels and the doings of our Saviour. They persisted in vice, in the seduction of nuns and the contemptuous treatment of monastic rights. Condemned by the judgment of God, and hurled from the heights of royal authority, they were overtaken by a speedy and awful death, and are now cut off from eternal light, and buried in the depths of hell and in the abyss of the infernal regions[1].' We have seen that in the letter written by Boniface to Eadburg, Ceolred is described as suffering torments in hell, and that King Aethelbald at a later date is depicted in the same predicament.

With his letter to Aethelbald Boniface forwarded two others to the priest Herefrith, probably of Lindisfarne[2], and to Ecgberht (archbishop of York, 732–66), requesting them to support him against Aethelbald. 'It is the duty of your office to see that the devil does not establish his kingdom in places consecrated to God,' he wrote to Ecgberht, 'that there be not discord instead of peace, strife instead of piety, drunkenness instead of sobriety, slaughter and fornication instead of charity and chastity[3].' Shortly afterwards he wrote to Cuthberht, archbishop of Canterbury (740–62), telling him of the statutes passed at the Synod of Soissons[4], and severely censuring the conduct of the layman, 'be he emperor, king or count, who snatches a monastery from bishop, abbot, or abbess.'

These admonitions show that the position of the religious houses and that of their rulers depended directly on the temper of the reigning prince. In the correspondence there are several letters from abbesses addressed to Boniface bearing on this point, which give us a direct insight into the tone of mind of these women. Their Latin is cumbersome and faulty, and biblical quotations are introduced which do not seem always quite to the point. The writers ramble on without much regard to construction and style, and yet there is a genuine ring about their letters which makes the distress described seem very real.

One of these letters was written by an abbess named Ecgburg, probably at an early period of Boniface's career[5]. Her reference to the remoteness of her settlement suggests the idea that it was Repton, and that she herself was identical with Ecgburg, daughter of Ealdwulf king of the East Angles, the abbess whom we have noticed in connection with Guthlac. If that be so her sister Wethburg, to whom she refers, may be identical with the young unnamed abbess whom Aelflaed sped on her journey to Rome.

---

[1] Epist. nr 59; written 745 (Hahn).   [2] Epist. nr 60.
[3] Epist. nr 61.   [4] Epist. nr 70; written after 748 (Hahn).
[5] Epist. nr 13, written 717–19 (Hahn).

'Since a cruel and bitter death,' she writes, 'has robbed me of him, my brother Osher, whom I loved beyond all others, you I hold dearer than all other men. Not to multiply words, no day, no night passes, but I think of your teaching. Believe me it is on account of this that I love you, God is my witness. In you I confide, because you were never forgetful of the affection which assuredly bound you to my brother. Though inferior to him in knowledge and in merit, I am not unlike him in recognizing your goodness. Time goes by with increasing swiftness and yet the dark gloom of sadness leaves me not. For time as it comes brings me increase of indignities, as it is written " Love of man brings sorrow, but love of Christ gladdens the heart." More recently my equally beloved sister Wethburg, as though to inflict a wound and renew a pang, suddenly passed out of my sight, she with whom I had grown up and with whom I was nursed at the same breast; one mother she and I had in the Lord, and my sister has left me. Jesus is my witness that on all sides there is sorrow, fear, and the image of death[1]. I would gladly die if it so pleased God, to whom the unknown is manifest, for this slow death is no trifle. What was it I was saying ? From my sister not a sudden and bitter death, but a bitterer separation, divides me ; I believe it was for her happiness, but it left me unhappy, as a corpse laid low, when adopting the fashion of the age she went on a pilgrimage, even though she knew how much I loved and cherished her, whom now as I hear a prison confines at Rome. But the love of Christ, which is strong and powerful in her, is stronger and more binding than all fetters, and perfect love casteth out fear. Indeed, I say, he who holds the power of divination, the Ruler of high Olympus, has endowed you with divine wisdom, and in his law do you meditate night and day[2]. For it is written : " How beautiful are the feet of them that preach the gospel of peace, and bring tidings of good things[3].") She has mounted by a steep and narrow path, while I remain below, held by mortal flesh as by irons upon my feet. In the coming judgment full of joy she, like unto the Lord, will sing : " I was in prison and ye came unto me[4]." You also in the future life, when the twelve apostles sit on their twelve seats[5], will be there, and in proportion to the number of those whom you have won by your work, will rejoice before the

---

[1] Jaffé, Ph., *loc. cit.*, footnote, p. 64, quotes the lines Virg. *Aen.*, II. 369–70, of which this sentence seems an adaptation.

[2] Comp. Psalm i. 2. [3] Romans x. 15. [4] Matth. xxv. 36.

[5] Comp. Matth. xix. 28.

tribunal of the eternal King, like unto a leader who is about to be crowned. But I living in the vale of tears as I deserve, shall be weeping for my offences, on account of which God holds me unfit to join the heavenly hosts. Therefore, believe me, the tempest-tossed mariner does not so much long for the haven, the thirsty fields do not long so much for rain, the mother on the winding shore does not so anxiously wait for her son, as I long to rejoice in your sight. But oppressed by sins and innumerable offences, I so long to be freed from imminent danger, that I am made desperate; adoring the footsteps of your holiness and praying to you from the depths of my heart as a sinner, I call to you from the ends of the earth, O beloved master; as my anxious heart prompts, raise me to the corner-stone of your prayer, for you are my hope and a strong tower invisible to the enemy. And I beg as consolation to my grief and as limit to the wave of my sorrow, that my weakness may be supported by your intercession as by a prop. I entreat that you will condescend to give me some comfort either in the form of a relic or of a few words of blessing, written by you, in order that through them I may hold your presence secure.'

By the side of this letter must be quoted another written by an Abbess Eangith, describing similar difficulties in a similar strain[1]. We do not know over which settlement Eangith presided, but her name and that of her daughter Heaburg of whom she speaks are inscribed in the Durham 'Liber Vitae[2].'

'Beloved brother in the spirit rather than in the flesh,' she writes, 'you are magnified by the abundance of spiritual graces, and to you alone, with God as our sole witness, we wish to make known what you see here spread out before you and blotted by our tears: we are borne down by an accumulation of miseries as by a weight and a pressing burden, and also by the tumult of political affairs. As the foaming masses of the ocean when the force of the winds and the raging fury of the tempest lash up the great sea, carry in and carry out again the heaving billows dashing over rocks, so that the keels of the boats are turned upwards and the mast of the ship is pressed downwards, so do the ships of our souls groan under the great press of our miseries and the great mass

---

[1] Epist. nr 14, written 719–22 (Jaffé). Haigh, D. H., 'On the monasteries of St Heiu and St Hild,' in *Yorkshire Archaeol. Journal*, vol. 3, p. 377, speaks of her as Cangith and holds her to have been abbess of Hackness.

[2] Birch, W. de Gray, *Fasti Monastici Aevi Saxonici*, 1872, p. 68.

of our misfortunes. By the voice of truth has it been said of the heavenly house: "The rain descended and the floods came, and the winds blew and beat upon that house[1]," etc.

'First and before all noteworthy of the things that affect us from without, must be mentioned the multitude of our offences and our want of full and complete faith, due not so much to care for our own souls but, what is worse and more oppressive, to care for the souls of those of either sex and of every age which have been entrusted to us. For this care involves ministering to many minds and to various dispositions, and afterwards giving account before the supreme tribunal of Christ both for obvious sins in deeds and words, and for secret thoughts which men ignore and God alone witnesseth; with a simple sword against a double-edged one, with ten thousand to meet twenty thousand warriors[2]. In addition to this care of souls we have difficulties in our domestic affairs, and various disagreements which the jealous enemy of all good has sown, namely, he who fills the impure hearts of men with malice and scatters it everywhere, but chiefly in the settlements of monks and nuns; but it is said "the mighty shall be mightily tormented[3]." Moreover the poverty and scantiness of our temporal possessions oppress us, and the smallness of the cultivated part of our estate; and the hostility of the king, for we are accused before him by those who envy us, as a wise man has said: "the bewitching of vanity obscureth good things[4]." Similarly we are oppressed by service due to the king and the queen, to bishop and prefect, officers and attendants. It would take long to enumerate those things which can be more easily imagined than described.

'To all these evils is added the loss of friends, connections, and relatives by alliance and by blood. I[5] have neither son nor brother, neither father nor father's brother, none but an only daughter who is bereft of all that was dear to her; and a sister who is old, and the son of our brother, who too is unhappy in his mind, for our king holds his family connections in great contempt. There is no one else for us to rely on; God has removed them all by one chance or another. Some have died in their native land, and their bodies lie in the grimy dust of the earth to rise again on the day of doom, when the Master's trumpet shall sound, and the whole race of man shall come forth from dark tombs to

---

[1] Matth. vii. 25. [2] Comp. Luc. xiv. 31.
[3] Wisdom vi. 7 (Vulgate). [4] Wisdom iv. 12 (Vulgate).
[5] There are some difficulties in this passage.

give account of themselves; when their spirits, borne upwards in angels' arms, shall abide with Christ; when all sorrow shall end, and envy be worn out, and grief and mourning shall vanish in sight of the saints. Again others have left their native shores, and trusted themselves to the wide seas, and have sought the threshold of the holy apostles Peter and Paul and of all those martyrs, virgins and confessors, whose number God alone knows.

'For these and other like causes, hardly to be enumerated in one day though July and August lengthen the days of summer, we are weary of our present life and hardly care to continue it. Every man uncertain of his purpose and distrustful of his own counsel, seeks a faithful friend whose advice he follows since he distrusts his own; and such faith has he in him that he lays before him and reveals to him every secret of his heart. As has been said, what is sweeter than having someone with whom one can converse as with oneself? Therefore on account of the pressing miseries we have now insisted on to the full, we needs must find a true friend, one whom we can trust more than ourselves; who will treat our grief, our miseries and our poverty as his own, who will sympathize with us, comfort us, support us by his words, and raise us up by wise counsel. Long have we sought him. And we believe that in you we have found the friend whom we longed for, whom we wished for, whom we desired.

'Would that God had granted to us that, as Habakkuk the prophet was sped with food into the lion's den to the seer Daniel[1], or that as Philip one of the seven deacons was sped to the eunuch[2], we also were sped and could come to the land and to the district where you dwell; or that it were possible for us to hear living words from your lips. 'How sweet are thy words unto my palate, O Lord, sweeter than honey to my mouth[3].'

'But since this is not vouchsafed to us and we are divided from you by a wide expanse of land and of sea and by the boundaries of many provinces, because of our faith in you referred to above we will tell you, brother Boniface, that for a long time we have entertained the design like so many of our friends, relatives and others, of visiting Rome, the mistress of the world, there to seek forgiveness of our sins as many others have done and are now doing; so especially I (wish to do) since I am advanced in age, and have erred more than others. Wala, at one time my abbess and spiritual mother, was acquainted with my wish and my

---

[1] Daniel xiv. 33 (Vulgate).   [2] Acts viii. 26.   [3] Ps. cxix. 103.

intention. My only daughter at present is young, and cannot share my desire. But because we know how many there are who scoff at this wish and deprecate this desire, and support their view by adducing what the canons of the synods enjoin, that wherever anyone has settled and taken his vow, there shall he remain and there serve God; for we all live in different ways and God's purposes are unknown, as the prophet says: 'Thy righteousness is like the great mountains, thy judgments are a great deep, O Lord[1]'; and because His sacred will and desire in these things is hidden,--therefore we two, both of us in our difficulty, call on you earnestly and reverently: be you to us as Aaron, a mountain of strength, let your prayer be our help, swing the censer of prayer with incense in sight of the Divine, and let the lifting up of your hands be as the evening sacrifice[2]. Indeed we trust in God and beg of your goodness that by supplication of mouth and inward prayer it may be revealed to you what seems for us wise and useful: whether we are to live at home or go forth on pilgrimage. Also we beg of your goodness to send back your answer across the sea, and reply to what we have scratched on these leaves in rustic style and with unpolished wording. We have scant faith in those who glory in appearance and not in heart[3], but faith in your love, your charity in God and your goodness.'

It is not known whether Eangith carried out her intention and went to Rome.

Boniface had another correspondence with an abbess named Bugga, but though Eangith states that her daughter Heaburg was sometimes called by that name, it is not probable that they were the same, for Boniface writing to Bugga makes no mention of Eangith's plan, which he would hardly have omitted to do if Heaburg had been his correspondent[4].

Bugga was afterwards abbess of a monastery in Kent. She too sent gifts to Boniface, and later entertained the idea of going to Rome. In early days the prelate wrote to her telling her how he had been mercifully led through unknown countries, how 'the Pontiff of the glorious see' Gregory II had inclined to him, and how he had cast down 'the enemy of the Catholic Church, Radbod,' the Frisian.

In reply she assures him of her continued affection and makes some remarks on books they have exchanged. The Passions of

---

[1] Ps. xxxvi. 6. [2] Cp. Ps. cxli. 2. [3] Cp. 2 Cor. v. 12.
[4] The name Bugga occurs frequently during this period.

the Martyrs which he has asked for she has not yet procured, but she will forward them as soon as she can. 'But you, my friend,' she writes, 'send me as a consolation what you promised in your kind letter, your extracts from the holy writings. And I beseech you to offer the oblation of the holy mass for one of my relatives whom I loved beyond all others. I send you by the bearer of this letter fifty gold coins (solidi) and an altar cloth, better gifts I cannot procure. They are truly signs of a great affection though of insignificant appearance[1].'

Bugga does not style herself abbess, but Boniface addresses her as such in acknowledging the receipt of her gifts and advising her about going to Rome. On another occasion he wrote to express concern at her troubles, which he heard from many people had not diminished since she retired from rule for the sake of quiet[2]. The letter in which he advises her about going to Rome is worth quoting[3].

'Be it made known to you, dearest sister,' he writes, 'regarding the advice which you asked for in your letter, that I do not presume to forbid you the pilgrim's journey, neither would I directly advise it. I will explain why. If you gave up the charge you had of the servants of God, of his virgins (ancillae), and your own monastic life, for the purpose of securing quiet and the thought of God, in what way are you now bound to obey the words and the will of seculars with toil and wearing anxiety? Still if you cannot find peace of mind in your home in secular life among seculars it seems right that you should seek in a pilgrimage freedom for contemplation, especially since you wish it and can arrange it; just in the way our sister Wethburg did. She told me in her letter that she had found the quiet she longed for near the threshold of St Peter. In reference to your wish she sent me a message, for I had written to her about you, saying that you must wait till the attacks, hostility and menaces of the Saracens who have lately reached the Roman States have subsided, and that God willing she would then send you a letter of invitation. I too think this best. Prepare yourself for the journey, but wait for word from her, and then do as God in his grace commands. As to the collection of extracts for which you ask, be considerate to my shortcomings. Pressing work and continuous travelling prevent my furnishing you with what you desire. As soon as I can I will forward them to please you.

[1] Epist. nr 16, written 720–22 (Jaffé); I think somewhat later.
[2] Epist. nr 86.   [3] Epist. nr 88.

'We thank you for the gifts and vestments which you have sent, and pray to God Almighty, to put aside a gift for you in return with the angels and archangels in the heights of heaven. And I beseech you in the name of God, dear sister, yea mother and sweet lady, that you diligently pray for me. For many troubles beset me through my shortcomings, and I am more distressed by uncertainty of mind than by bodily work. Rest assured that our old trust in each other will never fail us.'

Bugga carried out her intention and went to Rome, where she met Boniface, who was the Pope's guest about the year 737. He had achieved a signal success in reconverting the Hessians, and was now appointed to constitute bishoprics in Bavaria and to hold councils of Church dignitaries at regular intervals[1]. At Rome Bugga and Boniface walked and talked together, and visited the churches of the holy apostles. A letter from Aethelberht II, king of Kent, to Boniface refers to their meeting[2]. Bugga had come back to her old monastery and had given the king a description of her visit. She attained a considerable age, for she was advanced in years before her pilgrimage, and about twenty years later Bregwin, archbishop of Canterbury (759–765), wrote to Lul informing him of her death[3].

Boniface made provision at Rome for the women in whom he was interested. A certain deacon Gemmulus writes to him from Rome to inform him[4] that 'the sisters and maidens of God who have reached the threshold of the apostles' are there being cared for by himself and others as Boniface has desired.

The readiness with which Anglo-Saxon nuns went abroad eventually led to a state of things which cast discredit on religion. Boniface addressed the following remarks on these pilgrimages to Cuthberht of Canterbury in the letter written after the synod of Soissons[5].

'I will not withhold from your holiness,' he says, '... that it were a good thing and besides honour and a credit to your Church and a palliation of evils, if the synod and your princes forbade women, and those who have taken the veil, to travel and stay abroad as they do, coming and going in the Roman states. They come in great numbers and few return undefiled. For there are very few districts of Lombardy in which there is not some

---

[1] Epist. nrs 37, 38, 39.
[2] Epist. nr 103, written shortly after 740 (Hahn).
[3] Epist. nr 113. [4] Epist. nr 53. [5] Epist. nr 70.

woman of Anglian origin living a loose life among the Franks
and the Gauls. This is a scandal and disgrace to your whole
Church....'

The difficulty of exercising more control over those who chose
to leave their settlements was only partly met by stricter rules of
supervision. For there were no means of keeping back monk or
nun who was tired of living the monastic life. In the 9th century
Hatto bishop of Basel († 836) wrote to the bishop of Toul enjoining
that no one should be suffered to undertake a pilgrimage to Rome
without leave, and provisions of a much later date order that
houses shall not take in and harbour inmates from other settlements.

In this connection it is interesting to find Lul, who had settled
abroad with Boniface, excommunicating an abbess Suitha because
she had allowed two nuns to go into a distant district for some
secular purpose without previously asking permission from her
bishop[1]. The women who settled in Germany under Boniface were
brought under much stricter control than had till then been
customary in either France or England.

§ 2. Anglo-Saxon Nuns abroad.

Among the women who came to Germany and settled there
at the request of Boniface was Lioba, otherwise Leobgith, who
had been educated at Wimbourne in Dorset, at no very great
distance from Nutshalling where Boniface dwelt, and who left
England between 739 and 748. She was related to him through
her mother Aebbe, and a simple and modest little letter is extant
in which she writes to Boniface and refers to her father's death six
years ago; she is her parents' only child, she says, and would recall
her mother and herself to the prelate's memory.

'This too I ask for,' she writes in this letter, 'correct the rusti-
city of my style and do not neglect to send me a few words in
proof of your goodwill. I have composed the few verses which
I enclose according to the rules of poetic versification, not from
pride but from a desire to cultivate the beginnings of learning, and
now I am longing for your help. I was taught by Eadburg who
unceasingly devotes herself to this divine art.' And she adds four

---

[1] Epist. nr 126.

lines of verse addressed to God Almighty as an example of what she can do[1].

As mentioned above we are indebted for an account of Lioba's life to the monk Rudolf of Fulda († 865). From this we learn that Lioba at a tender age had been given into the care of the abbess Tetta at Wimbourne[2]. 'She grew up, so carefully tended by the abbess and the sisters, that she cared for naught but the monastery and the study of holy writ. She was never pleased by irreverent jokes, nor did she care for the other maidens' senseless amusements; her mind was fixed on the love of Christ, and she was ever ready to listen to the word of God, or to read it, and to commit to memory what she heard and read to her own practical advantage. In eating and drinking she was so moderate that she despised the allurements of a great entertainment and felt content with what was put before her, never asking for more. When she was not reading, she was working with her hands, for she had learnt that those who do not work have no right to eat.'

She was moreover of prepossessing appearance and of engaging manners, and secured the goodwill of the abbess and the affection of the inmates of the settlement. A dream of hers is described by her biographer in which she saw a purple thread of indefinite length issuing from her mouth. An aged sister whom she consulted about it, interpreted the dream as a sign of coming influence.

To Lioba, Tecla and Cynehild, Boniface addressed a letter from abroad, asking in the usual way for the support of their prayers[3]. Lioba's biographer tells us that when Boniface thought of establishing religious settlements, 'wishing that the order of either sex should exist according to rule,' he arranged that Sturmi, who had settled at Fulda, should go to Italy and there visit St Benedict's monastery at Monte Casino, and he 'sent envoys with letters to the abbess Tetta (of Wimbourne) begging her as a comfort in his labour, and as a help in his mission, to send over the virgin Lioba, whose reputation for holiness and virtuous teaching had penetrated across wide lands and filled the hearts of many with praise of her[4].'

---

[1] Epist. nr 23; the verse runs as follows:
> 'Arbiter omnipotens, solus qui cuncta creavit,
> In regno Patris semper qui lumine fulget,
> Qua jugiter flagrans sic regnat gloria Christi,
> Inlaesum servet semper te jure perenni.'

[2] *A. SS. Boll.*, St Lioba, Sept. 28, *Vita*, ch. 9.

[3] Epist. nr 91, written between 737–41 (Hahn).   [4] *Vita*, ch. 13.

This request shows that Boniface thought highly of the course of life and occupations practised in English nunneries and that he considered English women especially suited to manage the settlements under his care. In a letter written from Rome about 738 Boniface refers to the sisters and brothers who are living under him in Germany[1]. Parties of English men and women joined him at different times. One travelled under the priest Wiehtberht, who sent a letter to the monks of Glastonbury to inform them of his safe arrival and honourable reception by Boniface, and he requests that Tetta of Wimbourne may be told of this[2]. Perhaps Lioba, who was Tetta's pupil, was one of the party who travelled to Germany with Wiehtberht.

'In pursuance of his plan,' says Lioba's life[3], 'Boniface now arranged monastic routine and life according to accepted rule, and set Sturmi as abbot over the monks and the virgin Lioba as spiritual mother over the nuns, and gave into her care a monastery at the place called Bischofsheim, where a considerable number of servants of God were collected together, who now followed the example of their blessed teacher, were instructed in divine knowledge and so profited by her teaching that several of them in their turn became teachers elsewhere; for few monasteries of women (monasteria fœminarum) existed in those districts where Lioba's pupils were not sought as teachers. She (Lioba) was a woman of great power and of such strength of purpose that she thought no more of her fatherland and of her relations but devoted all her energies to what she had undertaken, that she might be blameless before God, and a model in behaviour and discipline to all those who were under her. She never taught what she did not practise. And there was neither conceit nor domineering in her attitude; she was affable and kindly without exception towards everyone. She was as beautiful as an angel; her talk was agreeable, her intellect was clear; her abilities were great; she was a Catholic in faith; she was moderate in her expectations and wide in her affections. She always showed a cheerful face but she was never drawn into hilarity. No one ever heard a word of abuse (maledictionem) pass her lips, and the sun never went down on her anger. In eating and drinking she was liberal to others but moderate herself, and the cup out of which she usually drank was called by the sisters 'the little one of our beloved' (dilectae parvus) on account of its smallness. She

---

[1] Epist. nr 34.   [2] Epist. nr 98, written 732–747 (Hahn).   [3] *Vita*, ch. 14.

was so bent on reading that she never laid aside her book except
to pray or to strengthen her slight frame with food and sleep.
From childhood upwards she had studied grammar and the other
liberal arts, and hoped by perseverance to attain a perfect knowledge of religion, for she was well aware that the gifts of nature
are doubled by study. She zealously read the books of the Old
and New Testaments, and committed their divine precepts to
memory; but she further added to the rich store of her knowledge
by reading the writings of the holy Fathers, the canonical decrees,
and the laws of the Church (totiusque ecclesiastici ordinis jura). In
all her actions she showed great discretion, and thought over the
outcome of an undertaking beforehand so that she might not
afterwards repent of it. She was aware that inclination is necessary for prayer and for study, and she was therefore moderate in
holding vigils. She always took a rest after dinner, and so did
the sisters under her, especially in summer time, and she would
not suffer others to stay up too long, for she maintained that the
mind is keener for study after sleep.'

Boniface, writing to Lioba while she was abbess at Bischofsheim, sanctions her taking a girl into the settlement for purposes
of instruction. Bischofsheim was on the Tauber a tributary of
the river Main, and Boniface, who dwelt at Mainz, frequently
conferred with her there. Lioba went to stay with Boniface at
Mainz in 757 before he went among the Frisians[1]; he presented
her with his cloak and begged her to remain true to her work
whatever might befall him. Shortly after he set out on his expedition he was attacked and killed by heathens. His corpse
was brought back and buried at Fulda, and Lioba went to pray
at his grave, a privilege granted to no other woman.

Lioba was also in contact with temporal rulers. Karl the
Great gave her presents and Queen Hildegard († 783) was so
captivated with her that she tried to persuade her to come and
live with her. 'Princes loved her,' her biographer tells us,
'noblemen received her, and bishops gladly entertained her and
conversed with her on the scriptures and on the institutions of
religion, for she was familiar with many writings and careful in
giving advice.' She had the supervision of other settlements besides her own and travelled about a good deal. After Boniface's
death she kept on friendly terms with Lul who had succeeded
him as bishop of Mainz (757–786), and it was with his consent

[1] Epist. nr 93.

that she finally resigned her responsibilities and her post as abbess
at Bischofsheim and went to dwell at Schornsheim near Mainz
with a few companions.   At the request of Queen Hildegard she
once more travelled to Aachen where Karl the Great was keeping
court.   But she was old, the fatigues of the journey were too much
for her, and she died shortly after her return in 780.   Boniface had
expressed a wish that they should share the same resting-place
and her body was accordingly taken to Fulda, but the monks there,
for some unknown reason, preferred burying her in another part
of their church.

It is noteworthy that the women who by the appointment
of Boniface directed convent life in Germany, remained throughout
in a state of dependence[1], while the men, noticeably Sturmi († 779)
whom he had made abbot at Fulda, cast off their connection with
the bishop, and maintained the independence of their monasteries.
Throughout his life Sturmi showed a bold and determined spirit,
but he was not therefore less interesting to the nuns of Boniface's
circle.   His pupil and successor Eigil wrote an account of his life
at the request of the nun Angiltrud, who is also supposed to have
come from England to Germany[2].

We know little concerning the other Anglo-Saxon women who
settled abroad, for there are no contemporary accounts of them.
The 'Passion of Boniface,' written at Mainz between 1000 and
1050, tells us that as Lioba settled at Bischofsheim so Tecla settled
at Kizzingen, where 'she shone like a light in a dark place[3].'   No
doubt this Tecla is identical with the nun of that name whom
Boniface speaks of in his letter to Lioba[4].   She has a place among
the saints[5], but it seems doubtful whether she founded the monastery at Kizzingen or the one at Oxenfurt.

The names of several other women are given by Othlon, a
monk of St Emmeran in Bavaria, who in consequence of a quarrel
fled from his monastery and sought refuge at Fulda.   While there,
between 1062 and 1066, he re-wrote and amplified Wilibald's life
of Boniface.   In this account he gives a list of the men who came

---

[1] Epist. nr 126; also Epist. nr 68, written 748 (from the Pope on the consecration of
abbot and abbess).

[2] *Vita St Sturmi* in Pertz, *Mon. Germ. Script.*, vol. 2, p. 365.

[3] In Jaffé, Ph., *Monumenta Moguntina*, 1866, p. 475.

[4] Comp. above, p. 135.

[5] *A. SS. Boll.*, St Tecla, Oct. 15, casts discredit on Tecla's settling at Kizzingen and
argues in favour of Oxenfurt.   Kizzingen existed in the 15 c.; nothing is known
concerning the later history of Oxenfurt.

into Germany from England, the correctness of which has been called in question. He then enumerates the women who came abroad and mentions 'an aunt of Lul called Chunihilt[1] and her daughter Berthgit[2], Chunitrud and Tecla, Lioba, and Waltpurgis the sister of Wilibald and Wunebald[3].' The only mention of Waltpurgis is her name, but he describes where the other women settled, some in the district of the Main, others in Bavaria.

This woman Waltpurgis has been the subject of many conjectures; writers generally do not hesitate to affirm that the sister of Wunebald and Wilibald is identical with the saint who was so widely reverenced. But St Waltpurgis, popularly called Walburg, is associated with customs and traditions which so clearly bear a heathen and profane character in the Netherlands and in North Germany, that it seems improbable that these associations should have clustered round the name of a Christian woman and a nun[4].

In face of the existing evidence one of two conclusions must be adopted. Either the sister of Wunebald and Wilibald really bore the name Waltpurgis, and the monk Wolfhard who wrote an account of a saint of that name whose relics were venerated at Eichstätt (between 882 and 912) took advantage of the coincidence of name and claimed that the Walburg, who bears the character of a pseudo-saint, and the sister of Wunebald and Wilibald were identical; or else, desirous to account for the veneration of relics which were commonly connected with the name Walburg, he found it natural and reasonable to hold that Walburg had belonged to the circle of Boniface, and identified her with the sister of Wunebald and Wilibald[5].

Nothing is preserved concerning this sister except a reference to her existence, which is contained in the accounts of the acts of Wilibald and Wunebald written by a nun at Heidenheim, whose name also is not recorded[6]. These accounts offer many points of

---

[1] Hahn, H., *Bonifaz und Lull, ihre angelsächsischen Correspondenten,* 1883, p. 138, footnote 4, considers her identical with the Cynehild of the correspondence.

[2] Two letters, nrs 148, 149, in the correspondence are written by 'Berthgyth,' apparently a nun in England who wished to go abroad, to her brother Baldhard, but judging by their contents ('I have been deserted by my parents,' etc.) it is improbable that she is identical with the nun referred to above.

[3] Jaffé, Ph., *Monumenta Moguntina,* 1866, p. 490.

[4] Comp. above, p. 25.

[5] Comp. the attempt to identify Chunihilt with St Gunthildis, *A. SS. Boll.,* Sept. 22.

[6] Edit. Canisius, H., *Thesaurus,* 1725, vol. 2; this anonymous nun is sometimes considered identical with the sister of Wilibald and Wunebald, and therefore with St Walburg.

interest. The nun who wrote them was of Anglo-Saxon origin; her style is highly involved and often falls short of the rules of grammar, but she had possession of interesting information, and she was determined to impart it. It has been noticed that her writing varies according to whether she is setting down facts or dilating on them; for she is concise enough when it is a question of facts only, but when it comes to description she falls into the spirit of Anglo-Saxon literature and introduces alliteration into her Latin and launches forth into panegyric. She came from England to Germany, as she tells us, shortly before the death of Wunebald (c. 765), and experiences of an unpleasant nature led her to expect that her writings would not pass without criticism.

'I am but a woman,' she says[1], 'weak on account of the frailty of my sex, neither supported by the prerogative of wisdom nor sustained by the consciousness of great power, yet impelled by earnestness of purpose,' and she sets to work to give a description of the life of Wilibald and the journey which he made to Palestine, parts of which she took down from his dictation, for at the close of her account she says that she wrote it from Wilibald's narrative in the monastery of Heidenheim in the presence of deacons and of some of Wilibald's pupils who were witnesses to the fact. 'This I say,' she adds, 'that no one may again declare this to be nonsense.'

The account she gives of Wilibald's experiences contains one of the earliest descriptions written in northern Europe of a journey to Palestine, and modern writers have commented on it as a curious literary monument of the time. Interest in descriptions of the Holy Land was increasing. Besides early references to such journeys in the letters of St Jerome who described how Paula went from Rome to Jerusalem and settled there in the 4th century, we hear how Adamnan came to the court of King Ealdfrith of Northumbria about the year 701 and laid before him his book on Holy Places[2] which he had taken down from the narrative of bishop Arculf who had made the pilgrimage, but of whom we know nothing more. But Adamnan's account is bald and its interest is poor compared to this description of the adventures of Wilibald and of what he saw on his travels.

The nun prefaces her account of the journey by telling us of Wilibald's origin. She describes how he fell ill as a child, how

---

[1] *Vita St Willibaldi* (also called Hodoeporicon), edit. Canisius, H., *Thesaurus*, 1725, vol. 2, ch. 2.

[2] Bede, *Hist. Eccles.*, bk 5, ch. 15.

his parents vowed him to a religious life if he were spared, and how in conformity with their promise they took him to the abbey of Waltham at the age of five, where Wilibald continued studying till manhood. We are not told to what his love of travel was due. He determined to go south and persuaded his father and his brother Wunebald to accompany him. We hear how they and their companions took boat and arrived at Rouen, how they travelled on till they reached Lucca where the father fell ill and died, and how the brothers pursued their journey to Rome where they spent the winter. We hear how the heat and bad air of summer drove them away from Rome and how, while Wunebald remained in Italy, Wilibald with a few companions pushed on by way of Naples and Reggio and reached Catania in Sicily, where he took boat for Ephesus and Syria. We get a good deal of information by the way on saints and on relics, and hear of the veil of St Agatha which stayed the eruptions of Mount Aetna, and of the Seven Sleepers of Ephesus. The travellers experienced all kinds of hardships; thrice they were cast into prison and liberated before their feet trod on holy ground. Then they visited Nazareth and Chana; they gazed upon Lake Tiberias, they bathed in the river Jordan, and finally they reached Jerusalem where they made a long stay, broken however by several long expeditions. Each site is described in turn, and its connection with scriptural history is pointed out. We hear a good deal about Jerusalem, about Mount Sion, the site of the Ascension of the Virgin, and about the site of the Nativity at Bethlehem. It was 'once a cave, now it is a square house cut into the rock,' over which a little chapel is built. We also hear of various monasteries where the travellers stayed in coming and going. Finally they travelled to Tyre, where they took boat to Constantinople. There they made a lengthy stay and then journeyed on to Italy and visited the Isle of Lipari, where Wilibald desired to get a glimpse of the crater, which is designated as hell, the thought of which called forth a fine piece of description from the nun.

'And when they arrived there they left the boat to see what sort of a hell it was. Wilibald especially was curious about what was inside the crater, and would have climbed the summit of the mountain to the opening; but he was prevented by cinders which rose from the black gulf and had sunk again; as snow settles falling from the sky and the heavenly heights in white thick masses, so these cinders lay heaped on the summit of the mountain and prevented Wilibald's ascent. But he saw a blackness and a terrible column of flame projected upwards with a noise like thunder from the pit, and he saw the flame and the smoky vapour rising to an immeasurable height. He also beheld pumice-stone which writers use[1] thrown up from the crater with the flame, and it fell into the sea and was again cast up on the shore; men there gathered it up to bring it away.'

When Wilibald and his companion Tidberht reached Rome they had been absent seven years, and their travels had made them personages of such interest that the Pope interviewed them. Wilibald at the Pope's suggestion agreed to join Boniface in Germany. Wunebald, the brother whom he had left in Italy, had met Boniface in Rome in 738 and had travelled back with him. Wilibald also settled in Germany and was made bishop of the new see of Eichstätt. Here he came across the nun, who was so fired by his account of his travels that she undertook to record them.

After she had finished this work she was moved to write a short account of the life of Wunebald[2]. It is written in a similar style and contains valuable historical information, but it has not the special interest of the other account. Wunebald on coming into Germany had first stayed at Mainz, then he travelled about with Boniface, and finally he settled at Heidenheim where he made a clearance in the midst of a wooded wilderness and dwelt there with a few younger men. He was active in opposing idolatrous customs, but does not appear to have been satisfied with his work. He died about the year 765, and his brother Wilibald, bishop of Eichstätt, and his sister, of whom mention is now made for the first time, came to his monastery to assist at the translation of his corpse. The sister took charge of his settlement, apparently for a time only, for the monastery at Heidenheim continued to be under the rule of an abbot and there is no evidence that women belonged to it.

It was from this sister that the nun received her information about Wunebald. The theory has been put forward that she was the same person as a nun who came to Heidenheim and was there miraculously cured. However that may be, this literary nun is the last Anglo-Saxon woman of whom we have definite information who came abroad in connection with Boniface. Her name is lost, it is as the anonymous nun of Heidenheim that she has come down to posterity.

[1] For erasing writing from parchment.
[2] *Vita St Wunebaldi*, edit. Canisius, H., *Thesaurus*, 1725, vol. 2.

CHAPTER V.

CONVENTS IN SAXON LANDS BETWEEN A.D. 800—1000.

'Nec scientia scibilis Deum offendit, sed injustitia sciéntis.' *Hrotsvith.*

§ 1. Women's Convents in Saxony.

SOME account has been given in the preceding chapters of the form which monastic settlements of women took among the Franks and the Anglo-Saxons during the first centuries after the acceptance of Christianity. Features similar to those which appear in France and England characterised the first period of monastic development among the continental Saxons, the last branch of the German race to accept Christianity as a nation. Here also we find highborn and influential women as abbesses at the head of establishments which were important centres of contemporary culture.

The convent in Saxon lands, as elsewhere, was a place of residence and a training school for women of the ruling classes. Girls came there to be educated, and either considered the convent as their permanent home or left it to be married; the widow frequently returned to it later in life. But some of the Saxon settlements of women gained an additional importance in the 10th and 11th centuries owing to their close connection with the political affairs and interests of the time. The abbess was frequently a member of the royal or imperial family. In one case she was appointed as the guardian of the Emperor, in another she became representative of the Emperor during his absence in Italy.

The story of the spread of monastic life into Saxony is closely connected with the history of the conquest of the country and the subsequent growth of national independence. The Saxons occupied the districts of northern Germany, Westphalia, Eastphalia and Engern, of which Westphalia bordered on lands occupied by the Franks. Between the 6th and the 9th centuries the Franks had sometimes fought against the Saxons and had sometimes made common cause with them against their mutual enemies the people of Thüringen. But the Saxons were warlike and ferocious, insensible to the influence of Christianity, and ready at any moment to begin hostilities. They became more and more dreaded by the Franks, who looked upon them as dangerous neighbours, and who attacked them whenever opportunity offered. Karl the Great († 814), king of the Franks, and Roman Emperor of the German nation, received the war against the Saxons as part of his heritage, but repeated inroads into Saxony and a cruelty bordering on vindictiveness were needed before he could speak of the conquest of the Saxons as an accomplished fact. In 785, after a prolonged struggle, Widukind, the Saxon leader in whom the spirit of Arminius lived, was finally defeated; and he and his followers accepted Christianity as part of their subjection.

The Frankish Emperor and the Church now united in extending a uniform system of government over the lands of the Saxons. The count (*graf* or *comes*) was made responsible for the maintenance of peace in the separate district (*gau* or *pagus*) entrusted to him, and bishoprics were founded as dependencies of the ancient archiepiscopal sees of Cöln and Mainz. At the same time colonies of monks migrated into the conquered districts from the west and south. Their settlements developed rapidly, owing to the favour which monastic life found with the newly converted Saxons.

The subjection of the Saxons was not however of long duration. The supremacy of the Western Empire culminated under the rule of Karl the Great; the union under one rule of many peoples who were in different stages of civilization was only possible at all through the rare combination of commanding qualities in this emperor; at his death the empire at once began to crumble away. This brought a returning sense of self-confidence to those peoples on whom the yoke of subjection had been forcibly thrust. Fifty years after Karl's death a warlike chief of the old type was established among the Saxons as duke (*herzog* or *dux*); a hundred years later and a Saxon duke was chosen king of the Germans by the united votes of Frankish and Saxon nobles. The supreme authority now passed from the Franks to the Saxons; a change which the Saxon historian of the 10th century associated with the transference of the relics of St Vitus from France to Saxon soil[1]. The present age seeks the explanation of the removal of the centre of authority in less romantic causes, and finds it in the altogether extraordinary aptitude which the Saxons showed for assimilating new elements of civilization, and for appropriating or remodelling to their own use institutions of rule and government into which they breathed a spirit peculiarly their own.

The history of the attainment to political supremacy by the Saxons helps us to understand the spirit which animated the Church and monastic institutions of the time. The bishoprics which Frankish overlordship had established were soon in the hands of men who were Saxons by birth, and a similar appropriation took place in regard to monastic settlements. Corvei, a religious colony founded on Saxon soil by monks from La Corbie in northern France, a lifetime after the conversion numbered Saxon nobles among its inmates. Settlements of women were also founded and rapidly gained importance, especially in the eastern districts where they rivalled the episcopal sees in wealth and influence.

A reason for the favour with which monastic life was regarded during the period of political subjection lay in the practical advantages which these settlements offered. The nobleman who turned monk was freed from the obligations thrust upon him by the new régime; he was exempt from fighting under the standard of his conqueror, and the property which he bestowed on the religious settlement was in a way withdrawn from the enemy. But when the people regained their independence the popularity of the convent still remained. For the Saxons were quick in realizing the advantages of a close union between religion and the state, and the most powerful and progressive families of the land vied with each other in founding and endowing religious settlements.

The political interest of the period centres in the career of Liudolf, who was styled duke by his people, but count by the Emperor. Liudolf rapidly rose to greatness and became the progenitor of a family which has given Germany many remarkable men and her first line of kings. His son Otto († 912) was renowned like his father for personal valour, and success in every way favoured the undertakings of his grandson Heinrich the Fowler († 936), first king of the Saxon line. Heinrich became the favourite hero of the national poet on account of the triumphs he gained over the Slavs

---

[1] Widukind, *Annalium libri tres*, year 924.

and Magyars, who at this time threatened the lands occupied by Germans at every point between the Baltic and the Adriatic. Again Heinrich's successes were reflected in those of his son Otto I († 973), surnamed the Great, who added the lustre of imperial dignity to his father's firmly established kingship. Emulating the fame of Karl the Great, Otto was crowned emperor by the Pope in Rome. During the reign of his son, Otto II († 982), and of his grandson, Otto III († 1002), the Saxon court remained the meeting-place of representatives of the civilized world. It was there that envoys were received from England and Italy, and it was from thence that messengers were sent out to Constantinople and Cordova. The elective crown of the German Empire remained hereditary in the Saxon dynasty for over a hundred years, and it is with this period that the Germans associate the first development of their national life on national soil[1].

At this time the kingdoms founded in other parts of Europe by peoples of the German race were much enfeebled. During the 9th and 10th centuries the Frankish princes were wanting in that unity of purpose which alone could prevent the appropriation of fruitful tracts of their territory by the vikings. In England a period of returning difficulties had followed the reign of King Aelfraed, so brilliant in many ways. The personal valour of his children, the intrepid Lady Aethelflaed (†918) and King Eadward (†925) her brother, had not stayed the social changes which prepared the way for the rule of the Dane. It is in Saxony only that we find the concentration and consolidation of power which make the advance and attitude of a nation conspicuous in history. The sword was here wielded to good purpose and likewise the pen. The bishoprics of Hildesheim, Halberstadt, and Magdeburg had become centres of artistic activity, and the monastery of Corvei rivalled the time-honoured settlements of St Gallen and Fulda in intellectual importance. The Saxon historian Widukind († after 973) was at work in Corvei in the 10th century; this author is for Saxon history what Gregory is for Frankish and Bede for Anglo-Saxon history. Monasteries for women, especially those of Herford, Gandersheim, and Quedlinburg, had rapidly developed and exerted a social and intellectual influence such as has rarely fallen to the lot of women's religious settlements in the course of history.

The first religious house for women of which we have definite

---

[1] Giesebrecht, W., *Geschichte der deutschen Kaiserzeit*, 4 ed. 1873, vol. 1.

information is Herford, which was situated close to Corvei in Westphalia and had originally been founded as a dependency of it. Two small settlements for women existed at an early period in Eastphalia, but our knowledge of them is slight. The story is told that the heathen Saxon Hessi, having been defeated by Karl the Great in 775, went to live in the monastery of Fulda, and left his daughter Gisela in possession of his property, which she devoted to founding two little monasteries (monasteriola) for her daughters. This information is preserved in an account of Liutberg, a Saxon girl of noble parentage who was brought up in one of these little monasteries, but afterwards left it, as she preferred to dwell as a recluse in a neighbouring cell. Here she was visited by Theotgrim, bishop of Halberstadt († 840), and by the writer to whom we owe our account of her[1]. Wendhausen, one of the little monasteries spoken of in this account, was in existence a century later, for an attempt was then made to transfer its inmates to Quedlinburg. The fame of Liutberg's virtues was great during her lifetime but apparently did not secure her recognition as a saint. The cell in which she had lived was afterwards granted to Quedlinburg by charter (958).

We have abundant information about Herford, the dependency of Corvei. In 838 a certain Tetta was abbess, who came from Soissons and regulated the settlement at Herford on the plan of the house she had left[2]. The Saxon element asserted itself here also. In 854 the abbess was Addila, who was of Saxon parentage and probably the widow of a Saxon nobleman. Again in 858 we hear of another abbess, Hadewy, probably the niece of Warin, who was abbot of Corvei and a relation of Duke Liudolf. During her rule the relics of the woman-saint Pusinna were sent to Herford by the Saxon nobleman Kobbo as a gift to his sister the abbess Hadewy. The Saxons had no traditions or relics of early Christians who had lived among them, and so they were obliged to import relics to form a centre for their worship. King and bishop alike set an extraordinary value on relics and paid exorbitant prices for them. So great an importance was attached to the arrival of the relics of Pusinna at Herford that a contemporary monk wrote a detailed account of the event[3]. But it is characteristic of the author's dispo-

---

[1] Ex Vita Liutbergae in Pertz, *Mon. Germ. Script.*, vol. 4, p. 158 (Potthast, *Wegweiser*, written about 870).

[2] Dümmler, E., *Geschichte des ostfränkischen Reichs*, 1865, vol. 1, p. 348.

[3] Translatio St Pusinnae in *A. SS. Boll.*, April 23 (Potthast, *Wegweiser*, written probably by a monk of Corvei between 860–877).

sition that he tells us nothing of the life and the works of Pusinna, who but for this account is unknown to history.

A side-light is thrown on the material prosperity and the national sympathies of the settlements of Corvei and Herford in 889. Egilmar, bishop of Osnabrück (885–906), lodged a complaint with the Pope, contending that these settlements, besides appropriating other rights, drew so many tithes from his diocese that his income was reduced to a quarter of what it should be. But Egilmar got scant reward for his pains, no doubt because those in authority at Corvei and Herford were family connections of Duke Liudolf, whom it was felt dangerous to cross. For the Saxon duke had gained in influence as the Franks relaxed their hold on Saxon affairs, and while he nominally remained a dependent, pressure from outside was not brought to bear on him. In refusing to interfere in Egilmar's behalf, which would have involved his coming into conflict with Liudolf, the Pope was acting in accordance with the policy which the Franks pursued in Saxon lands[1].

At an early date the abbey of Herford was renowned as an educational centre, and it long maintained its reputation. Hathumod, a daughter of Duke Liudolf, was educated there previous to becoming abbess at Gandersheim, as we shall see later on. A hundred years later Queen Mathilde († 968) of the race of the warrior Widukind, and wife of Heinrich the Fowler, was brought up at Herford, her grandmother being abbess at the time.

The foundation of Gandersheim in Eastphalia followed upon that of Herford. Gandersheim was founded by Duke Liudolf and remained the favourite settlement of the women of his family; we shall return to it later on. Two other important abbeys ruled by women in connection with royalty were Essen and Quedlinburg. Essen was founded by Altfrid, bishop of Hildesheim (847–874), a Saxon by birth[2], and Quedlinburg at the instigation of Queen Mathilde, who as mentioned above had been educated at Herford. For centuries the abbess of Quedlinburg remained a person of marked importance, in her influence both on politics and on matters social and literary. Essen and Quedlinburg afterwards became centres of art industry; all these early monastic foundations maintained their importance down to the time of the Reformation.

The favour found by these institutions is explained when we

---

[1] Dümmler, E., *Geschichte des ostfränkischen Reichs*, 1865, vol. 2, p. 336.
[2] Luentzel, *Geschichte der Diöcese und Stadt Hildesheim*, 1858, vol. 1, p. 22.

come to consider the uncertainty of the times and the changeful political events which accompanied the growth of Saxon independence. The age, judged by a later standard, may well be called an age of violence. For the country was in the hands of a number of overlords who were frequently at war together, and who dwelt in isolated castles in a thickly wooded district in which only a patch here and there had been brought under cultivation.

The monotony of life in the castles or burghs of this period can hardly be exaggerated. Means of communication were few and occasions for it were rare. When the master and his men were absent, engaged in some private broil, or else summoned by the arrière-ban to attend the duke or the king, weeks and months would go by without a reminder of the existence of the world outside; weeks and months when the arrival of a traveller offered the one welcome diversion. The young nobleman followed his father to camp and to court, where he tasted of the experiences of life; the young noblewoman stayed at home, cut off from intercourse with those of her age and standing, and from every possibility of widening her mental horizon.

It is with the daughters of these families that the religious house first found favour. Settlements such as Herford, Gandersheim, Essen, and Quedlinburg offered the companionship of equals, and gave a domestic and intellectual training which was the best of its kind. Later ages were wont to look upon the standard of education attained at Gandersheim and Quedlinburg as exemplary. The word college (collegium), which early writers often apply to these settlements in its modern sense of a learning and a teaching body, aptly designates their character. For the religious settlement was an endowed college where girls were received to be trained, and where women who wished to devote themselves to learning and the arts permanently resided.

The age at which girls were received in these settlements can be determined by inference only; some were given into their care as children, others joined them later in life. Probably here as elsewhere girls came at about the age of seven, and remained till the age of fourteen, when they left if marriage was to be their destiny. The responsibilities of married and of unmarried life were undertaken at this period by persons of extreme youth. Hathumod was made abbess of Gandersheim when she was between twelve and thirteen years of age; and Mathilde, as abbess of Quedlinburg, at the age of twelve received her dying grandmother's injunctions together with valuable documents[1], but in her case the chronicler notes that she had developed early[2].

It remains an open question at what period in history the inmates of these settlements took vows. Fritsch, who has written a detailed history of the abbey of Quedlinburg, holds that its inmates never took a permanent vow, since not a single case of the defection of a nun is on record[3], but this view is disproved by accounts of consecrations during the early period in other houses. Luther at the time of the Reformation noted that the nuns of Quedlinburg were bound by no vow[4]. Probably the inmates took vows at first, and the custom afterwards lapsed. Harenberg, to whom we owe many learned dissertations on Gandersheim, says that the women there lived at first according to the rule of St Benedict; but after the 12th century became Austin canonesses[5]. Engelhausen, a writer of the 15th century, speaking of the inmates of Saxon houses generally, says that they lived as Austin canonesses[6]. Early writers in speaking of the inmates of Saxon convents use the familiar terms nuns (sanctimoniales) and virgins (virgines); the term canoness (canonissa), which designates a woman who took residence without a permanent vow, came into general use only at a later date[7]. It seems simplest therefore throughout to retain the familiar term nun when speaking of the inmates of Saxon settlements, though it must be understood with a reservation, for we are not certain of the exact meaning of the word at different periods.

Engelhausen, the writer referred to above, adds that abbeys for women in Saxony were founded 'in order to help the noblemen who fought for the faith of Christ and were killed by the heathens; so that their daughters might not be reduced to begging (mendicare) but might live in these monasteries (monasteria), and when they had attained a marriageable age, might leave to be married.'

The range of subjects taught in the Saxon nunnery was wide. It included the study of religious as well as of classical writers. Spinning, weaving, and embroidery were also taught and practised. We shall see later on that the nuns assembled at Quedlinburg

---

[1] Vita Mathildis Reg. (in Pertz, *Mon. Germ. Script.*, vol. 4, p. 283 ff.), c. 26.

[2] *Annales Quedliburgenses*, year 999.

[3] Fritsch, *Geschichte des Reichstifts Quedlinburg*, 1826, vol. 1, p. 45.

[4] Luther, *An den Adel christl. Nation*, 1520, edit. Knaake, vol. 6, p. 440.

[5] Harenberg, *Historia Ecclesiae Gandersh.*, 1734, vol. 1, p. 529.

[6] Engelhausen, *Chronicon* (in Leibnitz, *Scriptores rer. Brunsv.* 1707, vol. 2), p. 978.

[7] Comp. below, ch. 6, § 1.

wove large and elaborate hangings. Reference is also made to
the study of law, and it is said that Gerberg II, abbess at Gandersheim († 1001), instructed her niece Sophie in convent discipline
and in common law. An early chronicle in the vernacular says
that the princess Sophie, a woman of determined character, so
mastered these subjects that she was able to enter into disputation
with learned men and successfully opposed them[1].

Where the inmate of a convent was consecrated to the office
of nun, this was done by the bishop of the diocese; but a curious
story is told in connection with the consecration of the above-
named princess Sophie[2]. Sophie was the daughter of the emperor
Otto II, and had been educated at Gandersheim, but she refused
to be consecrated by the bishop of Hildesheim, who usually performed this office at the convent, and declared that she must have
the archbishop of Mainz, whose dignity was more in keeping with
her station. The compromise that both prelates should assist at
the consecration was at last agreed upon. But Sophie was not
satisfied. She left Gandersheim for the court of her brother,
and only returned at the death of the abbess, whom she succeeded.
Endless quarrels occurred during the term of her rule. On one
occasion she allowed her nieces, Sophie and Ida, who were consecrated nuns, to depart on a visit to her friend the archbishop
of Mainz, but when they sent word from Mainz that they did
not intend to return to Gandersheim, she applied to her old enemy
the bishop of Hildesheim, and forced him to interfere with the archbishop and bring back her nuns. They returned, but only for a time,
for they were appointed abbesses at other convents.

It is interesting to note how large a number of princesses of
the ruling dynasty were unmarried, and remained in convents.
Five daughters of Duke Liudolf spent their lives at Gandersheim,
of whom only one as far as we know had been betrothed. At
a later period Mathilde, the only daughter of Otto I, was from her
cradle upwards appointed to become abbess of Quedlinburg; and
her cousin Gerberg, daughter of Heinrich, duke of the Bavarians
(† 955), was abbess of Gandersheim. In the next generation
Mathilde, daughter of Prince Liudolf († 957), was abbess at
Essen († 1011), and her two cousins, Adelheid and Sophie, the

---

[1] Luentzel, *Geschichte der Diöcese und Stadt Hildesheim*, 1858, vol. 1, p. 67, quoting
'Reimchronik,'

> 'Dat Bog segt, dat se so vele Wisheit konde,
> 'Dat se ok wol gelerden Meistern wedderstunde.'

[2] Harenberg, *Historia Ecclesiae Gandersh.*, 1734, vol. 1, p. 626 ff.

daughters of Otto II, embraced the religious profession at the wish, it is said, of their mother. Adelheid was abbess at Quedlinburg (999–1040), and Sophie, the princess alluded to above, was abbess at Gandersheim (1001–1039). When Sophie died her sister Adelheid planned to unite in herself the rule of both houses, but death put a stop to her ambition[1]. The princess Mathilde, another daughter of Otto II, had married Ezo, son of the Palgrave of Lothringen, to whom she bore seven daughters; six of these embraced convent life and in course of time attained to the rank of abbess[2].

These details are not without significance. They suggest that it was probably for the interest of the royal family that its princesses should remain in the convent in preference to contracting matrimonial alliances which might involve their relatives in political difficulties. On the other hand they suggest that life in these settlements must have been congenial in more ways than one.

As abbess of one of the royal houses the princess certainly held a place of authority second to that of no woman in the land. To gather together a few items of this power : she held the abbey of the king and from the king, which precluded a dependent relation on lords spiritual or temporal, and made her abbey what is termed a free abbey (*freies reichstift*). Her rights of overlordship sometimes extended over many miles, and the property of Gandersheim is described as enormous[3].

As holding the place of a feudal lord the abbess had the right of ban ; she issued the summons when war had been declared and sent her contingent of armed knights into the field; and she also issued the summons to attend in her courts, where judgment was given by her proctor (*vogt*). In short she had the duties and privileges of a baron who held his property of the king, and as such she was summoned to the Imperial Diet (*reichstag*). She may have attended in person during early times, the fact ap-

---

[1] Luentzel, *Geschichte der Diöcese und Stadt Hildesheim*, vol. 1, p. 319.

[2] 'De fundatione Brunswilarensis' (in Pertz, *Mon. Germ. Scriptores*, vol. 11, p. 394 footnote); Adelheid was abbess of Nivelles, Mathilde of Villich and Diedenkirchen, Theofanu of Essen, Hedwig of Neuss ; Sophie and Ida, to whom reference has been made in the text, are said by Pertz to have presided over Gandersheim and St Maria at Cöln ; Sophie certainly did not become abbess at Gandersheim, perhaps she went to Mainz ; Ida probably presided over the convent of St Maria on the Münzenberg, a dependency of Gandersheim.

[3] Waitz, G., *Deutsche Verfassungsgeschichte*, 1868, vol. 7, p. 258.

pears doubtful; but in the 16th century she was only represented there[1].

Similar rights and privileges devolved on those abbesses in England who were baronesses in title of the land they held. But these abbesses never secured some of the rights enjoyed by their sisters in Saxony, for example the right of striking coin which the abbess of Quedlinburg secured under Otto I[2]. Coins also are extant which were struck by abbesses of Gandersheim, whose portraits they bear[3].

In addition to these advantages of position, the abbesses of the chief Saxon houses in the 10th and 11th centuries were in direct contact with the court and with politics. During the minority of Otto III, who was three years old when his father died in Italy (983), his mother Adelheid together with his aunt Mathilde, abbess of Quedlinburg, practically ruled the empire. Later when this emperor went to Italy for a prolonged stay in 997 the management of affairs was given to the abbess Mathilde, who is praised for the determined measures she took to oppose the invading Wends. In 999 she summoned a diet at Dornberg on her own authority[4].

The so-called free abbeys were under the obligation of entertaining the king and his retinue in return for privileges granted to them, and as the king had no fixed place of residence he stayed at his various palaces (palatia) in turn, and usually spent holiday time at one of the religious centres. Frequent royal visits to Quedlinburg are on record; the court was also entertained at Gandersheim. These visits brought a store of political information to the abbess of which she made use in her own way. Thus Mathilde, abbess of Quedlinburg, is thought to have supplied the annalist of Quedlinburg with the information which gives his chronicle its special value, and she was so far interested in the history of her own time that Widukind forwarded his history of the Saxons to her book by book for approval[5]. The abbess Gerberg of Gandersheim was similarly in contact with politics. As we shall see she supplied the nun Hrotsvith with the materials for writing the history of Otto the Great.

---

[1] Reichstage, 1548–1594.

[2] Fritsch, *Geschichte des Reichstifts Quedlinburg*, 1828, vol. 1, p. 259.

[3] Luentzel, *Geschichte der Diöcese und Stadt Hildesheim*, 1858, vol. 1, p. 67.

[4] Fritsch, *Geschichte des Reichstifts Quedlinburg*, 1828, vol. 1, p. 84.

[5] Ebert, Ad., *Geschichte der Litteratur des Mittelalters*, 1887, vol. 3, p. 429 footnote.

§ 2.   Early History of Gandersheim[1].

From these general remarks we turn to the foundation and early history of Gandersheim, one of the earliest and wealthiest of Saxon houses, which claims our attention as the home of the nun Hrotsvith. It was situated on low-lying ground near the river Ganda in Eastphalia and was surrounded by the wooded heights of the Harz mountains. It owed its foundation to Liudolf himself, the great Saxon duke and the progenitor of the royal house of Saxony. At the close of a successful political career, Liudolf was persuaded by his wife Oda to devote some of his wealth and his influence to founding a settlement for women in Eastphalia, where his property chiefly lay.

Oda was partly of Frankish origin, which may account for her seeking the aggrandisement of her family in a religious foundation at a time when there were very few in Saxon lands. It is note-worthy that this foundation was to be for women and that all the daughters of Liudolf and Oda went to live there. Information about the early history of Gandersheim is abundant. There are extant a life of Hathumod, its first abbess, which was written by her friend the monk Agius († 874), and an elegy on her death in which Agius tries to comfort her nuns for the loss they have sustained ; both these compositions are written in a very attractive style[2]. A century later the nun Hrotsvith was busy at Gandersheim describing the early history of the settlement in a poem in which she celebrates both it and the family of its founder[3]. In many ways this is the most beautiful and finished of the nun's com-positions ; a work which reflects credit alike on her powers as a poetess, and on the settlement with which her name and fame are indissolubly linked.

From these accounts we gather that Oda's mother, Ada, had already had a vision of the future greatness of her family. Hrots-vith tells how St John the Baptist appeared to her clad in a gar-ment made of camel's hair of bright yellow, his lovely face of shining whiteness, with a small beard and black hair. In giving

---

[1] Harenberg, *Historia Ecclesiae Ganders.*, 1734 ; also Luentzel, *Geschichte der Diö-cese und Stadt Hildesheim*, 1858, vol. 1, pp. 33 ff., 63 ff.

[2] Agius, *Vita et Obitus Hathumodae* (in Pertz, *Mon. Germ. Scriptores*, vol. 4, pp. 166–189).

[3] Hrotsvith, 'Carmen de Primordiis Coenobii Gandersh.,' in *Opera*, edit. Barack, 1858, p. 339 ff.

these details of the saint's appearance the nun was doubtless describing a picture she had before her at Gandersheim.

It was in 852 that a plan was formed for transferring a small congregation of women, who had been living at Brunshausen, to some property on the river Ganda. A suitable site had to be sought and a fitting centre of worship provided. Liudolf and Oda undertook a journey to Rome and submitted their scheme to Pope Sergius II (844–847), begging him for a gift of relics. They received from him the bodies of the saints Anastasius and Innocentius, which they carried back with them to Saxony.

On the night before All Saints' Day a swineherd in Liudolf's employ had a vision of lights falling from heaven and hanging in the air, which was interpreted as a heavenly indication of the site of the settlement. A clearance was accordingly made in the densely wooded district and a chapel was built.

It was at this time that Hathumod, the eldest daughter of Liudolf, was living in Herford. From childhood her bent had been serious, and her friend Agius tells us that 'of her own free will she desired to be admitted to serious studies to which others are driven even by force[1].' She left her father's residence for Herford, where she was so happy that in after years she often longed to be back there. In 852 at the age of twelve she was taken away to Gandersheim to preside over the new settlement. This settlement was to be an improvement on existing institutions of the kind, for Agius tells us that its members were not allowed to have separate cells or to keep servants. They slept in tenements (villula) in the neighbourhood till their 'spiritual mother' was able to provide them with a suitable dwelling. Curious sidelights are thrown on other religious institutions by the following remarks of Agius on the nuns of Hathumod's convent : ' They shared everything,' he says[2]; 'their clothes were alike, neither too rich nor too poor, nor entirely of wool. The sisters were not allowed to dine out with relatives and friends, or to converse with them without leave. They were not allowed like other nuns (sanctimoniales) to leave the monastery to stay with relatives or visit dependent estates (possessiones subjectae). And they were forbidden to eat except at the common table at the appointed times except in cases of sickness. At the same hour and in the same place they partook of the same kind of food. They slept together and came together to celebrate the canonical hours (ad

---

[1] Agius, *Vita et Obitus Hathumodae*, ch. 3.   [2] Ibid. ch. 5.

canonicos cursus orandi). And they set to work together whenever work had to be done.'

Agius draws a beautiful picture of the gentleness and dignified
bearing of Hathumod, who was at once strong and sensitive.
She was always greatly cheered by signs of goodness in others,
and she was as much grieved by an offence of a member of the
community as if she had committed it herself. Agius tells us
that she was slow in making friends but that she clung faithfully
through life to those she had made.

Her literary acquirements were considerable. 'No one could
have shown greater quickness of perception, or a stronger power
of understanding in listening to or in expounding the scriptures,'
he says[1], and the scriptures always remained her favourite reading.

It is difficult to form an idea of the standard of life in these
religious settlements. The age was rough and barbarous in many
ways, but the surroundings of the Saxon dukes did not lack a
certain splendour, and traces of it would no doubt be found in the
homes they made for their daughters. In these early accounts
nothing transpires about their possessions in books and furniture,
but it is incidentally mentioned that the abbess Hathumod owned
a crystal vessel in the form of a dove, which contained relics and
hung suspended by her bedside[2].

The plan was formed to build a stone church for Gandersheim
an unusual and difficult undertaking. No suitable stone, however,
could be found till one day, as Hathumod was praying in the
chapel, she was divinely moved to walk forth and follow a dove
which was awaiting her outside. The bird led the way to a
spot where the underwood was removed and masses of stone
which could be successfully dealt with were laid bare. 'It is the
spot barren through its huge masses of stone, as we know it now-
a-days,' Hrotsvith the nun wrote a hundred years later[3].

The densely-wooded character of the neighbourhood is frequently referred to by early and later writers. Lingering superstitions peopled the forest with heathen fantasies, with 'fauns
and spirits,' as Hrotsvith designates them. The settlement lay
in the midst of the forest and was at all times difficult of access,
but especially so in winter when the ground was covered with
snow. In the introduction to her history of Otto the Great
Hrotsvith likens her perplexity and fear in entering on so vast

---

[1] Agius, *Vita et Obitus Hathumodae*, ch. 9. [2] Ibid. ch. 15.
[3] 'Carmen de Primordiis Coenobii Gandersh.,' line 273.

a subject to the state of mind of one who has to cross the forest in mid winter, a simile doubtless suggested by the surroundings of the convent[1]. Her feelings, she says, were those of 'someone who is ignorant of the vast expanse of the forest which lies before him, all the paths of which are hidden by a thick covering of snow; he is guided by no one and keeps true to his direction only by noticing the marks pointed out to him; sometimes he goes astray, unexpectedly he again strikes the right path, and having penetrated half way through the dense interlacing trees and brush-wood he longs for rest and stops and would proceed no farther, were he not overtaken by some one, or unexpectedly guided by the footprints of those who have gone before.'

Neither Liudolf the founder of Gandersheim nor his daughter Hathumod lived to see the stone church completed. He died in 866, and the abbess in 874 at the age of thirty-two. She was surrounded by her nuns, among whom were several of her sisters, and her mother Oda, who had also come to live at Gandersheim. The monk Agius, who was a frequent visitor at the home, was often with her during her last illness, and after her death he composed an elegy in dialogue to comfort the nuns under the loss they had sustained. This poem is full of sweetness and delicacy of feeling, and is said to have been written on the model of the eclogues of Virgil. Alternate verses are put into the mouths of the nuns and of Agius; they describe their sorrow, and he dwells on the thoughts which might be a consolation to them. It opens in this strain:

'Sad were the words we exchanged, I and those holy and worthy sisters who watched the dying moments of the sainted abbess Hathumod. I had been asked to address them, but somehow their recent grief made it impossible for them to listen to me, for they were bowed down by sorrow. The thoughts which I then expressed I have now put into verse and have added somewhat to them. For they (the sisters) asked me to address them in writing, since it would comfort them to have before their eyes, and to dwell upon, the words which I then spoke in sadness. Yielding to their wish and entreaties, I have attempted to express the thoughts which follow. Thou, O reader, understand that I am conversing with them, and follow us if thou wilt in our lament.'

He then directly addresses the nuns and continues: 'Certainly we should weep for one who died before her time in the bloom

---

[1] 'Carmen de Gestis Oddonis I,' in *Opera*, edit. Barack, 1858, p. 302.

of youth. Yet grief also has its limits; your sorrowful weeping should be within bounds. 'Tis natural you should be unhappy, still reason commands moderation in all things, and I therefore entreat you, O beloved and holy sisters, to stay your weeping and your tears. Spare your energies, spare your eyesight which you are wearing out by excess of grief. "Moderation in all things" has been said wisely and has been said well, and God Himself commands that it should be so.' The nuns make reply in the following words: 'What you put before us is certainly true. We know full well that God forbids excess, but our grief seems not excessive, for it falls so far short of what her merit claims. We can never put into words the wealth of goodness which we have lost in her. She was as a sister to us, as a mother, as a teacher, this our abbess under whose guidance we lived. We who were her handmaids and so far beneath her shared her life as her equals; for one will guided us, our wishes were the same, our pursuits alike. Shall we not grieve and weep and lament from our hearts for her who made our joy and was our glory, and in whom we have lost our happiness? There can be no excess of tears, of weeping and of grief, for in them only we find solace now that we shall never more behold her sweet face.' Agius replies: 'I doubt not that your grief is well founded, or that your tears rightly flow. But weeping will not undo you altogether, for the body has powers of endurance; you must bear this great anguish, for it has come to you through the will of God. Believe me, you are not alone in this grief, I too am oppressed by it, I too am suffering, and I cannot sufficiently express to you how much I also have lost in her. You know full well how great was her love for me, and how she cherished me while she lived. You know how anxious she was to see me when she fell ill, with what gladness she received me, and how she spoke to me on her deathbed. The words she spoke at the last were truly elevating, and ever and anon she uttered my name.' Agius tries to comfort himself with dwelling on Hathumod's gentleness and sweetness, and urges the nuns as they loved their abbess in the flesh now to continue loving her in the spirit. This alone, he says, will help the work to grow and increase which she began and loved. 'To dwell on grief,' he says, 'brings weeping and weakness; to dwell on love cheers and brings strength. The spirit of your abbess is still among you, it was that which you most loved in her, and it is that which you have not lost.'

There is a curiously modern ring in much that the monk

urges.   His poem sets forth how the nuns at last took heart, and requested Agius to visit them again and help them with his advice, which he promised to do.

On her deathbed Hathumod in talking to Agius compared her monastery to a plant of delicate growth and deplored that no royal charter sanctioning its privileges had as yet been obtained[1].   This charter and further privileges were secured to the settlement during the abbacy of Gerberg I (874–897), sister and successor of Hathumod, a woman of determined character and full of enthusiasm for the settlement.   She was betrothed at one time to a certain Bernhard, against whose will she came to live at Gandersheim, and refused to leave it.   He had been summoned to war, and departed declaring that she should not remain in the convent after his return.   But opportunely for her wishes he was killed and she remained at Gandersheim.   She ruled as abbess more than twenty years and advanced the interests of the settlement in many ways.   The stone church which had been begun during Hathumod's rule was completed during that of Gerberg and was consecrated in 881, on All Saints' Day.   The bishop of Hildesheim officiated at the ceremony of consecration, many visitors came to assist, and the assembled nuns for the first time took part in the singing of divine service.

The abbess Gerberg was succeeded by her sister Christine, who ruled from 897 to 919.   Köpke, one of the chief modern historians of this period, considers that these three sisters, Hathumod, Gerberg and Christine, abbesses of Gandersheim, were among the most zealous advocates of culture and civilizing influences in Saxony during the 9th century[2].   The settlement became a centre of interest to the whole ducal family.   After the death of Liudolf his widow Oda, who is said to have attained the age of one hundred and seven years, dwelt there altogether. She outlived her son, Duke Otto, who died in 912 and was buried at Gandersheim, and it is said that she lived to hear of the birth of her great-grandson Otto (913), who was destined to become king and emperor.

After the death of the abbess Christine the settlement of Gandersheim drifts for a time into the background ; Quedlinburg, founded by Heinrich I at the instigation of his wife Mathilde, takes its place in ducal and royal favour.   Scant notices are pre-

---

[1] Agius, *Vita et Obitus Hathumodae*, ch. 11.
[2] Köpke, R., *Deutschlands älteste Dichterin*, 1869, p. 17.

served of the abbesses who ruled during the first half of the 10th century. We hear of the abbess Hrotsvith († 927) that she was distinguished like her namesake of later date for literary acquirements[1], and that she wrote treatises on logic and rhetoric which are lost. And 'what is more,' says an early writer[2], 'she forced the devil to return a bond signed with blood by which a youth had pledged away his soul.'

Her writings may have perished in the fire which ravaged the settlement without permanently interfering with its prosperity during the rule of Gerberg II (959–1001). Contemporary writers concur in praise of the learning, the powers of management and the educational influence of this princess, who was the daughter of Heinrich, duke of the Bavarians († 955). Heinrich for many years was the enemy and rival of his brother Otto I ; and the final reconciliation and lasting friendship between these princes formed an important episode in the history of the time. We do not know what prompted Gerberg to embrace convent life ; perhaps she became a nun at the wish of her father. She was appointed abbess at the age of nineteen when her father was dead and her mother Judith was ruling in Bavaria in the interests of her young son. Gerberg ruled at Gandersheim for forty-two years ; she has a special claim on our interest because she was the friend, teacher, and patron of the nun Hrotsvith.

§ 3. The Nun Hrotsvith and her Writings[3].

The nun Hrotsvith occupies a unique position in monastic life and among unmarried women generally. 'This fruitful poetic talent,' says the writer Ebert, 'which lacks not the inspiration and the courage of genius to enter upon new ground, evinces how the Saxon element was chosen to guide the German nation in the domain of art.' The literary work of Hrotsvith can be grouped under three headings. To the first belongs the writing of metrical legends which were intended for the perusal and the edification of inmates of convents ; to the second, the composition of seven dramas written in the style of Terence ; and to the third, the

---

[1] Harenberg, *Historia Ecclesiae Gandersh.*, 1734, p. 589.

[2] Meibom, H., *Rerum German. Script.*, 1688, vol. 1, p. 706, quoting Selneccer.

[3] Hrotsvith, *Opera*, edit. Barack, 1858; Ebert, Ad., *Allgemeine Geschichte der Litteratur des Abendlandes*, 1887, vol. 3, p. 285 ff.

writing of contemporary history in metrical form. Each kind of work has merits of its own and deserves attention. But while Hrotsvith as a legend writer ranks with other writers of the age, and as a historical writer is classed by the modern historian Giesebrecht with Widukind and Ruotger, as a writer of Latin drama she stands entirely alone. We have no other dramatic compositions except hers between the comedies of classic times and the miracle plays, which at first consisted only of a few scenes with bald dialogue.

It can be gathered from Hrotsvith's writings that she was born about the year 932; and the fact of her entering a nunnery is proof of her gentle birth. It is uncertain when she came to Gandersheim, probably at a very early age. She owed her education there partly to Rikkardis, to whom she refers in her writings, but chiefly to the abbess Gerberg, who, she says, was somewhat younger than herself.

Judging from Hrotsvith's writings she worked diligently and soon attracted attention beyond the limits of her convent. The following facts in regard to time are of importance. The first of her two sets of legends was put together and dedicated to Gerberg as abbess, that is after the year 959; she wrote and submitted part if not the whole of her history of Otto the Great to Wilhelm, archbishop of Mainz, before the year 968, in which the prelate died. How the composition of her dramas is related in point of time to that of the legends and the historical poems cannot be definitely decided; probably the dramas were written in the middle period of Hrotsvith's life. For the legends bear marks of being the outcome of early effort, while the historical poems, especially the one which tells of the early history of Gandersheim, were written in the full consciousness of power. We do not know the date of Hrotsvith's death; an early chronicle says that she wrote a history of the three Emperors Otto, in which case she must have lived till 1002, that being the year of Otto III's death. But the annalist to whom we owe this remark may have been misinformed; only a part of the history of the first emperor is extant, and we cannot argue from any references in her other works that she wrote a continuation of it[1]. The nun and her writings soon ceased to attract attention, and there are few references to her in any writings for nearly five hundred years. At the beginning of the 16th century, however, the humanist Conrad

[1] *Opera*, edit. Barack, Einleitung, p. 6.

Celtes came across a copy of her dramas, which seemed to him
so remarkable that he had them printed. And since then they
have repeatedly been published, and excellent translations have
been made of them into German and French[1].

In the introduction to her plays Hrotsvith appeals to the
judgment of powerful patrons, but she does not give their names;
in her history, as mentioned above, she asks for criticism from
Wilhelm, archbishop of Mainz, who was the illegitimate son of
Otto I, and a leading prelate of the time. This exhausts what we
know of friends outside the convent; probably the abbess Gerberg
was the chief critic throughout and had more influence on her than
any other. It was she who introduced Hrotsvith to the works,
classical and other, which she had herself studied under learned
men, and she was always ready to encourage her able pupil and
supply her with materials to work upon.

The library at Gandersheim, to which Hrotsvith had access,
contained the writings of a number of classical and theological
authors. Among the classical writers with whom the nun is
thought to have been directly acquainted were Virgil, Lucan,
Horace, Ovid, Terence, and perhaps Plautus; among the Christian
writers Prudentius, Sedulius, Fortunatus, Marianus Capella, and
Boethius[2]. Ebert, who has analysed the sources from which
Hrotsvith drew the subject matter of her legends and dramas,
considers that at this time Greek authors were read at Gandersheim in Latin translations only. Another writer, arguing from
the fact that the nun frequently uses words of Greek origin, considers that she had some knowledge of Greek[3]. This latter opinion
has little in its favour. However we know that Greek teachers
were summoned from Constantinople to instruct Hedwig, Gerberg's
sister, who was to have married the Emperor Constantine. The
match fell through, but the Saxon royal family aimed steadily at
securing an alliance with the court of Constantinople, and ultimately
attained this object by the marriage of Otto II to the Greek
princess Theofanu (971).

After Hrotsvith had mastered the contents of the library at
Gandersheim she was moved to try her hand at writing Latin
verse; she cast into metrical form the account of the birth and
life of the Virgin Mary contained in a gospel which in some

---

[1] Piltz, O., *Die Dramen der Roswitha*, no date; Magnin, *Théâtre de Hrotsvitha*, 1845.
[2] Köpke, R., *Deutschlands älteste Dichterin*, 1869, p. 28.
[3] Hrotsvith, *Opera*, edit. Barack, Einleitung, p. 54.

manuscripts is ascribed to St James, the brother of Christ[1]. The story is well told, and the incidents described follow each other naturally; the poem exceeds nine hundred lines in length. She supplements the original text with some amplifications of a descriptive nature and a panegyric on Christ, with which she closes the poem.

The diffidence Hrotsvith felt at first in writing is described in the introduction which she prefixed to the complete collection of her legendary poems and addressed to a wider public[2].

'Unknown to others and secretly, so to speak, I worked by myself'; she says, 'sometimes I composed, sometimes I destroyed what I had written to the best of my abilities and yet badly; I dealt with material taken from writings with which I became acquainted within the precincts of our monastery of Gandersheim through the help of our learned and kindly teacher Rikkardis, afterwards through that of others who taught in her place, and finally through that of the high-born abbess Gerberg, under whom I am living at present, who is younger than I am in years but more advanced in learning as befits one of royal lineage, and who has introduced me to various authors whom she has herself studied with the help of learned men. Writing verse appears a difficult and arduous task especially for one of my sex, but trusting to the help of divine grace more than to my own powers, I have fitted the stories of this book to dactylic measures as best I could, for fear that the abilities that have been implanted in me should be dulled and wasted by neglect; for I prefer that these abilities should in some way ring the divine praises in support of devotion; the result may not be in proportion to the trouble taken and yet it may be to the profit of some.'

The nun is filled with the consciousness that her undertaking is no mean one. 'Full well I know,' she says, addressing the Virgin, 'that the task of proclaiming thy merits exceeds my feeble strength, for the whole world could not celebrate worthily that which is a theme of praise among the angels.' The poem on the life of the Virgin is written in leonine hexameters, that is with rhymes at the middle and the end of the line. This form of verse was sometimes used at that period, and Hrotsvith especially in her later historical poems handled it with considerable skill.

Hrotsvith afterwards added to the account of the Virgin a

---

[1] 'Maria,' *Opera*, p. 7.
[2] *Opera*, edit. Barack, p. 2.

poem of a hundred and fifty lines on the Ascension of Christ[1]. In this, as she tells us, she adapted an account written by John the Bishop, which had been translated from Greek into Latin.

This poem also is simple and dignified, and gives proof of considerable power of expression on the part of the nun. Her vocabulary however has certain peculiarities, for she is fond of diminutives, a tendency which in the eyes of her editor is peculiarly feminine[2].

The poem on the Ascension closes with the following characteristic lines: 'Whoever reads this let him exclaim in a forbearing spirit: Holy King, spare and have mercy on the suppliant Hrotsvith and suffer that she who here has been celebrating thy glorious deeds may persevere further in holy song on things divine!'

The next subject which engrossed the nun's attention was the history of Gongolf[3], a huntsman and warrior of Burgundy, who lived in the time of King Pipin. He was credited with performing wonders such as calling up a fountain; he was a pious Christian and was put to a cruel death by his faithless wife and her lover. This poem is over five hundred lines in length and contains some fine descriptive passages. The version of the story Hrotsvith made use of being lost, we cannot tell how far she drew upon her own powers of narrative[4].

But the next legend she wrote left full scope for originality of treatment. It describes the experiences and martyrdom of Pelagius, a youth who had been recently (925) put to death by the Saracens at Cordova in Spain; the event, as she herself informs us, had been described to Hrotsvith by an eye-witness. The story opens with an enthusiastic description of the beauties of Cordova. Pelagius, the son of a king of Galicia, persuaded his father to leave him as hostage with the Caliph. But the Caliph, enamoured by the youth's physical beauty, persecuted him with attentions, and meeting with contempt ordered him to be cast down from the city walls. The young man remained unharmed, and was then beheaded and his head and body thrown into the river. Fishermen picked them up and carried them to a monastery, where their identity was ascertained by casting the head in the

---

[1] 'Ascensio Domini,' *Opera*, p. 37.
[2] *Opera*, edit. Barack, Einleitung, p. 48.   [3] 'Gongolf,' *Opera*, p. 43.
[4] Ebert, *Allgemeine Geschichte der Litteratur des Abendlandes*, 1887, vol. 3, p. 290.
[5] 'Pelagius,' *Opera*, p. 63.

fire, which left it untouched.   The head and body were then given solemn burial.

The next legend has repeatedly been commented on as the earliest account in verse of a pact with the devil and as a precursor of the many versions of the legend of Faust[1].   The 'Lapse and conversion of Theophilus[2]' may have had special attractions for Hrotsvith since the incident of the devil forced to return his bond was connected, as mentioned above, with her namesake Hrotsvith, abbess of Gandersheim.   The story of Theophilus which Hrotsvith expanded and put into verse had recently been translated from Greek into Latin, as Ebert has shown.   The story runs as follows.

Theophilus, nephew of a bishop of Cilesia (of uncertain date), had been educated in the seven liberal arts, but he held himself unworthy of succeeding his uncle, and considered the office of 'vice-domus' more suited to his powers.   His popularity however drew on him the hatred of the newly appointed bishop, who robbed him of his post.   Thirsting for revenge the young man went for advice to a certain Hebrew, 'who by magic art turned away many of the faithful,' and who led him at night through the town to a dark place 'full of phantasms that stood in white clothes holding torches in their hands' (line 99).   Their demon king was at first indignant that a Christian claimed his assistance and jeered at the Christians' ways, but at last he promised to help Theophilus on condition that he should sign an agreement by which he pledged himself to be one of the ghastly crew to all eternity. The young man agreed to the condition, and on his return home was favourably received by the bishop and reinstated in his dignity.   But his peace of mind had deserted him ; again and again he was seized by qualms of conscience and affrighted by agonising visions of eternal suffering which he forcibly describes in a monologue.   At last he sought to escape from his contract by praying to the Virgin Queen of heaven in her temple, and for forty days consecutively prayed to her to intercede in his favour with God.   The Virgin at last appeared to him, told him that he was free and handed him the fatal document.   On a festal day he confessed his wrong-doing before all the people and burnt the parchment in their presence.   In the very act of doing so he

---

[1] Ebert, *Allgemeine Geschichte der Litteratur des Abendlandes,* 1887, vol. 3, p. 295.

[2] 'Theophilus,' *Opera,* p. 79.

appeared as a changed man before their eyes and was instantly overtaken by death.

To this legend Hrotsvith attached a little prayer of eight lines which is a grace for use at meals. This prayer is in no way connected with the legend, and its presence here indicates that the legends were originally intended to be read aloud during meals in the refectory, and the reading to be closed with a prayer.

Having written so far Hrotsvith collected her legendary poems together with the poem on the Virgin and dedicated them in the form of a little book to her teacher, the abbess Gerberg. Evidently the stories attracted attention beyond the limits of the convent, and Hrotsvith was encouraged to continue in the path she had chosen. Accordingly she wrote a second set of legends, in composing which she was mindful of a wider public and that not exclusively of her own sex. For in the opening lines of the first of these legends which treats of the conversion of Proterius by Basilius, bishop of Caesarea, she begs that those who peruse this story 'will not on account of her sex despise the woman who draws these strains from a fragile reed[1].'

The story of this conversion, like that of Theophilus, treats of a pact with the evil one, but with a difference. For in the one story the man signs away his soul to regain his position, in the other he subscribes the fatal bond for the purpose of securing the hand of the bishop's daughter. The bishop however intercedes with God in his behalf and regains his liberty for him. The poem is neither so complete nor so striking as that of Theophilus.

Two more legends are grouped with it. One of them describes the Passion of Dionysius[2], who suffered martyrdom at Paris, and who at an early date was held identical with Dionysius the Areopagite. The hand of this saint had been given as a relic to King Heinrich the Fowler, and had been deposited by him at Quedlinburg—an incident which made the saint's name familiar in Saxon lands.

The passion of Dionysius is described according to a prose account written by Hilduin († 814), but Hrotsvith abbreviated and altered it[3]. She describes how Dionysius witnessed an eclipse of the sun at Memphis at the time when Christ was put to death, how he returned to Athens and there waited to hear something of the new god. The apostle Paul arrived and preached,

---

[1] 'Proterius,' *Opera*, p. 97.   [2] 'Dionysius,' *Opera*, p. 107.
[3] Ebert, *Allgemeine Geschichte der Litteratur des Abendlandes*, 1887, vol. 3, p. 300.

and Dionysius followed him to Rome. From Rome he was despatched into Gaul to preach the new faith, and while there he was first cast into the flames which did not burn him, and then thrown before wild beasts which refused to touch him. He was finally beheaded during the persecutions under Diocletian. In this poem there is an especially fine passage in which we hear how Dionysius after being beheaded rose to life and took up his head, which he carried away down the hill to the spot where he wished to be buried,—a story similar to that told of many saints.

The last legend which Hrotsvith wrote treats of the Passion of St Agnes, a virgin saint of Rome, whose fortitude in tribulation and stedfast adherence to Christianity and to the vow she had taken made her story especially suitable for a convent of nuns[1]. The story has often been put into writing from the 4th century downwards ; Hrotsvith took her account from that ascribed to Ambrosius († 397), which she followed closely. She prefaces it with an address to maidens vowed to God, who are exhorted to remain steadfast in their purpose. Like most of these legendary tales it is between four and five hundred lines in length.

Throughout her legends Hrotsvith, as she herself says in a few remarks which stand at the conclusion of the legends, was bent on keeping close to the original accounts from which she worked. 'I have taken the material for this book, like that for the one preceding it, from ancient books compiled by authentic authors (certis nominibus), the story of Pelagius alone is excepted.... If mistakes have crept into my accounts, it is not because I have intentionally erred but because I have unwittingly copied mistakes made by others[2].'

Ebert, commenting on the spirit of the legends generally, remarks on the masterly way in which the nun has dealt with her material, on her skill in supplying gaps left by earlier writers, on her deft handling of rhyme and rhythm, on the right feeling which guides her throughout her work, and on the completeness of each of her legends as a whole[3].

The lines in which the second set of legends are dedicated to Gerberg bear witness to the pleasure Hrotsvith derived from her work. 'To thee, lady Gerberg,' she says, 'I dedicate these stories, adding new to earlier ones, as a sinner who deserves benevolent indulgence. Rejoicing I sing to the accompaniment with dactylic

---

[1] 'Agnes,' *Opera*, p. 117. [2] *Opera*, p. 133.

[3] Ebert, *Allgemeine Geschichte der Litteratur des Abendlandes*, 1887, vol. 3, p. 301.

measures; do not despise them because they are bad, but praise in your gentle heart the workings of God[1].'

Having so far worked along accepted lines and achieved success therein, the nun of Gandersheim was moved to strike out a new path. Conscious of her powers and conscious of a need of her time, filled with admiration for the dramatic powers of classical writers while disapproving of their tendencies, she set to work to compose a series of plays on the model of Terence, in which she dramatised incidents and experiences calculated to have an elevating influence on her fellow-nuns.

How she came to write plays at all and what determined her in the choice of her subject, she has described in passages which are worth quoting in full. They show that she was not wanting either in spirit or in determination, and that her conviction that the classical form of drama was without equal strengthened her in her resolve to make use of that form as the vehicle for stories of an altogether different tenor. The interest of the plays of Terence invariably turns on the seduction of women and exposure of the frailty of the sex; the nun of Gandersheim determined to set forth woman's stedfast adherence to a vow once taken and her firm resistance to temptation. Whatever may be thought of these compositions, the merit of originality can hardly be denied to them. They were intended for perusal only, but there is nothing in the dialogue or mechanism that makes a dramatic representation of them impossible.

'There are many Christians,' says the nun[2], 'from whom we cannot claim to be excepted, who because of the charm of finished diction prefer heathen literature with its hollowness to our religious books; there are others who hold by the scripture and despise what is heathen, and yet eagerly peruse the poetic creations of Terence; while delighting in his flow of language, they are all polluted by the godless contents of his works. Therefore I "the well known mouthpiece of Gandersheim" have not hesitated in taking this poet's style as a model, and while others honour him by perusing his dramas, I have attempted, in the very way in which he treats of unchaste love among evil women, to celebrate according to my ability the praiseworthy chasteness of godlike maidens.

'In doing so, I have often hesitated with a blush on my cheeks through modesty, because the nature of the work obliged me to

---

[1] *Opera*, p. 95.   [2] *Opera*, p. 137.

concentrate my attention on and apply my mind to the wicked passion of illicit love and to the tempting talk of the amorous, against which we at other times close our ears. But if I had hesitated on account of my blushes I could not have carried out my purpose, or have set forth the praise of innocence to the fulness of my ability. For in proportion as the blandishments of lovers are enticing, so much greater is the glory of our helper in heaven, so much more glorious the triumph of those who prevail, especially where woman's weakness triumphs and man's shameless strength is made to succumb. Certainly some will allege that my language is much inferior, much poorer, and very unlike that of him whom I try to imitate. It is so, I agree with them. And yet I refuse to be reproached on this account as though I had meant to class myself with those who in their knowledge are so far above my insufficiency. I am not even so boastful as to class myself with the least of their pupils ; all I am bent on is, however insufficiently, to turn the power of mind given to me to the use of Him who gave it. I am not so far enamoured of myself that I should cease from fear of criticism to proclaim the power of Christ which works in the saints in whatever way He grants it. If anyone is pleased with my work I shall rejoice, but if on account of my unpolished language it pleases no one, what I have done yet remains a satisfaction to myself, for while in other writings I have worked, however insufficiently, only in heroic strophe (heroico strophio), here I have combined this with dramatic form, while avoiding the dangerous allurements of the heathen.'

Those passages in which Hrotsvith speaks of her modest hesitation are especially worthy of notice and will not fail to appeal to those women now-a-days, who, hoping to gain a clearer insight into the difficulties with which their sex has to contend, feel it needful to face facts from which their sensibilities naturally shrink. They will appreciate the conflicting feelings with which the nun of Gandersheim, well-nigh a thousand years ago, entered upon her task, and admire the spirit in which she met her difficulties and the courage with which she carried out her purpose, in spite of her consciousness of shortcomings and derogatory criticism.

As she points out, the keynote of her dramas one and all is to insist on the beauties of a steadfast adherence to chastity as opposed to the frenzy and the vagaries of passion. In doing so she is giving expression to the ideas of contemporary Christian teaching, which saw in passion, not the inborn force that can be applied to good or evil purpose, not the storage of strength which works for social advantage or disadvantage, but simply a tendency in human nature which manifests itself in lack of self-restraint, and the disturbing element which interferes with the attainment of calmness and candour.

As Hudson, one of the few English writers who has treated of this nun and her writings[1], remarks : ' It is on the literary side alone that Hrotsvitha belongs to the classic school.   The spirit and essence of her work belong entirely to the middle ages ; for beneath the rigid garb of a dead language beats the warm heart of a new era.   Everything in her plays that is not formal but essential, everything that is original and individual, belongs wholly to the christianised Germany of the 10th century.   Everywhere we can trace the influence of the atmosphere in which she lived ; every thought and every motive is coloured by the spiritual conditions of her time.   The keynote of all her works is the conflict of Christianity with paganism ; and it is worthy of remark that in Hrotsvitha's hands Christianity is throughout represented by the purity and gentleness of woman while paganism is embodied in what she describes as ' the vigour of men (virile robur).'

For the nun does not disparage marriage, far from it ; nor does she inculcate a doctrine of general celibacy.   It is not a question with her of giving up a lesser joy for a greater, but simply of the way to remain true to the higher standard, which in accordance with the teaching of her age she identified with a life of chastity.   Her position may appear untenable ; confusion of thought is a reproach which a later age readily casts on an earlier. But underneath what may seem unreasonable there is the aspiration for self-control.   It is this aspiration which gives a wide and an abiding interest to her plays.   For she is not hampered by narrowness of thought or by pettiness of spirit.   Her horizon is limited, we grant ; but she fills it entirely and she fills it well.

Passing from these generalities to the plays themselves, we find ourselves in a variety of surroundings and in contact with a wide range of personalities.   The transition period from heathendom to Christianity supplies in most cases the mental and moral conflicts round which centres the interest of these plays.

The plays are six in number, and the one that stands first is divided into two separate parts.   Their character varies considerably.   There is the heroic, the romantic, the comic and the un-

[1] Hudson, W. H., ' Hrotsvitha of Gandersheim,' *English Historical Review*, 1888.

relieved tragic element, and the two plays that stand last contain long disquisitions on scholastic learning. A short analysis of their contents will give the reader an idea of the manner in which Hrotsvith makes her conceptions and her purpose evident.

'Gallicanus,' the play that stands first[1], is in some ways the most striking of all. A complex theme is ably dealt with and the incidents follow each other rapidly; the scene lies alternately in Rome and on the battle-field. The Emperor Constantine is bent on opposing the incursions of the Scythians, and his general Gallicanus claims the hand of the emperor's daughter Constantia as a reward for undertaking so dangerous an expedition. Constantia is a convert to Christianity, Gallicanus is a heathen. In an interview with her father the girl declares she will sooner die than be united to a heathen, but with a mixture of shrewdness and confidence in her faith she agrees to marry him on his return on condition that the Christians John and Paul shall accompany him on his expedition, and that his daughters shall meanwhile be given into her keeping. The manner in which she receives the girls is at once proud and dignified. 'Welcome my sisters, Attica and Artemia,' she exclaims; 'stand, do not kneel, rather greet me with a kiss of affection.' There is no development of character in the course of the play, for Hrotsvith is chiefly bent on depicting states of mind under given conditions. The characters in themselves are forcibly drawn: witness the emperor's affection for his daughter, the general's strength and determination, Constantia's dignified bearing and the gentleness of the Christian teachers. The sequel of events bears out Constantia's anticipations. The daughters of Gallicanus are easily swayed in favour of Christianity and their father is converted. For Gallicanus is hard pressed by the Scythians on the battle-field and despairs of success, when the Christian teachers urge him to call upon their God for help. He does so, overcomes the Scythians and takes their leader Bradan prisoner. In recognition of his victory he is rewarded by a triumphal entry into Rome. But he is now a convert to Christianity; he describes to the emperor how Christ Himself and the heavenly host fought on his side, and he approaches Constantia and his daughters and thus addresses them: 'I greet you, holy maidens; abide in the fear of God and keep inviolate your virgin crown that the eternal King may receive you in His embrace.' Constantia replies: 'We serve Him the more readily if thou dost not oppose us.' Gallicanus:

---

[1] 'Gallicanus,' *Opera*, p. 143.

'I would not discourage, prevent or thwart your wishes, I respect them, so far that I would not now constrain thee, beloved Constantia, whom I have secured at the risk of my life.' But he admits that his resolve costs him much, and he decides to seek solace in solitude for his grief at having lost so great a prize.

The sequel to this play is short, and describes the martyrdom of the Christian teachers, John and Paul, who had accompanied Gallicanus on his expedition. Gallicanus is no more, the Emperor Constantius is dead, and Julian the Apostate reigns in his stead and cruelly persecutes the Christians. No woman appears in this part of the play. We first witness the martyrdom of the Christians who are put to death by Terentian, one of the emperor's generals. Terentian's son is then seized by a terrible illness, and his unhappy father goes to the grave of the martyrs, where he becomes a convert to Christianity and prays for their intercession with God in behalf of his son. His prayer finds fulfilment and the boy is restored to health. Hrotsvith took this story from the Acts and the Passion of the saints John and Paul, but, as Ebert has shown, the development is entirely her own[1]. Though working on the model of Terence the nun is quite indifferent to unities of time and place, and sacrifices everything to the exigencies of the plot, so that the transition from scene to scene is often sudden and abrupt.

The next play is 'Dulcetius, or the sufferings of the maidens Agape, Chionia and Irene[2].' It dramatises a story which was familiar in western Europe from an early date; Ealdhelm mentions it in his poem on Virginity. Its popularity is no doubt due to the juxtaposition of entirely divergent elements, the pathos of martyrdom being in close company with scenes of broad humour.

During the persecutions under Diocletian three youthful sisters are brought before the emperor, who thus addresses the eldest:

'*Diocletian.* The noble stock from which you spring and your extreme beauty demand that you should be connected with our court through marriage with high officials. This we incline to vouchsafe you if you agree to disown Christ and offer sacrifice to our most ancient gods.

Agape. O spare yourself this trouble, do not think of giving us in marriage. Nought can compel us to disown the name of Christ, or to debase our purity of heart.

---

[1] Ebert, *Allgemeine Geschichte der Litteratur des Abendlandes*, 1887, vol. 3, p. 316.
[2] 'Dulcetius,' *Opera*, p. 174.

Diocletian. What is the object of this madness?

Agape. What sign of madness do you see in us?

Diocletian. A great and obvious one.

Agape. In what?

Diocletian. In this, that casting from yourselves the observance of the ancient faith, you follow this new foolish Christian teaching.

Agape. Blasphemer, fear the power of God Almighty, threatening danger....

Diocletian. To whom?

Agape. To you and to the realm you govern.

Diocletian. The girl is crazy, let her be removed.'

He then interviews the other two, but with similar results; threats are of no avail and the girls are handed over to the general Dulcetius to be summarily dealt with. Dulcetius, however, is so powerfully impressed by their beauty, that he orders them to be placed in a chamber beyond the kitchen, hoping to take advantage of their helplessness and induce them to gratify his passion. He repairs at night to the chamber in spite of the warning of his soldiers, when a spell falls on him, he misses the room, and his reason so utterly forsakes him that he proceeds to fondle and caress the pots and pans which he seizes upon in his excitement. The girls are watching him from the next room through a chink in the wall and make merry over his madness.

'*Agape.* What is he about?

Hirena. Why, the fool is out of his mind, he fancies he has got hold of us.

Agape. What is he doing?

Hirena. Now he presses the kettle to his heart, now he clasps the pots and pans and presses his lips to them.

Chionia. How ludicrous!

Hirena. His face, his hands, his clothes are all black and sooty; the soot which clings to him makes him look like an Ethiopian.

Agape. Very fitting that he should be so in body, since the devil has possession of his mind.

Hirena. Look, he is going. Let us wait to see what the soldiers who are waiting outside will do when they see him.'

The soldiers fail to recognise their leader, they take to their heels. Dulcetius repairs to the palace, where the gatekeeper scoffs at his appearance and refuses him admittance, in spite of his insisting on his identity and speaking of himself as dressed in splendid attire. At last his wife who has heard of his madness comes forth to meet him. The spell is broken and he discovers that he has been the laughing-stock of the maidens. He then orders them to be exposed naked in the market-place as a punishment. But a divine power causes their garments to cling to them, while Dulcetius falls so fast asleep that it is impossible to rouse him. The Emperor Diocletian therefore entrusts the accomplishment of the maidens' martyrdom to Sisinnius. Two of the girls are cast into the flames, but their souls pass away to heaven while their bodies remain without apparent hurt. The third sister is threatened with shameful treatment, but before it is carried out she is miraculously borne away to a hill-top. At first the soldiers attempt in vain to approach her, but at last they succeed in killing her with arrows. The youthful, girlish traits which appear in both the mirth and the sorrow of the three sisters are well developed, and form a vivid contrast to the unrelieved brutality of Dulcetius and Sisinnius.

Quite a different range of ideas is brought before the reader in the next play, 'Calimachus,' which is Hrotsvith's nearest approach to a love tragedy[1]. She took its subject from an apocryphal account of the apostles, but as Ebert remarks she handles her material with considerable freedom[2]. The opening scene shows her power of immediately presenting a situation. The scene is laid in the house of Andronicus, a wealthy Ephesian. The youth Calimachus and his friends enter.

'*Calimachus.* A few words with you, friends!

Friends. We will converse with thee as long as thou pleasest.

Calimachus. If you do not mind, we will converse apart.

Friends. Thou biddest, we comply.

Calimachus. Let us repair to a secluded spot, that we may not be interrupted in our converse.'

They go and Calimachus explains how a heavy misfortune has befallen him; they urge him to unbosom himself. He confesses he is in love with a most beauteous, most adorable being, it is a woman, the wife of Andronicus; what shall he do to secure her favour? His friends declare his passion hopeless; Drusiana is a Christian and has moreover taken the vow of chastity; 'I ask for help, you give me despair,' Calimachus exclaims. In the next scene he confronts Drusiana and declares his passion. Drusiana

---

[1] 'Calimachus,' *Opera*, p. 191.

[2] Ebert, *Allgemeine Geschichte der Litteratur des Abendlandes*, 1887, vol. 3, p. 321.

repudiates his advances but she is intimidated by his threats, and gives utterance to her fears in a monologue in which she declares that she would rather die than yield to him. Sudden death cuts her down; and the apostle John is called in by her husband and undertakes to give her Christian burial. But the youth Calimachus is not cured of his passion. At the instigation of his companion, Fortunatus, he goes with him by night to the vault where she lies and would embrace the corpse, but a serpent of terrible aspect surprises the two young men and kills them. In the following scene the apostle is leading Andronicus to the vault: when they enter they come upon the serpent lying by the side of the youths. The apostle then explains to Andronicus what has happened and gives proof of his great power by awakening Calimachus from the dead. The young man confesses his evil intentions and explains how he came there at the suggestion of his companion. The apostle then recalls Drusiana to life, and she begs that Fortunatus also may be restored, but the apostle refuses on account of the man's wickedness. Drusiana herself then intercedes in his behalf and prays to God for his restoration. Her wish is fulfilled, Fortunatus comes back to life, but he declares he would sooner have died than have seen Drusiana happy and his friend a convert to Christianity. The wounds which the serpent had inflicted at once begin to swell, and he expires before their eyes, and the apostle explains that his jealousy has sent him to hell. A great deal of action is crowded into this play and we are abruptly carried on from scene to scene. It closes with some pious reflections on the part of the apostle.

There is considerable diversity of opinion among modern writers on the merits of the dramas we have discussed hitherto, but all concur in praise of the play called 'Abraham,' which dramatises the oft repeated story of a woman who yields to temptation and is reclaimed from her wicked ways. The interest in this play never flags and the scenes are worked out with a breadth of conception which gives the impression of assured strength[1].

Hrotsvith took the subject of this drama from an account, written in the 6th century by Ephrem, of the life of his friend, the hermit Abraham. The story was written originally in Greek and is preserved in that language; the translation into Latin used by Hrotsvith is lost[2]. The plot of the drama is as follows:

[1] 'Abraham,' *Opera*, p. 213.
[2] Ebert, *Allgemeine Geschichte der Litteratur des Abendlandes*, 1887, vol. 3, p. 323.

The devout hermit Abraham consults his friend the hermit Ephrem as to what he shall do with his niece, Maria, who is left to his care, and together they decide that she shall come and live in a cell near her uncle. Abraham throughout speaks directly and to the point, while Ephrem's talk is full of mystic allusions. He talks to the maiden of the beauties of the religious vocation and assures her that her name, Maria, signifies 'star of the sea,' and that she is therefore intended for great things. The maiden is surprised at his words and naïvely remarks that it would be a great thing 'to equal the lustre of the stars.' She comes to dwell in a cell close to that of the two hermits, but after a time she is enticed away and disappears from the sight of her uncle, who is deeply grieved at her loss. For several years he hears nothing from her; at last a friend comes and tells him that the girl has been seen in the city, and is there living in a house of ill fame. The old man at once decides to go forth to seek his niece and to reclaim her. He dons shoes, a traveller's dress and a large hat, and takes with him money, since that only can give him access to her. The scene then shifts from the sylvan solitude to the house where Maria is living. Abraham arrives and is received by the tavern-keeper, whom he asks for a night's lodging, offering him his 'solidus' and requesting to see the woman the fame of whose beauty has spread. This scene and the one that follows bring the situation before the reader admirably. Abraham is served with a meal and Maria enters, at sight of whose levity he scarce represses his tears. She entertains him, and he feigns a gaiety corresponding to hers, the tavern-keeper being present. Of a sudden she is overcome by the thought of the past, but he keeps up his assumed character. At last supper is over, and they retire into the adjoining chamber. The moment for disclosure has come, and Hrotsvith is seen at her best.

'*Abraham.* Close fast the door, that no one enter and disturb us.

Maria. Be not concerned, I have done so; no one will find it easy to get in.

Abraham. The time has come; away, deceitful clothes, that I may be recognised. Oh, my adopted daughter, joy of my soul, Maria, dost thou not know the aged man who was to thee a parent, who vowed thee to the heavenly king?

Maria. Oh woe is me! it is my father, my teacher Abraham, who speaks.

Abraham. What then has come to thee, my daughter?

Maria. Ah, wretchedness!

Abraham. Who was it that deceived thee? Who allured thee?

Maria. He who was the undoing of our first parents.

Abraham. Where is the noble life thou once wast wont to lead?

Maria. Lost, lost for ever!

Abraham. Where is thy virgin modesty, thy wondrous self-restraint?

Maria. Gone from me altogether.

Abraham. If thou dost not return to thine own self, what reward in the life to come canst thou expect for fasting, prayer, and watching, since fallen as from heaven's heights thou now art sunk in hellish depths?

Maria. Woe, woe is me!

Abraham. Why didst thou thus deceive me? why turn from me? Why didst thou not make known to me thy wretchedness, that I and my beloved Ephrem might work for thy repentance?

Maria. Once fallen into sinfulness, I dared not face you who are holy.

Abraham. But is there any one entirely faultless, except the Virgin's Son?

Maria. Nay, no one.

Abraham. 'Tis human to be frail, but to persist in wickedness is of the devil. Not he who falls of a sudden is condemned, but he who, having fallen, does not strive forthwith to rise again.

Maria. Woe unto me, wretch that I am!

(She sinks to the ground.)

Abraham. Why dost thou sink? why lie upon the ground? Arise and ponder what I am saying.

Maria. Fear casts me down, I cannot bear the weight of thy paternal admonition.

Abraham. Dwell only on my love and thrust aside thy fear.

Maria. I cannot.

Abraham. Think, was it not for thee I left my little hermitage, and so far set aside the rule by which I lived that I, an aged hermit, became a visitor to wantonness, and keeping silence as to my intent spoke words in jest that I might not be recognised? Why then with head bent low gaze on the ground? Why hesitate to give answer to my questions?

Maria. The accusations of my conscience bear me down, I dare not raise my eyes to heaven, nor enter into converse with thee.

Abraham. Be not afraid, my daughter, do not despair; rise from this depth of misery and fix thy mind on trust in God.

Maria. My sins in their excess have brought me to depths of desperation.

Abraham. I know thy sins are great, but greater than aught else is Heaven's power of grace. Put by thy grief and do not hesitate to spend the time vouchsafed to thee in living in repentance; divine grace overflows, and overflowing washes out the horrors of wrong-doing.

Maria. If I could entertain the hope of grace I should not be found wanting in repentance.

Abraham. Think of the weariness that I have suffered for thee; leave this unprofitable despair, nought in this world is so misleading. He who despairs of God's willingness to have compassion, 'tis he who sins hopelessly; for as a spark struck from a stone can never set aflame the ocean, so the bitterness of sin must ever fail to rouse sweet and divine compassion.

Maria. I know the power of grace divine, and yet the thought of how I have failed fills me with dread; I never can sufficiently atone.

Abraham. Thy feeble trust in Him is a reproach to me! But come, return with me to where we lived, and there resume the life which thou didst leave.

Maria. I would not disobey thee; if it be thy bidding, readily I yield.

Abraham. Now I see my daughter such as I would have her; I hope still to hold thee dearest among all.

Maria. I own a little wealth in gold and clothing; I abide by thy decision what shall be done with it.

Abraham. What came to thee in evil, with evil cast it from thee.

Maria. I think it might be given to the poor; or offered at the holy altars.

Abraham. I doubt if wealth acquired in wickedness is acceptable to God.

Maria. Besides this there is nothing of which the thought need trouble us.

Abraham. The dawn is breaking, the daylight shining, let us now depart.

Maria. Lead thou the way, dear father, a good shepherd to the sheep that went astray. As thou leadest, so I follow, guided by thy footsteps!

Abraham. Nay, I shall walk, my horse shall bear thee, for this stony road might cut thy tender feet.

Maria. Oh, that I ever left thee! Can I ever thank thee enough that, not by intimidation and fear, but by gentle persuasion alone, unworthy though I am, thou hast led me to repentance?

Abraham. Nought do I ask of thee but this, be now devoted to God for the remainder of thy life.

Maria. Readily I promise, earnestly will I persevere, and though the power fail me, my will shall never fail.

Abraham. It is agreed then—as ardently as before to vanity, be thou now devoted to the will divine.

Maria. Thy merits be my surety that the divine will shall be accomplished.

Abraham. Now let us hasten our departure.

Maria. Yea, hasten; for I loathe to tarry here.'

They return to the hermitage together, and Maria resumes her former mode of life in hope of redeeming the past. The drama closes with a scene between Abraham and Ephrem, who discourse on the beneficent change which familiar surroundings are already working in Maria; the angels sing rejoicing at the conversion of the sinner, says Abraham; and Ephrem adds that the repentance of the iniquitous causes greater joy in heaven than the perseverance of the just.

This play, currently known as 'Abraham,' but which would be more fitly named 'Maria,' marks the climax of Hrotsvith's power. In form it preserves the simple directness of the classic model, in conception it embodies the moral ideals of Christian teaching.

The last two plays of Hrotsvith are chiefly of historical interest for the learned disquisitions they contain; their dramatic value is comparatively small, and many of the scenes are in a way repetitions of scenes in other plays. In 'Paphnutius' we again have the story of a penitent woman, the hetaira Thais, who lived in the 6th century, but whose conversion has little of the interest which attaches to that of Maria. In 'Sapientia' we have a succession of scenes of martyrdom which recall those of the play 'Dulcetius.' The Lady Sapientia and her three daughters Fides, Spes and Caritas are put to death by order of the Emperor Hadrian, but the horrors of the situation are relieved by no minor incidents. The learned disquisitions in these plays are however extremely curious because they show on the one hand what store Hrotsvith set on learning, and on the other they give an idea of the method of study pursued at Gandersheim in those days.

The play 'Paphnutius[1]' opens with passages which Hrotsvith probably adapted from two works of Boëthius: 'On the teaching of Aristotle,' and 'On the study of music[2].' The philosopher Paphnutius dilates to his assembled pupils on man as the microcosm (minor mundus) who reflects in himself the world, which is the macrocosm (major mundus), and then explains that there is antagonism in the world, which is striving for concord in accordance with the rules of harmony. He explains how a similar antagonism exists in man and is represented by body and soul, which can also be brought into agreement. These thoughts, he says, have been suggested to him by the life of the hetaira Thais whose body and soul are ever at variance. Paphnutius further enlarges on the higher course of study known as the 'quadrivium' which includes arithmetic, geometry, music and astronomy[3], and discourses about music and the influence of harmony. His pupils, however, object to being taken along such devious paths and having such knotty questions propounded to them, and at last they quote Scripture in defence of their ignorance, saying that God has chosen the foolish that he may confound the wise. This rouses indignation in Paphnutius, who declares that 'he who advocates falsehood, be he a fool or a learned man, deserves to be confounded by God.' And he further utters words which are not devoid of a deeper significance: 'It is not the knowledge that man can grasp which is offensive to God, but the conceit of the learned.'

The learned disquisitions of the play 'Sapientia' are presented in a form still less attractive[4]. The Lady Sapientia, who speaks of herself as one of noble stock, and as the descendant of Greek princes, dilates on the relative value of numbers[5] to the emperor Hadrian till he tires of it and commands her to be gone.

It is sometimes alleged that these two later plays were the productions of earlier years, and that the nun added them to

---

[1] 'Paphnutius,' *Opera*, p. 237.

[2] Piltz, O., *Dramen der Roswitha* (no date), p. 178, refers to Boëthius, *In Categorias Aristotelis*, liber 1, 'de substantia'; and to *De musica*, liber 1.

[3] The ancient course of university study included the seven 'liberal arts' and was divided into the *Trivium* including grammar, dialectic and rhetoric, and the *Quadrivium* including arithmetic, geometry, astronomy and music. The *Trivium* was sometimes designated as *logic* and the *Quadrivium* as *physic*.

[4] 'Sapientia,' *Opera*, p. 27.

[5] Piltz, *Die Dramen der Roswitha*, p. 181, refers to Boëthius, *De Arithmetica*, liber 1, cc. 9–22.

her other more finished productions in order to equal the number
of the plays of Terence. However this may be, they were probably the two plays which she submitted to the criticism of three
outside but now unknown patrons with a letter in which she states
that she has taken threads and pieces from the garment of philosophy to add to the worth of her work. We render this letter in
full, since it throws an interesting light on what Hrotsvith thought
of her own powers. If it brought advice which led to the composition of the other plays, we must commend the judgment of
those who counselled her. But it is just possible that the approval which was accorded to the legends was denied to the plays,
—the absence of the name of the abbess Gerberg in connection
with them is remarkable,—and that, after writing a number of
dramas which found no appreciation, Hrotsvith was moved to
compose ' Paphnutius ' and ' Sapientia,' introducing learned disquisitions in hope of giving them a more solid value.

The letter runs as follows :

' To you, learned men[1], who abide in wisdom and are unenvious
of another's progress and well-disposed towards him as befits the
truly learned, I, Hrotsvith, though I am unlearned and lacking
in thoroughness, address myself; I wish you health and unbroken
prosperity. I cannot sufficiently admire your great condescension,
and sufficiently thank you for the help of your liberal generosity
and for your kindness towards me ; you, who have been trained in
the study of philosophy and have perfected yourselves in the pursuit
of knowledge, have held my writings, those of a lowly woman,
worthy of admiration, and have praised with brotherly affection
the power which works in me. You have declared that there is
in me a certain knowledge of that learning (scientiam artium) the
essence of which is beyond my woman's understanding. Till now
I have dared to show my rude productions only to a few of my
nearest friends, and my work along these lines would probably
have ceased, for there were few who understood my intentions,
and fewer who could point out to me in what I had failed, and
who urged me to persevere. But now that threefold approval comes
to me from you I take confidence and feel strengthened by
your encouragement to devote my energies to work where God
permits, and to submit this work to the criticism of those who
are learned. And yet I am divided between joy and fear, which

---

[1] ' who favoured and improved these works before they were sent forth,' additional
words of some manuscripts ; *Opera*, edit. Barak, p. 140 footnote.

contend within me; for in my heart I rejoice, praising God through whose grace alone I have become what I am; and yet I am fearful of appearing greater than I am, being perplexed by two things both of which are wrong, namely the neglect of talents vouchsafed to one by God, and the pretence to talents one has not. I cannot deny that through the help of the Creator I have acquired some amount of knowledge, for I am a creature capable of learning, but I acknowledge there is ignorance in me. For I am divinely gifted with abilities, but were it not for the untiring zeal of my teachers, they would have remained undeveloped and unused through my want of energy (pigritia). Lest this gift of God in me should be wasted through neglect I have sought to pluck threads and pieces from the garments of philosophy, and have introduced them into my afore-mentioned work (praefato opusculo), so that my own moderate knowledge may be enhanced by the addition of their greater worth, and God, who grants power, may be praised by so much the more as a woman's power is held to be inferior. This is the object of my writing, this alone the purpose of my exertions, for I do not conceal from myself that I am ignorant, and had it depended on myself alone, I should know nothing. But as you urge me on by the possibility of your approval and by your request proffered to me in writing, I now submit to your criticism this little work which I wrote with the intention of sending it to you but which I have hitherto kept concealed on account of its demerits, hoping you will study it with the intention of improving it as though it were your own work. And when you have altered it to a correct standard, send it back to me so that I may profit by your teaching in those points in which I may have largely failed.'

The productions of Hrotsvith in the domain of contemporary history consist of a poem on the emperor Otto the Great, and a history of the monastery of Gandersheim. The history of Otto is thought to have been over sixteen hundred lines in length[1], but only a fragment of about nine hundred lines is preserved. The nun received the materials for this history chiefly if not exclusively by word of mouth from the abbess Gerberg, whose family feeling it seems to reflect in various particulars, for among other distinctive traits, the quarrel between the father of Gerberg and his brother the emperor is passed over; it is rather a history of the members of the ruling family than a description of contemporary

---

[1] Ebert, *Allgemeine Geschichte der Litteratur des Abendlandes*, 1887, vol. 3, p. 305.

events[1]. This detracts from its historic, though hardly from its poetical value, which is considerable. Some of the episodes, such as that of the imprisonment and flight of Queen Adelheid in Italy, are admirably told. Adelheid was the widow of the king of the Langobards, and was afterwards married to Otto I. Her flight and imprisonment in Italy previous to her second marriage are unrecorded except by Hrotsvith.

The last work of the nun was probably that on the foundation and early history of Gandersheim, in which, as in the history of Otto, Hrotsvith enlarges more on persons than on events, and gives a detailed account of Duke Liudolf, his wife and daughters. Many details referred to above, in our chapter on the early history of the settlement, are taken from this account, which is in many ways the most finished and beautiful of Hrotsvith's compositions.

The interest in Hrotsvith's writings lay dormant for several centuries. It was revived at the close of the 15th century when the learned abbot Tritheim wrote of her, and the poet Celtes caused her dramas to appear in print. During the last thirty years many writers have treated of her, an appreciative and attractive account of her was written by Köpke[2], and different views have been expressed as to her merits as a poet, a dramatist and a historian[3]. Whatever place be ultimately assigned to Hrotsvith, the reader of her writings cannot fail to be attracted by her modesty, her perseverance, her loftiness of thought, and the directness of purpose which underlies all her work. She stands nearly alone in Saxony, and by her very solitariness increases our respect for her powers, and for the system of education which made the development of these powers possible.

---

[1] Ebert, *Allgemeine Geschichte der Litteratur des Abendlandes*, 1887, vol. 3, p. 311.
[2] Köpke, *Die älteste deutsche Dichterin*, 1869.
[3] Comp. *Allgemeine Deutsche Biographie*, article ' Roswitha.'

CHAPTER VI.

THE MONASTIC REVIVAL OF THE MIDDLE AGES.

'Pulchritudo certe mentis et nutrimentum virtutum est cordis munditia, cui visio Dei spiritualiter promittitur; ad quam munditiam nullus nisi per magnam cordis custodiam perducitur.'   *Anselm to the Abbess of St Mary's.*

§ 1. The new Monastic Orders.

IN this chapter I intend to give a description of the different monastic orders which were founded between the 10th and the 12th centuries, and to enter at some length into the reasons for their progress. A mass of heterogeneous information must be passed in rapid review with occasional digressions on outside matters, for it is only possible to understand the rapid progress of monasticism by recalling the relation in which it stood to other social developments.

As we cross the borderland which divides the centuries before the year 1000 from the period that follows, we become aware of great changes which about this time take definite shape throughout all social institutions. In the various strata of society occupations were becoming more clearly differentiated than they had ever been before, while those who were devoted to peaceful pursuits, whether in lay or religious circles, were now combined together for mutual support and encouragement.

In connection with religion we find the representatives of the Church and of monasticism becoming more and more conscious of differences that were growing up between them. Monasticism from its very beginning practically lay outside the established order of the Church, but this had not prevented bishop and abbot from working side by side and mutually supporting each other; nay, it even happened sometimes that one person combined in himself the two offices of abbot and bishop. But as early Christian times passed into the Middle Ages, prelates ceased to agree with headquarters at Rome in accepting monasticism as the means of securing a foot-hold for religion. The Church was now well established through-out western Europe, and her ministers were by no means pre-pared to side unconditionally with the Pope when he fell out with temporal rulers. The monastic orders on the contrary generally did side with him, and by locally furthering his interests, they became strongholds of his power.

The 12th century has been called the golden age of monasticism, because it witnessed the increased prosperity of existing monasteries and the foundation of a number of new monastic and religious orders. A wave of enthusiasm for the life of the religious settlement, and for the manifold occupations which this life now embraced, passed over western Europe, emanating chiefly from France, the country which took the lead in culture and in civilizing influences.

The 12th century, as it was the golden age of monasticism, was also the golden age of chivalry; the cloister and the court were the representative centres of civilized life. Under the influence of the system of mutual responsibility called feudalism, the knight by doughty deed and unwavering allegiance to his lord, his lady and his cause, gave a new meaning to service ; while the monk, devoted to less hazardous pursuits, gave a hitherto unknown sancti-fication to toil. The knight, the lady, the court-chaplain and the court-poet cultivated the bearings and the formalities of polite intercourse which formed the background of the age of romance, while in the cloister the monk and the nun gave a new meaning to religious devotion and enthusiasm by turning their activity into channels which first made possible the approximation of class to class.

This period knew little of townships as centres of intellectual activity, and their social importance remained far below that of cloister and court. The townsmen, whose possession of town land constituted them burghers, had won for themselves recognition as an independent body by buying immunities and privileges from bishop and king. But the struggle between them and the newer gilds, into which those who were below them in rank and wealth, formed themselves, was only beginning; the success of these newer gilds in securing a share in the government marks the rise of the township.

The diversity of occupation in the different kinds of gilds was anticipated by a similar diversity of occupation in the different monastic orders. The great characteristic of the monastic revival of the Middle Ages lay in the manifold and distinct spheres of activity which life offered inside the religious community. The studious, the educational, the philanthropic, and the agricultural element, all to some extent made part of the old monastic system. But through the foundation of a number of different orders which from the outset had separate aims, tastes which were widely dissimilar, and temperaments that were markedly diverse, met with encouragement in the religious settlement. The scholar, the artist, the recluse, the farmer, each found a career open to him ; while men and women were prompted to undertake duties within and without the religious settlement which make their activity comparable to that of the relieving officer, the poor-law guardian and the district nurse of a later age.

To gain a clear idea of the purposes which the new monastic and religious orders set before them, it will be best to treat of them severally in the chronological order of their foundation. Two lines of development are to be observed. There are the strictly monastic orders which sprang from the order of St Benedict, which they developed and amplified. These included the orders of Clugni, Citeaux, Chartreuse, and Grandmont, of which the last two took no account of women. On the other side stand the religious orders which are the outcome of distinctions drawn between different kinds of canons, when the settlements of regular canons take a distinctly monastic colouring. Among these the Premonstrant and the Austin orders are the most important, the members of which, from the clothes they wore, were in England called respectively White and Black Canons.

The importance of canonical orders, so far as women are concerned, lies in the fact that the 12th century witnessed the foundation of a number of religious settlements for both sexes, in which the men lived as canons and the women as nuns. The Premonstrant began as a combined order ; the orders of Fontevraud and of St Gilbert of Sempringham were of a similar kind. Bearing these distinctions in mind, we begin our enquiry with an analysis of the Cluniac and the Cistercian orders, which have their root directly in the monasticism of St Benedict.

As remarks in the previous chapters of this work will have shown, monasteries had sprung up during early Christian times independently of each other following a diversity of rules promulgated by various teachers, which had gradually been given up in favour of the rule of St Benedict. At the beginning of the 9th century this rule was largely prevalent in monasteries abroad, owing to councils held under the auspices of Karl the Great († 814)[1], and in England it gained ground through the efforts of Aethelwold, abbot of Abingdon and bishop of Winchester († 984). Some obscurity hangs about the subject, for a certain number of houses abroad, and among them some of the oldest and wealthiest, clung to the prerogative of independence and refused to accept St Benedict's rule, while in England, where this rule was certainly accepted in the 11th century, great diversity of routine either remained or else developed inside the different houses. This is evident from the account which Matthew Paris († 1259), a monk of St Albans, gives of the visitation of houses in the year 1232[2].

The order of Clugni[3] owes its origin to the desire of obviating a difficulty. As time wore on the rule of St Benedict had betrayed a weakness in failing to maintain any connection between separate monasteries. As there was no reciprocal responsibility between Benedictine settlements, a lay nobleman had frequently been appointed abbot through princely interference, and had installed himself in the monastery with his family, his servants and his retinue, to the detriment of the monastic property, and to the relaxation of discipline among the monks. The evil was most conspicuous abroad in the eastern districts of France and the western districts of Germany, and in 910 the order of Clugni was founded in Burgundy as a means of remedying it.

At first the order of Clugni was the object of great enthusiasm, and it was raised to eminence by a series of remarkable and energetic men. Powerful patrons were secured to it, master-minds found protection in its shelter. The peculiarities of its organisation consisted in the two rules that the abbot of the Cluniac house should be chosen during the lifetime of his predecessor, and that the abbots of different houses should meet periodically at a synod at which the abbot of Clugni should preside. The Pope's sanction having been obtained, the order remained throughout in close contact with Rome. In Germany especially this connection was prominent, and became an important political factor in the 11th century when the Cluniac houses directly supported the claim of Rome in the struggle between Pope and Emperor.

The order of Clugni took slight cognizance of women, and the

---

[1] Labbé, *Sacror. Concil. Collectio*, 1763, years 789, 804, 811; Helyot, *Histoire des ordres monastiques*, 1714, vol. 5, p. 146 ff.

[2] Matth. Paris, *Historia Major Angliae*, sub anno.

[3] Helyot, *Histoire des ordres monastiques*, 1714, vol. 5, pp. 184 ff. ; Ladewig, *Poppo von Stablo und die Klosterreform unter den Saliern*, 1883.

nunneries of the order were few and comparatively unimportant. A reason for this may be found in the nature of the order's origin, for the settlements of nuns had not been interfered with like the settlements of monks during the 9th and 10th centuries by the appointment of lay superiors, and were untouched by the consequent evils. If this be so the falling away from discipline, which called for correction in many houses of men, may justly be referred to a change thrust on them from without, not born from within.

In England the order of Clugni was not officially introduced till after the Norman Conquest, and then under circumstances which set a peculiar stamp on it. The seed which each order scattered broadcast over the different countries was the same, but the nature of the soil in which it took root, and the climate under which it developed, modified the direction of its growth.

During the 9th and 10th centuries England had been the scene of great social and political changes. The powerful kings who arose in Wessex and eventually claimed supremacy over all the provinces were unable to assert their authority to the extent of making the eastern provinces sink all provincial differences and jealousies, and join in organised resistance to the Danes. From the 9th century onwards, the entire seaboard of England, from Northumberland to the mouth of the Severn, had been exposed to the depredations of this people. Having once gained a foothold on the eastern coasts they quickly contracted alliances and adapted themselves to English customs, thus making their ultimate success secure.

The heathen invaders were naturally indifferent to the teachings of the Christian Church, and to the privileges of monasteries, and the scant annals of the period written before Knut of Denmark became king of England in 1016, give accounts of the destruction of many settlements. Some were attacked and laid waste, and others were deserted by their inmates. To realise the collapse of Christian institutions about this time, one must read the address which Wulfstan, archbishop of York (1002–1023), wrote to rouse the English to consciousness of the indignities to which their religion was exposed[1]. But the collapse was only temporary, bishoprics and abbacies stood firm enough to command the attention of the invader, and as the heathenism of the Dane yielded without a blow to the teaching of Christ, the settlements that were in the hands of abbot and monk rose anew.

[1] *Wulfstan*, edit. Napier, Arthur, Berlin 1883, p. 156.

However, it was only after the establishment of William of Normandy in England (1066) that the conditions of life became settled, and that the tide turned in favour of monasticism ; that is to say in favour of the monastic life of men, but not of women. Various reasons have been alleged for this difference : that the better position of the wife under Danish rule made women loth to remain in the convent, or that the spread of the system of feudal tenure excluded women from holding property which they could devote to the advantage of their sex. So much is certain, that during the reign of William many Benedictine houses for monks were founded or restored, but we do not hear of one for nuns.

In the wake of the Norman baron, the Norman prelate had entered this country, bringing with him an interest in the order of Clugni. It was William of Warren, son-in-law of the Conqueror, and earl of Surrey, who first brought over Cluniac monks, whom he settled at Lewes in Sussex. He did so at the suggestion of Lanfranc, a Norman monk of Italian origin, who had become archbishop of Canterbury (1070–1089). Before the close of William's reign Cluniac monks had met with patrons to build them four monasteries on English soil besides the house at Lewes.

The Norman barons continued to make liberal endowments to the order, but its popularity remained comparatively small, partly owing to the distinctly foreign character which it continued to bear[1]. Thus we find that after the accession of Henry II (1154), whose reign was marked by a rise in English national feeling, only one Cluniac house was added to those already in existence.

From the order of Clugni we pass to that of Citeaux[2], the foundation of which comes next in point of time, but which owed its existence to a different cause, and was characterised by widely dissimilar developments.

The story of the foundation of the order has been fully told by men who were under the influence of the movement ; the facts only of the foundation need be mentioned here. It originated in France when Robert, abbot of Molêmes, roused by the remonstrances of one Stephen Harding, an English monk living in his convent, left his home with a band of followers in 1098, in search of a retreat where they might carry out the rule of St Benedict in a worthier spirit. They found this retreat at Citeaux. From Citeaux and

---

[1] Tanner, T., *Notitia monastica,* edit. Nasmith, 1787, Introduction, p. ix.

[2] Helyot, *Histoire des ordres monastiques,* 1714, vol. 5, pp. 341 ff. ; *A. SS. Boll.,* St Stephanus abbas, April 17.

its daughter-house Clairvaux, founded in 1113 by the energetic Bernard, those influences went forth which made the Cistercian order representative of the most strenuous devotion to toil and the most exalted religious aspirations. While the order of Clugni in the 10th century secured the outward conditions favourable to a life of routine, devoting this routine chiefly to literary and artistic pursuits, the reform of Citeaux exerted a much wider influence. It at once gained extensive local and national sympathy, by cultivating land and by favouring every kind of outdoor pursuit.

The agricultural activity of the Cistercian has called forth much enthusiastic comment. Janauschek, a modern student of the order, describes in eloquent terms how they turned woods into fields, how they constructed water-conduits and water-mills, how they culti- vated gardens, orchards, and vineyards, how successful they were in rearing cattle, in breeding horses, in keeping bees, in regulating fishing, and how they made glass and procured the precious metals[1].

A comparison of their temper and that of the Cluniacs offers many interesting points; a comparison which is facilitated by a dialogue written by a Cistercian monk between 1154 and 1174 to exalt the merits of his order compared with those of the order of Clugni[2]. For while the Cluniac delighted in luxurious surround- ings, the Cistercian affected a simple mode of life which added to the wealth placed at his disposal by his untiring industry. While the Cluniac delighted in costly church decorations, in sumptuous vestments and in richly illuminated books of service, the Cistercian declared such pomp prejudicial to devotion, and sought to elevate the soul not so much by copying and ornamenting old books as by writing new ones; not so much by decorating a time- honoured edifice as by rearing a new and beautiful building.

Perhaps the nature of these occupations yields a reason why the Cistercian order at first found no place for women. At an early date Cardinal de Vitry (Jacobus di Vitriaco, † 1144), writing about the Cistercian movement, says that 'the weaker sex at the rise of the order could not aspire to conform to such severe rules, nor to rise to such a pitch of excellence[3].' In the dialogue referred to above, the Cluniac expresses wonder that women should enter the Cistercian order at all.

---

[1] Janauschek, L., *Origines Cisterciensium*, 1877.

[2] Dialogus inter Clun. et Cist. in Martène and Durand's *Thesaurus nov. Anecdot.* Paris, 1717, vol. 5, p. 1568.

[3] Jacopo di Vitriaco, *Historia Occidentalis*, 1597, c. 15.

The first Cistercian nunneries were founded at Tart in Langres and at Montreuil-les-Dames near Laon[1]. Hermann of Laon (c. 1150) describes 'how the religious of Montreuil sewed and span, and went into the woods where they grubbed up briars and thorns,'— an occupation which goes far to equalise their activity with that of the monks[2]. In Switzerland and Germany there is said to have been a pronounced difference in the character of Cistercian nunneries, due to the various conditions of their foundation. Some were aristocratic in tone, while others consisted of women of the middle class, who banded together and placed themselves under the bishop of the diocese, following of their own accord the rules accepted by the monks of Citeaux[3].

In Spain a curious development of the order of Citeaux is recorded, fraught with peculiarities which recall earlier developments.

In 1187 Alfonso VIII, king of Leon and Castille, founded an abbacy for nuns of the order of Citeaux at Las Huelgas near Burgos, the abbess of which was declared head over twelve other nunneries. In the following year the king sent the bishop of Siguenza to the general chapter at Citeaux to obtain leave for the abbesses of his kingdom to hold a general chapter among themselves. This was granted. At the first chapter at Burgos the bishops of Burgos, Siguenza and Placenza were assembled together with six abbots and seven abbesses, each abbess being entitled to bring with her six servants and five horses. The power of the abbess of Las Huelgas continued to increase. In the year 1210 she had taken upon herself the discharge of sacerdotal functions. In the year 1260 she refused to receive the abbot of Citeaux, whereupon she was excommunicated. After the year 1507 the abbess was no longer appointed for life, but for a term of three years only. Chapters continued to be held under her auspices at Burgos till the Council of Trent in 1545, which forbade women to leave their enclosures[4].

The date of the first arrival of monks of Citeaux in England was 1128, when William Giffard, bishop of Winchester († 1129), in early days a partisan of Anselm against Henry I, founded

---

[1] Helyot, *Histoire des ordres monastiques*, 1714, vol. 5, pp. 375, 468 ff.

[2] Hermannus, *De Mirac. St Mariae Laudun.* (in Migne, *Patrol. Cursus completus*, vol. 156), p. 1002.

[3] Brunner, S., *Ein Cisterzienserbuch*, 1881, p. 612.

[4] Helyot, *Histoire des ordres monastiques*, 1714, vol. 5, p. 376.

Waverley in Surrey for them[1]. Shortly afterwards Walter Espec, the most powerful baron in northern England, granted them land at Rievaulx in Yorkshire[2]. About the same time the foundation at Fountains repeated the story of Citeaux. A small band of monks, burning with the desire to simplify conventual life, left York and retired into the wooded solitude of Fountains, whence they sent to Bernard at Clairvaux asking for his advice[3].

These events fall within the reign of Henry I (1100–1135), the peacefulness of which greatly furthered the development of monastic life. The pursuits to which the Cistercians were devoted in England were similar to those they carried on abroad. Here also their agricultural successes were great, for they ditched, ridged and drained, wet land, they marled stiff soils and clayed poor ones. The land granted to them, especially in the northern counties, was none of the best, but they succeeded in turning wildernesses into fruitful land, and by so doing won great admiration. Similarly the churches built in this country under the auspices of these monks bear witness to great purity of taste and ardent imagination. The churches built by them were all dedicated to the Virgin Mary, who was the patron saint of the order.

All these early settlements of the Cistercian order were for monks, not for nuns, for Cistercian nunneries in England were founded comparatively late and remained poor and unimportant. If we look upon the Cistercians as farmers, builders and writers, this fact is partly explained. But there are other reasons which suggest why the number of Cistercian nunneries was at first small, and why the Cistercian synod shrank from accepting control over them.

Convents of women had hitherto been recruited by the daughters of the landed gentry, and their tone was aristocratic; but a desire for the religious life had now penetrated into the lower strata of society. Orders of combined canons and nuns were founded which paid special attention to women of the lower classes, but they encountered certain difficulties in dealing with them. It is just possible on the one hand that the combined orders forestalled the Cistercians in the inducements they held out; on the other, that the experience of the combined orders made the Cistercians cautious about admitting women.

---

[1] Birch, W. de Gray, *On the Date of Foundation ascribed to the Cistercian Abbeys of Great Britain*, 1870.

[2] Dugdale, *Monasticon*, ‘Rivaulx,’ vol. 5, p. 274.

[3] Ibid. ‘Fountains,’ vol. 5, p. 292, nrs I—XI.

Consideration of these facts brings us back to a whole group of phenomena to which reference was made in a previous chapter, viz. the disorderly tendencies which had become apparent in connection with loose women, the greater opprobrium cast on these women as time went on, and the increasing difficulties they had to contend with. The founders of the orders of combined canons and nuns tried to save women from drifting into and swelling a class, the existence of which was felt to be injurious to social life, by preaching against a dissolute life and by receiving all persons into their settlements regardless of their antecedents.

The earliest and in many ways the most interesting of these combined orders is that founded by Robert († 1117) of Arbrissel, a village in Brittany. Robert had begun life in the Church, but he left the clerical calling on account of his great desire to minister to the needs of the lower classes, and as a wandering preacher he gained considerable renown[1]. Men and women alike were roused by his words to reform their course of life, and they followed him about till he determined to secure for them a permanent abode. This he found in an outlying district at Fontevraud. He organised his followers into bands and apportioned to each its task. The men were divided into clerics, who performed religious service, and lay brothers, who did outdoor work. 'They were to use gentle talk, not to swear, and all to be joined in brotherly affection.' It appears that the women were all professed nuns[2]; unceasing toil was to be their portion, for they were to hold the industrious and hardworking Martha as their model and take small account of such virtues as belonged to Mary.

From every side workers flocked to the settlements, for Robert opened his arms to all. We are told that 'men of all conditions came, women arrived, such as were poor as well as those of gentle birth ; widows and virgins, aged men and youths, women of loose life as well as those who held aloof from men.' At first there was a difficulty in providing for the numerous settlers, but their labours brought profit, and gifts in kind poured in from outsiders, a proof that in the eyes of the world the settlements supplied an obvious need. Branch establishments were founded and prospered, so that in one cloister there were as many as three hundred women, in

---

[1] *A. SS. Boll.*, St Robertus, Feb. 25, contains two accounts of his life, the one by Baldric († 1130), the other by Andrea. Comp. also Helyot, *Hist. des ordres mon.*, 1714, vol. 6, pp. 83 ff.

[2] Differing from settlements of the Gilbertine order, in which there were lay sisters also.

another one hundred, and in another sixty. Robert returned to his missionary work, after having appointed Hersende of Champagne as lady superior of the whole vast settlement. Her appointment was decisive for the system of government,—Fontevraud remained under the rule of an abbess. It was for her successor, Petronille, that the life of the founder Robert was written soon after his death, by Baldric, bishop of Dol († 1130). Baldric repeatedly insists on the fact that no one was refused admission to these settlements. 'The poor were received, the feeble were not refused, nor women of evil life, nor sinners, neither lepers nor the helpless.' We are told that Robert attracted nearly three thousand men and women to the settlements; the nuns (ancillae Christi) in particular wept at his death.

The fact that Robert had the welfare of women especially at heart is further borne out by a separate account of the last years of his life, written by one Andrea, probably his pupil. Andrea tells how Robert at the approach of death assembled the canons or clerics of the settlement around him and addressed them saying: 'Know that whatever I have wrought in this world I have wrought as a help to nuns.' Fontevraud occupied a high standing, and we shall find that nuns were brought thence into England when the nunnery of Amesbury was reformed in the reign of King John. The order of Fontevraud made great progress in the course of the 12th century, and next to it in point of time stands the foundation of the order of Prémontré[1]. Fontevraud lies in the north-west of France, Prémontré in the east, and the efforts of Robert have here a counterpart in those of Norbert († 1134), who worked on similar lines. Norbert also left the clerical calling to work as a missionary in north-western Germany, especially in Westphalia, and he also succeeded in rousing his listeners to a consciousness of their ungodly mode of life. With a view to reform he sought to give a changed tone to canonical life and founded a religious settlement in the forest of Coucy, which he afterwards called Prémontré from the belief that the Virgin had pointed it out to him. His efforts were likewise crowned with success, for many settlements were forthwith founded on the plan of that of Prémontré. Hermann of Laon, the contemporary of Norbert, praises him warmly and remarks that women of all classes flocked to his settlements, and were admitted into the communities by adopting the cloistered life.

---

[1] Helyot, *Histoire des ordres monastiques*, 1714, vol. 2, pp. 156 ff. 'Leben des heil. Norbert' (written before 1155) transl. by Hertel in Pertz, *Geschichtsschreiber der deutschen Vorzeit.*

The statement is made, but may be exaggerated, that ten thousand women joined the order during Norbert's lifetime.

Norbert differed greatly in character from Robert; his personal ambition was greater, and his restless temperament eventually drew him into political life. He died in 1134, and in 1137 the chapter at Prémontré decided that the women should be expelled from all the settlements that had inmates of both sexes, and that no nuns should henceforth be admitted to settlements ruled by men. The reasons which led to this resolution are not recorded. The nuns thus rendered homeless are said to have banded together and dwelt in settlements which were afterwards numbered among Cistercian houses, thus causing a sudden increase of nunneries of this order. However a certain number of Premonstrant houses, occupied solely by nuns and ruled by a lady superior, existed previous to the decree of 1137. These remained unmolested, and others were added to them in course of time[1]. It can be gathered from a bull of 1344 that there were at that time over thirteen hundred settlements of Premonstrant or White Canons in existence in Europe, besides the outlying settlements of lay brothers, and about four hundred settlements of nuns[2]. The settlements of White Canons in England amounted to about thirty-five and were founded after the sexes had been separated. There were also two settlements of Premonstrant nuns in England[3].

A third order of canons and nuns, which in various ways is akin to the orders of Fontevraud and Prémontré previously founded abroad, was founded at the beginning of the 12th century in England by Gilbert of Sempringham. But as the material for study of this order is copious, and as it marks a distinct development in the history of women's convent life in England, it will be discussed in detail later[4].

The canons who belonged to the combined orders were regular canons, that is they owned no individual property, and further differed from secular canons in holding themselves exempt from performing spiritual functions for the laity. Erasmus at a later date remarked that 'their life is half way between that of monks and that of those who are called secular canons[5].'

---

[1] Helyot, *Histoire des ordres monastiques*, 1714, vol. 2, p. 175; Jacopo di Vitriaco, *Historia occidentalis*, 1597, ch. 15.

[2] Gonzague, *Monastère de Storrington*, 1884, p. 8.

[3] They were Brodholm and Irford.   [4] § 3 of this chapter.

[5] 'Peregrinatio Relig. ergo.'

As to the distinction between the two kinds, it appears that bands of canons who may fitly be termed regular had existed from an early period; but the subject is shrouded in some obscurity[1]. In the 11th century mention of them becomes frequent, especially in France, and at the beginning of the 12th century their position was defined by a decree published by Pope Innocent II at the Lateran Council (1139)[2]. By this decree all those canons who did not perform spiritual functions for the laity were designated as regular and were called upon to live according to the rule of life laid down by St Augustine in his Epistle, number 109. The terms Austin canon and regular canon were henceforth applied indiscriminately, but many independent settlements of unrecognised canons of an earlier date have since been included under this term.

A few words are here needed in explanation of the term canoness or Austin canoness, which is used in diverse ways, but is generally applied to women of some substance, who entered a religious community and lived under a rule, but who were under no perpetual vow, that is, they observed obedience and celibacy as long as they remained in the house but were at liberty to return to the world. These stipulations do not imply that a woman on entering a convent renounced all rights of property, an assumption on the strength of which the Church historian Rohrbacher interprets as applying to canonesses the entire chapter of directions promulgated at Aachen in 816, in the interest of women living the religious life[3]. But the terms used in these provisions are the ordinary ones applied to abbess and nun[4]. Helyot, who has a wider outlook, and who speaking of the canon explains how this term was at first applied to all living *in canone*, points out that uncertainty hangs about many early settlements of women abroad, the members of which were in the true sense professed[5]. It seems probable that they at first observed the rule of St Benedict, and afterwards departed from it, as has been pointed out above in connection with Saxon convents.

The tenor of the provisions made at Aachen shows that the monastic life of women in a number of early settlements abroad rested on a peculiar basis, and points to the fact that the inmates

---

[1] Helyot, *Histoire des ordres monastiques*, 1714, vol. 2, pp. 11 ff.

[2] Tanner, J., *Notitia Monastica* edit. Nasmith, 1787, Introd. XI.

[3] Rohrbacher, *Histoire universelle de l'église catholique*, 1868, vol. 6, p. 252.

[4] Labbé, C., *Sacror. Conc. Collectio*, 1763, year 816, part 2.

[5] Helyot, *Histoire des ordres monastiques*, 1714, vol. 2, p. 55.

of settlements founded at an early date were in some measure justified when they declared later that they had always held certain liberties, and insisted on a distinction between themselves and other nuns. The position of the inmates of some of these houses continued different from that of the members of other nunneries till the time of the Reformation. In England, however, this difference does not seem to have existed. The inmates of the few Austin nunneries, of which there were fifteen at the dissolution, though they are frequently spoken of as canonesses in the charters that are secured by them, appear to have lived a life in no way different from that of other nuns, while they were in residence, but it may be they absented themselves more frequently.

When once their position was defined the spread of the Austin Canons was rapid ; they combined the learning of the Benedictine with the devotional zeal of the Cistercian, and ingratiated themselves with high and low. Of all the settlements of the Austin Canons abroad that of St Victor in Paris stands first in importance. It became a retreat for some of the master minds of the age[1], and its influence on English thinkers was especially great[2]. Austin Canons came from France into England as early as 1108. At first their activity here was chiefly philanthropic, they founded hospitals and served in them; but they soon embraced a variety of interests. In the words of Kate Norgate speaking with reference to England[3]: 'The scheme of Austin Canons was a compromise between the old-fashioned system of canons and that of monkish confraternities ; but a compromise leaning strongly towards the monastic side, tending more and more towards it with every fresh development, and distinguished chiefly by a certain elasticity of organisation which gave scope to an almost unlimited variety in the adjustment of the relations between the active and the contemplative life of the members of the order, thus enabling it to adapt itself to the most dissimilar temperaments and to the most diverse spheres of activity.'

Their educational system also met with such success that before the close of the reign of Henry I two members of the fraternity had been promoted to the episcopate and one to the primacy. In the remarks of contemporary writers on religious settlements, it is curious to note in what a different estimation regular canons and

---

[1] Hugonin, 'Essai sur la fondation de l'école St Victor à Paris,' printed as an introduction to Hugo de St Victore, *Opera* (in Migne, *Patrologiae Cursus Compl.* vol. 175).

[2] Comp. below, ch. 9, § 1.

[3] Norgate, Kate, *History of the Angevin Kings*, 1887, vol. 1, p. 66.

monks are held by those who shared the interests of court circles. For the courtier, as we shall presently see, sympathised with the canon but abused and ridiculed the monk.

Throughout the early Christian ages the idea had been steadily gaining ground that the professed religious should eschew contact with the outside world, and it was more and more urged that the moral and mental welfare of monk and nun was furthered by their confining their activity within the convent precincts. Greater seclusion was first enforced among women; for in the combined orders the nuns remained inside the monastery, and were removed from contact with the world, while the canons were but little restricted in their movements. How soon habitual seclusion from the world became obligatory it is of course very difficult to determine, but there is extant a highly interesting pamphlet, written about the year 1190 by the monk Idung of the Benedictine monastery of St Emmeran in Bavaria, which shows that professed religious women in the district he was acquainted with went about as freely as the monks, and did not even wear a distinctive dress. The pamphlet[1] is the more interesting as Idung was evidently distressed by the behaviour of the nuns, but failed to find an authority on which to oppose their actions. He admits that the rule as drafted by St Benedict is intended alike for men and women, and that there are no directions to be found in it about confining nuns in particular, and in fact the rule allowed monks and nuns to go abroad freely as long as their superior approved. Idung then sets forth with many arguments that nuns are the frailer vessel; and he illustrates this point by a mass of examples adduced from classical and Biblical literature. He proves to himself the advisability of nuns being confined, but he is at a loss where to go for the means of confining them. And he ends his pamphlet with the advice that as it is impossible to interfere with the liberty of nuns, it should at least be obligatory for them when away from home to wear clothes which would make their vocation obvious.

No doubt the view held by this monk was shared by others, and public opinion fell in with it, and insisted on the advantages of seclusion. Many Benedictine houses owned outlying manors which were often at a considerable distance, and the management of which required a good deal of moving about on the part of the monks and nuns who were told off for the purpose. We shall see later that those who had taken the religious vow had pleasure as their object

---

[1] Idung, *De quatuor questionibus* in Pez, B., *Thesaurus anecdot. nov.* 1721, vol. 2.

as much as business in going about; but complaints about the
Benedictines of either sex are few compared with those raised
against the Cistercian monks. For the Cistercians in their capacity
of producers visited fairs and markets and, where occasion offered,
were ready to drive a bargain, which was especially objected to by
the ministers of the Church, who declared that the Cistercians lowered the religious profession in general estimation. Consequently
orders which worked on opposite lines enjoyed greater favour with
the priesthood ; such as the monastic order of Grandmont, which
originally demanded of its members that they should not quit their
settlement and forbade their owning any animals except bees ; and
the order of Chartreuse, which confined each monk to his cell, that
is, to a set of rooms with a garden adjoining[1]. But these orders did
not secure many votaries owing to their severity and narrowness.

Thus at the close of the 12th century a number of new religious
orders had been founded which spread from one country to another
by means of an effective system of organization, raising enthusiasm
for the peaceful pursuits of convent life among all classes of society.
The reason of their success lay partly in their identifying themselves
with the ideal aspirations of the age, partly in the political unrest
of the time which favoured the development of independent institutions, but chiefly in the diversity of occupation which the professed
religious life now offered. The success obtained by the monastic
orders however did not fail to rouse apprehension among the representatives of the established Church, and it seems well in conclusion
to turn and recall some of the remarks passed on the new orders by
contemporary writers who moved in the court of Henry II (1154–89).

It has been pointed out how the sympathies of court circles at
this period in England were with the Church as represented by the
priesthood ; courtier and priest were at one in their antagonism against
monks, but in sympathy with the canons. Conspicuous among these
men stands Gerald Barri (c. 1147–c. 1220), a Welshman of high
abilities and at one time court chaplain to the king. He hated all
monkish orders equally, and for the delectation of some friends whom
he entertained at Oxford he compiled a collection of monkish scandals
known as ' The Mirror of the Church[2],' in which he represents the
Cluniac monk as married to Luxury, and the Cistercian monk to
Avarice; but, in spite of this, incidental remarks in the stories he

---

[1] Helyot, *Histoire des ordres monastiques*, 1714, vol. 7, pp. 366, 406. Jacopo di
Vitriaco, *Historia Occidentalis*, 1597, c. 15.

[2] Giraldus Cambrensis, *Speculum Ecclesiae*, edit. Brewer, 1873.

tells give a high opinion of the Cistercian's industry, hospitality and unbounded charity. Gerald mentions as a subject for ridicule that the Cistercian monk lived not on rent, but on the produce of his labour, an unaristocratic proceeding which was characteristic of the order. Gerald's attitude is reflected in that of Ralph de Glanvil († 1190), justiciar of England during the reign of Henry II, a clever and versatile man of whom we know, through his friend Map, that he disliked all the monkish orders. But his enthusiasm for religious settlements was not inconsiderable, and several settlements of the Premonstrant or White Canons were founded by him.

The student of the period is familiar with the likes and dislikes of Walter Map († c. 1210), great among poets and writers of the age, who disliked all monks, but especially the Cistercians[1]. His friend Gerald tells how this hatred had originated in the encroachments made by the monks of Newenham on the rights and property of the church he held at Westbury. For the perseverance with which Cistercian monks appropriated all available territory and interfered with the rights of church and chapel, made them generally odious to the ministers of the Church; their encroachments were an increasing grievance. John of Salisbury, afterwards bishop of Chartres († after 1180), directly censured as pernicious the means taken by the monks to extend their power. He tells us they procured from Rome exemption from diocesan jurisdiction, they appropriated the right of confession, they performed burial rites; in short they usurped the keys of the Church[2]. By the side of these remarks it is interesting to recall the opinion of the monkish historian, William of Malmesbury, who a generation earlier had declared that the Cistercian monks had found the surest road to heaven.

All these writers, though lavish in their criticisms on monks, tell us hardly anything against nuns. The order of St Gilbert for canons and nuns alone calls forth some remarks derogatory to the women. Nigel Wirecker, himself a monk, giving vent to his embittered spirit against Church and monkish institutions generally in the satire of Brunellus, launches into a fierce attack against the tone which then prevailed in women's settlements[3]. He does not think it right that women whose antecedents are of the worst kind should adopt the religious profession and that as a means of preserving chastity they should systematically enjoin hatred of men.

---

[1] Map, W., *De Nugis Curialium* (written 1182–89), 1850, p. 38.

[2] John of Salisbury, *Polycraticus*, edit. Giles, bk. VII. chs. 21–23.

[3] Wirecker, N., *Brunellus*, 1662, p. 83.

A similar reference is contained in the poem in Norman French called the 'Order of Fair Ease,' which is a production of the 13th century, and which caricatures the different religious orders by feigning an order that unites the characteristic vices of all[1]. It is chiefly curious in the emphasis it lays on the exclusiveness of monasteries generally, representing them as reserved for the aristocracy. It contains little on nunneries and only a few remarks which are derogatory to the combined order of Sempringham.

These remarks were obviously called forth by the fact that the combined orders in particular admitted women from different ranks of life. For generally nunneries and their inmates enjoyed favour with churchman and courtier, whose contempt for the monk does not extend to the nun. In the correspondence of Thomas Beket, John of Salisbury, Peter of Blois and others there are letters to nuns of various houses which show that these men had friends and relatives among the inmates of nunneries. Indeed where members of the same family adopted the religious profession, the son habitually entered the Church while the daughter entered a nunnery. A sister of Thomas Beket was abbess at Barking, and various princesses of the royal house were abbesses of nunneries, as we shall presently see. They included Mary, daughter of Stephen (Romsey); a natural daughter of Henry II (Barking), and Matilda, daughter of Edward I (Amesbury); Queen Eleanor wife of Henry III also took the veil at Amesbury.

§ 2. Benedictine Convents in the Twelfth Century.

From this general review of the different orders we pass on to the state of nunneries in England during the 12th century, and to those incidents in their history which give some insight into their constitution.

Attention is first claimed by the old Benedictine settlements which still continued in prosperity and independence. Of these houses only those which were in connection with the royal house of Wessex remained at the close of the 10th century; those of the northern and midland districts had disappeared. Some were deserted, others had been laid waste during the Danish invasions; it has been observed that with the return of tranquillity under Danish rule, not one of the houses for women was restored. Secular monks or laymen took possession of them, and

---

[1] Goldsmid, *Political Songs*, vol. 2, p. 64.

when they were expelled, the Church claimed the land, or the settlement was restored to the use of monks. Some of the great houses founded and ruled by women in the past were thus appropriated to men. Whitby and Ely rose in renewed splendour under the rule of abbots; Repton, Wimbourne and numerous other nunneries became the property of monks.

Various reasons have been given for the comparatively low ebb at which women's professed religious life remained for a time. Insecurity during times of warfare, and displacement of the centres of authority, supply obvious reasons for desertion and decay. A story is preserved showing how interference from without led to the disbanding of a nunnery. The Danish earl Swegen († 1052), son of Earl Godwin, took away (vi abstractam) the abbess Eadgifu of Leominster in Herefordshire in 1048, and kept her with him for a whole year as his wife. The archbishop of Canterbury and the bishop of Worcester threatened him with excommunication, whereupon he sent her home, avenging himself by seizing lands of the monastery of Worcester. He then fled from England and was outlawed, but at a later period he is said to have wanted the abbess back. The result is not recorded, for Leominster as a women's settlement ceased to exist about this time[1]. There is no need to imagine a formal dissolution of the settlement. The voluntary or involuntary absence of the abbess in times of warfare supplies quite a sufficient reason for the disbanding of the nuns.

About the same time a similar fate befell the monastery of Berkley-on-Severn, in spite of the heroic behaviour of its abbess. The story is told by Walter Map how it was attacked and plundered at the instigation of Earl Godwin († 1053) and how in spite of the stand made by the abbess, a 'strong and determined' woman, the men who took possession of it turned it into a 'pantheon, a very temple of harlotry[2].' Berkley also ceased to exist[3].

The monasteries ruled by women, which survived the political changes due to the Danish invasion and the Norman Conquest, had been in connection with women of the house of Cerdic; with hardly an exception they were situated in the province of Wessex

---

[1] Freeman, *Norman Conquest*, 3rd edit. 1877, vol. 2, p. 609.

[2] Ibid. p. 554; Map, *De Nugis Curialium*, 1850, p. 201 (Freeman: Map like other Norman writers speaks very ill of Godwin).

[3] Dugdale, *Monasticon*, vol. 6, p. 1618 (p. 1619 he says in connection with the destroyed nunnery Woodchester that the wife of Earl Godwin built it to make amends for her husband's fraud at Berkley).

within the comparatively small area of Dorset, Wilts, and Hampshire. Chief among them were Shaftesbury, Amesbury, Wilton
(or Ellandune), Romsey, and St Mary Winchester (or Nunnaminster). With these must be classed Barking in Essex, one of
the oldest settlements in the land, which had been deserted at one
time but was refounded by King Edgar, and which together with
the Wessex nunneries, carried on a line of uninterrupted traditions
from the 9th century to the time of the dissolution.

The manors owned by these settlements at the time of the
Conquest lay in different shires, often at a considerable distance
from the monastery itself.

From the account of survey in the Domesday book we gather
that Shaftesbury had possessions in Sussex, Wiltshire, Dorset, and
Hampshire[1], and that Nunnaminster owned manors in Hampshire,
Berkshire, and Wiltshire[2]. Barking, the chief property of which
lay in Essex, also held manors in Surrey, Middlesex, Berkshire, and
Bedfordshire[3].

These monasteries were abbacies, as indeed were all houses for
nuns founded before the Conquest. The abbess, like the abbot,
had the power of a bishop within the limits of her own house and
bore a crozier as a sign of her rank. Moreover the abbesses of
Shaftesbury, Wilton, Barking, and Nunnaminster 'were of such
quality that they held of the king by an entire barony,' and by
right of tenure had the privilege at a later date of being summoned
to parliament, though this lapsed on account of their sex[4].

The abbess as well as the abbot had a twofold income; she
drew spiritualities from the churches which were in her keeping,
and temporalities by means of her position as landlord and landowner. The abbess of Shaftesbury, who went by the title of abbess
of St Edward, had in her gift several prebends, or portions of the
appropriated tithes or lands for secular priests. In the reign of
Henry I she found seven knights for the king's service, and had
writs regularly directed to her to send her quota of soldiers into
the field in proportion to her knights' fees; she held her own courts
for pleas of debts, etc., the perquisites of which belonged to her[5].

To look through the cartularies of some of the old monasteries,

---

[1] Dugdale, *Monasticon*, 'Shaftesbury,' vol. 2, p. 470.

[2] Ibid. 'Nunnaminster,' vol. 2, p. 451.   [3] Ibid. 'Barking,' vol. 1, p. 436.

[4] Ibid. 'Shaftesbury,' vol. 2, p. 472. The abbess does not even seem to have been
represented (as she was at the Diet abroad).

[5] Ibid. p. 472; and p. 473 footnote.

is to realise how complex were the duties which devolved on the ruler of one of these settlements, and they corroborate the truth of the remark that the first requirement for a good abbot was that he should have a head for business. Outlying manors were in the hands of bailiffs who managed them, and the house kept a clerk who looked after its affairs in the spiritual courts; for the management and protection of the rights and privileges of the property claimed unceasing care.

The Benedictine abbesses do not seem to have been wanting in business and managing capacity. At the time of the dissolution the oldest nunneries in the land with few exceptions were also the wealthiest. The wealth of some was notorious. A saying was current in the western provinces that if the abbot of Glastonbury were to marry the abbess of Shaftesbury, their heir would have more land than the king of England[1]. The reason of this wealth lies partly in the fact that property had been settled on them at a time when land was held as a comparatively cheap commodity; but it speaks well for the managing capacities of those in authority that the high standing was maintained. The rulers prevented their property from being wasted or alienated during the 12th and 13th centuries, when the vigour or decline of an institution so largely depended on the capacity of the individual representing it, and they continued faithful to their traditions by effecting a compromise during the 14th and 15th centuries, when the increased powers of the Church and the consolidation of the monarchical power threatened destruction to institutions of the kind.

It is worthy of attention that while all nunneries founded during Anglo-Saxon times were abbacies, those founded after the Conquest were generally priories. Sixty-four Benedictine nunneries date their foundation from after the Conquest, only three of which were abbacies[2]. The Benedictine prioress was in many cases subject to an abbot; her authority varied with the conditions of her appointment, but in all cases she was below the abbess in rank. The explanation is to be sought in the system of feudal tenure. Women no longer held property, nunneries were founded and endowed by local barons or by abbots. Where power from the preceding period devolved on the woman in authority, she retained it; but where new appointments were made the current tendency was in favour of curtailing her power.

---

[1] Dugdale, *Monasticon*, vol. 1, p. 472.   [2] They were Godstow, Elstow, Malling.

Similarly all the Cistercian nunneries in England, which numbered thirty-six at the dissolution, were without exception priories. The power of women professing the order abroad and the influence of the Cistercian abbesses in Spain and France have been mentioned—facts which preclude the idea of there being anything in the intrinsic nature of the order contrary to the holding of power by women. The form the settlement took in each country was determined by the prevailing drift of the time, and in England during the 11th and 12th centuries it was in favour of less independence for women.

Various incidents in the history of nunneries illustrate the comparatively dependent position of these settlements after the Conquest. At first Sheppey had been an abbacy. It had been deserted during the viking period; and at the instigation of the archbishop of Canterbury about the year 1130 nuns were brought there from Sittingbourne and the house was restored as a priory.

Amesbury again, one of the oldest and wealthiest abbeys in the land for women, was dissolved and restored as a priory, dependent on the abbess of Fontevraud. This change of constitution presents some interesting features. The lives of the women assembled there in the 12th century were of a highly reprehensible character; the abbess was accused of incontinence and her evil ways were followed by the nuns. There was no way out of the difficulty short of removing the women in a body, and to accomplish this was evidently no easy undertaking. Several charters of the time of King John and bearing his signature are in existence. The abbess, whose name is not on record, retired into private life on a pension of ten marks, and the thirty nuns of her convent were placed in other nunneries. A prioress and twenty-four nuns were then brought over from Fontevraud and established at Amesbury, which became for a time a cell to the foreign house[1]. This connection with France, at a time when familiarity with French formed part of a polite education, caused Amesbury to become the chosen retreat of royal princesses. During the wars with France under the Edwards, when many priories and cells were cut off from their foreign connection, Amesbury regained its old standing as an abbacy.

Several of the Benedictine nunneries founded after the Conquest

---

[1] Dugdale, *Monasticon*, 'Amesbury,' vol. 2, p. 333; Freeman, *History of the Norman Conquest* (3rd edit. 1877), vol. 2, p. 610; the event is dated 1177; perhaps the letters from John of Salisbury, *Epist.* edit. Giles, nrs 72, 74, are addressed to the abbess of Amesbury, who was deposed.

owed their foundation to abbacies of men.   Some were directly
dependent cells, like Sopwell in Hertfordshire, a nunnery founded
by the abbot of St Albans, who held the privilege of appointing
its prioress.   So absolute was this power that when the nuns
appointed a prioress of their own choice in 1330, she was deposed
by the abbot of St Albans, who appointed another person in her
stead[1].   Similarly the nunnery at Kilburn was a cell to Westminster, its prioress being appointed by the abbot of Westminster[2].
But as a general rule the priories were so constituted that the nuns
might appoint a prioress subject to the approval of the patron of
their house, and she was then consecrated to her office by the
bishop.

Various incidents show how jealously each house guarded its
privileges and how needful this was, considering the changes that
were apt to occur, for the charters of each religious house were the
sole guarantee of its continued existence.   From time to time they
were renewed and confirmed, and if the representative of the house
was not on the alert, he might awake to find his privileges en-
croached upon.   In regard to the changes which were liable to
occur the following incident deserves mention.   In the year 1192
the archbishop of York formed the plan of subjecting the nunnery
of St Clement's at York[3], a priory founded by his predecessor
Thurstan, to the newly-founded abbacy for women at Godstow.
Godstow was one of the few women's abbacies founded after the
Conquest, and owed its wealth and influence chiefly to its connection with the family of Fair Rosamond, at one time the mistress
of Henry II, who spent the latter part of her life there.   But the
nuns of St Clement's, who had always been free, would not obey
the abbess of Godstow, and they saved themselves from the archbishop's interference by appealing directly to the Court of Rome.

A curious incident occurred during the reign of Henry III
in connection with Stanford, a nunnery in Northamptonshire.
Stanford was a priory dependent on the abbot of Peterborough
who had founded it.   It appears that the prioress and her convent,
in soliciting confirmation of their privileges from Rome, employed
a certain proctor, who, besides the desired confirmation, procured
the insertion of several additional articles into the document, one
of which was permission for the nuns to choose their own prioress,
and another a release from certain payments.   When the abbot of

---

[1] Dugdale, *Monasticon*, 'Sopwell,' vol. 3, p. 362.
[2] Ibid. 'Kilburn,' vol. 3, p. 422.   [3] Ibid. 'St Clement's,' vol. 4, p. 323.

Peterborough became aware of these facts he threatened to complain to the Pope, whereupon the prioress with the nuns' approval carried all their charters and records of privileges to the archbishop of Canterbury, alleging that the proctor had acted against their order. They renounced all claim to privileges secretly obtained, and besought the primate to represent their conduct favourably to the Pope and to make peace between them and their patrons[1].

Both these incidents occurred in connection with Benedictine nunneries. The difficulties which occurred in Cistercian nunneries are less easy to estimate, as they were not daughter-houses to men's Cistercian abbacies, but in many cases held their privileges by a bull obtained directly from the Pope. Thus Sinningthwaite in Yorkshire[2], founded in 1160, held a bull from Alexander III which exempted the nuns from paying tithes on the lands they farmed, such exemption being the peculiar privilege of many Cistercian settlements. Other bulls secured by Cistercian nunneries in England are printed by Dugdale[3].

A few incidents are recorded in connection with some of the royal princesses, which illustrate the attitude commonly assumed towards professed nuns, and give us an idea of the estimation in which convents were held. Queen Margaret of Scotland we are told desired to become a nun; her mother and her sister Christina both took the veil, and her daughters, the princesses Matilda and Mary, lived at Romsey for some years with their aunt Christina. As Pope Innocent IV canonised (1250) Queen Margaret of Scotland a few words must be devoted to her.

Her father Edward, the son of Edmund Ironside († 1016), had found refuge at the Scottish court when he came from abroad with his wife Agatha and their children, a son and two daughters. Of these daughters, Christina became a nun; but Margaret was either persuaded or constrained to marry King Malcolm in 1070, and having undertaken the duties of so august a station as that of queen, she devoted her energies to introducing reforms into Scotland and to raising the standard of industrial art. We possess a beautiful description of her life, probably written by her chaplain Turgot[4], and her zeal and high principles are further

---

[1] Dugdale, *Monasticon*, 'Stanford,' vol. 4, p. 257.
[2] Ibid. 'Sinningthwaite,' vol. 5, p. 463.
[3] Ibid. 'Swine,' vol. 5, p. 494, nr 2; 'Nun-Cotham,' vol. 5, p. 676, nr 2.
[4] *A. SS. Boll.*, St Margaret, June 10.

evidenced by her letters, some of which are addressed to the primate Lanfranc.

Margaret's two daughters, Matilda and Mary, were brought up in the convent, but it is not known when they came to Romsey in Wessex; indeed their connection with Wessex offers some chronological difficulties. Their mother's sister Christina became a professed nun at Romsey in 1086[1]; she may have lived before in a nunnery in the north of England[2], and there advocated her niece Matilda's acceptance of the religious profession as a protection against the Normans. If this is not the case it is difficult to fix the date of King Malcolm's scorn for her proposal that Matilda should become a nun[3]. King Malcolm was killed fighting against William Rufus in 1093, Queen Margaret died a few days afterwards, and the princesses Matilda and Mary, of whom the former was about thirteen, from that time till 1100 dwelt at Romsey in the south of England. In the year 1100, after the violent death of Rufus, Henry, the younger of his brothers, laid claim to the English crown. A union with a princess, who on the mother's side was of the house of Cerdic, appeared in every way desirable. According to the statement of William of Malmesbury (✝ c. 1142) Henry was persuaded by his friends, and especially by his prelates, to marry Matilda. 'She had worn the veil to avoid ignoble marriages,' says William, who lived close to the locality and was nearly a contemporary, 'and when the king wished to marry her, witnesses were brought to say she had worn it without profession[4].' This is borne out by the historian Orderic Vitalis (✝ 1142), whose information however is derived at second hand, for he enlarges on the princesses' stay with the nuns at Romsey, and on the instruction they received in letters and good manners, but he does not say that they were actually professed[5].

The fullest account of the event is given by Eadmer (✝ 1124), who was nearly connected with the primate Anselm, and he naturally puts the most favourable construction on Matilda's conduct. According to him she wished to leave the convent and went before Anselm to plead her cause.

'I do not deny having worn the veil,' the princess said. 'When I was a child my aunt Christina, whom you know to be a deter-

---

[1] *Dict. of Nat. Biography*, Christina.

[2] Brand, *History of Newcastle*, vol. 1, p. 204.

[3] Freeman, *History of William Rufus*, vol. 2, pp. 596, 682.

[4] Will. of Malmesbury, *Gesta Reg.* (Rolls Series), pp. 279, 470, 493.

[5] Orderic Vitalis, *Eccles. Hist.*, transl. by Forester, 1847, vol. 3, p. 12.

mined woman, in order to protect me against the violence of the Normans, put a piece of black cloth on my head, and when I removed it gave me blows and bad language. So I trembling and indignant wore the veil in her presence. But as soon as I could get out of her sight I snatched it off and trampled it under-foot[1].' In a lively way she goes on to describe how her father seeing the veil on her head became angry and tore it off, saying he had no intention other than that she should be married. Anselm, before complying with the wish of the princess, convened a chapter at Lambeth, but after hearing their decision, he declared Matilda free and united her in marriage to the king.

Anselm's behaviour is doubtless faithfully represented by Eadmer. Curiously enough later historians, Robert of Gloucester, Matthew Paris and Rudbone († c. 1234), represent Matilda as unwilling to leave the cloister to be married; and in one of these accounts she is described as growing angry, and pronouncing a curse on the possible offspring of the union. Walter Map goes so far as to say that the king took to wife a veiled and professed nun, Rome neither assenting nor dissenting, but remaining passive.

Perhaps the validity of the union was afterwards for political reasons called in question. At any rate Mary, Matilda's sister, also left the convent to be married to Eustace, Count of Boulogne, without objection being raised.

That Matilda did not object to leaving the cloister, we have conclusive proof in her great and continued affection for Anselm as shown in her letters to him. These letters and the charitable deeds of the queen, throw light on the Latinity of the Romsey pupil and on the tastes she had imbibed there.

We shall have occasion to return to Matilda again in connection with the philanthropic movement of the age, and we shall find her founding the hospital of St Giles in the soke of Aldgate, and bringing the first Austin Canons from France into England[2].

All her life she retained a taste for scholarly pursuits, and patronised scholars and men of letters. Her correspondence with the primate Anselm[3] yields proof of her own studies and the freedom with which she wrote Latin.

In one of these letters, written shortly after her marriage

---

[1] Eadmer, *Historia* (Rolls Series), p. 122.

[2] Comp. below, ch. 8, § 2.

[3] Anselm of Canterbury, *Epistolae* (in Migne, *Patrol. Cursus completus*, vol. 159), the numeration of which is followed in the text.

(bk 3. 55), Matilda urges the primate in strong terms to abstain from the severe fasting he practises, quoting from Cicero 'on Old Age,' and arguing that as the mind needs food and drink, so does the body ; she at the same time admits the Scriptures enjoin the duty of fasting, and Pythagoras, Socrates and others urge the need of frugality. Anselm in his answer incidentally mentions having joined her to the king in lawful wedlock.

Matilda's next letters are less fraught with learning, and in unaffected terms express grief at Anselm's voluntary exile, which was the outcome of his quarrel with the king. She is saddened by his absence and longs for his return (3. 93); she would act as intercessor between him and her husband (3. 96), and she writes to the Pope on Anselm's behalf (3. 99). The queen both read and admired Anselm's writings, and compares his style to that of Cicero, Quintilian, Jerome, Gregory and others (3. 119) with whom her reading at Romsey may have made her acquainted.

Anselm is not slow in answering that the king's continued bitterness is to him a source of grief, and in expressing the desire that the queen may turn his heart. It is good of her to wish for his return, which, however, does not depend on himself; besides 'surely she wishes him to act in accordance with his conscience.' In one of these letters he accuses the queen of disposing otherwise than she ought of the churches which are in her keeping (3. 57, 81, 97, 107, 120, 128).

Anselm's continued absence from Canterbury, which was due to the quarrel about investiture, was felt to be a national calamity, and many letters passed between him and those among the Church dignitaries who sided with him against the king.

Among Anselm's correspondents were several abbesses of Wessex settlements, who seem to have been in no way prejudiced against him on account of the approval he gave to Matilda's leaving the cloister. He writes in a friendly strain to another Matilda, abbess of St Mary's, Winchester (Winton), thanking her for her prayers, urging her to cultivate purity of heart and beauty of mind as an encouragement to virtue, and begging her to show obedience to Osmund (bishop of Winchester) in affairs temporal and spiritual (3. 30). To Adeliz, also abbess at St Mary's (3. 70), he writes to say she must not be sorry that William Giffard has left his appointment as bishop of Winchester, for his going is a reason for rejoicing among his friends, as it proves his steadfastness in religious matters. He also writes to Eulalia, abbess (of Shaftesbury), who was anxious for him to come back, and begs her to pray that his return may prosper (3. 125).

The references to the Benedictine nunneries of Wessex contained in this correspondence are supplemented by information from other sources.

In the early part of the 12th century a girl named Eva was brought up at a convent, but which she left to go to Anjou, since she preferred the life of a recluse there to the career which was open to her in the English nunnery. Her life abroad has been described in verse by Hilarius († c. 1124) who is the earliest known Englishman who wrote religious plays. After studying under Abelard Hilarius had taken up his abode at Angers, near the place where Eva dwelt, and was much impressed by her piety and devotions[1].

From his poem we gather that Eva had been given into the care of the nuns at St Mary's, Winchester (Winton), a place which he designates as 'good and renowned.' The girl's progress in learning was the subject of wonder to the abbess and her companions, but when Eva reached the age at which her enrolment as a member of the community was close at hand, 'she turned' in the words of the poet, 'from success as though it had been a sinful trespass,' and left the nunnery to go abroad.

Her admirer Hilarius has celebrated other women who were devoted to religious pursuits. He addresses one of them as 'Bona,' and praises her for caring little for the religious garb unless good works accompany it. The meaning of her name and that of other religious women whom Hilarius also addresses, such as 'Superba,' and 'Rosa,' gives him an opportunity for compliments on the virtues these names suggest. His poems, though insignificant in themselves, add touches to our knowledge of women who adopted the religious profession.

In the wars which ensued after the death of Henry I (1134) the nunneries of Wessex witnessed the climax and the end of the struggle. The Empress Matilda, daughter of Henry I and Queen Matilda, who claimed the crown on the strength of her descent, finding the sympathies of London divided, approached Winchester, and was received by two convents of monks and the convent of nuns who came forth to meet her. The Empress for a time resided at St Mary's Abbey, and there received a visit from Theobald,

---

[1] Hilarius, *Versus et ludi*, edit. Champollion-Figeac, 1838, p. 1. (Champollion prints Clinton, which he no doubt misread for Winton.)

archbishop of Canterbury[1]. During the fighting which followed
the nunnery of Wherwell was burnt[2], and perhaps St Mary's Abbey
at Winchester was destroyed[3]. Matilda finally yielded to Stephen,
and left England on condition that her son Henry should succeed
to the crown.

The nunnery of Romsey continued its connection with royalty,
and we find the daughter of Stephen, Mary of Blois, established
there as abbess previous to her marriage. Her case again throws
curious side-lights on the foundation of convents and the possibilities open to women who adopted the religious profession.

The princess Mary had come over from St Sulpice in France
with seven nuns to Stratford at Bow (otherwise St Leonard's,
Bromley in Middlesex), when the manor of Lillechurch in Kent
was granted to the nunnery there by King Stephen for her own
and her companions' maintenance[4]. But these women, as the
charter has it, because of the 'harshness of the rule and their
different habits' could not and would not stay at Stratford, and
with the convent's approval they left it and removed to Lillechurch, which was constituted by charter a priory for them. Mary
removed later to Romsey where she became abbess some time
before 1159[5], for in that year her brother William, the sole surviving heir of Stephen, died, so that she was left heiress to the
county of Boulogne. She was thereupon brought out of the
convent at the instigation of Henry II, and married to Matthew,
son of the Count of Flanders, who through her became Count of
Boulogne. Thomas Beket, who was then chancellor, not primate,
was incensed at this unlawful proceeding, and intervened as a
protector of monastic rule, but the only result of his interference
was to draw on himself the hatred of Count Matthew[6]. It is said
that Mary returned to Romsey twelve years later. Her daughters
were, however, legitimised in 1189 and both of them married.

Various letters found here and there in the correspondence
of this period show how women vowed to religion retained their
connection with the outer world. Among the letters of Thomas
Beket there is one in which he tells his 'daughter' Idonea
to transcribe the letter he is forwarding, and lay it before the

---

[1] Milner, J., *History of Winchester*, 1823, vol. 1, p. 212.

[2] Dugdale, *Monasticon*, 'Wherwell,' vol. 2, p. 634.

[3] Ibid. 'St Mary's Abbey,' vol. 2, p. 452.

[4] Ibid. 'Lillechurch,' vol. 4, p. 378, charter nr 2.

[5] Ibid. 'Rumsey,' vol. 2, p. 506.

[6] Norgate, Kate, *History of the Angevin Kings*, 1887, vol. 1, p. 469.

archbishop of York in the presence of witnesses[1]. It has been mentioned that a sister of Thomas Beket was in 1173 abbess at Barking.

Again, among the letters of Peter of Blois († c. 1200), chaplain to Henry II, are several addressed to women who had adopted the religious profession. Anselma 'a virgin' is urged to remain true to her calling; Christina, his 'sister,' is exhorted to virtue, and Adelitia 'a nun' is sent a discourse on the beauties of the unmarried life[2].

§ 3. The Order of St Gilbert of Sempringham[3].

The study of the order of St Gilbert, which is of English origin, shows how in this country also sympathy with convent life was spreading during the 12th century, and how, owing to the protection afforded to peaceful and domestic pursuits by the religious houses, many girls and women of the middle classes became nuns. From an intellectual point of view the order of St Gilbert has little to recommend it, for we know of no men or women belonging to the order who distinguished themselves in learning, literature or art. As a previous chapter has indicated, its purpose was chiefly to prevent women from drifting into the unattached and homeless class, the existence of which was beginning to be recognised as prejudicial to society.

The material for the study of the order is abundant. We have several accounts of the life and work of Gilbert, besides minute injunctions he drafted to regulate the life of his communities, and there are references to him in contemporary literature. The success of his efforts, like that of the men who founded combined orders of canons and nuns abroad, was due to the admission of women into his settlements regardless of their class and antecedents. Like Robert of Arbrissel his interest centred in women, but he differed from him in giving the supreme authority of his settlements into the hands of men. For the settlements which afterwards became double originated in Gilbert's wish to provide for women who

---

[1] Beket, *Epistolae* (in Migne, *Patrol. Cursus compl.*, vol. 190), nr 196.

[2] Petrus Blesiensis, *Epistolae*, edit. Giles, letters nrs 35, 36, 55, 239.

[3] *A. SS. Boll.*, St Gilbert, Feb. 4, contain two short lives; Dugdale, *Monasticon*, vol. 6 inserted between pp. 946, 947, contains a longer account, the 'Institutiones,' and various references to Gilbert; *Dict. of Nat. Biography* refers to a MS. account at Oxford, Digby, 36, Bodleian.

sought him as their spiritual adviser.   It was only in consequence
of the difficulties he encountered that canons were added to the
settlements.

Helyot likens the order of St Gilbert to that of Norbert, the
founder of the order of Prémontré[1], but here too there are marked
points of difference, for in disposition and character Gilbert was as
unlike Norbert as he was to Robert ; he had neither the masterfulness of the one nor the clear-sighted determination of the other.
The reason of his popularity lies more in his gentleness and per-
suasiveness, and these qualities made him especially attractive to
women.

Gilbert was a native of Lincolnshire, born about 1083, the son
of a wealthy Norman baron and an English woman of low rank.
His ungainly appearance and want of courtly bearing rendered him
unfit for knightly service.   He was sent to France for his education
and there attained some reputation as a teacher.   After his return
home he devoted his energies to teaching boys and girls in the
neighbourhood.   His father bestowed on him two livings, one of
which was at Sempringham.   His chief characteristic was pity for
the lowly and humble, and this attracted the attention among others
of Robert Bloet, bishop of Lincoln († 1123).   For a time Gilbert
acted as a clerk in Bloet's house, and after his death remained
with his successor Alexander († 1148) in a like capacity.   With
Alexander he consulted about permanently providing for those
of the lower classes whom his liberality was attracting to Sempringham.

The first step taken by Gilbert was to erect suitable dwellings
round the church of St Andrew at Sempringham for seven women
whom he had taught and who had devoted themselves to religion
under his guidance, and as they were not to leave their dwelling
place, lay sisters were appointed to wait on them.   He also provided
dwellings at Sempringham for the poor, the infirm, for lepers, and
orphans.

The order of Gilbert is held to have been established before
1135, the year of King Henry I's death[2].   The author of his life
in Dugdale likens Gilbert's progress at this time to the chariot of
Aminadab ; to it clung clerics and laymen, literate and illiterate
women, and it was drawn by Master Gilbert himself.

Gilbert had entered into friendly relations with the Cistercian

---

[1] Helyot, *Histoire des ordres mon.*, 1714, vol. 2, p. 190.
[2] *Dict. of Nat. Biography.*

monks who were then gaining ground in Yorkshire, and William, first abbot of Rievaulx († 1145–6), was among them. He had a good deal to do with Ailred († 1166), a notable north-country man who came from Scotland to live at Rievaulx, and afterwards became abbot successively of Revesby and Rievaulx.

At this time there were no nunneries in the north of England, for the great settlements of the early English period had passed away and no new houses for women had been founded. The numbers of those who flocked to Gilbert were so great that he felt called upon to give them a more definite organisation. His friendship with Cistercian monks no doubt turned his eyes to Citeaux, and the wish arose in him to affiliate his convents to the Cistercian order. Having placed his congregations under the care of the Cistercians, he set out for Citeaux about 1146.

But his hopes were not fulfilled. At Citeaux he met Pope Eugenius III († 1153) and other leading men. He cemented his friendship with Bernard of Clairvaux and entered into friendly relations with Malachy, bishop of Armagh († 1148), who had introduced the Cistercian order into Ireland. But the assembly at Citeaux came to the conclusion that they would not preside over another religious order, especially not over one for women[1], and Gilbert was urged to remain at the head of his communities and Bernard and Malachy presented him with an abbot's staff.

He returned to England, burdened with a responsibility from which he would gladly have been free, and obliged to frame a definite rule of life for his followers. As one account puts it, 'he now studied the rules of all religious orders and culled from each its flowers.' The outcome of his efforts was the elaborate set of injunctions which now lie before us.

From these injunctions we can see how Gilbert's original plan had expanded, for his settlements consisted of bands of canons, lay-brethren, nuns, and lay-sisters. One set of rules is drafted for the canons who observed the rule of St Augustine and performed religious service for the double community, and a separate set for the laymen who acted as servants. And similarly there is one set of rules for the nuns who lived by the rule of St Benedict, and another for their servants the lay-sisters.

These rules suggest many points of similarity to the combined settlements of canons and nuns previously founded abroad, but there are also some differences.

---

[1] *A. SS. Boll.*, St Gilbert, Feb. 4, *Vita*, nr 2, ch. 3; Dugdale, *Vita*, p. xi.

In the Gilbertine settlements the dwellings of the men and women were contiguous, and the convent precincts and the church were divided between them. The men's dwelling was under the rule of a prior, but three prioresses ruled conjointly in the women's house. The arrangements in both convents were alike, and the duties of prior and prioress similar, but in all matters of importance the chief authority belonged to the prior who was at the head of the whole settlement. The property owned by Gilbertine settlements apparently consisted largely of sheep, and among the men we note a number of shepherds and a 'procurator' who bought and sold the animals. The ewes were regularly milked and the wool was either used in the house for making clothes, or sold. The lay-sisters were appointed to spin and weave and the nuns to cut out and make the garments.

There was one cellar and one kitchen for the whole settlement, for the cellaress in the women's house acted as caterer both for the canons and the nuns. Domestic duties fell to the share of the women. They cooked the canons' food as well as their own and handed the meals into the men's quarters through a hole in the wall with a turn-table, through which the plates and dishes were returned to them. They also made clothes for the whole establishment.

At the daily chapter held in the women's house the prioresses presided in turn, with a companion on either side. The cellaress reported to the prioress, who settled the allowances and gave out the food. She received information also from the 'scrutatrices,' the nuns whose duty it was to go the round of the house and report disorders, and according to whose reports she imposed the various penances.

We also hear in the women's house of a librarian ('precentrix[1]'), who had the keys of the book-case ('armarium'), which was kept locked except during reading time when the nuns were allowed the use of the books. There was to be no quarrelling over the books; the nun like the canon was directed to take the one allotted to her and not to appropriate that given to another. Simplicity of life was studied. Pictures and sculpture were declared superfluous and the crosses used were to be of painted wood. Only books for choir use were to be written in the convent, but while this holds good alike for the women and for the men, there is this further prohibition with regard to the nuns, that talking in Latin was to be avoided.

---

[1] The 'precentrix' is strictly speaking the leader of the choir. Cf. below ch. 10 § 2.

' Altogether,' says the rule[1], ' we forbid the use of the Latin tongue unless under special circumstances.'

The cooking was done by the nuns in turn for a week at a time in compliance with a regulation contained in the rule of St Benedict. The librarian also had her week of cooking, and when she was on duty in the kitchen, gave up her keys to another nun. We hear also of the mistress appointed to teach the novices, and of the portress who guarded the approaches to the house.

The injunctions drafted for the canons and the lay members of the settlement are equally explicit. Directions are also given about tending the sick, who were to be treated with tenderness and care.

Girls were admitted into the company of the nuns at the age of twelve, but several years passed before they could be enrolled among the novices. At the age of twenty the alternative was put before the novice of joining the nuns or the lay-sisters. If she decided in favour of the latter she could not afterwards be promoted to the rank of nun ; she was bound to observe chastity and obedience while she remained in the house, but she was not consecrated. A certain amount of knowledge of the hymns, psalms and books of service was required from the novice before she could make profession.

The scheme of life worked out by Gilbert met with success and numerous patrons were found to endow settlements on the plan of that at Sempringham. As the chronicler says, ' many wealthy and highborn Englishmen, counts and barons, seeing and approving of the undertaking the Lord had initiated and holding that good would come of it, bestowed many properties ("fundos et praedia') on the holy father (Gilbert) and began to construct on their own account numerous monasteries in various districts.'

The greater number of these settlements were situated in Lincolnshire and Yorkshire, but judging by the extant charters the conditions and purposes of their foundations were not always the same. Sometimes the grant is made conjointly to men and women, sometimes reference is made to the prior only. In the earlier charters the women are especially noticed, in the later ones more account is taken of the men. As time went on the order gradually ceased to have any attraction for women, and at the time of the dissolution several foundations originally made for men and women were occupied only by canons.

---

[1] Dugdale, *Institutiones*, p. lxxxii.

Gilbert himself did not accept a position of authority in his order but became a canon at Bullington, one of its settlements.   He appears to have been influential in wider circles and we find him several times at court.   King Henry II visited him, and both the king and Queen Eleanor made grants of land to the order.   Henry regarded Gilbert with so much favour that when he was summoned before the King's Court in London on the charge of having supported Beket in his exile, the king sent a message from abroad ordering his case to be reserved for royal judgment, which practically meant his acquittal[1].

Rapidly as the number of Gilbertine houses increased, the order did not remain entirely free from trouble, for even in Gilbert's lifetime distressing incidents happened which justified to some extent the scornful remarks of contemporary writers.   One of these difficulties arose sometime between 1153 and 1166 in connection with a girl at Watton.   A full account of the affair was written and forwarded to Gilbert by Ailred, abbot of Rievaulx[2].   This account illustrates pointedly the readiness of the age to accept a miraculous rendering of fact, and gives a curious insight into the temper of a community of nuns.   Indeed such violence of conduct, and details of such behaviour as are here described show that the barbarity of the age, which so often strikes us in connection with camp and court, was reflected in the monastery.

Watton was among the older Gilbertine houses and had been founded before 1148 by a nobleman Eustace Fitz-John on property which had belonged to a nunnery during the early English period[3]. The settlement was among the larger Gilbertine houses ; it owned property to the extent of twenty acres.

The girl had been placed under the care of the nuns of Watton at the suggestion of Murdach, abbot of Fountains († 1153), and had given endless trouble by her unbecoming levity and hopeless laziness.   'She is corrected by word of mouth but without result, she is urged by blows but there is no improvement,' writes Ailred, who speaks of her as a nun without telling us that she had actually made profession.

She made the acquaintance of one of the lay-brothers who were engaged in repairing the women's dwelling.   The two contrived to

---

[1] *Dict. of Nat. Biography.*

[2] Ailred, *Opera* (in Migne, *Patrol. Cursus comp.*, vol. 195), p. 789.   'De sancti-moniali de Wattun.'

[3] Oliver, G., *History of Beverley and Watton*, 1829, p. 520 ff.; cf. above, p. 91.

meet frequently out of doors until at last the nun's condition became obvious. Her fellow-nuns were so incensed at this discovery that they treated her with barbarous cruelty and would have put her to death had not the prioress intervened and had her chained and imprisoned. The anger of the nuns now turned against the lay-brother who had brought disgrace on their convent, and with a mixture of cunning and deceit they managed to discover him and have him terribly mutilated. 'I do not praise the deed, but the zeal,' says Ailred ; 'I do not approve of bloodshed, but for all that I praise the virgins' hatred of such wickedness.' The esprit de corps among the nuns and their indignation evidently went far in his eyes to excuse behaviour which he would not describe as he did if he had not felt it altogether reprehensible.

Meanwhile the nun overcome by contrition was awaiting her delivery in prison ; there she had visions of abbot Murdach who had died some years before. He first rebuked her, but then miraculously relieved her of her burden and restored her to her normal condition. The nuns though greatly surprised were convinced of the truth of the statement concerning the miraculous doings of Murdach because they found the nun's chains loosened. The prior of Watton sent for Ailred to enquire more closely into the matter. Ailred came, collected all possible evidence, and was convinced that there had been divine intervention on the girl's behalf. He wrote an account of what had happened to Gilbert, with these words as preface : 'to know of the Lord's miracles and of his proofs of divine love and to be silent about them were sacrilege.' What became of the girl we are not told. For trespasses such as hers the rule of Gilbert decreed life-long incarceration, but the canon for a like trespass suffered no punishment beyond being expelled from the settlement.

The old age of Gilbert was further troubled by the evil conduct of two men, Gerard a smith, and Ogger a carpenter. He had taken them into the order out of charity, but they greatly abused his kindness, appropriated the revenues of the order, and encouraged dishonesty and sexual irregularities. Their behaviour was productive of such results that it called forth a letter from Beket to Gilbert in which he says 'the greater our love, the more we are troubled and perturbed by hearing of things happening in your order, which are a grievance not only before the eyes of men but before the eyes of God.'

However letters in defence of Gilbert were written by Roger

archbishop of York († 1181), Henry bishop of Winchester († 1171) and William bishop of Norwich († 1174), who treat the occurrence as a misfortune and praise the order generally in the warmest terms. Praise from other quarters is not wanting, which shows that Gilbert's work was considered remarkable, especially with regard to the influence he had over women. William of Newburgh wrote of him : ' As far as this is concerned, in my opinion he holds the palm above all others whom we know to have devoted their energies to the control and government of religious women[1].'

Gilbert lived to an advanced age. Walter Map, writing between 1182 and 1189, speaks of him as over a hundred and well-nigh blind. He was buried at Sempringham, where his tomb became the goal of many pilgrimages and the scene of many miracles. He was canonised a saint of the Church by Pope Innocent II in 1202. One of the accounts of his life, written shortly after his death, says that the order at that time numbered thirteen conventual churches and contained seven hundred men and fifteen hundred women.

The East Riding Antiquarian Society has recently begun excavating on the site of Watton Priory, one of the oldest Gilbertine settlements, and has ascertained many particulars about the inner arrangements of this house[2]. It has found that the church, built on the foundations of a Norman church which had been destroyed by fire in 1167, was divided throughout its entire length by a substantial partition wall nearly five feet thick. The church served for both sexes of the community, which were kept separate by this partition. In some places remains of this wall were found up to the height of four feet; this was part of the solid foundation upon which, above the height of the eye, was erected an open arcade which made it possible for the whole community to hear the sermon preached on festal days from the pulpit. The parts into which the church was divided were of unequal size. Dr Cox, the president of the Society, who read a paper on the Gilbertine statutes, said that the full complement of the double house at Watton consisted of a hundred and forty women and seventy men, and that the larger part of the church was appropriated to the women and the smaller to the men.

It was further shown by the excavations that the dividing wall had in one place an archway, covering the door which was opened for the great processions of both sexes which took place on the four-

---

[1] Dugdale, *Monasticon*, vol. 6, p. xcviii.
[2] Report in *Athenaeum*, Oct. 7, 1893.

teen great festivals of the year and at funerals. Remains were also found of an opening in the wall with a turn-table, so arranged that articles could be passed through without either sex seeing the other. Through this the chalice, when the canons' mass was over, would be passed back and restored to the custody of the nuns; no doubt this was constructed on the same plan as the opening through which the food was passed.

The cloister of the nuns lay on the north side of the transept and must have been about a hundred feet square, an alley of ten feet wide surrounding it. It is thought that the stone of which the house was built must have been brought up the Humber from Whitby. An early writer tells us that the nuns' dwelling at Watton was connected by an underground passage with the holy well at Kilnwick, and that the nuns by means of these waters performed wonderful cures[1].

---

[1] Oliver, G., *History of Beverley and Watton*, 1829, p. 531.

CHAPTER VII.

ART INDUSTRIES IN THE NUNNERY.

'Spernere mundum, spernere nullum, spernere sese,
Spernere sperni se, quatuor haec bona sunt.' *Herrad.*

§ 1. Art Industries generally.

FROM consideration of the nuns of different orders we turn to
enquire more closely into the general occupations and productive
capacities of nuns during early Christian times and the Middle
Ages. It seems worth while collecting the information scattered
here and there on the work done by these women, since the group-
ing together of various notices gives some, though necessarily an
incomplete, idea of the pursuits to which nuns were devoted when
not engaged in religious service. The work done, as we shall see,
includes art productions of every kind, weaving, embroidery,
painting and illuminating as well as writing, which during the
period under consideration must be looked upon as an art.

From the first monastic life had been dominated by the idea that
idleness is at the root of all evil. In a well ordered religious house
the times for work and for leisure, for eating, sleeping and for attendance at divine service were fixed by custom and were enforced by
routine; we shall treat later of the way in which the day was divided
by the canonical hours. The purpose of the ordinary settlement,
beyond observing the hours, was to educate girls, to train novices
and to provide suitable occupation for the nuns of the convent.
In all houses reading and copying books of devotion was included
among the occupations, and in some, the cultivation of art in
one or more of its branches. Between the 8th and the 14th
century religious settlements were the centres of production in
handicrafts and in art industry; to study the art of this period, it
is necessary to study the productions of the monasteries.

A sense of joint ownership united the members of each of the religious settlements, and this was especially true of the older Benedictine houses which have fitly been likened to small republics. To the convent inmate the monastery was the centre of his interests and affections, and the house's possessions were in a sense his own. He was proud of them and proud if he could add to their store. Increased communication with the south and the east brought books, materials and other beautiful objects which the inmates of the religious settlement zealously copied and multiplied. During times of political and social unrest, while states were in their making, the goldsmith, the scribe, the illuminator, and the embroiderer, all found protection and leisure in the religious house. The so-called dark ages, the centuries between 800 and 1200, cease to be dark as soon as one enquires into the contents of monastic libraries, and the monotony of convent routine ceases to appear monotonous on entering one of the old treasuries and reflecting on the aims and aspirations which were devoted to producing this wealth in design and ornamentation, the bare fragmentary remains of which are to us of to-day a source of unending delight and wonder.

Some of the houses ruled by women like so many of those ruled by men became important centres of culture, where the industrial arts were cultivated, and where books were prized, stored and multiplied. Nuns as well as monks were busy transcribing manuscripts, a task as absorbing as it was laborious, for the difficulties in the way of learning to write can hardly be overestimated considering the awkwardness of writing materials and the labour involved in fabricating parchment, ink and pigment. But as the old writer with a play on the words *armarium*, bookcase, and *armatorium*, armoury, remarks, 'a monastery without its book-case is what a castle is without its armoury.' And all houses, whether for monks or nuns, took rank as centres of culture in proportion to their wealth in books.

Of the books over which the early scribe spent so much time and trouble, comparatively speaking only a few survive. All books are worn out by use, especially books of devotion ; many were destroyed when printing came in and parchment was handy to the book-binder ; many when the Reformation destroyed convents. The early scribe usually omitted to add his name to the book he was copying. In the books which are preserved the names of men scribes are few, and the names of women scribes fewer still, though they do occasionally occur. Wattenbach, a student of manuscripts and of the mediæval art of writing, has collected a number of names of women whom he has found mentioned as scribes. He gives them, adding the remark that other books no doubt were written by nuns where mention of the fact is omitted[1].

It will be profitable to recall these names and examine the references to work done by nuns as calligraphists and miniature painters, for here and there women attained great proficiency in these arts. The amount of writing done in women's houses compared with that done by men was no doubt small, for it was not in this direction that the industry of the nun lay. But what remains shows that where scope to activity was given talents of no mean kind were developed.

In some departments of art industry, especially in weaving church hangings, and embroidering altar cloths and church vestments, nuns greatly distinguished themselves. In his comprehensive work on church furniture Bock is eloquent on the industry of nuns. He first praises their early proficiency in the art of weaving and passes on to the art of embroidery. ' This art also,' he says, ' was chiefly cultivated in religious houses by pious nuns up to the 12th century. The inmates of women's establishments were especially devoted to working decorations for the altar. Their peaceful seclusion was spent in prayer and in doing embroidery. What work could seem worthier and nobler than artistic work intended for the decoration of the altar? It is in the nunnery that the art of design as well as the technique of weaving were brought to their highest perfection[2].'

Owing to the perishable material of this work the amount which was done of course far exceeded what has been preserved. We often come across remarks on such work, rarely across remains of it, and we are obliged to take on trust the praise bestowed by early writers as so little exists by which we can judge for ourselves. But enough remains to bear out the praise which contemporaries bestow on the beauties of hangings and vestments manufactured by nuns, and to give us the highest opinion of their industry and their artistic skill.

Among women generally embroidery has always had votaries, and in the nunnery it found a new development. During early Christian ages nuns worked large hangings for decorating the basilica walls, and short hangings for the square altar ; and when the Gothic style took the place of the earlier Byzantine in architecture,

---

[1] Wattenbach, W., *Schriftwesen im Mittelalter*, 2nd edit. 1875, p. 374.
[2] Bock, F., *Geschichte der liturg. Gewänder*, 3 vols. 1866–71, vol. 1, p. 214.

rendering such hangings superfluous, they devoted their energies to working church vestments and furniture.

The proficiency acquired by the girl in the convent was not lost if she returned to the world. We hear a good deal of badges and standards worked by ladies at baronial courts during the age of romance, and their work was no doubt influenced by what had been evolved in church decoration.

In studying the art industry of the convent, we needs must treat of work produced with the brush and the pen side by side with work produced with the needle. At two periods in history, the 8th and 13th centuries, England takes the lead in art industry, and at both periods there is reference to excellent work done by nuns.

A former chapter has mentioned how Eadburg, the friend of Boniface, was at work in her monastery in Thanet in the 8th century, transcribing scriptural writings on parchment in gold lettering, an art in which she excelled[1]. Among the gifts sent to Boniface by lady abbesses in England vestments and altar-cloths are mentioned which had without a doubt been worked in the houses over which these ladies presided if not actually made by themselves[2].

The importance and the symbolical meaning which early Christians attached to death supplies the reason why the abbess of Repton in Mercia sent a winding-sheet to St Guthlac during his lifetime[3]. Cuthberht of Lindisfarne was wrapped in a shroud which his friend Aelflaed, abbess of Whitby, had sent[4]. Both were of linen, for early Christians, who were content to wear rough woollen clothes during their lifetime, thought it permissible to be buried in linen and silk. Thus we read that Aethelthrith the abbess of Ely sent to Cuthberht a present of silk stuffs which she decorated with gold and jewels and which were shown at his resting-place at Durham till the 12th century[5]. The silk robe on which the body of Wilfrith (✝ 709) had been laid was sent as a present to an abbess Cynethrith[6].

About this time silk, which had been rarely seen north of the Alps, was frequently sent from the east and was greatly prized. It has been mentioned in a previous chapter how Radegund at Poitiers received a gift of silk from a relation in Constantinople[7], and

---

[1] Cf. above, p. 122.	[2] Cf. above, pp. 122, 132.

[3] Cf. above, p. 109.	[4] Cf. above, p. 106.

[5] Michel, F., *Étoffes de soie au moyen âge*, 1852, vol. 2, p. 339, contains this and other references.

[6] Eddi, *Vita Wilfredi*, c. 65 (it is unknown over which house she presided).

[7] Cf. above, p. 63.

among the charges brought by the turbulent Chrodield against the
abbess Leubover was that she had appropriated part of an altar-
cloth to make a robe for her niece. Caesarius of Arles in his
rule for women forbade their working embroidery except for purposes of church decoration. Repeated complaints were made
during the early ages in England against nuns for wearing embroidery and silks. The council of Cloveshoe of the year 747
censures the undue attention given to dress. 'Time shall be
devoted more to reading books and to chanting psalms than to
weaving and decorating (plectendis) clothes with various colours in
unprofitable richness[1].' But to control the standard of clothes
remained a standing difficulty in all convents, and especially in
those of women[2].

Apart from personal decoration the arts of weaving and
embroidering were encouraged in every way. 'Towards the 10th
century the art of making large hangings had so far progressed
in England,' says Bock, 'that large scenes with many figures were
represented[3].'

Inside the cloister and out of it the art flourished, and the
mention of gifts of hangings becomes frequent. Thus Ealdhelm in
his 'Praise of Virginity' (c. 7) speaks of hangings made by the
nuns, while reference is made to secular women at the time of the
Conquest who did remarkable work. Among them were Alwid
and Liwid who practised the air of embroidery and taught it[4].
Emma, otherwise Aelfgifu (†1052), after her marriage to King
Knut, made a gift of hangings and vestments to the abbey of Ely,
some of which were embroidered with gold and jewels on silk,
others of green and purple colour were of such splendour that
their like could not be found elsewhere in England[5]. Again,
Aelflaed, the wife of Edward the Confessor (†1066), made hangings
with pictures of the apostles for Frithstan of Winchester.

'We know,' says Michel in his work on silk and the use of it in
embroidery[6], 'that the women of England, long before the Conquest,
worked assiduously at weaving and embroidering, and that they
were as distinguished in this branch of art as men were in others.'
Unfortunately no specimens of the work done in religious settle-

---

[1] Haddon and Stubbs, *Councils and Ecclesiastical Documents*, 1869.
[2] Cf. above, pp. 103, 115, 198, and below, ch. 11, § 1.
[3] Bock, F., *Geschichte der liturg. Gewänder*, 1866, vol. 1, p. 142.
[4] Michel, F., *Étoffes de soie pendant le moyen âge*, 1852, vol. 2, p. 340.
[5] Wharton, *Anglia Sacra*, vol. 1, p. 607.
[6] Michel, F., *Étoffes de soie pendant le moyen âge*, 1852, vol. 2, p. 338.

ments during this early period have been preserved, so far as I am aware. We do not know what artist designed and executed the famous Bayeux tapestry which is worked in woollen cross-stitch on a strip of linen; but it was certainly not the work of nuns.

The references to weaving and embroidering during the later period are fewer, but a certain amount of the work done in England has been preserved, though the clue as to where and by whom it was done is generally wanting. While weaving and embroidery were throughout important branches of home industry, art-needle-work seems to have owed its higher development to nuns.

In connection with the prioress Christina of Mergate we hear that she had worked three mitres and several pairs of sandals in wonderful work (operis mirifici) as a present for Pope Hadrian IV (†1159), who was of English origin, and perhaps known to her. Her work was carried to Rome by the abbot of St Albans, who had affronted Hadrian in early days and wished to propitiate him; we hear that the Pope was so delighted with the work that he could not refuse the present[1].

England was, indeed, at this time famous for its embroidery, and her products were much admired abroad. In the words of Prof. Middleton:

'Another minor branch of art, in which England during the 13th century far surpassed the rest of the world, was the art of embroidering delicate pictures in silk, especially for ecclesiastical vestments. The most famous embroidered vestments now preserved in various places in Italy are the handiwork of English embroiderers between 1250 and 1300, though their authorship is not as a rule recognized by their present possessors. The embroidered miniatures on these marvellous pieces of needlework resemble closely in style the illuminations in fine Anglo-Norman manuscripts of the 13th century and in many cases have obviously been copied from manuscript miniatures[2].'

A conclusion to be possibly drawn from this is that some of the early work which has come back to this country from Italy may in reality be English. There is no doubt it is curiously like the work done in England[3]. In a footnote to the above passage Prof. Middleton points out that the Popes of the period, on sending the

---

[1] Dugdale, *Monasticon*, 'St Albans,' vol. 2, p. 186 footnote.

[2] Middleton, J. H., *Illuminated MSS.*, 1892, p. 112.

[3] For example in the South Kensington Museum, nr 594–1884, Italian chasuble; nr 1321–1864, panel of canvas, from Bock's Collection (*Descriptive Catalogue of Tapestry and Embroidery*, 1888).

pall to a newly elected English archbishop, suggested that they
would like in return embroidered vestments of English work, 'opus
anglicum,' a term at one time applied to work done in a special
style[1]. Its peculiarity seems to have consisted in the working of
figures in coloured floss silk on a piece of material, generally linen ;
on this the silk was worked in close-lying chain stitches, which,
following the contours of face and drapery, entirely covered the
material just as the strokes of a brush in a miniature cover the
parchment. The background to these figures was also covered
with coloured floss silk, but this was not worked in chain stitch but
in various styles of straight close-lying stitches in diaper pattern.
Prof. Middleton, in the passage quoted above, says that the embroiderer copied the miniature painter; in composing scenes and
arranging figures this would of course be the case. But considering
the styles of some of the backgrounds, it seems possible that in his
turn the miniature painter borrowed from the embroiderer, by
taking the idea of filling up the background to his figures with
lines and diagonal patterns, which lines and patterns had been
suggested to the embroiderer by the texture of the stuff he was
covering. Gold and silver threads were liberally used in the 'opus
anglicum[2],' and even jewels may have been introduced[3]. The general
effect was that of a shining, glossy picture, and the care and industry
needed to produce it exceeded even that required in miniatures.

The English monk Matthew Paris (†1259) describes an incident
illustrating at once the excellence of the embroidery done in
England and the rapacity of Pope Innocent IV. The Pope he
tells us was struck by the splendour of the embroidery worn by the
English clergy who came to Rome in the year 1246, and asked
where it was made. 'In England,' he was told. He replied,
'England is really a storehouse of delight; truly it is an
inexhaustible fountain, and where there is so much, much can be
taken.' And he sent letters to the abbots of the Cistercian houses
in England, ordering them to forward to him gold embroidery of

---

[1] Bock, F., *Geschichte der liturg. Gewänder*, 1866, vol. 1, p. 209, suggests that gold
plaques may have been sewn into the work.

[2] Cf. South Kensington Museum, nr 28–1892, a number of fragments of textile linen
worked over in coloured silks and gold thread with scenes taken from the life of the
Virgin. English work of the 14th century (*Descriptive Catalogue of Tapestry and
Embroidery*, 1888).

[3] Michel, F., *Étoffes de soie pendant le moyen âge*, 1852, vol. 2, p. 337, points out that
the expression 'opus anglicum' was applied also to the work of the goldsmith ; comp.
Ducange, *Glossarium*, 'Anglicum.' ' Loculus ille mirificus...argento et auro gemmisque,
anglico opere subtilitater ac pulcherrime decoratus.'

this kind, 'as though they could get it for nothing.' Curiously enough it was supplied to them by London merchants[1].

A certain number of pieces of early English embroidery now form part of the collection of art-needlework on view at South Kensington. Among them is a cope, nine feet seven by four feet eight; it is considered a splendid example of the 'opus anglicum,' and as is suggested 'may have been worked by the nuns of some convent which stood in or near Coventry[2].' There was no nunnery in Coventry in the Middle Ages, the nearest nunnery of importance would be the one at Wroxhall. 'This handsome cope,' says Dr Rock, 'so very remarkable on account of its comparative perfect preservation, is one of the most beautiful among the several liturgic vestments of the olden period anywhere to be now found in Christendom[3].' It is made of linen entirely covered with embroidery in floss silk. The space is divided up into barbed interlacing quatrefoils, of which in the present state of the cope there are fifteen. These enclose pictures representing Michael overcoming Satan, the Crucifixion, the risen Christ, Christ crowned as King, Christ in the garden, the death of the Virgin, her burial, and single figures of the apostles which are placed in the quatrefoils along the lower edge of the cope. Among them are St Philip, St Bartholomew, St Peter and St Andrew. Other pictures of the apostles are wanting, for the lower edge in some places is cut away. The faces, hands and coloured draperies of these figures are worked in coloured floss silk in the way described above, and the background of all the quatrefoils is in diaper pattern, worked in short straight stitches in a dark green colour. The spaces between the quatrefoils were filled with crimson silk which has faded to a rich brown, and in each of these spaces stands a winged angel, those nearest Christ standing on a wheel. Their faces and draperies are worked in similar style to those of the other figures, and the dividing bands which mark off the quatrefoils are worked in a variety of stitches; sometimes loose threads are laid on and sewn over, sometimes gold thread is worked in. In spite of many colours having faded the effect of the work is splendid; no textile fabric of any period exceeds it in evenness and finish, to say nothing of beauty of design.

---

[1] *Historia Major Angliae*, sub anno.

[2] South Kensington Museum, nr 83–1864 (*Descriptive Catalogue of Tapestry and Embroidery*, 1888).

[3] Ibid. p. 168.

The edge of the cope in one place is mended by cutting and sewing together. A band of embroidery which represents a succession of armorial bearings worked in small cross-stitch is carried right round it. This band is considered to be fifty years later in date than the cope, and is somewhat different in style. Its addition suggests that some accident happened to the cope, perhaps by fire, and that a piece had to be cut away and a new finish given to the edge.

At the time of the dissolution this cope was in the possession of the nuns of Sion, a house founded under peculiar circumstances as late as the 15th century. Its inmates left England in a body and carried the cope away with them in their wanderings. They finally settled at Lisbon, where the house continued to be recruited by English women. At the beginning of this century they returned to England, and the cope was acquired by the Museum authorities.

In looking at this piece of work it is distressing to think of the way in which the property of monasteries in England was appropriated, scattered, and destroyed at the dissolution. In no European country was the heirloom of mediæval art so uniformly effaced and defaced. The old inventories give some idea of the art treasures that had accumulated in monasteries in the course of centuries, but very few fragments were saved from the rapacity of Henry VIII and his agents.

From England we pass to Germany to consider the remains of decorative work done by nuns in various departments of art between the 8th and the 14th centuries. Influence from two sides gave a new direction to art-industry ; on one side was the influence of Roman art due to contact with France; on the other the influence of Byzantine art due to intercourse with the East.

A high standard of work was soon attained in France ; and at Bourges, early in the 7th century, we hear of the abbess Eustadiola making many gifts to her settlement, vases of gold and silver ornamented with jewels, crosses, candelabra and chalices. 'Also she made holy vestments,' says her biographer[1], 'and decked the altar with costly hangings which with her own hands and through the help of her women she embellished with embroidery and with gold fringes ; besides the hangings with which she decorated the walls.'

This active interest spread from France into the convents of the Low Countries during the 8th century, in one of which the sisters Harlind and Reinhild did excellent work, which is highly

---

[1] *A. SS. Boll.*, St Eustadiola, June 8. Vita, ch. 3.

praised. They were contemporaries of Boniface and Willibrord, who visited and consecrated them in their settlement at Maaseyck.

There is extant an account, written between 850 and 880, of the education they received and the work to which they were devoted[1]. We learn from this account that Harlind and Reinhild showed a serious disposition at a youthful age, and that their parents were persuaded to send them to the religious house for women at Valenciennes on the river Schelde, where, in the words of the 9th century writer, 'they were instructed in reading, in chanting (modulatione), in singing the psalms and also in what now-a-days is deemed wonderful, in writing and in painting (scribendo atque pingendo), a task laborious even to men. Likewise they were carefully trained in every department of work such as is done by women's hands, in various designs, in different styles; so that they attained a high standard of excellence in spinning, weaving, designing, sewing, and embroidering with gold and jewels on silk[1].'

When their education was finished the girls returned to their parents, but they found no scope for their energies at home and decided to devote themselves to religion. Their parents agreed to found a settlement for them at Maaseyck, where at first they had twelve women with them. But many noble as well as free-born girls placed a black veil on their heads, as the biographer says, and came to them hoping to be taken into the settlement.

We hardly need to be told that these gifted sisters abhorred idleness and were devoted to work. Their energies were given to weaving, embroidering and writing. Among other things they had woven with their own hands short curtains, intended no doubt for the altar, which were splendidly embroidered with a variety of designs[2]. These, in the words of their biographer, 'the holy women embroidered with God and his saints ornate with gold and jewels, and left them behind them in their house. The four gospels, which contain the words and actions of Jesus Christ our Lord, they transcribed with commendable zeal. Likewise a book of psalms, such as we call a psalter, they worked (stylo texuerunt), as well as many other holy writings, which to this day remain in that same place, and are resplendent in new and shining gold, and glowing

---

[1] *A. SS. Boll.*, SS. Herlindis et Renild, March 22, ch. 5 (videlicet nendo et texendo, creando ac suendo, in auro quoque ac margaritis in serico componendo).

[2] Ibid. ch. 12 (palliola...multis modis variisque compositionibus diversae artis innumerabilibus ornamentis).

with jewels, so that the work might almost have been done to-day.'

Thus writes the 9th century chronicler. It seems from a remark made by Stadler that some of the vestments they made were sent as a present to Boniface, and samples of their work, it is not stated of what kind, are preserved to this day in the little church of Maaseyck[1].

A previous chapter has dealt with the rapid development of women's houses in Saxony in the 10th and 11th centuries. References to the encouragement of art in these convents are numerous; they became storehouses of wealth, partly through gifts bestowed on them by their abbesses and partly owing to the industry of the nuns. The marriage of Otto II with a Greek princess brought Greek decorative work into fashion, and workmen came from Greece into Germany, where they were patronised by bishops and lady abbesses.

Thus at Essen, one of the great Saxon abbacies for women, the art treasury to this day contains the celebrated bronze candelabra made at the command of the abbess Mathilde († 1011)[2], and a golden crucifix of Greek workmanship of great beauty which, as its inscription says, was the gift of the abbess Theofanu (1039–1054)[3]. This abbess was the granddaughter of Otto II and his Greek wife, and her appointment to the abbacy marks a great advance in the prosperity of the house. The treasury at Essen also contains a Bible cover carved in ivory, which represents the abbess Theofanu depositing a book at the feet of the Virgin[4].

An account of the great power and wealth of the abbey at Quedlinburg has already been given. Its treasury (zither) still contains many interesting specimens of early art industry collected in the days of its prosperity[5]. The splendid cloak worked with figures from the Apocalypse belonging to Otto III was probably made under the direction of his aunt Mathilde, abbess of Quedlinburg († 999). Somewhat later we hear of another sumptuous cloak which the Empress Kunigund († 1040) had made for her husband Heinrich II, and of the wonderful embroidery done in gold on purple by Heinrich's sister Gisela († 1037), the wife of Stephen, king of Hungary,

---

[1] Stadler and Heim, *Vollständiges Heiligenlexicon*, 1858, 'Harlindis.'

[2] *Zeitschrift für Christl. Archaeologie*, edit. Schnuetgen, 1856, 'Münsterkirche in Essen,' 1860, Beiträge.

[3] Labarte, *Arts industriels au moyen âge*, 1872, vol. 1, p. 341.

[4] Ibid. vol. 1, p. 84.

[5] Fritsch, *Geschichte des Reichstifts Quedlinburg*, 1828, vol. 2, p. 326.

which seems to have been embroidered in imitation of a painting on stuff preserved at a Benedictine convent near Raab. To the present day this embroidery forms part of the Hungarian coronation robes[1]. It is not directly stated where this work was made, but the general excellence of the work done by nuns[2], and the connection of Saxon princesses with convents, suggest the possibility that the work was done in convents.

One of these Saxon princesses, Hedwig († 994), sister of the abbess Gerberg and duchess of Swabia, gave the monks of St Gallen some vestments which she had embroidered herself[3]. Among them was a white stole (stola) on which were worked in gold a series of pictures representing the 'Marriage of Philology to Mercury,' a subject taken from a story by Martianus Capella, a writer of the 5th century, whose works were much read in nunneries. The story was afterwards translated into German by Notker († 1022), a monk of St Gallen.

A peculiar interest attaches to Agnes, abbess of Quedlinburg (1184–1203). She encouraged art industry in all its branches and under her the nuns made large curtains for church decoration. Some of these are still in existence, and Kugler, the art student, considers them as of great value in the study of the art industry of that period. Agnes herself wrote an account of the property she bequeathed to the monastery, and in it she mentions a golden cup, several silken covers (dorsalia), and hangings[4]. Her chronicler credits her with writing and illuminating with her own hands books for divine service; and a copy of the gospels, said to have been written by her, is still preserved[5]. But the great work of her life was the manufacture of wall-hangings, which she and her nuns worked together. One set was intended for the Pope, but was never forwarded to him. Like the vestments made by Hedwig, the subject taken for them was the 'Marriage of Philology to Mercury.'

One curtain still exists measuring twenty-four feet by twenty; it is of a coarse woollen material, into which large figures are woven, which Kugler thinks must have been designed by two different

---

[1] Bock, F., *Geschichte der liturg. Gewänder,* 1866, vol. 1, p. 155.

[2] Schultz, A., *Höfisches Leben zur Zeit der Minnesinger,* 1889, cites many passages from the epics which refer to embroidery worn by heroes and heroines. A piece of work of special beauty described vol. 1, p. 326, had been made by an apostate nun.

[3] Ekkehard IV., c. 10, in Pertz, *Mon. Germ. Scriptores,* vol. 2, p. 123.

[4] Erath, *Codex diplom. Quedliburg.,* 1764, p. 109.

[5] Brunner, S., *Kunstgenossen der Klosterzelle,* 1863, vol. 2, p. 555.

hands. 'While some of the work,' he says[1], 'is in no way superior to other pictorial representations of the time, and only here and there in details shows superior skill, other parts though retaining the peculiar style of Byzantine art, show a grace and dignity in the arrangement of the figures, and a perfection in the drawing of drapery, which in works of such an early period arouse admiration in the beholder.' In his handbook on painting Kugler further says that we probably have in them the nearest approach of the art of the time to full perfection.

In describing the curtain he tells us of a manly bearded figure with raised hand, probably intended for the writer Martianus himself; near him stands Mercury half covered by a well-draped toga, a very youthful figure in accordance with the author's description. These and other figures hold scrolls on which their names are woven, but owing to the worn state of the hanging some of the names are gone and some are illegible. Three female figures are designated as 'Manticen,'—whom Mercury would have married had she not preferred Apollo; 'Sichem,'—a name standing for Psyche, whom Cupid had already enticed away according to Martianus; and 'Sophia,'—whom Mercury likewise desired to marry but in vain. All these figures are described by Kugler as splendid, especially that of 'Sichem' whose pose and drapery he pronounces most beautiful.

A crowned figure of a man comes next, with a scroll bearing the words 'happy in wealth' (qua felix copia talis), whom Kugler supposes to be Hymenaeus, and a man and woman joining hands, who are designated as Mercury and Philology. Similar allegorical figures fill the other parts of the curtain. In Kugler's estimation the figures of 'Prudentia' and 'Fortitudo' are strikingly grand; while others, 'Justitia,' 'Temperantia,' and 'Philologia' with her mother 'Pronesis,' are of inferior design.

There is another set of hangings preserved at Halberstadt, which, if the remark of an early chronicler may be believed, was also the work of the abbess Agnes and her nuns[2]. Kugler however, apparently unacquainted with this statement, places these hangings at a somewhat earlier date, since they are of less finished workmanship, but he admits that 'in spite of their faded colours and their roughness of design, a certain severe dignity cannot be

[1] Kugler, F., *Kleine Schriften*, 1853, vol. 1, pp. 635 ff.; part of the hanging is given by Muentz, E., *Tapisseries, broderies et dentelles*, 1890, plate 2.

[2] Fritsch, *Geschichte des Reichstifts Quedlinburg*, 1828, vol. 1, p. 121.

denied to these figures which with wide-open eyes stare at the beholder[1].'

We have a description of these curtains from Büsching, who travelled in quest of monastic treasures in the beginning of this century[2]. They measure three-and-a-half by fifteen feet. On the centre piece a king (God?) is represented on a throne, with one hand raised, the other holding a sceptre; Cato and Seneca, each bearing a written scroll, sit on either side. Next to them come six apostles, sitting two and two under a canopy, each bearing a scroll with his name—another instance of how readily art in the 12th century grouped together figures of Christian and classical origin, where it was an object to unite the conceptions of religion and philosophy; then Christ, pictured under a rainbow arch, which is supported by angels. On Christ's further side come the other six apostles similarly arranged, and then follow scenes illustrating Old Testament history, such as Jacob's dream; Abraham visited by angels; the sacrifice of Isaac;—in these scenes the figures are comparatively small and of inferior design to the larger ones. Judging from Büsching's description, the style of the tapestry is the same as that of the manuscript illustrations of the time. The background is uniformly of one colour, and the contours of the figures and their draperies are in thick brown outline, the intervening spaces being filled with different colours. Kugler compares the pictorial effect of these hangings with that of the miniatures contemporaneously painted in the abbey of Hohenburg under the abbess Herrad, of whose work we shall speak presently. They recall the dignified and somewhat sombre character of Byzantine art.

There is plenty of information from the Continent to show that nuns belonging to houses of different religious orders were equally industrious at the loom and with the needle.

Thus at Göss, formerly a Benedictine nunnery near Loeben in Steier, the church still treasures a complete set of vestments, 'ornatus integer,' worked by the nuns between 1275 and 1300 during the rule of 'abbatissa Chunegundis.' Bock describes them as most curious and beautiful, worked on linen with coloured silks in a design of fantastic animals and flowers[3].

Again at Wienhausen near Celle several ancient wall-hangings are preserved which were woven by the nuns of the Cistercian settlement there, and show their industry and skill, and the readi-

[1] Kugler, F., *Kleine Schriften*, 1853, vol. 1, p. 540.

[2] Büsching, F. G., *Reise durch einige Münsterkirchen*, 1819, p. 235.

[3] Bock, F., *Geschichte der liturg. Gewänder*, 1866, vol. 1, p. 227.

ness with which secular subjects were treated in the convent. On one which dates from the 14th century the story of Tristan and Isold is represented; on another hunting scenes; and on a third the figures of the prophets[1].

At Heiningen near Wolfenbüttel, a house of Austin nuns, the inmates wove hangings with allegorical figures which are still in existence. At Lüne, Wende, Erfurt and at the Cistercian house of Ebsdorf wall-hangings were made which are still preserved, and show the ability of the nuns who worked at the loom between the 13th and 15th centuries[2]. We are indebted to Bock for a comprehensive treatise on church decoration and vestments. He also made a large collection of specimens of such work, but it has apparently been scattered. Some part of it has been acquired by the authorities at the South Kensington Museum where it is at present on view.

From these examples of art-needlework and tapestry, we must turn to the art of writing and decorating books. We hear of a woman calligraphist in connection with one of the ancient monasteries in Bavaria, the fame of whose industry was carried on through centuries[3]. The monastery of Wessobrunn had been founded in the 8th century; it included a community of nuns as well as of monks, the dwelling allotted to the nuns being spoken of as the Parthenon, a term sometimes applied to a religious house for women in these districts. In the words of the monkish historian who wrote about 1513: 'the dwellings of the monks were where they are now, but those of the nuns where the parish church now stands.' Here between the years 1057 and 1130 Diemud the nun was active as a scribe, the amount of whose work in the estimation of many 'exceeded what could be done by several men.' She had become a professed nun at an early age and 'was most skilful in the art of writing; for while she is not known to have composed any work of her own, yet she wrote with her own hand many volumes in a most beautiful and legible character both for divine service and for the library of the monastery, which volumes are enumerated in a list written by herself in a certain *plenarius.*' This list which is extant includes works to the number of forty-five, which were highly prized during the nun's lifetime and had a considerable market value. We find in the list 'a Missal with Gradual

---

[1] Bock, F., *Geschichte der liturg. Gewänder*, 1866, vol. 3, pp. 201 ff.

[2] Ibid. 1866, vol. 3, p. 202.

[3] Hefner, *Oberbair. Archiv*, 1830, vol. 1, p. 355.

and Sequences' given to the bishop of Trier, and a 'book of Offices with the Baptismal Service,' given to the bishop of Augsburg. A 'bibliotheca,' that is, a Bible, in two volumes, written by Diemud, was given by the monastery of Wessobrunn in exchange for an estate at Peissenburg. Besides these works the list mentions another Bible in three volumes, books containing the gospels and lessons, writings of Gregory and Augustine, and the Ecclesiastical History of Eusebius. In course of time these books were scattered, lists of those which remained at Wessobrunn being made from time to time. At the sequestration of the monastery at the beginning of the 19th century only fifteen volumes written by Diemud remained, which were taken to Munich. They are said to be of rare beauty, distinguished by highly ornate initial letters and by small writing which is most elegant[1]. An example of this writing was reproduced by Hefner in the hope that it might lead to the identification of other books written by Diemud which may have found their way into other libraries and be still in existence.

Contemporaneously with Diemud we find another Bavarian nun, Leukardis, active as a scribe at Mallersdorf; she is said to have been of Scottish origin and she knew Scotch (or Irish?), Greek, Latin, and German, and did so much good work that the monk Laiupold, who was also devoted to writing, established an anniversary in her memory[2].

The nuns of Admunt in Bavaria are also spoken of as devoted to transcribing, and Wattenbach comments on the neat and elegant way in which they mended the parchment leaves of their manuscripts with coloured silken thread[3].

Again a manuscript written for Marbach about the year 1149 by Gutta von Schwarzenthan is described as splendid. It contains the martyrology of Usuard, the Rule of St Augustine with the comments of Hugo of St Victor, the constitutions of Marbach and a homily for every day in the year[4]. We hear of Emo, abbot of Wittewierum (1204–34), a Premonstrant house which contained men and women, that 'not only did he zealously encourage his canons (clericis) to write, acting as their instructor, but taking count of the diligence of the female sex he set women who were clever at writing to practise the art assiduously[5].' Wattenbach

---

[1] Westermayer in *Allgemeine Deutsche Biog.*, article 'Diemud'; *Catalogus Cod. Lat. Bibliothecae Reg. Monac.*, vol. 7, 1881, nrs 140, 146—154.

[2] Wattenbach, W., *Schriftwesen im Mittelalter*, 2nd edit. 1875, p. 374.

[3] Ibid. p. 177.   [4] Ibid. p. 304.   [5] Ibid. p. 374.

considers that nuns were especially clever in copying books for choir use, and in decorating them.

These notices must suffice. They prove that women leading cloistered lives took an active interest in art-industry in all its branches and that productiveness in their houses was controlled by the same causes which led to the development and decay of art-industry in the houses of men. Excellent work was done in Benedictine houses during early Christian times, that is between the 8th and the 11th centuries; the revival of monastic life in the Middle Ages gave a new impulse to art-industry and the highest degree of excellence was reached in the first half of the 14th century. After that there are signs of a steadily accelerated decline. The reason of this, as a later chapter will show, lies chiefly in the changed conditions of life outside the convent, which made it easier for artisans in the townships to practise those arts and crafts which had hitherto been practised in religious settlements. Writing, decorating, and book-binding[1], as well as weaving and embroidering[2], were taken up by secular workers and were practised by them on a far larger scale; the spread of education in lay circles and the greater luxury in home surroundings having created a new taste and a new market for artistic productions. The taste of this wider public naturally influenced the character of the work which was produced; cheapness and splendour, if possible the combination of the two, were the qualities chiefly aimed at. These are valuable qualities no doubt in their way, but insistence on them had a discouraging effect on the productiveness of the convent. During the 14th and 15th centuries convents gave up their artistic pursuits. The self-denying industry and unobtrusive earnestness which set the stamp of excellence on the productions of the old hand-worker were no more, for the spirit which looked upon the production of things beautiful as a matter of religion had died out.

§ 2. Herrad and the 'Garden of Delights.'

A work produced at Hohenburg, a nunnery in Elsass, in the 12th century confirms the belief that given favourable conditions it is possible for women to produce good work and to help to accumulate knowledge. Herrad, the abbess of this house, conceived

---

[1] Middleton, J. H., *Illuminated MSS.*, 1892, p. 216.
[2] Michel, F., *Étoffes de soie pendant le moyen âge*, 1852, vol. 2, p. 350.

the idea of compiling for the use of her nuns an encyclopædic work which should embody, in pictures and in words, the knowledge of her age. The importance of this work has long survived the attainment of its original purpose, for with its hundreds of illustrations and its copious text it has afforded a wealth of information on the customs, manners, conceptions and mode of life of the 12th century, to which many students of archæology, art and philology have gone for instruction and for the illustration of their own books. 'Few illuminated manuscripts had acquired a fame so well deserved as the "Garden of Delights," the *Hortus Deliciarum*, of Herrad,' says the editor of the great collection of reproductions of the pictures which illustrated her work[1]. For the work itself is no more. The MS. was destroyed in the fire which broke out in the library of Strasburg when that city was bombarded by the Germans in 1870, and with it perished a complete copy of the text. Our knowledge of the work is therefore limited to the remarks of those who had studied it and to those portions of it which had been copied or transcribed previous to its destruction. The 'Society for the Preservation of the Monuments of Elsass' is at present collecting and publishing a reproduction of all existing tracings and copies of the pictures or of parts of them, and this collection already numbers nearly two hundred. They are mere fragments of course of the work itself, and yet they are of the highest interest. For Herrad's 'Garden of Delights' with its apt illustrations gave a complete picture of life in its domestic and out-of-door aspects as it presented itself in the 12th century. It showed what conceptions and ideas were then attractive to nuns and their estimation of knowledge, and it has given greater insight than any other production into the talents, the enthusiasm and the industry which were found at this period in a nunnery.

The religious settlement at Hohenburg[2] was an ancient foundation situated on the flat summit of a spur of the Vosges mountains, which here rise abruptly to a height of over two thousand five hundred feet from the wide expanse of the valley of the Rhine below. The wooded heights on either side of the Rhine were the favourite haunts of missionaries in early times, who settled there and appropriated sites in close proximity to the castles or strongholds of the landed gentry. At one time there were as many as

---

[1] *Reproductions par la Société pour la conservation des monuments de l'Alsace*, Sept livraisons containing Plates 1–53 inclusive (till 1895).

[2] Silbermann, J. A., *Beschreibung von Hohenburg*, 1781.

sixty religious settlements in the Rhine valley between Basel and
Mainz and over a hundred castles or burgs. The nunnery of
Hohenburg was of high rank among these religious settlements
owing to its extensive property and to its commanding situation.
The summit of the hill was surrounded by an ancient wall dating
from pre-Christian times which is still known as the heathen wall;
it enclosed a wide clearance of fields and meadows, and the
numerous buildings of the convent settlement. This height was
the goal of numerous pilgrimages and had various associations
dating from heathen times. It is at the present day a favourite
health resort on account of its aspect and romantic surroundings.

From historical information recently collected by Roth[1] we
gather that a religious settlement of women existed on the Hohenburg as early as the 9th century. Judith, the wife of Ludwig the
Pious (†840), took some interest in it. Legendary lore has spun
many webs about the religious settlements in the Rhine district including that of Hohenburg, and the majority of modern historians
have taken no trouble to unravel them. Legend[2] tells us that a holy
maiden St Odilia fled from the persecution of a cruel father and came
to the Hohenburg, where she settled and gathered many women about
her. Various stories more or less fanciful are told of her. She was
cured of blindness and baptized by Archbishop Hildulf of Trier and
Bishop Erhard of Regensburg—who are unknown to history; she
was carried down the river in a chest and educated at the convent
of Beaume or Palma; and she has been given as a relative to St
Leodgar bishop of Autun (†678) and as a daughter to Eticho duke
of the Allemanni. Besides these stories we find the name Odilia
locally associated with a cave, a well, three linden-trees and a stone
of peculiar shape which are obviously heathen survivals, and
encourage the view that Odilia is the representative of some pre-
Christian divinity. Roth has shown that the name Odilia is
nowhere on record in these districts before the 10th century, and
it occurs in connection with Hohenburg only in the 11th century,
that is three or four hundred years after the saint's reputed foundation of the house. When Pope Leo IX (1048–1054), who was an
Alsatian, visited his home he was presented with a rhymed
'responsarium' on the local saints of the district. Among them
was Odilia, who at that time was directly associated with the
nunnery. A hundred years later when the convent was better

[1] Roth, K. L., 'Der Odilienberg' in *Alsatia*, 1856, vol. 1, pp. 91 ff.
[2] Comp. above, pp. 22, 24.

known through the influence and activity of its abbesses Relind and Herrad, St Odilia was looked upon as the daughter of Duke Eticho and the founder of the house—this will be shown from pictures preserved in Herrad's work.   But evidently this abbess had no knowledge of the saint's blindness and sufferings, nor of her connection with St Leodgar and other prelates, which are all described in her legend written another hundred years later.

In the year 1154 Relind[1], abbess of Berg, a nunnery near Neuburg on the Danube, was appointed abbess at Hohenburg in accordance with the wish, it is said, of the emperor Friedrich Barbarossa (1152–1190).   Her influence was most beneficial; many daughters of the surrounding gentry came to study under her, and among them Herrad of the family of Landsperg.   The term nun must be applied to these women with a reservation; some writers speak of them as Austin canonesses on account of the liberties they enjoyed.   In Herrad's 'Garden' the picture of her nuns represents them wearing clothes that differ little from those worn by women in other walks of life.   Their dresses are of different colours, their cloaks are generally brown, and their veils are always brilliantly coloured, some red, some purple[2].   The only detail of dress which they have in common is a white turban or head-dress, over which the veil is thrown.   They wear no wimples.   The establishment of the house under Herrad's rule consisted of forty-seven nuns and thirteen novices (or lay sisters?) who are represented as wearing clothes similar to those of the nuns.

Herrad's admission to the house furthered its prosperity in every way, for besides literary and artistic abilities she had considerable powers of management.   She succeeded Relind as abbess in 1167, and in 1181 she founded a settlement of Austin canons at Truttenhausen, and later another at St Gorgon, both of which are situated not far below the summit of the hill.   The canons of these settlements took it in turn to read mass in the women's chapel.   Roth speaks of other improvements which Herrad carried out with the help of her diocesan, the bishop of Strasburg.

The consecration of a church at Niedermünster, situated below the Hohenburg, also falls within the term of Herrad's rule.   A second nunnery was founded there as a dependency, which was separated from the parent house probably during Herrad's lifetime,

---

[1] Wiegand, in *Allgemeine Deutsche Biographie*, article 'Relind.'

[2] It is possible but hardly probable that the miniaturist in colouring the picture gave free play to his fancy.

owing to the efforts of the abbess Edelind (1195–1200), who according to Gérard was also of the family of Landsperg[1]. The claim of this abbess to the attention of posterity rests on her having been the possessor of a still extant chased case several feet high, which she had made to hold a fragment of the Holy Cross which a camel was alleged to have brought to Niedermünster of its own accord in the time of Karl the Great. This case is covered with many figures worked in relief and is praised by art students as a curious example of early metal work[2].

The history of Hohenburg and Niedermünster in the sequel offers much that is interesting. For while the nuns at Niedermünster accepted the rule of St Benedict, the nuns on the Hohenburg persisted in their independent course. At Niedermünster a stone monument is still to be seen which experts declare to be 13th century work, and which gives a clue to the association of St Odilia with Leodgar, to whom the church at Niedermünster was dedicated. Three sides of this monument are covered with figures. On one stands St Leodgar ; on the next St Odilia with long tresses, and Duke Eticho ; on the third the Virgin, also with long tresses, and below her the abbesses Relind and Herrad holding a book. Both these abbesses are designated by name, and wear convent garb and wimples utterly different from the clothes worn by them in the pictures of Herrad's book[3].

From these general remarks we turn to the great work of Herrad's life, to which she herself gave the title of the 'Garden of Delights.' It consisted of 324 parchment leaves of folio size, which contained an account of the history of the world founded on the Biblical narrative, with many digressions into the realm of philosophy, moral speculation, and contemporary knowledge—and with numerous pictures in illustration of it.

The book was so arranged that the pictures stood alongside of the text ; and the pages of the work which were devoted to illustrations were in most cases divided into three sections by lines across, so that the pictures stood one above the other. The figures in each picture were about four inches high. There were, however, a certain number of full-page illustrations with larger figures, and it is among these that the greatest proofs are given of Herrad's imaginative powers and the range of her intellectual abilities.

---

[1] Gérard, Ch., *Les artistes de l'Alsace*, 1872, p. 92.

[2] Ibid. ; Engelhardt, *Herrad von Landsperg und ihr Werk*, 1818, p. 16, footnote.

[3] The monument is represented in Schoepflin, *Alsatia Illustrata*, 1751, vol. 1, ad pag. 797.

Engelhardt, to whom we are indebted for the fullest description of the ' Garden of Delights,' made tracings of a number of pictures and copied their colouring[1]. He comments on the brilliant smoothness and finish of the original miniature paintings. Only the silver, he says, was tarnished ; the gold was undimmed and all the colours preserved their full brilliancy, when he had the work before him in the early part of this century. According to him the method of painting was as follows. First the figures were drawn in dark outline, then the colouring was filled in bit by bit ; shadows and high lights were next laid on, and then the dark outlines were again gone over.

The question has naturally arisen whether Herrad did the whole of the work herself. The text which stood at the beginning and at the end of it referred to her as its sole author. Students are generally agreed that the outline drawing and the writing were entirely her work, but the colours may or may not have been laid on by her. For the work was wonderfully complete in plan and execution—the conception of one mind, which laboured with unceasing perseverance to realize the conception it had formed.

The style in which the pictures were drawn has likewise been the occasion of much comment. We are here on the border-land between the conventional Byzantine and the realistic Gothic styles. ' We see very clearly,' says Woltman[2], ' how the new ideas which scholastic learning and poetry had generated required new modes of expression, and led to conceptions for which the older art yielded no models and which had to be taken from real life.' In most cases Herrad no doubt had a model before her and adhered to the traditional rendering, but where the model was wanting she may have drawn on her powers of imagination and supplied details from her surroundings. Thus incidents of Biblical history are represented by her in a manner familiar to the student of early Christian art. A grave and serious dignity which recalls the wall mosaics at Ravenna characterizes the figures of God, Christ, Mary, and the angels; Engelhardt has pointed out the close similarity of Herrad's picture of the Annunciation to that contained in a Greek MS. of the 9th century[3]. But in other cases Herrad either composed herself or else drew from models which were nearer to her in time and place.

---

[1] Engelhardt, *Herrad von Landsperg und ihr Werk*, 1818, with sheets of illustrations, which in a few copies are coloured.

[2] Woltman, in *Allgemeine Deutsche Biographie*, article ' Herrad.'

[3] Engelhardt, *Herrad von Landsperg und ihr Werk*, 1818, Vorwort p. xi.

Thus the picture of the sun-god Apollo represents him in a heavy mediaeval cart drawn by four horses, and the men and women in many pictures are dressed in the fashion of the time. The pictures drawn from real life especially delight the archæological student. A water-mill grinding corn, men at the plough, soldiers on the march and fighting, are drawn with minute exactness and with considerable skill. Some of these scenes are powerfully realistic in spite of a certain awkwardness in the figures; for example, that of a traveller who is waylaid by robbers, coupled with the story of the good Samaritan, which is illustrated by à series of pictures. In the first of these a man is depicted lying by the roadside; in the second we see him on a horse which is led by the Samaritan, and in the third he has arrived at the inn and is being lifted down from the horse.

Herrad executed her work between 1160 and 1170, but additional entries were made as late as 1190. This period falls in the reign of the emperor Friedrich Barbarossa (1152–1190), which followed upon that of the luckless Konrad III, and was one of comparative quiet and prosperity in Germany. The power of the Pope had passed its climax, there was schism in the Papacy, which was greatly aggravated by the line of conduct Friedrich adopted, but the scene of their struggle had shifted to the cities of northern Italy. We shall see later on that political changes were watched with much interest in some nunneries, and that the conduct of the Emperor, the Pope, and the bishops was keenly criticised among nuns. It is difficult to tell how far events affected Herrad. The prose narrative which her work contained, as far as we know, has perished and we have no definite clue to her interpretation of contemporary affairs, but probably she was content to devote her energies to rearranging and interpreting the intellectual wealth of the age without entering into party conflicts. The illustrations of the 'Garden of Delights' which have been preserved are invaluable for the study of contemporary life, but they contain no information as to contemporary events.

The study and enjoyment of the work in its original form were facilitated by the addition to the picture of the name of every person and every implement in Latin or in German, sometimes in both; and in many cases an explanatory sentence or a moral maxim was introduced into the picture, so that the nun who studied the work naturally picked up Latin words and sentences. Through the industry of Engelhardt all these sentences and words have been preserved, and the coupling of implements with their names forms a valuable addition to our knowledge of terms as applied in early mediaeval times. The book also originally contained a continuous history in Latin for more advanced students, but unfortunately that is lost. Engelhardt says that it described the history of the world from the Creation to the coming of Antichrist, with many extracts from various writers. He enumerates twenty writers from whose works Herrad quotes. Among them are Eusebius Pamphili († c. 350), Jerome († 420), Isidor of Seville († 636), Bede († 735), Frechulf († 838), and others who were her contemporaries, such as Petrus Lombardus († 1164) and Petrus Comestor († 1198). When quoting from secular writers the abbess invariably made mention of the fact. In one instance she remarked that 'all these things have been described by philosophers by aid of their worldly wisdom (per mundanam sapientiam), but this was the product of the Holy Spirit also.'

The attitude which Herrad assumed towards learning generally can be studied in the pictures which deal with abstract conceptions. They are usually of folio size and contain illustrations which are instructive to the student of mediaeval scholasticism. Two pictures introduced into the history of the Tower of Babel which illustrate the falling away from true faith deserve especial attention. The one is a representation of the 'Nine Muses'; on it female heads of quaint dignity in medallions are arranged in a circle. The other represents the 'Seven Liberal Arts,' in accordance with the mediaeval interpretation of the teaching of Aristotle[1]. On it Philosophy, a female figure, is seated in the centre of the picture wearing a crown with three heads. These heads are designated as 'ethica, logica, phisica'; by means of these three branches of learning philosophy adds to her powers of insight. Socrates and Plato, who are designated as 'philosophers,' sit below, and from the figure of Philosophy 'seven streams of wisdom flow which are turned into liberal arts' as the text explains. These arts are personified as female figures in 12th century dress, and are so arranged that each figure stands in a separate division forming a circle round Philosophy and the philosophers. The Liberal Arts are robed in different colours, and each holds an emblem of her power. 'Grammar,' dressed in dark red, has a book and a birch rod; 'Geometry,' in light red, has a measuring rod and a compass; 'Arithmetic,' in light blue, holds a string of alternate white and black beads; 'Music,' dressed in

---

[1] Cf. above, p. 180.

purple, has a lyre, a zither and a hurdy-gurdy; 'Astronomy,' in dark green, holds a measure and looks up at the stars; 'Rhetoric,' in dark blue, has a stilus and a writing-tablet (tabula); and 'Dialectic,' in light green, holds the head of a howling dog. Each figure is encircled by a sentence explaining the special nature of her power. In the lower part of the picture are four men, seated at desks, with books, pens and penknives, engaged in reading and writing. These are the 'poets or magi, who are filled with a worldly spirit'; black birds appear to be whispering in their ears.

The whole of this picture is doubtless traditional; its admission into the work shows that Herrad's conception of 'profane' learning was one of distinct appreciation. The idea conveyed by means of the pictures to the young women students was by no means superficial or derogatory to learning. On the contrary, we see them under the influence of a teacher through whom their respectful attitude towards the means and modes of knowledge was assured.

Another picture of folio size, called 'The Ladder to Perfection,' shows that Herrad accepted a critical attitude towards the members of religion. A ladder is drawn diagonally across the page and a number of figures are seen ascending it on their way towards heaven. The highest rung has been reached by Christian love (Caritas) personified as a woman to whom a crown is proffered from heaven. Below her stand the representatives of different branches of the religious profession and laymen arranged in order of excellence, and with each is given a picture of the temptation which prevents him from ascending further up the ladder. Among these the hermit (heremita) stands highest, but he is held back by the charms of his garden. Below him stands the recluse (inclusus), whose temptation is slothfulness, which is represented by a bed. Then comes the monk (monachus), who leans towards a mass of gold; 'he is typical of all false monks,' says Herrad, 'whose heart is drawn from duties by the sight of money, and who cannot rise above greed.' The nun (sanctimonialis) and the cleric (clericus) have reached the same rung on the ladder. She is the representative of false nuns who yield to the temptation of persuasion and gifts, and return to their parents, never attaining the crown of life; he is drawn away by the allurements of the table, and by a woman (amica) who stands below. There are also figures of a lay woman and a soldier who are respectively attracted by the charms of a city and of war.

They are absorbed by vanities, and we are told 'rarely reach the crown of life through contemplation.' The picture is further crowded with demons who are attacking and angels who are defending the people on the ladder. The devil lurks below in the form of a dragon ready to seize upon those who fall.

In further illustration of Herrad's attitude towards the clergy, Engelhardt cites a passage from her work in which she severely censures the customs which the clergy tolerate in church on festal days. In company with laymen and loose women they eat and drink, and indulge in jokes and games which invariably end in uproariousness. 'How worthy of praise,' she exclaims, 'if the spiritual princes of the Church (principes ecclesiae spirituales) restored the evangelical teaching of early times in the place of such customs[1].'

From these general remarks we turn to the pictures which illustrate the Biblical narrative in a number of scenes containing a store of imagery and a wealth of design. We cannot but admire the ready brush of the abbess and the courage with which she grappled with difficulties, drawing with equal skill human figures and divine personifications, dramatic incidents and allegorical combinations.

The pictures which illustrated the Creation were led up to by a number of diagrams and digressions on astronomy and geography, with lists of technical terms in Latin and their German equivalents. Among these was a picture of the signs of the zodiac and a 'computus' or table for determining the festal days of the year. The desire to fix the date of incidents of Old and New Testament history absorbed much attention at this period, and Herrad's table of computation was looked upon as so important that it was recently used by Piper as the starting-point for an investigation on the Calendar generally[2]. In Herrad's table the date of Easter was worked out for a cycle of 532 years, that is from 1175 till 1706; leap-years were marked, and the day of the week on which Christmas fell was given for the whole period.

The history of the Biblical narrative opens with a picture illustrating the creation of the animals. The lion, the elephant, the unicorn and the giraffe are most fantastic, but the ox, the ass, the horse, the domestic fowl, the sylvan animals of northern latitudes,

---

[1] Engelhardt, *Herrad von Landsperg und ihr Werk*, 1818, p. 104.
[2] Piper, F., *Kalendarien und Martyrologien der Angelsachsen*, 1862.

and fish, are drawn with tolerable correctness.   God is represented in classical robes moving slowly across a wave of the waters.   In another picture He is depicted in a simpler manner seated and fashioning the small figure of Adam, which He holds between His knees.   Again He is seen breathing life into Adam's nostrils, and then holding in His hand a rib out of which projects the head of Eve, while Adam is lying asleep on the ground.   There is a series of pictures illustrating the temptation and expulsion from Paradise.   A full-sized one gives the Tree of Life, which has many ramifications out of which human faces are peeping.   Adam and Eve are throughout pictured as of the same height and are several times drawn in the nude.   There is a very graceful picture in which Adam is seen delving while Eve spins.

Poems on the First Man and on the Fall accompanied by musical notation are here introduced.   The poems are preserved, the music is apparently lost ; it is not stated whether Herrad wrote the music herself.

The story of Noah and his sleeping in the vineyard, and the building of the Tower of Babel, are illustrated by scenes details of which are presumably drawn from real life.   Here we see wooden vats and buckets, the various implements used in the vintage, pictures of masons at work dressed in short kirtles, and the various implements and arrangements for building.

After the pictures on secular learning above referred to the thread of Biblical narrative is resumed, and there are many scenes from the lives of the patriarchs, such as Jacob giving his blessing, a picture of Jacob's dream, Pharaoh seated on his throne with sumptuous surroundings, and the passage over the Red Sea, in which the soldiers are clad in chain-mail and march with standards borne aloft.   Soldiers similarly accoutred are drawn in one picture fighting under the leadership of Joshua ; in another picture they are seen attacking a city, a scene taken from the story of the assault of Dan.   The adoration of the golden calf gave occasion for a picture which also illustrates contemporary manners.   Men and women dressed in the costume of the day are seen joining hands in a ring and dancing round the idol.   We also have pictures of the Holy Ark and of the Tabernacle ; the seven-branched candlestick is most elaborately drawn, and the twelve tribes of Israel are grouped in medallions around it.

The next remarkable picture is the burial of Moses.   In a solitary rocky surrounding God lays the patriarch in his grave, while a demon holds him by the legs and is pushed away by an angel. The demon was obviously a living reality to Herrad, and he frequently appears in her pictures with his wide mouth, long nose, pointed ears and green-coloured body, a figure grotesque rather than terrible. When the moment of death is represented he invariably puts in an appearance and claims the soul, which in one case escapes from the dying person's mouth in the shape of a small black demon. In another picture the soul is wrapped in swaddling clothes and is borne aloft by angels. This was a pre-Christian conception, that life is a small living thing which dwells inside a human being and escapes at death. On classic soil one comes across escaping life represented as a babe ; in German folk-lore it is often a mouse or a toad.

The story of Goliath and of David is also illustrated. David is a diminutive figure wearing a kirtle, Goliath is huge and clad in chain-mail. Another picture represents David playing on the harp. There were also a number of scenes from the books of Kings, of Job, and of Tobit ; none of these have as yet been reproduced. A picture of the prophets has, however, been published, in which a number of figures of different ages are depicted in different attitudes standing side by side. One of the most curious and dramatic pictures is the full-page illustration of Jonah being cast up by the fish. The fish is a carp of huge size, but it is designated as a whale.

The New Testament pictures follow on the Old Testament, but between them stand several which illustrate their unity. One is an allegorical figure with two heads, the one the head of Moses, the other that of Christ. There is also a picture in folio size of the mystic family of Christ. At the bottom is Abraham, who holds the mystic vine which grows upwards and divides into beautiful twisted ramifications forming circles, and in these are arranged the heads of patriarchs, kings, and groups of other members of Christ's family. A picture of Leviathan is extremely curious. He is depicted floating below. God stands above with a rod and line, and uses the cross as a fish-hook, dragging out of the huge creature's mouth the heads of the prophets which are strung to- gether in a row.

The history of Christ was led up to by an account of the birth of John the Baptist. The Nativity was celebrated by several poems, the words of which have come down to us; the music which accom- panied them is apparently lost. Among the most realistic pictures preserved is that of the 'Murder of the Innocents'; agony is characteristically expressed in the attitude and faces of the mothers who watch the soldiers fulfilling their task.

Other pictures, copies of which have been preserved, illustrate the arrival of the three kings and Christ's baptism. In this latter picture the Jordan is personified as a river-god sitting in the water; the doors of heaven above are wide open and a dove drawn in the accepted style is descending. Christ's parables gave the abbess many occasions for depicting scenes taken from real life, many of which in their simplicity are truly delightful. Biblical stories were supplemented by incidents taken from legendary history, which were likewise accompanied by pictures, few of which seem to have been preserved. The story of the healing power of the statue of Christ, the legend of the Vernacle, and the story of the True Cross were all illustrated. There was Adam planting the Tree of Life, King Solomon fetching its wood to Jerusalem and making a bridge over the river with it, and the Queen of Sheba coming on a visit and hesitating to cross the bridge.

The pictures of the story of the Agony, the Resurrection, and the Acts of the Apostles met with great praise from all who saw them. There were folio-sized pictures setting forth the Universality of the Church, and the Contending of Virtues and Vices[1]. Of this latter series several pictures have just appeared in reproduction; some are arranged in pairs, facing each other. The chief Vices, each with a band of attendants, are depicted confronting and then overcome by the chief Virtues; all are represented as women. Thus Pride, 'Superbia,' seated on horseback on a lion's skin and brandishing a spear, is leading a band of women, who are clad in chain-mail with robes flowing about their feet and carrying spears, against a band of Virtues similarly attired but carrying swords. A most interesting picture is that of Luxury, 'Luxuria,' who is seen with fourteen attendant Vices riding in a sumptuous four-wheeled car; Luxury is in front throwing violets. She is confronted by a band of Virtues led by Temperance, 'Temperantia,' who are in front of the horses and hold up their hands in reprobation. On the next picture the car of Luxury is smashed, the horses are overturned, and she herself is under the wheels. Of her attendants 'Voluptas' has cast aside her rings and ornaments and is caught in a briar-bush, 'Amor' has thrown away bow and quiver, and 'Avaritia' is

---

[1] Apparently following the 'Psychomachia' of Prudentius, a Christian poet of the 5th century.

seizing upon what the others have dropped. On another picture Liberality, 'Largitas,' has stripped Rapine and Avarice, and has transfixed Avarice with a spear.

Some of the pictures which illustrate Solomon in his glory and Solomon's Vanity of Vanities have also been preserved. Among them is Solomon lying on a sumptuous couch and surrounded by his warriors. A representation of two mannikins occurs among the Vanities; these mannikins were moved by threads, exactly like a modern toy. The pictures illustrating the experiences of the Church, the position of her members from Pope to cleric, the means of repentance, and the coming of Antichrist, all roused the enthusiasm of those who saw them; none of these have till now been reproduced. Gérard, who was probably the last to see and handle the work of Herrad, was especially struck by the pictures of the Last Judgment and of Heaven and Hell. His descriptions of them were lying in the library at the time of the bombardment, and were only rescued by the devotion of a friend[1]. On the strength of these pictures he numbers Herrad among the most imaginative painters the world has known. Engelhardt also was greatly struck by them. He describes a picture of Hell in the following terms (p. 51):

'A mass of rocks was arranged so as to make a framework to this picture, in the chasms of which rocks flames were flaring and the condemned were seen suffering torments. Rivers of flame divided the inner part of the picture into four divisions. In the lowest of these, at the bottom of Hell, sat Lucifer or Satan in chains holding Antichrist in his lap. Next to him a demon carried along a covetous monk, whose punishment was then represented: he lay on his back without clothes and a demon poured molten gold into his mouth. In the second division counting from below two boiling caldrons hung suspended: in the one were Jews, in the other soldiers (the text says 'milites vel armati'). Demons stood by holding men of either kind ready to add them to those already in the caldrons; other demons were stirring the caldrons with forks. In front of the Jews' caldron a demon was depicted holding a naked sinner to whom he administered punishment by beating him. In the division above this a usurer had hot gold poured into his hand; a slanderer was made to lick a toad; an eaves-dropper had his ears pinched; a vain woman was assisted at her toilet by demons (they seemed to be lacing her); the woman

[1] Gérard, Ch., *Les artistes de l'Alsace*, 1872, Introd. p. xix., p. 46, footnote.

who had murdered her child was forced to devour it. The following peculiar picture filled the highest division: a rope was drawn
through chasms in the rocks so as to form a swing; on this a grinning
demon sat swinging. At the ends of the rope which hung on the
other side of the rocks two sinners were hanging bound head and
foot so as to balance each other; demons held them by the hair.
Another sinner hung suspended by his feet, with a block of stone
hanging from his neck on which a demon was swinging. Sensual
pleasures personified were wound around and bitten by snakes, and
a man who had committed suicide was depicted plunging a knife
into his own body.'

These pictures illustrated with forcible directness conceptions
which were current throughout the religious world and served as
a means of teaching the lesson of reward and punishment in the
world to come. Later on in treating of mysticism we shall again
see these conceptions stimulating the imaginative powers of women
living in convents.

Copies of the last pages of the 'Garden of Delights,' which
are devoted to a representation of the Hohenburg and of its
convent of women, have fortunately been preserved. Here we
see the settlement as it presented itself to Herrad and the thoughts
she associated with it. The picture is the size of two folio pages.
High above in the centre stands Christ in front of the convent church,
holding in His right hand a golden staff which is touched by the
Virgin and St Peter, and the end of which is supported by Duke
Eticho, whom Herrad looked upon as the father of St Odilia. St John
the Baptist and St Odilia are seen standing on the other side of
Christ. A green hill is represented below roughly studded with
bushes or brambles,—this is the hill of the Hohenburg. On one
slope of it Duke Eticho is seated, and he hands the golden key of
the convent to St Odilia, who advances towards him followed by
a band of women. Relind, Herrad's teacher and predecessor, also
stands on the hill with her hand resting on a cross on which are
inscribed verses addressed to the nuns. The fact that she restored
the church and the discipline at Hohenburg, which had fallen entirely into decay, is commemorated in a sentence which is placed on
the other side of her. Over against her stands Herrad herself, who
also holds verses addressed to the nuns. And between these two
abbesses all the members of Herrad's congregation are drawn, six
rows of women's heads placed one above the other. There is no
attempt at portraiture, but the name of each nun and each novice

is added to her picture. Among these names are those of families of the surrounding landed gentry, from which we gather that the nunnery was chiefly for the upper classes. The nuns in the picture address lines to Christ begging Him to number them among the elect.

Such in rough outline was the 'Garden of Delights,' the loss of which is greatly to be deplored, both from the point of view of culture in general, and from that of women in particular. But even in its fragments the work is a thing to dwell upon, a monument which bears the stamp of wide knowledge and lofty thought. It shows how Herrad found her life's interest in educating the young women given into her care, how anxious she was that they should be right-minded in all things, and how she strove to make their studies delightful to them. The tone which she took towards her congregation is apparent from the words in which she directly addressed them. For besides occasional admonitory words, two long poems, one at the beginning, the other at the end of the work, are devoted to the admonition of the nuns. Herrad's poems are composed in different metres; some have the dignity of the hexameter, some the easier flow of shorter-lined dactylic verse. The poems addressed to her nuns are of the latter kind. Their incisive rhythm and ringing rhyme, in which their value chiefly lies, make a translation difficult. Still a version of the first of these poems in English prose will help to give the reader some idea of the tone of the abbess; the form of address is necessarily determined by the mode of expression of the 12th century, the meaning of the original is by no means always clear.

This is: 'The rhyme of Herrad, the abbess, in which she lovingly greets the young maidens (virgunculas) of the Hohenburg and invites them to their weal to faith and love of the true Bridegroom.

'Hail, cohort of Hohenburg virgins, white as the lily and loving the Son of God, Herrad, your most devoted, your most faithful mother and handmaiden sings you this song. She greets you times countless and daily prays that in glad victory you may triumph over things that pass. O, mirror of many things, spurn, spurn those of time, and garner virtues, Band of the true Bridegroom. Press on in the struggle to scatter the dread foe, the King of Kings aids you for His desire is towards you. He Himself strengthens your soul against Satan; He Himself will grant the glory of His kingdom after victory. Delights await you, riches are destined for you, the court of heaven proffers you countless joys. Christ prepares espousals wondrous in delights, and you may look for this prince if you preserve your chastity. Mean time put around you noble circlets (?) and make your faces to shine fair, freed from mental strife. Christ hates spot or stain, He abhors time-worn lines (of vice); He desires beauteous virgins and drives forth women who are unchaste. With a dove-like faith call upon that your Bridegroom, that your beauty may become an unbroken glory. Living without guile, be admonished by praisegiving, so that you may complete your best works of ascent. Do not hesitate amidst the doubtful currents of the world, the truthful God holds out rewards after danger. Suffer hardships now, despising the world's prosperity, be now fellow of the cross, hereafter sharer of the kingdom. Steer across the ocean freighted with holiness, till you leave the bark and land in Sion. May Sion's heavenly castle with its beauteous halls be your home when the term of life is past. May there the virgin Ruler, Mary's Son, receive you in His embrace and lift you up from sadness. Setting aside all the wiles of the mean tempter, you will be abundantly glad, sweetly rejoicing. The shining Star of the Sea, the one virgin Mother will join you to her Son in bond eternal. And by your prayer do not cease to draw me with you to the sweetest Bridegroom, the Son of the Virgin. As He will be partner of your victory and of your great glory, He will draw you from earthly things. Farewell, chaste band, you my exceeding joy, live without offence, ever love Christ. May this book prove useful and delightful to you, may you never cease to ponder it in your breast. May forgetfulness not seize you like the ostrich (more Struthineo)[1], and may you not leave the way before you have attained. Amen.'

This address in verse was followed by these lines in prose— 'Herrad, who through the grace of God is abbess of the church on the Hohenburg, here addresses the sweet maidens of Christ who are working as though in the vineyard of the Lord ; may He grant grace and glory unto them.—I was thinking of your happiness when like a bee guided by the inspiring God I drew from many flowers of sacred and philosophic writing this book called the 'Garden of Delights'; and I have put it together to the praise of Christ and the Church, and to your enjoyment, as though into a sweet honeycomb. Therefore you must diligently seek your salvation in it and strengthen your weary spirit with its sweet honey

---

[1] Probably with reference to Job xxxix., 14–15.

drops ; always be bent on love of your Bridegroom and fortified by spiritual joys, and you will safely pass through what is transitory, and secure great and lasting happiness. Through your love of Christ, help me who am climbing along a dangerous uncertain path by your fruitful prayer when I pass away from this earth's experiences. Amen.'

Thus far we have followed Herrad in her work and in her relations towards her nuns ; the question naturally arises, What inner experiences prompted her to her great undertaking and in what spirit did she carry it through? It has been noticed that a sombreness is characteristic of certain parts of the work, and is peculiar to some of her poems also. Two short verses which occur in the work seem to reflect her mental state. The one urges great liberality of mind. It discusses the basis of purity, and comes to the conclusion that purity depends less on actions than on the spirit in which they are done. The other follows the mind through its several stages of development and deserves to be chronicled among the words of wisdom. It runs as follows: 'Despise the world, despise nothing, despise thyself, despise despising thyself, —these are four good things.'

CHAPTER VIII.

PROPHECY AND PHILANTHROPY.

'Pauper homo magnam stultitiam habet quando vestimenta sua scissa sunt, semper in alium aspiciens, considerans quem colorem vestimentum illius habeat, nec suum a sorde abluit.' *Hildegard.*

§ 1. St Hildegard of Bingen[1] and St Elisabeth of Schönau[2].

FROM the peaceful pursuits of mediaeval nuns we turn to some of the women who were interested in the problems of the day, and whose minds were agitated by current difficulties which they sought to solve in their own way. In Germany in the early Middle Ages the struggle between Pope and Emperor, and the interference in temporal matters of prelates in their character as dependents of the Pope, gave rise to a prolonged struggle. Much criticism, reflection and speculative energy were brought to bear on the relations between monarchical and ecclesiastical power, on the duties of the ministers of the Church, and on the Pope's efficiency in controlling them. It is at least curious to find among the voices that are raised in criticism and protest, those of two nuns, who in consideration of the services they have rendered to the faith are estimated as saints. The present chapter proposes to deal in outline with the writings of St Hildegard of Bingen (1098–1178) and of St Elisabeth of Schönau (c. 1129–1165). These two women differed somewhat in their points of view, but they were equally zealous in supporting the Pope's authority, and were equally in-

---

[1] Hildegardis, *Opera*, 1882 (in Migne, *Patrol. Cursus Compl.*, vol. 197, which contains the acts of the saint reprinted from *A. SS. Boll.*, St Hildegardis, Sept. 17; her life written by Godefrid and Theodor; the 'Acta Inquisitionis'; the article by Dr Reuss, and the fullest collection of the saint's works hitherto published).

[2] Roth, F. W., *Die Visionen der heil. Elisabeth und die Schriften von Ekbert und Emecho von Schönau*, 1884.

spired by the belief that the Church could and should maintain a lofty and universal standing and act as a regenerator to society. The exhortations of these women were very popular, and in the year 1158, when they were in the full exercise of their power, the annalist wrote, 'in these days God made manifest His power through the frail sex, in the two maidens Hildegard and Elisabeth, whom He filled with a prophetic spirit, making many kinds of visions apparent to them through His messages, which are to be seen in writing[1].'

The attitude of these women and the tone of their writings were the direct outcome of contemporary events. They were deeply moved by the instability of social conditions and shared the belief of other great reformers of the age, that what was needed to remedy social evils was a livelier faith in the truths of religion and a higher standard of morality in conduct.

The 12th century is the age when national feeling in the different countries of Europe first asserted itself strongly, and when consciousness of solidarity within made possible the apprehension of ideas which lie beyond the pale of immediate personal and national advantage. The conception of knighthood, hitherto determined only by land ownership and loyalty to a lord, was given a new interpretation, and the order of Knights Templars was founded, which held knighthood to be based upon devotion to the cause of religion and loyalty to the Saviour. Similarly love of war, which till then had expended itself in self-protective and aggressive warfare, was turned into a new channel, and the thought of the Crusade roused peoples of different nationalities to fight side by side, inspired by a common cause and actuated by a common interest. The authority of the Pope as a temporal ruler had reached its climax, and there were threatening signs of its decline, but when this power, like the conception of knighthood, received the new interpretation, its importance had never been more distinctly emphasized.

The Popes who ruled between 900 and 1000 had been absorbed by party squabbles in Rome and had done little to raise the dignity of their office in other lands. But a change had come through Hildebrand, who nominally served, but practically ruled, five Popes before he himself sat in the chair of St Peter as Gregory VII (1073–1085). Owing to his influence the papal power rapidly increased and took a universal colouring, for, by

---

[1] 'Annales Palidenses' in Pertz, *Mon. Germ. Script.* vol. 16, p. 90.

identifying himself with all the wider and higher interests of humanity, the Pope succeeded in winning for himself the recognition of his supreme authority in matters both spiritual and temporal.   There was something grand and inspiring in this conception of the Pope as the universal peace-maker, and of Rome as the central and supreme court of appeal of the civilized world, but it could not last.   In proportion as national life in the different countries struggled into being, this overlordship of the Pope was felt to weigh heavily and to hamper development, and criticisms arose concerning his right to interfere in matters that did not appertain directly to the Church.   At the time we are speaking of—the second half of the 12th century—there were indications of a distinction drawn between 'sacerdotium' and 'imperium,' between priestly and imperial status considered as the rightful basis of power, with a consequent loss of prestige to the Church.   The position of the Papacy was moreover seriously affected by continued schism.   As a check to this loss of prestige, those who were in favour of papal supremacy urged that the Church must be strengthened in its members, and they sought an increase of influence in a reform of the life of the clergy generally.

It has been mentioned above how from the 10th century onwards a direct connection had grown up between the Pope and the monastic centres, and how the founders of new religious orders had by a like direct connection secured a safeguard against wilful interference with their prerogatives by prince and prelate.   Outside Italy it was in the monastery that the Pope throughout the 12th century found his chief advocates, that his spiritual supremacy was most earnestly emphasized, and that the belief was fostered that through his influence a re-organization of society could be obtained.

In this connection no figure of the age is more remarkable than that of Bernard of Clairvaux[1] († 1153), 'the simple monk, clad in plain clothes, weakened by fasting,' whose power is felt in religious and lay circles alike.   The secret of Bernard's influence lay in the fact that he was in one direction the mouthpiece of the ideal aspirations of his age—he emphasized the spiritual side of religion and insisted on the great social and moral advantages to be obtained by accepting spiritual direction as a guide in practical matters.   By doing so he at once increased the reverence felt for religion and gave it a practical value.   His very success

---

[1] Neander, *Der heil. Bernard und seine Zeit*, 1848.

commands admiration, repellent as his narrowness appears in some particulars. It is true that he diminished schism by persuading King Louis VI of France to recognise Pope Innocent II (1130–43), that he won over the German Emperor Lothar († 1137) to the same course; it is true that he founded the order of the Knights Templars, gave a new impulse to the order of Citeaux, and preached the Crusade; but it was he who declared the writings of Abelard († 1142) false, and who had Arnold of Brescia expelled from Paris on the charge of heresy.

Socially and politically speaking the state of affairs in the German Empire during the first half of the 12th century had taken a deplorable turn through the choice of Konrad († 1152) as emperor. His vacillating policy left party hatred rampant between the rival houses of Welf (Guelph) and Hohenstaufen. On the slightest provocation this hatred broke out in warfare; it was checking all possibility of material progress and prosperity when the thought of a crusade offered a welcome diversion to these turbulent elements. For the first crusade few recruits had been drawn from any districts except the northern provinces of France, but the second assumed very different proportions. As early as 1145 Pope Eugenius was granting indulgences to those who joined it, while Bernard took up the idea and preached it with great success all along the Rhine. Disastrous as the undertaking itself proved to those who took part in it, its immediate effects on the countries from which the crusaders were drawn were most beneficial. After speaking of the terrible contentions which for years had set the ruling powers in Poland, Saxony and Bohemia at strife, Bishop Otto III of Freising († 1158) continues in this strain: ' Suddenly, through the counsel of the Most High, a speedy change was effected; and in a short time the turmoils of war were quieted, the whole earth seemed restored to peace, and unnumbered bands from France and from Germany received the Cross and departed to fight against its enemies.'

When these crusaders had been sped on their way—a motley crowd in which figured emperor and king, adventurous knight, venturesome woman, and vagrants of every kind and of both sexes—Pope Eugenius, whose position at Rome was insecure and who had been staying at Clairvaux with Bernard, journeyed to Trier at the request of the archbishop to meet in council the prelates of the neighbouring districts. Among them was Heinrich, archbishop of Mainz (1142–53), who together with Wibald, abbot

of Corvei, had been appointed representative of the emperor during
his absence. It was on this occasion that some of Hildegard's
writings were first submitted to the Pope, probably at the request
of Archbishop Heinrich. Judging from what Hildegard says herself,
Heinrich and the church at Mainz had accepted her writings,
saying that 'they had come through God and through that power
of prophecy by which the prophets had anciently written[1].'

These writings were exhortations to faith and piety set forth in
the form of revelations. Hildegard had been at work on them
for the past six years, and they form the first part of the book
'Scivias' (that is 'Sci vias,' Know the ways[2]), as it now lies before us.
The life of Hildegard, written shortly after her death, tells us that
Bernard 'with the consent of others urged the Pope that he should
not suffer so obvious a light to be obscured by silence, but should
confirm it by authority[3].'

The time was ripe for the kind of literature which comes under
the heading of prophecies. At the time of the Second Crusade
leaflets containing one of the so-called Sibylline prophecies had had
a wide circulation and had greatly inflamed men's minds as to
coming events[4]. Simultaneously with Hildegard the abbot Giovanni
Gioachimo († after 1215) foretold coming events, so that later writers
often cited Hildegard and Joachim side by side. There was something earnest and yet undefined, something fiery and suggestive in
these writings, which appealed to the restless imagination of the
age, for they were largely founded on the Apocalypse, and like the
Apocalypse admitted of many interpretations. Their very vague-
ness repels the exact thinker, but attracts the mind that is conscious
of quickened sensibilities and roused emotions, without being able
to guide them into practical channels.

Bernard of Clairvaux unhesitatingly accepted the divine origin
of Hildegard's writings, and in a letter to her, which seems to have
been written while the Pope's decision was pending, he addressed
her in most respectful terms[5]: 'They tell us that you understand
the secrets of heaven and grasp that which is above human ken
through the help of the Holy Spirit,' he wrote among other things.
'Therefore we beg and entreat you to remember us before God
and also those who are joined to us in spiritual union. For the

[1] *Opera* (*Vita*, c. 17), p. 104.   [2] *Opera*, 'Scivias, pp. 383–738.
[3] Ibid. (*Vita*, c. 5), p. 94.
[4] Giesebrecht, W., *Geschichte der deutschen Kaiserzeit*, vol. 4, p. 505.
[5] *Opera* (Epist. nr 29), p. 189.

spirit in you joining itself unto God, we believe that you can in great measure help and sustain us.' Hildegard—with a mixture of self-assurance, and eagerness to justify that assurance, which is thoroughly characteristic of her—replied to Bernard in ecstatic terms[1], praised him for having preached the Cross and spoke of him as the eagle who gazes into the sun.

The correspondence[2] of Hildegard is voluminous, for from the time when her writings first gained approval from the Pope, many lay princes and dignitaries of the Church, bishops and abbots, abbesses and nuns, wrote to her, generally asking for her good opinion or for advice, but sometimes propounding questions of speculative interest, to which Hildegard in reply sent sometimes a few sentences, sometimes a long disquisition. It is largely owing to this correspondence that the fame of the abbess has spread beyond the confines of Germany. Linde, one of the few modern students who has treated of Hildegard, enumerates many manuscript copies of these letters which are preserved in the libraries of German cities, in Paris, London and Oxford. The genuineness of the letters has been questioned on the ground that all those addressed to Hildegard are curiously alike, but Linde, after examining a number of manu-script copies, came to the conclusion that the letters were genuine[3]. In their present arrangement the letters do not stand in chrono-logical order but according to the rank of the correspondents, so that those written by Popes to Hildegard with their replies stand first, then come those written by archbishops, bishops, emperors, and so on. With few exceptions there is only one letter from each corre-spondent, an arrangement which suggests the work of a scribe, who for the sake of uniformity may in some instances have selected from or summarized his material. The letters printed by Migne are a hundred and forty-five in number, but Linde refers to a few more in his list with the remark that parts of the correspondence exist separately and are sometimes cited as separate works[4].

These letters of Hildegard's, as well as her other writings, contain many references to herself; she never fails to inform us of the circumstances which led her to begin a work. She tells us that she was middle-aged when she first wrote an account of her visions, but that she had been subject to these visions from her earliest childhood, and that the mental agonies she went

---

[1] *Opera* (Responsum), p. 189.   [2] Ibid. 'Epistolae,' pp. 1–382.
[3] Linde, *Handschriften der königl. Bibliothek in Wiesbaden*, 1877, pp. 19 ff.
[4] Ibid. pp. 53 ff.

through before she sought relief in writing were ever present to her mind.

Moreover we are in possession of an account of her life written between 1181 and 1191, of which the first part is by Godefrid, who introduces extracts from the book 'Scivias.' The second and third parts are by Theodor, who uses an autobiography of Hildegard of which we have no other mention. It appears from the Acts of Inquisition of the year 1233 which were drafted to establish Hildegard's claim to canonization, that both these monks had stayed with Hildegard.

Summarizing the contents of these different accounts and the information which the voluminous writings of the abbess supply, we gather that Hildegard, at the time when the Pope's attention was first drawn to her, was between forty and fifty years of age; that she was a daughter of one of the landed gentry, and that she had been given into the care of the nuns of Disibodenberg at the age of seven and had made profession at fourteen. Disibodenberg[1], situated on the river Nahe, was a monastery of some importance and has preserved annals extending from 831 to 1200 which contain useful contributions to contemporary history. The house was under the rule of an abbot, but a convent of nuns had been lately added to it when Hildegard came there; this convent was under the rule of the 'magistra' Jutta, sister of Meginhard, Count of Sponheim. From Jutta Hildegard received her training, which included a knowledge of books of devotion, scripture and music. Apparently she could not write German[2], and in Latin her acquaintance with grammatical inflection and construction was limited[3], so that when she began to write she availed herself of the help of a monk and afterwards of that of some nuns of her convent who helped her to polish (limare) her sentences.

During the years she spent at Disibodenberg she seems to have been devoted to nursing[4], and the consecration of a chapel in the infirmary about this time leaves us to infer that there were in this monastery special conveniences for the sick[5]. In the year 1136 she succeeded Jutta as lady superior, and at once formed the plan of leaving Disibodenberg and settling some distance away

---

[1] Schneegans, W., *Kloster Disibodenberg*; Schmelzeis, *Das Leben und Wirken der heil. Hildegardis*, 1879, pp. 45 ff.

[2] *Opera* (Responsum to Bernard), p. 190.

[3] Ibid. (*Vita* c. 14), p. 101.   [4] Ibid. (*Vita* c. 19), p. 105.

[5] Schmelzeis, *Das Leben und Wirken der heil. Hildegardis*, 1879, p. 53.

on the Rupertsberg near Bingen on the Rhine, in a convent foundation of her own. But at first Kuno (✝ 1155), abbot of Disibodenberg, opposed her going and cast doubts on the vision in which she declared she was divinely directed to do so[1], while many who did not belong to the monastery, and among them the parents of girls who had been given into her care, disapproved of their daughters being taken to a distant and desolate neighbourhood[2]. But Hildegard persisted, for the accommodation at the monastery was insufficient for herself and her numerous pupils, and besides as abbess at the Rupertsberg she would have a very different standing. She fell ill, and then, chiefly through the intercession of friends outside who made grants of land and helped her towards the erection of new buildings, the abbot was brought to agree to her wishes. Among others Heinrich, archbishop of Mainz, advocated her going, and about the year 1147 she removed to the new settlement with eighteen young women. We have a description of the influence she exerted over these girls, her spiritual daughters, when they were still at Disibodenberg. In the new home Hildegard adopted the rule of St Benedict, but she met with opposition, for some of the young women objected to the greater restrictions put upon them by the new rule, and the abbess needed the help and support of the better and wiser ones amongst them to overcome the difficulty. After the labour of moving Hildegard fell ill and lay prostrate for several years, till she was strengthened and restored by visions of the work that still lay before her.

The Acts of Inquisition tell us that there was accommodation on the Rupertsberg for fifty professed nuns (dominae), seven poor women and two priests[3], but the independence of the nunnery was not easily secured and Hildegard repeatedly travelled to Disibodenberg to settle matters. The men's convent continued to supply priests to the women on the Rupertsberg, but as late as 1170 difficulties occurred in regard to their appointment, and we find Hildegard writing to Pope Alexander begging him to admonish the abbot of Disibodenberg in her behalf[4].

A considerable portion of 'Scivias' was written before Hildegard removed to the Rupertsberg. She has described in the introduction to the book how she was led to write it[5].

[1] *Opera* (*Vita* c. 21), p. 106.   [2] Ibid.
[3] Ibid. (Acta Inquisitionis), p. 136.   [4] Ibid. (Epist. nr 4), p. 154.
[5] *Opera*, p. 383.

'It was in my forty-third year, when I was trembling in fearful anticipation of a celestial vision, that I beheld a great brightness through which a voice from heaven addressed me: "O fragile child of earth, ash of ashes, dust of dust, express and write that which thou seest and hearest. Thou art timid, timid in speech, artless in explaining, unlearned in writing, but express and write not according to art but according to natural ability, not under the guidance of human composition but under the guidance of that which thou seest and hearest in God's heaven above; what thus thou hearest proclaim, like a listener who understanding the words of his teacher, as this teacher wills and indicates, so gives expression to his words according to the power of his speech. Thus thou, O child of earth, proclaim what thou seest and hearest, and put it in writing, not as thou or others will it, but as He wills who knows, sees and disposes of all in the depths of His mysteries." Again I heard a voice from heaven, saying: "Speak these wonderful things, write them in thy unlearned way, proclaim them." And it happened in the year 1141 of Christ's incarnation, when I was forty-two years and seven months old, that a fiery light of great brilliancy streaming down from heaven entirely flooded my brain, my heart and my breast, like a flame that flickers not but gives glowing warmth, as the sun warms that on which he sheds his rays. Then of a sudden I had the power of explaining Scripture, that is the Psalter, the Gospels and the other Catholic books both of the Old and of the New Testament (Psalterium, Evangeliorum et aliorum catholicorum tam Veteris quam Novi Testamenti volumina), though I did not understand the inflections of words, their division into syllables, their cases and tenses. I had been conscious from earliest girlhood of a power of insight, and visions of hidden and wonderful things, ever since the age of five years, then and ever since. But I did not mention it save to a few religious persons who followed the like observances with myself; I kept it hidden by silence until God in His grace willed to have it made manifest.'

In this strain she tells how her visions came to her, not when she was asleep or when she was dreaming or in any way excited, but in the most serious of moods. They had for years perturbed her, and she had shrunk from putting them into writing, when a sudden illness came upon her and made her alter her mind. Then in her own words, 'a noble high-born girl and the man whom I had secretly sought and consulted, were witnesses to how I set my hand to the task'—that is to the composition of 'Scivias.'

It would lead us too far to give a summary of the contents of this extraordinary book; it is divided into three parts, the first containing the account of six, the second of seven, and the third of thirteen visions, all of which seem to have taken place in the following way. Hildegard is confronted by a bright light, which radiates over some wonderful piece of imagery, a mountain, an abyss, some beast, man, or building, or part of the firmament, which, with the figures that throng around, she minutely describes, and then she gives an explanation of the allegorical meaning of this picture vouchsafed to her from God in heaven. The real and the unreal alike supply material for these visions, which show great powers of imagination; in their allegorical application they dwell upon the Creed, the Scriptures, the Incarnation, the Trinity, and life hereafter, and other questions of doctrinal and theological interest. The descriptions are highly coloured throughout, but their application is often very obscure. A translation of the opening passages of one of the visions, which turns on the pro-, tection afforded to the faithful against the wiles of the devil, will give some idea of the character of their imagery[1].

'Then I saw a shining light, wide and high as a mountain, which spreading upwards flashed into many tongues of fire (linguas). And outside it stood a number of men clad in white, in front of whom, like a veil, transparent crystal extended from their breasts downwards to their feet. But before this band, in their pathway, lay a dragon (vermis) of huge size and length, of such terrible and threatening aspect as cannot be expressed. On his left was as it were a market-place where the riches of this world lay heaped, wealth delightful to the eye, where buying and selling went on; some people passed by this place in a great hurry without buying, while others drew near slowly and stayed to buy and sell. The dragon was black and hairy, and covered with venomous excrescences, of which five kinds extended from his head over his body to his feet in the shape of rings; one was green, one white, one red, one yellow, one black, and all were equally charged with deadly venom. His head was broken, causing his left jaw to hang down. His eyes were red and flashed fire; his ears were round and furred; his nostrils and mouth were those of a dragon (vipera), he had the hands of a man, the feet of a dragon, and below a short horrible tail. And his neck, hands and feet were bound by a chain

---

[1] *Opera* (lib. 2, visio 7), p. 555.

and this chain was fixed to the abyss, and held him so fast that he could not move away to suit his wicked will. From his mouth poured forth four streams of flame, of which one rose aloft, a second spread towards the children of this world, a third towards the company of just men, the last towards the abyss. The flames which rose aloft threatened those who aspired to heaven, who move in three ranks, one touching the sky, the other betwixt heaven and earth, the third close to earth, and all were crying, "We are striving to reach heaven." But some of them, although touched by the flames, fell not, others barely kept their footing, yet others falling again to earth, gathered themselves up and went forth anew.—The flames which spread towards the children of this world reached some and burnt them to utter blackness, of others they took hold, turning them hither and thither; yet others burst away, and striving towards those who were nearing heaven shouted out aloud: "Ye faithful ones, give us help!" But some remained as though spell-bound.—The flames which ran to the company of the just covered some with blackness; the company of the just moved in six ranks, and those whom the cruel flames wounded not were tainted by the poison of the dragon which issued from the green, white, red, yellow, and black parts of its body.—The flames which sought the abyss carried various punishments to those who had not been cleansed by baptism, who ignored the true faith and worshipped Ṣatan instead of God. And I further saw arrows pouring from the dragon's mouth, black smoke issuing from his body, steaming liquid bubbling from his sides, and excretions going out from the lower part of his body, like to frogs that are disastrous to man, and which bring infection to many. And a black mist with foul odour going forth contaminated all.

'But lo and behold the men shining in brilliancy advanced towards this dragon to fight and vex it, whom it could harm neither by fire nor by poison. And I heard a voice from heaven saying unto me: "God, who disposes all in wisdom, summons His faithful band to the glory of their heritage; the old deceiver lies in wait and tries his evil powers, but he is overcome, his presumption is defeated; they attain their heavenly heritage, and he suffers eternal disgrace. Therefore dost thou behold a shining light, wide and high as a mountain, flashing upwards into many tongues of fire, which is the justice of God, as it glows in the faith of believers, setting forth the breadth of His holiness, the height of His glory, by which glory are declared the wondrous powers of the divine Spirit."'

All the visions of the first two parts of the book are written in this vague indefinite strain, but in the third Hildegard, conscious of the evils that had come upon the Church through the schism in the Papacy, became more outspoken in her views, and enlarged on the true faith being shaken, on Holy Scripture being disregarded, and on the great works of learned men being neglected. She says definitely that there can be no life where the head is severed from the limbs; and such, in her estimation, is the condition of the Church while schism continues. In common with a current view, she expected that things would go from bad to worse till the coming of Antichrist, whose appearance and influence she describes in eloquent and impressive imagery[1]. The apprehensive tone of these descriptions is in agreement with the growing consciousness of wickedness and personal responsibility, which assumed such proportions during the latter half of the 12th century, and made the minds of many prepared for the altruistic doctrines spread abroad by the orders of friars.

The last vision of the book 'Scivias' lays stress upon the final revolution and reconciliation which will follow the reign of Antichrist and the times of trouble, and in this vision occur passages in dialogue, cast into dramatic form and called a symphony (symphonia), which rank among the finest productions of their kind[2]. The subject of this improvised drama is 'the Progress of the Soul on her way to heaven.' It opens with a lament of those Souls who are still confined in the body, whereupon one Faithful Soul (Fidelis anima), who is set free, raises her voice in supplication, calling on the Virtues or Divine Powers (Virtutes) for assistance. They respond and promise help, when Divine Knowledge (Scientia Dei) raises her voice and adds to the consciousness of helplessness in the Faithful Soul, who is now importuned on one side by Pride or the Devil (Diabolus) and on the other by Humility (Humilitas), both of whom are striving to gain possession of her. But the Virtues urge her to hold by Humility and the Devil is put to flight, whereupon the Virtues guide the Faithful Soul upwards to Heaven where she is finally received by Victory (Victoria). The whole ends with a hymn in praise of Christ which is sung by the Virtues.

It is probable that only the first and second parts of the work 'Scivias' were laid before the Pope in 1146. He wrote to Hildegard as abbess of the Rupertsberg, and the letter is short and

---

[1] *Opera* (lib. 3, visio 11), p. 709.   [2] *Opera* (lib. 3, visio 13), p. 733.

curt[1].   He refers to her wonderful powers and then continues: 'We congratulate ourselves in this grace of God, and we congratulate thee, but we would have thee reminded that God resisteth the proud, but giveth grace to the lowly.   Take good care of this grace which is within thee in order that what thou art spiritually (in spiritu) urged to proclaim, thou mayest proclaim with caution.'   And he adds words to the effect that he confirms the settlement she has founded.

The whole of the lengthy reply[2] which Hildegard sent to this letter was written in an admonitory tone, for she considered herself the chosen mouthpiece of God though characterizing herself as a poor lowly woman.   'The light stays with me and glows in my soul as it has done since my childhood,' she says to the Pope, 'therefore I send thee these words, a true admonition from God.' A mass of imagery follows, powerful and direct, but not always clear in its application.

In one place she writes: 'A jewel lies on the road, a bear comes, and deeming it beautiful puts out his paw and would treasure it in his bosom' (the bear is the German Emperor)[3].   'But suddenly an eagle snatches the jewel, wraps it in the covering of his wings and bears it upwards to the royal palace' (the eagle represents the Pope, the palace the kingdom of Christ).   'The jewel gives out much light before the king, so that he rejoices and out of love of the jewel gives to the eagle golden shoes' (the insignia of papal authority), 'and praises him for his goodness. Now do thou, who art sitting in the place of Christ in care of the Church, choose the better part; be as the eagle overcoming the bear, that with the souls entrusted to thee thou mayest decorate the palace of the Church; so that with golden shoes thou mayest rise aloft and be removed from thine enemies.'

Other images follow.   It is told how the valleys overtop the hills and then the hills overtop the valleys, with the obvious application that no order is maintained in the Church, since the lower clergy presume upon and the higher abuse their powers; each one neglecting to do his duty, and class being envious of class.   'The poor man is very foolish who, when he knows that his garment is soiled, looks at others and reflects on the appearance of their clothes, instead of washing and cleaning his own.... Therefore, do thou, great shepherd called upon to follow Christ, supply

---

[1] *Opera* (Epist. nr 1), p. 145.   [2] *Opera* (Responsum), p. 145.
[3] This interpretation is given by Schmelzeis, *Das Leben und Wirken der heil. Hildegardis*, 1879, p. 157.

a light to the hills, a rod to the valleys. Give to the teachers precepts, bring unto the lowly discipline.' And further, ' Make all things pure and have thine eyes everywhere.'

After settling near Bingen Hildegard completed the book 'Scivias' and then engaged on the compilation of two books on medicine, one of which has never been published[1]. The other is usually called ' Physica ' ; its amplified title runs, ' On the nature of man, of the various elements and of various creatures and plants, and on the way in which they are useful to man[2].' This book, of which the printing press issued several editions in the 16th century, has been characterised by the scientist Virchow as an early ' materia medica, curiously complete considering the age to which it belongs[3].' Haeser, in his history of medicine, also points out the importance of the work, saying that 'it contains descriptions of the medicinal properties of the best-known animals, plants and minerals, together with directions how to improve accepted remedies against illness in man and beast[4].' He considers that the book has an historical value because it is an independent German treatise based chiefly on popular experience, for no writer except Isidor of Seville († 636) is made use of in it. In this connection it has been further commented on by Jessen[5].

The book consists of a collection of terse bits of description, of sensible advice, and of old-world superstitions. It is so arranged that a description is given first of plants (230 in number), and then of elements (14), trees (60), stones (26), fishes (37), birds (72), animals (43), and lastly of metals (8). The German term for each object is given and its health-giving or obnoxious properties are mentioned. Thus the description of the mulberry tree is followed by the information that a decoction of its leaves forms an efficacious remedy in cases of skin disease, and after the description of prunes comes the information that they are good for a dry cough. When treating of the pig Hildegard states that pork is indigestible and should be avoided in cases of sickness. While some descriptions are excellent and obviously based on direct observation, as for example that of the properties of soda, others are entirely fabulous,

---

[1] Jessen, ' Ueber die medic. naturhist. Werke der heil. Hildegardis,' in *Kaiserl. Acad. der Wissenschaften*, Wien, *Naturwissensch. Abth.* vol. 45 (1862), pp. 97 ff.

[2] *Opera*, ' Physica,' pp. 1117–1352.

[3] Virchow, R., ' Zur Geschichte des Aussatzes, besonders im Mittelalter,' in *Archiv für pathol. Anatomie*, vol. 18, p. 286.

[4] Haeser, H., *Lehrbuch der Geschichte der Medizin*, 1875, vol. 1, p. 640.

[5] Jessen, *Botanik der Gegenwart und Vorzeit*, 1864, pp. 120–127.

such as that of the unicorn. We get the savour of primitive
leechcraft in the statements that carrying about a dead frog is
good for the gout, that drinking water out of a cypress bowl rids
one of devils and fantasies, and that eating raven's flesh should
be avoided since it encourages thieving propensities. In regard
to diagnosis of disease Hildegard's ideas are necessarily vague.
The illnesses referred to are chiefly indigestion, fevers, coughs,
delusions and leprosy. Several kinds of leprosy are distinguished,
and the chief remedies prescribed are baths in decoctions of leaves
and other less savoury preparations.

In the light of information such as is contained in this book,
the wonderful cures which Hildegard and many other early saints
are said to have effected take a new meaning. It is generally
allowed that the fame of monasteries as curative centres is
founded on a basis of fact which consists in their healthy situation, abundance of pure water, and regular diet. But evidently
there is more than this. When we look through the 'Physica,'
compiled under Hildegard's direction if not directly by her, we
feel that, if we could only see behind the veil of the miraculous
through which all religious writers persist in looking at the alleviation of physical and mental suffering, we should be brought
face to face with much judicious treatment and with the application
of a considerable amount of medicinal knowledge.

During the early part of her stay on the Rupertsberg Hildegard also wrote a book of Latin texts for hymns (before 1153)
which are accompanied by musical notation[1],—certain 'Expositions
of the Gospels' (before 1157) for the use of her nuns, which have
not been printed[2],—an explanation 'of the rule of St Benedict[3],'—
and another 'of the symbol of St Athanasius[4].' In the opening
sentences of this last work she describes the difficulties she had to
contend with in founding the nunnery, and admonishes the nuns to
guard against division and discord when she is no more. Another
work entitled 'Vitae meritorum,' consisting of moral admonitions,
was written between 1158 and 1162, but has not been printed[5]. A

---

[1] Linde, *Handschriften der königl. Bibliothek in Wiesbaden*, 1877, p. 83; an
example of the musical notation as an appendix in Schmelzeis, *Das Leben und Wirken
der heil. Hildegardis*, 1879.

[2] Linde, *Handschriften der königl. Bibliothek in Wiesbaden*, 1877, p. 78, 'Exposi-
tiones Evangeliorum.'

[3] *Opera*, 'Explanatio regulae St Benedicti,' pp. 1053–1069.

[4] Ibid. 'Explanatio symboli St Athanasii,' pp. 1066–1093.

[5] Linde, *Handschriften der königl. Bibliothek in Wiesbaden*, 1877, p. 38.

series of questions was forwarded to her by Guibert of Gembloux and was the occasion of a lengthy reply, sent to him in the form of a letter[1]. Hildegard also either invented or perpetuated in writing a glossary of words of a secret language, each term accompanied by its equivalent in Latin or in German, sometimes in both. Scholars look upon this work as containing words invented by members of the convent to be used in the presence of strangers for the purpose of secret communication[2].

These writings give proof of Hildegard's active interest in her convent, though at the same time she remained keenly alive to events outside. The choice of Friedrich Barbarossa (1152–1190) as successor to Konrad proved favourable in many respects to German lands, but the position of the Papacy was further jeopardised when Friedrich fell out with Pope Hadrian (1154–59). After the death of this Pope Friedrich did not support his legitimate successor Alexander III (1159–81), but the successive Antipopes, Victor IV (✝ 1164), Paschalis III (✝ 1168) and Calixtus III (resigned 1178). The cities of northern Italy tried to secure autonomy, and plotted against the Emperor. Again and again their rebellion obliged him to cross the Alps and devote himself to their subjection, while several of his powerful German prelates at home, by no means convinced of the rightfulness of his cause, sided with Pope Alexander, some secretly, some openly, against the Antipope and the Emperor. Hildegard joined this party and charged the Emperor with being partly responsible for the continued schism and for the diminished authority of the Church. With these views she wrote a letter full of adulation to Eberhard, archbishop of Salzburg (1147–1164), who adhered to Alexander[3], and sent dark forebodings of impending disaster to Arnold, archbishop of Mainz (1153–1160[4]). It would lead too far to dwell upon the numerous letters written during these years by the abbess who, believing herself to possess a miraculous insight into things, wrote sometimes in a threatening, sometimes in an admonitory, and sometimes in an encouraging strain. The outside world generally, including many clever and cultivated men, held her to be divinely enlightened. Arnold II, archbishop of Cöln (1151–1156), wrote to entreat her to send him her writings whatever their state[5]. The abbot of Elwangen

---

[1] *Opera*, 'Solutiones triginta octo quaestionum,' pp. 1038–1053.
[2] Linde, *Handschriften der königl. Bibliothek in Wiesbaden*, 1877, p. 79.
[3] *Opera* (Epist. nr 12), p. 164.   [4] Ibid. (Epist. nr 6), p. 157.
[5] Ibid. (Epist. nr 11), p. 163.

wrote saying that she could 'speak of the present, uncover the past, and foresee the future[1],' and the provost and clergy of Trier wrote to consult her in their trouble, and declared her 'filled by the Holy Ghost and acquainted with things which are hidden from mankind generally[2].'

Many powerful prelates, abbots and abbesses sought confirmation of their views or advice in tribulation from the learned abbess. Her fame spread beyond the confines of Germany, for we find the patriarch of Jerusalem addressing a letter to her, in which he said that he was living in sad straits and begged for her prayers, and Hildegard, evidently influenced by his exalted position, urging him to remain steadfast and assuring him that while his faith is firm he need not despair[3].

Among the letters which refer to convent matters we note one addressed to Heinrich, the archbishop of Mainz. In early days he had supported Hildegard, but at a later date he advocated against her wish the promotion of one of her nuns to the post of abbess in another convent, thus drawing on himself Hildegard's scorn and anger. The nun was Hiltrud of Sponheim, who had helped Hildegard to put ' Scivias' into writing and whose loss was a serious matter to her. She vented her anger by attacking the bishop and threatening him with ruin. 'The rod you raise is not raised in the interest of God,' she wrote to him[4], and ended her letter with these words : 'your days are numbered, remember how Nebuchadnezzar fell and lost his crown. Many others who presumed that they would attain to heaven have likewise fallen.' In point of fact Heinrich was soon afterwards charged with wasting the goods of the Church, was deposed and died in exile.

Another nun, who had also helped Hildegard with her writing and left her against her wish, was Richardis, sister of Hartwich, bishop of Bremen (1148–1168). The correspondence includes a letter from Hartwich to Hildegard, telling her that his sister died shortly after accepting her post as abbess, that she always regretted having left Hildegard and would have returned to her if she had lived. Hildegard in reply speaks warmly of the virtues of Richardis, and says that she finds comfort in the thought that God has removed her from the vanities of this world[5].

Abbesses of many convents, convinced of Hildegard's being

---

[1] *Opera* (Epist. nr 62), p. 281.

[2] Ibid. (Epist. nr 49), p. 253.

[3] Ibid. (Epist. nr 22), p. 178.

[4] Ibid. (Epist. nr 5), p. 156.

[5] Ibid. (Epist. nr 10), p. 161.

divinely inspired, wrote to her for advice concerning personal matters. Thus the abbess of Altwick near Utrecht asked if she were justified in resigning her post and becoming a recluse, and Hildegard in reply urged her not to yield to temptation but to remain in charge of her flock[1]. The abbess Sophie of Kizzingen had the same wish but was likewise advised to persevere in her vocation[2]. Among numerous other letters from the superiors of convents there is one from the abbess Adelheid of Gandersheim († 1184) who had been educated by Hildegard and who wrote begging for news and saying that she was shortly coming on a visit[3].

Among the letters bearing on Hildegard's religious attitude is one addressed to Philip von Heinsberg, an earnest adherent of Pope Alexander. He afterwards became archbishop of Cöln, and Hildegard wrote warning him of the dangers to be apprehended from a sect of heretics, doubtless the so-called Cathari, of whom more later[4]. This sect were at the time in possession of a well-planned organization in the Rhine districts, and aroused serious apprehension in religious circles. The archbishop of Cöln, Reinald von Dassel (1159–1167), disputed with them; Ekbert, a monk of Schönau to whom we shall return, directly attacked their doctrines, and in 1163 a number of them were burnt to death at Cöln. It is interesting to note what fears they inspired and how their doctrines were interpreted. In the eyes of Hildegard there is no doubt as to their being altogether evil.

The situation of the Rupertsberg near the Rhine, the highway of communication in those days, kept Hildegard in touch with the outside world. She received many visitors and took frequent journeys. We hear of her going to Cöln, Trier, Würzburg, Bamberg and to many monasteries in the neighbourhood, but the story that she went as far as Paris and Tours is unfounded—the result of a misinterpreted passage in the account of her life[5]. Personal acquaintance with Hildegard seems only to have confirmed the belief in her superior abilities and her direct converse with the Godhead—a curious illustration of the credulity of the age, with its craving for signs and wonders.

Her clear-sightedness and consciousness of prophetic power in-

---

[1] *Opera* (Epist. nr 100), p. 321.   [2] Ibid. (Epist. nr 101), p. 322.
[3] Ibid. (Epist. nr 96), p. 317.   [4] Ibid. (Epist. nr 48), p. 243 ; cf. below, p. 281.
[5] Ibid. (*Vita*, c. 44), p. 122; also p. 142 (Reuss here misunderstands the *Acta Inquisitionis*, p. 138), comp. Schmelzeis, *Das Leben und Wirken der heil. Hildegardis*, 1879, pp. 538 ff.

creased with age, and there is the strongest evidence of them in her last important work, which bears the title of ' The Book of Divine doings[1].' It was written between 1163 and 1170, ' when the apostolic see was most seriously oppressed,' and for imaginative- ness, breadth of knowledge and power of generalization ranks highest among Hildegard's works.

The leading idea of this book is to establish parallels, sometimes between things divine and human, sometimes between the physical and the spiritual world, sometimes between the facts of the Biblical narrative and their allegorical meaning, with a view to glorifying God in His works. It contains vivid bits of description, valuable glimpses of contemporary scientific knowledge, and occasional brilliant similes, but the conceptions among which it moves are so entirely those of a past age that it is often difficult to grasp their import.

Thus in the first vision there is the description of the creation of man in the image and the likeness of God, which is supposed to account for the complexity of the human being. In another vision the heavenly spheres are set forth according to the accepted astro- nomical theory, and their movements within each other and mutual interdependence are described. In each of these spheres resides a spiritual influence, such as divine grace, good works, or repentance, and as the heavenly spheres influence each other, so these spiritual influences control and determine the nature of man. Many of the parallels are extremely curious, such as those between things physical and physiological, in which the external influences of wind, weather and the constellations are treated in connection with the humours of the human body. For the humours in the human body are so disposed that their undue pressure on heart, lungs or liver upsets the balance of the constitution and produces stomachic disorders, fevers, pleurisy, leprosy, etc., thus showing that these illnesses are indirectly the outcome of physical surroundings.

The learned abbess also draws parallels between the configura- tion of the surface of the earth with its heights and depths, and human nature with its heights of virtue and depths of vice[2]. Forced as some of these comparisons appear to modern ideas, the language in which they are given shows considerable appreciation of pheno- mena in nature. Hildegard amplifies her book by disquisitions on passages in Job, the Psalms, St John, and the Apocalypse, which bear on the relation of light to life, of the spirit to the word, and of

---

[1] *Opera*, ' Liber divinorum Operum,' pp. 739–1037.
[2] Ibid. (visio 4), pp. 807 ff.

mental to physical darkness. The moments of the Creation are explained in their allegorical application, and give rise to comparisons such as this[1]: that the firmament of faith, like the firmament of nature, is illumined by two kinds of light; the greater light, like that of day, comes through prelates and spiritual teachers, the lesser light, like that of night, through kings and secular princes. In another passage man is likened to the soul and woman to the body, for the soul is of heaven and the body of earth, and their combination makes human life possible[2]. The wickedness which preceded the Flood, the falling away from the true faith, and the manner in which God chastised man by means of water and fire, are described in very impressive language, and together with a description of the Plagues of Egypt, lead up to the last vision, which enlarges on the evils of the time and on coming events. Here again as in 'Scivias' we have a description of impending changes, of threatening disaster, and of the results of the coming of Antichrist; it is perhaps as emphatic in the way of prophecy as anything that has ever been written. Contemporaries were powerfully impressed by this part of the book; even to later ages it appeared truly remarkable. Again and again in times of trouble and difficulty men have gone to it and found corroboration of the changes which were taking place around them. The reader can judge for himself how men's minds at the time of the Reformation were likely to be affected by the perusal of passages such as those which follow, in which the collapse of the German Empire—that is the Roman Empire of the German nation—and the Papacy, and their falling asunder had been described three hundred years before by the abbess of the Rupertsberg[2].

'In the days to come the Emperors of the Roman See, forfeiting the power by which they had up to that time firmly upheld the Roman Empire, will become feeble in all their glory, so that the empire that has been given into their hands by divine power will gradually become enfeebled and fail, until they themselves, becoming sordid, feeble, servile and criminal in their practices, will be altogether useless, and yet they will claim to be respected by the people; but being indifferent to the people's welfare, they cannot be respected or held high. Then the kings and princes of the

---

[1] *Opera* (visio 5, c. 36), p. 934.
[2] Ibid. (visio 5, c. 43), p. 945.
[3] Ibid. (visio 10, c. 25), p. 1026.

various peoples, who before were subject to the Roman Empire, will cut themselves off from it and refuse to be ruled by it. And thus the Roman Empire will sink to decay. For each clan and each people will set up a king unto themselves whom they will respect, alleging that the greatness of the Roman Empire was previously more an encumbrance to them than an advantage. But after the Imperial sceptre in this way has been divided, never to be restored, then the dignity of the Apostolic See (infula) will be impaired also. For neither princes nor other men, of the religious or the lay orders, will uphold any religion in the name of the Apostolic See, and they will violate the dignity of that name. They will appoint unto themselves other teachers and archbishops under some other name in the various districts, so that the Apostolic See (apostolicus), impaired in its standing through collapse of its dignity, will barely maintain its hold on Rome and on a few adjoining districts. This will come about partly through the irruptions of war, partly through the common consent and unity of religious and lay folk, who will demand of each secular prince that he fortify and rule his kingdom and his people, and of whatever archbishop or other spiritual teacher who is appointed that he exert discipline over those who are subject to him, lest they again experience the evils which by divine decree they experienced once before.'

Various interpretations have in the course of time been given to Hildegard's prophecies, and a number of pamphlets, some consisting of amplified passages of her works, some entirely spurious, have circulated under her name. In the 13th century she was held to have indicated the threatened downfall of the Dominican friars[1], and even in England in the 'Creed of Piers Ploughman' we are called to 'hearken to Hildegard[2].' At the time of the Reformation the attention genuine passages from her writings attracted was very considerable, and again in the 17th century they were interpreted as foretelling the downfall of the Jesuits[3]. Even in the course of the present century, passages taken from Hildegard's writings have been explained as foretelling the revolt of Belgium[4].

Hildegard lived to the advanced age of eighty-two. Her last writings, which were purely legendary, were a life of St Rupert, the

---

[1] Linde, *Handschriften der königl. Bibliothek in Wiesbaden,* 1877, pp. 95 ff.

[2] Line 1401.

[3] Cf. *The Nunns prophesie...concerning the rise and downfall of...the...Jesuits,* 1680.

[4] *Prédictions sur la révolution de la Belgique.* Amsterdam, 1832.

patron saint of her nunnery[1], and a life of St Disibodus, patron
saint of the monastery she had left[2]. As for Disibodus Wattenbach says that 'there is no mention of him previous to the 12th
century[3].' Indeed Grimm has explained the name 'Disiboden'
as a height hallowed to holy women (idisi), in which case, if an
early Christian dwelt there at all, he must have taken his name
from the height. In 1178 Hildegard passed away after a short
illness, and soon after her death an enquiry was instituted with
a view to her official canonization. In spite of renewed efforts
this was not accomplished, but her name was placed on the
Roman Martyrology and she is reckoned among the accepted
saints of the Church[4].

Surely it is curious that no attempt has hitherto been made
to submit the writings and influence of Hildegard to a detailed
critical examination. The few accounts which tell of her, such
as that of Schmelzeis[5], are dictated solely by the wish to show how
divine grace was made manifest in her. The reprint of her chief
works and a descriptive account of the extant manuscript copies
of her writings, and of genuine and supposititious works[6], have
now brought the material for such an enquiry within reach of the
student, and made it possible to obtain an analysis of the aims and
character of a woman whose influence and popularity were far-
reaching, and on whom later ages in recognition of her powers
have bestowed the epithet of the 'Sibyl of the Rhine[7].'

It remains to cast a glance at the writings of Elisabeth, the
nun at Schönau, who contemporaneously with Hildegard was held
to be divinely inspired, and who, 'while Hildegard acted as adviser
to Emperor and Pope, in humbler wise influenced the clergy and
the people[8].' In later ages the names of Hildegard and Elisabeth
were frequently coupled together, and their efforts to rouse the
representatives of the Church to greater consciousness of their
responsibilities were looked upon as a proof of God's wish to
restore the supreme influence of the Church. The nun Elisabeth
dwelt in the women's convent which was attached to the Bene-

---

[1] *Opera*, 'Vita St Rupertis,' pp. 1081–1092.
[2] Ibid. 'Vita St Disibodi,' pp. 1093–1116.
[3] Linde, *Handschriften der königl. Bibliothek in Wiesbaden*, 1877, p. 75, footnote.
[4] *Opera*, p. 90; *A. SS. Boll.* St Hildegardis, Sept. 17.
[5] Schmelzeis, *Das Leben und Wirken der heil. Hildegardis*, 1879.
[6] Linde, *Handschriften der königl. Bibliothek in Wiesbaden*, 1877.
[7] *Opera*, p. 140, footnote.
[8] Roth, F. W. E., *Die Visionen der heil. Elisabeth* etc. 1884, Vorwort, p. cv.

dictine monastery of Schönau in the diocese of Trier. She went there in 1141 at a youthful age, and in 1157 she became lady superior (magistra). Her brother Ekbert († 1184) while a canon at Bonn frequently visited her, and it was through her persuasion that he finally became a monk at Schönau. He was a writer of some importance, well known for his exhortations against the heretic Cathari; he had been educated with Reinald von Dassel, afterwards archbishop of Cöln, and with him adhered to the cause of the Emperor and the Antipope Victor. Elisabeth was inspired by similar political sympathies. For unlike Hildegard, who was an ardent supporter of Pope Alexander, Elisabeth was favourably inclined towards his opponent Pope Victor—a preference which laid her open to calumny.

The 'Visions' of Elisabeth came to her between 1152 and 1160, and we are told that they were sent her in the first place for her own comfort, direction and enlightenment. They are grouped together in three books, but there is a later work entitled 'On the ways of God,' which is sometimes referred to as a fourth book of the visions[1]. She also wrote 'Revelations on the holy band of Virgins at Cöln.' Her collected works fill the smaller half of a moderately sized volume.

It is supposed that Elisabeth was helped by her fellow-nuns to put the visions of the first books into writing, and that her brother Ekbert assisted in their circulation. The manuscript from which they were published contains an introduction by Ekbert written after he had become abbot at Schönau (1167), in which he says he has collected (conscripsi) these writings and other things that have reference to them, and that he has translated into Latin what happened to be in German[2].

The first book of the 'Visions' contains short accounts of how on certain festal days during religious service Elisabeth, who was delicate and apt to get excited at the mention of certain saints, asserts she saw them before her bodily. It is described how she was liable at any time to fall into trances, in which she lost consciousness of what happened around her. In the second and third books the accounts of the visions are fuller and more elaborate; they contain interesting bits of imagery and symbolism, and give us occasional glimpses of the daily life in the convent. It is curious to note how the fancied visions of the nun were in various

---

[1] Roth, *Die Visionen der heil. Elisabeth* etc. 1884, Vorwort, pp. cvii. ff.

[2] Ibid. 'Liber Visionum primus,' Prologus, p. 1.

particulars accepted by her contemporaries as manifestations of
the divine will.   The party in the Church, who were desirous of
establishing the 'Assumption of the Virgin' as a recognised festival,
greeted Elisabeth's vision of this incident[1] with enthusiasm.   Other
festivals of the Church, for example that of Corpus Christi, owed
their general acceptance to inspired visions of nuns.   For the
emotional yearning of the age found relief in representations of
religious ideas, and the Church readily ministered to the desire
by elaborating the cult of relics and saint-worship.

It is thought that Elisabeth's book 'On the ways of God[2]' was
written after she became acquainted with the 'Scivias' of Hildegard, and her title looks like an imitation[3].   This work consists
also of visions, but these are given in the form of admonitions
(sermones) addressed to different classes of society; the work is
wonderfully complete in plan and execution.   In simple and direct
language men are urged to mend their ways, and to listen to the
admonitions which the Angel of the Lord has vouchsafed to them
through the mouth of the nun.

In this book Elisabeth sees the summit of a lofty mountain,
on which stands a man whose face is luminous, whose eyes shine
like stars and from whose mouth goes forth a sword.   She sees
three paths leading up this hill; one is blue, another green, and
the third purple.   The blue path indicates the use of contemplation,
the green of action, and the purple of martyrdom.   But afterwards
other paths appear which also lead up the hill towards heaven:
these are the paths of married people (conjugatorum), of celi-
bates (continentium), of prelates (prelatorum), of widows (vidua-
torum), of hermits (heremitarum), of young people (adolescentum
et juvenum) and of children (infantum).

'I was resting on my bed but not asleep,' says Elisabeth,
speaking of those who have chosen a life of contemplation[4], 'when
the Angel (spiritus) of the Lord visited me of a sudden and in-
inspired me to speak as follows: "Give heed, you, who have
renounced worldly pleasures and who have chosen to follow in the
footsteps of Him who has summoned you into His beauteous light
and who Himself calls you His chosen sons, appointing you to the
end of time to judge the tribes of Israel.   Consider among yourselves in what way you should live in humility, obedience, love,

---

[1] Ibid. 'Liber Visionum secundus,' c. 31, p. 53; Anlage, p. 153.
[2] Ibid. 'Liber Viarum Dei,' pp. 88–122.
[3] Ibid. Vorwort, p. cix.   [4] Ibid. 'Liber Viarum Dei,' c. 10, p. 92.

and without murmuring, without disparagement, jealousy and pride, and take heed that you keep yourselves from other vices! Love one another, that your Father in heaven be not blasphemed in you and be not roused to anger at your leaving your path, the path of contemplation!" Then the Angel (angelus) of the Lord followed up his utterances by saying: "If there be among you wranglings, quarrels, disparagements, complaints, anger, hatred and jealousy, spiritual pride (extollencia oculorum), desire for advancement, boasting, ribaldry, gluttony, laziness, incontinence, idleness and such like, in all of which you walk on, sons of this world, what place do you give to divine contemplation?" And again he spoke and said: "This exhortation of God is addressed to you who have chosen to serve God whether in the clerical or in the monastic profession. You have chosen the best part, but take heed lest it slip from you. Studiously avoid the sinfulness of those who outwardly bear the semblance of religion, but shame its worth by their actions. With their lips they honour God; by their ways they blaspheme Him. Some of them strive for knowledge of the law, but they know not how to apply it. They turn their back on truth, and yet they boast of moving in the path of contemplation. They make the law of God and their advocacy of it serve their pride, avarice and desires, and from those who dwell in Jesus Christ they boldly snatch wealth and honours, and cherish their foulness. The sanctuary of God, and places to be hallowed by angels, they visit with pride and pollution, and raise the adorable treasures of Christ's sacrament in irreverent ministration with impure hearts. They jeer at him who rebukes them and sadden him with contempt and persecution. Those among them who are less wicked, are yet hateful before the Lord. For they walk about with the semblance of humility, but their hearts are far removed from it. They multiply words, but of what use are these when in their hearts they oppose God, neglect brotherly love, envy and disparage others, and wrangle about position? They profess contempt of the world, but worship that which is of the world, strut about boldly, and yield to every gust of their desires. They have cast aside the customs of their fathers; they engage in the business of this world and fill the Church with wranglings. Thus religion suffers contempt, and faith is divided. But why should I enlarge on such doings, saith the Lord? A shout is raised against them, but they listen not and repudiate my voice of admonition in contempt....."'

And it is not only those of the religious profession whom the nun admonishes. The address to married people[1] is especially interesting, not only on account of her conception of the mutual obligations of husband and wife, claiming obedience from the wife and respect for his wife's feelings from the husband, but because she vehemently attacks women's love of dress and men's love of indulgence. The Angel of God informs Elisabeth that now-a-days men in large numbers degrade their desires to the level of women's folly, and are foolish enough to adapt themselves to women's stupidity. 'The love of dress, which thou dost hate and despise in the women of the world who come to thee, has grown apace on earth, and has become a madness, and brings down the wrath of God. They delight in walking about, their steps hampered by the mass of their garments, and they try to wear out to no profit what the poor sorely need. O wretchedness, O blindness!'

It is in the course of this exhortation that Elisabeth consults the Angel about the heretic Cathari[2], who she states are said to reject marriage while teaching at the same time that only those marriages are valid where both parties have preserved their virginity. The Angel cannot deny that such marriages are most acceptable to God, but declares that they are rare. Yet he announces that the leaders of that sect are of Satan. 'Then,' the nun continues, 'I said, "Lord, what and of what kind is their faith?" He answered: "Their faith is contemptible, their works are worse." And I said: "Yet they have the appearance of just men and are praised as men of good works." "Truly," he replied, "they put on an appearance of just and innocent living, through which they attract and convert many, and yet inwardly they are full of the worst madness."' Considering that nothing is known of these early dissenters except what their opponents have preserved, these remarks are interesting as showing that though Hildegard treated the Cathari with unhesitating contempt Elisabeth was perplexed about them.

Another exhortation addressed to the ministers of the Church is eloquent in its attacks on the overbearing conduct of the clergy, and on the way they neglect their flocks. Widows are then admonished to cultivate peace of mind and to reflect only on spiritual joys, and hermits are urged not to carry their self-denying practices to extremes, since immoderate fasting is pro-

---

[1] Roth, *Die Visionen der heil. Elisabeth* etc. 1884, 'Liber Viarum Dei,' c. 13, p. 100.
[2] Ibid. p. 104.

ductive of no good results. The book seems originally to have
ended here, for the last two exhortations are evidently the result
of an afterthought. In the first of these young people are recommended to cultivate seriousness of mind, and the second treats
of young children, but only in a vague way, for their parents are
said to be chiefly responsible for their behaviour. The book ends
with a paragraph to the effect that the angel appeared and addressed the bishops of Trier, Cöln and Mainz telling them to
amend their ways and accept the contents of the book. 'Read
them, and hearken to their divine admonitions,' it says[1], 'and
receive them with an equable mind. Do not think they be the
fabrications of a woman, for they are not ; they have come through
God, the Almighty Father, who is the source and origin of all
goodness.'

It must have been some time after she had begun to write
visions that Elisabeth wrote the following letter to Hildegard. It
is preserved in the third book of her visions, and also in the correspondence of Hildegard, together with the reply sent to it[2].

'What you said had been revealed to you concerning me, I now
write to confirm ; a cloud of distrust has come over my mind owing
to the foolish sayings of some people who are ever talking of me ;
they are not true. The talk of the people I can easily bear, but not
of those who wear clerical garb, they bitterly oppress my spirit. For
goaded on, at whose instigation I know not, they ridicule the grace
of God that is within me, and do not hesitate rashly to condemn
what they do not understand. I hear that certain letters written in
their spirit are circulating under my name. They accuse me of
having prophesied concerning the Day of Judgment, which I surely
never have presumed to do, as knowledge of its advent is denied to
mortal man.' She goes on to explain how the angel of God had
repeatedly appeared to her, saying that the time for contrition and
repentance had come, and how she had spoken of this to others. But
now a letter is circulated, full of threats against the abbot. In her
distress she begs that Hildegard will accept this explanation, offer
prayers in her behalf and write her some words of consolation.

In her reply to this letter Hildegard admits Elisabeth's power
of prophecy. She also is a trumpet through which the blasts of
divine admonition become audible. Another letter addressed to
Hildegard by Elisabeth shows that they remained in communi-

---

[1] Roth, *Die Visionen der heil. Elisabeth* etc. 1884, 'Liber Viarum Dei,' c. 20, p. 122.
[2] Ibid. pp. 70, 178.

cation[1], though their different church and political sympathies naturally precluded a closer connection.

The last book Elisabeth wrote added greatly to her fame. It consists of 'Revelations on the holy band of virgins of Cöln[2],' the companions and fellow-martyrs of St Ursula, the origin of which legend is shrouded in some obscurity[3]. The story current in Elisabeth's time in various versions states that in the 3rd century Ursula, a British princess, went on pilgrimage to Rome with 11,000 virgin companions, and that on their journey homewards these virgins together with many followers were murdered at Cöln, either by the Huns or some other heathen tribes. The name Ursula, however, does not occur in any of the ancient martyrologies, and therefore may be a latter-day addition to the story, while the extraordinary number of her companions is held to have originated through misreading an inscription which refers to eleven martyred virgins (XI M. V.). History speaks of virgin martyrs at Cöln at an early date.

In 1156 a quantity of bones were found in an ancient cemetery outside Cöln, and this led to the revival of the story, which now assumed gigantic proportions. The relics of one of the virgins named Cordula were brought to Schönau by Ekbert. Elisabeth's imagination was roused, the progress of St Ursula, various incidents of her journey and the character of many of her companions, were made manifest to her in a series of visions by St Verena, also one of the band, who repeatedly appeared to Elisabeth and divinely enlightened her on various points in dispute. With the help of this saint Elisabeth felt enabled to explain how Pope Cyriacus (otherwise unknown to history) came to be of the party; how it was that archbishops, cardinals and a king of England accompanied these women, and what caused one of the band to bury, with some of the dead, tablets inscribed with their names, which tablets had come to light at Cöln. The whole account, which Elisabeth promulgated in good faith, and which her contemporaries had no hesitation in accepting as genuine, forms a most interesting example of mediaeval religious romance. It teems with chronological and historical impossibilities: apart from these it bears the stamp of truthfulness. It is pure romance, but it is romance set forth in a

---

[1] Ibid. p. 74.

[2] Ibid. 'De Sacro Exercitu Virginum Coloniensium,' pp. 123–153.

[3] Ibid. Vorwort, pp. cxi ff. Roth discusses the history of the development of this legend.

spirit of conviction and with a circumstantiality of detail thoroughly convincing to the uncritical mind.

Throughout the Rhine district these visions were greeted with acclamation. They were welcome for two reasons; they increased the interest and traffic in the relics at Cöln, and they fell in with current traditions and encouraged the revived local worship of the three women-saints. The names of these were now connected with that of St Ursula[1], and the legend of St Ursula became the centre of many floating traditions, and has proportionately attracted the attention of the hagiologist and the folk-lore student. Eleven thousand became the accepted number of Ursula's followers and the compilers of the *Acta Sanctorum* have actually succeeded in making out a list containing over seven hundred names[2].

In literature the version of the legend as told by Elisabeth was accepted in preference to earlier versions, and became popular not only in Germany, but also in England and France, especially in Normandy. In England both the legend and the visions were known as early as 1181 through Roger, a monk of the Cistercian abbey at Forde in Devonshire. It is thought that he came into personal contact with Elisabeth at Schönau, and references are sometimes made to him as the compiler of the 'Visions' and as the author of the legend of the band of 11,000 virgins[3].

Elisabeth died in 1164 at the early age of thirty-six, and her brother Ekbert, who was staying with her at the time, wrote a full account of the last days of her life to three nuns of the convent of St Thomas at Andernach[4]. In this letter he describes Elisabeth's thoughtful care and tenderness to her companions on her deathbed, and says that she was more than a sister to him and that his grief is proportionally greater. Like Hildegard Elisabeth has never been officially canonized, but her name also was inscribed in the Roman Martyrology compiled by Gregory VIII, by which she became a recognised saint of the Church[5].

A later age witnessed other notable nuns who were divinely inspired and who were acknowledged to be so by their contemporaries, but, as we shall see later, their communings with God and the saints were chiefly directed to intensifying mystic and

---

[1] Comp. above, p. 40.

[2] *A. SS. Boll.*, St Ursula, Oct. 21.

[3] Roth, *Die Visionen der heil. Elisabeth* etc. 1884, Vorwort, p. cxxiv; Hardy, Th. D., *Descriptive catalogue of MS. material*, 1858, vol. 2, p. 417.

[4] Roth, *Die Visionen der heil. Elisabeth* etc. 1884, p. 253.

[5] *A. SS. Boll.*, St Elisabetha, June 18.

devotional feelings in themselves.   They have neither the hold on
outside events nor the wide outlook which give such a deep interest
to the writings of St Hildegard of Bingen and St Elisabeth of
Schönau.

§ 2.   Women-Saints connected with Charity and Philanthropy.

The last section showed how earnestly the religious teachers
of the 12th century advocated a stricter practice of the precepts
of religion.   The practical outcome of this advocacy was an increased consciousness among those of the upper and authoritative
classes of society of the needs and sufferings of humbler folk, and
an extraordinary development of pity and tenderness for suffering
generally.   It can be noticed that everywhere there sprang into
life the desire to help those who were in distress, and to cultivate
that love and sympathy which is indifferent to rank, degree and
antecedents, and especially so with regard to the diseased, despised
and shunned.

The representative figures of this movement during the 13th
century are St Francis of Assisi († 1226) and St Elisabeth of
Thüringen († 1231), whose fame will abide wherever the precepts
of Christianity in the direction of unselfishness and charitable zeal
are cherished.   The tendency to renounce all worldly possessions,
which was a feature of the 13th century, culminated in them,
and their example was followed by many men and women who
on account of their altruistic sympathies are numbered among
the saints.   Since the practical outcome of their efforts carries
in itself the beginnings of our modern charitable institutions of
hospital, almshouse and infirmary, their work is well worth a somewhat detailed account, but such an account must necessarily be
preceded by a few general remarks on the development of charitable
zeal in the course of history.

From the earliest period Christian teachers had championed
the cause of the poor and afflicted, and had upheld the sanctity
of human life as such, whether in the aged, the crippled, or the
unborn.   Moreover the Church throughout ministered to poverty
by almsgiving, and looked upon the destitute as having a special
claim on her care.   At two distinct periods in history these self-
imposed duties were specially requisite—at the breaking up of

the Roman Empire, and at the collapse of the feudal system. For under the Roman social system slavery had been a safeguard against vagrancy, but when slavery was discontinued the class of homeless outcasts became numerous. And again under the feudal system men belonged to the soil they were born on, but in proportion as serfdom ceased, beggars, and especially the diseased, increased to a great extent. In both instances efforts to stay the consequent evils to society were made by all professing Christians, but the attitudes of the 5th and the 12th centuries have distinct points of difference which it is well to bear in mind.

Glancing back along the vistas of time to the 5th century we find Severin bishop of Noricum († 482) instituting a regular and far-reaching system of charitable relief which has been described by his disciple Eugippius[1]. In connection with Magnericus of Trier († 596), the famous opposer of idolatrous practices, the newly-developed virtues of this period are thus summed up by his biographer, the monk Eberwein († 1047)[2]: 'With him (Magnericus) the hungry found bread, the traveller found shelter, the naked found clothing, the weary found rest, and the stranger found hopefulness.' We see that the efforts of these men were directed to ministering to poverty but not to disease, for the prevalent attitude of Christian society towards disease continued for some centuries strongly self-preservative. The poor were fed, but the diseased were shunned, especially those who were visibly disfigured, and who included the vast class of those who from the 11th century were currently spoken of as lepers (leprosi).

The homogeneity of the disease *lepra* in this application has been called into question, and it has been shown that the 'lepers' of the Middle Ages included those suffering from cutaneous eruption brought on by St Anthony's fire, from gangrene of the limbs, such as comes through protracted use of bread containing rye spurred or diseased with ergot, and from other diseases which produce visible disfigurement. Scant provision was made for such people during early Christian ages, and lepers were numbered among social outcasts, not from fear of contagion—that was a comparatively late idea—but simply from a wish on the part of society to be spared a sorry sight. The diseased member of a family was a visible burden to his relations, and finding himself despised and shunned by his associates he took refuge with

---

[1] *A. SS. Boll.*, St Severinus, Jan. 8.
[2] *A. SS. Boll.*, St Magnericus, July 25, *Vita*, c. 49.

outlaws, who herded together and lived in a state of filth, misery and moral degradation terrible to recall.

It is in the treatment of these unfortunate people that the 12th century witnessed a revolution. The efforts of a few large-souled individuals overcame the general disgust felt towards disease, the restraints of a more barbarous age were broken through, the way to deal with the evil was pointed out, and gradually its mitigation was accomplished. The task these people set themselves, as so often happens in the course of social reform, absorbed them so entirely that they thought no sacrifice too great when it was a question of carrying out their ideas. It seems therefore rather gratuitous on the part of the modern scientist to say that a 'halo of morbid exaggeration surrounded the idea of leprosy in the mediaeval religious mind. We live in a time of saner and better proportioned sentiment,' etc.[1] In point of fact an evil is removed only by putting it for a time into strong relief, when it comes to be rightly dealt with and so is gradually checked. In early Christian times nothing was done for diseased people and lepers, but in the 12th and 13th centuries first individuals, then the masses, became interested in them. It mattered little that vagrants of the worst kind felt encouraged to call themselves lepers because as such they could excite more pity, could gain admission into hospitals, or were allowed to solicit alms under royal patronage. The movement once set going in the right direction steadily did its work : and the class of lepers so prominent in the 11th and 12th centuries were rapidly disappearing by the end of the 13th[2].

From the earliest period monasteries and church centres offered some alleviation for the sick and distressed, but their resources were at first intended for the relief of those who belonged to the settlement. The peaceful pursuits and regular occupations of the monk naturally prolonged his term of life, and as Christianity set great store by a peaceful and happy death, when feebleness and sickness crept on the member of a convent he was relieved from his duties and tended in an outhouse by a brother told off for the purpose. The guest-house of the settlement, called *hospitalis*, generally stood near this outhouse for the sick, but sometimes it was identical with it, and the pilgrims and travellers who were ill were nursed with the convent inmates. While these combined houses for guests and invalids, attached to convents, were numerous

[1] Creighton, C., *History of Epidemics in England*, vol. 1, 1891, p. 85.
[2] Ibid. p. 97.

from the first, the foundation of shelters intended primarily for strangers took place comparatively late. Among them must be numbered the shelters designated as hospitals (hospitales), founded in outlying districts for the reception of pilgrims (pro susceptione peregrinorum) such as the Pope urged Karl the Great († 814) to keep up in the Alps[1]. Pilgrims were always an object of solicitude to the Church, and it was in their interest that the earliest independent road-side shelters and hospitals in cities were founded. These shelters and hospitals often consisted of no more than the protection of a roof, and the proctor, or brothers and sisters who voluntarily took charge of the house, secured the needful sustenance for themselves and those seeking their aid by going about begging.

The impulse to found these rests or hospitals naturally emanated from Rome, from a very early date the site of pilgrimages, but a new impulse was given to the movement by the foundation of two important guest-houses at Jerusalem in the 11th century, when that city also was a frequent resort of pilgrims. Of these two guest-houses or hospitals[2], one was intended for men and placed under the management of men, the other was for women and placed under the management of women. They were arranged according to an elaborate system which is interesting in many ways. The men were divided into three classes—the knights who looked after the interests of the house, the priests who attended to the sick, and the lay-brothers who assisted in the same work. The knights formed themselves into the religious order of St John, from the name of the church near which their headquarters lay. Similarly the women's house, which was near the chapel of St Mary Magdalen, consisted of ladies, nuns and lay servants. The fact that St John and St Mary Magdalen were so often adopted as patron saints of similar houses elsewhere was due to the chance connection of these saints with the hospitals at Jerusalem.

Looking after pilgrims and nursing the sick constituted the chief work of the order at Jerusalem, but after the conquest of that city in 1187, when the knights removed to Malta and the ladies to Spain, the care of those not belonging to their body ceased to hold the foremost place. But the existence of the hospitals at Jerusalem and the attention they had attracted in the different

---

[1] Muratori, *Antiquitates Italiae*, 1738. Pope Hadrian I to Karl the Great, vol. 3, p. 581.

[2] Salles, F., *Annales de l'ordre de Malte, ou des hospitaliers de St Jean de Jérusalem*, 1889.

countries of Europe, where grants of land had been made for their support, indirectly stimulated efforts in favour of the foundation of similar shelters or hospitals.

The first idea of independent hospitals came into England from Rome, when Archbishop Lanfranc († 1089), a native of Italy, founded two hospitals in the true sense of the word, one inside, one outside Canterbury. The one situated inside the city walls is described by the historian Eadmer († 1124) in the following terms[1]. 'He divided it into two parts; men who were sick in various ways inhabited the one, women the other part. He gave to them clothes of his own and daily sustenance; and ordered that there should be servants and masters who were to take care they should want nothing; the men had no access to the women, nor the women to the men.' A chapel was built on the other side of the way and given into the care of canons, who were to attend to the spiritual needs of the sick and to see to their burial after death.

The other hospital founded by Lanfranc was at Herbaltown, in the woods of Blean, a mile away from Canterbury; it was for those who were afflicted with scrofula (regia valetudine fluentibus), and who at a later date, in the confirming charter of Henry II, are styled lepers (leprosi)[2].

These accounts of Lanfranc's foundations are especially interesting as they give us some of the earliest well-authenticated indications of a changed attitude towards lepers, and anticipate the efforts made in their behalf in the 12th century by the founders of the orders of combined canons and nuns, and in the 13th century by a number of women who on this account are numbered among the saints. These women, as we shall see, not only felt interested in these unfortunate beings but unhesitatingly tended them with their own hands. They knew nothing of the disgust usually felt towards wretchedness and poverty, and found their life's happiness in vanquishing sordidness and filth. In the eyes of some of their contemporaries they were chiefly bent on seeking sorry sights and coveting painful experiences, but, apart from the appreciation they found among those to whom they directly ministered, others were generous enough to recognise the heroism of their efforts.

Among these women must be numbered Matilda († 1118) the

---

[1] Dugdale, *Monasticon*, 'Hospital of St Gregory,' vol. 6, p. 615, nr 1.

[2] Dugdale, *Monasticon*, 'Herbaldoun,' vol. 6, p. 653; Creighton, C., *History of Epidemics*, vol. 1, 1891, p. 87.

wife of Henry I of England, the daughter of St Margaret and the sister of St David of Scotland, whose education and marriage have been discussed above in connection with Romsey. Highly as Matilda was esteemed by her contemporaries, she has never been accepted as a saint, and no day is given to her in the Calendar. This omission is perhaps due to the fact that she left her nunnery against the wishes of some of the clergy, perhaps owing to her husband's quarrels with the Pope, for Matilda was beloved by high and low and early writers are unanimous in praise of her. Map speaks of her as the holy queen Matilda (sanctae Matildis reginae)[1].

This estimate is based on the fact that Matilda was so moved by pity towards lepers that she overcame the repugnance commonly felt towards them. A well-authenticated story is told of how her brother David, coming into her apartment, found it full of lepers. She proceeded to lay aside her robe and with a towel girt about her washed and dried their feet and then kissed them, and when her brother objected she replied that in kissing the feet of lepers she was kissing the feet of the Eternal King. Ailred of Rievaux recounts the story, which he had from David, who repeatedly spoke of it to him[2].

This generous disposition is borne out by the fact that soon after her marriage Matilda founded the hospital of St Giles in the East for the maintenance of forty lepers, a chaplain, a clerk and a messenger[3]. It was commonly known for a long time afterwards as the hospital of Matilda. It was founded in 1101, and Matthew Paris saw it a hundred and fifty years later and made a sketch of it which is still extant[4]. With the exception of the house founded by Lanfranc in Herbaltown, the inmates of which were not styled lepers at the time, the hospital of St Giles, the foundation of 'good Queen Maud,' was the first institution of its kind in England and for a long time remained quite the most important.

But we must study the records of foreign countries to find the majority of those women who were actively beneficent to the sick, and who for this reason are officially accepted as saints. Probably leprosy, or the diseases collected under this designation, showed greater virulence on the Continent than they ever did in England,

---

[1] Map, W., *De Nugis Curialium*, 1850, p. 228.
[2] Ailred, *Opera* (in Migne, *Patrol. Cursus Completus*, vol. 195), p. 368.
[3] Dugdale, *Monasticon*, ' St Giles in the Fields,' vol. 6, p. 635.
[4] Creighton, C., *History of Epidemics in England*, vol. 1, 1891, p. 88.

and the miseries of those who were repulsively disfigured were extreme, when in the first half of the 13th century a small group of women personally related to each other took pity on them. The field of their labours was in Central and South Germany and the adjoining countries, which were at that time brought under German influence.

All the women who were actuated by this new philanthropic spirit were members, either by birth or marriage, of the powerful and influential family of the Counts of Andechs and Meran[1]. The scientist Virchow has remarked that this family, which was once most prosperous and widely spread, practically extinguished itself through its extreme ascetic tendencies[2]. Its men joined the Crusades, and any who returned dedicated their sons to the celibacy of the bishopric and their daughters to that of the cloister; and in this way the family ceased to exist after a few generations.

Whence the first impulse towards charitable deeds came to them we know not, but we find them sometimes taking the initiative in philanthropic enterprises, and sometimes uniting their efforts to those of others who were working on similar lines to their own. Some members of the family acted as patrons to the Cistercian order, —others invited and encouraged the settlement of the Teutonic or Red Cross Knights in their lands. Others again were strongly attracted by the teachings of the Dominican and Franciscan friars, who were very influential in the first half of the 13th century. Various tendencies were represented in the different countries of Europe by the followers of St Francis of Assisi. This divergence arose partly because the rule of life promulgated in 1209 was supplanted by another in 1221, and partly from the varied interests of each country. In South Germany it was the influence of the Franciscans which primarily encouraged charitable zeal and self-denial.

Hedwig, daughter of Count Berthold, of the family of Andechs and Meran, first claims our attention on account of her charitable deeds. She married Heinrich the Bearded (✝ 1238), first duke of Silesia, Poland and Croatia. These districts were occupied by people of the Slav race, and it was at this time that they were first brought into contact with German influence and civilization. Christianity had been introduced in the 12th century, but there

---

[1] Hormayr, 'Die Grafen von Andechs und Tyrol,' *Sämtl. Werke*, vol. 3.

[2] Virchow, R., 'Zur Geschichte des Aussatzes, besonders in Deutschland,' in *Archiv für pathol. Anatomie*, vol. 18, article 2, p. 311.

were very few churches, and the conditions of life were unsettled and insecure owing to the continued feuds of the barons. Heinrich checked internal dissensions with a high hand; he was zealous in introducing German law and in encouraging German immigration, and in this way gave solidarity to this part of the Empire. His marriage with the daughter of a family which was among the wealthiest and most influential in South Germany is a proof of his German sympathies.

Hedwig is the recognised patron saint of Silesia. Grünhagen says[1]: 'If we call to mind how far the numerous churches and charitable foundations which are referred to the Duchess Hedwig influenced civilization at that period, how the monks and nuns whom Hedwig summoned spread German culture in these districts; if we further remember how powerfully at that time the example of unselfish piety and sympathy, emanating from the throne, took hold of the mind of the people; we shall be obliged to accept as well founded the veneration Hedwig generally enjoyed, although we may not feel attracted by the traits of exaggerated asceticism insisted on by her legend.'

Hedwig[2] was born in 1174 and sent for her education to Kizzingen, an ancient convent foundation situated in Franken on property belonging to her family. In 1186, when not yet thirteen, she was taken from the convent to be married. She brought with her into Silesia a dower of thirty thousand marks, which was forthwith devoted to religious and charitable purposes, for Hedwig appears throughout to have been filled by the belief, which she shared with her husband, that religious settlements and colonies were alone capable of introducing culture and establishing civilization in the land.

The monastic orders had only recently gained a foothold in these districts. In 1139 a band of Benedictine monks had settled near Breslau, the centre of the country, and in 1175 at the instigation of Boleslaus, the father of Hedwig's husband, some Cistercians had come to Leubus. These Cistercians were now helpful in constructing a nunnery at Trebnitz near Breslau, which Hedwig founded soon after her marriage. She summoned thither nuns from the Cistercian nunnery at Bamberg, where her sister Mathilde, afterwards abbess of Kizzingen, was being educated, and entrusted the rule

---

[1] *Allgemeine deutsche Biographie*, article 'Hedwig.'

[2] Stenzel, G. A. H., *Scriptores rerum Siles.*, Breslau 1835, 'Vita St. Hedwigis' vol. 2, pp. 1–114; also *A. SS. Boll.*, St Hedwig, Oct. 17.

of the new convent to Pietrussa († 1214), a nun from the convent of Kizzingen. The abbess and convent of Trebnitz are mentioned as early as 1202. The house was intended to promote education among girls of both noble and lowly parentage, and among them was Agnes, daughter of the king of Bohemia, of whom we shall hear more. It soon numbered a hundred inmates, and at the time when Hedwig's life was written, that is towards the close of the 13th century, it contained a hundred and twenty women.

This life of Hedwig, written some time after her death, emphasizes the ascetic habits which she embraced, and in agreement with later descriptions and pictures represents her as an emaciated person worn thin by self-denial and fasting. On the other hand the representation of her on her sarcophagus, which is of an earlier date, represents her as a vigorous, massive and comely woman[1]. The account of her life shows that she advocated new ideas throughout. ' By marrying,' it says, ' she followed her parents' will rather than her own, as is clearly manifest from what followed, for she checked herself by self-restraint. Bound by the sacrament she was determined to live her married life as the apostle has taught, keeping his precepts of marriage worthily. She hoped to secure eternal life by giving birth to children, yet she wished also to please God by chastity, and with her husband's consent practised self-restraint. Whenever she was aware that the duties of motherhood were beginning, she avoided her husband's proximity, and firmly denied herself all intercourse until the time of her confinement. She did so from the time of first becoming a mother, that is at the age of thirteen years and thirteen weeks, and under like circumstances ever behaved in the same way. When she had become the mother of three sons, Boleslaus, Konrad, and Heinrich, and of three daughters, Agnes, Sophie, and Gertrud, she altogether embraced a life of chastity. The like observation of chastity in marriage which Mother Church has sanctioned she pressed upon every one she could.' Her conduct appears to have had her husband's sanction. Heinrich's sympathies are apparent in his granting property to the Cistercians for a monastery called after him Heinrichsau, in founding an important hospital in Breslau dedicated to the Holy Ghost, and in making a foundation for canons at Neumarkt, where he

---

[1] *Verein für das Museum schles. Alterthümer*, edit. Luchs, H., 1870. Also Luchs, H., *Schlesische Fürstenbilder*, 1872.

erected an important leper hospital[1]. During one of the wars which he engaged in, he was taken prisoner by the heathen Prussians, and the story is told how his wife, indifferent to every danger, went to him and procured his release.

It was in connection with the lepers who were sheltered at Neumarkt that Hedwig's conduct appeared especially wonderful to her contemporaries. Her biographer tells us that she had taken into her special care the leprous women who lived there, 'so that she sent them money, food and game (ferinas) several times a week, and gave them liberally clothes and other necessaries of life, taking care of them as though they had been her own daughters. With wonderful tenderness she attended upon those who were afflicted with bodily ills, and her affections melted towards the poor and infirm, whom she tended with great love and helpfulness.'

A series of paintings in miniature were executed at an early date which set forth the work of the pious Hedwig and of which a copy made in 1353 is extant[2]. It forms a valuable monument of early painting, and in archaeological interest compares favourably with the work of Herrad. In these pictures we repeatedly see Hedwig in the company of the Trebnitz nuns. In one picture she leads the nuns into the convent, in another she shows them the church, and in a third she waits on them. They are represented as surrounding her in her trials and at her death, and as laying her in her tomb. In these pictures the nuns wear grey or blue gowns and a black headdress, no wimples (which are worn by lay women), and they do not seem to share the same dwelling, but to inhabit separate small huts which are pictured standing side by side round the church. Hedwig herself wears simple clothing but no convent garb. In these pictures a legendary reading is given to some incidents of her life. For example she is represented as surrounded in her hours of tribulation by hairy and grotesque demons.

A large number of these pictures show Hedwig's charitable zeal. There is one in which she is depicted urging upon her husband the cause of the poor; again she makes the gift of a house to them; she washes and kisses the feet of lepers; she feeds the sick, who are seen lying in bed; she gives food to the poor; she ministers to a prisoner; and she distributes gifts among

---

[1] Virchow, R., 'Zur Geschichte des Aussatzes, besonders in Deutschland,' in *Archiv für pathol. Anatomie*, vol. 18, article 2, p. 275.

[2] Wolfskron, *Bilder der Hedwigslegende*, 1846.

pilgrims.   Men who are in the stocks and doomed to death also rouse her pity; and she insists on feeding the poor with her own hands before she can be persuaded to sit down to meals.   In these pictures we note the scarred and blotched appearance of those who are designated as lepers, the wretched appearance of the poor, and the curiously low type of countenance of all the beggars.

In her family relations Hedwig was most unfortunate, and one can but hope that her charitable zeal brought her solace or that the different basis on which family life then rested made her feel the sad fate of her relations less acutely than she would otherwise have done.   Her sister Agnes married Philippe Auguste, king of France (1180–1223), but she was repudiated in consequence of the Pope's attack on the validity of her marriage, and died in misery in 1201.   Her other sister Gertrud, who was the mother of St Elisabeth of Thüringen, married Bela III of Hungary, and was assassinated in 1214.   Hedwig's daughter Gertrud was betrothed to Otto von Wittelsbach, who in consequence of political intrigues was tempted to murder Philip, king of Swabia, in 1208.   Heinrich and Ekbert, Hedwig's two brothers, were accused of being his accomplices, and the consequence was that Heinrich saw his castle destroyed and lived for years in banishment, and Ekbert, who was bishop of Bamberg (1203–37), was obliged to fly, though he was afterwards reinstated in his see.   When Otto the king-murderer was dead, Gertrud, his prospective bride, entered the nunnery at Trebnitz, where she afterwards succeeded Pietrussa as abbess.

In the year 1216, however, Hedwig had the joy of seeing her son Heinrich, who reigned conjointly with his father, married to Anna, a princess of Bohemia, whose tendencies were quite in accordance with her own.   Indeed Anna's zeal was carried yet a step farther in the direction of self-imposed lowliness and humility, she readily submitted to bodily chastisement.   She has no place among the saints, but we are in possession of an early account of her[1] which speaks in great praise of her charitable deeds.   Conjointly with her husband Anna made several religious foundations, and greeted the Dominican and Franciscan friars as brothers in the Lord.   Inmates of the nunnery of the order of St Francis, which she had founded at Breslau, spoke with enthusiasm of her goodness and charity.   She too nursed the leprous with her own hands, distributed food among the poor, and was to 'forlorn children and orphans a protector and a mother.'

[1] Stenzel, G. A. H., *Scriptores rer. Siles.*, 1835, 'Vita Annae ducissae Sil.' vol. 2, p. 127.

History has preserved an account of the courageous manner in which she opposed the Tartars, at whose invasion of Breslau, she, her mother-in-law Hedwig, and Gertrud, the abbess of Trebnitz, fled to Crossen. Anna's husband was killed by the enemy and his head was set on a stake outside the town to induce her to surrender, but in vain. After the defeat of the Tartars the women returned to Breslau, where they found their nunnery utterly deserted. The nuns had fled, and years passed before the settlement regained its standing—Hedwig bestowed her property Schawoine on it in the hope that this would help it to recover.

Hedwig spent the last years of her life in close connection with Trebnitz. She died in 1243 and as early as 1267 was canonized by Pope Clement IV. Her daughter-in-law, Anna, lived to a great age, and to the end of her days remained interested in her convent and charitable foundations. In 1253 she founded a hospital at Kreuzberg on the model of one previously founded by her cousin St Elisabeth. This hospital and the one founded at Neumarkt by Hedwig are still in existence, but the nunneries founded by these women have long since passed away.

The movement Hedwig had inaugurated in Silesia forthwith made itself felt in wider circles, and we find the princess Agnes of Bohemia, Anna's sister, who had lived for several years at Trebnitz, advocating after her return to Prague practices similar to those with which she had come into contact in Silesia. Agnes also is a saint of the Church[1], and her fame rests on her charitable works and on her indifference to position and possessions in comparison with the relief of suffering humanity. She is moreover a virgin saint. For she was to have married the emperor Friedrich II († 1250) against her wish, when her father opportunely died, leaving her free to remain single. She then devoted her patrimony, which was considerable, to founding a nunnery at Prague together with an important hospital.

Agnes was supported at home by her brother, the king of Bohemia, and by the bishop of Prague. Pope Gregory IX († 1241) wrote to her praising her resolution to remain unmarried, and Clara, the friend of St Francis, wrote to her from Assisi to encourage her in her devotions. Clara's letters are extant, and afford an interesting glimpse of the aims which these women set before them. In one letter Clara praises Agnes for refusing marriage with the 'Caesar,'

---

[1] *A. SS. Boll.*, St Agnes de Bohemia, March 6, print two accounts, of uncertain date.

and advises her rather to follow blessed poverty and devote herself to the mortification of the flesh.   Again she addresses Agnes as a second Rachel, admonishing her to turn her thoughts to eternity, and likening her to the holy St Agnes with the blessed lamb[1].

The Bohemian princess was further encouraged in her aims by the gift of a prayer-book, a veil, a platter and a drinking-cup which Clara had used.   The accounts we have of Agnes, consisting of a longer and a shorter record lately printed from MSS preserved at Prague, give a full description of the willing humility this holy woman practised in the convent and of the tenderness she showed towards the sick.

'There you might see her,' says the longer account[2], 'the daughter of Premislaus III, king of Bohemia, lighting with her own hands the fire for the sisters ; the sister of Wenceslaus IV, king of Bohemia, cleaning out the dirty rooms ; the intended spouse of the emperor Friedrich II perspiring in the kitchen like any lowly maid. And while she did so, not by angry expression or stern face did she resent it ; filled with joy she worked as a servant of Christ and proved it to those who saw her by the sweet expression she wore.   She behaved in this way not only to those who were healthy, but she gladly extended her kindness to those who were ill ; she spread soft beds for them, she carefully removed all that could distress eyes and nose, she prepared food with her own hands, and cooked it that it might be served to taste, with untiring energy, that the sick might be freed from ill, pains diminish, illness yield and health return.   Such were her occupations inside the convent (parthenon), but she was not confined by walls.   Throughout Prague her doings were apparent.'   We find her visiting women who were sick or in trouble, and collecting, mending and washing the garments of lepers with her own hands.

Agnes lived till 1282 and is accepted as a saint, but has never been officially canonized.   The hospital she founded at Prague is still in existence.

The fame of these women, great and abiding as it is in the countries they lived in, has not penetrated much beyond the districts which knew them during their lifetime.   It is different with another woman-saint of the period who, within the span of a short life, acquired such fame that she ranks among the holy followers of Christianity who are the possession of all countries

---

[1] *A. SS. Boll.*, Ibid., print these letters.
[2] *A. SS. Boll.*, Ibid., *Vita* I, ch. 32.

and of all ages. St Elisabeth, landgravine of Thüringen, a princess
of Hungary, combined in a rare degree those qualities of love,
devotion, and unselfish zeal which make Christian virtue in one
aspect so attractive. The tendencies of those among whom her lot
was cast and her own sad personal experiences throw her loveable
qualities into even greater relief. All the qualities in Matilda,
Hedwig, Anna, and Agnes which made them beloved and venerated appear to meet in Elisabeth. A loving wife, a pious mother,
a faithful widow, the comforter of the sick and the protector of the
poor, she stands on the threshold of a new era, indifferent to the
prejudices of her age, regardless of its derogatory criticism, intent
only on carrying into effect the promptings dictated by a keener
sense of sympathy with suffering and a closer appreciation of the
needs of others than her contemporaries could generally grasp.
No woman-saint has attained a fame at all to be compared with
hers. It has been computed that before the middle of this century
over a hundred versions of her story were in existence, a number
which has since been more than doubled. Of these accounts some
are in Latin, others in French, English, Italian and Hungarian, the
mass of them being of course in German. Many painters, and
among them some of the greatest Italian masters, Botticelli, Fra
Angelico, Orcagna, Memmi and Taddeo Gaddi, have been eager to
depict incidents of her life or to introduce her into their pictures[1].

The bulk of the literature which celebrates the name and
fame of Elisabeth has scant importance from the historical point
of view, which seeks a reasonable basis for her fame. For most
versions of her story were dictated more by the wish to dwell on
her piety than to encourage discerning appreciation of her character.
Among the legendary accounts composed in her praise there is a
poetical version of her life in mediaeval German, which extends over
four thousand five hundred lines and contains much that is attractive[2]. There is also in existence a modern German prose version
of her story which has considerable charm[3]. But the climax of
beauty of legendary narrative is reached in her case by the account
of her life written in French in the middle of this century by

---

[1] Montalembert, C., *Histoire de Ste Elisabeth de Hongrie, duchesse de Thuringe*,
edition de luxe 1878, with preface by Gautier, contains reproductions of some of those
pictures; Potthast, A., *Wegweiser*, enumerates a number of accounts of the life of St
Elisabeth.

[2] Rieger, L., prints this ‘Leben der heil. Elisabeth’ in *Literarisch. Verein*, 1843,
and discusses early MS accounts of her life.

[3] Justi, C. W., *Elisabeth, die Heilige*, 1797.

Montalembert[1].   It is widely read in unadorned and in sumptuous editions in the French original and in its German translation.   On the other hand its exuberance of religious colouring and legendary character have called forth an account based solely on contemporary records, which, drawn with a firm hand in clear outline, gives a picture of Elisabeth's life less fantastic, it is true, but more discerning and more truly beautiful[2].   In the light of this work it becomes possible to fit the form of Elisabeth to the background of her age, and, by thus placing her, to appreciate to some extent her great and lasting importance.   In a history of the development of philanthropic endeavour and charitable work no woman's figure more fitly represents the beauty of unselfish devotion.

Born at Presburg in Hungary in 1207, Elisabeth was related both to St Hedwig of Silesia and to St Agnes of Bohemia.   For her father King Andreas II of Hungary (✝ 1235) was uncle to Agnes, while her mother Gertrud was sister to Hedwig, so that Elisabeth was cousin to one saint and niece to the other.   Her mother Gertrud, like Hedwig in Silesia, had become the centre of a small German party in Hungary, with which their two brothers Count Heinrich of Andechs and Bishop Ekbert of Bamberg sought refuge after the murder of the king of Swabia referred to above. After several years Bishop Ekbert was enabled to return to his see chiefly owing to the influence exerted in his behalf by Hermann, landgrave of Thüringen; it was no doubt owing to this connection that his niece, the princess Elisabeth, at that time a child of four, was betrothed to the son of the landgrave.   This took place some time in the year 1211, and she was carried from Hungary to the Wartburg in Thüringen, there to receive her education.

At this period the customs at the court of Hungary were comparatively speaking uncivilized, and struggles were frequent. In 1214 Gertrud, Elisabeth's mother, was assassinated, a victim of the revolt of the Hungarians against German ascendency.   Thüringen and the Wartburg on the contrary were the seat of the greatest refinement of which the age of romance in German lands proved capable.   Landgrave Hermann, a prince of uncertain politics, but a zealous patron of art, had drawn thither the lyric poets of the age, whose brilliant assemblies and contests in the eyes of posterity are surrounded with the halo of a tournament in song.

[1] Montalembert, C., *Histoire de Ste Elisabeth de Hongrie*, 1836, 7th edit. 1855.

[2] Wegele, F. X., ' Die heil. Elisabeth von Thüringen' in Sybel, *Historische Zeitschrift*, 1861, pp. 351–397, which I have followed in the text.

But the temper of this gay throng had apparently no charm for the Hungarian girl, who was chiefly conscious of the levity and laxity which characterized it; conscious too that this outward brilliancy could not compensate for the hollowness which lurked beneath. A serious girl, though lively at times, she did not win general favour, least of all that of the landgravine Sophie, her prospective mother-in-law. When the news came of reverses at the Hungarian court, Sophie would have broken off the match and sent Elisabeth home or would have placed her in a nunnery. But at this juncture the attraction which Ludwig, the betrothed of Elisabeth, felt towards her asserted itself. He was conscious of a decided preference for the girl, and so he informed the noble knight Vargila, who had conducted Elisabeth from Presburg and who all along remained the staunch advocate of her interests.

Young Ludwig of Thüringen, a gentle and loveable character, of strict political integrity, is regarded as a saint on account of his numerous religious foundations and his tragic end. His chaplain has left an account of his life which throws much light on his relations to Elisabeth. He was left heir to his father's dominions in 1216, was declared of age by the emperor Friedrich II, and, in spite of the advice of his courtiers and against his mother's wish, clung to Elisabeth and married her in 1221, he being twenty and she fourteen years old at the time.

The happy married relations of the youthful pair are established beyond a doubt. Incidents are told and points insisted on by kinsfolk and friends which prove affection and tenderness on both sides, and directly contradict the statements of interested religious writers of a later date who maintain that life in a convent would have been more to Elisabeth's taste. On the contrary, whatever thoughts Elisabeth may have had afterwards on the superiority of a life of sacrifice to a life of domestic happiness, during these years she appears as the devoted wife and loving mother who combines the fulfilment of domestic duties with charitable zeal. There is a story told of her that she used to leave the Wartburg, her babe in her arms, and descend into the town of Eisenach, where she would visit the poor and the sick. Her dress on these occasions would be of a simple woollen material, and on her return she would take it off and have it given to some poor person. We hear that she frequently travelled about with her husband, and that she was sorely grieved at being separated from him when, on the summons of the emperor, he went to Italy. It was during his absence there

in the spring of 1226 that the famine occurred during which
Elisabeth distributed food with so lavish a hand that the granaries
of the castle were emptied and she herself was severely censured
by the court party, which had no sympathy with her philanthropy.
The number of those whom she fed is sometimes quoted as three
hundred, sometimes as nine hundred. The number may be exaggerated, but this much is certain, that Elisabeth's conduct
attracted attention beyond her immediate neighbourhood. She
had also opened at Eisenach a hospital or infirmary for twenty-four
sick people, whom she partly tended herself. Writers of a later
date tell us that at the suggestion of Cardinal Ugolino, afterwards
Pope Gregory IX, St Francis of Assisi, hearing of Elisabeth's
charitable work, sent her his old cloak as a sign of appreciation;
but the story needs corroborative evidence.

When Ludwig returned from Italy his courtiers were loud in
their complaints of his spendthrift wife, but he listened to them
with good-humoured indifference. 'Let her continue giving to the
poor if God so wills it,' he said, 'if but the Wartburg and the
Neuburg remain to us.' He evidently appreciated and shared her
philanthropic zeal; for he founded a shelter (xenodochium) for
the poor, the weak and the infirm at Reinhardsbrunn, assisted
his wife in founding a hospital at Gotha, and encouraged brothers
of the nursing order of St Lazarus to settle in that part of the
country[1]. The interest Elisabeth felt in social outcasts evidently
touched a sympathetic chord in his kindly nature, even when this
interest was carried to an extreme, the meaning and social fitness
of which it is not easy to appreciate. For example, the story is
told that Elisabeth when staying at Neuburg tended a leper with
her own hands and had him placed on her husband's bed, an action
which greatly shocked Sophie, her mother-in-law. The legend-
writer of later date,—not satisfied with the strong impulsiveness of
feeling which alone renders such an action possible and even under
certain conditions raises it above criticism, and at the same time
unable to grasp the reasonableness of Sophie's point of view,—tells
us that the leper suddenly assumed the form of Christ, a miracle
by which her doubts were confounded.

In 1227 Ludwig, in answer to a summons from the emperor,
took the cross and left for Italy, never to return. His biographer
says that having received the cross he kept it in his pocket instead

[1] Virchow, R., 'Zur Geschichte des Aussatzes, besonders in Deutschland,' in *Archiv
für pathol. Anatomie*, vol. 18, article 2, p. 313.

of displaying it on his coat, for fear of distressing his wife, who was about to give birth to their third child. But Elisabeth came across it by chance and was bowed down by grief at the thought of losing him. Together with others she started him and his followers on their journey, and travelled on with him yet another day's journey to delay the dreaded moment of separation. On her return to the Wartburg she devoted herself to her charitable work with increased zeal, and her inclination to self-denial became more accentuated owing to contact with members of the Franciscan order.

The attempt of the Franciscan friars to gain a foothold in Germany had at first been frustrated. Ekbert, bishop of Bamberg, Elisabeth's uncle, was the first to give them a gracious reception. From Bamberg they spread into the adjoining districts, and Elisabeth's favour enabled them to build a chapel at Eisenach. Konrad, one of these friars, had been nominated inquisitor by Pope Innocent III, and coming to Eisenach in 1226 soon won the affections of Ludwig and Elisabeth. At a later date Konrad of Marburg drew popular hatred on himself by his extreme rigour and anti-heretical teaching, and suffered a violent death (1233). But in earlier years he had gained much sympathy by preaching the views of St Francis on the renunciation of worldly goods and on practising unlimited charity[1]. When Ludwig departed to the south, he entrusted Konrad with considerable authority, which he turned to account by strengthening the ascendency he had gained over Elisabeth. She accepted him as her guide in all things, and upheld his views that to levy taxes is an evil and that each person should earn the food he requires by the work of his own hands. To carry this into practice she refused to accept any tribute and tried to earn money herself. Within a short time, however, came the news that Ludwig had died in Italy from a fever before setting sail for the East. The news came to Elisabeth as an overpowering shock. 'Dead!' she exclaimed, 'dead! so henceforth to me is the world and all things pleasant it contains.' Trials now came thick upon her. Her husband's brother, Hermann, with a usurper's determination, seized Ludwig's possessions and expelled Elisabeth, whom he had always looked upon with disapproval. She was forced to fly from the Wartburg with her children, and in the depth of a severe winter she paced the streets of Eisenach, seeking refuge with those

---

[1] *Allgemeine deutsche Biographie*, article ' Konrad von Marburg.'

she had formerly befriended, but no one dared to harbour her. At last her aunt Mathilde, abbess of Kizzingen, sent for her and for her two faithful waiting-women, perhaps for the children also. Elisabeth would gladly have accepted a permanent home in the convent, but her uncle Ekbert interfered. He appointed a more suitable dwelling-place—and urged upon her the desirableness of a second marriage. Elisabeth refused, and we hardly need the assurance of the legend-writer that it was because she had taken the vow of chastity, considering how recently her husband had died. However in the meantime the band of Ludwig's followers returned home bringing with them their leader's corpse, and a rapid change of affairs took place in the Wartburg. Hermann the usurper was forced to yield, Elisabeth was reinstated in her rights, and was fetched back to the castle by the noble Vargila. But her stay there was not of long duration. Her position was intolerable, and she felt that nothing could bring her solace short of the renunciation of all prerogatives of station and wealth. She would have become a recluse had not the Franciscan friar Konrad prevented this excess of humility. As it was she went to the Franciscan chapel at Eisenach, publicly renounced the world and its claims, and removed to Marburg in Hessen where she would be near Konrad and devote herself to a life of sacrifice. She refused to live in the castle, and with the two waiting-women, who throughout remained faithful to her, dwelt in a hut on the hillside, devoting all her property to constructing a hospital in the town, where she spent most of her time waiting on the sick and infirm.

Her conduct at Marburg filled the people with amazement as it had done at Eisenach, and numbers pressed thither to see her and to be tended by her. Considering that she only spent about two years there, the impression she made must have been extra-ordinary, for the undying memory of her fame continues to this day among the people. We hear a good deal of the asceticism she practised under Konrad's guidance during these last years of her life; how she submitted to bodily chastisement, how she admitted that her own children were not dearer to her than those of others, how she expressed regret at ever having been married, and how she suffered her faithful waiting-women, who like herself had adopted the grey dress of the order of St Francis, to be removed out of her sight. She died in 1231 at the early age of twenty-four. In accordance with the general wish she was canonized within a few years of her death by Pope Gregory IX in 1235. Immediately

after her death hospitals constructed on the plan of that at Marburg and acknowledging St Elisabeth as their patron saint sprang
up in many cities.   With all these facts before us we cannot deny
to her the achievement of lasting social importance.   To this day
hospitals in Germany founded both under Catholic and Protestant
auspices are often dedicated to her.

The loving tribute of a later age has perpetuated her fame in
many ways.   It has struck medals in her memory, has surmounted
fountains by her statue, and has reared to her memory the minster
of Marburg, one of the finest monuments of German mediaeval
architecture.   In spite of the ravages of time and the robberies
perpetrated during warfare her sarcophagus there remains a wondrous achievement of the art of the goldsmith.   It is still an object
of pious admiration and devout pilgrimage, both to the faithful
believer and to the appreciative student of history and art.

Our age has witnessed a great spread of philanthropic interest
and charitable zeal among women of the educated classes ; a wave
of feeling, similar to that which swept over mankind in the 13th
century, bears down all other considerations when there are outcasts to be rescued and suffering to be alleviated.   Nursing the
sick has become a distinct and a respected profession ; the administration of charity, an education in itself, is absorbing some of the
best energies of the community, and women who seek to rescue
suffering humanity are at last enabled to do so by the guiding
hand of science.   Certainly circumstances have changed.   We live
no longer in an age when the leper need display his sores to arouse
pity, nor where almsgiving *per se* has a social value.   And yet now
as then the success of charitable work depends on unselfish
devotion and goodness of heart in the individual, and it is in this
sense that the charitable work of the women-saints of the past
retains its meaning.   It is not by imitating their deeds that a later
age walks worthily in their footsteps and pays them the tribute of
reverence, but by accepting and furthering the spirit in which these
deeds were done.

CHAPTER IX.

'Die tumpheit behaget ir alleine selbe,
die weisheit kan niemer volle leren.'

(Mechthild the beguine.)

§ 1.   Mystic writings for women in England.

THE last chapter, in dealing with some of the women who
distinguished themselves in the cause of charity and philanthropy,
has suggested in what direction the determining feature of the
religious life of women in the 13th century must be sought.
Outward events, stirring political changes, and awakening confidence in national strength, had largely increased human sympathies and widened the mental horizon. In regard to women,
who sought their vocation outside the circle of home, this had
led on the one hand to efforts for alleviating human want and
human suffering, on the other to a stirring of the imagination in
the direction of speculation on the value and the help afforded by
religious belief.

The different beauties of the active and the contemplative life
had all along been realized, and were currently represented by
the figures of Mary and Martha, types of divergent tendencies
which were attractive in different ways. The busy Martha with
her charitable devotion was the ideal of many women, since
rescuing the needy, assisting the helpless, and ministering to the
sick constituted the vocation of women in a special sense. But
a peculiar charm of a different kind hung at all times round the
thoughtful and studious Mary, who set the claims and realities
of life at nought compared with the greater reality of the eternal

life hereafter. At the beginning of the 13th century, when the increase in religious enthusiasm deepened yearnings for the apprehension of the divine, men in their individual capacities began to seek a personal and closer communion with God. The absorption by things spiritual as contrasted with things material took a new departure. On one side was the learned thinker who, trained in the knowledge of the schools, sought to fathom his own powers and through them the powers of mankind so as to transcend the limits of sensible existence, and who gave a new development to mysticism in its technical sense. On the other side was the large number of those who, no longer satisfied with the mediation of appointed ministers of the Church, sought a personal relation to God, the effect of which on themselves would be moral regeneration. It was in connection with these that a number of writings were composed which represent mysticism in its popular sense: the steps by which the divine can be approached, set forth under the form of an allegory.

The allegorical mysticism of the Middle Ages culminates in Dante (1260–1321). It is well to bear this in mind in the presence of minor lights. For while there is much that is strangely fascinating in the 13th century mystic, and touches of simple good faith and of honest directness of purpose abound, the conditions under which he works and the language in which he expresses himself cannot pass without criticism. Cloistered seclusion, estrangement from the outside world, the cult of asceticism, and insistence on the emotional side of life, if judged by the standard of to-day, are not conducive to mental and moral welfare. Moreover a later age always finds it difficult to understand that an earlier one had its own notions in regard to the fitness and beauty of the surroundings it made for itself. But productive genius at all times freely makes for itself surroundings that cannot be called absolutely healthy. It needs a certain effort to realise on what ground the 13th century mystic stands. But when once we are able to follow him, moving in his world is like walking in an enchanted garden, —enchanted to us, but real to him, where each growing sentiment and each budding thought has its peculiar charm.

It is the same with regard to the language in which the mystic expresses himself. The close communion he seeks with the Godhead leads him to use terms which are directly adopted from those which express the experiences and feelings of ordinary life. There is in him no shrinking from holding God and the saints as personalities, and no hesitation in expressing desire for things spiritual in language currently used for expressing the promptings of desire for things of this world ; for he is a realist in the view he takes of God and the saints. The old interpretation of the Song of Solomon supplied him with a model after which to form his conceptions, and by a further adaptation it led every nun to greet her bridegroom in Christ and every monk to greet his bride in the Virgin. Outside the convent the age of romance had brought a new element into the relations of the sexes and had accepted years of service and continued wooing as the steps which led to the consummation of desire. This idea transferred to spiritual relations now caused the mystic to dwell on the steps by which the Divine can be approached. The poetry of romance and the poetry of mysticism have much in common ; both appear to have been the outcome of the same sentiments differently applied in convent and court. And as the language of real life made it possible for the mystic to formulate his feelings, so his religious aspirations in their turn helped to spiritualise the relations of real life.

It deserves special attention that some of the writings of these early mystics are in the vernacular and include some of the most beautiful productions in Middle English and in early German. Their philological interest has recently led to their publication, but their social importance is equally great. For in them we see how the high estimation of virgin purity, which was in the fore-ground of the moral consciousness of the age, was advocated by the leaders of thought and came to influence the lives of individual women, and how the asexual existence which hitherto had been accepted as praiseworthy was extolled as virtue in itself.

Again it is difficult for a later age to rate this conception at its just value, for the depreciation of the relationship of sex is to the modern mind not only misplaced but misleading. It is only when we think of the gain this depreciation has helped to secure in self-control and self-respect that it appears at all reasonable.

Of the early productions of the mystic school, which are distinctly moral in tendency and personal in tone, none offer greater attractions than works written in England during the first half of the 13th century for the use of women who were vowed to religion. All these writings, some of which will here be considered, are in the vernacular, and owing to their measured grace and tone of delicate refinement are among the most attractive

monuments of Middle English. They are chiefly productions of
the south of England where the Saxon element had been preserved
in its integrity. Scholars have remarked how a certain roughness
of diction and a heroic element opposed to softness of sentiment
lingered on in the north and precluded the utterance of gentler
strains, while the south used a language of combined vigour and
grace and became the cradle of lyric poetry. Moreover the south
at this period cultivated the qualities which give to a movement
its moral stamina. We find loyalty to the king coupled with
distaste for court pleasures, and strong religious feeling combined
with that insistence on nationality which precluded servile submission to the Pope. The south was also in connection with the
best intellectual forces of the age as represented by the growing
schools at Oxford, and Oxford in its turn was in direct touch
with Paris, which remained throughout the 12th century the most
important centre of learning and education in Europe.

A few words must be given to this connection and its results,
for it was in Paris that the master-minds of Oxford acquired that
enthusiasm for study which, applied to the realities of life, became
zeal for reform and desire for moral regeneration.

Two lines of study are apparent in Paris. There is the mysticism of the school of St Victor, represented by men of such
mental calibre as Hugo († 1141), a native of Germany, and his
pupil Richard († 1173), a native of Scotland. The combined
influence of these two men on the English mind was very great,
for many productions of the English mystical school were inspired
by or adapted from their Latin mystical works. The writings
of Richard translated into English are frequently found in manuscripts by the side of the works of the later English mystics,
Richard Rolle († 1349), and Walter Hylton († 1395).

On the other hand Paris was the first to experience the vivifying
influence of the renewed study of Greek philosophy, especially
of the Aristotelian *corpus*, together with its comments by Arabian
philosophers, especially with those of Averroes (fl. 1150). Jews
from the south of France had introduced these writings, which,
repeatedly condemned but as often advocated, had the effect on
speculative minds of the introduction of a new science[1]. Christian
theology, rising to the occasion, adopted their metaphysical views,
though so radically divergent from its own, and the result was the

---

[1] Hauréau, *Histoire de la philosophie scolastique*, 1850, vol. 1, pp. 319 ff.

birth of scholastic philosophy. But where the incompatibility of the union was felt scholars left the halls of discussion and turned their energies to grappling with the problems of active life.

In Oxford as early as 1133 Robert Pullen, who had studied in Paris, was lecturing on week days and preaching on Sundays to the people, and during the course of the 13th century a number of men who had won the highest distinctions at the university,— such as Edmund Rich († 1240), Adam Marsh († 1257–8), and Robert Grosseteste (afterwards bishop of Lincoln, † 1253), followed in his footsteps. Their efforts fell in with those of the newly founded orders of friars, and they greeted as brothers in the spirit the twelve Dominicans who arrived at Oxford in 1221 and the Franciscans who came in 1224. These maintained an utter distrust of learning, which led to much argument between them and the students, but all alike were zealous in working for the welfare of the uneducated classes.

We are indebted to Thomas de Hales[1] for one of the earliest and most beautiful poems written for the use of a nun. He was a native of Hales in Gloucestershire, studied both at Oxford and Paris, and was under the influence of the Franciscan movement. Wadding says in his annals of the Franciscan order that ' Thomas de Hales, created a doctor of the Sorbonne, was most celebrated and is known not only in England, but also in France, Germany, and Italy.' Thomas was on friendly terms with Adam Marsh who had become a Franciscan friar, and he joined this order himself as is apparent from the superscription of his English poem[2]. Various facts suggest possibilities as to his career, for Hales in Gloucestershire was the home also of Alexander de Hales († 1245) who went to Paris and spent his energies in compiling a work on scholasticism which secured him the title of *doctor irrefragabilis.* Moreover in 1246 Hales became the seat of a Cistercian monastery founded by Henry III.'s brother, Richard, earl of Cornwall, who was intimately connected with the circle of men at Oxford and a friend and patron of the Franciscans. It is possible that Thomas owed encouragement to the learned Alexander or to Earl Richard. The year 1250 is accepted as the date when he flourished, but his English poem was probably written somewhat earlier. This is suggested by the praise bestowed in it on King Henry and his

---

[1] *Dictionary of National Biography*, article ' Hales, Thomas.'

[2] 'A luve ron,' edit. Morris, *Old English Miscellany*, p. 93, for the Early Engl. Text Soc. 1872.

wealth, which could hardly have been accorded later than 1240, for it was then that the king began to alienate his people's affection by tampering with the coinage and by countenancing foreign influences at court and in the Church, in compliance with the wishes of his wife, Eleanor of Provence.

The poem of Thomas is called a *Luve Ron*, that is a love song; it consists of twenty-six rhymed stanzas with much alliterative assonance. Falling in with the tendencies of the age it treats of the happiness in store for women who accept Christ as their spouse. Thomas describes how he came to advise a nun in her choice of a lover. As the translation of the poem into modern English rhyme sacrifices much of its directness, the stanzas which follow have been rendered as prose.

> 'A maid of Christ bade me earnestly to make her a love-song,
> That she might best learn how to take a faithful lover,
> Most faithful of all, and best suited to a free woman;
> I will not refuse her, but direct her as best I can.
>
> Maiden, thou must understand that this world's love is rare,
> In many ways fickle, worthless, weak, deceiving,
> Men that are bold here pass away as the winds blow;
> Under the earth they lie cold, fallen away as meadow grass.
>
> No one enters life who is certain to remain,
> For here man has many sorrows, neither repose nor rest;
> Towards his end he hastens, abiding but a short time,
> Pain and death hurry him away when most he clings to life.
>
> None is so rich nor yet so free but he soon must go;
> Gold and silver, pomp and ermine give him no surety;
> Swift though he be, he cannot escape, nor lengthen his life
>   by a day,
> Thus, thou seest, this world as a shadow glides past.'

The poet then enlarges on the transitoriness of terrestrial love. Where are Paris and Helen, Amadis, Tristram, and others famous for their love? 'They have glided from this world as the shaft that has left the bow-string.' Wealth such as King Henry's, beauty such as Absalom's availed them nought. But the poet knows of a true king whose love abides.

> 'Ah sweet, if thou knewest but this one's virtues!
> He is fair and bright, of glad cheer, mild of mood,

Lovely through joy, true of trust, free of heart, full of wisdom;
Never wouldst thou regret it if once thou wert given into
    his care.

He is the richest man in the land as far as men have the
    power of speech,
All is given into his hand, east, west, north and south.
Henry the king holds of him and bows to him.
Maiden, to thee he sends the message that he would be beloved
    by thee.'

The beauty of this lover, Christ, is thus described, and the fairness of his dwelling, where hate, pride and envy enter not, and where all rejoice with the angels. 'Are not those in a good way who love such a lord?' the poet asks. In return for the bliss Christ grants, He asks only that the maiden keep bright the jewel of maidenhood which He has entrusted to her. The poem ends thus:

'This poem, maiden, I send thee open and without a seal,
Bidding thee unroll it and learn each part by heart,
Then be very gracious and teach it faithfully to other maidens.
Who knows the whole right well will be comforted by it.

If ever thou sittest lonely, draw forth this little writing,
Sing it with sweet tones, and do as I bid thee.
He who has sent thee a greeting, God Almighty, be with thee,
And receive thee in his bower high up in heaven where He sits.
And may he have good ending, who has written this little song.'

From this poem we turn to the prose works written at this period for religious women, which are inspired by the same spirit of earnest devotion, and contain thoughts as tender, refined, and gentle as the poem of Thomas de Hales. The prose treatise known as the *Ancren Riwle*[1], the rule for recluses, is by far the most important of these works, and from the present point of view deserves close attention, for it gives a direct insight into the moral beauties of the religious attitude, and enables us to form some idea of the high degree of culture and refinement which the 13th century mystic attained.

A few words of criticism on the purpose of the book and on its authorship are here necessary. We have before us a work written not for the regular inmates of a nunnery, not for nuns who lived

[1] Edit. Morton for the Camden Soc. 1853.

under the rule of a prioress or abbess, but for religious women who, after being trained in a nunnery, left it to continue a chaste and secluded life outside. The Church at all times gave most honour to those monks and nuns who were members of a convent and lived under the rule of a superior, but it did not deny the credit of holy living, or the appellations monk and nun, to those who either alone or with a few companions devoted themselves to religion, and dwelt sometimes near a chapel or sanctuary, sometimes in a church-yard. From the earliest times the people had held such male and female recluses in special reverence, and the Church, yielding to popular feeling, accepted them as holy, and in some instances countenanced their being ranked as saints.

With reference to the distinction made from the earliest period between the different classes of those who professed religion, and their respective claims to holiness, it seems well to quote from the introductory chapter of the rule of St Benedict. The following passages occur in all the prose versions of the rule known to me, whether written for the use of men, or adapted to the use of women.

The Anglo-Saxon version of the rule of St Benedict made in the 10th or 11th century, which is based on the version written by Aethelwold about the year 961, runs thus[1]: 'There are four kinds of monks, *muneca;* the first kind are those in monasteries, *mynstermonna,* who live under a rule or an abbot. The second kind are the hermits, *ancrena,* that is settlers in the wilds (*westen-setlena*), who, not in the first fervour of religious life, but after pro-bation in the monastery, have learned by the help and experience of others to fight against the devil, and going forth well armed from the ranks of their brethren to the single-handed combat of the wilderness, are able without the support of others to fight by the strength of their own arm and the help of God against the vices of the flesh and their evil thoughts. A third and most bane-ful kind of monk are the self-appointed ones, *sylfdemena,* who have been tried by no rule nor by the experience of a master, as gold in the furnace, but being soft as lead and still serving the world in their works, are known by their tonsure to lie to God. These, in twos or threes or even singly without a shepherd, not enclosed in the Lord's sheepfold, follow the enjoyment of their will instead of a rule; whatever they think fit or choose to do they call holy, and what they like not they condemn as unlawful. There is a fourth

---

[1] 'Die angelsächsischen Prosabearbeitungen der Benedictinerregel,' edit. Schröer, 1885 (in Grein. *Bibliothek der angels. Prosa,* vol. 2), p. 9.

kind of monk called wandering, *widscrithul,* who spend all their life wandering about, staying in different cells for three or four days at a time, ever roaming, given up to their own pleasures and the evils of gluttony, and worse in all ways than the self-appointed ones.'

In the English versions of the rule for women, two of which, drafted respectively in the 13th and in the 15th century, are extant, the same distinctions are drawn between different kinds of nuns. The 13th century version states[1] that there are the nuns living in a monastery under an abbess, *mynecene,*—a kind of nun called *ancre* or recluse,—the self-appointed nuns,—and the wandering nuns who are declared altogether evil.

The difference between the nun and the *ancre* is made clear by these passages. The *ancre* or recluse, called in Latin *inclusa,* is the nun who after receiving a convent education lives a holy life away from the nunnery, and it is for *ancren* or nuns of this kind that the book we are about to discuss was written. Fortunately the work does not stand alone as an exhortation to women recluses. We are in possession of a letter from Ailred of Rievaulx, written between 1131 and 1161, and addressed to his sister (sic), which was written for a similar purpose though covering very much narrower ground, and contains advice analogous to that contained in the *Ancren Riwle.* The original is in Latin[2], and in this form it was probably known to the author of the *Ancren Riwle,* who refers to it, saying how Ailred had already insisted that purity of life can be maintained only by observing two things, a certain hardness of bodily life and a careful cultivation of moral qualities.

The letter of Ailred is in the form of a series of short chapters and is divided into two parts, the first of which (c. 1–20) treats of the outward rule. It gives advice as to whom the *inclusa* should converse with, and whom she should admit into her presence; it tells her that she should not own flocks, which leads to buying and selling; that she should live by the work of her hands, not accepting as a gift more food than she needs for herself and her servants; and that she must not do as some recluses do, who busy themselves with 'teaching girls and boys and turn their cells into a school.' It also directs her about divine service, and about her food and clothes.

Having so far dealt with outward things Ailred (c. 21–46)

---

[1] Schröer, *Winteney Version der Regula St Benedicti,* 1888, p. 13.

[2] 'De vita eremetica' (in Migne, *Patrol. Cursus Compl.,* vol. 32, by an oversight it is included among the works of St Augustine), p. 145.

dwells on the inward life, on virginity, on the dangers of temptation and on the beauties of humility and love. His sentences are short and are illustrated by quotations from scripture, by reference to the holy virgin St Agnes, and by remarks on the respective merits of Mary and Martha. The concluding chapters (c. 47–78) are found also in the works of Anselm, archbishop of Canterbury († 1109)[1], and appear to have been borrowed from him.

The letter of Ailred proves that the conduct of the recluse was attracting attention in the 12th century. Part of his letter was translated into Middle English by one Thomas N. in the 13th century, about the same time when the *Ancren Riwle* was drawn up, and in its superscription it is designated as the 'information' which Ailred, abbot of Rievaulx, wrote for his sister the *inclusa*[2]. In this translation, however, the opening parts of the work which treat of the outward rule (c. 1–20) are omitted, evidently because the translation was intended not for recluses but for nuns, to whom directions about domestic matters, such as buying, selling, clothing and eating, would not apply.

Further evidence can be adduced to show that women recluses in the 13th century occupied public attention to an increasing degree. Hitherto they had been left to dwell where they pleased, supported by chance gifts from the people, but in the 13th century it became usual to leave them legacies. A mass of information on the subject has been collected by Cutts[3], who describes how women recluses occupied sometimes a range of cells, sometimes a commodious house; and how they kept one or more servants to run on their errands. In 1246 the bishop of Chichester issued an injunction which shows that his attention had been drawn to these women, and that in his mind there was a distinct difference between them and regular nuns. Under the heading 'On recluses' (*inclusis*) it says[4]: 'Also we ordain that recluses shall not receive or keep any person in their house concerning whom sinister suspicions may arise. Also that they have narrow and proper windows; and we permit them to have secret communication with those persons only whose gravity and honesty do not admit of suspicion. Women recluses should not be entrusted with the care of church vestments;

---

[1] Anselm, *Opera* (in Migne, *Patrol. Cursus Compl.*, vol. 158), 'Meditationes' (nr 15–17), pp. 786 ff.

[2] Edit. Koelbing, *Englische Studien*, vol. 7, p. 304.

[3] *Scenes and characters of the Middle Ages*, 1872, pp. 93—151.

[4] Wilkins, D., *Concilia*, 1737, vol. 1, p. 693.

if necessity compels it, we command it to be done with caution, that he who carries them may have no communication with the recluses.'

Taking these various remarks into consideration and comparing them with what is said in the *Ancren Riwle* itself, the author of which keeps clear in his mind the difference between recluse and nun, I think the idea that this work was originally written for the Cistercian nunnery at Tarent in Dorsetshire, as is usually alleged[1], will be abandoned. This assumption is based on the superscription of a Latin copy of the book, which states that Simon of Ghent wrote it for his sisters the anchoresses near Tarent (apud Tarente). But the theory that the book was originally in Latin, and that it was written by Simon, archdeacon at Oxford in 1284, and bishop of Salisbury between 1307–1315, has long been abandoned. The idea that it was written for the nunnery at Tarent may also be discarded, for Tarent was a house founded by Ralph de Kahaines in the time of Richard I. Therefore at the time when Simon lived, and doubtless also at the time when the book was written (1225–1250), the settlement must have consisted of more than three women recluses and their servants. Women recluses might be living at Tarent as elsewhere, since Simon forwarded the book to recluses there, but they would not be members of the Cistercian convent. It may be noticed in passing that the other Latin copy of the rule, which was destroyed by fire in 1731, had a superscription saying that Robert Thornton, at one time prior, gave it to the recluses (*claustralibus*) of Bardney, which is a Benedictine abbey for men in Lincolnshire.

To relinquish the idea that the *Ancren Riwle* was written originally for the Cistercian nunnery at Tarent is to relinquish also the supposition[2] that it is the work of Richard Poor, dean of Salisbury, and afterwards bishop successively of Chichester and Durham († 1237), for the theory of his authorship rests only on his interest in this nunnery, to which he added a chapel and where his heart lies buried. A fuller knowledge of the English writings of the time may reveal by whom and for whom the book was written. The dialect proves it to be the production of a native of the south-western part of England, while its tone reveals a connection with Paris and Oxford. The writer must have had a high degree of culture, and was familiar with French, with court poetry,

---

[1] Brink, B. ten, *Early English Literature*, trans. Kennedy, 1883, p. 205.

[2] First advanced by Morton, *Ancren Riwle*, Introd. pp. xii—xv; it is supported neither by tradition nor by documentary evidence.

and with the similes so frequent in the stories of romance. He had a sound theological training, with a knowledge of the works of Jerome, Augustine, Gregory, Anselm, and notably of Bernard, from whom he frequently quotes. He had strong religious sympathies, but imperfect sympathy with the established church,—these latter facts tend to prove that he was in some measure connected with the friars. His references to 'our lay brethren,' and his description of the 'hours' as said by them, may serve as a clue to his identification[1].

The *Ancren Riwle* or rule for recluses, fills a moderately sized volume and is extant in eight manuscript copies, of which five are in English, that is four in the dialect of the south and one in that of the north,—two in Latin, and one in French. The work is divided into eight parts, a short analysis of which will give an idea of the importance of the book and of the wide range of its author's sympathies. As he says himself the book was written for three sisters who in the bloom of their youth had forsaken the world to become anchoresses, but he expects it will be read by others. He assumes that his readers know Latin and French as well as English, a fact which in itself proves that like the *ancren* referred to above, the *ancren* here addressed had received their education in a nunnery.

In the short introduction which precedes the work the author says he will accede to the request of the women who have importuned him for a rule.

'Do you now ask what rule you recluses should observe?' he asks (p. 5)[2]. 'You should always keep the inward rule well with all your might and strength for its own sake. The inward rule is ever alike; the outward varies.... No recluse by my advice shall make profession, that is promise to keep anything commanded, save three things, obedience, chastity and stedfastness; she shall not change her home save by need, such as compulsion, fear of death or obedience to her bishop, or her master (herre). For she who undertakes anything and promises to do it at God's command, is bound to it and sins mortally in breaking her promise by will or wish. If she has not promised she may do it and leave it off as she will, as of meat and drink, abstaining from flesh and fish and other like things relating to dress, rest, hours and prayers. Let her say as many of these as she pleases, and in what way she

---

[1] Dalgairns, Introd. to Hylton, *Scale of Perfection*, 1870, thinks it possible that the author was a Dominican friar.

[2] Comp. throughout *Ancren Riwle*, edit. Morton for the Camden Soc. 1853.

pleases. These and other such things are all in our free choice to do or let alone whenever we choose, unless they are promised. But charity, that is love, and meekness and patience, truthfulness and keeping the ten ancient commandments, confession and penitence, these and such as these, some of which are of the old law, some of the new, are not of man's invention.'

He then goes on to tell them that if asked to what order they belong, they must say, to the order of St James, who was God's apostle (and who wrote a canonical epistle). He dilates upon early Christian hermits and recluses, saying that they were of the order of St James, for in his mind St James the apostle is identical with St James the hermit.

He then describes the contents of his work, saying the first part only shall treat of the outward rule, all the others of the inward.

The first part accordingly (pp. 15–48) is on religious service, and in it the women are advised what prayers they shall say and at what time of the day: 'Let everyone say her hours as she has written them,' and as a guide take what 'hours' are kept by 'our lay brethren.' The sick, the sorrowful, prisoners, and Christians who are among the heathen shall be called to mind. The tone which the author occasionally takes has the full personal ring of 13th century mysticism. (p. 35) 'After the kiss of peace in the mass, when the priest consecrates, forget there all the world, and there be entirely out of the body, there in glowing love embrace your beloved spouse (leofman) Christ, who is come down from heaven into the bower of your breast, and hold him fast till he have granted all that you wish.' Several prayers follow, one in Latin on the adoration of the cross, and several in English which are addressed to the sweet lady St Mary.

Outward observances being disposed of, the author then advises the women how to keep guard over the heart, 'wherein is order, religion and the life of the soul,' against the temptations of the five senses (pp. 48–117). The different senses and the dangers attending them are discussed, sometimes casually, sometimes in a systematic manner. In connection with Sight we get interesting details on the arrangement of the building in which the recluses dwelt. Its windows are hung with black cloth on which is a white cross. The black cloth is impervious to the wind and difficult to see through; the white of the cross is more transparent and emblematic of purity, by the help of which it becomes safe to look abroad. Looking abroad, however, is generally attended with danger. 'I write more particularly for others,' the author here remarks, 'nothing of the kind touches you, my dear sisters, for you have not the name, nor shall you have it by the grace of God, of staring recluses, whose profession is unrecognisable through their unseemly conduct, as is the case with some, alas !'

Speech too should be wisely controlled, talking out of church windows should be avoided, and conversation generally should be indulged in only through the 'house' window and the parlour window. 'Silence always at meals,' says the author, and quotes from Seneca and Solomon on the evil effects of idle prattling. Hearing, that is listening too readily, also has its dangers, for it leads to spreading untruths. 'She who moves her tongue in lying makes it a cradle to the devil's child, and rocketh it diligently as a nurse.' In passages which show a keen insight into human nature and which are dictated by a wise and kindly spirit, the author among other examples describes how anyone seeking the recluse's sympathy for bad ends would approach her in plaintive strains, deploring that he is drawn to her, and assuring her that he desires nothing but her forgiveness, and thus by engrossing her thoughts more and more, would perturb her mind by rousing her personal sympathy.

The sense of Smell also has its dangers ; but in regard to the fifth sense, Feeling, there is most need, the author thinks, of comfort, 'for in it the pain is greatest, and the pleasure also if it so happen.' The sufferings of Christ are analysed and it is shown how he suffered in all his senses but especially in feeling.

The next part of the work (pp. 118–177) contains moral lessons and examples. The peevish recluse finds her counterpart in the pelican which kills her own young ones when they molest her. Like the bird, the recluse in anger kills her works, then repents and makes great moan. There are some fine passages on the effects of anger which is likened to a sorceress (uorschup-pild) and transforms the recluse, Christ's spouse, into a she-wolf (wulvene). That women devotees often behaved very differently from what they ought is evident from these passages, for false recluses are likened unto foxes who live in holes and are thievish, ravenous and yelping, but 'the true recluses are indeed birds of heaven, that fly aloft and sit on the green boughs singing merrily ; that is, they meditate, enraptured, upon the blessedness of heaven that never fadeth but is ever green, singing right merrily ; that is in such meditation they rest in peace and have gladness of

heart as those who sing.' In one passage, where the flight of
birds is described, it says, 'the wings that bear the recluses
upwards are good principles, which they must move unto good
works as a bird that would fly moveth its wings.' From dumb
animals wisdom and knowledge can be learnt, says the author,
giving as an example the eagle, which deposits in his nest a
precious stone called agate, which wards off harm, and thus Jesus
Christ should be cherished to keep off evil. In another passage
the author plays on the words *ancre* and anchor, saying that the
ancre or recluse is anchored to the Church as the anchor to the
ship, that storms may not overwhelm it. The reasons for
solitary life are then enumerated under separate headings, and
passages from the Old and the New Testament are freely quoted
in illustration and corroboration of the statements made.

The fourth part of the book (pp. 178-298) dilates on temptation,
in regard to which the writer holds that greater holiness brings
increased difficulties. 'As the hill of holy and pious life is greater
and higher, so the fiend's puffs which are the winds of temptation
are stronger thereon and more frequent.' Patience and meekness
are chiefly required to resist the troubles of sickness, and wisdom
and spiritual strength must resist grief of heart, anger and wrath.
Again the recluses for whom the book is written are assured that
they have least need to be fortified against temptations and trials,
sickness only excepted.

The imagery in which the author goes on to describe the seven
chief sins is graphic and powerful. They are personified as the
Lion of Pride, the Serpent of Envy, the Unicorn of Wrath, the
Bear of Sloth, the Fox of Covetousness, the Swine of Gluttony, and
the Scorpion of Lust, each with its offspring. Of the Scorpion's
progeny we are told that 'it doth not become a modest mouth
to name the name of some of them,' while the Scorpion itself
is a kind of worm, that has a face somewhat like that of a woman,
but its hinder parts are those of a serpent. It puts on a pleasant
countenance and fawns upon you with its head but stings with
its tail. Again, the sins are likened to seven hags (heggen), to
whom men who serve in the devil's court are married. The description of these men as jugglers, jesters, ash-gatherers and devil's
purveyors, gives interesting details on the characters in real life
by which they were suggested. Of the comforting thoughts
which the recluse is to dwell upon the following give a fine
example.

'The sixth comfort is that our Lord, when he suffereth us to be tempted, playeth with us as the mother with her young darling : she fleeth from him and hides herself, and lets him sit alone, look anxiously around calling Dame, dame ! and weep awhile, and then she leapeth forth laughing with outspread arms and embraceth and kisseth him and wipeth his eyes. Just so our Lord leaveth us sometimes alone, and withdraweth his grace and comfort and support, so that we find no sweetness in any good we do, nor satisfaction of heart ; and yet all the while our dear father loveth us none the less, but doeth it for the great love he hath for us.'

In times of tribulation the recluse is directed to meditate on God and His works, on the Virgin and the saints, and the temptations they withstood, such as are related in an English book on St Margaret. Again and again the writer, who does not tire of this part of his theme, dwells on the various sins separately, and on the best way of meeting them.

The next part of the book (pp. 298–348) is devoted to an analysis of the use and the manner of confession, the theory and practice of which in the Church of Rome are ancient, but which the religious enthusiasm of the Middle Ages elaborated into a hard and fast system. That self-introspection and analysis are helpful in developing and strengthening conscientiousness no one will deny, but the habitual disclosure of one's thoughts and criticisms of self to another, though it may still afford support to some, has ceased to appear generally advisable. Granted that the practice in the past served a good purpose, the advice given in this book for recluses appears dictated by a strong sense of fitness and moderation. The author considers confession powerful in three directions : it 'confoundeth the devil,' it gives us back all the good we have lost, and it 'maketh us children of God.' Under these headings there is a long and systematic elaboration of the sixteen ways in which confession should be made, viz. it should be accusatory, bitter, complete, candid, and it should be made often, and speedily, humbly and hopefully, etc. Stories out of the Bible and parables of a later age are introduced in corroboration of each injunction. Under the heading of candid confession the words to be used in self-accusation are interesting, because it is obvious that a higher moral standard is claimed from women than from men. The person who has committed sin is to address the father confessor (schrift feder) in these words : ' I am a woman, and ought by right to have been more modest than to speak as I have spoken, or to do as I have done; and therefore my sin is greater than if a man had done it, for it became me worse.' From the Gospels and the Fathers the writer adduces strings of wise sayings which bear on the points he would impress upon his readers. This fifth part of the book, he says, belongs to all men alike, not to recluses in particular, and he ends by admonishing the sisters in this way : ' Take to your profit this short and concluding summary of all mentioned and known sins, as of pride, ambition, presumption, envy, wrath, sloth, carelessness, idle words, immoral thoughts, any idle hearing, any false joy or heavy mourning, hypocrisy, the taking too much or too little meat or drink, grumbling, being of morose countenance, breaking silence, sitting too long at the parlour window, saying hours badly or without attention of heart or at a wrong time, any false word or oath, play, scornful laughter, wasting crumbs, or spilling ale or letting things grow mouldy or rusty or rotten ; leaving clothes not sewed, wet with rain, or unwashed ; breaking a cup or a dish, or carelessly looking after any thing which we own and should take care of; or cutting or damaging through heedlessness.' These in the writer's eyes are the likely sins among the recluses whom he addresses and against which he warns them to be on their guard. If they have committed them they must forthwith confess, but trivial faults should be wiped away by prayers said before the altar the moment the recluse is conscious of them.

Passing from the subject of Confession to that of Penance (pp. 348–383) the author as he says borrows much from the Sentences of Bernard, the general drift of which is in favour of self-discipline and implies mortification of the flesh. In this context comes the reference to Ailred's (Seint Aldret's) advice to his sister, who also was directed to give the body pain by fasting, watching, and discipline, by having coarse garments and a hard bed, and by bearing evil and working hard. But here again the recluses addressed are told that in the eyes of their adviser they incline rather to over-much self-denial than to over-much self-indulgence.

The seventh part of the book (pp. 384–410) treats of the pure heart or of love and is attractive in many ways. The sentiments developed and the pictures described give one the highest opinion of the feelings of which the age was capable, as reflected in this writer's innermost being. The beautiful parable where Christ woos the soul in guise of a king is well worth repeating, for there we see the courtly attitude, which the age of romance had developed in real life, receiving a spiritual adaptation.

'There was a lady who was besieged by her foes within an earthly castle, and her land was all destroyed and herself quite poor. The love of a powerful king was however fixed upon her with such boundless affection that to solicit her love he sent his messengers one after the other, and often many together, and sent her trinkets both many and fair, and supplies of victuals and help of his high retinue to hold her castle. She received them all as a careless creature with so hard a heart that he could never get nearer to her love. What would'st thou more? He came himself at last and showed her his fair face, since he was of all men the fairest to behold, and spoke so sweetly and with such gentle words that they might have raised the dead from death to life. And he wrought many wonders, and did many wondrous deeds before her eyes, and showed her his power and told her of his kingdom, and offered to make her queen of all that he owned. But all availed him nought. Was not this surprising mockery? For she was not worthy to have been his servant. But owing to his goodness love so mastered him that he said at last: "Lady, thou art attacked, and thine enemies are so strong that thou canst not without my help escape their hands that thou mayest not be put to a shameful death. I am prompted by love of thee to undertake this fight, and rid thee of those that seek thy death. I know well that I shall receive a mortal wound, but I will do it gladly to win thy heart. Now I beseech thee for the love I bear thee that thou love me at least after my death, since thou would'st not in my lifetime." Thus did the king. He freed her of her enemies and was himself wounded and slain in the end. Through a miracle he arose from death to life. Would not that same lady be of an evil kind if she did not love him above all things after this?'

'The king is Jesus Christ, the Son of God, who in this wise wooed our Soul which the devils had beset. And He as a noble wooer, after many messengers and many good deeds, came to prove His love and showed through knighthood that He was worthy of love, as sometime knights were wont to do. He entered in a tournament, and as a bold knight had His shield pierced everywhere in the fight for His lady's love.'

The likeness between the shield and Christ's body is further dwelt upon. The image of His crucified form hangs suspended in church, as 'after the death of a valiant knight, men hang up his shield high in church to his memory.'

There is more on the theme of love that is very fine. The ideas generated by knighthood are obviously present to the mind of the writer.

Interesting also is his classification of the different kinds of love. The love of good friends (gode iueren) is first mentioned, but higher than that is the love between man and woman, and even higher still that between mother and child, for the mother to cure her child of disease is ready to make a bath of her blood for it. Higher again is the love of the body to the soul, but the love which Christ bears to His dear spouse, the soul, surpasses them all.

'Thy love,' says our Lord, 'is either to be freely given or it is to be sold, or it is to be stolen and to be taken with force. If it is to be given, where could'st thou bestow it better than on me? Am I not of all the fairest? Am I not the richest king? Am I not of noblest birth? Am I not in wealth the wisest? Am I not the most courteous? Am I not the most liberal of men? For so it is said of a liberal man that he can withhold nothing; that his hands are perforated as mine are. Am I not of all the sweetest and most gentle? Thus in me all reasons thou may'st find for bestowing thy love, if thou lovest chaste purity; for no one can love me save she hold by that.—But if thy love is not to be given but is to be sold, say at what price; either for other love or for something else? Love is well sold for love, and so love should be sold and for nought else. If thy love is thus to be sold, I have bought it with love surpassing all other. For of the four kinds of love, I have shown thee the best of them all. And if thou sayest that thou wilt not let it go cheaply and askest for more, name what it shall be. Set a price on thy love. Thou canst not name so much but I will give thee for thy love much more. Wouldest thou have castles and kingdoms? Wouldest thou govern the world? I am purposed to do better; I am purposed to make thee withal queen of heaven. Thou shalt be sevenfold brighter than the sun; no evil shall harm thee, no creature shall vex thee, no joy shall be wanting to thee; thy will shall be done in heaven and on earth; yea, even in hell.'

And in a further development of this idea all imaginable good, Croesus' wealth, Absalom's beauty, Asahel's swiftness, Samson's strength, are held out as a reward to the soul who responds to the wooing of Christ and gives herself entirely into His keeping. 'This love,' says the author in conclusion, 'is the rule which governs the heart.'

The last part of the book (pp. 410–431) appears to be appended as an after-thought, as it treats once more of domestic matters. 'I said before at the beginning,' says the author, 'that ye ought not, like unwise people, to promise to keep any of the outward rules. I say the same still, nor do I write them save for you alone. I say this in order that recluses may not say that I by my authority make new rules for them. Nor do I command that they shall hold them, and you may change them whenever you will for better ones. Of things that have been in use before it matters little.' Practical directions follow which throw a further light on the position and conduct of the recluse, and which in many particulars are curiously like the injunctions which form the opening part of the letter of Ailred. The recluses shall partake of Communion on fifteen days of the year; they shall eat twice a day between Easter and Roodmass (September 14), during the other half year they shall fast save on Sundays; and they shall not eat flesh or lard except in sickness. 'There are recluses,' says the writer, 'who have meals with their friends outside. That is too much friendship; for all orders it is unsuitable, but chiefly for the order of recluses who are dead to the world.' A recluse shall not be liberal of other men's alms, for housewifery is Martha's part and not hers. 'Martha's office is to feed and clothe poor men as the mistress of a house; Mary ought not to intermeddle in it, and if any one blame her, God Himself the supreme defends her for it, as holy writ bears witness. On the other hand a recluse ought only to take sparingly that which is necessary for her. Whereof, then, may she make herself liberal? She must live upon alms as frugally as ever she can, and not gather that she may give it away afterwards. She is not a housewife but a Church ancre. If she can spare any fragments to the poor, let her send them quietly out of her dwelling. Sin is oft concealed under the semblance of goodness. And how shall those rich anchoresses who are tillers of the ground, or have fixed rents, do their alms privately to poor neighbours? Desire not to have the reputation of bountiful anchoresses, nor, in order to give much, be too eager to possess more. Greediness is at the root of bitterness: all the boughs that spring from it are bitter. To beg in order to give away is not the part of a recluse. From the courtesy of a recluse and from her liberality, sin and shame have often come in the end.'

This idea, that the recluse shall follow the example of Mary and not that of Martha, occurs also in Ailred's letter, though it is more briefly stated (c. 41 ff.).

'You shall possess no beast, my dear sisters,' says the author of the *Ancren Riwle*, 'except only a cat. A recluse who has cattle appears as Martha was.' She thinks of the fodder, of the herds-man, thoughts which bring with them traffic. 'A recluse who is a buyer and seller (cheapild) selleth her soul to the chapman of hell.' Ailred similarly warned his 'sister' against keeping flocks (c. 5 ff.). But the author of the *Riwle* allows the recluse to keep a cow if need be. 'Do not take charge,' he says, 'of other men's things in your house, nor of their property, nor of their clothes, neither receive under your care the church vestments nor the chalice, unless compelled thereto, for oftentimes much harm has come from such caretaking.' The clothes the sisters wear shall be warm and simple, 'be they white, be they black; only see that they be plain and warm and well-made.' He warns them against severe discipline by the use of hair-cloth and hedgehog-skins, and against scourging with a leathern thong. He desires them to have all needful clothing, but forbids wearing rings, brooches, ornamented girdles and gloves. The recluse shall 'make no purses to gain friends therewith, nor blodbendes[1] of silk; but shape and sew and mend church vestments, and poor people's clothes.' The point Ailred in his rule strongly insisted upon, the command that the recluse shall not keep a school as some recluses do, is reiterated by the author of the *Ancren Riwle*, for the excitement it brings and the personal affection it creates between teacher and pupil are felt to be fraught with danger. If there be a girl who needs to be taught, the recluse shall cause her to be instructed by her servant, for she shall keep two servants, the one to stay at home, the other to go abroad, 'whose garments shall be of such shape and their attire such that their calling be obvious.' The recluse shall read the concluding part of this book to her women once a week, but she herself is to read in it daily if she have leisure.

Such in brief outline is the *Ancren Riwle*, a book which above all others gives an insight into the religious life as appre-

---

[1] That is bands or ligatures to be used after the letting of blood.

hended in the 13th century in England; a book which, written
for women—the number of whom can never have been great,
contains much that remains wise and instructive to this day,
owing to its wide outlook and liberal spirit. It gives the very
highest opinion of the author's gentleness and refinement, and
of the exalted sentiments of the women he was addressing.

This is not the place to dwell on the numerous spiritual love-
songs which were written in English at this period under the
influence of mystic tendencies; but it must be pointed out that
those which breathe the love of a woman's soul to Christ were
presumably written in the interest of nuns. Among them is one
in prose, entitled the 'Wooing of Our Lord[1],' written by its author
for his 'sister,' which has a certain likeness to the 'Ancren Riwle,'
and on this ground has been ascribed to the same author. Probably it is a paraphrase of part of it, but it has none of the
harmonious flow of the treatise itself, and its tone is so much
more emotional, that it looks like the production of a later age.

The idea of the exaltation of virginity at this period further
led to the re-writing in English of the legends of women-saints
whose stories turn on the might of virginity in conflict with the
evil powers of this world. Among them the legends of St Margaret, St Juliana and St Cecilia, are extant in a manuscript of
about the year 1230. Their authorship is unknown, but they
were evidently written in the first place for religious women.

In conclusion a few words must be said on a treatise written
about the same time called 'Holy Maidenhood' (Hali Meidenhad),
the interest of which lies in the fact that while advocating the
same cause as the writings discussed above, it is quite untouched
by their spirit[2]. Here also the advantages of the love of Christ
over love for earthly things are enlarged on, and the superiority
of the 'free' maiden over her who has embraced family life is
upheld. But this is done in a broad familiar strain and with
repeated fierce attacks on marriage.

The author ornaments his treatise with Biblical quotations, but
he possesses none of the courtly grace and elegance of diction of
Thomas de Hales and the author of the *Ancren Riwle*. In form
the treatise answers to its drift, for it is written in an alliterative
homely style which gives it a peculiar interest from the philological

---

[1] *Old English Homilies*, First Series, edit. Morris, 1867, p. 268.

[2] *Hali Meidenhad*, edit. Cockayne, for the Early English Text Soc., 1866.

point of view. Looked at from the religious standpoint it yields a curious example of what the tone and temper would be of one who, grasping the moral drift of the age, remained a stranger to its tenderer strains. At the same time its author is not without considerable insight into the realities of life and has a sense of humour usually absent in mystic writings. The following passage which dwells on some of the annoyances of married life give a good example of this (p. 37).

'And how I ask, though it may seem odious, how does the wife stand who when she comes in hears her child scream, sees the cat at the flitch, and the hound at the hide? Her cake is burning on the stone hearth, her calf is sucking up the milk, the earthen pot is overflowing into the fire and the churl is scolding. Though it be an odious tale, it ought, maiden, to deter thee more strongly from marriage, for it does not seem easy to her who has tried it. Thou, happy maiden, who hast fully removed thyself out of that servitude as a free daughter of God and as His Son's spouse, needest not suffer anything of the kind. Therefore, happy maiden, forsake all such sorrow for the reward reserved to thee as thou oughtest to do without any reward. Now I have kept my promise, that I would show that to be glozed over with falsehood, which some may say and think of as true: the happiness and sweetness which the wedded have. For it fares not as those think who look at it from the outside; it happens far otherwise with the poor and the rich, with those who loathe and those who love each other, but the vexation in every case exceeds the joy, and the loss altogether surpasses the gain.'

The writer then recommends Christ as a spouse and gives a graphic description of pride, which he considers a power equal to that of the devil. He has such a lively horror of pride and thinks its effects so baneful that, should the maidenhood he has been extolling be touched by it, its prerogative, he says, forthwith breaks down. 'A maid as regards the grace of maidenhood surpasses the widowed and the wedded, but a mild wife or meek widow is better than a proud maiden,'—a distinction which is curious and I believe stands alone at this early period. The saints Catharine, Margaret, Agnes, Juliana and Cecilia are quoted as maidens of irreproachable meekness.

The treatise 'Hali Meidenhad' exists in one copy only, and there is no evidence as to how much it was read. Its obvious purpose is to encourage girls to become nuns, and this not so

much on account of the beauties of convent life, as because of the
troubles in worldly life they would escape by doing so.

§ 2.   The Convent of Helfta and its Literary Nuns[1].

The mystic writings with which the present chapter has hitherto
dealt are works written for nuns, not by them, for of all the English
mystic writings of the 13th century, womanly though they often
are in tone, none can claim to be the production of a woman.   It
is different on the Continent, where the mystic literature of the
13th century is largely the production of nuns, some of whom have
secured wide literary fame.   Their writings, which were looked upon
by their contemporaries as divinely inspired, are among the most
impassioned books of the age.   They claim the attention both of
the student of art and the student of literature.   For strong natures
who rebelled against the conditions of ordinary life, but were shut
out from the arena of intellectual competition, found an outlet for
their aspirations in intensified emotionalism, and this emotionalism
led to the development of a wealth of varying imagery which subsequently became the subject-matter of pictorial art.   In course
of time the series of images offered and suggested by Scripture
had been supplemented by a thousand floating fancies and a mass
of legendary conceits, which were often based on heathen conceptions; and the 13th century mystic first tried to fix and interpret
these in their spiritual application.   His endeavours may appear
to some a dwelling on fruitless fancies, but since this imagery in
its later representations, especially in painting, has become a thing
of so much wonder and delight, the writers who first tried to
realise and describe these conceptions deserve at least respectful
attention.

The convent of Helfta near Eisleben in Saxony stands out
during the 13th century as a centre of these mystic tendencies
and of contemporary culture, owing to the literary activity of its
nuns.   All the qualities which make early mysticism attractive,—
moral elevation, impassioned fervour, intense realism and an
almost boundless imagination,—are here found reflected in the

---

[1] Comp. *Revelationes Gertrudianae ac Mechtildianae*, edit. Oudin, for the Benedictines
of Solesmes 1875, 2 vols., which contain the works of these three nuns; Mechthild
von Magdeburg, *Offenbarungen, oder Das Fliessende Licht der Gottheit*, edit. Gall
Morel, 1869; Preger, W., *Geschichte der deutschen Mystik im Mittelalter*, 1874, vol. 1,
pp. 70—132.

writings of three women, who were inmates of the same convent, and worked and wrote contemporaneously.

The convent to which these women belonged was of the Benedictine order. It had been founded in 1229 by Burkhardt, Count von Mansfeld, and his wife Elisabeth, for the use of their two daughters and for other women who wished to join them in a religious life. So many of the daughters of the Thuringian nobility flocked thither that the convent was removed in 1234 to more spacious accommodation at Rodardesdorf, and again in 1258 to a pleasanter and more suitable site at Helfta.

The convent was then under the abbess Gertrud[1] of the noble family of Hackeborn, whose rule (1251–1291) marks a climax in the prosperity and influence of the house. The convent numbered over a hundred nuns, and among them were women distinguished in other ways besides writing. In the annals of the house mention is made of Elisabeth and Sophie, daughters of Hermann von Mansfeld;—the former was a good painter, and the latter transcribed numerous books and held the office of prioress for many years before she succeeded Gertrud as abbess. Reference is also made to the nun Mechthild von Wippra († c. 1300), who taught singing, an art zealously cultivated by these nuns.

This enthusiasm for studies of all kinds was inspired in the first place by the abbess Gertrud, of whose wonderful liberality of mind and zeal for the advance of knowledge we read in an account written soon after her death by members of her convent[2]. She was endlessly zealous in collecting books and in setting her nuns to transcribe them. 'This too she insisted on,' says the account, 'that the girls should be instructed in the liberal arts, for she said that if the pursuit of knowledge (studium scientiae) were to perish, they would no longer be able to understand holy writ, and religion together with devotion would disappear.' Latin was well taught and written with ease by various members of the convent. The three women writers who have given the house lasting fame were Mechthild,—who was not educated at the convent but came there about the year 1268, and who is usually spoken of as the beguine or sister Mechthild,—the nun and saint Mechthild von Hackeborn, the sister of the abbess Gertrud, who was educated in the convent and there had visions between 1280 and 1300,—and Gertrud—known in literature as Gertrud the Great. Her

---

[1] *Revelationes,* etc. edit. Oudin, vol. 1, Praefatio.
[2] Ibid. vol. 1, pp. 497 ff.

name being the same as that of the abbess caused at one time a confusion between them.

The writings of these nuns were composed under the influence of the same mystic movement which was spreading over many districts of Europe, and therefore they contain ideas and descriptions which, forming part of the imaginative wealth of the age, are nearly related to what is contemporaneously found elsewhere. In numerous particulars the writings of these nuns bear a striking resemblance to the imagery and descriptions introduced into the Divine Comedy by Dante. Struck by this likeness, and bent upon connecting *Matelda* of the *Purgatorio* with a real person, several modern students have recognised her prototype in one of the writers named Mechthild[1].

The writings of both these women are anterior in date to the composition of the Divine Comedy, and as they were accepted by the Dominicans, certainly had a chance of being carried into distant districts. But there is no proof that Dante had either of these writers in his mind when he wrote in the *Purgatorio* of Matelda as appearing in an earthly paradise to the poet on the other side of the river Lethe.

> ' A lady all alone, she went along
> Singing and culling flower after flower,
> With which the pathway was all studded o'er.
> " Ah, beauteous lady, who in rays of love
> Dost warm thyself, if I may trust to looks,
> Which the heart's witnesses are wont to be,
> May the desire come unto thee to draw
> Near to this river's bank," I said to her,
> " So much that I may hear what thou art singing." '

It is she who makes the triumph of the Church apparent to the poet while Beatrice descends to him from heaven.

Without entering into this controversy, it is interesting to note the similarity of the visions in which Mechthild von Hackeborn describes heaven, and those which Mechthild of Magdeburg draws of hell, to the descriptions of the greatest of Italian poets.

In order to gain an idea of the interests which were prominent at the convent at Helfta it will be well to treat of the lives, history

---

[1] Comp. Preger, 'Dante's Matelda,' Acad. Vortrag, 1873; Paquelin and Scartazzini, 'Zur Matelda-Frage' in *Jahrbuch der Dante Gesellschaft*, Berlin, 1877, pp. 405, 411; Lubin, *Osservazioni sulla Matilda svelata*, 1878.

and writings of its three women writers in succession,—the beguine Mechthild,—the nun Mechthild,—and the nun Gertrud. Their characters and compositions bear marked points of difference.

Mechthild the beguine[1] was born about 1212 and lived in contact with the world, perhaps at some court, till the age of twenty-three, when she left her people and came to Magdeburg to adopt the religious life. She was led to take this step by a troubled conscience, which was no doubt occasioned by her coming into contact with Dominican friars. At this time they were making a great stir in Saxony, and Mechthild's brother Balduin joined their order. Mechthild lived at Magdeburg for many years in a poor and humble way in a settlement of beguines, but at last she was obliged to seek protection in a nunnery, because she had drawn upon herself the hatred of the clergy.

The origin and position of the bands of women called beguines[2] deserve attention, for the provisions made for them are evidently the outcome of a charitable wish to provide for homeless women, and to prevent their vagrancy and moral degradation. The name given to these women lies in great obscurity. It is sometimes connected with a priest of Liège (Lüttich) Lambert le Bègue (the stammerer, † 1172), a reformer in his way whose work recalls that of the founders of orders of combined canons and nuns, and who was very popular among women of all classes and advocated their association. Many settlements of beguines were founded in the towns of Flanders and Brabant, some of which have survived to this day ; and in German towns also the plan was readily adopted of setting aside a house in the town, for the use of poor women who, being thus provided with a roof over their heads, were then left to support themselves as best they could, by begging, or by sick nursing, or by the work of their hands. These women were not bound by any vow to remain in the house where they dwelt, and were not tied down to any special routine. This freedom led to different results among them. In some instances they were attracted by mysticism ; in others they advocated ideas which drew on them the reproach of heresy and gave rise to Papal decrees condemning them ; in others again they drifted into ways which were little to their credit and caused them to be classed with loose women.

---

[1] *Allgemeine Deutsche Biographie*, article 'Mechthild' by Strauch, Ph.

[2] Keller, L., *Die Reformation und die älteren Reformparteien*, 1885, pp. 29 ff.; also Hallman, E., *Geschichte des Ursprungs der Beguinen*, 1843.

In one of the houses allotted to these women in Magdeburg Mechthild spent the years between 1235 and 1268, and during that time, under the encouragement of the Dominican friars, she wrote prayers, meditations, reflections on the times, and short accounts of spiritual visions, some in prose, some in verse, which had a wide circulation. The fact of their being written in German at a time when writings of the kind in German were few, was the cause of their being read in lay as well as in religious circles. These writings were afterwards collected, presumably in the order of their composition, by a Dominican friar who issued them under the title of 'The Flowing Light of Divinity.' Six of the seven books into which the work is divided were composed before Mechthild went to Helfta, and the visions and reflections she wrote after her admission were grouped together in the seventh book. These writings were originally issued in the German of the north, but the only German copy now extant is a south German transcript, which was written for the mystics of Switzerland. The work was translated into Latin during Mechthild's lifetime by a Dominican friar, but his collection only contains the first six books, the contents of which are arranged in a different order. Both the German and the Latin versions have recently been reprinted[1].

Among these writings were several severely critical and condemnatory of the clergy of Magdeburg, who resented these attacks and persecuted Mechthild. On this account she sought admission at Helfta, which was not far distant from Halle, where her special friend the Dominican friar Heinrich was living[2]. The nuns at Helfta were on friendly terms with the Dominicans, who frequently visited them[3], and it appears that the nun Gertrud the Great knew of the writings of the beguine and advocated her admission to the nunnery. She came there in 1268 and lived there for about twelve years; passages in the writings of her fellow nuns refer to her death and burial[4].

With regard to her writings we are struck by their diversified contents, by their variety in form, and by their many-sided sympathies. The 'Flowing Light of Divinity' (Fliessende Licht der

---

[1] Mechthild von Magdeburg, *Offenbarungen, oder Das Fliessende Licht der Gottheit*, edit. Gall Morel, 1869; the abridged Latin version in *Revelationes*, etc. edit. Oudin, vol. 2, pp. 423–710.

[2] Heinrich not to be confounded with Heinrich who translated her work.

[3] *Revelationes*, etc. edit. Oudin, vol. 2, pp. 298, 329, 332, etc.

[4] Ibid. vol. 1, p. 542; vol. 2, pp. 325, 330.

Gottheit), consists of a collection of shorter and longer compositions, some in poetry, some in prose, which may be roughly classed as spiritual poems and love-songs, allegories, visions, and moral reflections or aphorisms. Against mysticism the charge has been brought that it led to no activity in theological thought and did not produce any religious reformation, but surely enquiries into the nature of the soul and its relation to God such as these are full of speculative interest, and have played no small part in paving the way towards a more rational interpretation of the position of man with regard to faith, to merit, to retribution and to the other great questions of dogma.

Turning first to the poems which treat of spiritual love, many are in dialogue, a form much used by the Minnesingers of the age but rarely by its religious poets. Among them is a dialogue[1] between the Soul and the queen Love, who sits enthroned. The Soul accuses Love (spiritual love of course) of robbing her of a liking for the goods of this world, but Love justifies herself by saying that she has given to the Soul instead all that constitutes her true happiness. In another dialogue[2] the Soul exclaims in wonder at Love, who in eloquent strains describes the power that is within her. By this power she drove Christ from heaven to earth; is it then to be wondered at that she can capture and hold fast a soul?

One of the longer pieces[3], less complete in form but more complex in ideas, describes how a call comes to the Soul, and how she urges her servants the Senses to help her to adorn herself to go forth to the dance, that her craving for joy may be satisfied. The Soul justifies her desire in strains such as these:

' The fish in the water do not drown, the birds in the air are not lost,
  The gold in the furnace does not vanish but there attains its glow.
  God has given to every creature to live according to its desire,
  Why then should I resist mine?'

The Soul then describes the various experiences which led to her union with Christ, which she expresses in passionate strains suggestive of the Song of Solomon.

---

[1] Mechthild, *Offenbarungen*, etc. edit. Gall Morel, p. 3 ' Wie die minne und die kuneginne zesamene sprachen.'

[2] Ibid. p. 6 ' Von den megden der seele und von der minne schlage.'

[3] Ibid. p. 18 ' Von der minne weg,' etc.

Again, we have the Soul[1] complaining to Love of the ties which bind her to the body, and Love directs her how to overcome them. Understanding too discourses with the Soul[2], and the Soul admits the greater capacities of Understanding, but she insists that Understanding owes to her the capacity both of contemplation and spiritual enjoyment. In other poems like points of abstract interest are touched upon. One of the most curious of these productions is a dialogue in which Understanding converses with Conscience[3] and expresses surprise at Conscience, whose attitude is one of proud humility. Conscience explains that her pride comes through her contact with God, and that her humility is due to her contrition at having done so few good works.

The question of how far good works are necessary to salvation, in other words justification by faith *versus* justification by works, is a thought prominent in the beguine's mind, and gives the key-note to a curious and interesting allegory on admission to the communion of the saints[4]. A poor girl longing to hear mass felt herself transported into the church of heaven, where at first she could see no one. Presently youths entered strewing flowers,— white flowers beneath the church tower, violets along the nave, roses before the Virgin's altar, and lilies throughout the choir. Others came and lighted candles, and then John the Baptist entered bearing the lamb, which he set on the altar and prepared to read mass. John the Evangelist came next, St Peter and so many more of heaven's inmates that the poor girl felt there was no room left for her in the nave of the church. She went and stood beneath the tower among people who wore crowns, 'but the beauty of hair, which comes from good works, they had not. How had they come into heaven? Through repentance and good intention.' There were others with them so richly clad that the girl felt ashamed of her appearance and went into the choir, where she saw the Virgin, St Catherine, holy Cecilia, bishops, martyrs and angels. But suddenly she too was decked with a splendid cloak, and the Virgin beckoned to her to stand by her side. Prompted by the Virgin she then took part in the religious service and was led to the altar, where John the Baptist let her kiss the wounds of the lamb. 'She

---

[1] Mechthild, *Offenbarungen*, p. 43 'Wie die minne vraget,' etc.

[2] Ibid. p. 38 'Wie die bekantnisse und die sele sprechent zesamne,' etc.

[3] Ibid. p. 232 'Wie bekantnisse sprichet zu dem gewissede.'

[4] Ibid. p. 30 'Von der armen dirnen' (I have retained the designation 'saint' where it is used in the allegory).

to whom this happened is dead,' says the writer, 'but we hope to find her again among the choir of angels.'

This allegory was severely censured, and in a later chapter[1] Mechthild says that a 'Pharisee' argued that it was forbidden for a layman, like John the Baptist, to hold mass. Mechthild's arguments in reply to the charge are somewhat involved, but she boldly declares that John, who was in close communion with God, was better fitted in some respects to say mass than Pope, bishop or priest.

With Mechthild, John the Baptist, John the Evangelist and St Peter, patron saint of the Dominicans, stand foremost among the saints of heaven. There is a beautiful account[2] of a Soul who found herself in company with God and the saints, who each in turn explained how they had helped to bring her there.

Glimpses of heaven and hell are frequent in these writings, and a full description of hell[3] and one of paradise[4] deserve special attention from the point of view of mediæval imagery. Hell is here characterised as the seat of Eternal Hatred, which is built in the deepest depths from stones of manifold wickedness. Pride, as shown in Lucifer, forms the foundation-stone; then come the stones of disobedience, covetousness, hatred and lewdness, brought thither through acts of Adam. Cain brought anger, ferocity, and warfare, and Judas brought lying, betrayal, despair and suicide. The building formed by these stones is so arranged that each part of it is occupied by those who were specially prone to the various sins. In its depths sits Lucifer, above him Christians, Jews and heathens, according to the kind of crime committed by each. The horrors of their sufferings recall those pictured by Herrad, and at a later period by Dante and Orcagna. The usurer is gnawed, the thief hangs suspended by his feet, murderers continually receive wounds, and gluttons swallow red-hot stones and drink sulphur and pitch. 'What seemed sweetness here is there turned into bitterness. The sluggard is loaded with grief, the wrathful are struck with fiery thongs. The poor musician, who had gleefully fed wicked vanity, weeps more tears in hell than there is water in the sea.' Many horrible and impressive scenes, such as the mediæval mind loved to dwell upon, are depicted.

The picture drawn of paradise is correspondingly fair. Ac-

---

[1] Mechthild, *Offenbarungen*, p. 210 'Da Johannes Baptista der armen dirnen messe sang.'
[2] Ibid. p. 46 ' Wie sich die minnende sele gesellet gotte,' etc.
[3] Ibid. p. 82 ' Von der helle,' etc.
[4] Ibid. p. 270 ' Ein wenig von dem paradyso.'

cording to the beguine there is an earthly and a heavenly paradise. Regarding the earthly paradise she says: ' There is no limit to its length and breadth. First I reached a spot lying on the confines of this world and paradise. There I saw trees and leaves and grass, but of weeds there were none. Some trees bore fruit, but most of them sweet-scented leaves. Rapid streams cut through the earth, and warm winds blew from the south. In the waters mingled earth's sweetness and heaven's delight. The air was sweet beyond expression. But of birds and animals there were none, for God has reserved this garden for human beings to dwell there undisturbed.' In this garden Mechthild finds Enoch and Elias who explain what keeps them there. Then she sees the higher regions of paradise in which dwell the souls who are waiting to enter the kingdom of God, ' floating in joy as the air floats in the sunshine,' says Mechthild; and she goes on to explain how on the Day of Judgment paradise will altogether cease to exist and its inhabitants will be absorbed into heaven.

The beguine's writings contain various references to herself and her compositions, and considerable praise of the Dominican friars. In one place[1] she describes how she was told that her writings deserved to be burnt, but she turned in prayer to God as was her wont from childhood, and He told her not to doubt her powers for they came through Him. ' Ah Lord,' she exclaimed in reply, ' were I a learned man, a priest, in whom thou hadst made manifest this power, thou would'st see him honoured, but how can they believe that on such unworthy ground thou hast raised a golden house?......Lord, I fail to see the reason of it.' But the attacks against her roused her to anger, and she closes the poem with a stern invective against those who are false.

Another passage contains an autobiographical sketch of Mechthild's early experiences[2]. She says that when she was twelve years old she felt drawn to things divine, and from that time to the present, a period of thirty-one years, she had been conscious of God's grace and had been saved from going astray. ' God is witness,' she continues, ' that I never consciously prayed to be told what is written in this book; it never occurred to me that such things could come to anyone. While I spent my youth with friends and relations to whom I was most dear, I had no knowledge of such things. Yet I always wished to be humble, and

---

[1] Mechthild, *Offenbarungen*, p. 52 ' Von diseme buche,' etc.
[2] Ibid. p. 90 ' Dis buch ist von gotte komen,' etc.

from love of God I came to a place (Magdeburg) where with one exception I had no friends.' She describes how at that time two angels and two devils were her companions, and were to her the representatives of the good and evil tendencies of which she was conscious. The devils spoke to her of her physical beauty, promised fame 'such as has led astray many an unbeliever,' and prompted her to rebellion and unchastity. Obviously her passionate nature rose against the mode of life she had adopted, but the thought of Christ's sufferings at last brought her comfort. She was much perturbed by her power of writing. 'Why not give it to learned folk?' she asked of God, but God was angered with her, and her father-confessor pressed upon her that writing was her vocation. In another impassioned account she describes how she was oppressed by a devil[1].

In the third book of her writings Mechthild says[2] that God pointed out to her the seven virtues which priests ought to cultivate, and we gather from this that she did not consider the clergy devout or pure-minded. In further passages[3] she dilates on the duties of prelate, prior and prioress, and severely attacks the conduct of a deacon of Magdeburg. Even more explicit in its severity to the priesthood is an account[4] of how God spoke to her, and told her that He would touch the Pope's heart and make him utter a prayer, which is given, and in which the Pope declaims against the conduct of his clergy who are 'straightway going to hell.' In the Latin translation God's admonition is amplified by the following passages: 'For thus says the Lord: I will open the ear of the highest priest and touch his heart with the woe of my wrath, because my shepherds of Jerusalem have become robbers and wolves before my very eyes. With cruelty they murder my lambs and devour them. The sheep also are worn and weary because you call them from healthy pastures, in your godlessness do not suffer them to graze on the heights on green herbs, and with threats and reproof prevent their being tended with healthful teaching and healthful advice by those men who are supported by faith and knowledge. He who knows not the way that leads to hell and would know it, let him look at the life and

---

[1] Mechthild, *Offenbarungen*, p. 110 'Von einer vrowe, etc.'

[2] Ibid. p. 68 'Von siben dingen die alle priester sollent haben.'

[3] Ibid. p. 171 'Wie ein prior, etc.'; p. 177 'Von der regele eines kanoniken, etc.'; p. 178 'Got gebet herschaft.'

[4] Ibid. p. 198 'Wie böse pfafheit sol genidert werden.'

morals of the base and degenerate clergy, who, given to luxury and
other sins, through their impious ways are inevitably going the way
to hell[1].'

The friars, it is said, must come to the rescue and reform the
world, and Mechthild being especially inclined to the Dominicans
dwells on their usefulness to true faith in a number of passages[2].
There is a long description of how God saw that His Son, with
the apostles, martyrs, confessors and virgins, was unable to lead
back the people who had gone astray, and therefore He sent into
the world two other children, that is the two orders of friars,
to save them. In another vision[3] God explains to Mechthild
the special purpose for which He has lately sent five new saints
into the world, one of whom is Elisabeth of Thüringen 'whom I
sent,' said the Lord, 'to those wretched ladies who sit in castles
with much unchastity, puffed up with conceit, and so absorbed
by vanities that they ought to be cast into the nether regions.
Many a lady however has now followed her example in what
measure she would or could.' The other saints are Dominic,
who has been sent to reclaim unbelievers,—Francis, who has
come as a warning to covetous priests and conceited laymen,—
a new St Peter, the Martyr († 1252),—and the sister Jutta von
Sangershausen. History tells us of Peter that he was appointed
inquisitor against the heretics in Lombardy and murdered at their
instigation[4]; and of Jutta that, having lost her husband in 1260,
she placed her children in convents and went among the heathen
Prussians where she tended the leprous till her death four years
afterwards[5]. From later passages in the writings of Mechthild,
written after she had come to live at Helfta[6], it appears that she felt
that faith was not increasing in the world ; perhaps she was disappointed in her exalted anticipations of the influence of the friars.

The writings of Mechthild of this later period are more mystic
and visionary than those of earlier days. She is distressed at
the troublous times that have come to Saxony and Thüringen,

---

[1] *Revelationes*, etc. edit. Oudin, vol. 2, p. 524.

[2] Mechthild, *Offenbarungen*, p. 115 'Von sehs tugenden St Domenicus'; p. 116
'Dur sehszehen ding hat got predierorden liep'; ibid. 'Von vierhande crone bruder
Heinrichs'; p. 154 'Von sehsleie kleider, etc.'

[3] Ibid. p. 166 'Von funfleie nuwe heligen.'

[4] *A. SS. Boll.*, St Peter of the Dominican Order, April 29.

[5] Ibid., St Jutta vidua, May 5, appendix.

[6] Mechthild, *Offenbarungen*, p. 256 'Wie ein predierbruder wart gesehen.'

and tells[1] how she fell ill and was so perturbed that she lost the power of prayer for seventeen days. Many prayers and visions, some of great sweetness and beauty, were the production of these later days. A long allegory called the 'Spiritual Convent or Ghostly Abbey[2]' shows the high opinion she had of life in a nunnery. In this poem the inmates of the convent are personified as the Virtues, an idea occasionally used during the Middle Ages, and one which at a later date in England, as we shall hear afterwards[3], was handled in a very different manner, the convent inmates being represented as the Vices. In Mechthild's convent Charity is abbess, Meekness is chaplain, Peace is prioress, Kindliness is sub-prioress, and among the inmates of the convent there is Hope the singing-mistress, and Wisdom the schoolmistress 'who with good counsel carefully instructs the ignorant, so that the nunnery is held holy and honoured.' Bounty is cellaress, Mercy sees to the clothes, Pity tends the sick, and Dread sits at the gate. The provost or priest is Obedience, 'to whom all these Virtues are subject. Thus does the convent abide before God,' the poem ends, '...happy are they who dwell there.'

The writings of Mechthild offer many more points of interest. Not the least curious among her compositions are the amplified descriptions of Biblical history, as of the Creation, the Nativity, and the early experiences of the Virgin[4], which enter minutely into the feelings and emotions of those immediately concerned and give them an allegorical and spiritualised application. Short spiritual poems are also numerous, but so much depends on their form that a translation cannot convey their chief beauty. Their general drift is exemplified by the two following[5].

'It is a wondrous journeying onwards, this progress of the Soul, who guides the Senses as the man who sees leads him who is blind. Fearlessly the Soul wanders on without grief of heart, for she desires nought but what the Lord wills who leads all to the best.'

And again[6], 'My Soul spake to her Spouse: Lord, thy ten-

---

[1] Mechthild, *Offenbarungen*, p. 243 'Von der not eines urluges.'

[2] Ibid. p. 249 'Von einem geistlichen closter.'

[3] Comp. below, ch. 11, § 1.

[4] Mechthild, *Offenbarungen*, p. 68 'Von dem angenge aller dinge'; p. 107 'Von der heligen drivaltekeit, etc.'; p. 147 'Von sante marien gebet, etc.'

[5] Ibid. p. 14 'In disen weg zuhet die sele, etc.'

[6] Ibid. p. 16 'Von der pfrunde trost und minne.'

derness is to my body delightful ministration; thy compassion is to my spiritual nature wondrous comfort; and thy love is to my whole being rest eternal.'

Thoughts such as these are found scattered up and down in the beguine's writings, and give one a high estimation of her poetic power, her ready imagination and her mastery of language. Her vigorous nature guided into the channel of spiritual aspirations frequently filled her poems with a passionate eloquence.

In conclusion may stand a few of the beguine's moral reflections, which, if they are not borrowed from elsewhere, argue well for her power of condensing thoughts into short sentences; but here also it is not easy to find the exact words in which to render the chief points of these reflections[1].

'Vanity does not stop to think what she is losing;
Perseverance is laden with virtues.
Stupidity is ever self-sufficient;
The wisest never comes to the end of what he would say.
Anger brings darkness unto the soul;
Gentleness is ever sure of attaining grace.
Pride would ever raise herself aloft;
Lowliness is ever ready to yield...
Sluggishness will never gain wealth;
The industrious seeks more than his immediate advantage.'

And the following,—which are the product of a later period and have in them the ring of a deeper experience[2]—'None knows how firm he stands, until he has experienced the prompting of desire; none how strong he is, until hatred has attacked him; none how good he is, before he has attained a happy end.'

From the writings of the beguine Mechthild we pass to those of her companion at Helfta, the nun Mechthild von Hackeborn. Her 'Book of Special Grace[3]' consists entirely of visions or revelations described by her and put into writing by her fellow-nuns; it was widely read, and gave rise to similar productions in other nunneries. There are many early manuscript copies of the book in existence; it was originally written in Latin, but has been translated into German, English, Italian and French, and has repeatedly been printed.

---

[1] Mechthild, *Offenbarungen*, p. 98 'Von zwein ungeleichen dingen, etc.'
[2] Ibid. p. 214 'Bekorunge, die welt und ein gut ende prüfent uns.'
[3] 'Liber Specialis Gratiae,' in *Revelationes*, etc. edit. Oudin, vol. 2, pp. 1–421.

The visions are so arranged that those contained in the first part of the book have reference to festal days of the Church, to Christ, Mary and the saints. The second part treats of the manifestations of divine grace of which Mechthild was conscious in herself, and the third and fourth describe how God should be praised and what is conducive to salvation or 'soul-hele.' In the fifth part Mechthild holds converse with those who have departed this life, chiefly members of the convent, for the belief that it was possible to hold communion with the souls of the departed was readily accepted at Helfta as in other religious houses.

A sixth and seventh part were added to Mechthild's book after her death by her fellow-nuns and contain information about her sister, the abbess Gertrud, and details about Mechthild's death and the visions other nuns had of her.

The nun Mechthild von Hackeborn, who was nine years younger than her sister Gertrud, had come to the house as a child on a visit with her mother, and was so much attracted to it that she remained there. She is described by her fellow-nuns as a person of tender and delicate refinement, whose religious fervour was remarkable, and these characteristics are reflected in her writings. She was often suffering, noticeably at the time when her sister, the abbess Gertrud, died (1291). She is praised for her lovely voice, and references to music and singing in her visions are frequent. It is not quite clear when her fellow-nuns began to put her visions into writing, presumably between 1280 and 1300, and authorities also differ on the year of her death, which the Benedictines of Solesmes accept as 1298[1], whereas Preger defers it till 1310[2].

In the description of her visions Mechthild von Hackeborn appears throughout as a person of even temper and great sweetness of disposition, one who was not visited by picturesque temptations, troubles and doubts, and who therefore insisted chiefly on the beautiful side of things; for hell with its torments and the whole mise-en-scène of the nether regions have no meaning and no attraction for her. In her revelations Christ, the Virgin, and other members of the vast hierarchy of heaven enter as living realities. She is particularly fond of the angels, whom she loves to picture as the associates of men on earth and in heaven. In conformity with the conceptions of her age Christ is to her the wooer of the soul,

---

[1] *Revelationes*, etc. edit. Oudin, vol. 2, p. 727.

[2] Preger, W., *Geschichte der deutschen Mystik im Mittelalter*, 1874, vol. 1, p. 87.

the chosen bridegroom, who combines all that makes humanity attractive and divinity sublime. Christ and the Virgin love to confer with Mechthild, or rather with her Soul,—the terms are used indiscriminately,—and enter into converse with her whenever she seeks enlightenment. Flowers and precious stones, the splendour of vestments, and occasionally some homely object, supply her with similes and comparisons.

The following descriptions occurring in visions will give some idea of the spirit in which Mechthild wrote[1].

'After the feast of St Michael...she saw a golden ascent divided into nine grades, crowded by a multitude of angels, and the first grade was presided over by angels, the second by archangels and so on upwards, each order of angels presiding over one grade. She was divinely informed that this ascent represented the abode of men in this way,—that whoever faithfully, humbly, and devotedly fulfils his duty to the Church of God, and for God's sake, to the infirm, to the poor and to travellers, abides in the first grade, consorting with the angels. Again, they who by prayer and devotion are closer to God and in nearness to Him, are devoted to knowledge of Him, to His teaching and help, are in the next grade and are the companions of the archangels. Those again who practise patience, obedience, voluntary poverty, humility, and bravely perform all virtues, mount to the next grade with the Virtues. And those who, opposing vice and greed, hold the fiend and all his suggestions in contempt, in the fourth grade share the triumph of glory with the Powers. Prelates who fully respond to the duties the Church has entrusted to them, who watch day and night over the salvation of souls and discreetly give back twofold the talent entrusted to them,—these in the fifth grade hold the glory of heaven as a recompense of their work with the Pre-eminences. Again, those who with complete submission bow before the majesty of the Divine, and who out of love for Him love the Creator in the created, and love themselves because they are fashioned after the image of God, who conform to Him as far as human weakness permits, and, holding the flesh subservient to the spirit, triumph over their mind by transferring it to things celestial, these glory in the sixth grade with the Rulers. But those who are steadfast in meditation and contemplation, who embracing pureness of heart and peace of mind make of themselves a temple meet for God, which

---

[1] *Revelationes*, etc. edit. Oudin, vol. 2 ('Liber Specialis Gratiae,' bk 1, ch. 30, De angelis), p. 102.

truly may be called a paradise, according to Proverbs (viii. 31) " my delights were with the sons of men," and about which it is said (2 Cor. vi. 16) " I will dwell in them and walk in them," these dwell in the seventh grade with the Enthroned. Those who outstrip others in knowledge and apprehension, who by a singular blessedness hold God in their minds as it were face to face and give back what they have drawn from the fountain of all wisdom, by teaching and explaining to others, these abide in the eighth grade of the ascent together with the Cherubim. And those who love God with heart and soul, who place their whole being in the eternal fire which is God itself, love Him not with their own but with divine love being the chosen ones of God, who see all creatures in God and love them for His sake, friends as well as enemies, those whom nothing can divide from God nor stay in their ascent—for the more their enemies attack them the more they grow in love,—those who, fervent themselves, awake fervour in others, so that if they could they would make all mankind perfect in love, who weep for the sins and faults of others, because, indifferent to their own glory, they seek but the glory of God, these shall for evermore dwell in the ninth grade with the Seraphim, between whom and God there is nought in closer nearness to Him.

'During mass she (Mechthild) saw that a large number of angels were present, and each angel in guise of a lovely youth stood by the side of the maiden entrusted to his care. Some held flowering sceptres, others golden flowers. And as the maidens bowed they pressed the flowers to their lips in sign of everlasting peace. Thus angels assisted at the entire mass.

'And as the maidens advanced to partake of the communion, each of the angels led her who was entrusted to his care. And the King of Glory stood in the place of the priest surrounded by shining splendour, on His breast an ornament in the shape of a branched tree, and from His heart, in which lies hidden the wealth of wisdom and knowledge, flowed a stream which encompassed those who advanced with a flood of heavenly joy.'

In the preceding passages we see Mechthild in the state of rapture called forth by the moments of celebration and service; the extracts which follow describe one of the divine visitations which came to her as a special manifestation of grace[1].

---

[1] *Revelationes*, etc. edit. Oudin, vol. 2 (' Liber Specialis Gratiae,' bk 2, ch. 2, De vinea domini), p. 137.

'On a certain Sunday, while they were singing the *Asperges me, Domine*, she said "Lord, in what wilt thou now bathe and cleanse my heart?" Straightway the Lord with love unutterable bending to her as a mother would to her son, embraced her saying : "In the love of my divine heart I will bathe thee." And He opened the door of His heart, the treasure-house of flowing holiness, and she entered into it as though into a vineyard. There she saw a river of living water flowing from the east to the west, and round about the river there were twelve trees bearing twelve kinds of fruit, that is the virtues which the blessed Paul enumerates in his epistle : love, joy, peace, long-suffering, gentleness, goodness, benignity, meekness, faith, modesty, temperance, chastity[1]. This water is called the river of love ; thereunto the soul entered and was cleansed of every stain. In this river there were numerous fish with golden scales, which signified those loving souls which, separated from earthly delights, have plunged themselves in the very well-spring of all good, that is, into Jesus. In the vineyard palm-trees were planted, some of which stood erect, while others were bent to the ground. The palms that stand erect are those who despised the world with its flowers, and who turned their minds to things divine ; and the palms that are bent down are those wretched ones who lie in the earthly dust of their misdeeds. The Lord in likeness of a gardener was digging in the earth, and she said : "O Lord, what is thy spade?" And He answered : "My fear."—Now in certain places the earth was hard, in others soft. The hard earth signified the hearts of those who are hardened in sin and who know not how to be corrected either by advice or by reproof ; the soft earth the hearts of those who are softened by tears and true contrition. And our Lord said : "This vineyard is my Catholic Church, in which for thirty-three years I laboured with my sweat ; do thou labour with me in this vineyard." And she said : "How?" To whom the Lord replied : "By watering it." And straightway the Soul ran eagerly to the river and set a vessel filled with water on her shoulders, and as it was heavy, the Lord came and helped her, and its burden was lightened. And the Lord said : "Thus when I give grace to men, do all things performed or borne for my sake seem light and easy. But if I withdraw my grace, then do all things seem burdensome." Moreover round about the palms she saw a multitude of angels like unto a wall...'

In a similar strain the visions of Mechthild proceed, always

---

[1] Cf. Gal. v. 22-3, to which Mechthild adds.

gentle and rarely impassioned but shining with the glow of end-lessly changing imagery.　There is no limit to the pictures which rise before her mental eye or to the points which suggest analogy with things divine[1].

'To rouse the piety of believers in relation to the glorious image of our Saviour Jesus Christ, on the Sunday *Omnis terra* (the second after Epiphany), that is on the day when the expo-sition at Rome of the image of Christ takes place, she was granted this vision.　On a mountain overgrown with flowers she beheld our Lord seated on a throne of jasper decorated with gold and red stone.　The jasper which is green is typical of the power of eternal divinity, gold represents love, and the red stone the suffer-ings which He endured through love of us.　The mountain was surrounded by beautiful trees covered with fruit.　Under these trees rested the souls of the saints, each of whom had a tent of cloth of gold, and they ate of the fruit with great enjoyment.　The hill is emblematic of the mortal life of Christ, the trees are His virtues, love, pity and others.　The saints rest under different trees according as they adhered to the Lord's different virtues; those who followed Him in charity, eat of the fruit of the tree of charity; those who were full of pity, eat of the fruit of the tree of pity, and so on accord-ing to the virtue each has practised.

'Then those who were ready to honour the holy face with a special prayer approached the Lord, carrying on their shoulders their sins, which they laid at His feet; and they were forthwith transformed into jewels of glowing gold (xenia aurea).　Those whose repentance had come out of love, because they were sad at having offended God without having been punished, saw their sins changed into golden necklaces.　Others who had redeemed them by saying the psalms and other prayers, had them trans-formed into golden rings such as are used at festivals (Domini-calibus).　Those who had made restitution for their sins by their own efforts, saw before them lovely golden shields; while those who had purified their sins by bodily suffering, beheld them as so many golden censers, for bodily chastisement before God is like the sweetness of thyme.'

The following is an example of a homely simile[2].

---

[1] *Revelationes*, etc. edit. Oudin, vol. 2 ('Liber Specialis Gratiae,' bk 1, ch. 10, De veneratione imaginis Christi), p. 31.

[2] Ibid. vol. 2 ('Liber Specialis Gratiae,' bk 2, ch. 23, De coquina domini), p. 165.

'On a certain occasion she was conscious of having received an unusual gift through the Lord's bounty, when feeling her inadequacy she humbly said : " O bounteous King, this gift, does it befit me who deem myself unworthy of entering thy kitchen and washing thy platters?" Whereupon the Lord: "Where is my kitchen and where are the platters thou wouldst wash?" She was confounded and said nothing. But the Lord, who puts questions not that they may be answered but that He may give answer unto them Himself, made her rejoice by His reply. He said : " My kitchen is my heart which, like unto a kitchen that is a common room of the house and open alike to servants and masters, is ever open to all and for the benefit of all. The cook in this kitchen is the Holy Ghost, who kindly without intermission provides things in abundance and by replenishing them makes things abound again. My platters are the hearts of saints and of chosen ones, which are filled from the overflow of the sweetness of my divine heart."'

From a passage in these books[1] we learn that a large number of Mechthild's visions had been put into writing by her fellow-nuns before she was made acquainted with the fact. For a time she was sorely troubled, then she gained confidence, reflecting that her power to see visions had come from God, and indeed she heard a voice from heaven informing her that her book should be called the ' Book of Special Grace.'

She had all her life been distressed by physical suffering. During her last illness she was generally unconscious and her fellow-nuns crowded about her praying that she would intercede with God in their behalf.

Neither of the Mechthilds makes any reference in her writings to the nun Gertrud, but Gertrud's works contain various references to her fellow-nuns[2], and it is surmised that Gertrud helped to put the nun Mechthild's visions into writing before she wrote on her own account. A passage in her own book of visions[3] refers to revelations generally, and the Lord explains to her how it is that visions are sometimes written in one, sometimes in another language. This idea may have been suggested by the fact that the beguine Mechthild's writings were in German and the nun Mechthild's in Latin.

---

[1] *Revelationes*, etc. edit. Oudin, vol. 2 (bk 2, ch. 43, De nomine et utilitate hujus libri), p. 192.

[2] Ibid. vol. 1, pp. 46, 269.   [3] Ibid. vol. 1, p. 218.

Gertrud was very different from both of these writers in disposition[1]. Probably of humble origin, she had been given into the care of the convent as a child (in 1261), and in her development was greatly influenced by the sisters Gertrud the abbess, and the nun Mechthild von Hackeborn. Of a passionate and ambitious nature, she devoted all her energies to mastering the liberal arts, but in consequence of a vision that came to her at twenty-five, she cast them aside and plunged into religious study. She mastered the spirit and contents of Holy Writ so rapidly that she began to expound them to others. Then she made extracts and collections of passages from the Fathers, out of which we are told she made many books. The influence of her personality was such that 'none conversed with her who did not afterwards declare they had profited by it.' The admiration she aroused among her fellow-nuns was so great that they declared that God had compared her to the nun Mechthild and that He said: 'In this one have I accomplished great things, but greater things will I accomplish in Gertrud[2].' As a proof of her industry we are told[3] that she was occupied from morning till night translating from Latin (into German), shortening some passages, amplifying others 'to the greater advantage of her readers.' From another passage it appears that she compiled a poem (carmen) from the sayings (dictis) of the saints[4], and as an illustration of her moral attitude we are told that when she was reading the Scriptures aloud and 'as it happened,' passages occurred which shocked her by their allusions, she hurried them over quickly or pretended not to understand them. 'But when it became needful to speak of such things for some reason of salvation, it was as though she did not mind, and she overcame her hesitation[5].' Her great modesty in regard to her own requirements is insisted on by her biographer. Many bore witness to the fact that they were more impressed by her words than by those of celebrated preachers, for she frequently moved her audience to tears[6]. In addition the writer feels called upon to mention a few incidents that happened to Gertrud, giving them a miraculous rendering, no doubt from a wish to enhance her worth.

The information about Gertrud is supplied by the first part of her book called 'The Legacy of Divine Piety[7],' which as it does

---

[1] *Revelationes*, etc. edit. Oudin, vol. 1, pp. 1 ff. on her life.   [2] Ibid. vol. 1, p. 14.
[3] Ibid. vol. 1, p. 23.   [4] Ibid. vol. 1, p. 227.   [5] Ibid. vol. 1, p. 27.
[6] Ibid. vol. 1, p. 39.
[7] 'Legatus Divinae Pietatis' in *Revelationes*, etc. edit. Oudin, vol. 1, pp. 1 ff.

not mention Gertrud's death, seems to have been written while she was alive, perhaps as a preface to a copy of her revelations. It was only after many years of study and literary activity that she determined to write down her personal experiences, and these accounts, written between 1289 and 1290, form the second part of the book as it stands at present and constitute its chief and abiding interest.

The admiration bestowed on the 'Legacy of Divine Piety' was almost greater than that given to the writings of the nun Mechthild. The perusal of a chapter will show Gertrud's attitude of mind. Starting from the occasion when she first became conscious of a living communion with God, she describes how step by step she realised an approximation to things divine, such as reverence, love, and the desire of knowledge alone can secure. She speaks of experiencing in herself a deeper religious consciousness which reacted in making her feel herself unworthy of the special attention of her Creator, and she continues in this strain[1]:

'If I look back on what the tone of my life was before and afterwards, in truth I declare that this is grace I am grateful for and yet unworthy of receiving. For thou, O Lord, didst grant unto me of the clear light of thy knowledge to which the sweetness of thy love prompted me more than any deserved correction of my faults could have done. I do not recall having felt such happiness save on the days when thou didst bid me to the delights of thy royal table. Whether thy wise forethought had so ordained, or my continued shortcomings were the reason of it, I cannot decide.

'Thus didst thou deal with and rouse my soul on a day between Resurrection and Ascension when I had entered the courtyard at an early hour before Prime, and sitting down by the fishpond was enjoying the beauties of the surroundings which charmed me by the clearness of the flowing water, the green of the trees that stood around, and the free flight of the birds, especially the doves, but above all by the reposeful quiet of the retired situation. My mind turned on what in such surroundings would make my joy perfect, and I wished for a friend, a loving, affectionate and suitable companion, who would sweeten my solitude. Then thou, O God, author of joy unspeakable, who as I hope didst favour the beginning of my meditation and didst complete it, thou didst inspire me with the thought that if, conscious of thy grace, I flow back to be joined to thee like the water; if, growing in the knowledge of virtue like unto

---

[1] 'Legatus Divinae Pietatis' in *Revelationes*, etc. edit. Oudin, vol. 1, p. 61.

these trees, I flower in the greenness of good deeds; if, looking down on things earthly in free flight like these doves, I approach heaven, and, with my bodily senses removed from external turmoil, apprehend thee with my whole mind, then in joyfulness my heart will make for thee a habitation.

'My thoughts during the day dwelt on these matters, and at night, as I knelt in prayer in the dormitory, suddenly this passage from the Gospel occurred to me (John xiv. 23), "If a man love me, he will keep my words; and my Father will love him, and we will come unto him, and make our abode with him." And my impure heart felt thee present therein. O would that an ocean of blood passed over my head that my miserable inadequacy were washed out now that thou hast made thy abode with me in dignity inscrutable! Or that my heart snatched from my body were given to me to cleanse with glowing coal, so that, freed of its dross, it might offer thee if not indeed a worthy abode, yet one not altogether unworthy. Thus, O God, didst thou show thyself from that hour onwards, sometimes kindly, sometimes stern, in accordance with my improved or neglectful way of life; though I must admit that the utmost improvement to which I sometimes momentarily attained, had it lasted all my life, never had made me worthy of the least part of the sustenance which I received in spite of many sins and, alas! of great wickedness. For thy extreme tenderness shows me thee more grieved than angered by my shortcomings, a proof to me that the amount of thy forbearance is greater when thou dost bear with me in my failings, than during thy mortal life, when thou didst bear with the betrayer Judas.

'When I strayed in mind, tempted away by some deceitful attraction, and after hours, or alas! after days, or woe is me! after weeks, returned to my heart, always did I find thee there, so that I cannot say that thou hast withdrawn thyself from me from that hour, nine years ago, till eleven days before the feast of John the Baptist, save on one occasion, when it happened through some worldly dispute, I believe, and lasted from Thursday (the fifth feria) to Tuesday (the second feria). Then on the vigil of St John the Baptist, after the mass *Nec timeas etc.*, thy sweetness and great charity came back to me, finding me so forlorn in mind that I was not even conscious of having lost a treasure, nor thought of grieving for it, nor was desirous of having it returned, so that I cannot account for the madness that possessed my mind, unless indeed it so happened because thou didst wish me to experience in myself these words of St Bernard: "We fly and thou pursuest us; we turn our back on thee, thou comest before us; thou dost ask and art refused ; but no madness, no contempt of ours makes thee turn away who never art weary, and thou dost draw us on to the joy of which it is said (1 Cor. ii. 9), 'Eye hath not seen, nor ear heard it, neither has it entered into the heart of man."'

These passages must suffice. Anyone desirous of following Gertrud through the further experiences which guided her to the knowledge of God and gave her an insight into the working of spiritual love must turn to her writings, which bear the reader onwards in continuous flow, and with much self-analysis and self-realisation give evidence of the conscious joy which develops into rapture in the presence of the Divine. A passage contained in the last chapter of the book describes Gertrud's hopes regarding her work, and fitly summarises her aspirations[1].

'Behold, beloved God,' she writes, 'I here deposit the talent of thy most gracious friendship, which, entrusted to me, the lowliest and least worthy of thy creatures, I have set forth to the increase of thy power; for I believe and dare affirm that no reason prompted me to write and speak but obedience to thy will, desire for thy glory, and zeal for the salvation of souls. I take thee to witness that I wish thee praise and thanks, for thy abundant grace withdrew itself not from me on account of my unworthiness. And herein also shalt thou find praise, that readers of this book will rejoice in the sweetness of thy bounty, and, drawn to thee, learn greater things through it ; for as students progress from first learning the alphabet to acquaintance with logic (logica), by means of the imagery here described they will be led to taste of that hidden divine sustenance (manna) which cannot be expressed even by allegory....Meanwhile in accordance with thy faithful promise and my humble request, grant to all who read this book in lowliness that they rejoice in thy love, bear with my inadequacy, and feel true contrition themselves, in order that from the golden censers of their loving hearts a sweet odour may be wafted upwards to thee, making full amends for my carelessness and shortcomings.'

Before the personal interest of this portion of the book the other parts written by fellow-nuns fade into insignificance. They contain accounts of Gertrud's thoughts on various occa-

---

[1] *Revelationes*, etc. edit. Oudin, vol. 1, p. 113.

sions, and are chiefly interesting for the comments they contain on various accepted saints; we here see what thoughts were suggested to the Helfta nuns by the personalities of St Benedict, St Bernard, St Augustine, St Dominic, St Francis, St Elisabeth, and others. Thus the feast of St John the Apostle gives rise to an account of him[1] sitting in heaven, where he keeps the holy record, and writes in different colours, sometimes in red, sometimes in black, sometimes in letters of gold—a simile which recalls the art of writing. The 'Legacy of Divine Piety' of Gertrud has repeatedly been printed in the original Latin, sometimes in conjunction with the 'Book of Special Grace' of the nun Mechthild, and, like the revelations of Mechthild, the writings of Gertrud have been translated into German and English. Both in their original form and in selections the writings of these nuns are used as books of devotion among Catholics to this day, but neither Gertrud nor Mechthild have till now been given a place in the *Acta Sanctorum.*

Gertrud outlived her distinguished contemporaries at Helfta; she died in 1311[2], her thoughts having been engrossed by the anticipation of death for some time before. During these last years of her life she composed a number of prayers called 'Spiritual Exercises'[3] for the use of her fellow-nuns, the religious fervour of which has perhaps rarely been surpassed.

They are written in rhyme but in varying rhythm; perhaps they are best designated as rhymed prose. Only the original Latin can give an idea of their eloquence, but, in the interest of the general reader I have added one in English prose. It is one of the series designated as 'a supplication for sinfulness and a preparation for death.' There is one prayer for every canonical hour; the following[4] is intended for repetition after the hour of prime, 'when the Soul holds converse with Love and Truth; and when the thought of eternal judgment, at which Truth will preside, causes the Soul to beseech Love to help her to secure Jesus as her advocate.'

'And thus shalt thou begin to effect a reconciliation with God.

'O shining Truth, O just Equity of God, how shall I appear before thy face, bearing my imperfections, conscious of the burden

---

[1] *Revelationes*, etc. edit. Oudin, vol. 1, p. 351.

[2] Preger, W., *Geschichte der deutschen Mystik im Mittelalter*, 1874, vol. 1, p. 78.

[3] 'Exercitia Spiritualia,' in *Revelationes*, etc. edit. Oudin, vol. 1, pp. 617–720.

[4] Ibid. pp. 701 ff.

of my wasted life, and of the weight of my great negligence? Woe, woe is unto me; I did not make the payment of a Christian's faith and of a spiritual life there where the treasures of love are stored, that thou mightest receive it back with manifold increase of interest. The talent of life entrusted to me, not only have I left it unused; but I have forfeited it, debased it, lost it. Where shall I go, whither shall I turn, how can I escape from thy presence?

'O Truth, in thee undivided abide justice and equity. In accordance with number, weight and measure dost thou give judgment. Whatever thou dost handle is weighed in truly even scales. Woe is unto me, a thousand times woe, if I be given over to thee with none to intercede in my behalf! O Love, do thou speak for me, answer for me, secure for me remission. Take up my cause, that through thy grace I may find eternal life.

'I know what I must do. The chalice of salvation I will take; the chalice, Jesus, I will place on the unweighted scale of Truth. Thus, thus can I supply all that is wanting; thus can I outweigh the balance of my sins. By that chalice can I counterbalance all my defects. By that chalice I can more than counterpoise my sins.

'Hail, O Love, thy royal bondservant Jesus, moved in His inmost being, whom thou didst drag at this hour before the tribunal, where the sins of the whole world were laid on Him who was without spot or blemish, save that out of pity of me He charged Himself with my sins,—Him the most innocent, Him the most beloved, condemned for love through my love of Him and suffering death for me, Him I would receive from thee to-day, O Love Divine, that He may be my advocate. Grant me this security that in this cause I have Him as my defender.

'O beloved Truth! I could not come before thee without my Jesus, but with Jesus to come before thee is joyful and pleasant. Ah Truth, now sit thee on the seat of judgment, enter on the course of justice and bring against me what thou wilt, I fear no evil, for I know, I know thy countenance cannot confound me, now that He is on my side who is my great hope and my whole confidence. Verily, I long for thy judgment now Jesus is with me, He the most beloved, the most faithful, He who has taken on Himself my misery that He may move thee to compassion.

'Ah, sweetest Jesus, thou loving pledge of my deliverance, come with me to the judgment court. There let us stand together side by side. Be thou my counsel and my advocate. Declare what thou hast done for me, how well thou hast thought upon me, how lovingly thou hast added to me that I might be sanctified through thee. Thou hast lived for me that I may not perish. Thou hast borne the burden of my sins. Thou hast died for me that I might not die an eternal death. All that thou hadst thou gavest for me, that through the wealth of thy merit I might be made rich.

'Verily in the hour of death judge me on the basis of that innocence, of that purity which came to me through thee when thou didst make atonement for my sins with thine own self, judged and condemned for my sake, so that I, who am poor and destitute in myself, through thee may be wealthy beyond measure.'

CHAPTER X.

SOME ASPECTS OF THE CONVENT IN ENGLAND DURING THE LATER MIDDLE AGES.

'All that wons in religioun
aw to haue sum ocupacioun,
outher in kirk or hali bedes,
or stodying in oder stedes;
ffor ydilnes, os sais sant paul
es grete enmy unto the soul.'

Rule of St Benedict translated into English for the use of women,
1400–1425 (ll. 1887 ff.).

§ 1.   The External Relations of the Convent.

FROM consideration of affairs on the Continent we return once more to England, to consider the external relations of the convent and the purposes these institutions fulfilled during the later Middle Ages. Speaking generally the monasteries maintained their standing unimpaired till the beginning of the 14th century; then their character began to change and for quite a century they ceased to be attractive to progressive and original minds. The range of occupations cultivated by their inmates was restricted, and these inmates gradually came to regard everything with indifference except their own narrow religious interests.

The previous chapters have shown that monasteries at different periods had served a variety of purposes and had inaugurated progress in various directions; but after the year 1350 few if any new developments are recorded. As agricultural centres they continued prosperous on the whole; the abbot and the abbess retained their character as good landlords; charity and hospitality continued to be practised by them. But as intellectual centres the monasteries had found their rival in the growing townships. The townships at the beginning of the 14th century were so well established that they were able to protect and further pursuits and industries which had hitherto flourished under the protection of monastic centres. Book-learning and science were cultivated in a more liberal spirit at the universities, where the friars of different orders had established houses ; and the arts and crafts flourished on more fruitful soil under the protection of the town. The progress of the English nation during the 14th and 15th centuries is uncontested ; but little of it, if any, was due to the influence of monks. On the whole monasteries continued to be favourably regarded by the nation, and the system of which they formed part was not attacked, but while the friar freely moved from city to city and for a while became the representative of learning and art, the monk bound to his convent home showed an increasing want of intellectual activity.

The change was part of the great revolution which was taking place in feudal institutions generally. The age of chivalry was a thing of the past, and though the romantic ideas it had engendered had not ceased to influence mankind, they no longer possessed the transforming power of innovation. Similarly, mysticism which had been so largely cultivated inside convent walls had done its work in ushering in a spiritualised interpretation of religion; during the 14th century it was spread abroad and popularised by the friars, who gave it a new development, the monk's interest in it seemed to cease. But the ceremonial and ritual which the mystic had helped to elaborate, and the many observances by which the Catholicism of the Middle Ages had secured a hold on the concerns of daily life, continued in undisturbed prominence,—with this difference, that from elevating the few the ritual had now come to impress the many.

It is often insisted on that during the later Middle Ages monasteries were homes of superstition and idolatry, and that practices in devotional ritual and in the cult of the miraculous were kept up by them to the extent of making them a hindrance to moral and intellectual development, and obnoxious to the advocates of more liberal and advanced views. The fact must be taken as part of the conservative attitude of these houses, which had strengthened their hold on outside attention by obser-vances with which their existence was indissolubly bound up. Certainly a later age may be excused for condemning what had become a mischief and a hindrance; but it is well to recall that it was precisely those usages and tendencies which a later period condemned as superstitious, that had been elaborated at an early period by leaders in thought, who saw in them the means of setting forth the principles of the Christian faith. And the elaborate cult, the processions and imagery of mediæval Christianity, have a deeply significant side if we think of them in connection with the poetic, pictorial, dramatic and architectural arts of the later Middle Ages.

Convents retained some importance for the education of women during these ages. Attention must be given to them in this connection, though the standard of tuition they offered was not high. Compared with the level they had reached during an earlier period convents showed signs of retrogression rather than of advance, and compared with what was contemporaneously attained at the universities, the training women received in the convent was poor in substance, cramped in method, and insufficient in application. But, as far as I have been able to ascertain, a convent education remained the sole training of which a girl could avail herself outside the home circle. For the universities absolutely ignored the existence of woman as a being desirous or capable of acquiring knowledge, and the teaching at the mediæval university was so ordered that students ranged in age from the merest boyhood to manhood. These centres then, by ignoring the existence of women, appropriated to men not only the privileges of a higher education, but also all knowledge from its rudiments upwards.

The standard of education in the average nunnery was deteriorating because devotional interests were cultivated to the exclusion of everything else. In early Christian times we saw monk and nun promoting intellectual acquirements generally, but the separation of the sexes, and the growing feeling in favour of the stricter confinement of nuns within convent precincts, advocated by a later age in the interests of a stricter morality, more and more cut off the nun from contact with secular learning. In the 12th century we saw Queen Matilda, the pupil of a Wessex house, writing fluent Latin and speaking not only of the Fathers of the Church but quoting from classical writers of whom she evidently knew more than the name. But in the later Middle Ages the class of writers who were read in the convent was restricted; service books, the legends of the saints, theological works, and some amount of scripture, comprised the range of the nun's usual studies. The remarks of contemporary writers bear out the inferences to be drawn from such a narrowed curriculum of study. The nun is represented as a person careful in her devotions, pious in her intent, of good manners and gentle breeding, but one-sided in the view she takes of life.

The author of the *Ancren Riwle*, as mentioned above, left us to infer that the women he was addressing were acquainted with English, French, and Latin, and their education must have been given them in convents. His work was written in the early half of the 13th century. In all convents down to the Reformation Latin continued to be studied to some extent, if only so far as to enable the nun to repeat her prayers, to follow mass and to transcribe a book of devotion. The lady superior, by the terms of her appointment and on account of the duties of her station, was bound to have some knowledge of it. But at the same time one comes across remarks which lead one to suppose that Latin was falling into disuse in nunneries, especially in the south of England, and that French was taking its place. Corroboration of this view is afforded by a list of injunctions sent by the bishop of Winchester to the convent at Romsey, in consequence of an episcopal visitation in 1310; they were drawn up in Latin, but a literal translation into French was appended for the greater convenience of the nuns[1]. The rules and ordinances prescribed by Archbishop Walter Reynolds to the convent of Davington in Kent about the year 1326 were written in French[2], and so were the set of rules forwarded by the abbot of St Albans to the convent of Sopwell in 1338[3]. On the other hand injunctions written in Latin were sent to Godstow in Oxfordshire in 1279 and to Nun-Monkton in Yorkshire in 1397.

French down to the middle of the 14th century was the language of the upper classes as well as the legal language[4], and many literary products of the time are in French. A 'Life of St Katherine' written in Norman French by Clemence, a nun at Barking, is extant in two MSS. Only its opening lines have been published in which the nun informs her readers that she has translated this life from Latin into 'romans[5].' Letters written by ladies superior during this period were usually in French. Thus the prioress and convent of Ankerwyke in Buckinghamshire addressed a petition to King Edward III. in French[6], and the abbess of Shaftesbury in

---

[1] Dugdale, *Monasticon*, 'Rumsey,' vol. 2, p. 507 footnote.

[2] Ibid. 'Davington,' vol. 4, p. 288.

[3] Ibid. 'Sopwell,' vol. 3, p. 365, charter nr 7.

[4] Jusserand, J., *Histoire littéraire du Peuple Anglais*, 1894, pp. 121 ff., 235 ff.

[5] *Romania*, edit. Meyer et Paris, vol. 13, p. 400.

[6] Dugdale, *Monasticon*, 'Ankerwyke,' vol. 4, p. 229, charter nr 4.

1382 petitioned King Richard II. in the same language[1]. Various documents and year-books which were kept in religious houses show that entries made during the early period were in Latin, but in the 14th century French frequently occurs. In the 15th century both Latin and French were abandoned and the use of English became general. The documents of Barking, a most important Benedictine nunnery, are partly in Latin, partly in French, and partly in English[2]. The extant charters of Legh or Minchenlegh in Devonshire are exclusively in Latin, but the rubrics of the 14th century are in French[3]. In the register of Crabhouse[4], an Austin settlement of nuns in Norfolk, all three languages are used.

In the nunneries of the south of England French maintained itself longest, but it was Norman French, which continued in use after the change abroad which made the French spoken on this side of the Channel (except that of court circles) sound unfamiliar to a Frenchman. In the Prologue to his *Canterbury Tales*, written about 1386, Chaucer introduces a prioress who was one of the pilgrims *en route* for Canterbury, and remarks on the kind of French which she spoke (l. 124):

> 'And Frenche she spake full fayre and fetisly
> After the scole of Stratford atte Bow,
> For Frenche of Paris was to hire unknowe.'

Evidently he is referring to the French which was generally in use at the nunneries. Stratford, otherwise St Leonard's, Bromley, was situated in Middlesex.

English was first heard at the opening of the session at Westminster in 1363, and in 1404 French was unintelligible to the English ambassadors in Flanders. I have come across few French documents relating to nunneries which are later than the year 1400; in fact a petition in French written in 1433 by the prioress of Littlemore in Oxfordshire stands almost alone[5].

There is extant a highly interesting rhymed version of the rule of St Benedict written for the use of nuns in the English dialect of the north between 1400 and 1425[6]. It is not the earliest version

---

[1] Dugdale, *Monasticon*, 'Shaftesbury,' vol. 2, p. 471, charter nr 21.

[2] Ibid. 'Barking,' vol. 1, p. 441.

[3] Ibid. 'Legh,' vol. 6, p. 333, footnote *t*. MS. Harleian 3660.

[4] Bateson, M., 'Register of Crabhouse Nunnery' (no date), *Norfolk and Norwich Archæol. Society*.

[5] Dugdale, *Monasticon*, 'Littlemore,' vol. 4, p. 490, charter nr 14.

[6] Koelbing, *Englische Studien*, vol. 2, pp. 60 ff.

in English made for the use of nuns; there is a translation, known as the Winteney version, which was written for them and is preserved in a copy of the 13th century; and it is possible that the earliest Benedictine rule in Anglo-Saxon for monks was adapted from a version in the vernacular written for women[1]. However the author of the rhymed version of the 15th century is conscious of women's comparative ignorance of Latin. He prefaces his rule with the reason which prompted him to make it. 'Monks and learned men,' he says, 'may know the rule in Latin and gather from it how to work, serving God and Holy Church; it is for the purpose of making it intelligible to women who learnt no Latin in their youth that it is here set into English that they may easily learn it...'

The name of this translator is unknown. On the ground of certain passages referring to singing in choir (line 1188 ff.) it has been supposed, but with slight probability, that the translation was the work of a woman.

Another proof of the growing unfamiliarity with Latin in nunneries is afforded by the introduction to the register of Godstow, which was one of the wealthier English Benedictine nunneries. This register was written under the abbess Alice Henley, who is known to have been ruling in the year 1464, and consists of 126 folio leaves of vellum. According to Dugdale[2] it comprises 'an account of the foundation of the house, an A. B. C. of devotion, a kalendar of the year, and all the charters of the house translated into English.' The translator has left an introduction to his work which in modern English runs as follows: 'The wise man taught his child to read books gladly and to understand them well, for lack of such understanding has often caused negligence, hurt, harm and hindrance, as experience proves; and since women of religion in reading Latin books are excused from much understanding where it is not their mother tongue, therefore if they read their books of remembrance and of gifts written in Latin, for want of understanding they often take hurt and hindrance; and since for want of truly learned men who are ready to teach and counsel them, and for fear also of publishing the evidence of their titles which has often caused mischief, it seems right needful to the under-

---

[1] This supposition is based on certain peculiarities in the language of the rule for men. Cf. 'Die angelsächsischen Prosabearbeitungen der Benedictinerregel,' edit. Schröer, 1885 (in Grein, *Bibliotek der angels. Prosa*, vol. 2) Einleitung, p. xviii.

[2] Dugdale, *Monasticon*, 'Godstow,' vol. 4, p. 357, charter nr 23.

standing of these religious women that they have besides their Latin books some written in their mother tongue, by which they may secure better knowledge of their property and more clearly give information to their servants, rent-gatherers and receivers in the absence of their learned counsellors; therefore I, a poor brother, and 'wellwyller' to the abbess of Godstow Dame Alice Henley and to all her convent, which are for the most part well learned in English books...have undertaken to make this translation for them from Latin into English.'

I have come across very few references to books which have come from nunneries. A celebrated manuscript in Latin, which contains a collection of the lives of the saints and is written on vellum, belonged to the convent at Romsey[1]; a copy of 'The life of St Katherine of Alexandria' by Capgrave (in English verse of the 15th century), which has lately been printed, is designated as belonging to Katherine Babington, subprioress of Campsey in Suffolk[2]; and the famous Vernon manuscript which contains the most complete collection of writings in Middle English on salvation or 'soul-hele' probably came from a nunnery.

The inventories taken of the goods and chattels belonging to convents at the time of the dissolution contain few references to books. Probably only books of devotion were numerous, and these were looked upon by the nuns as their personal property like their clothes, and were taken away with them when they left. The inventory of the nunnery of Kilburn mentions that two copies of the *Legenda Aurea*, the one written, the other printed, were kept in the chamber of the church[3]. In connection with Sion, the only house in England of the order of St Bridget, we shall hear of a splendid collection of books, all I believe of a devotional character.

An inventory of the goods of the comparatively insignificant priory of Easebourne in Sussex, which never numbered more than five or six nuns, was taken in the year 1450 and shows what books of devotion were then in its possession. The following are enumerated: two missals, two breviaries, four antiphonies, one large *legenda* or book of the histories of the saints, eight psalters, one book of collects, one *tropon* or book of chants, one French Bible, two *ordinalia* or books of divine office, in French, one book of the

---

[1] Lansdowne MS. 436.
[2] *Early English Text Soc.*, nr 100. Arundel MS. 396.
[3] Dugdale, *Monasticon*, 'Kilburn,' vol. 3, p. 424.

Gospels, and one martyrology[1]. It is in accordance with the exclusively pious training shown by the possession of books such as these that Chaucer lets his prioress, when called upon to contribute a tale, recount the legend of a boy-martyr who was murdered at Alexandria, and the nun who was with her tell the legend of St Cecilia. The prioress in this case did not fail to impress her hearers, while the monk, who was also of the party and told of worthies of biblical and of classical repute, roused no interest.

In the eyes of Chaucer the prioress was a thoroughly estimable person. 'Madame Eglentine,' whose smiling was 'ful simple and coy,' and who spoke French fluently, was distinguished also for elegance of manners at table. She neither dropped her food, nor steeped her fingers in the sauce, nor neglected to wipe her mouth, and throughout affected a certain courtly breeding which went well with her station.

> ' And sikerly she was of grete disport,
> And ful plesant, and amiable of port,
> And peined hire to contrefeten chere
> Of court, and ben estatelich of manere,
> And to ben holden digne of reverence.'

Her sensitiveness was so great that she wept on seeing a mouse caught in a trap, and the death of one of the small dogs she kept caused her great grief. She could not bear to see one of them beaten, for in her 'all was conscience and tendre herte.' The only ornament she wore was a brooch which was attached to her beads and on which were inscribed the words *Amor vincit omnia.* The poet's designating her companion as the 'other nun,' suggests that the prioress in this case was a nun herself, that is that she was not the superior of a priory, but prioress and member of a convent which was under an abbess.

Education in a nunnery at this period secured the privilege of being addressed as 'Madame,' the title of a woman of the

---

[1] Blaauw, W. H., 'Episcopal visitations of the Benedictine nunnery of Easebourne' in *Sussex Arch. Collections*, vol. 9, p. 12. According to Bradshaw, H., 'Note on service books' (printed as an appendix in Middleton, J. H., *Illuminated Manuscripts*, 1892) the missal was used for celebration of the mass; while the breviary contained the services for the hours, including the *antiphony* (anthems to the psalms)—the *legenda* (long lessons used at matins),—the psalter (psalms arranged for use at hours),—and the collects (short lessons used at all the hours except matins). In the list above, these are enumerated as separate books. He further says that the *ordinale* contained general rules for the right understanding and use of the service books. It is noteworthy that this is in French in the list of books at Easebourne.

upper classes. Directions in English about the consecration of nuns which were in use in the diocese of Lincoln about the year 1480 are in existence[1]. In these the bishop at the conclusion of the service is directed to offer words of advice to the newly professed nuns, which begin as follows: 'Daughters and virgins, now that you are married and espoused to Him that is above king and 'kaysor,' Jesus Christ, meet it is and so must you from henceforth in token of the same be called 'madame or ladye[1].'

Judging from a passage in Chaucer (l. 3940) this privilege was apparently kept by those who had been educated in a nunnery and returned to the world. The reeve tells about the miller's wife who was 'come of noble kyn; she was i-fostryd in a nonnerye,' and on account of her kindred and the 'nostelry' she had learned, no one durst call her but 'Madame.'

It remains to note how far the standing of nunneries was directly affected in the later Middle Ages by external social and political changes. Various conditions combined to curtail the privileges of religious houses, which when once lost were never recovered.

The reign of Edward I (1272–1307) was marked by many legal innovations. One of the first acts of the king was to appoint a commission to enquire into jurisdictions, and a general survey of the whole kingdom was taken to obtain correct knowledge of the rights by which property was held. Local and manorial rights were throughout called into question, which in many instances resulted in their being curtailed to the advantage of the king. In common with other holders of property, the heads of monasteries incurred direct losses, especially the heads of smaller settlements, where the property was not so well managed and the superior could not afford to have a legal adviser.

Among those cited before the justices in eyre were the abbesses and prioresses of convents of various orders, who as we gather from the account of these pleas[2] sometimes appeared in person, sometimes through an attorney, to justify their claims and to seek re-establishment of their rights. The superiors of smaller settlements, whose property lay near their house, generally appeared in person, but the superiors of larger houses, where the jurisdiction over property which lay at a distance was called into question,

---

[1] Maskell, W., *Monumenta Ritualia*, 1882, vol. 3, p. 357 footnotes.
[2] *Placita de Quo Warranto* published by Command.

appeared by an attorney. Thus the abbess of Barking which lies in Essex appeared by an attorney at Bedford and in Buckinghamshire, but in Essex she appeared in person to defend certain rights connected with property she held at Chelmsford[1]. The abbess of Malling in Kent appeared by attorney at Canterbury, where she secured renewal of her rights before the king's justiciaries not only to liberties and franchises of the most extensive kind in East and West Malling, but to the holding of a market twice a week, and of three fairs in the year[2].

On the other hand we find the prioress of Stratford appearing in person before the judges in eyre at the Stone Cross, bringing her charters with her[3]. The prioress of Wroxhall at first refused to answer the summons to appear at Warwick. Afterwards she appeared in person and succeeded in establishing her claim to her possessions in Hatton and Wroxhall together with many privileges and immunities which had been confirmed to her priory by Henry II, Richard I, John and Henry III, as appears in the charters granted by those monarchs[4].

But not all were so successful. The prioress of Redlingfield in Suffolk also came in person to justify a right which was held to belong to the crown, but which she claimed that she and all her predecessors had held time out of mind. But as she could show no special warrant, William de Gyselham prayed judgment for the king. A day was appointed for further hearing of the case at Westminster, but no further proceedings appear[5]. Frequently a case was adjourned to Westminster and we hear no more of it; sometimes also the king's attorney did not choose to prosecute his suit further.

A closer analysis of these pleas helps us to understand the various and complicated rights, immunities and privileges which abbess and prioress had acquired in common with feudal lords at an early period, and which the larger houses retained with few abatements down to the time of the dissolution. The study of these rights shows that a considerable business capacity and no small amount of attention were required to protect a settlement against deterioration and decay.

---

1 *Placita de Quo Warranto*, pp. 11, 97, 232, 233.
2 Dugdale, *Monasticon*, 'Malling,' vol. 3, p. 381, charter nr 5.
3 Ibid. 'Stratford,' vol. 4, p. 119, charter nr 3.
4 Ibid. 'Wroxhall,' vol. 4, p. 88.
5 Ibid. 'Redlingfield,' vol. 4, p. 25, charter nr 2.

The number of religious houses[1] for women which existed at this period, including those of all orders, was close upon a hundred and thirty. Their number can be estimated only approximately, because some fell to decay and were abandoned as we shall see later, while, regarding Gilbertine settlements, it is unknown at what period nuns ceased to inhabit some of them. The number of monasteries for men including those of all monkish and canonical orders, at the same period was over four hundred; while the friars, the number of whose houses fluctuated, at the time of the dissolution owned about two hundred houses.

Of the settlements of nuns eighty-two belonged to the order of St Benedict, and twenty-seven (including two houses which had been founded by the order of Cluni) to Cistercian nuns. Fourteen houses were inhabited by Austin nuns or canonesses (including Sion), and two by nuns of the order of Prémontré.

In England only the orders of friars of St Francis and St Dominic had houses for women attached to them. The nuns of the order of St Clare, called also Poor Clares or Nuns Minoresses, had been established in connection with the Franciscan friars, and owned three houses, of which the house in London, known as the Minories, was of considerable importance. Only one house of Dominican nuns existed in England. The nuns both of the Dominican and the Franciscan orders differed in many particulars from other nuns and are usually spoken of not as nuns but as sisters[2]. They observed strict seclusion, and as a rule took no interest in anything save devotion. A set of rules for the nuns of St Clare was written by St Francis himself, and gives a fair idea of the narrow interests to which women who embraced religion under his auspices were confined[3].

Regarding the wealth of the settlements of different orders, the houses of the Benedictine order owned most property and drew the largest incomes; the houses owned by monks were throughout wealthier than those owned by nuns. Judging by the computations made at the time of the dissolution the Cistercian houses for men, and the houses of Austin and of Premonstrant Canons, were comparatively rich, whereas the houses of Cistercian and of Premonstrant nuns were poor, but the income of the Austin nunnery,

---

[1] Gasquet, A., *Henry VIII and the English Monasteries*, 1888, appendices to vols. 1 and 2.

[2] The word 'mynchyn' was I believe never applied to them.

[3] Holstenius, *Codex regularum*, 1759, vol. 3, p. 34.

Buckland in Somersetshire, compared favourably with that of the wealthier Benedictine houses for women. We shall have occasion to speak more fully of the house of Sion, which was of the order of St Bridget, and the wealth of which at the time of the dissolution exceeded that of any other nunnery.

§ 2. The Internal Arrangements of the Convent.

At this point of our enquiry it seems well to pause for a while to describe the inner arrangements of a nunnery as they present themselves during the later Middle Ages, the offices which fell to the several members of the convent, and the daily life of the nun. The material at the disposal of the student lies scattered in the convent registers, in the accounts of visitations, and in contemporary literature, and is supplemented by the study of ruins. The inventories of monasteries made during the reign of Henry VIII at the time of the dissolution (c. 1536–1538) further add to this information. For no religious settlement for women was founded after the death of Edward III (1377) with the sole exception of Sion, and no important changes were made in the routine of existing houses, so that the state of things which survived at the dissolution may be taken with slight reservations as supplementing our information concerning the arrangements during the earlier period.

Regarding the position and duties of the lady superior, it has been mentioned before[1] that comparatively few of the Benedictine nunneries had the standing of abbeys, most of them being priories, and that the abbesses of four houses had the additional title of baroness by reason of the property they held of the king. They were called upon to fulfil duties in accordance with their station, and like secular barons found knights for the king's service. In 1257 Agnes Ferrar, abbess of Shaftesbury, was summoned to Chester to take part in the expedition against Llewellin ap Griffith, and again in 1277 Juliana Bauceyn was summoned for a like purpose[2].

The lady superior of a house in the 14th and 15th centuries was frequently seen outside the convent; pleasure as well as business might take her from home. It has been mentioned that the heads of convents sometimes appeared in person before the justices in eyre. Dame Christina Basset, prioress of the Bene-

---

[1] Cf. above, p. 204.
[2] Dugdale, *Monasticon*, ' Shaftesbury,' vol. 2, p. 473.

dictine nunnery of St Mary Prée in Hertfordshire, in the account of her expenditure between 1487-1489 had the following entry made : ' when I rode to London for the suit that was taken[1].' In 1368 the bishop of Sarum, in whose diocese Shaftesbury was, granted a dispensation to Joan Formage to go from her monastery to one of her manors to take the air and to divert herself[2]. Complaints were made of the too frequent absence of their prioress by members of the Benedictine nunnery of Easebourne, at the visitation in 1441, when it was alleged that the prioress was in the habit of riding about and staying away on pretence of business more often than was deemed advantageous to the convent[3].

After her election by the convent, the lady superior made profession of canonical obedience to the bishop of her diocese and in some cases waited upon the patron of her house. The nunnery of St Mary's, Winchester, was one of the houses that held of the king. In 1265 Eufemia was received by Henry III, and her successor Lucia went to Winchester castle to be presented[4]. In houses which held of the king it was part of the royal prerogative that on his coronation the king should recommend a nun to the convent. In connection with Shaftesbury we find this on record in the first year of Richard II (1377-1399) and again in the first of Henry V. In 1428, several years after the accession of Henry VI, who became king when a child, a royal mandate was issued to the abbess of Shaftesbury to admit Joan Ashcomb as a nun[5]. And in 1430 the same king nominated Godam Hampton to be received as a nun at Barking[6].

All the versions of the Benedictine rule known to me speak of the head of the monastery as the abbot, and in the Winteney version, which was written for nuns in the 13th century, the head of the women's house is accordingly designated as abbess[7]. But, probably because the number of abbesses was comparatively small, the translator of the rule of St Benedict, in the rhymed English version of the 15th century, speaks throughout of the prioress as head of the nunnery[8]. It is the prioress (l. 337 ff.) who is to be honoured inside

---

[1] Dugdale, *Monasticon*, ' St Mary Prée,' vol. 3, p. 353, charter nr 9.

[2] Ibid. 'Shaftesbury,' vol. 2, p. 474.

[3] Blaauw, W. H., 'Episcopal Visitations of the Benedictine Nunnery of Easebourne,' *Sussex Archæol. Collections*, vol. 9, p. 7.

[4] Dugdale, *Monasticon*, ' St Mary Winchester,' vol. 2, p. 452, footnote.

[5] Ibid. 'Shaftesbury,' vol. 2, p. 473.   [6] Ibid. ' Barking,' vol. 1, p. 441, charter nr 8.

[7] Schröer, *Winteney Version der regula St Benedicti*, 1888, p. 16.

[8] Edit. Koelbing, *Englische Studien*, vol. 2, pp. 60 ff. (line references in the text throughout this section are to this version).

the abbey (sic) and out of it wherever she goes or rides, who shall be law in herself, who shall have no pride in her heart but ever love God, and who is responsible as a shepherd or herdsman for the women given into her care. All these injunctions are given in other versions of the rule to the abbot or abbess. It further says that the prioress shall not favour any one nun by letting her travel more than the rest,—a command evidently added by the translator. In another passage (l. 2116 ff.) closely following the original text it is enjoined that the prioress shall liberally entertain guests, but if it happens that there be none, she shall invite some of the older sisters to dine with her.

A detailed account is preserved of the formalities of the appointment of a prioress to the convent of St Radegund's at Cambridge[1]. This settlement, founded about the middle of the 12th century, had experienced many vicissitudes, but was comparatively prosperous in the year 1457, when the death of the prioress, Agnes Seyntel, on September 8th, left its twelve inmates without a head. We gather from a charter that the first step taken after her demise was that the subprioress, Matilda Sudbury, and the convent sent information to the bishop of Ely asking for permission to appoint a successor. This being granted the nuns assembled on Sept. 23rd and fixed the 27th as the day of the election. On this day all the nuns were present at mass, and then three of them were chosen arbiters (*compromissarias*). These were Joan Lancaster, Elizabeth Walton and Katherine Sayntlow, who took the oath and gave their votes, and then they administered the oath to the other nuns, who gave their votes also. The form of administration of the oath and the oath itself are both given in Latin. The nuns were adjured 'by the Father, the Son and the Holy Ghost, at the peril of their soul, according to God and their conscience, to name and choose her as prioress who was most needful to the priory.' The form of oath corresponds to this adjuration.

The votes being then counted it was found that a majority of seven were in favour of the appointment of Joan Lancaster, whereupon Elizabeth Walton, being called upon by the others, declared the result of the election. The *Te Deum* was then sung and the prospective prioress, reluctantly in this case it seems, was led to the chief altar of the convent church, where she was left,

---

[1] Shermann, A. J., *Hist. Coll. Jesus Cantab.*, edit. Halliwell, 1840, p. 16.

while the result of the election was proclaimed to the people outside 'in the vulgar tongue.' All this happened before noon, when the nuns returned to the chapter-house and called upon Elizabeth Walton and Katherine Sayntlow to draw up the deeds of the election, and to lay them before the newly appointed prioress, who was requested to affirm her election at four o'clock in the vestibule of the church. After much persuasion Joan Lancaster yielded and accepted the election. The words of her speech are given; in them she declares that she is a free woman and legitimate, born in lawful wedlock, and therefore entitled to proffer her consent and assent. Eleven nuns put their signatures to this document, one of whom designates herself as subprioress and president, another as leader of the choir, *succentrix*, another as cellaress, *celeraria*, and another calls herself treasurer, *thesaurissa*.

In connection with the Benedictine convent of Langley, in Leicestershire, a further formality is recorded at the election of a new prioress. The permission of the patron of the house having been obtained, the nuns proceeded to elect a new prioress, and a page with a white staff sent by the patron guarded the door of the priory till the election was made. 'For which in right of his master he was to have his diet but nothing more[1].'

The form of consent by which an abbess accepted office is entered in the register of Bishop Lacy of Exeter. In 1449 Johan or Jane Arundell was appointed abbess of the Austin settlement of Legh or Canonlegh, in Devonshire[2]. Her consent is drawn up in English, and in it she speaks of herself as sister Johan Arundell, *mynchyn*, an ancient word for nun which continued in use in the south of England till the time of the dissolution.

A previous chapter has shown that the appointment of a prioress in those nunneries which were cells to an abbey, depended on the abbot[3]. In the houses which were independent and elected their own head, a licence from the bishop had to be secured. And if the nuns neglected to secure this licence before electing a superior difficulties were apt to occur. In the case of Catesby, a Benedictine house in Northamptonshire, such difficulties are repeatedly recorded. At the death of the prioress Johanna de Northampton (1291), the cellaress of the house was elected in her stead by the nuns; but the election having been made without a licence, the

---

[1] Dugdale, *Monasticon*, 'Langley,' vol. 4, p. 220.
[2] Maskell, W., *Monumenta Ritualia*, 1882, vol. 3, p. 358 footnote.
[3] Cf. above, p. 206.

bishop of Lincoln declared it void. Afterwards however he confirmed it in consideration of the merits of the person elected. At her death similar neglect on the one side was followed by similar opposition on the other; the bishop first declared the election void and then confirmed it. The relation of Catesby to the diocesan continued to be a source of difficulties. In 1444 the prioress Agnes Terry was suspended from the conduct of all business relating to the revenues of the house during the bishop's pleasure, and a commission was granted to the abbot of St James in Northampton to inspect the accounts of the nunnery[1].

Sometimes neglect of the administration of the property of the house was the cause of the voluntary or forced resignation of a superior. Love of finery is represented as the cause of the ruin of the prioress Juliana of Bromhall in Berkshire, into whose conduct an enquiry was instituted in 1404. It was found on this occasion that she 'had injured the convent and her own character in that she had converted to her nefarious use, alienated and wasted chalices, books, jewelry (*jocalia*), the income and possessions' of the priory[2]. She resigned, but it is not recorded whether she remained in the house. In several instances a deposed lady superior did remain in the convent. Thus Margaret Punder, prioress of Flixton, an Austin convent, resigned because of complaints of her negligence, but she remained in the house as a member of the convent[3].

The dignitaries of the Church took upon themselves to protect the abbess or prioress against violation of her rights by laymen; under social arrangements which made the nunnery the one place of safety for the unmarried daughters of the gentry, it is obvious that ecclesiastical and lay authorities would be of one mind in severely punishing those who failed to respect the nun's privileges.

In 1285 a knight carried off two nuns from the settlement at Wilton, 'which coming to the archbishop's ears he first excommunicated him, and subsequently absolved him on these conditions,— first that he should never afterwards come within a nunnery or be in the company of a nun; then that on three Sundays running he should be whipped in the parish church of Wilton, and likewise three other days in the market and church of Shaftesbury; that he should fast a certain number of months; that he should not

---

[1] Dugdale, *Monasticon*, 'Catesby,' vol. 4, p. 635.
[2] Dugdale, *Monasticon*, 'Bromhall,' vol. 4, p. 506.
[3] Jessopp, A., *Visitations of the Diocese of Norwich* (1492–1532), pp. 185, 190, 318.

wear a shirt for three years; and lastly that he should not any more take the habit and title of a knight, but wear apparel of a russet colour until he had spent three years in the Holy Land[1].'

Where an abbess was at the head of a nunnery, the prioress and sub-prioress, and sometimes a second prioress and sub-prioress were appointed by her; where the settlement was ruled by a prioress it was she who appointed the sub-prioress. This is in accordance with the written rule of St Benedict, where the abbot nominates the *praepositus* or provost whose duties correspond to those of the prioress or sub-prioress[2]. The rhymed version of the rule, in which the prioress is treated as chief in authority, says the sub-prioress (l. 1406 ff.) shall be appointed by the prioress, 'for if it were done otherwise strife and debate might easily arise.' This provision was dictated by the feeling that, if chosen by the convent, the person second in authority might presume. For this reason 'the sub-prioress, sexton and other such officers shall not be chosen but appointed as the prioress desires,' and if the sub-prioress does wrong and refuses to mend her ways 'out of the flock she shall be fled.'

The duties of the person second in authority consisted in seeing that the hours of divine service were rightly kept. A manuscript now at Oxford, written in English, which came from Barking nunnery gives directions as to the formal appointment of the prioress in that house[3]. It belongs to the end of the 14th century. Barking it will be remembered was one of the chief abbeys for women. The manner in which the abbess appointed the person second to her in authority is described in the following passage: 'When a prioress is to be made, the abbess shall commend the rule to her, enjoining that she be helpful to her and maintain religion in accordance with the rule. And she shall set her in her seat. And then shall come the chaplain with incense towards her. And the abbess and she shall go before the convent into the choir. And then shall they go to St Alburgh, and the convent shall say the *Levavi* (Ps. 121, *Levavi oculos meos*, 'I lifted up my eyes'); and the prioress shall lie prostrate, and the abbess shall say the prayers aforesaid with the orison *Oremus*, etc. Then shall the prioress go to the choir; the chapter mass being *Spiritus Domini*. And the same day shall be given to the convent a

---

[1] Dugdale, *Monasticon*, 'Wilton,' vol. 2, p. 317.

[2] Benedictus, *Regula*, c. 65 (in Migne, *Patrol. Cursus Compl.* vol. 66).

[3] Dugdale, *Monasticon*, 'Barking,' vol. 1, p. 437, footnote *k*.

pittance or allowance of good fish. And when she dies, she must give to the convent...' Here the manuscript closes abruptly.

In houses of the Benedictine order the lady superior of the house, whether abbess or prioress, usually dwelt apart from the convent in a set of chambers or a small house of her own, where she received visitors and transacted business. In some of the largest houses the prioress, sub-prioress and sexton also had establishments of their own as we shall see presently. In Cistercian houses the arrangements seem to have varied, but in the majority of houses of the order, usually among Austin nuns and always among the nuns of St Clare, the head of the house lived in closer contact with the members of her convent and took her meals at the same table as the nuns.

The lady superior managed all the business of the house and presided at the meetings of the convent, the members of which fulfilled a number of functions which we will pass in rapid review. The full complement of offices was of course found in the larger houses only; in the smaller houses several posts were frequently held by one and the same person. Reference is most frequently made to the offices of sexton, cellaress, and chaplain,—these seem to have existed in almost every house.

The rhymed version of St Benedict's rule gives the following injunctions about the duties of the sexton (l. 1521 ff.):—She shall ring the bells to all the services night and day, and keep the ornaments of the church, the chalice, books, vestments, relics, and wax and annual rents. She shall preserve the vessels of the altar and keep them clean.'

Other versions of the rule, as far as I am aware, contain nothing about these duties. The sexton at Barking at the time of the Reformation was responsible for the receipt of considerable sums[1].

Duties of great importance devolved on the cellaress, who managed the receipts and expenditure appertaining to the food; certainly no light task and one that required considerable powers of management. On this point the versified rule of St Benedict closely follows the original rule. We are told (l. 1467 ff.) that the cellaress 'shall be chosen by counsel out of the community'; she shall be wise and gentle and of mild ways, not hard like a shrew, nor slow nor mean in her dealings (grochand in hir dede), but gladly do her office and take special care of young children, poor guests

---

[1] Dugdale, *Monasticon*, 'Barking,' vol. 1, p. 445 Computus.

and others that ask at her door, knowing that on the day of judgment she will have to render account.

Fortunately we are in possession of an extremely interesting document written in English about the year 1400. It came from Barking nunnery, and enables us to form some idea of the duties devolving on the cellaress[1]. It is entitled 'Charthe longynge to the office of the celeresse,' and describes the duties of buying and selling, illustrating the economic condition of the house no less than the standard of living at that convent. From the manuscript the inference can be drawn that more than one cellaress was appointed at a time. The one whose duties are described in the 'Charthe' provides and deals out the food, and manages the receipts from the home farm. The 'Charthe' opens with injunctions how the cellaress, when she comes into office, must look after what is owing to the office by divers farmers and rent-gatherers and see that it be paid as soon as may be. A list follows of the sums she receives annually from various sources,—farms and rent for various tenements in London and elsewhere. She receives 'of the canons of St Paul's in London for a yearly rent by the year 22 shillings; and of the prior of the convent of St Bartholomew's in London by the year 17 shillings.' The following entries are curious. 'She should receive yearly of a tenement in Friday Street, London, but it is not known where it stands, 23 shillings and four pence; and she should receive 30 shillings of the rent of Tyburn, but it is not paid.'

A list follows of the things she is to be charged with, from which it is evident that the duties of selling as well as of buying devolved on her. She is to be charged with the ox-skins she sells, also with the 'inwards' of oxen, and with tallow and messes of beef; 'and all these be called the issues of the larder.' If she sells hay from any farm belonging to her office, she must charge herself with it or let it be called ' the foreign receipt.'

She is then directed as to the stores she has to provide, which may be grouped under the headings of grain, flesh, fish, and condiments.

The grains include malt, of which she provides three quarters yearly for the 'tounes' of St Alburgh and Christmas, and she pays twenty pence to the brewer of each 'toune';—and wheat, of which a quarter and seven bushels are required, which go to the allowance or pittance of the four men and dames resident in the monastery,

---

[1] Dugdale, *Monasticon*, charter nr 15.

for making 'russeaulx,' perhaps some kind of cake, during Lent, and for baking eels on Shere Tuesday (Tuesday preceding Good Friday). She provides two bushels of peas every year in Lent, and one bushel of beans for the convent against Midsummer. Both peas and beans are evidently dried.

Under the heading 'buying of store' the only item she is mentioned as providing is twenty-two oxen a year, which she evidently feeds on her pasture. Another passage tells us that 'she shall slay but every fortnight if she be a good housewife.' A passage further on refers to her buying pigs and possibly sheep. Geese and fowls she apparently received from her own farm.

She buys fish in large quantities, principally herrings, some white,—that is fresh or slightly salted, some red,—that is salted, by the cade or by the barrel. A note at the end of the 'Charthe' states that a cask or 'cade of herrings is six hundred herrings,' 'the barrel of herrings is one thousand herrings.' Seven cades of white herrings and three barrels of the same she buys for Lent.

Also she must provide eighteen salt fish and fourteen or fifteen salt salmon for the convent in Lent. Eels are mentioned, but not that she bought them; no doubt they were caught on the convent property.

Of condiments the cellaress has to provide almonds, twelve lbs. for Lent; figs, three pieces[1] and twenty-four lbs.; raisins, one piece; rice, twenty-eight lbs.; and mustard eight gallons. There is no mention of salt or of sugar as being provided for the nuns.

We are next informed of the cellaress' expenses in money. Here the peculiar word 'russeaulx' figures again, variously spelt. All the ladies of the convent, who at the time numbered thirty-six, are in receipt of 'ruscheauw sylver,' payable sixteen times in the year, 'but it is paid only twice now, at Easter and at Michaelmas.' The ladies also receive twopence each for crisps and crumcakes at Shrovetide. Wherever there is question of paying money or providing food in portions, the cellaress has to give double to the chief officers of the house, such as the prioress, the cellaress, etc., which suggests that they had a double ration either to enable them to feed their servant, or perhaps a visitor.

The cellaress further pays five annuities called 'anniversaries,' namely, to Sir William, vicar, to Dame Alice Merton, to Dame Maud, the king's daughter, to Dame Maud Loveland, and to

---

[1] I am unable to ascertain the quantity indicated by the 'piece.'

William Dunn, who are residing in the monastery. William Dunn moreover receives twelve gallons of good ale with his annuity.

In 'offerings and wages' the cellaress shall pay twelve pence to the two cellaresses; to the steward of the household what time he brings money home from the courts 20 pence, and again at Christmas 20 pence; to my lady's (the abbess') gentlewoman 20 pence; 'to every gentleman 16 pence and to every yeoman as it pleases her to do, and grooms in like case.' The abbess receives a sugar-loaf at Christmas; her clerk is paid thirteen shillings and fourpence, her yeoman cook 26 shillings and eightpence for their wages. Her groom cook and her pudding wife (grom coke and poding wief) receive the gift of one gown a year of the value of two shillings.

A description follows of the food which the cellaress has to provide for the convent on special days in the year. 'A pece of whete' and three gallons of milk for 'frimete on St Alburgh's day'; four bacon hogs twice in winter, 'and she must buy six grecys (young pigs), six sowcys (perhaps 'sowkin,' diminutive for young female hog, or else 'sowthes,' Middle English for sheep) for the convent and also six inwardys and 100 (?) egges to make white puddings'; also bread, pepper and saffron for the same puddings, also three gallons of good ale for 'besons.' Other directions follow which are perplexing, such as 'mary bones to make white wortys'—can it be marrowbones to make white soup, or does 'bones' stand for buns? Again we hear of 'cripcis and crumcakes,' chickens, bonnes (buns?) at Shrovetide, and of '12 stubbe elles and 60 shafte[1] elles,' to bake for the convent on Shere Thursday. When the abbess receives a bottle of Tyre (wine) at Easter time the convent receives two gallons of red wine. The convent receives three gallons of ale every week. Regarding the wine it is well to recall that grapes were grown to some extent in mediæval England, and that after the dissolution, a vineyard of five acres is scheduled as part of the possessions of Barking nunnery[2].

A paragraph is devoted to the giving out of eggs. The thirty-seven ladies sometimes receive money instead of eggs, 'ey sylver,' as it is called; in one case the alternative is open to the cellaress of giving thirty-two eggs or of paying twopence. Butter also forms an important item in the 'Charthe'; it is given out in 'cobbets,' three cobbets going to a dish.

---

[1] I am unable to ascertain the difference between 'stubbe' and 'shafte.'

[2] Rogers, Th., *Six Centuries of Work and Wages*, 1884, p. 101.

It likewise falls to the cellaress to hire pasture, to see to the mowing of her hay, to see that all manner of houses within her office be duly repaired, not only within the monastery but without, on her farms and manors.

The 'Charthe' returns to directions about food, and mentions among other things pork, mutton, geese, hens, bacon and oatmeal.

The following passages will give some idea of the language in which these directions are couched.

'And the under-celaress must remember at each principal feast, that my lady (the abbess) sits in the refectory, that is to wit five times in the year, at each time shall (she) ask the clerk of the kitchen (for) supper eggs for the convent, at Easter, Whitsuntide, the Assumption of Our Lady, at St Alburgh, and at Christmas; at each time to every lady two eggs, and each (person receiving) double that is the prioress, celaress and kitchener...'

'Also to remember to ask of the kitchen at St Alburgh's time, for every lady of the convent half a goose...also to ask at the said feast of St Alburgh of the said clerk for every lady of the convent one hen, or else a cock.' The manuscript, which is corrected in several places and has additions made by another hand, closes abruptly.

It is interesting to compare the directions about food found in the rule of St Benedict with the high standard of living suggested by the 'Charthe' of Barking. The rhymed version says (l. 1620) that she who is seeing to the kitchen shall provide each day two kinds of 'mete,' so that she who will not eat of one kind may take the other. The convent is also to be supplied with two kinds of pottage (thick soup?) daily. If they have apples of their own growing they shall partake of them; also each lady is to be given a pound of bread each day, which is to serve her for her three meals. The rule adds words to the effect that the 'celerer' may give an extra allowance of food if she sees need though always with caution for fear of gluttony. In regard to drink, wine and ale shall be 'softly' tasted.

It appears probable from this 'Charthe' to the cellaress that the office of Kitchener at Barking was a permanent appointment, which is curious considering that in an ordinary way the members of the convent were bound to serve in the convent kitchen as cook, each for the term of a week. The injunction is repeated in every version of the Benedictine rule known to me. According to the rhymed version of the north the nun who has served her term in the kitchen is directed to leave the kitchen and the vessels clean for her who succeeded her in office. When her time is up she shall kneel before the assembled members of the convent saying, 'Blessed be the Lord that has never failed me,' whereupon the nun who is to act as cook shall say, 'Lord, to my helping take thou heed.' But this injunction was evidently disregarded in the wealthier houses at a later date, for in connection with St Mary's, Winchester, we read of a convent-cook and an under convent-cook[1]. A nun of Campsey, an Austin house consisting at the time of a prioress and eighteen nuns, complained at the visitation of the house in 1532 of the unpunctuality of the meals, which she ascribed to the fault of the cook (culpa coci),—using a term which suggests that the cook in this case was a man[2].

An appointment in the nunnery which has led to some controversy is that of chaplain, it being alleged by some writers that the chaplain of the convent was necessarily a man. Certainly in most houses, especially in the wealthier ones, there were men chaplains; for example at the nunnery of Shaftesbury, where men chaplains are mentioned by the side of the abbess in various early charters and played an important part[3]. Again at St Mary's, Winchester, at the time of the dissolution, men chaplains were among those who are described as resident in the monastery[4]; at Kilburn nunnery the fact that the chaplain who dwelt on the premises was a man is evident from the arrangement of the dwellings,—three chambers which lie together being designated as set apart for the chaplain and the hinds or herdsmen[5]. But the fact that the chaplain's office could be and was held by a woman is established beyond a doubt by the following information. In consequence of an episcopal visitation (1478) of the Benedictine convent of Easebourne, injunctions were sent to the prioress, one of which directs that 'every week, beginning with the eldest, excepting the sub-prioress, she shall select for herself in due course and in turns one of her nuns as chaplain (capellanissam) for divine service and to wait upon herself[6].' This injunction is in accordance with

---

[1] Dugdale, *Monasticon,* 'St Mary's, Winchester,' vol. 2, p. 451, charter nr 4.

[2] Jessopp, A., *Visitations of the Diocese of Norwich* (1492–1532), p. 290.

[3] Dugdale, *Monasticon,* 'Shaftesbury,' vol. 2, p. 472.

[4] Ibid. 'St Mary, Winchester,' vol. 2, p. 451, charter nr 4.

[5] Ibid. 'Kilburn,' vol. 3, p. 424.

[6] Blaauw, W. A., 'Episcopal Visitations of the Benedictine Nunnery of Easebourne,' *Sussex Arch. Collections,* vol. 9, p. 15.

the words of Chaucer, who says that the prioress who was on a
pilgrimage to Canterbury had with her a nun who acted as
chaplain to her (l. 163):

> 'Another Nonne also with hire hadde she
> That was hire chapelleine, and preestes thre.'

In the accounts of visitations in the diocese of Norwich between 1492 and 1532 the designation chaplain applied to an
inmate of a nunnery appears in the Benedictine house of Redlingfield, in the Austin priory of Campsey and in others. In
Redlingfield at the visitation of 1514 the complaint is made against
the prioress that she does not change her chaplain, and at Flixton
in 1520 it is alleged that the prioress has no chaplain and sleeps
by herself in her chamber away from the dormitory[1]. At Elstow
in Bedfordshire at the time of the surrender Katheryne Wyngate
adds the designation 'chapellain' to her name[2], and among the
nuns of Barking who were still in receipt of their pension in 1553
was Mathea Fabyan who is styled chaplain (capellan)[3]. How far
the woman chaplain performed the same offices as the man
chaplain seems impossible to tell ; probably she recited the inferior
services in the chapel of the nunnery.

In the rhymed version of the rule of St Benedict the office
of chaplain is passed over, but in the poem of the 'Spiritual Convent' written by the beguine Mechthild, of which a former chapter
has given an account, the chaplain is a woman. And similarly the
English version of this poem called the 'Ghostly Abbey' which is
attributed to John Alcock, bishop of Ely († 1500), refers to women
chaplains. It says God had ordered His four daughters to come
and dwell in the abbey ; Charity was made abbess and to her
Mercy and Truth were to be as 'chapeleyns,' going about with
her wherever she goes. He bade also that Righteousness should
be with Wisdom who was prioress, and Peace with Mekeness who
was sub-prioress, Charity, Wisdom and Mekeness having chaplains
because they were 'most of worship[4].'

I have found very little information about the arrangements
made in the nunnery for the young people who boarded with and
were taught by the nuns, and hardly a clue is to be had as to

---

[1] Jessopp, A., *Visitations of the Diocese of Norwich* (1492–1532), p. 138.

[2] Dugdale, *Monasticon*, 'Elstow,' vol. 3, p. 411, charter nr 8.

[3] Ibid. 'Barking,' vol. 1, p. 438, footnote *b*.

[4] 'Here begynneth a matere' etc. (by John Alcock (?)), printed by Wynkyn de
Worde (1500), last page but one.

the number of those who might stay in one house at the same time. The only allusion on this point is to St Mary's, Winchester, where twenty-six girls, mostly daughters of knights, were staying at the time of the dissolution. Rogers refers to a roll of expenditure of the Cistercian priory, Swine, in Yorkshire, on which he says are enumerated a number of young persons, daughters of the surrounding gentlefolk, who lived 'en pension' in this small community[1]; and Rye has compiled a list of those who boarded at Carrow at different times[2]. From 'The Death of Philip Sparrow,' a poem written by John Skelton († 1529), we gather that the girl who is represented as intoning the lament over a tame bird, lived and boarded with the 'Nuns Black' at Carrow, where her sparrow was devoured by the cat, whereupon she took out a sampler and worked the sparrow in stitches of silk for her solace[3]. Apparently not only girls, but boys also, were given into the care of nuns, for injunctions forwarded to Romsey in 1310 by the bishop of Winchester forbade that boys and girls should sleep with the nuns or be taken by them into the choir during divine service[4]. Injunctions sent to Redlingfield in 1514 also directed that boys should not sleep in the dormitory[5]; and Bishop Kentwode in the directions he sent to St Helen's in London ordered that none but 'mayd learners' should be received into that nunnery[6]. In the year 1433 Catherine de la Pole, abbess of Barking, petitioned Henry V. for a sum of money due to her for the maintenance of Edward and Jasper Tudor, sons of Catherine, the queen dowager, by Owen Tudor. It seems that these boys were receiving their education at this abbey[7]. But the popularity of the convent even as an educational establishment began to decrease at the close of the 14th century. Judging from the Paston Letters it was no longer customary in Norfolk to send girls to board with the nuns; they were sent to stay away from home with some other country family.

Other offices held by members of the convent are as follows: *thesaurissa*,—the nun bursar who was responsible for the revenues coming through the Church; the *precentrix* and *succentrix*,—the

---

[1] *Six Centuries of Work and Wages*, 1884, p. 166.
[2] Rye, W., *Carrow Abbey*, 1889, p. 48 ff.
[3] Skelton, *Poetical Works*, 1843, vol. 1, p. 51, 'Phyllyp Sparowe.'
[4] Dugdale, *Monasticon*, 'Rumsey,' vol. 2, p. 507, footnote *p*.
[5] Jessopp, A., *Visitations of the Diocese of Norwich* (1492—1532), p. 140.
[6] Dugdale, *Monasticon*, 'St Helen's,' vol. 4, p. 551, charter nr 3.
[7] Ibid. 'Barking,' vol. 1, p. 437, footnote *m*.

leaders and teachers of the choir, who are sometimes mentioned together (Campsey); the *cameraria* or chambress,—who saw to the wardrobe; the *infirmaria* or keeper of the infirmary,—who took charge of the sick nuns; the *refectuaria*,—who had the care of the refectory or dining hall; the *elemosinaria*,—who distributed alms; the *magistra noviciarum*,—who taught the novices. The *cantarista* occurs in connection with Sheppey; no doubt she is identical with the *precentrix* of other places. The further designations of *tutrix*, or teacher, occurs in connection with Shaftesbury, and *eruditrix*, instructress, in connection with Thetford; I have not come across these terms elsewhere.

All these appointments were made by the superior of the house and declared in the presence of the convent, and all except those of chaplain and kitchener seem to have been permanent. The chaplain was probably changed because it was a privilege to go about with the abbess, and the kitchener because of the hard work her duties involved. On the death of the abbess often the prioress, sometimes the cellaress, was appointed to succeed her, but not necessarily so.

Having so far treated of the duties of the convent inmates, we will examine the form of admission for novices and the daily routine of the nun.

According to the rhymed rule of St Benedict (l. 2155) the girl who was old enough to be admitted as nun into a religious community was granted entry as a novice and after two months had 'the law' read to her, and then the question was put if she wished to stay or to go. If she stayed, it was for six months; after which, if still desirous of being received, she proffered her petition to the abbess. If after twelve months she still persisted in her resolution, she was received as a member of the convent and pronounced these words before the altar : ' Suscipe me, domine, secundum eloquium tuum, et vivam. Et non confundas me in expectatione mea.' The formal profession or consecration was undertaken by the bishop, who visited the nunnery periodically, but as these visits were often years apart, it is probable that the declaration made before the superior of a house and the priest constituted a novice a member of a convent, and for all practical purposes made her a nun. Fosbroke is of opinion that the girl who entered at the age of twelve made profession after she had passed a year in the community : he adds that she was consecrated by the bishop when she had reached the age of twenty-five and not before[1]. But it is impossible to draw a line between profession and consecration, as the 'non-professed' nun was invariably the nun who had not been installed by the bishop. In 1521 at the visitation of Rusper the settlement consisted of the prioress, one professed nun and two nuns entered on the list as not professed, of whom one declared that she had lived there awaiting profession for twelve years, the other for three[2]. Women who had been professed at one house were sometimes inmates of another; and I have not found any remark which leads to the inference that this was thought objectionable. A nun residing at Rusper was afterwards prioress of Easebourne. The record of a visitation at Davington in Kent (1511) shows that the convent contained four inmates, of whom two were professed nuns. The one, professed at Cambridge, had been there for twenty years; the other, professed at Malling, had been there for ten. The other two inmates entered on the list as not professed were girls of ten and fifteen[3].

The consecration of nuns was a very ancient and solemn rite. Several forms of the office as celebrated in England are in existence[4]. One comes from the monastery of St Mary's, Winchester, and is contained in a manuscript written probably soon after 1500; the directions are in English, but the words in which the bishop addressed the maidens and their answers are in Latin. Another manuscript written about 1480 contains the office as used in the diocese of Lincoln, with prayers in English and rubrics in Latin; it contains also various directions and addresses omitted in the other manuscript. A third is throughout in English.

These forms of consecration show that after the celebration of the office of high mass in church the prospective nuns entered, each bearing a habit, a veil, a ring and a scroll. The form of interrogation they were put through and the prayers they recited during the installation are given. The declaration was made by the nuns in Latin and runs as follows: ' I, sister..., promise steadfastness (stabilitatem), continuance in virtue (conversionem morum meorum), and obedience before God and all His saints.' We

---

[1] Fosbroke, *British Monachism*, 1843, p. 176.

[2] Way, A., 'Notices of the Benedictine Priory of St Mary Magdalen, at Rusper,' *Sussex Arch. Collections*, vol. 5, p. 256.

[3] Bateson, M., 'Visitations of Archbishop Warham in 1511,' in *English Hist. Review*, vol. 6, 1891, p. 28.

[4] Maskell, W., *Monumenta Rit.*, 1882, vol. 3, p. 331, 'The order of consecration of Nuns,' from Cambridge Fol. Mm. 3. 13, and Lansdown MS., 388; p. 360 'The manner to make a Nun,' from Cotton MS., Vespasian A. 25, fol. 12

also have the declaration of four nuns who were installed by the bishop of Ely at Chatteris, which is couched in similar terms[1]. The nun in this case made her promise 'in accordance with the rule of St Benedict in this place, Chatteris, built in honour of St Mary, in the presence of the reverend father in Christ, William, bishop of Ely,' adding 'I subscribe this with my own hand,' whereupon she made the sign of the cross on the scroll which she carried in her hand and from which she had read her declaration. The form of declaration made at Rusper in Sussex in the year 1484 is similar, but the nun further promises 'to live without property (sine proprio)' of her own[2].

For several days after her consecration the nun lived in retirement, strictly observing the rule of silence. She then resumed her ordinary duties in church, cloister, refectory and dormitory. She usually kept within the convent close, but she was not altogether cut off from intercourse with the outside world. The rhymed rule of St Benedict of the north, transcribing the passages which refer to the monk's going abroad if need be, adapts them to the use of the nun (l. 2450), 'when a sister is going to her father, mother, or other friends, she shall take formal leave of the convent.' And if she is away on an errand (l. 1967), she shall not stay away for a meal though invited to do so unless she has asked leave before going. And again (l. 1957) if she be away during Lent and cannot attend service in church she shall not forget to keep the hours by saying her prayers. And again (l. 2094), when nuns go away into the country they shall wear 'more honest' clothes (that is clothes more clearly showing their profession), which they can take off on coming home for simpler ones. From passages such as these we gather that nuns sometimes stayed away from their convent, leave of absence having been procured; and that besides pilgrimages and business, friendly intercourse with their relatives might take them away from the convent for a time.

The day at the convent was divided by the canonical hours, stated times fixed by ecclesiastical law for prayer and devotion[3]. The hours since the 6th century were seven in number, viz. matins, prime, tierce, sext, none, vespers or evensong, and compline.

---

[1] Dugdale, *Monasticon*, 'Chatteris,' vol. 2, p. 614.

[2] Way, A., 'Notices of the Benedictine Priory of St Mary Magdalen at Rusper,' *Sussex Arch. Collections*, vol. 5, p. 256.

[3] Comp. Smith and Cheetham, *Dictionary of Christian Antiquities*, 1875, article 'Hours of Prayer.'

During winter a night office was said in church at the eighth hour, that is at two o'clock in the morning, when the *matutinae laudes* were sung, but the time for that was variable. 'Then shall they rise to sing and read, and after that she who has need may have meditations' (Rhymed rule, l. 1166). Between Easter and winter however the rule says 'that the nuns shall unto matins rise when the day begins to dawn that they their letters well may know.' Injunctions sent to Easebourne in 1524 direct the prioress to hold matins at the sixth hour, that is at midnight. Matins were followed by a period of rest, probably till five o'clock, when the nuns rose and assembled in the choir to celebrate the office of prime. This was followed by business transacted in the chapter house, by a meal and by work. According to the prose versions of the Benedictine rule children were taught between prime and tierce.

At tierce a short chapter-mass was sung followed by continued study; 'from terce to sext the nuns shall read lessons' (l. 1905). At eight the nuns assembled in the choir for the celebration of High Mass, the principal service of the day, after which came the chief meal. This was served in the refectory; 'the convent when they sit at meat for to read shall not forget' (l. 1739); and while reading went on 'if any of them need aught softly with signs they shall it crave' (l. 1754). The time of the meal was moveable. In summer the nuns were to eat at the sext, but on Wednesdays and Fridays they were to fast till nones, that is noon, except 'they swink and sweat in hay or corn with travail great' (l. 1768), when the time might be altered at the will of the superior. Between December and Lent they always ate at nones. If they eat early 'then shall they sleep and silence keep' (l. 1910) till nones, from which time till evensong work was resumed.

About three o'clock, vespers, that is evensong, once more assembled the convent inmates in church. The celebration of evensong partook of the solemnity of the celebration of high mass. In the monks' houses at high mass and at vespers the youths who were supported there for the purpose attended and joined the brethren in their choral service. In the nuns' houses the arrangements for the girls who dwelt with the nuns were similar, at least in some cases. After vespers came supper, and then 'the nuns could sit where they would and read lessons of holy writ or else the lives of holy men' (l. 1791), until the tolling of the bell summoned them to the chapter-house, where they joined their superior. Compline completed the religious exercises of the day. After this the nuns retired to the dormitory, where silence unbroken was to be observed. Inside the dormitory, curtains, in some houses if not in all, were hung so as to separate bed from bed.

The celebration of the hours formed at all times the great feature of monastic life, and in itself involved a considerable amount of labour, especially during the later period, when the ritual of service had become very elaborate. Indolence and ease might creep in between whiles, deterioration might take place in the occupations of the nuns between hours, but the observance of the hours themselves constituted the nun's privilege and her *raison d'être*, and was at all times zealously upheld.

§ 3. The Foundation and Internal Arrangements of Sion[1].

Before leaving the subject of women's convent life in England in the later Middle Ages, it will be interesting to devote some attention to the foundation and interior arrangements of Sion, a convent founded under peculiar circumstances at a time when it was no longer usual to found or endow religious settlements. The information relating to Sion has been characterised as the most valuable record we possess of monastic life in the 15th century. It refers to one short period only and bears out what has already been put forward with regard to other nunneries. The interests of the women who joined this convent centred round devotional practices and a highly elaborated convent routine.

The settlement of Sion belonged to the order of St Bridget of Sweden, and was the only house of its kind in England. It was situated in beautiful surroundings near Isleworth on the Thames, and was so richly endowed that at the time of the dissolution its income far exceeded that of any other nunnery, not excepting the time-honoured settlements of Shaftesbury and Barking. It was the only English community of women which escaped being scattered at the time of the Reformation. Its convent of nuns removed to Holland, but returned to the old house for a time after the accession of Queen Mary. At the close of her reign the nuns again went abroad and after various vicissitudes settled at Lisbon, where the convent continued to be recruited from English homes

---

[1] Aungier, G. J., *History and Antiquities of Syon*, 1840; *Myroure of Oure Ladye*, Early English Text Soc., 1873, Introduction by Blunt, J. H.

till the beginning of this century.   Then the nine sisters of which the convent consisted came to England, and settled at Chudleigh, near Newton-Abbot, in Devonshire.

A few words in passing must be devoted to the nun and saint Bridget[1] of Sweden, founder of the order which took her name— a woman of acquirements and influence.   She was born of a kingly race in 1304, and from the house of a powerful father passed to that of a powerful husband; but the responsibilities of a large household and the care of a family of seven children did not draw her attention from social and political affairs.   She was strongly imbued with the need of reform in religion, and believed in the possibility of effecting a change by encouraging monasticism. A large part of her property and much of her time were devoted to enlarging the religious settlement of Wadstena.   She then went on a pilgrimage to Santiago in Spain, after which husband and wife separated, each to embrace convent life.   Bridget, or Birgitta as her people called her, dwelt at Wadstena, which she reformed according to rules which she believed she had received direct from heaven.   She also wrote some 'Revelations,' which in their strong invective recall the Revelations of St Hildegard of Bingen with this difference, that St Bridget with open directness spoke of the dangers which she thought were gathering around Sweden. The tone of these writings brought her into difficulties.   She escaped from them by removing to Rome in 1350, where she lived for over twenty years.   Here she was looked upon as the representative of the Church party which strongly censured the Pope for continuing to dwell at Avignon.   This party looked upon Bridget as the chosen mouthpiece of God.   Her power of prophecy was generally recognised after her threatening visions about the state of things in Sweden had proved true.   Settlements on the plan of that of Wadstena rapidly multiplied during her lifetime in Sweden and in North Germany.   It was partly owing to her influence that the first attempt was made to translate the Bible into Swedish, and she is looked upon by the Swedes as one of that faithful band who worked for their national regeneration.   She died in 1372 and was officially canonised a saint in 1391[2].

A great feature of the order of St Bridget was that its settlements consisted of a double community of men and women who combined for purposes of divine service, but were otherwise separate,

[1] Hammerich, *Den hellige Birgitta*, 1863.

[2] *A. SS. Boll.*, St Birgitta vidua, Oct. 8.

each community having its own conventual buildings separately enclosed. The convent of nuns, according to Bridget's stipulation, numbered sixty women including the abbess, and in accordance with a fanciful notion, such as one comes across in the Middle Ages, these women had associated with them thirteen priests, who represented the apostles, four deacons who represented the great doctors of the Church, and eight lay brothers; the lady abbess was at the head of this double community. The order in its development abroad endeavoured to influence all classes. It encouraged charity, promoted education and collected books. But in England its tone fell in with that of other nunneries in the 15th century; the interests of Sion were entirely devotional and its large library seems to have contained religious works only.

I am not aware of any mention of Bridget in contemporary English literature previous to the introduction of her order into this country, which took place at the beginning of the 15th century. In the year 1406 Philippa, daughter of Henry IV, was sent to Lund in Sweden to be married to King Eric XIII (1382–1445), under whose rule the crowns of Sweden, Denmark and Norway were united. The princess travelled under the charge of Henry, third Baron Fitzhugh, who held an important position at the court of Henry IV; he was made Constable of England at the coronation of Henry V, and seems to have been on terms of intimacy with both these monarchs. By some means Fitzhugh's attention was drawn to the monastery of Wadstena, the chronicle of which records his visit to it. He volunteered to found a branch of the order of St Bridget in England, and promised the gift of a manor, Hinton near Cambridge, on condition that some of the order took possession of it within three years.

In consequence of Fitzhugh's visit and offer a priest and two deacons professing the order of St Bridget were elected at Wadstena in 1408, and sent to England. Blunt considers it probable[1] that it was by the advice of Fitzhugh that Henry V about this time devoted manors at Sheen and Isleworth to religious purposes. Carthusian monks were settled at Sheen, nuns of St Bridget were settled at Isleworth,—and the two settlements were called respectively Bethlehem and Sion. In February of 1415 Henry V in the presence of the bishop of London laid the foundation stone of a building destined for the nuns near Twickenham, and in March the royal charter was drawn up and signed. By this the members

---

[1] *Myroure of Oure Ladye,* Introd. p. xiv.

of the new settlement were bound 'to celebrate Divine Service for ever for our healthful estate while we live and for our souls when we shall have departed this life, and for the souls of our most dear lord and father (Henry IV) late king of England, and Mary his late wife, etc.' Before the close of the year four consecrated Swedish sisters, three novices and two brothers arrived in England from Wadstena. They were sent by the king and queen of Sweden and were sped on their way by the archbishop of Lund and other dignitaries.

The settlement at Sion had been granted an income of a thousand marks, to be drawn from the royal exchequer until the permanent endowments made to it should amount to that sum. In 1418 Pope Martin V received the house under his special protection ; the first profession or monastic engagement took place two years later. Twenty-four nuns, five priests, two deacons and four lay brothers pronounced their vows before archbishop Chicheley of Canterbury (1420). And before the close of Henry's reign (1422) the house was endowed with manors and spiritualities, scattered over the land from Kent to the Lake district, which were chiefly appropriated from the possessions of alien priories.

The appropriation of alien priories forms an interesting episode in the history of English monasticism, for it constitutes a prelude to the dissolution of monasteries generally. While men were becoming critical of religious institutions owing to the spread of Lollard doctrines, the Lancastrian kings appropriated the lands and the revenues of alien priories and made use of them to fortify the Church and monasticism, thus counteracting influences which in the first instance had made the appropriation of these houses possible.

The number of alien priories in England is differently quoted as a hundred and a hundred and forty[1]. Most of them had been founded soon after the Conquest, when the gift of a manor on English soil to a foreign house had brought over from France a few monks and nuns, who after defraying the expenses of their houses remitted any surplus revenue or else forwarded a sum of money in lieu of it to the parent house. When the relations between France and England became strained it appeared advisable to sever the connection between the foreign house and its English colonies. Edward I, when he determined on war with France, appropriated the revenues of alien priories for a time, and his

---

[1] Gasquet, A., *Henry VIII and the English Monasteries*, 1888, vol. 1, p. 42.

successors frequently did the same; the dangers to which these cells were exposed causing some foreign houses to sever the connection by selling their English property.

The alien cells occupied by nuns were very few. Amesbury, which had ·been constituted a cell to Fontevraud, regained its independent standing during the wars with France[1]; Westwood[2], another cell of Fontevraud, and Levenestre or Liminster in Surrey, a cell of Almanache in Normandy, were dispersed, and the abbess of Almanache treated for the sale of the property[3].

After many attempts to interfere with foreign cells Henry V resolved on their final sequestration (1414), and it was part of the property thus appropriated which was bestowed on the houses called Bethlehem and Sion.

The chief information we have on the conventual life of the women assembled at Sion is contained in a set of 'additional rules' written in English 'for the sisters of the order of St Saviour and St Bridget'[4]. The same rules exist in a manuscript of contemporaneous date adapted to the use of the brothers, whose duties, save in a few particulars, were similar. They acted as priests and confessors to the double community. The chapel had a double chancel, each with its separate stalls; it was divided by a 'crate' or grille which did not prevent the brothers and sisters from being visible to each other during divine service. The gate of this grille was kept locked, and was only opened for the entrance and departure of the clergy when they said mass at the altar of the sisters' chapel. The lay brothers of the settlement acted as labourers, and had no part in the government of the house.

The additional rules for the sisters are grouped together in fifty-nine chapters, and contain most elaborate directions not only as to the occupation, behaviour and special duties of the various inmates of the convent, but for exigencies of every kind. After directions about the holding of the Chapter, lists of defaults are worked out, grouped under the headings of light, grievous, more grievous and most grievous (c. 1–7). 'A careful consideration of this code of "defaultes" and their penalties,' says Blunt[5], 'leads to the conclu-

---

[1] Dugdale, *Monasticon*, 'Amesbury,' vol. 1, p. 333.

[2] Ibid. 'Westwood,' vol. 6, p. 1004.

[3] Ibid. 'Levenestre,' vol. 6, p. 1032.

[4] Aungier, G. J., *History and Antiquities of Syon*, 1840, p. 249 ff., from Arundel MS. nr 146 (chapter references throughout the text in this chapter are to this reprint).

[5] *Myroure of Oure Ladye*, Introd. p. xxxv.

sion that it was intended as an exhaustive list of *possible* crimes, and that it offers no ground for believing that the Sisters of Sion were ever guilty of them or ever incurred the severer punishments enjoined in connection with them.' Among 'light defaults' we note such as neglect in religious observance and in washing; among 'grievous defaults,' despising the common doctrine as taught by the holy fathers, and going unconfessed for fourteen days. 'More grievous defaults' are such as sowing discord, theft, and using sorcery or witchcraft; 'most grievous defaults' are manslaughter, fleshly sin, and blasphemy. We gather from the directions that one mode of severe punishment was imprisonment, whereas 'discipline' was administered regularly by the sisters to each other. The power of the abbess over the members of the convent was absolute; she is spoken of in these rules sometimes as sovereign, sometimes as majesty. It was she who decreed punishment and penance, and when the bishop enjoined correction in consequence of an enquiry, she decided upon and administered it. Twenty-eight questions, which the bishop on the occasion of his visitation was allowed to put to the abbess and the convent, are given (c. 10). They refer to devotional duties, to the observance of fasts, etc. One question (nr 10) enquires of the sisters how they are occupied when they are not at divine service or at conventual observances; another (nr 18) if there be an inventory or register of the books of the library, and how they and other books of study are kept; again another (nr 26) enquires as to the state of the infirmary.

A caution against slander suggests a curious idea of equity. If any sister bring an accusation against another before the bishop, she shall not be heard 'unless bound to the pain if she fail in proof, that she whom she accuses shall have, if she be found guilty.'

Among the men who necessarily had access to the women's conventual buildings, physicians, workmen and labourers are enumerated.

The election of a new abbess (c. 12) was effected by the sisters alone within three days of the occurrence of a vacancy. It was not managed in quite the same way as elsewhere. The prioress proposed a name, and if the sisters voted unanimously in favour of it, the election was called 'by the way of the Holy Ghost.' But if they did not agree, they named a candidate and the ballot was repeated till a sufficient majority was obtained. The election was not valid unless confirmed by the bishop. When the abbess pronounced the words of her 'obedience' she was supported by a learned man of law or notary, besides the confessor of the house and two brothers. The confessor was appointed at the discretion of the abbess herself, the 'sadder' or elderly sisters and the brothers ; but the other appointments were made by the abbess alone (c. 13). She appointed the sisters to office and could remove them. As elsewhere, she was obliged to do so in the chapter-house in the presence of the convent.

The rules of keeping silence, the year of proof, and the instruction and profession of novices, are fully discussed (c. 15). The account of how the sisters were professed is supplemented by Aungier[1]. He gives an additional description of the ceremony in church, probably of somewhat later date, and of the interrogatory through which the bishop put the prospective nun. The first question which he put was to this effect: 'Art thou free and unfettered by any bond of the Church, or of wedlock ; of vow, or of excommunication?' to which she made answer, 'I am truly free.' The bishop then asked : 'Does not shame, or perchance grief of worldly adversity, urge thee to a religious profession, or perhaps the multitude of thy debts compel thee?' To which she answered : 'Neither grief nor shame incites me to this, but a fervent love of Christ ; and I have already paid all my debts according to my power,' etc. I have not met with similar questions in any other place.

In the additional rules directions are also given about singing and keeping the hours and the festivals (c. 18–44). The day at Sion was divided by the seven 'hours' in the usual way. At the hours in chapel the 'sadder' or elder sisters sang together with the younger ones or 'song-sisters.' The 'observance of the altar' at both masses belonged to the brothers ; it was so arranged that the brothers' service came first and the sisters' began when that of the brothers ended. In addition to the usual hours and masses two ceremonies were daily observed at Sion. One was the singing of the psalm *De Profundis* at an open grave to which the whole convent wended its way after tierce. The other consisted of a prayer addressed to Mary in chapel before evensong, from which none of the sisters was to absent herself except for an important reason.

A number of festivals were celebrated at Sion with special

---

[1] Aungier, G. J., *History and Antiquities of Syon*, 1840, pp. 312 ff., from Additional MS. nr 5208.

services and processions (c. 29). Among them were the feast of the Circumcision, the translation of St Bridget and the day of St John the Baptist 'when their feasts fall on Sunday and not else'; also Palm Sunday, St Mark's day, Rogation Sunday, St Peter and St Paul, St Anne's, Michaelmas, all the feasts of Our Lady and all the principal or high double feasts of the year. On these occasions the sisters walked two and two in procession, and the sister who was sexton bore the 'image of our lady' after the cross, and two torches were carried on either side a little before the image. The additional rules contain directions to the sisters on the arrangement of divine service on these occasions, and further directions in the rule for the brothers minutely describe the elaborate ritual which took place.

The additional rules also contain a full description of the duties of each appointment in the convent (c. 45). The choir in church was led by a *chauntres* and *subchauntres* who should be 'cunning and perfect in reading and singing.' It was the duty of the *ebdomary*, or weekly appointed nun (c. 46), to be one of the first in choir; she was 'to abstayn and withdrawe herself from alle thynges that wyke that myght lette her to performe her office.' When the abbess did not execute the service the ebdomary began the *Invitatory*; and she always gave the third blessing after the abbess had read the third lesson. She also fulfilled the office of the abbess at the principal feasts, except in such things as belonged exclusively to the abbess.

We hear also of the duties of the sexton, *sexteyne* (c. 48), who kept the church ornaments and the altar 'whole and sound, fair, clean and honest,' and who saw to the washing of altar-cloths, *awbes* or surplices. She was not allowed to touch or wash the hallowed *corporas* or cloths with bare hands, but was obliged to wear linen gloves, and in starching the cloths she was directed to use starch made of herbs only. The sexton had in her keeping wax, lamps, oil and all other things belonging to the church; she had to provide for the church *syngynge* or communion *brede, sudarys*, wax-candles, tallow-candles, wax rolls, tapers, torches, mats, *uattes*, and *roundlettes*; and she provided for the *penners*, pens, ink, inkhorns, tables, and all else that the abbess asked of her. Also she opened and shut the doors and windows of the sisters' choir and common places, lighted and extinguished tapers and candles, and snuffed them 'in such wise and in such time that the sisters be not grieved with the savour.'

It was the duty of the sexton to ring the bells in the women's part of the house; the ringing of a bell regulated throughout the life of those assembled at Sion. It roused the brothers and sisters from sleep, summoned them to church, called them to meals, and ever and anon gave notice for a devotional pause in whatever occupation was going on at the moment. When one of the community passed away from life the large or curfew bell was tolled continuously.

Another appointment in the women's convent was that of the *legister* or reader at meals (c. 50), who was directed to read out distinctly and openly, that all might understand, whatever the abbess or chauntress had assigned. On one day of the week she read out the rule. Absolute silence reigned during meals. If any-one had a communication to make, this was done by means of signs, used also at other times when silence was to be observed. A curious 'table of signs used during the hours of silence by the sisters and brothers in the monastery of Sion' was drawn up by Thomas Betsone[1], one of the brothers. Together with other tables of the kind, it suggests the origin of the method by which the deaf and dumb were formerly taught.

At Sion the abbess had her meals with the sisters, sitting at a high table while they sat at side tables (c. 51–52), and the servitors or lay sisters waited. When they had done the sisters wiped their knives and spoons on the napkins (without washing them?); they were to guard against spotting the cloth, and spilling the food, and were directed to put away their cups and spoons honest and clean (without washing them?) into the 'coffyns' which were kept underneath the table, or in some other place ordered by the abbess. At the end of a meal the sisters swept together the crumbs with their napkins, and then, at a sign from the abbess, they bore the food away to the serving-house. The youngest sister took the first dish, and each one carried away something according to age. The language in which the utensils are described presents some difficulties. They carried away the drink and then 'the garnapes that they sette on, ther pottes and cruses, after thys, brede, hole, kytte, cantelles, ande crommes, and laste of alle salt,' ending evermore with the abbess or president, and inclining to each sister as they took them up and they again to them.

The behaviour of the sisters to each other and to the abbess in the refectory, the dormitory, the chapter-house, etc. was carefully

---

[1] Aungier, G. J., *History and Antiquities of Syon*, 1840, pp. 405 ff. 'A table of signs.'

regulated (c. 53). The sisters when they met the abbess bowed to her, 'for love without reverence is but childish love.' The desire for refinement in bearing and behaviour is manifested throughout by these directions, and some of them are curious. Thus the sister who washed her hands was directed not to 'jutte up' the water on another, nor to spit in the lavatory, nor to presume to go without her veil and crown upon her head, except only in her cell, washing-house, etc. Judging from this reference to cells, the dormitory at Sion was divided by partitions or curtains, so that each sister practically had a room to herself.

Many details are then given concerning the duties of the prioress and other appointments. The nuns appointed to enquire into shortcomings are here designated as *serchers* (c. 55). The treasurer and her fellow kept the muniments of the monastery and its possessions in gold and silver in the treasury, in a large chest to which there were two keys, one kept by the treasurer and the other by her fellow (c. 56). These sisters also provided and paid for all necessary medicines, spices and powders, etc.

Duties of no small importance devolved on the *chambres*, or mistress of the wardrobe, who saw to the raiment of the sisters and the brothers, both in regard to linen and to woollen clothes, shaping, sewing, making, repairing and keeping them from 'wormes,' and shaking them with 'the help of other sisters.' I transcribe in the original spelling the things she is told to provide: '*canuas for bedyng, fryses, blankettes, shetes, bolsters, pelowes, couerlites, cuschens, basens, stamens, rewle cotes, cowles, mantelles, wymples, veyles, crownes, pynnes, cappes, nyght kerchyfes, pylches, mantel furres, cuffes, gloues, hoses, shoes, botes, soles, sokkes, mugdors* (sic), *gyrdelles, purses, knyues, laces, poyntes, nedelles, threde,—waschyng bolles and sope,—*(written in the margin) and for all other necessaries, as directed by the abbess, which shall not be over curious but plain and homely, without wearing of any strange colours of silk, gold or silver, having all things of honesty and profit and nothing of vanity after the rule, their knives unpointed and purses being double of linen cloth, and not silk.'

In illustration of the office of the chambress, Blunt has published a document preserved in the Record Office, which contains the account of Dame Bridget Belgrave, chambress at Sion from Michaelmas 1536 to Michaelmas 1537, the year preceding the dissolution[1]. This shows that the chambress provided

---

[1] *Myroure of Oure Ladye*, Introd. p. xxvi.

the material for the dress of the sisters and other items. She buys *russettes*, white cloth, *kerseys*, fryce, Holland cloth and other linen cloth mostly by the piece, which varies in the number of its yards; she provides soap, calf-skins, thread, needles and thimbles; she purchases new spectacles and has old ones mended. Among many other items of interest we find fox-skins, paper, and pins of divers sorts; she sets down a sum for burying poor folks, and 'expences at London,' from which we gather that she had been there; and pays 'rewards' and 'wages' to the *grome*, the *skynner*, and the *shumakers*.

The duties of the cellaress stand next in the additional rules (c. 56), and they recall the complex duties belonging to the same post at Barking. Blunt has also illustrated these duties by publishing the accounts, rendered by Dame Agnes Merrett, for the last year preceding the dissolution[1]. This cellaress also charged herself with various sums received for hides, calf-skins and wool-felles or sheep-skins. She received payment for boarding My Lady Kyngeston and her servants, and sister Elizabeth Nelson. She received rent from various tenants and managed the home farm at Isleworth. We hear of her buying horses, cattle, hogs and peacocks for its storing. Its dairy was managed by paid servants. This cellaress, like her fellow at Barking, purchased provisions and fish for the use of the convent, but her entries are more numerous and infer a higher standard of living, perhaps due to the fact that these accounts are more than a hundred years later than the 'charge of the cellaress at Barking.' The cellaress at Sion also bought salt salmon, herrings by the barrel, and red herrings by the 'caade'; also *stubbe* eels. She further bought spices, fruits, sugar, nutmegs, almonds, currants, ginger, isinglass, pepper, cinnamon, cloves, mace, *figge doodes* (sic), *topnettes* (sic), great raisins, prunes, saffron and rice. Her 'foreign payments' include seed for the garden, boat-hire, and expenses at London, by which we see that she too, like the chambress of the house, had been there. Among her other expenses are *rewards* to the 'clerke of the kechyn,' the 'baily of the husbandry,' the 'keper of the covent (convent) garden,' and the 'cookes.' Members of the convent were deputed by the abbess to look after the sick (c. 57), and the writer insists upon the need of gentleness and patience in dealing with them.

'Often change their beds and clothes,' he says, 'give them medicines, lay to them plaisters and minister to them meat and

---

[1] *Myroure of Oure Ladye*, Introd. p. xxix.

drink, fire and water, and all other necessaries night and day, as need requires after the counsel of the physicians, and precept of the sovereign ; do not be squeamish in washing and wiping them by avoiding them, be not angry nor hasty, nor impatient though one have the vomit, another the flux, another the frenzy, and now sings, now cries, now laughs, now weeps, now chides, now is frightened, now is wroth, now well apayde, for there be some sickness vexing the sick so greatly and provoking them to ire that the matter drawn up to the brain alienates the mind.   And therefore those in attendance should have much patience with them, that thereby they may secure an everlasting crown.'

Aungier has also reprinted lists of the capabilities of indulgence granted to Sion, and of the pardons secured by those who offered prayers in the chapel there[1].   This shows one of the means by which money was secured to religious houses in the 15th century. Indulgences were granted at Sion on almost every festival in the year.   By 'devoutly giving somewhat to the reparation of the said monastery' and offering prayers on Midlent Sunday, the visitor at Sion might secure pardon extending from a hundred days to 'clean remission of all sin except in the points which are reserved to the Pope.'   To give alms on the feast of St Bridget, the patron saint of the house, secured to him who sought help 'pardon and clean remission in all cases reserved and unreserved,' according to the wording of the document.   This power, as the manuscript informs us, had been granted 'by diverse holy fathers, popes at Rome, archbishops, bishops, cardinals and legates.'   Aungier supplements it by printing a document which came from Norfolk on the capa- bilities of pardon possessed by different religious houses[2].   There are entries in this referring to the 'pardoun of beyds' of the Charterhouse of Mount Grace and of the Charterhouse at Sheen, and to the pardon of beads at Sion and at the 'Crossed Friars' beside London Tower.

A number of devotional books were written for the nuns at Sion ; some in Latin, some in English.   A few of the service books of the house have been preserved.   Among them is the Martyrology which was in daily use among the brothers and which contains historical memoranda, accounts of the saints, the records of the

---

[1] Aungier, G. J., *History and Antiquities of Syon*, 1840, p. 421, 'Indulgentia monas- terii de Syon,' MS. Ashmol. nr 750 ; p. 422, 'The Pardon of the monastery of Shene which is Syon,' MS. Harleian 4012, art. 9.

[2] Ibid. p. 426, footnotes.

deaths of the sisters, brothers and benefactors of the house between 1422 and 1639, and extracts from religious writers. This martyrology accompanied the women's convent on their wanderings, and since their return it has been acquired by the British Museum[1]. A translation of it into English was made by Richard Whytford († 1542), a brother of Sion, 'for the edificacyon of certayn religyous persones unlerned that dayly dyd rede the same martiloge in Latyn not understandynge what they redde[2].' Whytford wrote other religious books, among them the 'Pype or Tonne of Perfection'; the 'Fruyte of redempcyon,' which is now held to be by 'Simon, the anker of London,' has been attributed to him.

Among other books written for the nuns is a curious discourse in English by Thomas Fishbourne, father confessor in 1420, to which is added a portion of the gospel of St Peter ad Vincula[3]. It contains a discussion on the nature of pardons and indulgences, particularly of those procured at Rome. Symon Wynter, another brother of the house (1428), wrote a treatise for them in praise of the Virgin (Regina Coeli)[4]; and Thomas Prestius wrote instructions for the novices[5]. The house owned a large library, to the celebrity of which Sir Richard Sutton added by a splendid work printed at his expense by Wynkyn de Worde in 1519 and called in honour of the monastery 'The Orchard of Syon[6]'.

The most important work in English however compiled for the nuns was a devotional treatise on divine service with a translation into English of the Offices, called the 'Mirror of Our Lady,' first printed in 1530, the authorship of which is attributed by its latest editor, Blunt, to Thomas Gascoigne (1403–1458)[7]. Gascoigne was an eminent divine, at one time Chancellor of the University of Oxford; he caused the life of St Bridget to be translated into English and bequeathed most of his books by will to the sisters at Sion. The Offices in this book are amplified, and Blunt was much struck by the similarity of many passages to the Book of Common Prayer. The purpose of the writer is expressed in the following words[8]:

'As many of you, though you can sing and read, yet you cannot

---

[1] *Myroure of Oure Ladye*, Introd. p. xlv.   B. M. Addit. MS., nr 22285.

[2] Printed by Wynkyn de Worde (?), 1526; reprinted for the Bradshaw Society, 1893.

[3] Aungier, G. J., *History and Antiquities of Syon*, 1840, p. 529. MS. Harleian 2321, fol. 17 ff.

[4] Ibid. p. 527.   [5] Ibid. p. 527.   [6] Ibid. p. 526.

[7] *Myroure of Oure Ladye*, Introd. p. ix.   [8] Ibid. p. 2.

see what the meaning thereof is…I have drawn your legend and all your service into English, that you see by the understanding thereof, how worthy and holy praising of our glorious Lady is contained therein, and the more devoutly and knowingly sing it and read it, and say it to her worship.'

The 'Mirror of Our Lady' is very instructive with regard to the just estimation of the position and feelings of religious women during the later Middle Ages. There is much in it that is eloquent, refined, and beautiful, but its insistence on detail is sometimes wearisome. The style of the writer is fitly illustrated by the following passages, which are taken from the introductory treatise on the reading of religious books[1]. The wording of the original is retained as closely as possible, but the spelling is modernized.

'Devout reading of holy books is called one of the parts of contemplation, for it causes much grace and comfort to the soul if it be well and discreetly used. And much reading is often lost for lack of diligence, that it is not intended as it ought to be. Therefore if you will profit in reading you must keep these five things. First you ought to take heed what you read, that it be such thing as is speedwell for you to read and convenient to the degree you stand in. For you ought to read no worldly matters nor worldly books, namely such as are without reason of ghostly edification or belong not to the need of the house ; you ought also to read no books that speak of vanities and trifles, and much less no books of evil or occasion to evil. For since your holy rule forbids you all vain and idle words in all times and places, by the same it forbids you reading of all vain and idle things, for reading is a manner of speaking. The second, when you begin to read or to hear such books of ghostly fruit as accord for you to read or to hear, that then you dispose yourselves thereto with meek reverence and devotion…The third that you labour to understand the same thing that you read. For Cato taught his son to read so his precepts that he understand them. For it is, he says, great negligence to read and not to understand. And therefore when you read by yourself alone you ought not to be hasty to read much at once but you ought to abide thereupon, and sometimes read a thing again twice or thrice or oftener till you understand it clearly. For St Austin said that no man should ween to understand a thing sufficiently in any wise by once reading. And if you

[1] *Myroure of Oure Ladye,* pp. 65 ff.

cannot understand what you read, ask of others that can teach you. And they that can ought not to be loth to teach others....The fourth thing that is to be kept in reading is that you dress so your intent that your reading and study be not only for to be cunning or for to be able to speak it forth to others, but principally to inform yourself and to set it forth in your own living....The fifth thing is discretion. So that according to the matter you arrange your reading. For you must understand that different books speak in different wise. For some books are made to inform the understanding and to tell how spiritual persons ought to be governed in all their living that they may know how they shall live and what they shall do, how they shall labour in cleansing their conscience and in getting virtues, how they shall withstand temptation and suffer tribulations, and how they shall pray and occupy themselves with ghostly exercise, with many such other full holy doctrines.... Other books there be that are made to quicken and to stir up the affections of the soul, as some that tell of the sorrows and dreads of death and of doom and of pains, to stir up the affection of dread and of sorrow for sin. Some tell of the great benefits of our Lord God, how He made us and bought us and what love and mercy He shewed continually to us to stir up our affections of love and of hope in Him. Some tell of the joys of heaven, to stir up the affections of joy to desire thitherward. And some tell of the foulness and wretchedness of sin, to stir up the affections of hate and loathing thereagainst.'

CHAPTER XI.

MONASTIC REFORM PREVIOUS TO THE REFORMATION.

'For sum (nunnes) bene devowte, holy, and towarde,
And holden the ryght way to blysse;
And sum bene feble, lewde, and frowarde,
Now god amend that ys amys!'

(*From ' Why I cannot be a nun,*' l. 311.)

§ 1. Visitations of Nunneries in England.

THE changes which came over convent life towards the close
of the Middle Ages and modified its tenor can be studied in the
efforts made to reform monastic life in the centuries preceding the
Reformation. Both in England and abroad the heads of many
houses were zealous in removing abuses which their predecessors
had suffered to creep in, and in checking tendencies the deteriorating effect of which now first came to be realized. The bull promulgated by Pope Benedict XII in 1336 with a view to reforming
the Benedictine order had been accepted with a reservation in
England and had left matters in Germany practically untouched.
But in the 15th century a movement in favour of reform was inaugurated within the religious orders themselves; it was increased
by pressure brought to bear on monastic houses from without.
For the prelates of the Church as well as others were eager to
interfere with monastic settlements, all the more as such interference frequently tended to the increase of their own prerogative.
But in spite of the devoted earnestness of many individuals and
the readiness of convents to accept correction, the movement failed
to restore its former glory to an institution which in common with
other influential institutions of the Middle Ages appeared doomed
to decay.

The attempts of the monastic orders to restore vigour to
themselves, and the efforts of the Church to promote monastic

reform, were largely furthered by the desire to counteract the dangers to the established religion which threatened from the spread of heretical teaching.

In England a critical attitude towards monastic institutions and the Church was the outcome of Wyclif's († 1384) influence. It was checked for the time being by the alliance of the Church with the Lancastrian kings (after 1399) in favour of a reactionary policy. Several monasteries were endowed by these kings, among them houses of Carthusian monks and Sion, as mentioned above. Reforms were instituted and the prelates of the Church eagerly resumed their powers of visitation. By so doing they succeeded in checking monastic abuses, which continued to exist for a longer period on the Continent and there assumed much greater proportions.

In Germany, owing partly to its scattered provinces, partly to the want of concerted action between the dignitaries of Church and State, monasteries throughout the 14th century were left to drift in the way they listed, often in the direction of indifferentism, often in that of positive evil. The abuses of convent life at the beginning of the 15th century were far greater there than in England, and the efforts at reform were proportionally greater and more strenuous. In Germany also the effort to counteract the effect of heretical doctrines by way of reform was decisive. For, as we shall see later on, monastic reforms on a large scale were instituted immediately after the Church Council at Constance (1415) which condemned Hus to the stake.

The accounts of visitations instituted by the diocesan give us an insight into the abuses which threatened life in the nunnery at different periods. The diocesan was bound to visit the religious settlements situated within his diocese periodically, with the exception of those which had secured exemption through the Pope. For some time before the movement in favour of monastic reform began, these visitations appear to have taken place at irregular intervals and at periods often many years apart. But afterwards they became frequent, and called forth injunctions which give us an idea of the abuses which needed correction. Later still these powers of visitation of the diocesan were extended by means of special permits secured from Rome. Towards the close of the 15th century we find the prelates of the Church eager to interfere with monasteries, and regain a hold on those which had been removed from their influence.

The visitation of a religious house in all cases was so conducted that the diocesan previously sent word to the convent announcing his arrival. After assisting at mass in the chapel, he repaired to the chapter-house and there severally interrogated the superior of the house and its inmates as to the state of affairs. Their depositions were taken down in writing and were discussed at headquarters. A list of injunctions rectifying such matters as called for correction was then forwarded in writing to the superior of the house.

Among the earliest injunctions forwarded to a nunnery which I have come across are those sent to Godstow after a visitation held in 1279 by John Peckham, archbishop of Canterbury[1]. The first part treats of the celebration of the divine offices and of the part novices are to take in the singing. The feast of St John which is celebrated by childish festivities (puerilia solemnia), no doubt in accordance with an ancient folk custom, is not to be extended to a second day. Directions are then given about going outside precincts and staying away on business. The nuns are directed not to converse with the neighbouring students at Oxford (scholares Oxonii) unless they have permission to do so from the abbess, and to knit no bonds of friendship with them, 'because such affection often brings harmful thoughts.'

The attraction which the students at Oxford exerted on the nuns of Godstow has a counterpart at a later date in the effect which intercourse with the students at Cambridge had on the nuns of St Radegund's. When John Alcock, bishop of Ely († 1500), proposed the dissolution of this nunnery he urged that the nearness of the university had led to the demoralisation of the prioress and the nuns[2].

In the directions forwarded to Godstow we also find it enjoined that secular and religious visitors shall dine in the guest-house (hospitalaria communi) or in the chamber of the abbess, and on no account within the convent precincts with the nuns. Directions are also given as to the wearing of simple clothes, in which matter 'the rule of Benedict' (sic) shall be observed. These directions are not easy to understand. 'Linings of dyed woollen (imposterum burneto[3]),' say they, 'shall not be worn ; nor red dresses (rugatas tunicas) nor other unseemly clothes wide at the sides.'

Archbishop Peckham, who reformed abuses at Godstow, ad-

---

1 Dugdale, *Monasticon,* 'Godstow,' vol. 4, p. 357, Charter nr 16.
2 Ibid. 'St Radegund's,' vol. 4, p. 215, Charter nr 3.
3 Ducange, 'burnetum, pannus ex lana tincta confectus.'

dressed a mandate to the abbess of Romsey in 1286 against a certain prebendary William Shyrlock, who seems to have been one of the residential canons of the place. He is not to presume to enter the cloister or the church while suspicions are entertained against him, and the nuns are not to converse with him in the house or elsewhere, for he is accused of living a dishonest and dissolute life[1]. No aspersion in this case is cast on the doings of the nuns.

A serious scandal is said to have occurred about the year 1303 in the Cistercian nunnery of Swine in Yorkshire, but details concerning its nature are not forthcoming. In consequence of an enquiry into the state of the house the prioress resigned, and her successor also absented herself, it is alleged, on account of some scandal[2].

The nunneries which were cells to abbeys of men were exempt from the visitation of the diocesan; they were inspected by the abbot of the parent house, who enquired into abuses and enjoined corrections. A mandate of this description which was forwarded to Sopwell nunnery, a cell of St Alban's, by the abbot in 1338 is in existence. The nuns are directed to observe silence in the church, the cloister, the refectory, and the dormitory. No sister shall hold converse with secular persons in the parlour unless she is wearing a cowl and a veil; and tailors and others who are employed shall work in some place assigned to them outside the convent precincts[3].

Among the injunctions sent to Chatteris in Cambridgeshire in the year 1345 the following are worth noticing: Nuns shall not keep fowls, dogs or small birds (aviculae) within the convent precincts, nor bring them into church during divine service, and they shall not, from a wish to reform them, take into their employ servants who are known for their bad ways[4].

In April of the year 1397 a visitation of the nunnery of Nun-Monkton in Yorkshire was conducted by Thomas Dalby, archdeacon of Richmond, who acted for the archbishop of York[5]. He accused the prioress Margaret Fairfax of allowing various kinds of fur to be worn in her house, especially grey fur. He also objected to the wearing of silk veils and to the prioress herself acting as treasurer (bursaria) of the house, and charged her with having

---

[1] Dugdale, *Monasticon*, ' Rumsey,' vol. 2, p. 507, footnote *p*.
[2] Ibid. 'Swine,' vol. 5, p. 493.   [3] Ibid. ' Sopwell,' vol. 3, p. 362, charter nr 7.
[4] Ibid. ' Chatteris,' vol. 2, p. 614, charter nr 11.
[5] Ibid. ' Nun-Monkton,' vol. 4, p. 192, charter nr 2.

alienated its property to the value of a hundred marks. He censured her for entertaining John Munkton, and inviting him to dinner in her chamber, and for allowing the use of unusual vestments and clothes; for too readily receiving back nuns who had disgraced their profession (lapsae fornicatione); and for allowing nuns to receive gifts from friends to support them. He also complained that John Munkton behaved badly, had dallied (ludit) with the prioress at meals in her chamber, and had been served there with drink.

Injunctions were forwarded in the following July to rectify these matters, and directing the prioress to have no communication with *Dominus* John Munkton, William Snowe or Thomas Pape, except in the presence of the nuns. The usual vestments were to be worn in church, and the nuns were enjoined not to wear silk garments (paneis), silk veils, precious furs, finger rings, and embroidered or ornamental *jupes*, in English called gowns, like secular women. They were not to neglect the commemoration of the dead under penalty of being deprived of special clothes (carentiae camisarum?) for two whole weeks.

The general tenor of these injunctions argues a want of management on the part of the lady superior and a tendency to luxury among the nuns. As time wore on complaints about mismanagement of revenues became more frequent, but they were accompanied by evidence of increasing poverty, especially in the smaller houses, which shows that the lady superior was labouring under difficulties for which she was not altogether responsible.

A serious blow was dealt to the monastic system by the Black Death, which began in 1349. It produced a temporary collapse of discipline and indifference to religion[1], and resulted in changes in the state of agriculture and the position of the labourer, which affected the poorer and smaller houses in a disastrous manner.

Thus we read about Thetford, a small Benedictine nunnery in Norfolk[2], that the nuns' revenues had much decreased through mortality and inundation since 1349, and that when Henry V levied a tax on religious houses, Thetford, which consisted at the time of a prioress and nine nuns, was excused on the plea of poverty. The increasing poverty of the house is evident from accounts of visitations between 1514 and 1520[3]. On one occasion

---

[1] Gasquet, A., *The Great Pestilence*, 1893, Introd. p. xvi.
[2] Dugdale, *Monasticon*, 'Thetford,' vol. 4, p. 475.
[3] Jessopp, A., *Visitations of the Diocese of Norwich*, 1492–1532, pp. 90, 155.

the nuns declared they were short of service books; on another that the prioress received illiterate and deformed persons (indoctae et deformes) into the house; and again that there was great poverty and that the few novices had no teacher.

Again we read of Malling in Kent that it was excused from payments in 1404; in 1349 the bishop of Rochester had found it so decayed as to be hardly capable of restoration[1]. Two abbesses had died of the pestilence; there were only eight inmates left in the house, four of whom were professed and four non-professed.

Malling recovered itself, but not so Wyrthorp in Northampton-shire, where Emma de Pinchbeck and many of the Austin nuns fell victims to the pestilence[2]. The archbishop appointed Agnes Bowes as prioress, but the convent was beyond recovery. In 1354 Sir Th. Holland, the patron of the house, petitioned that it should be united to the nunnery at Stamford, to which its prioress and the one remaining nun removed[3]. In the royal licence which secured this change it is stated 'that the convent being poorly endowed was by the pestilence which lately prevailed reduced to such poverty that all the nuns but one on account of penury had dispersed.' In the course of the 14th century other nunneries complained of insufficient revenue and poverty, among them Seton in Cumberland[4], St Sepulchre's at Canterbury in 1359[5], and Rusper and Easebourne which were both situated in Sussex.

In a few cases accounts are preserved of successive visitations to the same nunnery extending over a number of years, which afford a valuable record of part of the life-history of the house. The visitations conducted between 1442 and 1527 at Rusper and at Easebourne are most instructive as showing the gradual collapse which many of the smaller houses experienced.

The chief complaint made during the visitation of Rusper in 1442 was that the prioress of the house had failed to render account to the sisterhood during the term she had held office[6]. She was consequently enjoined by the bishop of Chichester to produce an account year by year and submit it to him and to the sisterhood. Some thirty years later in 1478 upon enquiry it was found that

[1] Dugdale, *Monasticon*, 'Malling,' vol. 3, p. 382; Gasquet, A., *The Great Pestilence*, 1893, pp. 104, 106.   [2] Gasquet, p. 137.

[3] Dugdale, *Monasticon*, 'Wyrthorp,' vol. 4, p. 266.

[4] Ibid. 'Seton,' vol. 4, p. 226, charter nr 2.

[5] Ibid. 'St Sepulchre's,' vol. 4, p. 413, footnote *l.*

[6] Way, A., 'Notices of the Benedictine Priory of St Mary Magdalen at Rusper,' *Sussex Archæol. Collections*, vol. 5, p. 244; Dugdale, *Monasticon*, 'Rusper,' vol. 4, p. 586.

the convent was in debt, and the bishop asked for an inventory of the house, which was drawn up for him. The community at this time consisted of the prioress and five nuns, four of whom are entered as professed, one as non-professed.

Again in 1484 the bishop visited Rusper, and three nuns were consecrated on this occasion. But the house had entered on a downward course of poverty and decay. In 1485 Rusper was exempted from paying subsidy on the plea of poverty. During the visitation of 1521 the nuns referred their pecuniary poverty to the onerous expenses caused by the too frequent visits of friends and relations who came to stay with the prioress, while the prioress herself referred the poverty to other reasons, but agreed that the house was fast going to ruin. No complaints were made at the visitation three years later (1524), except against a certain William Tychen, who sowed discord. Again in 1527 the prioress and nuns deposed that all was well in the house, but that its poverty was extreme and that it was on the brink of ruin.

The accounts of the visitations to Easebourne[1] are even more instructive, for there the deteriorating effects of mismanagement and poverty were increased by want of discipline and quarrelsomeness among the nuns. In 1414 the community consisted of the prioress and six or seven nuns. In 1437 and 1439 its poverty was already so great that letters patent were secured on the plea of insufficient revenue, exonerating the prioress and her convent from certain payments called for by the clergy. In 1441 the house was in debt to the amount of £40, and here also the convent cast the blame of mismanagement on the head of the house, referring the debts to 'costly expenses of the prioress, who frequently rides abroad, and pretends she does so on the common business of the house, though it is not so, with a train of attendants much too large, and tarries long abroad, and she feasts sumptuously both at home and abroad.... And while she does so the members of the convent are made to work like hired workwomen, and they receive nothing whatever for their own use from their work, but the prioress takes the whole profit.'

In reply to their complaints the bishop forbade the prioress to compel the sisters to continual work; 'and if they should wish of their own accord to work, they shall be free to do so, but yet so that they may receive for themselves the half part of what

[1] Blaauw, W. H., 'Episcopal Visitations of the Priory of Easebourne,' *Sussex Archæol. Collections*, vol. 9, pp. 1–32; Dugdale, *Monasticon*, 'Easebourn,' vol. 4, p. 423.

they gain by their hands; the other part shall be converted to the advantage of the house and unburdening its debts.' But discharging those debts was no easy matter. The prioress was commanded to sell her costly fur trimmings for the advantage of the house, and if she rode abroad to spend only what was needful, and to content herself with four horses. The administration of temporal goods was taken from her altogether and given to 'Master Thomas Boleyn and John Lylis, Esquire.' But under their management the debt of £40 had increased in nine years to £66; and in 1475, as again in 1485 and 1489, the house had to be excused from payments. Rumours of an unfavourable character about what went on in the house now reached the bishop, and before the next visitation in 1478, the prioress Agnes Tauke was summoned to Chichester, where she promised on her oath before the bishop and others to resign her office if called upon to do so.

The deposition made by her nuns during the ensuing visitation confirmed the unfavourable rumours; two nuns had left the priory ostensibly for their health and were abroad in apostasy. One nun referred this conduct to neglect on the part of the prioress, another to that of the chaplain, John Smyth, who confessed to having sealed or caused to be sealed a licence to one of the nuns to go out of the priory after having had criminal intercourse with her. Other complaints were made against the prioress, 'that she had her kinsmen staying with her for weeks at the priory and gave them the best food, while the nuns had the worst'; also that she was herself of bad character. But these recriminations were not accepted by the bishop. The desire of Agnes Tauke to improve matters was accepted as genuine and she was not called upon to resign.

Discontent however remained a standing characteristic of the nuns at Easebourne. At the visitation of 1521 the prioress deposed that the nuns lived honestly and religiously according to the rule of St Augustine (sic) and were sufficiently obedient to her, but the nun sexton blamed the prioress for 'not making up any account annually as she ought in presence of the sisters concerning her administration of goods,' and another nun deposed that she neglected to provide for the sisters the sum of thirteen shillings and four pence in money to which they were entitled. Again in 1524 the prioress deposed that all was well, but the sub-prioress complained of disobedience, both among the professed and the non-professed nuns, who on their side complained of harshness of treatment. The bishop believed the complaints of the latter and blamed the behaviour of the sub-prioress, who submitted to correction.

The recriminations of the nuns at Easebourne recall a picture drawn about this time by Langland (c. 1390) in the *Vision of Piers the Ploughman,* in which Wrath personified as a friar describes how he stirred up quarrels in a nunnery. In its earliest version the poem omits these passages ; and Langland, so ready to abuse and ridicule monk and friar, is chary in his references to nuns. In the later versions of his poem (text B and C) 'Wrath' is described as acting first as gardener and then as cook in a nunnery, where in the character of 'the prioress' potager and of other poor ladies,' he 'made them broths of various scandals.' Among the stories he set going was

... 'that Dame Johane was a bastard
And Dame Clarice a knight's daughter, a cuckold was her sire,
And Dame Purnell a priest's concubine, she will never become
  prioress,
For she had a child in cherry time, all our chapter it wist.'

In consequence the nuns fall to quarrelling among themselves and end with attacking one another bodily. The picture, even if overdrawn, proves, in conjunction with the temper of the nuns at Easebourne, that peaceableness no longer formed the invariable concomitant of convent life during the 15th century.

Various particulars in the history of men's houses corroborate the fact that considerable changes were going on inside the monastic body during the 15th century.

Reference has been made to the fluctuations in the history of alien priories. Some of the foreign houses, aware of the dangers to which their English colonies were exposed, advocated the sale of their property in England. Numerous grammar-schools and colleges profited by the change or owed their foundation directly to it. As early as 1390 William Wykeham bought estates of alien priories for New College, his foundation at Oxford. Waynfleet, bishop of Worcester, who in 1415 founded St Mary Magdalen College at Oxford, annexed to it Sele, an alien priory which had been admitted to denizenship[1]. It is noteworthy that some religious houses about this time dissolved of their own accord. Thus the master and brethren of St John's hospital at Oxford obtained leave from Henry VI to convey their house to Wayn-

---

[1] Dugdale, *Monasticon,* 'Sele,' vol. 4, p. 668.

fleet[1]. The Austin priory of Selborne, which 'had become a desert convent without canons or prior,' was likewise annexed to St Mary Magdalen College, a change which was ratified by a bull from Innocent VIII in 1486[2].

It has already been said that a change of attitude towards religious institutions on the part of the public was the direct outcome of the spread of Wyclif's teaching. In 1410 Sir John Oldcastle, the so-called leader of the Lollards, who was burnt for heresy eight years later, made a proposal in the House of Commons which is curious in various ways. It was to the effect that their temporalities should be taken from bishop, abbot and prior, and the revenues of their possessions employed to pay a standing army, to augment the income of the noblemen and gentry, to endow a hundred hospitals and to make small payments to the clergy[3]. No notice in this case was taken of the donors or representatives of the settlement, to whom land and tenements upon default, or neglect of those to whom they were granted, otherwise reverted. The proposal was accompanied by a list of monasteries which might be appropriated, but the proposal was summarily quashed.

The Church Council held at Basel (from 1418), at which English prelates also were present, was emphatic in urging the need of monastic reform. It would be interesting to ascertain if this was prompted solely by the feeling that the recognised abuses of convent life lowered religion in general estimation, or if suspicions were entertained that religious houses might be harbouring unorthodox elements. Great efforts at reform were made within the Benedictine order; chapters were held by the abbots at regular intervals and the system of visitations formulated for mutual supervision and control by the various monasteries once more received attention. We shall see this system in full operation on the Continent. In England we have accounts of several chapters of Benedictine abbots held between 1422 and 1426, in which reports of extensive visitations were given[4]. The chapter of 1473 appointed the abbot of St Albans (Alboin, 1464–1476) to visit at Glastonbury, and the abbot of Eynsham to visit at St Albans[5].

Churchmen on all sides were eager to promote monastic reforms

---

[1] Dugdale, *Monasticon*, 'St John's,' vol. 6, p. 678.
[2] Ibid. 'Selbourne,' vol. 6, p. 510.
[3] Gasquet, A., *Henry VIII. and the English Monasteries*, 1888, vol. 1, p. 52.
[4] Wilkins, D., *Concilia*, 1737, vol. 3, pp. 413, 419, 462.
[5] Dugdale, *Monasticon*, 'St Albans,' vol. 2, p. 205.

and interfere with monastic privileges. In 1418 Pope Martin V
sent a bull to the archbishop of Canterbury bidding him hold
visitations regularly[1]. But the story of the gradual encroachment
of the Church on monastic privilege and property is less striking
in England than abroad, for the independent spirit of individual
houses was less strong, and convents generally, especially those of
women, seem to have yielded without opposition to the claims
made by energetic churchmen. Some monasteries of men, however, resented interference and maintained their rights. An episode
in this struggle deserves attention, as it reflects unfavourably on
two nunneries which were dependencies of the abbey of St Albans.
There was a long-standing jealousy between the lord abbot of St
Albans and the lord primate of Canterbury, renewed by a quarrel
between Abbot Wallingford and Archbishop Bourchier, which had
been decided in favour of the former. The abbey enjoyed exemption from episcopal visitation, not only for itself but for its
dependencies or cells, among which were the nunneries of Sopwell
and St Mary Prée. In 1489 Archbishop Morton of Canterbury
secured a Papal bull[2] which empowered him to visit all the
monasteries of his diocese, those subject to his visitation and
those exempt from it. And this, as the document says, 'not only
because the former strictness of life is abandoned...but also because
life is luxurious and dissolute.'

In consequence of the authority conferred by this bull the
primate penned a letter[3] to the abbot of St Albans containing
charges of a serious nature. After a few opening sentences it
continues in the following strain:

'... Moreover, among other grave enormities and wicked crimes
of which you are accused and for which you are noted and de-
famed, you admitted a certain married woman named Elena
Germyn, who some time ago wrongfully left her husband and
lived in adultery with another man, to be sister and nun in the
house or priory of Pré, which you hold to be in your jurisdiction;
and there you appointed her prioress notwithstanding her husband
was living and is alive now. Further, brother Thomas Sudbury,
your fellow-monk, publicly and notoriously and without inter-

---

[1] Wilkins, D., *Concilia*, 1737, vol. 3, p. 390.   [2] Ibid. 1737, vol. 3, p. 630.
[3] Ibid. Year 1490, vol. 3, p. 632. Froude without taking into consideration the
circumstances under which this letter was penned takes its contents as conclusive evidence
of the abuses of the monastic system at the time of the Reformation. Comp. *History of
England*, 1893, vol. 2, p. 304; *Life and Letters of Erasmus*, 1894, p. 18.

ference or punishment from you, associated and still associates
with this woman on terms of intimacy, like others among your
brethren and fellow-monks who had access and still have access
to her and to others elsewhere as to a brothel or house of ill fame.
And not only in the house of Pré but also in the nunnery of
Sopwell, which you contend is under your jurisdiction also, you
change the prioresses and superiors (praesidentes) again and again
at your will and caprice, deposing good and religious women and
promoting to the highest dignity the worthless and wicked, so
that religion is cast aside, virtue is neglected, and many expenses are
incurred by reprehensible practices through your introducing certain
of your brethren who are thieves and notorious villains to preside
there as guardians to manage the goods of the priories, which
more correctly speaking are wasted, and those places which were
religious are rendered and reputed profane and impious, and so
far impoverished by your doings and the doings of those with
you as to be brought to the verge of ruin.

'Similarly in dealing with other cells of monks which you say
are subject to you within the monastery of the glorious proto-
martyr Alban, you have dilapidated the common property in its
possessions and jewels; you have cut down, sold and alienated
indiscriminately copses, woods, underwood, oaks and other forest
trees to the value of 8000 marks and more; while those of your
brethren and fellow-monks, who, as is reported, are given over
to all the evils of the world, neglecting the service of God, and
openly and continually consorting with harlots and loose women
within the precincts and without, you knowingly defend instead
of punishing them; others too you protect who are covetous of
honour and promotion and bent on ministering to your cupidity,
and who steal and make away with chalices and other jewels of
the church, going so far as to extract sacrilegiously precious stones
from the very shrine of St Alban.'

This letter is dated 1490, and is addressed to William, presumably William Wallingford, as he became abbot in 1476; it
is however confidently asserted that he died in 1484. But this
date may need revision. For he was succeeded by his prior
Thomas Ramryge, who was not elected till 1492; 'at all events
this period of eight years is very obscure,' says the historian of
St Albans[1]. Concerning William Wallingford we know that the

---

[1] Newcome, P., *History of the Abbacy of St Albans*, 1793, p. 399.

chapter of Benedictine abbots held at Northampton in 1480 appointed him to visit all the monasteries situated in the diocese of Lincoln, but that he deputed two of his convent to do so[1]. His successor Ramryge wrote a book ' on the doings of the abbots, monks and benefactors of the monastery of St Albans' in which Wallingford appears of a character very different from that suggested by Morton's letter. 'Prudent and wise in the management of his abbey and resolute in the defence of its rights,' says Dugdale on the authority of Ramryge, ' he was successful too in resisting the claims of Archbishop Bourchier (Morton's predecessor) which upon appeal to Rome were decided in his favour.' He completed the high altar at St Albans and set up a printing-press in his monastery between 1480 and 1486.

In face of this evidence the language used by Morton appears somewhat violent. Unfortunately no additional information is forthcoming from the nunneries of St Mary Prée and Sopwell. We have an account rendered by the prioress Christina Basset of Prée for the year 1485–1486, four years previous to the date of Morton's letter, entries in which show that Christina Basset had succeeded Alice Wafer, who had been deposed for mismanagement of the revenues, but continued to live in the convent[2]. About Sopwell we only know that Wallingford appointed a commission in 1480 to set aside the prioress Joan Chapell on account of old age and infirmity in favour of Elizabeth Webb, one of the nuns[3].

It were idle to deny that the state of discipline in many houses was bad, but the circumstances under which Morton's letter was penned argue that the charges made in it should be accepted with some reservation.

It remains to cast a glance on the views expressed on the state of monasteries in general literature in the 15th century, from which we gather that the religious settlement was fast sinking in popular estimation. Two poems in this connection deserve especial attention, the 'Land of Cockayne,' a spirited satire on monastic life generally, written about 1430, and a poem of somewhat later date preserved in fragments only, which has been published under the title, 'Why I cannot be a nun.'

---

[1] Dugdale, *Monasticon*, 'St Albans,' vol. 2, p. 206, footnote *c*; 'the Book of Ramryge,' MS. Cotton. Nero D. VII.

[2] Dugdale, *Monasticon*, 'St Mary de Pree,' vol. 3, p. 353, charter nr 9.

[3] Ibid. 'Sopwell,' vol. 3, p. 363.

The 'Land of Cockayne'[1] describes in flowing rhyme a country 'of joy and bliss,' where flow rivers of oil, milk, honey and wine, and where stands a fair abbey of white and grey monks. Their house in accordance with the popular fancy is a delightful abode constructed out of food and sweetmeats with shingles of 'flour-cakes,' and the cloister is of crystal with a garden in which spices and flowers grow. The monks dwell here in the greatest comfort; some are old, some are young; at times they are engaged in prayer, at times they seek diversion away from home. Another abbey, 'a fair nunnery,' stands at no great distance, the inmates of which live in the like ease and carelessness. Here too there is a river of milk, the nuns wear silken clothing, and when it is hot they take a boat and go to bathe in the river. They here meet the monks and disport themselves together, throwing off all restraint.

Clever and much to the point as this poem appeared to the laymen who had come to look upon convent life as a life of idleness and self-indulgence, its historical importance is exceeded by the poem, 'Why I cannot be a nun[2].' It is generally spoken of as the production of a woman on the ground of its reflecting a woman's experiences, but there is no direct evidence on the point; its author writes as one unattached to a nunnery, and by the remark that he knows more than he chooses to tell is perhaps concealing his ignorance.

It consists of an adaptation to a different purpose of the story of the 'Ghostly Abbey,' which was peopled with personified Virtues[3], and to which reference has been made in previous chapters of this work. Here personified Vices are described as having taken possession of the abbey. The poem is divided into two parts, of which it seems doubtful through the state of the manuscript which ought to come first. As it stands printed it begins abruptly with a description of how commissioners received the charge to ride all over England to seek out nunneries and enquire into their state. They visited the houses of Kent and are represented as returning to the father of the writer, who asks them how they have sped and how the nuns fared

---

[1] 'Land of Cockayne,' in *Early English Lives of Saints*, etc., Philological Society, 1858, p. 156.

[2] 'Why I cannot be a nun,' in *Early English Lives of Saints*, etc., Philological Society, 1858, p. 138.

[3] Comp. above, pp. 339, 377.

(l. 28). When he has heard their report he tells his daughter, who wishes to become a nun, that he will have none of it. The girl is sore aggrieved; she deplores her ill-luck and continues in this strain:

> 'Then it befell on a morn of May
> In the same year as I said before,
> My pensiveness would not away
> But ever waxed more and more.
> I walked alone and wept full sore
> With sighings and with mourning.
> I said but little and thought the more
> But what I thought no man need hear.
> And in a garden I disported me
> Every day at divers hours
> To behold and for to see
> The sweet effect of April flowers.
> The fair herbs and gentle flowers
> And birds singing on every spray;
> But my longing and sadness
> For all this sport would not away.'

She kneels to Jesus, the king of heavenly bliss, and tells Him how she is destitute of good counsel and would commit her cause to Him. She then falls asleep and a fair lady appears to her, who calls her by name (Kateryne, l. 122), and who on being asked says her name is Experience, and that she has come with the help of Christ Jesus, adding 'such things as I shall show thee I trust shall set thy heart at rest.' She takes the girl by the hand and leads her through a meadow fair and green to a house of 'women regular,' a cloister, 'a house of nuns in truth of divers orders old and young, but not well governed,' for here self-will reigns instead of discipline. 'Perhaps you would like to know who was dwelling here; of some I will tell you, of others keep counsel; so I was taught when I was young,' says the writer. The first lady they encounter in the house is Dame Pride, who is held in great repute, while poor Dame Meekness sits alone and forsaken. Dame Hypocrite sits there with her book, while Dame Devout and her few companions have been put outside by Dame Sloth and Dame Vainglory. In the convent remain Dame Envy 'who can sow strife in every state,' Dame Love-Inordinate, Dame Lust, Dame Wanton and Dame Nice, all of whom take scant heed of God's service.

'Dame Chastity, I dare well say, in that convent had little cheer, she was often on the point of going her way, she was so little beloved there; some loved her in their hearts full dear, but others did not and set nothing by her, but gave her good leave to go.' Walking about under the guidance of Experience the writer also comes upon Dame Envy who bore the keys and seldom went from home. In vain she sought for Dame Patience and Dame Charity; they were not in the convent but dwelt outside 'without strife' in a chamber where good women sought their company. Meanwhile Dame Disobedient set the prioress at nought; a fact especially distressing to the writer, 'for subjects should ever be diligent in word, in will, in deed, to please their sovereign' (l. 273). Indeed she declared, when she saw no reverence, she would stay in the house no longer. She and Experience left and sat down on the grass outside the gates to discuss what they had seen. Experience explained that for the most part nuns are such as they have seen (l. 310); not all, she adds; 'some are devout, holy and blessed, and hold the right way to bliss, but some are weak, lewd, and forward; God amend what is amiss.' She passed away and the writer awakes, convinced that she certainly does not care to go and live in a nunnery. 'Peradventure,' the writer adds, 'some man will say and so it really seems to him that I soon forsook the perfect way for a fantasy or a dream, but dream it was not, nor a fantasy, but unto me welcome information (gratius mene).'

The other part of the poem advises the 'ladies dear,' who have taken the habit which is a holy thing, to let their lives correspond with their outward array. The writer enlarges on the good conversation and the virtues of the holy women who were professed in the past, and enumerates as models of virtuous living a number of women saints chiefly of English origin.

Productions such as this clearly show in what direction the estimation of religious houses and their inmates was tending. The nature of devotional pursuits and keeping the houses was not yet called into question, but apart from its religious significance the nunnery had little to recommend it. As places of residence these houses still attracted a certain number of unmarried women, and as centres of education still exerted some influence, but the high standard they had at one period maintained was a thing of the past.

§ 2. Reforms in Germany.

The history of monastic reform on the Continent previous to the Reformation supplies us with many interesting particulars both of the position of monasteries generally and of the convent life of women. Though religious settlements had been little interfered with before the Church Council at Constance, extensive reforms were undertaken subsequent to it in order to secure a return of discipline. The movement was inaugurated from within the religious orders, and led to the union of different houses into so-called congregations. But its peaceable character was soon marred by the introduction of political and party interests. Thirty years after the first convent reforms, it was no longer a question of how far the well-being and right living of monk and nun should be secured, but how far religious settlements could be made amenable to external interference and who should have the right of interfering with them.

For this complication the instability of political life is partly responsible. The authority of the Pope had greatly decreased, and, at the beginning of the 15th century, the Emperor no longer kept the balance between the contending parties. The prelates of the Church, many of whom were independent temporal princes, had succeeded in allying themselves to the impoverished, but influential, nobility. In South Germany especially the Church was becoming more and more aristocratic; birth, not merit, secured admission and promotion in the ecclesiastical body. The townships were generally opposed to the Church and the nobility; they emphatically insisted on their rights, but their combined efforts to make their influence felt in the constitution had signally failed. Apart from them stood the princes and minor potentates, who tried to coerce the nobility, in many cases succeeded in depriving their prelates of their rights, and availed themselves of the general relaxation of authority to promote their own selfish ends.

To these different representatives of power the monastery became debatable ground, where the diocesan, the township and the prince of the land in turn claimed the right of interference and where in many instances their interests clashed. The greater settlements, which held directly from the Emperor, were not drawn into the conflict; it was round the lesser ones that contention chiefly raged.

One of the most interesting movements in the direction of monastic reform is associated with the Benedictine monk Johannes von Minden († 1439) who, as representative of the abbot of the house of Reinhausen near Göttingen, was present at the general chapter of Benedictine abbots held near Constance in 1417[1]. Johannes returned to his convent burning with reformatory zeal, which his abbot and fellow-monks would not countenance. He left his convent and after many hardships was enabled by the help of a rich patroness to settle at Bursfeld, where he realized some of his ideas[2]. His views agreed with those of Johannes Rode († 1439), a Carthusian, who had become abbot of the Benedictine monastery of St Matthias at Trier, and the joint efforts of these men resulted in a scheme of mutual supervision and control of different houses by means of periodical visitations undertaken by members of the Benedictine order. The settlements which agreed to the innovation joined in a union or so-called congregation, to which Bursfeld gave its name. The union or congregation of Bursfeld was eventually joined by one hundred and thirty-six monasteries of men and sixty-four of women. The purpose of the union was not to attempt any new departure, but to guarantee the maintenance of discipline as a means of securing the return of prosperity.

The nunnery of Langendorf, near Weissenfels in Saxony, was incorporated into the union of Bursfeld, and a comprehensive scheme of rules[3], which gives us an insight into the tone and tendency of the German mediæval nunnery on the reformed plan, was drawn up for its use. The rules recall those contemporaneously drafted for the monastery of Sion in England. We have in them similar directions concerning an elaborate ritual, similar exhortations to soberness of living and gentleness of manner; the information on convent life and daily routine is equally explicit; and we hear of the different appointments inside the convent, and of the several duties of its members. There is also an exhaustive list of possible failings and crimes, followed by directions as to correction and punishment. Cats, dogs and other animals are not to be kept by the nuns, as they detract from seriousness; if a nun feels sleepy during hours, she shall ask leave to withdraw rather than fall asleep; if a nun dies of an infectious disease, her

---

[1] Möhler, J. A., *Kirchengeschichte*, edit. 1867, vol. 2, pp. 612 ff.

[2] Comp. Leuckfeld, *Antiquitates Bursfeldenses*, 1713; Pez, *Bibliotheca ascetica*, vol. 8, nrs 6 ff.

[3] Discussed in Klemm, G. F., *Die Frauen*, vol. 4, p. 181, using *Ordinarius* preserved at Dresden (MS. L. 92).

corpse shall not be carried into church, but the burial service shall take place outside. No member of the convent shall be chosen abbess unless she has attained the age of twenty-nine,—a provision which I have not come across elsewhere. The abbess has under her the same staff of officers whose duties have already been described. There is the prioress, the sub-prioress, the teacher of the novices, the cellaress, the chauntress, the sub-chauntress, the sexton, the keeper of books, the chambress, the infirmaress, the portress and others. We are told how novices made profession and how the hours of the Virgin were to be kept. We are also informed of the occupations of the nuns between hours, and learn that they were active in many ways. There are references to the transcribing of books, to binding books, to preparing parchment, and also to spinning and weaving; but the transcribing of books is pronounced the more important work, since it is more akin to spiritual interests. Further we hear about visits paid by the nuns, and about the reception of visitors. Only professed religious women were to be received on a visit inside the convent precincts; other visitors were to dwell and take their meals outside.

In the case of this nunnery it is unknown how far the convent showed readiness to join the congregation of Bursfeld, or how far it was persuaded or coerced into doing so. The movement in favour of monastic reform entered on a new stage with the advent of the zealous and influential reformer, Johann Busch († after 1479), the promoter of the congregation of Windesheim. The work of Busch is the more interesting as he has left a detailed account of it. His book 'On monastic reform' describes the changes he advocated and the means by which he effected them during a contest of over thirty years[1]. He was a native of Zwolle in the Netherlands and entered the Austin convent of Windesheim, where he attracted so much attention that he was summoned to Wittenberg in Saxony (1437), and there conducted monastic reforms at the desire of the prior. He remained in Saxony for many years, residing sometimes at one place, sometimes at another, and pursued his plans so ardently that he occasionally transcended the limits of his authority[2]. His success in persuading convents to reconsider their tenor of life and in inducing lay princes and prelates to assist him in his efforts was so great that Cardinal Cusanus, of whom we shall hear

---

[1] Busch, J., *Liber de reformatione monasteriorum* (written between 1470–1475), edit. Grube, 1887.

[2] *Deutsche Allgemeine Biographie*, article 'Busch, Joh.'

more, pronounced him especially fitted to act as a monastic reformer (1451). His book contains a detailed account of his work
in connection with about twenty nunneries. His great merit and
that of the congregation of Windesheim was the introduction of
German devotional books.

From these and other descriptions we gather that many
nunneries willingly accepted the proposed changes in so far as they
were designed to raise the standard of teaching and to improve
the system of discipline, but that opposition was made where the
changes tended to interfere with the position and prestige of the
settlement. In some cases a compromise was effected by the
energetic and intelligent conduct of the lady superior; in others
the direct refusal of the nuns to conform resulted in open force
being brought to bear on them. Scenes were enacted which recall
the turbulence of early Christian times, and show how strong a
sense of independence still lived in some convents.

Among the Austin nunneries which gave Busch endless trouble
was that of Derneburg, near Hildesheim, where he was appointed
to visit as father confessor between 1440 and 1442[1]. The nuns
there were in the habit of dining out continually, and when exception was taken to this, gave as an excuse that relatives and
friends were always ready to entertain them at meals, but refused
to furnish contributions in kind towards the support of the convent.
Busch got over this difficulty by pleading with the lay people, but
his action in the matter still further roused the rebellious spirit of
the nuns. On one occasion his life was attempted at their instigation; on another, when he went to inspect their cellar, they locked
him in and left him there. As a consequence of this he refused
from that time forward to be the first to go on any tour of inspection. His efforts to impress these nuns were in vain, and
finally he asked for the assistance of the bishop of Hildesheim and
the abbot of the Cistercian house of Marienrode; as a consequence
the rebels were conveyed away from Derneburg to other convents,
and their house was given into the hands of Cistercian nuns.
Similar difficulties occurred at Wennigsen, at Mariensee and at
Werder, where the Duke of Hannover interfered in the most
arbitrary manner[2]. At Wienhausen the abbess and convent refused to conform to the rule of St Benedict, though the additional
authority of their diocesan and of Duke Otto of Brunswick was

---

[1] Busch, *Liber de reformatione monasteriorum*, 'Derneburg,' p. 588.
[2] Ibid. 'Wennigsen,' 'Mariensee,' 'Werder' pp. 555 ff.

brought to bear on them[1]. Forcible measures were resorted to in this case also. The abbess was deposed and she and her nuns were carried away in a chariot to other nunneries, and nuns from the reformed house of Derneburg were installed in their place.

At the Cistercian nunnery of St Georg, near Halle, the nuns at first declared that they were exempt from the visits of the diocesan, and refused admission to the delegates. After prolonged opposition they yielded to Busch[2]. At Heiningen the nuns pleaded poverty as an excuse for staying away from home[3]. Many settlements complained of poverty and insufficient revenue, among which was Frankenberg, near Goslar[4]. The nuns of Dorstad earned money by taking pupils from outside the precincts[5], and other houses, among them that of Neuwerk, received girls and boarded and educated them. Busch however forbade their doing so on the ground that intercourse with secular interests was harmful. At Neuwerk, which was a Cistercian nunnery at Erfurt[6], the wealth of the community in vessels, vestments, and books was quite a revelation to Busch. The house owned thirty books of devotion (the convent at the time consisted of thirty inmates), a number which appeared to Busch so considerable that he did not insist on the nuns adopting the service-book in use at Windesheim, as this change would have rendered their books useless to them.

The nuns at Neuwerk readily accepted the proposed reforms, and received nuns from the reformed nunnery of Heiningen who dwelt with them for three years and helped them to restore their system of religious discipline and teaching. The abbess Armengard von Rheden, of the wealthy Benedictine nunnery of Fischbeck on the Weser[7], also agreed to receive nuns from a reformed house into her establishment as teachers.

Full details are preserved of the reform of the nunnery of Marienberg[8] near Helmstädt in Saxony, the prioress of which, Helena von Iltzen, hearing of the work of Busch, sought his assistance in matters of reform. Her house is said to have belonged to no order in particular. When she applied to Busch he was resident provost (after 1459) of the Austin canonry of Sülte near Hildesheim. He travelled to Bronopie, a nunnery

---

[1] Busch, *Liber de reformatione monasteriorum*, 'Wienhausen,' p. 629.

[2] Ibid. 'St Georg in Halle,' p. 568.   [3] Ibid. 'Heiningen,' p. 600.

[4] Ibid. 'Frankenberg,' p. 607.   [5] Ibid. 'Dorstad,' p. 644.

[6] Ibid. 'Neuwerk,' p. 609.   [7] Ibid. 'Fischbeck,' p. 640.

[8] Ibid. 'Marienberg,' p. 618.

situated outside Campen on the confines of Holland, to consult with the prioress, who accordingly deputed two nuns of her convent, Ida and Tecla, and one lay sister Aleydis, to repair with him to Marienberg. Of the two nuns Ida had been chosen for her knowledge of religious service, Tecla for her powers of instruction. Busch describes how he travelled across Germany with these women in a waggon drawn by four horses, and how on their arrival at Marienberg Ida was appointed to act as sub-prioress, and Tecla as teacher, and how the prioress of the house reserved to herself the management of temporal affairs only. Tecla is described as well versed in grammar (grammatica competenter docta); she instructed the inmates of the house in scholastic knowledge (scientiis scholasticalibus) with such success that her pupils after three years were able to read Holy Writ, and readily composed letters and missives in correct Latin (litteras sive missas in bona latina magistraliter dictarent). 'I have seen and examined these myself,' says Busch.

After three years the illness of Ida made the nuns desirous of returning to their own convent, and Busch again undertook to escort them. A proof of the affection they had won during their stay and of the regret that was felt at their departure is afforded by the letters which passed between them and their friends. They were staying for some nights at the nunnery of Heiningen on their journey home when two letters reached them. In one the nuns wrote describing their grief. 'When we see your empty places in the choir, the refectory, and the dormitory, we are filled with sorrow and weep.' And they wish that the distance which separates them were not so great, then at least they might go to visit their friends. When Tecla's pupils (the letter says) entered the schoolroom for their lessons on the Saturday, they wept so much that the prioress, who was in great grief herself, was constrained to try to comfort them. The other letter, a short one specially addressed to Tecla, was written by these pupils: this accompanied the longer letter, and in it they assured her of their continued admiration and devotion. Ida, Tecla and Aleydis in reply sent two letters to Marienberg. A longer one was addressed by them to the convent collectively, and a shorter one by Tecla to her pupils, in which she praises them for having written such a good Latin letter and assures them that she is glad to think of her stay with them, since it has been productive of such good results.

The nunnery of Marienberg, which had so readily accepted reforms, acted as advocate of similar changes to other houses. Busch tells us that the nunnery of Marienborn situated not far from it, and the nunnery at Stendal in Brandenburg, accepted reforms at its instigation[1].

In the records of Busch comparatively few charges of a coarse nature are brought against nunneries, but he adds an account of two nuns who were in apostasy, and who were persuaded by him to return to their convents. One had left her convent and had adopted lay clothing[2]; the story of the other, Sophie, an illegitimate daughter of Wilhelm, duke of Brunswick, reads like a romance[3]. The girl had been stowed away in the convent of Mariensee by her relatives for convenience, but indifferent to vows unwillingly accepted, she ran away and for seven years lived in the world, tasting few of the sweets of life and much of its bitterness. At last, broken in spirit by the loss of her child, she was persuaded by Busch to come and live in the convent of Derneburg, the members of which received her with tender pity for her sufferings and treated her with loving care. Finally she agreed to return to the nunnery she had originally left, glad of the peace which she found there.

Some of the nunneries on which pressure was brought to bear by the monastic reformers altogether ceased to exist. The historian of the diocese of Speyer (Rheinbayern) tells us that the Benedictine nunnery of Schönfeld was interfered with in 1443 and fell into decay, and that its property was appropriated; that the Cistercian nunnery of Ramsen also ceased to exist, owing to feuds between Count Johann II of Nassau and the abbot of Morimund, who both claimed the right of interference; and that the dissolution of Kleinfrankenthal, a settlement of Austin nuns situated in the same diocese, was declared in 1431 by Pope Eugenius IV on account of the evil ways of the nuns[4].

The historian of the reforms undertaken in the diocese of Trier notifies many important changes[5]. He considers that the nuns in many convents had drifted away from the former strictness of

---

[1] Busch, *Liber de reformatione monasteriorum*, 'Marienborn,' 'Stendal,' p. 622.

[2] Ibid. pp. 664 ff.　　　　　　　　[3] Ibid. pp. 659 ff.

[4] Remling, F. X., *Urkundl. Geschichte der Abteien und Klöster in Rheinbayern*, 1836, 'Schönfeld,' vol. 1, p. 165; 'Ramsen,' vol. 1, p. 263; 'Kleinfrankenthal,' vol. 2, p. 79.

[5] Marx, J., *Geschichte des Erzstifts Trier*, 1860, vol. 3, p. 466 (Benedictine nunneries, pp. 457–511, Cistercian nunneries, pp. 579–593).

discipline and lived as Austin canonesses, returning to the world
if they chose to get married. Many of these settlements now
accepted stricter rules of life, and among them were the nunnery
of Marienberg (diocese of Trier), the abbess of which, Isengard
von Greiffenklau (✝ 1469), had come under the influence of Johannes Rode—and Oberwerth, which owed reform to its abbess
Adelheid Helchen (1468–1505).

On the other hand Elisabeth von Seckendorff, abbess of the
time-honoured nunnery of St Walburg at Eichstätt, refused to
see that a changed condition of things demanded reform. The
bishop of Eichstätt made his power felt; she was deposed, and
Sophie was summoned from the nunnery of St Maria at Cöln, and
made abbess in her stead (1456–1475)[1].

We have detailed accounts of reforms in South Germany from
the pen of another contemporary writer, Felix Fabri (✝ 1502),
a Dominican friar of Ulm[2]. He télls us how Elisabeth Krelin
(✝ 1480), abbess of the important Cistercian nunnery, Heggbach,
a woman of great intelligence and strong character, effected reforms
in her house on her sole responsibility. These changes were
productive of such good results that many nuns left the houses
to which they belonged and came to live under her. Gredanna
von Freyberg (✝ 1481), abbess of the ancient and wealthy Benedictine nunnery of Urspring, hearing of these changes, came on
a visit to Heggbach, where she made friends with the abbess, and
when she left she was bent on carrying out similar changes in her
own convent. But here she met with opposition. Her nuns, who
were members of the nobility, aware that the changes advocated
meant interference with the liberty they enjoyed, divided for and
against her, and those who were against her appealed to their
relatives for support. Gredanna in vain asked for help from the
abbot of the monastery of St Georg in the Black Forest to which
her house was allied; he dared not interfere, and it was only when
the archduchess Mechthild of Austria called upon him to do so,
that he summoned nuns from the reformed nunnery of St Walburg
at Eichstätt and with them and some monks came to Urspring.
But the rebellious nuns, nothing daunted, shut themselves up in
the outlying buildings of the infirmary, which they barricaded;
the soldiers were called out but from a religious dread refused

---

[1] Brusch, C., *Chronol. Mon. Germ.*, 1682, p. 508.
[2] Fabri, F., *De Civitate Ulmensi*, edit. Veesenmeyer, Liter. Verein, Stuttgart, 1889,
pp. 180 ff.

to attack them. Nothing remained short of placing these 'amazons' as Fabri calls them in a state of siege; the pangs of hunger at last forced them to yield. The reforms which Gredanna then effected were productive of such beneficial results that the house regained a high standing.

The reform of Söflingen near Ulm[1], an account of which we also owe to Fabri, affords one more of many examples of the tyranny of interference. This house belonged to the order of St Clare, and like all the houses of this order was subject to the Franciscan friars, who had the exclusive right of control over them.

The Franciscans of Ulm having accepted reforms in consequence of the papal bull of 1484, the town authorities of Ulm called upon the nuns to do the same, and Fabri relates how 'a number of burghers accompanied by religious doctors of various orders, by noblemen, their followers, and by members of the town-gilds, armed and unarmed, marched upon Söflingen in a great crowd, as though to fight for the glory of God.' They conveyed with them a new abbess and a number of nuns of the reformed order of St Clare, whom they meant to instal at Söflingen. But here they were met by open defiance. The lady superior, Christine Strölin († 1489), shouted that she could not and would not be deposed, and her nuns vented their indignation in threats and blasphemy. Not by promises, not by threats, could they be persuaded to leave their lady superior. They rushed through the buildings, snatched up coffers and boxes, and followed Christine out of the house. Their loyalty and unanimity in defending their rights awaken feelings in their favour which are confirmed when we find the bishop of the diocese disapproving of the forcible measures resorted to by the citizens; endless quarrels and discussions ensued. The abbess Christine, after staying at various places, returned to Söflingen and was reinstated in her rights, on condition of adopting certain reforms; some of her nuns came back with her, but others refused to do so and went to live in other nunneries.

Details concerning the 'reform' of one other nunnery are worth recording because they show how a representative of the Church openly attempted to curtail the privileges of a powerful nunnery. The struggle of the nunnery of Sonnenburg in the Tyrol with the Cardinal Legate Nicolas Cusanus († 1464), bishop of Brixen, has been the subject of close historical enquiry, as its importance far

---

[1] Fabri, F., *De Civitate Ulmensi*, pp. 202 ff.

exceeds the interests of those immediately concerned[1]. In this struggle the representative of the Pope came into open conflict with the prince of the land, Sigmund, archduke of Austria and duke of Tyrol, who defied the Cardinal and obliged him to flee the country and seek refuge at Rome. The quarrel which began over the nunnery ended with the ban of excommunication being pronounced against Sigmund, and with his appeal to a Church Council against the authority of the Papal Curia.

Sonnenburg was the wealthiest and most influential Benedictine settlement of women in the land. It was in existence as early as the 11th century and had extensive powers of jurisdiction which repeatedly brought its abbess into conflict with her rival in power, the bishop of Brixen. Against him she had sought and secured the protection of the archduke; but at the time of the appointment of Cusanus as bishop, the settlement of a matter of temporal administration between herself and the bishopric was pending. Cusanus had obtained from Rome exceptional powers of monastic visitation, powers such as were conferred at a later date on the Cardinal Legate Ximenes in Spain and on the Cardinal Legate Wolsey in England. By virtue of these powers Cusanus at once transferred the affair with the abbess from the temporal domain to the spiritual, and in his character of monastic visitor and reformer sent a manifesto to the abbess and nuns to the effect that after the coming festival of Corpus Christi they were on no account to absent themselves from the convent or to receive visitors. The abbess, Verena von Stuben, and her convent, which consisted at the time of seven nuns, ignored this command, obedience to which would have cut off intercourse with the archduke and made attention to the pending matter of business impossible. More closely pressed, the abbess gave an evasive answer and lodged a complaint with Sigmund, in which she and the convent declared themselves ready to accept the desired change (p. 66[2]) but said that they were convinced that such a course at the present moment would be fatal to their position. It was clear to them that Cusanus was bent on their ruin. The archduke to whom they appealed declared that the prelate was transgressing the limits of his authority, and intimated to him that he would not have the temporalities of the

---

[1] Jäger, A., *Der Streit des Cardinals N. von Cusa mit dem Herzoge Sigmund von Oesterreich*, 1861, 2 vols. (the struggle over Sonnenburg is in vol. 1).

[2] Ibid. vol. 1 (page references in the text throughout this section are to the above account).

house interfered with,—a decision to which Cusanus for the moment deferred.

The documents relating to the further progress of this quarrel are numerous. A kind of chronicle was kept at Sonnenburg written partly by the nuns, partly by the abbess, into which copies of over two hundred letters and documents were inserted. It bears the title 'On what occurred between Cardinal Cusanus and the abbess Verena,' and is now in the library at Innsbruck[1].

Foiled in his first attempt to gain control over Sonnenburg, Cusanus now devoted his attention to other religious communities. He took under his protection a number of recluses, called sylvan sisters, 'Waldschwestern' (p. 63), and having secured further powers from Rome, attempted to interfere with the convent of Minoresses or Poor Clares at Brixen (p. 87). But these nuns, though they were low-born and uneducated, were as stubborn as their high-born and learned sisters on the Sonnenburg; Verena's conduct may have given them the courage to oppose the Cardinal. Their lady superior was forcibly removed at his instigation, but they appealed against him at Rome, and though their opposition was censured, Cusanus was directed to place the matter in the hands of the Franciscans at Nürnberg, who declared themselves willing to institute the desired reforms. Nuns from the convent of St Clare at Nürnberg were despatched to Brixen, and the tone of the house was raised without its privileges being forfeited.

On the strength of his increased visitatorial powers Cusanus (1453) returned to the charge at Sonnenburg, but its inmates would give no official declaration of their intentions (p. 90). Accordingly the bishop of Eichstätt was summoned to hold a visitation there, but he was refused admission by the nuns. However a second deputation came which could not be warded off, and the convent gave the desired information; the result of which was that injunctions were forwarded confining the authority of the abbess to the control of the nuns, and practically despoiling her of her property. Strict seclusion was to be observed, and the house was to be furnished with a key, which was to be given to a person appointed by Cusanus. The management of the monastic property was to be in the hands of a bailiff who was to render account to the bishop direct, not to the abbess. Scant wonder that the abbess Verena, indignant at the order and despairing of help from without, offered to resign. Her offer delighted

---

[1] Jäger, A., *Der Streit des Cardinals N. von Cusa* etc., 1861, Vorwort, p. x.

the legate, who forthwith despatched Afra von Velseck to undertake the management of affairs at the convent, with the command
that she was to take no step without previously consulting him
(p. 94). It seems that Cusanus entertained the idea of appropriating the temporalities of the nunnery altogether, and transferring
them to the use of monks, who were to be subject to his friend and
ally, the abbot of Tegernsee (p. 95). He afterwards gave up the
plan, 'since the nobility,' as he wrote (p. 127), 'look upon this house
as a home for their daughters and are opposed to my plan.'

At this juncture things took an unexpected turn. Verena
consulted with her friends in the matter of the pension on which
she was to retire (p. 109); and Cusanus was angered by the objections they raised to his proposals. There was a stormy interchange of letters between him and the abbess (p. 124), which
ended in Verena's resuming her authority, and in Afra's deposition. Cusanus sent an armed escort to fetch away his protégée
and threatened excommunication to the convent. In vain was a
complaint against him sent by the nuns to Rome; Cusanus had
anticipated them. The Pope censured the nuns' conduct, affirmed
Cusanus' authority, and cast imputations on the character of the
abbess, which were indignantly resented in a second letter forwarded to the Pope by the nuns.

The archduke Sigmund now tried to interfere in the interest
of peace. A second visitation was undertaken, and a list of injunctions was drawn up for the nuns (p. 133). Among these we
note that nuns from a reformed convent were to come and live as
teachers at Sonnenburg; the abbess was henceforth to have no
separate household, she was forbidden to go out without asking
leave from the diocesan, she was not to go on pilgrimages or visit
health resorts, and she was not to be present at weddings.

But the abbess and the convent refused to accept these injunctions, and they were accordingly placed under an interdict.
The hospital belonging to the house and its property were confiscated, the chaplains were forbidden to celebrate mass, and the
ban of excommunication was pronounced against the nuns and
was reiterated by the priest of the nearest church on feast days
and on Sundays. This was a great humiliation to the nuns and
helped to lower them in general estimation.

Sigmund was absent at the time. Soon after his return Pope
Nicolas V, the patron of Cusanus, died (1455), and his successor
Calixtus III warned the Cardinal against pushing things to

extremes (p. 161). Sigmund also pleaded in favour of the nuns
that they were staying within precincts, and that Verena was an
estimable woman. Cusanus in answer contended that what he
had done, he had done with the sanction of Rome, and that he
had excommunicated and deposed Verena solely on account of
her disobedience ; and he then acknowledged that she was a
thoroughly honest and excellent manager. In his letters to the
abbot of Tegernsee, written about the same time, he speaks of
Verena as a very Jezebel who is full of wiles against him (p. 153).
' Maybe she will pretend obedience to deceive me,' he wrote among
other things, ' but the devil of pride has her soul in his possession
and will prevent her from really humbling herself.' But the relations between Sigmund and his bishop were becoming strained
in other respects. The first breach of the peace occurred when
the abbess came to Innsbruck to seek support. Cusanus despatched
a deacon to prevent her being received, and Sigmund had the deacon
cast into prison.

The nuns on the Sonnenburg were in a sorry plight. They
dared not leave the house, the usual tithes were not brought to
them and there had been no ingathering of the produce of their
own harvest, for Cusanus threatened excommunication to anyone
having intercourse with them or looking after their interests. They
were nigh upon starvation (p. 277), and had recourse to an unlawful step. They took a band of armed men into their service and
directed them to gather the tribute due to them. But the soldiers
sent by the archbishop put these men to flight and then stormed the
cloister. The nuns fled into the adjoining woods and found refuge
in a house. ' But we were betrayed and had to fly again,' they
wrote in their chronicle ; ' during three days we were pursued and
sought by the troops, repeatedly we were so near to them that we
saw them and they saw us. But the Virgin Mary helped us to
escape from them.' Afra von Velseck had been put in possession
of their empty house, but Cusanus could not support her ; fearful
of Sigmund he had fled from his bishopric and repaired to Rome.
The archduke conducted the nuns back and begged Verena to
resign, offering her a house near Innsbruck (p. 309). An envoy
was accordingly despatched to Rome to proffer terms of submission
to Cusanus if only he would take the ban of excommunication
from the nuns. The bishop at last yielded to the Pope's command, though with a sufficiently bad grace. ' I send you a copy
of Verena's letter to me,' he wrote to the envoy Natz, ' she tells

lies as usual.' And on the margin of her letter, as a comment on her declaration that she had repeatedly sought absolution, he added the words, 'this is a lie.'

Penance in its extreme form was undergone by the convent (p. 311), but as Cusanus persistently denied to Sigmund the right of appointing a new abbess, many letters passed before the conditions of peace were settled and ratified. The correspondence, as Jäger remarks (p. 315), throws an interesting light on the character of the women concerned. Verena, who throughout maintained a proud dignity, retired from the convent on a pension; Afra, who had resorted to various intrigues, finally renounced all claims, and Barbara Schöndorfer came over from Brixen and was installed as abbess.

Thus ended the quarrel about the privileges of Sonnenburg, which lasted six years and led to the curtailment of many of its rights. The story proves the inability of convents to preserve their independence, and shows how their weakness was made the excuse for interference from without to the detriment of the abbess in her position as landowner.

It remains to enquire how far the improvements effected in monastic life by peaceful and by forcible means were lasting, and in what position the nunnery stood at the beginning of the 16th century.

Some valuable information is given on the general state of monasticism by a number of addresses delivered by Tritheim, abbot of Sponheim († 1516), before the assembled chapter of Benedictine abbots between 1490 and 1492[1]. Tritheim takes high rank among the older humanists; he was an enlightened man according to the notions of his age, and collected a wonderful and comprehensive library of books in many languages at Sponheim. His interest in necromancy afterwards brought reproach on him and he left his convent, but at the time when he pleaded before the assembled abbots he was full of enthusiasm for his order and full of regrets concerning it. In his address 'on the ruin of the Benedictine order,' he pointed out how effectually the Bursfeld and other congregations had worked in the past, but the beneficial results they effected had passed away and little of their influence remained. If only those who are vowed to religion, says Tritheim, would care more for learning, which has been made so much more

---

[1] Tritheim, *Opera pia et spiritualia*, edit. Busaeus, 1604, 'Orationes,' pp. 840-916.

accessible by the invention of printing, the outlook would not be so utterly hopeless.

In these addresses Tritheim takes no account of nunneries, but we can discover his attitude towards nuns in an address to a convent[1], the keynote of which is that the women assembled there should cultivate love, lowliness and patience under tribulation. The address is gentle and dignified, but it shows that Tritheim, in common with other men of the time, attached importance to nunneries chiefly for the piety they cultivated. His belief in this respect is shared by the zealous reformer Geiler von Kaisersberg († 1500), who preached many sermons before the nuns of the convents of St Mary Magdalen (Reuerinnen), and of St Stephan at Strasburg, and who likewise saw the beauty of a nun's vocation only in her devotional and contemplative attitude. We gather from his sermons, many of which are preserved in the form in which they were written out by nuns[2], that a clear line of demarcation existed in his mind between reformed and unreformed convents, and that while emphatic in denouncing the ungodly ways of the inmates of unreformed houses, life in a reformed house was comparable in his eyes to Paradise. Geiler's efforts as a reformer were so far crowned by success that the convent of St Mary Magdalen to which he had devoted his efforts, outlived the attacks to which it was exposed at the time of the Reformation.

The fact that Tritheim insists only on the devotional attitude of nuns is the more noticeable as he visited at the convent of Seebach, the abbess of which, Richmondis van der Horst, was equally praised for her own abilities and the superior tone she maintained in her convent. For instances were not wanting which show that intellectual tastes were still strong in some nunneries and that women living the convent life were themselves authors and took a certain amount of interest in the revival of classical learning, as we shall see later.

Thus Butzbach (called Premontanus, † 1526), a pupil of Hegius, who became a monk at Laach and was an admirer of Tritheim, was in correspondence with Aleydis Ruyskop († 1507), a nun at Rolandswerth, who had written seven homilies on St Paul in Latin and translated a German treatise on the mass into Latin. He dedicated to her his work on 'Distinguished learned women,' which he took from the work of the Italian Benedictine Jacopo of Ber-

---

[1] Tritheim, *Opera*, etc., Epist. nr 3, p. 921 (written 1485).

[2] Geiler, *Predigten Teutsch*, 1508; *Seelen-Paradies*, 1510, etc.

gamo, but from delicacy of feeling he omitted what Jacopo had inserted in praise of women's influence as wives and mothers[1]. In this work Butzbach compares Aleydis to Hrotsvith, to Hildegard and to Elisabeth of Schönau.   He also wrote to Gertrud von Büchel, a nun who practised the art of painting at Rolandswerth, and he refers to Barbara Dalberg, niece of the bishop of Worms, who was a nun at Marienberg, and to Ursula Cantor, who, he declares, was without equal in her knowledge of theology.

But in spite of these instances and others, a growing indifference is apparent, both among the advocates of the new culture and in the outer world generally, to the intellectual occupation of women, and the training of girls.   In their far-reaching plans for an improved system of education the humanists leave girls out of count, and dwell on their qualities of heart rather than on their qualities of mind.   That the training of the mental faculties must be profitable in all cases for women does not occur to them, though the idea is advanced with regard to men.

At the close of the 15th century Wimpheling († 1528) wrote a work on matters of education entitled *Germania*.   It is a conception of ideal citizenship, and in it he insists that the burghers of Strasburg must let their sons receive a higher education and learn Latin in the 'gymnasium,' of which he gives his plan, regardless of the vocation they intend to embrace.   Only a short chapter[2] of the book refers to the training of girls.   Their parents are cautioned against placing them in nunneries, which in the writer's mind are little better than brothels.   He advises their being trained at home for domestic life and made to spin and weave like the daughters of Augustus.

Similar tendencies are reflected in the works of Erasmus († 1536). His Colloquies or Conversations introduce us to a number of women under various aspects ; and the want of purpose in convent life, the danger of masterfulness in wives, the anomalous position of loose women, and the general need there was of cultivating domestic qualities, are all in turn discussed.

Two Colloquies turn on the convent life of women.   In the first[3] a girl of seventeen declares herself averse to matrimony, and

---

[1] Information on those works of Butzbach which are not published is given in the second supplementary volume, pp. 439 ff. of Hutten, U. v., *Opera*, edit. Böcking, 1857.

[2] Wimpheling, *Germania*, transl. Martin, E., 1885, ch. 77.

[3] Erasmus, *Colloquies*, transl. Bailey, edit. Johnson, 1878, 'The Virgin averse to Matrimony,' vol. 1, p. 225.

expresses her intention of becoming a nun. The man who argues
with her represents to her that if she be resolved to keep her
maidenhood, she can do so by remaining with her parents and
need not make herself from a free woman into a slave. ' If you
have a mind to read, pray or sing,' he says, ' you can go into your
chamber as much and as often as you please. When you have
enough of retirement, you can go to church, hear anthems, prayers,
and sermons, and if you see any matron or virgin remarkable for
piety in whose company you may get good, or any man who is
endowed with singular probity from whom you can gain for your
bettering, you can have their conversation, and choose the preacher
who preaches Christ most purely. When once you are in the
cloister, all these things, which are of great assistance in promoting
true piety, you lose at once.' And he enlarges on the formalities
of convent life, ' which of themselves signify nothing to the advancement of piety and make no one more acceptable in the eyes of
Christ, who only looks to purity of mind.' The girl asks him if
he be against the institution of monastic life. He replies, ' By no
means. But as I will not persuade anyone against it who is
already in it, so I would undoubtedly caution all young women,
especially those of a generous temper, not to precipitate themselves
unadvisedly into that state from which there is no getting out
afterwards, and the more so because their chastity is more in danger
in the cloister than out of it, and you may do whatever is done
there as well at home.'

His arguments however are in vain ; the girl goes into a
convent. But the next Colloquy, called the ' Penitent Virgin[1],'
describes how she changed her mind and came out again. She
was intimidated by the nuns through feigned apparitions, and when
she had been in the house six days she sent for her parents and
declared that she would sooner die than remain there.

Another Colloquy[2] shows how masterfulness in a wife destroyed
all possibility of domestic peace and happiness ; yet another[3] how
a woman of loose life was persuaded to adopt other ways on purely
reasonable grounds. Again we have a young mother who is persuaded to tend her child herself, since the promotion of its bodily
welfare does much towards saving its soul[4]. The most striking

---

[1] Erasmus, *Colloquies*, ' The Penitent Virgin,' vol. 1, p. 237.
[2] Ibid. ' The Uneasy Wife,' vol. 1, p. 241.
[3] Ibid. ' The Young Man and Harlot,' vol. 1, p. 291.
[4] Ibid. ' The Lying-in Woman,' vol. 1, p. 441.

illustration however of the fact that in the eyes of Erasmus the position of woman was changing is afforded by the 'Parliament of Women[1],' in which a great deal of talk leads to no result. Cornelia opens and closes the sitting, and urges that it is advisable that women should reconsider their position, for men, she says, are excluding women from all honourable employments and making them 'into their laundresses and cooks, while they manage everything according to their own pleasure.' But the assembled women dwell on irrelevant detail and harp on the distributions of class in a manner which shows that those qualities which made their participation in public affairs possible or advisable were utterly wanting among them. Erasmus passes no remarks derogatory to women as such, and yet he leaves us to infer that they cannot do better than devote their attention exclusively to domestic concerns.

Judging by his writings and those of others who were active in the cause of progress, there was a growing feeling that the domestic virtues needed cultivation. A change in the position of women was not only imminent but was felt to be desirable, and probably it was in conformity with what women themselves wished. Both in England and on the Continent the idea that virginity was in itself pleasing to God was no longer in the foreground of the moral consciousness of the age; it was felt that the duties of a mother took higher rank, and that the truest vocation of woman was to be found in the circle of home. This view, as we shall see presently, tallied with the views taken by the Protestant reformers and prepared the way for the dissolution of nunneries.

[1] Erasmus, *Colloquies*, 'The Assembly or Parliament of Women,' vol. 2, p. 203.

CHAPTER XII.

THE DISSOLUTION.

'In church, chapell and priory
Abby, hospitall and nunry,
    Sparing nother man nor woman,
Coopes, albes, holy ornamentes,
Crosses, chalecys, sensurs and rentes,
Convertyng all to usys prophane.'

The Blaspheming English Lutherans, verse 33.

'The Abbaies went doune because of there pride,
And made the more covetus riche for a tyme,
There leivenges dispercid one everi syde,
Where wonce was somme praier, now placis for swyne.'

Quoted by Furnival from Douce MS 365, l. 95.

§ 1. The Dissolution in England.

THE movement of the 16th century commonly spoken of as the Reformation was the forcible manifestation of a revolution in thought which had long been preparing. This period may fitly be likened to a watershed between the socialistic tendencies of the Middle Ages and the individualistic tendencies which have mainly prevailed since. It forms the height which limits average modern conceptions, but which can be made the standpoint from which a more comprehensive view of things past and present becomes possible. Like other great epochs in history it is characterised by a sense of assurance, aspiration, and optimism,—and by wasted possibilities which give its study an ever renewed interest. The political, social, and intellectual changes which accompanied the Reformation are especially interesting nowadays when the standards which were then formulated are felt to be no longer final. The progressive thought of to-day, heretical though the assertion may sound to some, has become markedly insensible to the tenets which the reformers of the 16th century propounded and in which Protestantism found its strength and its safeguard. While paying due deference to the courage of the men who heralded what was advance if measured by such needs as they realised, the thinker of to-day dwells not so much on the factors of civilisation which those men turned to account as on those which they disregarded ;—he is attracted by Erasmus, not by Luther, and looks more to him who worked in the interest of reform than to him who worked in the interest of the Reformation.

Among the important social changes effected by the Reformation the dissolution of the monasteries forms a small but a significant feature, a feature pregnant with meaning if considered in the light of the changing standards of family and sex morality. For those who attacked the Church of Rome in her fundamentals, while differing in points of doctrine, were at one in the belief that the state of morality needed amendment, and that marriage supplied the means of effecting the desired change. In open antagonism to principles which formed the groundwork of monasticism, they declared celibacy odious and the vow of chastity contradictory to scriptural teaching and in itself foolish and presumptuous.

The language in which Luther, Bullinger and Becon inculcated these principles is often offensive to modern ears. Their views are wanting in good taste, but consistency cannot be denied them. For these men were logical in condemning the unmarried state at every point, attacking it equally in the priest, the monk, the nun and the professed wanton. The changed attitude towards loose women has repeatedly been referred to in the course of this work, and it has been pointed out how such women, at one time not without power, had been steadily sinking in general estimation. Society, bent on having a clear line drawn between them and other women, had interfered with them in many ways, and had succeeded in stamping them as a class, to its own profit and to their disadvantage. But even at the close of the Middle Ages these women retained certain rights, such as that of having free quarters in the town, which the advocates of the new faith openly attacked and summarily swept away. Zealous if somewhat brutal in the cause of an improved morality, they maintained that marriage was the most acceptable state before God and that a woman had no claim to consideration except in her capacity as wife and mother.

The calling of the nun was doomed to fall a sacrifice to this

teaching. Her vocation was in antagonism to the doctrines of
the party of progress, and where not directly attacked was regarded with a scarcely less fatal indifference. It has been shown
that great efforts were made before the Reformation to reform
life in nunneries, but various obstacles, and among them a growing
indifference to the intellectual training and interests of women,
were in the way of their permanent improvement. The nun was
chiefly estimated by her devotional pursuits, and when the rupture
came with Rome and these devotional pursuits were declared
meaningless, individuals who were driven from their homes might
be pitied, and voices here and there might be raised deploring the
loss of the possibilities secured by the convent, but no active efforts
were made to preserve the system, nothing was attempted to save
an institution, the *raison d'être* of which had vanished.

Previous to the Reformation the efforts of churchmen on the
Continent to reform convent life had led in several instances to the
disbanding of a convent. In England like results ensued from
the conduct of churchmen, who in their efforts to regenerate society
by raising the tone of religion, rank with the older humanists
abroad. These men had no intention of interfering with the
institution of monasticism as such, but were bent on removing
certain abuses. Among them were John Alcock, bishop of Ely,
Fisher, bishop of Rochester, and Cardinal Wolsey; they appropriated a number of decayed convents on the plea of promoting
religious education, and their action may be said to have paved
the way towards a general dissolution.

Among the monasteries dissolved by them were several belonging to nuns, and the fact is noteworthy that wherever the property
of women was appropriated, it was appropriated to the use of
men. Considering that the revenues of these houses had been
granted for women and had been administered by women for centuries, this fact appears somewhat regrettable from the woman's
point of view. But no blame attaches on this account to the men,
for their attitude was in keeping with progressive thought generally
and was shared by women themselves. Thus Margaret Beaufort
(† 1509) the mother of Henry VII, whose college foundations
have given her lasting fame, seems never to have been struck by
the thought that advantages might accrue from promoting education among women also. She founded Christ's College at Cambridge, planned the foundation there of St John's, and instituted
divinity professorships both at Oxford and at Cambridge. But

her efforts, in which she was supported by Fisher, bishop of Rochester, were entirely devoted to securing an improved education for the clergy.

The nunnery of St Radegund's at Cambridge was among the first establishments appropriated in the interest of the higher religious education of men on the plea of decay and deterioration. It had supported a convent of twelve nuns as late as 1460, but in 1496 it was dissolved. The change was effected by John Alcock, bishop of Ely († 1500), a man of liberal spirit who ranks high among contemporary ecclesiastics. The king's licence[1] for the dissolution of the house contains words to the effect that it had fallen into decay owing to neglect, improvidence, and the dissolute dispositions of the prioress and convent, which were referable to the close proximity of Cambridge. The house had only two inmates, of whom one had been professed elsewhere and the other was a girl. The bishop asked leave to declare the house dissolved in order to appropriate its possessions and revenues to the foundation of a college of one master (magister), six fellows (socii) and a certain number of students (scolares). These numbers show that the property of the house was not inconsiderable. The sanction of Pope Alexander III having been obtained[2], the nunnery of St Radegund was transformed into Jesus College, Cambridge[3].

This instance paved the way for others. The suppression of the smaller monasteries for the purpose of founding and endowing seats of learning on a large scale was advocated by Cardinal Wolsey soon after his accession to power. He was advanced to the chancellorship in 1513 and was nominated cardinal by the Pope in 1515, and among the first houses which he dissolved

---

[1] Dugdale, *Monasticon*, 'St Radegund's,' vol. 4, p. 215, charter nr 3.

[2] Gasquet, F. A., *Henry VIII and the English Monasteries*, 1888, vol. 1, p. 62.

[3] At a meeting of the Cambridge Antiquarian Society (reported in the *Academy*, Feb. 23, 1895), Mr T. D. Atkinson read a paper on 'The Conventual Buildings of the priory of St Radegund,' illustrated by a plan showing such of the college buildings as were probably monastic, and also the position of some foundations discovered in the previous summer. According to this paper the present cloister occupies the same position as that of the nuns, and the conventual church was converted into a college chapel by Alcock. The college hall which is upstairs is the old refectory, the rooms below being very likely used as butteries, as they still are. The present kitchen is probably on the site of the old monastic kitchen, and very likely the rooms originally assigned to the Master are those which had been occupied by the prioress. Further details of arrangement were given about the dormitory, the chapter house, the calefactory and common-room, etc., from which we gather that the men who occupied the nunnery buildings, put these to much the same uses as they had served before.

were the two nunneries of Bromhall in Berkshire and Lillechurch in Kent.

In a letter about Bromhall addressed to the bishop of Salisbury[1] Wolsey directs him to 'proceed against enormities, misgovernance and slanderous living, long time heretofore had, used, and continued by the prioress and nuns.' The nuns were to be removed 'to other places of that religion, where you best and most conveniently bestow them, especially where they may be brought and induced unto better and more religious living.' Henry VIII asked in a letter to the bishop that the deeds and evidences of the convent 'by reason of the vacation of the said place' might be delivered to his messenger[2]. It is not clear whether the inmates returned to the world or were transferred to other nunneries. In 1522 it was found that the prioress Joan Rawlins had resigned, her only two nuns had abandoned the house, and it was granted to St John's College, Cambridge, by the interest and procurement of Fisher, bishop of Rochester[3].

Full information is preserved about the charges brought against the nuns at Lillechurch. From records at Cambridge we learn on what pleas proceedings were taken. The house formerly contained sixteen nuns, but for some years past there had been only three or four. It stood in a public place, that is on the road to Rochester, and was frequented by clerics, and the nuns were notorious for neglect of their duties and incontinence. Moreover the foundations at Cambridge made by Margaret Beaufort needed subsidizing, and public feeling was against the house. Depositions were taken in writing from which we see that the prioress was dead, and that one of the three inmates had yielded to temptation some eight or nine years before. In answer to the question: 'Alas, madam, how happened this with you?'—she replied: 'And I had been happy I might have caused this thing to have been unknown and hidden.'—Together with her two companions she agreed to sign the form of surrender (dated 1521), which was worded as follows. 'Not compelled by fear or dread, nor circumvented by guile or deceit, out of my own free will, for certain just and lawful reasons (I) do resign and renounce all my right, title, interest and possession that I have had and now have in the aforesaid monastery.' We do not know what became of these

---

[1] Fiddes, 'Life of Card. Wolsey,' 1726, *Collect.*, p. 100.

[2] Ibid. p. 99.

[3] Dugdale, *Monasticon*, 'Bromhall,' vol. 4, p. 506.

women. Their house was given over to Bishop Fisher, and by letters patent it also passed to St John's College, Cambridge[1].

Regarding the charges of immorality brought against the inmates of convents in this and in other instances, it has been repeatedly pointed out by students that such accusations should be received with a reservation, for the occurrence may have taken place before the nun's admission to the house. The conventionalities of the time were curiously loose in some respects; the court of Henry VIII could boast of scant respect even for the conjugal tie, and a woman of the upper classes who disgraced herself naturally took refuge in a convent, where she could hope in some measure to redeem her character. The fact that Anne Boleyn, who was averse to the whole monastic system, at one time thought of retiring into a nunnery, is quoted as a case in point[2].

The readiness of Wolsey to dissolve decayed convents and to appropriate their property grew apace with his increase of power. In no case is it recorded that he was deterred by opposition. In 1524 he appropriated St Frideswith's, a house of Austin canons at Oxford, and made it the nucleus of his great college[3]. His legatine powers being further extended by a bull of the same year and the royal consent being obtained[4], twenty small convents were dissolved by him during the next few years[5]. Among them we note two nunneries, Wykes in Essex, and Littlemore in Oxfordshire[6]. But little is known of the number and character of their inmates at the time. Two further bulls[7] were obtained by Wolsey from Pope Clement (1523–34) for diminishing the number of monasteries and suppressing houses of less than twelve inmates. Gasquet, to whom we are indebted for a detailed account of the dissolution, shows that Clement, who was hard pressed by the Lutheran agitation at the time, only reluctantly yielded to Wolsey's request[8].

[1] Dugdale, *Monasticon*, 'Lillechurch,' vol. 4, p. 379, footnote *e*.

[2] Gairdner, J., *Letters and papers of the reign of Henry VIII*, Rolls Series, vol. 10, Preface, p. 43, footnote, and nr 890.

[3] Dugdale, *Monasticon*, 'St Frideswith's,' vol. 2, p. 138. Fiddes, 'Life of Card. Wolsey,' 1726, *Collect.*, p. 95.

[4] Wilkins, D., *Concilia*, 1737, 'Bull' (Sept. 1524), vol. 3, p. 703; 'Breve regium,' ibid. p. 705.

[5] Dugdale, *Monasticon*, 'St Frideswith's,' vol. 2, p. 138, footnote *x*.

[6] Ibid. 'Wykes,' vol. 4, p. 513; 'Littlemore,' vol. 4, p. 490, nr 12.

[7] Rymer, *Foedera*, 'Bulla pro monasteriis supprimendis,' vol. 6, p. 116; 'Bulla pro uniendis monasteriis,' p. 137.

[8] Gasquet, A., *Henry VIII and the English Monasteries*, 1888, vol. 1, pp. 101 ff.

Wolsey's proceedings in the matter, however, roused considerable local dissatisfaction and brought censure on him from the king. ' They say not that all that is ill gotten is bestowed on the colleges,' Henry wrote to him on the eve of his fall, ' but that the college is the cloak for covering mischiefs.' The king's ire was further roused by the cardinal's accepting the appointment of Isabel Jordan as abbess of Wilton, a house which was under royal patronage, and where the acceptance of the abbess belonged to the king. Anne Boleyn was in the ascendant in Henry's favour at the time, and wanted the post for someone else. But on enquiry at Wilton the unsuitability of this person became apparent. ' As touching the matter of Wilton,' Henry wrote to Anne, ' my lord cardinal has had the nuns before him and examined them, Master Bell being present, who has certified to me that for a truth she has confessed herself (which we would have abbess) to have had two children by sundry priests, and further since has been kept by a servant of Lord Broke that was, and not long ago ; wherefore I would not for all the world clog your conscience nor mine to make her ruler of a house who is of such ungodly demeanour, nor I trust, you would not that neither for brother nor sister I should so stain mine honour and conscience[1].' It is evident from this letter that whatever the character of the women received into the house might be, the antecedents of the lady superior were no matter of indifference. In this case the king's objection to one person and the unsuitability of the other led to the appointment of a third[2].

From the year 1527 all other questions were swallowed up by the momentous question of the king's divorce. Wolsey, who refused to comply with his wishes, went into retirement in 1529 and died in the following year. The management of affairs then passed into the hands of those who in this country represented the ruthless and reckless spirit of rebellion which had broken loose abroad. However several years passed before the attempt to appropriate the revenues of monasteries was resumed.

In the intervening period of increasing social and political un-

---

[1] Blunt, *The Reformation of the Church of England*, 1882, vol. 1, p. 92, footnote, says that the lady in question was ' Eleanor the daughter of Cary who had lately married (Anne's) sister Margaret.'

[2] Dugdale, *Monasticon*, ' Wilton,' vol. 2, p. 317, gives the correspondence. The abbess who succeeded to Isabel Jordan was probably Cecil Bodman or Bodenham, of whom more p. 441.

rest we note the publication, some time before 1529, of the 'Supplication for beggars,' with which London was flooded[1]. It was an attack on the existing religious and monastic orders by the pamphleteer Simon Fish († c. 1530). Based on the grossest misrepresentations this supplication, in a humorous style admirably suited to catch popular attention, set forth the poverty of the people, the immorality of those who were vowed to religion, and the lewdness of unattached women, and declared that if church and monastic property were put to a better use these evils would be remedied. The king, who was on the eve of a rupture with Rome, lent a willing ear to this 'supplication,' and it so fell in with the general belief in coming changes that the refutation of its falsehoods and the severe criticism of Luther written in reply by Thomas More passed for the most part unheeded[2].

Another incident which reflects the spirit of the time in its contrarieties and instability, is the way in which Elizabeth Barton, of the parish of Aldington, the so-called Maid or Nun of Kent, rose to celebrity or notoriety. Her foresight of coming events had been received as genuine by many men of distinction, but her visions concerning the king's projected divorce were fiercely resented by the king's partisans. Bishop Fisher wept tears of joy over her, Wolsey received her as a champion of Queen Katherine's cause, and even Thomas More showed some interest in her, while Cromwell accused her of rank superstition and induced Henry to take proceedings against her[3]. She had been a servant girl, but at the instigation of the clergy at Canterbury had been received into St Sepulchre's nunnery, where she lived for seven years and was looked upon with special favour by the Carthusian monks of Charterhouse and Sheen, and the inmates of the monastery of Sion. At the beginning of 1533 the king was married to Anne, and in the autumn of the same year Elizabeth Barton was accused of treasonable incitement and made to do public penance. Later a bill of attainder was brought in against her, and as Gasquet has shown[4], she was condemned without a hearing and executed at Tyburn with several Carthusian monks who were inculpated with

---

[1] Fish, S., 'A Supplicacyon for the Beggers,' republished *Early Engl. Text Soc.*, 1871.

[2] More, Th., 'The Supplycacyon of Soulys,' 1529 (?).

[3] Wright, Th., *Three chapters of letters on the Suppression* (Camden Soc., 1843), nrs 6–11.

[4] Gasquet, A., *Henry VIII and the English Monasteries*, vol. 1, pp. 110–150.

her on the charge of treason.   Henry also made an attempt to get rid of Bishop Fisher and of Sir Thomas More by causing them to be accused of favouring her 'conspiracy,' but the evidence against them was too slight to admit of criminal proceedings. It was on the charge of declaring that Henry was not the supreme head of the Church that Fisher suffered death (June, 1535), and on the yet slighter charge of declining to give an opinion on the matter, that More was executed a fortnight later[1].

The parliament of 1533 had passed the act abolishing appeals to the Court of Rome, and among other rights had transferred that of monastic visitation from the Pope to the king.   In the following year a further division was made,—the king claimed to be recognised as the head of the Church.   It was part of Henry's policy to avoid openly attacking any part of the old system ; gradual changes were brought about which undermined prerogatives without making a decided break.   Cromwell was appointed vicegerent in ecclesiastical matters, and it was on the plea of securing the recognition of the king's supremacy that he deputed a number of visitors or agents to conduct monastic visitations on a large scale, and to secure all possible information about religious houses.   His plan and the way in which it was carried out struck a mortal blow at the whole monastic system.

The agents employed by Cromwell were naturally laymen, and the authority of the diocesan was suspended while they were at work.   Great powers were conferred on them.   A list of the instructions they received is in existence ; and we gather from it that monks and nuns were put through searching interrogatories concerning the property of their house, the number of its inmates, its founders and privileges, its maintenance of discipline, and the right conduct of its inmates.   The agents then enjoined severance from the Pope or any other foreign superior, and directed those who had taken the vow, whether men or women, henceforth to observe strict seclusion.   A daily lesson in scripture was to be read ; the celebration of the hours was to be curtailed; profession made under the age of twenty-four was declared invalid ; and 'other special injunctions,' says the document, might 'be added by the visitors as the place and nature of accounts rendered (or comperts) shall require,' subject to the wisdom and discretion of Cromwell[2].

---

[1] Gairdner, J., *Letters and Papers* etc., vol. 8, Preface, pp. 33 ff.
[2] Wilkins, D., *Concilia*, 1737, vol. 3, p. 755.

The character of the visitors engaged in this task has been variously estimated. Among them was Dr Legh († 1545) who is described by a contemporary as a doctor of low quality. He wrote to Cromwell (July, 1535) recommending himself and Layton († 1544) for the purpose of visitation[1]. Layton had previously acted for Cromwell in conducting visitations at Sheen and Sion in the affair of Elizabeth Barton. Legh afterwards complained that he did not act as he himself did in regard to enforcing injunctions[2], but Legh, even in the eyes of his companion John ap Rice, another visitor with whom he had started for the western countries, was needlessly severe. 'At Laycock (nunnery),' wrote ap Rice[3], 'we can find no excesses. Master (Legh) everywhere restrains the heads, the brethren and sisters from going forth ; and no women of what estate soever are allowed to visit religious men's houses and vice versa. I think this is over strict, for as many of these houses stand by husbandry they must fall to decay if the heads are not allowed to go out.'

We have seen, in connection with matters on the Continent, that the heads of houses who were landowners felt it impossible to conform to the rule of always keeping within the precincts. The injunction in this case gave rise to a number of letters of complaint addressed by the heads of monasteries to Cromwell[4]. Cecil Bodman, abbess of Wilton, wrote to him as follows[5].

'Dr Legh the king's visitor and your deputy, on visiting my house, has given injunction that not only all my sisters but that I should keep continually within the precincts. For myself personally I am content; but as the house is in great debt, and is not likely to improve without good husbandry, which cannot be exercised so well by any other as by myself, I beg you will allow me, in company with two or three of the sad (serious) and discreet sisters of the house, to supervise such things abroad as shall be for its profit. I do not propose to lodge any night abroad, except by inevitable necessity I cannot return. I beg also, that whenever any father, mother, brother, sister, or nigh kinsfolk of my sisters, come unto them, they may have licence to speak with them in the hall in my presence. Wilton, 5 Sept.' (1535).

Another injunction which was felt to be a calamity was the

---

[1] *Dict. of Nat. Biography*, article 'Legh, Sir Thomas.'

[2] Wright, *Three chapters* etc., p. 56.

[3] Gairdner, J., *Letters* etc., vol. 9, nr 139.

[4] Ibid. Preface, p. 20.   [5] Ibid. vol. 9, nr 280.

order declaring that profession made under twenty-four was invalid.
'No greater blow could have been struck at the whole theory of
religious life,' says Gasquet[1], 'than the interference with the vows
contained in the order to dismiss those who were under twenty-four
years of age or who had been professed at the age of twenty. The
visitors, it is clear, had no scruple about their power to dispense
with the solemn obligations of the monastic profession. They
freely extended it to any who would go, in their idea that the
more they could induce to leave their convents, the better pleased
both the king and Cromwell would be.'

How far inmates of convents availed themselves of the permission to go is difficult to establish. Margaret Vernon, abbess
of Little Marlow in Buckinghamshire, who was left with only one
nun, did not feel unwilling to give up her house, and wrote to
Cromwell as follows[2].

'After all due commendations had unto your good mastership,
with my most humble thanks for the great cost made on me and
my poor maidens at my last being with your mastership, further-
more may it please you to understand that your visitors have been
here of late, who have discharged three of my sisters, the one is
dame Catheryn, the other two are the young women who were
last professed, which is not a little to my discomfort; nevertheless
I must be content with the king's pleasure. But now as touching
mine own part, I most humbly beseech you so special a good
master unto me your poor bedewoman, to give me your best
advice and counsel what way shall be best for me to take, seeing
there shall be none left here but myself and this poor maiden;
and if it will please your goodness to take this house into your
own hands either for yourself, or for my own (master) your son,
I would be glad with all my heart to give it into your mastership's
hands, with that you will command me to do therein. Trusting
and nothing doubting in your goodness, that you will so provide
for us that we shall have such honest living that we shall not be
driven by necessity either to beg or to fall to other inconvenience.
And thus I offer myself and all mine unto your most high and
prudent wisdom, as unto him that is my only refuge and comfort
in this world, beseeching God of His goodness to put in you His
Holy Spirit, that you may do all things to His laud and glory.
By your own assured bedewoman M(argaret) V(ernon).'

---

[1] Gasquet, *Henry VIII* etc., vol. i, p. 273.
[2] Wright, *Three chapters of letters*, p. 55.

Some time afterwards she was in London, trying to get an interview with Cromwell, and eventually she became governess to his son[1]. The property of her nunnery, together with that of Ankerwyke in Buckinghamshire, and several monasteries of men, was granted by Henry in 1537 to the newly founded abbey of Bisham, but at the general dissolution it fell to the crown[2].

Another petition touching the matter of dismissing youthful convent inmates was addressed to Cromwell by Jane G(o)wryng[3], in which she begs that four inmates of her house, whose ages are between fifteen and twenty-five and who are in secular apparel may resume their habits or else have licence to dwell in the close of the house till they are twenty-four. Also she wishes to know if two girls of twelve and thirteen, the one deaf and dumb, the other an idiot, shall depart or not. Again a letter was addressed to Cromwell, asking that a natural daughter of Cardinal Wolsey might continue at Shaftesbury till she be old enough to take the vow[4]

Modern writers are agreed that the effect of these visitations was disastrous to authority and discipline within the convent, not so much through the infringement of privileges as through the feeling of uncertainty and restlessness which they created. Visitation was dreaded in itself. With reference to Barking nunnery Sir Thomas Audley wrote to Cromwell: 'I am informed that Dr Lee is substituted by you to visit all the religious houses in the diocese of London. My suit at this time to you is that it may please you to spare the house at Barking[5].'

In point of fact the visitations were conducted in a manner which left those immediately concerned in no doubt as to the ultimate object in view. In court circles likewise men were aware that the monastic system was threatened by dangerous and far-reaching changes. While Cromwell's agents were on their tours of inspection Chapuys, the French ambassador (Sept. 1535) wrote as follows[6]: 'There is a report that the king intends the religious of all orders to be free to leave their habits and marry. And if they will stay in their houses they must live in poverty. He intends

---

[1] Gasquet, *Henry VIII* etc., vol. 1, p. 276 ; Ellis, H., *Original Letters*, Series 3, vol. 3, p. 11, says that after resigning at Little Marlow she became abbess at Malling.

[2] Dugdale, *Monasticon*, 'Little Marlow,' vol. 4, p. 419; 'Ankerwyke,' vol. 4, p. 229.

[3] Gairdner, J., *Letters and Papers* etc., vol. 9, nr 1075 (her house is unknown).

[4] Ellis, H., *Original Letters*, Series 1, vol. 2, p. 91.

[5] Wright, *Three chapters* etc., p. 74.

[6] Gairdner, J., *Letters and Papers* etc., vol. 9, nr 357.

to take the rest of the revenue and will do stranger things still.' And two months later he wrote that the king meant to exclude the abbots from the House of Lords for fear of their opposition to his intentions regarding the spoliation of monasteries[1].

The one merit Cromwell's visitors can claim is despatch, for in six months, between July 1535 and February 1536, the information on the monasteries was collected throughout the country and laid before Parliament. Gasquet has shown that the House of Lords was the same which had been packed for passing the act of divorce, and that the king, bent on carrying his purpose, bullied the Commons into its acceptance[2].

The preamble to the bill is couched in strong terms and begins as follows[3]: 'Forasmuch as manifest sins, vicious, carnal, and abominable living is daily used and committed amongst the little and small abbeys, priories, and other religious houses of monks, canons and nuns, where the congregation of such religious persons is under the number of twelve persons, whereby the governors of such religious houses and their convent spoil, destroy, consume and utterly waste, as well their churches, monasteries, priories, principal houses, farms, granges, lands, tenements and hereditaments, as the ornaments of their churches and their goods and chattels, to the high displeasure of Almighty God, slander of good religion, and to the great infamy of the king's highness and the realm, if redress should not be had thereof,'...and it goes on to say that since visitations have produced no results, and bad living continues, the Lords and Commons, after deliberation, have resolved to put the possessions of these religious houses to a better use, and that the king and his heirs shall for ever enjoy all houses that are not above the clear annual value of £200 in like manner as the heads of houses at present enjoy it, but that the king by 'his most excellent charity' is pleased to grant pensions to those whom he deprives.

Touching the evidence on which action was taken writers of the Elizabethan era speak of the so-called Black Book, the existence of which has since been disproved[4]. Latimer in a sermon preached in 1549 refers to the 'enormities' which were brought to the knowledge of the house; we hold a clue to these

---

[1] Gairdner, J., *Letters and Papers* etc., vol. 9, nr 732.
[2] Gasquet, A., *Henry VIII* etc., vol. 1, p. 293.
[3] Wright, *Three chapters* etc., p. 107.
[4] Ibid. p. 114; Gasquet, *Henry VIII* etc., vol. 1, p. 303.

in the letters forwarded by Cromwell's agents when on their tours of inspection, and in their 'comperts' or accounts rendered. The condensed accounts (comperta compertorum) rendered by Layton and Legh for the province of York including one hundred and twenty monasteries are extant, as also two other reports, one on twenty-four houses in Norfolk, another on ten[1].

It has been remarked that the evidence collected differs according to the character of the informers; the reports of Tregonwell for example are by no means so full of scandal as those of Layton and Legh. Moreover Layton and Legh gave a specially bad character to houses in the north where, as we shall see later on, both the people and the gentry were in favour of their continuance. It should also be noted that the state of the lesser houses which fell under the act was not uniformly worse than that of the larger. Many difficulties of course stood in the way of the men who collected evidence. They were received with suspicion and hatred, which their proceedings were not likely to dissipate, and they naturally lent a willing ear to any one who gave information of the character required. It has been shown that in several instances their reports were directly contradicted by those made by the leading men in the different counties, who after the passing of the act were appointed to make a new and exact survey, so that, considering the evidence forthcoming from both sides, it seems reasonable to accept that while the mode of life within convents no longer compared favourably with the mode of life outside them, their standard had not fallen so low, as to render these institutions uniformly despicable.

An example of how the visitors were received is afforded by a letter from Layton to Cromwell, in which he describes how after meeting Legh in the north they visited Chicksand, a Gilbertine house in Bedfordshire[2]. The nuns here at first refused to admit him, and when he forced an entrance the two prioresses would not admit the accusations made against two of their nuns, 'nor the parties concerned, nor the nuns, only one old beldame.' He tried intimidation and was told by the prioress 'that they were bound by their religion never to confess the secret faults done among them except only to their visitor of religion, and to that they were sworn every one of them at their first admission.'

A similar esprit de corps was manifested by a house of Gilber-

---

[1] Gairdner, J., *Letters and Papers* etc., vol. 10, nr 364.

[2] Wright, *Three chapters* etc., p. 91.

tine canons[1]. Layton in the same letter gives a bad character
to the nunnery of Harwold, in Bedfordshire, which was inhabited
by Austin canonesses[2], and the inmates of which had been foolish
enough to sign a Latin document in favour of Lord Mordaunt
without knowing what it contained.

The accusations brought by the visitors can be summarised
under two headings, superstitions and scandalous living. The
accounts of superstitions are full of most interesting particulars
for the student of art and of folklore; the properties which were
attached to relics, the character of the images and paintings which
were held in reverence, and the construction of saint-images, will
amply repay study[3]. The instances of scandalous living recorded
are numerous and affect alike the inmates of men's and of women's
houses. Coloured as they may be to suit the temper of inquisitor
and informer, there is no denying that they point to an advanced
state of monastic decay.

It has been estimated that the lesser houses including those
of monks and nuns which fell under the act numbered about three
hundred and eighty; they were to surrender to the crown within a
year. Of these the women's houses, owing to their comparative
poverty, were relatively more numerous than those of the men. Out
of about one hundred and thirty nunneries which existed at this
period only fifteen were exempt through having a yearly income
exceeding £200, but in addition to these over twenty by some
means or other secured a reprieve.

As the act abolishing the lesser houses was based on the
assumption of their corruption, the heads of some of the houses
which bore a good character asked leave on this ground to remain.
Among those who wrote to Cromwell in this sense was Jane
Messyndyne, prioress of a convent of about ten nuns at Legbourne
in Leicestershire, who pleaded that no fault had been found with
her house[4]. 'And whereas,' she wrote, 'we do hear that a great
number of abbeys shall be punished, suppressed and put down
because of their misliving, and that all abbeys and priories under

---

[1] Ellis, H., *Original Letters*, Series 3, vol. 3, p. 38.

[2] Dugdale, *Monasticon*, 'Harwold,' vol. 6, p. 330.

[3] Ellis, H., *Original Letters*, speaks of the image of Our Lady of Caversham which
was plated all over with silver, Series 1, vol. 2, p. 79; of that of St Modwen of Burton
on Trent with her red cowl and staff, Series 3, vol. 3, p. 104; of the 'huge and great
image' of Darvellgathern held in great veneration in Wales, Series 1, vol. 2, p. 82;
and of others, which were brought to London and burnt.

[4] Wright, *Three chapters* etc., p. 116.

the value of £200 be at our most noble prince's pleasure to suppress and put down, yet if it may please your goodness we trust in
God you shall hear no complaints against us neither in our living
nor hospitality keeping.' But petitions such as hers apparently
passed unheeded, for in the autumn of the same year (Sept. 1536),
the process of dissolution was going on at her house[1].

There seems no doubt that in many cases where the lesser
houses were allowed to remain bribery was resorted to, perhaps
backed by the intervention of friends. Payments into the Royal
Exchequer were made by a large proportion of the lesser houses
which continued unmolested, and among them were a number of
nunneries which paid sums ranging from £20 to £400[2]. Among
these was Brusyard in Bedfordshire, a small settlement of nuns of
the order of St Clare, the abbess of which wrote to Cromwell
seeking his intervention[3]; she ultimately secured a reprieve and
paid the sum of £20[4]. Alice Fitzherbert, abbess of the nunnery
of Polesworth in Warwickshire, to which an exceptionally good
character was given, bought a reprieve for £50, on the intervention
it is said of friends[5]. Again the abbess of Delapray, who is
characterised as a very sickly and aged woman, secured a reprieve
and paid £266. The agent Tregonwell had reported well of Godstow[6]. Its inmates all bore a good character excepting one who,
some thirteen years ago, had broken her vow while living in
another convent, had been transferred to Delapray by the bishop
of Lincoln and had since lived virtuously. Margaret Tewkesbury
the abbess wrote to Cromwell begging him to accept a little fee
and to forward the letter she enclosed to the king[7]. Her convent
was allowed to remain.

The attempt of the prioress of Catesby to save her house
in a similar manner was fruitless. The house bore an excellent
character according to Tregonwell[8], and his opinion was confirmed
by the commissioners who came down later (May, 1536) to take
an exact survey. 'We found the house,' they wrote to Cromwell[9],
'in very perfect order, the prioress a wise, discreet, and religious

[1] Gasquet, A., *Henry VIII* etc., vol. 2, p. 47.   [2] Ibid. Appendix I.
[3] Gairdner, J., *Letters and Papers* etc., vol. 9, nr 1094.
[4] Gasquet, A., *Henry VIII* etc., vol. 2, App. I.
[5] Wright, *Three chapters* etc., p. 139.
[6] Ellis, H., *Orig. Letters*, Series 3, vol. 3, p. 37.
[7] Ibid. p. 116.   [8] Ibid. p. 39.
[9] Wright, *Three chapters* etc., p. 129.

woman with nine devout nuns under her as good as we have seen. The house stands where it is a relief to the poor, as we hear by divers trustworthy reports. If any religious house is to stand, none is more meet for the king's charity than Catesby. We have not found any such elsewhere....' But the recommendation was insufficient and Joyce Bykeley, 'late prioress,' addressed herself directly to Cromwell.—'Dr Gwent informed you last night,' she wrote[1], 'that the queen had moved the king for me and offered him 2000 marks for the house at Catesby, but has not yet a perfect answer. I beg you, in my great sorrow, get the king to grant that the house may stand and get me years of payment for the 2000 marks. You shall have 100 marks of me to buy you a gelding and my prayers during my life and all my sisters during their lives. I hope you have not forgotten the report the commissioners sent of me and my sisters....' But her letter was of no avail. Somehow she had incurred the king's displeasure[2], and the order to dissolve her convent was not countermanded.

The sums paid by some nunneries appear enormous compared with their yearly income. Thus the convent of Pollesloe, with a yearly income of £164, paid the sum of £400 into the Royal Exchequer; Laycock, with an income of £168, paid £300, and the nuns of St Mary at Chester, with an income of £66, paid £160; other sums paid are given by Gasquet[3].

Among the lesser houses reprieved was St Mary's, Winchester, one of the nunneries dating from the Anglo-Saxon period, but which in course of time had decreased. The report of the commissioners who came down to take stock of the contents of the settlement provides us with many interesting particulars[4]. The number of persons residing in the monastery at the time was over a hundred. The abbess Elizabeth Shelley presided over a convent of twenty-six nuns, twenty-two of whom were professed and four novices. The nuns are designated in this report by the old term 'mynchyns.' With the exception of one who desired 'capacity,' that is liberty to return to the world, they all declared their intention of going into other houses. Five lay sisters also dwelt there, thirteen women-servants and twenty-six girls, some of whom were the daughters of knights receiving their education. Of the

---

[1] Gairdner, J., *Letters and Papers* etc., vol. 10, nr 383 (1536).
[2] Wright, *Three chapters* etc., p. 136.
[3] Gasquet, A., *Henry VIII* etc., vol. 2, App. 1.
[4] Dugdale, *Monasticon*, 'St Mary's,' vol. 2, p. 451, charter nr 4.

women-servants one belonged to the abbess who lived in a house of her own with her gentlewoman; the prioress, sub-prioress, sexton, and perhaps one other nun, lived in separate houses and each had her servant. There were also a number of priests and other men designated as officers of the household. Among them was a general receiver and his servant, a clerk and his servant, a gardener (curtyar), a caterer, a bottler (botyler?), a cook, an undercook, a baker, a convent cook, an under convent cook, a brewer, a miller, several porters and 'children of the high altar,' and two men enjoying corrodies, that is free quarters and means of subsistence. The yearly income of this vast establishment was assessed at £179, and the house therefore came under the act. But the abbess, Elizabeth Shelley, who is described as a person of spirit and talent, found means to avert the storm. The sum of £333 was paid by her into the Royal Exchequer[1], and (in August 1536) letters patent were obtained by which the abbey was refounded with all its property excepting some valuable manors[2].

Other convents which at the same time secured a licence to remain[3] were the Benedictine convent of Chatteris with Anne Seton[4] as prioress; the Austin convent of Gracedieu in Leicestershire; the convent of the order of St Clare of Dennis; also the nuns of St Andrew's, Marricks in Yorkshire under Christabel Cooper, and of St Mary's, Heyninges, in Lincolnshire under Joan Sandford[5]. No payment is recorded in connection with any of these houses so far as I have been able to ascertain.

Among the reprieves that of the Austin nuns or White Ladies at Gracedieu is noteworthy, as the report of Cromwell's agents (Feb. 1536) had charged two of its inmates with incontinence, and among other superstitions countenanced by the convent, mentioned their holding in reverence the girdle and part of the tunic of St Francis which were supposed to help women in their confinement[6]. But the special commissioners a few months later spoke of the prioress Agnes Litherland and her convent of fifteen nuns in the highest terms, describing them as of good and virtuous con-

---

[1] Gasquet, A., *Henry VIII* etc., vol. 2, App. I.
[2] Gairdner, J., *Letters and Papers* etc. vol. 11, nr 385 (20).
[3] Ibid. (22, 23, 35).
[4] Dugdale, *Monasticon*, 'Chatteris,' vol. 2, p. 614, calls her 'Anne Gayton.'
[5] Gairdner, J., *Letters and Papers*, vol. 11, nr 519 (11); nr 1217 (26).
[6] Ibid. vol. 10, nr 364.

versation and living, and saying that all of them desired their house to remain[1].

The convent of Dennis, which secured a licence at the same time, was one of the few settlements of nuns of St Clare, the abbess of which, Elizabeth Throgmerton, was renowned for her liberal sympathies. In 1528 a wealthy London merchant was imprisoned for distributing Tyndale's books and other practices of the sort, and he pleaded among other reasons for exculpation that, the abbess of Dennis wishing to borrow Tyndale's *Enchiridion*, he had lent it to her and had spent much money on restoring her house[2]. Legh in a letter to Cromwell[3] described how on visiting Dennis he was met by the weeping nuns, who were all ready to return to the world, a statement in direct contradiction to the fact that the house was not dissolved.

The work of dissolution began in April 1536 and continued without interruption throughout the summer. Gasquet holds that the women suffered more than the men by being turned adrift[4]. 'Many things combined to render the dissolution of conventual establishments and the disbanding of the religious more terrible to nuns than to monks. A woman compelled to exchange the secluded life of a cloister with all its aids to piety for an existence in the world, to which she could never rightly belong, would be obviously in a more dangerous and undesirable position than a man.'

By a provision of the act those who were professed were to receive pensions, but the number of inmates of the lesser houses to whom they were granted was comparatively small[5]. Moreover pensions were not apportioned with regard to the needs of subsistence, but to the wealth of the house, so that even those who received them were in a great measure thrown on their own resources. The number of professed nuns, as is apparent from the accounts given of St Mary's, Winchester, and other houses, was relatively small compared with the number of servants and dependents. These in some cases received a small 'award' but were thrown out of employment, while the recipients of alms from the house were likewise deprived of their means of living,

[1] Gasquet, A., *Henry VIII* etc., vol. 2, p. 206; Gairdner, J., *Letters and Papers* etc., vol. 10, Preface, p. 46.

[2] Dugdale, *Monasticon*, 'Dennis,' vol. 6, p. 1549.

[3] Ellis, H., *Orig. Letters*, Series 3, vol. 3, p. 117.

[4] Gasquet, A., *Henry VIII* etc., vol. 2, p. 203.   [5] Ibid. vol. 2, pp. 449 ff.

and went to swell the ranks of those who were dissatisfied with the innovation. While the process of dissolution was going on (July 1536) Chapuys the French ambassador wrote as follows[1]: 'It is a lamentable thing to see a legion of monks and nuns who have been chased from their monasteries wandering miserably hither and thither seeking means to live; and several honest men have told me that what with monks, nuns, and persons dependent on the monasteries suppressed, there were over 20,000 who knew not how to live.' His estimate may have reference to the ultimate effect of the act[2]. The immediate results of the suppression were, however, disastrous throughout the country, and the dissatisfaction which the suppression caused went far to rouse the latent discontent of the northern provinces into open rebellion.

It was in Lincolnshire, in October, that the commissioners first met with opposition. From here a rising spread northwards to Scotland, and under the name of the 'Pilgrimage of Grace' drew votaries from the lay and religious classes alike. The insurgents claimed among other things that the innovations in religion should be disowned, and that despoiled monasteries should be restored. They pursued the visitors Layton and Legh with unrelenting hatred on account of their extortions; Legh was in danger of his life and barely escaped their fury[3]. The rising assumed such proportions that the king was seriously alarmed; an army was sent to the north, strenuous efforts were made to win over the powerful northern barons, and concessions were made and rescinded with much shameful double-dealing. Beyond the effect it had on religious houses, the story of the rebellion, on which a new light has recently been thrown by the publication of letters which passed at the time[4], does not concern us here. Wherever the insurgents spread they seized on despoiled monasteries and reinstated their superiors and inmates; among other houses the nunnery of Seton in Cumberland was restored for a time[5]. But in proportion as the king regained his authority, terrible bloodshed followed; the representatives of the chief families and the abbots who had joined in the rising were hanged, burnt, or beheaded, and their property confiscated by attainder. Cromwell, who was

---

[1] Gairdner, J., *Letters and Papers* etc., vol. 11, nr 42.
[2] Ibid. vol. 11, Preface, p. 12.
[3] Gasquet, A., *Henry VIII* etc., vol. 2, pp. 84 ff.
[4] Gairdner, J., *Letters and Papers* etc., vols. 11, 12.
[5] Dugdale, *Monasticon*, 'Seton,' vol. 4, p. 226.

still on the high road to prosperity, availed himself of the rebellion
to institute a general suppression, which was speedily and summarily carried into effect. In the autumn of 1537, the fear of
systematic revolt being quelled, the suppression began and extended over the whole of 1538 and 1539. No further evidence
was collected, no act was passed till April 1539, when a provision
was made by which all monasteries which were dissolved or surrendered fell to the king[1]. The commissioners came down on
each house in succession, beginning with the less wealthy and
influential ones, and used every means to secure a free surrender.
Even then a certain reticence in the proceedings was observed
which went far to blind contemporaries to the vastness of the
ultimate object in view, for every effort was made to keep up the
fiction that Henry was doing no more than correcting abuses
and accepting free surrenders. But the study of documents proves
things to have been otherwise. The promise of a pension was
held out on condition of a voluntary surrender, but where hesitation was shown in accepting, the effect of threats of deprivation
was tried. The visitor Bedyll wrote that he advised the monks
of Charterhouse rather to 'surrender than abide the extremity
of the king's law[2],' and many of the forms of surrender which are
extant remain unsigned. On others the name of the superior is
the only signature, on others again the names of the superior and
the members of the convent are entered in the same hand. Considering the helpless position in which religious houses were placed,
it seems a matter for wonder that any opposition was made.

It is interesting to find that as late as (Jan.) 1538, two years
after the passing of the first bill, the heads of houses were asked
to believe that there was no wish for a general suppression[3],
and that a grant of continuance was made (May 1538) to the
nunneries of Kirkless and Nunappleton in Yorkshire[4]. In Yorkshire there was a strong feeling in favour of nunneries,—'in which
our daughters (are) brought up in virtue,' as Aske, one of the
leaders of the rebellion, put it[5], and owing doubtless to the opposition made by the rebels, a number of lesser nunneries in the
north which came under the act escaped dissolution. Among

---

[1] Gasquet, A., *Henry VIII* etc., vol. 2, p. 340.
[2] Gairdner, J., *Letters and Papers* etc., vol. 12, pt 2, nr 27.
[3] Gasquet, A., *Henry VIII* etc., vol. 2, p. 279.
[4] Gairdner, J., *Letters and Papers* etc., vol. 13, pt 1, nr 1115 (19), nr 1519 (44).
[5] Gasquet, A., *Henry VIII* etc., vol. 2, p. 222.

them besides Kirkless and Nunappleton were Swine and Nun-Kelyng; there is no evidence that they secured a licence at the time. The fact that Kirkless remained and gained a reprieve in 1538 is the more noticeable as the commissioners had in the first instance reported unfavourably on the state of the house[1].

In February 1538 a courtier wrote to Lord Lisle[2], 'the abbeys go down as fast as they may and are surrendered to the king,' adding the pious wish: 'I pray God send you one among them to your part.' For the property of religious houses which were appropriated to the king was now frequently granted to courtiers, or to those who were quick enough to avail themselves of their opportunities in the general scramble.

Several of the agents who had previously conducted visitations were among those who carried on the work of the dissolution. Among them London († 1543) has been characterised as 'the most terrible of all the monastic spoilers'; his letters remain to show in what spirit he stripped the houses of their property, seized relics and defaced and destroyed everything he could lay hands on[3]. There is a letter extant which Katherine Bulkeley, abbess of Godstow, wrote to Cromwell complaining of him[4]. He came down to her house (Nov. 1537), ostensibly to hold a visitation, but really bent on securing a surrender.

'… Dr London, which as your lordship does well know was against my promotion and has ever since borne me great malice and grudge like my mortal enemy, is suddenly come unto me with a great rout with him and here does threaten me and my sisters saying that he has the king's commission to suppress my house in spite of my teeth. And when he saw that I was content that he should do all things according to his commission and showed him plain that I would never surrender to his hand being my ancient enemy, now he begins to entreat me and to inveigle my sisters one by one otherwise than I ever heard tell that any of the king's subjects have been handled, and here tarries and continues to my great cost and charge, and will not take my answer that I will not surrender till I know the king's gracious commandment and your lordship's…' and more to the same purpose.

---

[1] Gairdner, J., *Letters and Papers* etc., vol. 10, nr 364.
[2] Ibid. vol. 13, pt 1, nr 235.
[3] Ellis, H., *Orig. Letters*, Series 3, vol. 3.
[4] Wright, *Three chapters* etc., p. 229.

London on the following day wrote to Cromwell[1] asking that the 'mynchyns' or nuns of her house, many of whom were aged and without friends, should be generously dealt with (in the matter of a pension). Stories were current[2] at the time about insults to which the nuns were exposed by the agents. Although it seems probable that there was no excessive delicacy used in their treatment, no direct complaints except those of the abbess of Godstow have been preserved.

The last pages of the history of several of the great abbeys are full of traits of heroism ; one cannot read without sympathy of the way in which for example the abbot of Glastonbury identified himself with the system to which he belonged, and perished with it rather than be divided from it. The staunch faith of the friars no less commands respect. The heads of women's houses naturally made less opposition. However Florence Bannerman, abbess of Amesbury, refused every attempt to bribe or force her into a surrender. After considerable delay she was deposed in December 1539, and was succeeded by Joan Darrell who surrendered the house at the king's bidding[3], and accepted the comparatively high pension of £100.

To some of the heads of houses it seemed incredible that the old system was passing away for ever, and they surrendered in the belief that their deprivation was only temporary. Elizabeth Shelley, abbess of St Mary's, Winchester, who in 1535 had saved her house, accepted the surrender but continued to dwell at Winchester with a number of her nuns, and when she died bequeathed a silver chalice which she had saved to the college in the city on condition that it should be given back to St Mary's if the convent were restored[4]. The fact that she succeeded in carrying away a chalice appears exceptional, for the inmates of convents who were expelled seem as a rule to have taken with them nothing except perhaps their books of devotion.

The story of the dissolution repeats itself in every convent. The inventory of the house having been taken, the lead was torn from the roofs, and sold together with the bells ; the relics and pictures were packed in sacks and sent up to London to be burnt.

---

[1] Wright, *Three chapters* etc., p. 227.

[2] Gasquet, A., *Henry VIII* etc., vol. 2, p. 225.

[3] Ibid. 456.

[4] Dugdale, *Monasticon*, 'St Mary's,' vol. 2, p. 451; Gasquet, A., *Henry VIII* etc., vol. 2, p. 476.

The plate and jewels of the house, the amount of which was considerable in the houses of men and in some of women (for example in Barking) were also forwarded to London to be broken up and melted; in a few instances they were sold. The house's property in furniture, utensils and vestments was sold there and then. The superiors and convent inmates were then turned away, and the buildings that had so long been held in reverence were either devoted to some profane use or else left to decay.

The inventory taken at the dissolution of the ancient Benedictine nunnery of Wherwell in Hampshire has been preserved among others, and shows how such a house was dealt with[1]. There is a list of the inmates of the convent and of the pensions granted to them; the abbess in this case received a yearly pension of £40, and her nuns' pensions ranged from £3. 6s. 8d. to £6. We then get a list of the dwellings of which the settlement was composed. The houses and buildings 'assigned to remain' were as follows: 'the abbess' lodging with the houses within the quadrant, as the water leads from the east side of the cloister to the gate, the farmery, the mill and millhouse with the slaughter-house adjoining, the brewing and baking houses with the granaries to the same, the barn and stables in the outer court.' The list of dwellings 'deemed to be superfluous' follows. 'The church, choir, and steeple covered with lead, the cloister covered with tiles and certain gutters of lead, the chapter house, the refectory (ffrayter), the dormitory, the convent kitchen and all the old lodgings between the granary and the hall door covered with tiles.' Then follow accounts of the lead and bells remaining, of the jewels, plate and silver 'reserved for the king's use,' and of the ornaments, goods and chattels which were sold. We further gather that the debts of the house were paid and that rewards and wages were given to the chaplain, officers and servants before they were turned away.

As mentioned above the pensions given differed greatly, and the heads of wealthy houses were allowed considerable sums. Thus Elizabeth Souche, abbess of Shaftesbury, the yearly income of which house was taxed at £1166, received £133 a year and all her nuns to the number of fifty-five were pensioned. Dorothy Barley, abbess of Barking, a house taxed at £862, received a yearly pension of £133; while Elizabeth Shelley, abbess of St

---

[1] Dugdale, *Monasticon*, 'Wherwell,' vol. 2, p. 634.

Mary's, Winchester, received only £26 a year. The prioress of St Andrew's, Marricks, a small house, received £5 annually, and her nuns a pension of from twenty to forty shillings each. Gasquet points out that a large number of those who were pensioned died during the first few years after the surrender[1]. Probably many of them were old, but there is extant a pension roll of the year 1553 (reign of Philip and Mary) from which can be gathered that a certain number of pensioned monks and nuns were then alive and continued to draw their pensions. Gasquet further remarks that only a few of the nuns who were turned away are known to have married[2]; considering that hardly any are known to have left their convents voluntarily, and that many of the younger ones were turned away through the act of 1535, this seems only natural.

Eye-witnesses as well as Cromwell's agents have left descriptions which give a striking picture of the brutality of the proceedings[3]. But the hardships to which the convent inmates were exposed, the terrible waste of their property, and the senseless destruction of priceless art treasures, must not blind us to the fact that the breaking up of the monastic system was but an incident in one of the most momentous revolutions within historic record. The dissolution of the monasteries at the time of the Reformation, to be rightly estimated, must be considered as part of a wider change which was remoulding society on an altered basis.

It is interesting to compare the view taken of monastic life at the time of the dissolution with the attitude taken towards convents in the following period. Some writings, as for example Lindesay in the play of the *Three Estates*, acted in the North in 1535[4], severely censure the inclinations which are fostered in the convent.

But strong as the feeling against convents and their inmates was in some instances at the time of the Reformation, when the system was once removed little antagonism remained towards those who had represented it. The thought of the nun, fifty years after she had passed away in England, roused no acrimony. Shakspere had no prejudice against her, and Milton was so

---

[1] Gasquet, A., *Henry VIII* etc., vol. 2, p. 481.

[2] Ibid. p. 479.

[3] Ellis, H., *Orig. Letters*, Series 3, vol. 3, p. 34, gives an interesting account.

[4] Lindesay, *Ane Satyre of the thrie Estaits*, edit. by Hall for the Early Engl. Text Soc., 1869, pp. 420 ff.

far impressed in her favour that he represented 'Melancholy' under the form of a 'pensive nun, devout and pure,—Sober, steadfast and demure.' It was only at a much later period that the agitation raised by the fear of returning 'Popery' caused men to rake up scandals connected with convents and to make bugbears out of them.

The losses incurred by the destruction of the convents were not however slow in making themselves felt; but as indifference towards women's intellectual interests had made part of the movement, a considerable time went by before the loss of the educational possibilities which the convent had secured to women was deplored. 'In the convents,' says Gasquet[1], 'the female portion of the population found their only teachers, the rich as well as the poor, and the destruction of these religious houses by Henry was the absolute extinction of any systematic education for women during a long period.' While devotion to domestic duties, exclusive of all other interests, continued to be claimed from women, the loss of their schools was a matter of indifference to society in general. But in proportion as shortcomings in women were felt, the thought arose that these might be due to want of training. The words in which the divine, Fuller (✝ 1661), expressed such thoughts in the 17th century are well worth recalling. The vow of celibacy in his eyes remained a thing of evil, but short of this the convents had not been wholly bad.

'They were good she schools wherein the girls and maids of the neighbourhood were taught to read and work; and sometimes a little Latin was taught them therein. Yea, give me leave to say, if such feminine foundations had still continued, provided no vow were obtruded upon them, (virginity is least kept where it is most constrained,) haply the weaker sex, besides the avoiding modern inconveniences, might be heightened to a higher perfection than hitherto hath been attained[2].'

---

[1] Gasquet, A., *Henry VIII* etc., vol. 2, p. 221.
[2] Fuller, Th., *Church History*, edit. Brewer, 1845, vol. 3, p. 336.

§ 2.   The Memoir of Charitas Pirckheimer.

A memoir is extant from the pen of the abbess of a convent
at Nürnberg.   It was written (1524–28) during the stormy period
following upon the outbreak of the Lutheran agitation, and it
helps us to realize the effect which the rupture with Rome had
on a convent of nuns.   Charitas Pirckheimer, the author of this
memoir, was the sister of Wilibald Pirckheimer († 1530), a well-
known humanist, and through him she was in touch with some
of the leading representatives of learning and art of her day.   She
was well advanced in life and had many years of active influence
behind her when the troubles began of which she has left a graphic
description.

An examination of the contents of her memoir must stand as
a specimen of the effects which the Reformation had on women's
convent life on the Continent, effects which varied in almost every
town and every province.   For the breaking up of the monastic
system abroad had none of the continuity and completeness it had
in England.   The absence of centralised temporal and spiritual
authority left the separate townships and principalities free to
accept or reject the change of faith as they chose.   The towns
were ruled by councils on which the decision in the first place
depended, and in the principalities the change depended on the
attitude of prince and magnate, so that the succession of the prince
of a different faith, or the conquest of one province by another,
repeatedly led to a change of religion.   In some districts the first
stormy outbreak was followed by a reaction in favour of Rome,
and convents which had disbanded were restored on a narrowed
basis; in others the monastic system which had received a severe
shock continued prostrate for many years.   But even in those
districts where the change of faith was permanently accepted, its
influence on conventual establishments was so varied that an
account of the way in which it put an end to nunneries lies beyond
the scope of this work.   It must suffice to point out that some
convents, chiefly unreformed ones, disbanded or surrendered under
the general feeling of restlessness; and that others were attacked
and destroyed during the atrocities of the Peasants' War.   The
heads of others again, with a clearsightedness one cannot but admire,
rejected Romish usages and beliefs in favour of the Lutheran faith,
and their houses have continued to this day as homes for unmar-

ried women of the aristocracy. Others were suffered to remain under the condition that no new members should be admitted, but that the old ones should be left in possession of their house till they died. To this latter class belonged the convent of St Clara at Nürnberg which we are about to discuss.

The convent dated its existence from the year 1279, in which several nuns from Söflingen, near Ulm, joined a number of religious women who were living together at Nürnberg, and prevailed upon them to adopt the rule of St Clara and place themselves under the guardianship of the Franciscan friars who had settled in Nürnberg in 1226[1]. It has been mentioned above that the nuns of this order, usually designated as Poor Clares, did not themselves manage that property of theirs which lay outside the precincts; they observed strict seclusion and were chiefly absorbed by devotional pursuits. Under the influence of the movement of monastic reform described in a previous chapter, Clara Gundelfingen (1450–1460), abbess of the house at Nürnberg, had greatly improved its discipline, and nuns were despatched from thence to convents at Brixen, Bamberg and other places to effect similar changes. There was another convent of nuns at Nürnberg dedicated to St Katherine which was under the supervision of the Dominican friars, but the convent of St Clara was the more important one and seems to have been largely recruited from members of wealthy burgher families. In 1476 it secured a bull from the Pope by which its use was altogether reserved to women who were born in Nürnberg.

Charitas Pirckheimer came to live in the house (1478) at the age of twelve. She was one of a family of seven sisters and one brother; all the sisters entered convents, excepting one who married, and they were in time joined by three of the five daughters of their brother[2]. These facts show that the women of most cultivated and influential families still felt convent life congenial. The Dominican writer Nider († 1438), speaking of convent life in the districts about Nürnberg, remarks that he had nowhere else found so many virtuous, chaste and industrious virgins[3]. Of the members of the Pirckheimer family who became nuns, Clara († 1533) joined her sister Charitas and acted as secretary to her for many years; her letters show her to have

[1] Binder, F., *Charitas Pirckheimer*, 1878, pp. 14 ff.   [2] Ibid. pp. 67 ff.
[3] Nider, Jos., *Formicarius*, bk. 1, ch. 4 (p. 8, edit. 1517).

been of a lively and sanguine disposition[1]. Walpurg, another sister, lived as a nun in the convent of St Clara at Münich ; Katharina became prioress at Geisenfeld, and Sabina and Euphemia entered the ancient Benedictine settlement of Bergen near Neuburg, of which they successively became abbesses. Sabina (1521–29), like her sister Charitas, was a great admirer of Albrecht Dürer, whom she consulted on the subject of illuminations done at her house[2]. A number of her letters remain to show that she held opinions of her own on some points of doctrine and watched the progress of affairs at Nürnberg with interest[3]. Her sister Euphemia (1529–47), who succeeded her, experienced even greater hardships than Charitas, for when Palgrave, Otto Heinrich of Neuburg, accepted the Protestant faith (1544), she and her nuns were expelled from their convent, and spent several years staying first at one place then at another, till the victory which the emperor Karl V won at Mühlberg (1547) made it possible for them to return to Bergen.

Charitas on entering the house at Nürnberg found herself among the daughters of family friends and relations. She contracted a lasting friendship with Apollonia Tucher, who was afterwards elected to the office of prioress, which she held for many years. Apollonia was nearly related to Anton Tucher († 1524), one of the wealthiest and most influential men of the town, and to Sixtus Tucher († 1507), a learned divine who was made provost of the church of St Lorenz, and in this capacity instructed the nuns of St Clara and provided them with religious literature. Scheurl († 1542), a nephew of Apollonia and a distinguished jurist, who came to settle at Nürnberg, greatly admired Charitas. We shall return to him later on.

Felicitas Grundherrin, another nun, who was made portress in 1503, wrote letters to her father which throw an additional light on the conduct and the experiences of the nuns during the period of religious contention. There were sixty inmates at that time, and among them we find the chief families of the town represented.

We are not informed at what age Charitas made profession.

---

[1] Muench, E., *Charitas Pirkheimer, ihre Schwestern und Nichten*, 1826, contains some of Clara's letters.

[2] Binder, F., *Charitas Pirkheimer*, p. 67.

[3] 'Briefe der Aebtissin Sabina,' edit. Lochner in *Zeitschrift für hist. Theologie*, vol. 36, 1866.

In 1494 she was joined by her sister Clara, and a few years later, when we first hear of her and her sister in connection with their brother, she was engaged in teaching the novices.

The career of Wilibald Pirckheimer, a man of considerable literary ability, is interesting, as it forms the centre of the intellectual and artistic life of Nürnberg, which at that time was achieving some of its greatest triumphs. The friend of Albrecht Dürer and of the leading humanists, he was himself full of enthusiasm for the revived interest in classic culture, and filled with that liberal appreciation of merit regardless of origin and nationality which is one of the attractive traits of the movement. In compliance with the taste of his age he had studied in Italy, and shortly after his return to Nürnberg, on the occasion of their father's death (1501), he lent his sisters, Charitas and Clara, a copy of the hymns of the Christian poet Prudentius, and an unnamed portion of Jerome's works, for their comfort and perusal ; Charitas thanked him for the loan in a Latin letter in which we get our first glimpse of her[1]. She says that she has been interested to find among the hymns some which are habitually sung in the choir and the authorship of which was unknown to her, and she begs she may keep Jerome's writings for some time longer, as they afford her so much delight. She refers to the frequent loans of books from her brother and assures him how much she depends on him for her education, begging him to visit and further instruct her. She has some knowledge of scripture, she says, but barely enough to instruct the novices.

In the year 1487 Celtes († 1508), a celebrated Latin scholar and poet, was crowned poet laureate by the Emperor Friedrich III at Nürnberg, and received at his hands the doctor's degree and a laurel wreath. Afterwards he travelled about in Germany, rousing interest in the revival of classical studies wherever he went, and encouraging those who were interested in learning to band together in societies (sodalitates) for the purpose of editing and publishing the classics. During a stay at a monastery in Regensburg (1501) he had come across the forgotten dramas of the nun Hrotsvith. They seemed to him so worthy of attention that he had them published at Nürnberg in a beautiful illustrated edition. We do not know if he was previously acquainted with

---

[1] Pirckheimer, B., *Opera*, edit. Goldast, 1610, p. 345; Binder, F., *Charitas Pirkheimer*, p. 52.

Charitas; but he sent her a copy of the dramas, and she wrote a grateful reply[1]. She begins by deploring the news she has heard that Celtes has been attacked and plundered by robbers. 'A few days ago,' she writes, 'I received the interesting writings of the learned virgin Hrotsvith, sent to me by you for no merits of my own, for which I express and owe you eternal gratitude. I rejoice that He who bestows powers of mind (largitor ingenii) and grants wisdom to men who are great and learned in the law, should not have denied to the frail and humbler sex some of the crumbs from the tables of wisdom. In this learned virgin the words of the apostle are verified that God chooses the humble to confound the strong....'

Celtes was charmed by this letter, and was inspired to compose a Latin ode[2] in praise of Charitas. In it he addressed her as the crown and star of womanhood, praised her for her knowledge of Latin, in which she worthily followed in the steps of a learned father and a learned brother, and enlarged on the pleasure her letter had brought. With the ode he sent a copy of a work on the city of Nürnberg lately published by him, and Charitas in reply sent a long letter which is most instructive in regard to the light it throws on her general attitude towards humanist culture[3]. While delighted by the gifts and the attentions of so distinguished a man as Celtes, she felt critical towards the heathen element in him, which seemed to her incompatible with the claims of a higher morality. The letter is too long to reproduce in full, but the following are some of its most noteworthy passages. 'I am your unworthy pupil, but a great admirer of yours and a well-wisher for your salvation, and as such I would earnestly and with all my heart entreat you not indeed to give up the pursuit of worldly wisdom, but to put it to higher uses, that is to pass from heathen writings to holy scripture, from what is earthly to what is divine, from the created to the Creator....Indeed neither knowledge nor any subject of investigation which is from God is to be contemned, but mystic theology and a good virtuous life must be ranked highest. For human understanding is weak and may fail us, but true faith and a good conscience never can. I therefore put before you, most learned doctor, when you have enquired into all under the sun, that the wisest of men said, Vanity of vanities....In the same

---

[1] Pirckheimer, *Opera*, edit. Goldast, 1610, p. 341; Binder, F., *Charitas Pirkheimer*, p. 81.

[2] Pirckheimer, *Opera*, p. 343; Binder, F., *Charitas Pirkheimer*, p. 84.

[3] Pirckheimer, *Opera*, p. 342; Binder, F., *Charitas Pirkheimer*, p. 85.

friendly spirit I would beg you to give up celebrating the unseemly tales of Jupiter, Venus, Diana, and other heathen beings whose souls are burning in Gehenna and who are condemned by right-minded men as detestable and deserving of oblivion; make the saints of God your friends by honouring their names and their memory, that they may guide you to the eternal home when you leave this earth.'

At the end of her letter she begged to be excused writing in this strain in words which suggest that her brother had urged her to speak out her mind, and a further letter of hers addressed to Wilibald says that she is forwarding to him a copy of her letter to Celtes[1]. She begs he will not bring him to the grating without sending her word previously, and expresses the belief that Celtes will not take umbrage.

We hear no more of their intercourse. Celtes soon afterwards left Nürnberg, and when Helena Meichnerin, abbess of the convent, resigned on account of some complaints of the town council, Charitas was chosen abbess (1503). Her acceptance of the post was made conditional by the Franciscan friars on her giving up her Latin correspondence[2], and there can be no doubt that this prohibition was primarily aimed at her intercourse with men like Celtes, who was known to be very lax in his morality, and whose sympathies in regard to learning were in direct opposition to the narrow religious views of the friars. Charitas conformed, but Wilibald's anger was roused, and he wrote to Celtes: 'You know that my sister Charitas has been chosen abbess. Imagine, those soft-footed men ($\chi\nu\lambda\acute{o}\pi o\delta\epsilon\varsigma$) have forbidden her to write Latin for the future. Observe their caution, not to say roguery[3].'

Charitas apparently wrote no more Latin letters, but her brother's friends continued to take an interest in her. Wilibald had a sincere regard for her abilities and frequently wrote of her to his friends. Other members of the humanist circle sought her out. Scheurl, the young jurist mentioned above, sent her from Bologna a copy of his ' Uses of the mass' (Utilitates missae) with a flattering letter which was presented to her by the provost Tucher (1506)[4]. It is overflowing with youthful enthusiasm, and says that of all the women he has met there are only two who are distinguished by abilities and intellect, knowledge and wealth,

[1] Pirckheimer, *Opera*, p. 344; Binder, F., *Charitas Pirkheimer*, p. 87.
[2] Binder, F., *Charitas Pirkheimer*, p. 88.   [3] Ibid. p. 220, note 26.
[4] Pirckheimer, *Opera*, p. 340; Binder, F., *Charitas Pirkheimer*, p. 89.

virtue and beauty, and are comparable to the daughters of Laelius
and Hortensius and to Cornelia, mother of the Gracchi; the one
is Cassandra (Fedele, poetess[1]) in Venice, the other is Charitas in
Nürnberg.   He expatiates on the merits of the Pirckheimer family
generally, and says Charitas is following the example of her relatives
in preferring a book to wool, a pen to the distaff, a stilus to a needle.
At a later stage of his career (1515) Scheurl wrote that it was usual
for men who were distinguished in mind and power to admire and
respect the abilities, learning and moral excellence of this abbess[2].

In 1513 Wilibald published an edition of Plutarch's essay 'On
retribution' which he had translated from Greek into Latin, and
dedicated it to his sister Charitas in a long and flattering epistle[3].
Mindful no doubt of the influences about her and referring to
difficulties in his own career, he spoke in the highest terms of the
Stoic philosophers and of the help their writings afforded.   'Accept
this gift on paper which, if I judge rightly, will not be displeasing
to you,' he says, 'and carefully peruse the writings of this pagan
author (gentilis).   And you will soon see that the philosophers
of antiquity did not stray far from the truth.'   Charitas was able
to appreciate this point of view and admitted in her reply that he
had sent her a jewel more precious than gold and silver[4].   Speaking
of Plutarch she confessed that 'he writes not like an unbelieving
heathen but like a learned divine and imitator of Christian perfection.   It is a wonderful circumstance which has filled me with
joy and surprise.'   But she thought her brother's praise of her
excessive.   'I am not learned myself, only the friend of those who
are learned; I am no writer, I only enjoy reading the writings of
others; I am unworthy of so precious a gift, though in truth you
have done well and wisely in placing the word Charitas at the
head of your work.   For Charity is the virtue which makes all
good things to be shared, and that Charity which is the Divine
Spirit itself will reward you here and in the life to come, where
honest efforts will be fully requited.'

A short time afterwards Pirckheimer dedicated to his sister
Clara, who was now teaching the novices, a 'Collection of the

---

[1] Born in Venice in 1465, was acquainted both with Latin and Greek, and studied
history, philosophy and theology. She disputed at Padua in public, wrote several learned
treatises, and was much admired and esteemed.

[2] Binder, F., *Charitas Pirkheimer*, p. 96.

[3] Pirckheimer, *Opera*, p. 230; Binder, F., *Charitas Pirkheimer*, p. 55.

[4] Pirckheimer, *Opera*, p. 344; Binder, F., *Charitas Pirkheimer*, p. 58.

Moral Sentences of Nilus.' It was a translation from Greek and Latin, and the title was ornamented with a design by Dürer[1]. He sent it 'to prevent her feeling any jealousy of her sister.' Clara shared her sister's tastes and was herself an ardent reader. When the New Testament edited by Erasmus appeared, Pirckheimer wrote to him that his sisters, who zealously read his writings, took great delight in this book also, and he says that they had greater insight into it than many men who were proud of their learning. They would have written themselves, he adds, if they had not felt shy of so great a man. Erasmus on one occasion compared the daughters of Sir Thomas More to the sisters of Wilibald Pirckheimer. Some writings of the humanist Reuchlin were also perused by them[2].

Wilibald further dedicated to Charitas his edition of the works of Fulgentius (1519), in a long preface in which he describes the difficulty he had had in procuring the manuscript from the library of his friend Tritheim, how he had despaired of deciphering it till the learned Cochlaeus came to his rescue, and how sure he felt that his sister would look upon the book as a treasure[3]. The translation of the sermons of Gregorius Nazianzenus, an important undertaking, he also accomplished mainly for the use of his sisters[4].

Besides their devotional and intellectual interests, the nuns at St Clara made their own clothes, and seem to have had some ability in sewing, for when the imperial robes which were kept at Nürnberg were to be carried to Aachen for the coronation of the Emperor Karl V, they were first given into the hands of the nuns to be looked over and mended[5].

An interesting light is thrown on the less serious side of the character of Charitas by an amusing German letter which she wrote to Dürer and two envoys of Nürnberg who were staying at Augsburg in 1518 on the occasion of the Imperial Diet. From there they had sent her a missive penned in a jovial hour, and Charitas in reply wrote[6]: 'I received your friendly letter with special delight and read it with such attention that my eyes were often brim full, but more from laughing than any other emotion. Many thanks to you that in spite of your great business and your amusements you should have taken the trouble to give directions

---

[1] Binder, F., *Charitas Pirkheimer*, p. 65, footnote.   [2] Ibid. p. 66.
[3] Pirckheimer, *Opera*, p. 247; Binder, F., *Charitas Pirkheimer*, p. 61.
[4] Binder, F., *Charitas Pirkheimer*, p. 62.   [5] Ibid. p. 35.
[6] Thausing, M., *Dürer's Briefe* etc., 1872, p. 167.

to this little nun about cloister-life, of which you have a clear mirror before you at present....' And she begs the envoy Spengler to study accounts with a view to advising her how to waste everything till nothing remains, and begs Dürer, 'who is such a draughtsman and genius,' to give his attention to the buildings, so that when she has the choir rebuilt he may help and advise her how to introduce larger windows so that the nuns' eyes may be less dim.

From these various notices we conclude that time passed not unpleasantly or unprofitably with the abbess of St Clara before those contentions began which followed upon the attack made on the established religion by Luther. In Nürnberg, as in most other cities, the feeling was general that the life of the prelacy was degenerate and that the Papacy was a hotbed of abuse. Luther's opposition to the Pope was therefore greeted with acclamation both by the enlightened men of the town, who felt that the tyranny of the Church was a stumblingblock in the way of progress, and by the people, who readily seized the idea that the means were now given them to break through class tyranny. Wilibald Pirckheimer was among those who without hesitation sided with the Lutheran agitation, but Charitas thought otherwise. The abbess of the convent of St Clara at Eger forwarded to her some of the fierce attacks on Luther from the pen of Emser († 1527), and Charitas was so delighted with them that she had them read out aloud to the nuns during meals, and was prompted to write a letter to their author[1].

This letter became a source of great annoyance to her. It fell into the hands of Emser's enemies, and was published with an abusive running comment on Charitas[2]. Even Wilibald was annoyed and declared she would have done better not to have written it. He strongly supported the Lutheran agitation at the time, and Eck, who suspected him of having written the attack on himself, entitled 'Eccius Dedolatus,' for personal reasons inscribed Wilibald's name on the Papal ban. There is extant from Wilibald's pen a fragment in which he expresses doubts as to the rightfulness of convent life generally[3], but he gradually modified his views. The violence and narrowness of the representatives of the party of progress in Nürnberg were little to his taste. On the plea of ill-health he withdrew from the council, and took no part in the stormy discussions of 1523, when the rupture with Rome was

---

[1] Binder, F., *Charitas Pirkheimer*, p. 105.   [2] *Eyn Missyve oder Sendbrief* etc., 1523.
[3] Pirckheimer, *Opera*, p. 375.

declared complete and decisions arrived at, momentous for the future of the new faith not only in Nürnberg, but in Germany generally.

At this juncture the memoir of Charitas[1] begins. She describes the effect of the Lutheran teaching; how ceremonies are being abolished, rules and vows declared vain, so that many monks and nuns are leaving their cloisters, putting off convent garb and marrying and otherwise doing as they choose.

'These various reasons brought us many troubles and difficulties,' she writes (p. 2), 'for many powerful and evil-minded persons came to see the friends they had in our cloister, and argued with them and told them of the new teaching, how the religious profession was a thing of evil and temptation in which it was not possible to keep holy, and that we were all of the devil. Some would take their children, sisters and relatives out of the cloister by force and by the help of admonitions and promises of which they doubtless would not have kept half. This arguing and disputing went on for a long time and was often accompanied by great anger and abuse. But since none of the nuns by God's grace was moved to go, the fault was laid on the Franciscans, and everyone said they encouraged us, so that it would be impossible to convince us of the new belief while we had them as preachers and confessors.'

The friars had long been odious for their determined class feeling, religious intolerance, and encouragement of superstitions; it was obvious that the advocates of change would direct their attacks against them. Charitas, fully aware of the emergency, assembled the nuns and put before them the danger of being given over to 'wild priests and apostate monks,' and with their consent decided to hand in a 'supplication' to the town council. This council was presided over by three leading men (triumviri), of whom one named Nützel was the so-called representative (pfleger) of the convent, another named Ebner had a daughter among the nuns, and the third, Geuder, was the brother-in-law of Charitas. She consulted Wilibald on the matter of the supplication, but forthwith wrote and despatched a letter to each of these three men, begging and claiming the protection of her privileges.

The supplication itself (p. 12) was carefully worded, and re-

---

[1] 'Pirkheimer, Charitas': *Denkwürdigkeiten aus dem Reformationszeitalter,* herausg. Höfler, C., *Quellensammlung für fränk. Geschichte,* vol. 4, 1852 (page references in the text to this edition).

quested that the connection between the Franciscans and the nuns might not be severed, contradicting the charges which were brought against the former. They do not forbid the nuns to read the Evangels and other books, Charitas says,—'if they did so we should not obey them.' The nuns have the Old and the New Testament in daily use in the German and the Latin versions. Charitas denies despising the married state or retaining nuns by force. 'But as we compel no one, so too we claim not to be compelled, and to remain free in mind as well as in body. But this cannot be if we are given over to strange priests, which would be destruction to our community....,' and more to a like purpose.

The supplication was handed in at the beginning of 1524, but after considerable delay the councillors postponed giving a definite reply to it. In the meantime Charitas was much annoyed by the mother of one of her nuns who tried to persuade her daughter to leave the convent, and finding her words of no avail, appealed to the town council (p. 19) for an order to take her 'out of this prison' as she called it, into which she had sent her nine years before at the age of fourteen. Charitas also sent in a statement of the case (p. 28), but again no reply was vouchsafed her.

The letters which Clara wrote to her brother about this time help us to realise the situation. All her letters are undated, but in one she thanks Wilibald for his advice about the supplication, and says that if divine service should really be abolished she means to devote herself more to reading, for 'the dear beloved old writers surely were no fools[1].' In another she thanks him for the loan of books and says a work of Erasmus (probably *De libero arbitrio*) has pleased the sisters by its moderation. As to Charitas 'she finds great comfort in her beloved old Cyprian, in whose writings she reads day and night. She sends greetings and the message that she prefers Cyprian to all these new evangelists who strut about in cut garments and golden chains[2].'

Though Clara did not lose her cheerfulness, Charitas, who saw further, was full of apprehension. From what her sister says she regretted the severe tone of her letter to Geuder[3]. On other occasions also she was led to indignant utterances which she afterwards regretted[4].

---

[1] Muench, E., *Charitas Pirckheimer* etc., 1826, p. 104.

[2] Binder, F., *Charitas Pirkheimer*, p. 125, from an unpublished letter.

[3] Muench, E., *Charitas Pirckheimer* etc., p. 110.

[4] Ibid., p. 118 (on a letter written to Nützel).

A gap occurs at this period in her memoir which she resumed writing in March 1525, after the religious disputation had taken place at Nürnberg. After many stormy scenes, 'the preachers of the Evangel,' as they called themselves, decided to carry out their intentions without waiting for the decision of a Church Council. The immediate result of the decision was an attack on all religious houses. But in the convent of St Clara the determined and reckless energy of the reformers was matched by indignant protest and unyielding opposition on the part of the abbess.

Charitas has described in full (p. 33) how a deputation from the town council asked to be admitted into her house, and how they informed her and the assembled nuns that their connection with the Franciscans was at an end; a 'reformed' preacher had been appointed to preach in the church of the nuns, and they were left the choice among several men who would act to them as confessors. Much argument followed, but Charitas maintained that her house and the Franciscans had always been closely connected. 'If we yield it is only to force and we turn to God,' she said, 'and before Him we lodge a protest and declare that we are forced against our will, and that we reject and discountenance all your proposals.' The· assembled nuns rose to their feet to shew their approval of her speech, and the deputation in vain tried the effect of persuasion. Charitas scorned the idea of having anything to do with apostate monks; and the deputation retired after blaming the women for behaving in a most ungrateful manner. A second visit led to similar results; Charitas abode by her decision, the nuns wept, and the deputation retired after venting their indignation in threats.

The hopes of the convent now centred in Nützel, their representative in the town council, and Charitas with her brother's approval wrote to him (p. 41) begging him to come to her. But the first words Nützel spoke dispelled every hope of assistance from that quarter; he blamed the nuns for opposing the council, and urged the advisability of their giving way. Charitas was most indignant and declared she was well aware that it was intended to force them to this new belief, but that they were agreed that neither in life nor in death would they listen to what the Church had not previously countenanced. She called upon the prioress to read out a second petition to the council asking to have their father confessor back or else to be left without one. She wanted Nützel to take charge of this petition, but he was only angered, and taking Charitas aside, represented to her that her opposition was a serious matter ; her example was encouraging other women's convents to opposition, which would relent if she did.   He said that by resigning and disbanding the convent bloodshed would be averted, and he spoke in praise of the new preacher.   But Charitas remained unmoved.   As he was leaving the house his daughter and the other nuns, whose fathers were members of the town council, went down on their knees to him imploring protection.   He refused to listen, but was so far impressed that he never slept all the following night, as his wife afterwards told the nuns (p. 54).

The convent's opposition to their plans was a source not only of annoyance but of apprehension to the town authorities.   The peasants' rising was spreading in the direction of Nürnberg, and as popular feeling was against religious houses the argument that dissolving the house might help to avert a danger was not altogether unfounded.   Nützel in a long expostulation (p. 55) shortly afterwards tried to impress this view on the abbess, but Charitas urged (p. 59) that other reasons besides hatred of the friars had roused the peasants to rebellion, and complained that the ill-feeling against her house was largely due to the reformed preachers, who declared they would not rest till they had driven monks and nuns out of the town (p. 62).   Rightly or wrongly she held that Poliander, the reformed preacher who was now preaching in the convent church, had been promised a reward if he persuaded her or her nuns to leave the convent (p. 67), and that his want of success aggravated his hatred of them.   It was in vain that Nützel wrote in praise of him (p. 67).   Charitas now looked upon Nützel as a dangerous enemy, and her sister Clara wrote to Wilibald[1] begging him to advise the convent how to get rid of the man.   In another letter[2] she said that Charitas was seriously afraid of him.

In place of the Franciscans a number of reformed preachers now preached before the nuns and the people in the convent church.   Among them was Osiander, formerly a Carthusian, whose violence at a later period was censured and resented by his Protestant brethren ; and the nuns were obliged to attend and to listen to a torrent of abuse and imprecation by him and others. 'I cannot and will not detail,' says Charitas in her memoir (p. 70), 'how they perverted Holy Writ to a strange meaning, how they

---

[1] Muench, E., *Charitas Pirckheimer* etc., p. 106.   [2] Ibid. p. 109.

cast down the doctrines of the Church and discarded all ceremonies; how they abused and reviled all religious orders and
classes, and respected neither Pope nor Emperor, whom they
openly called tyrant, devil, and Antichrist; how roughly and in
what an unchristian-like spirit and against all brotherly love they
abused us and charged us with great wickedness, for the purpose of
rousing the people, whom they persuaded that an ungodly set like
ourselves should be destroyed, our cloister broken open, ourselves
dragged out by force, since we represented a despicable class,
heretics, idolatrous and blasphemous people, who were eternally
of the devil.'

One might be tempted to look upon this description as an
exaggeration were it not for a letter from Wilibald Pirckheimer
to Melanchthon, in which he describes the outrages to which the
nuns were exposed in similar terms. ' The preachers scream, swear,
and storm, and do everything in their power to rouse the hatred
of the masses against the poor nuns; they openly say that as
words were of no avail, recourse should be had to force,' and he
wonders the cloister has not yet been attacked[1].

Under the pressure of popular opinion and increasing restlessness the Austin monks gave over their house, and they were followed by the Carmelites, the Benedictines, and the Carthusians.
The Dominicans hesitated; the Franciscans refused to go. Charitas
expresses wonder that the 'spiritual poison,' as she calls it, which
the preachers several times a week tried to infuse into the nuns,
took no effect, and that none of them expressed a desire to leave
the convent (p. 85).

Things had now come to such a pass that convents outside
the city disbanded before the peasants' rising; and nuns from
Pillenreuth and Engelthal sought refuge in the town with the
nuns of St Clara (p. 86). These lived in daily fear of their house
being stormed, for the people shouted and swore at them from
below, threw stones into the choir, smashed the church windows,
and sang insulting songs in the churchyard outside. But the
nuns, nothing daunted, continued to keep the hours and to ring
the bells, though they were every moment prepared for the worst.
Clara in a letter to Wilibald described her own and her sister's
fears in eloquent terms[2]; and the nun Felicitas Grundherrin wrote

---

[1] Pirckheimer, *Opera*, p. 374.
[2] Muench, E., *Charitas Pirckheimer* etc., p. 108.

to her father entreating him to abide by the old faith[1]. In these
days the nuns seem to have read a good deal of pamphlet literature, but they failed to see anything beyond an encouragement
to violence and disorder in the whole Lutheran movement.

A further attempt was made by the council to coerce the
convent. A number of injunctions were sent to the abbess which
were to be carried out within a month (p. 88). The first of these
commanded her to absolve the nuns from their vow that they
might enjoy 'Christian freedom'; another that she should send
the young nuns home though they refused, 'since children should
obey their parents.' The deputies who laid these injunctions before
the abbess assured her that the council was prepared to restore
to the nuns what they had brought to the convent; that they
would give money to those who had brought nothing, and provide
a dower for those who married. To these arguments Charitas
replied that the nuns had made a vow not before her but before
God, that it was not in her power to dispense them from it and
that she would not urge them to disobedience. With a touch of
bitterness she added that their mothers were continually at the
convent grating urging them to go (p. 87). For the matrons of
the town especially sided with the reformed preachers and cried
shame on convent life. 'If it were not for the women and the
preachers things would not be so bad,' Clara wrote on one occasion
to Wilibald[2], and on another she spoke of the sharp tongues and
violent behaviour of the women.

The deputation further claimed that the nuns should take off
their convent clothes (p. 93), the sight of which they said gave
umbrage. 'We are continually told,' Charitas replied, 'that our
vows and our clothes threaten to cause a rising, but it is your
preachers, to whom we are forced to listen, who try to provoke
one by abusing and condemning us from the pulpit and charging
us with vices and impurity to humour the people.' The command
was also given to do away with the convent grating; and it was
backed by the threat that if Charitas failed to comply with it
the town authorities would throw open the house to all visitors.
The heaviness of this blow was such that after the deputation
had left Charitas summoned the nuns and asked their intentions
severally. In the eyes of the whole convent throwing open the
house involved turning it into a public resort of bad character.

[1] Binder, F., *Charitas Pirkheimer*, p. 118.
[2] Ibid. p. 150, from an unpublished letter.

They felt they must yield or leave the house altogether, but they promised to abide by the decision of Charitas if she would stay and advise them. The intrepid abbess decided to do away with the grating at one window, declaring that they acted against the rule under protest and only temporarily. On the other points she sought the advice of learned men outside, but they advised compromise, for, to give her own words (p. 95), 'they said all chance was gone of gaining anything by opposition; we must yield if we did not want the house to go to ruin. People now did things by main force regardless of justice or equity, fearful neither of Pope nor Emperor, nor even of God except in word ; things were such that these people said, What we will must be done, thus and not otherwise, declaring themselves more powerful than the Pope himself.'

In the meantime the feelings against the nunnery were by no means unanimous. Geuder, the brother-in-law of Charitas, was emphatic at the council meeting in denouncing the throwing open of convents, which in his eyes also meant turning them into disreputable houses[1]. But no amount of opposition made by him and others could prevent a scene from being enacted in the convent chapel, which was afterwards looked upon as disgraceful, not only by those who provoked it, but by outsiders whether partisans of the Lutheran movement or not. The repeated attempts to persuade the nuns to leave having failed and Charitas refusing to bid them go, two of the chief councillors, one of them Nützel, the representative of the convent's interests, and the widow of a councillor who had long clamoured for her daughter's release, repaired to the convent with a number of other persons, claimed to be admitted, and declared they had come to fetch their daughters away. The three nuns, who were between nineteen and twenty-three years of age, tried to hide, but Charitas bade them come forth, and they then sought refuge with her in the convent chapel. She has described in full how the young women besought her to protect them, how their parents and others abused and reviled them, and how in spite of their protests, their indignation and their tears, their relations at last resorted to violence. Four persons seized each nun and dragged and pushed her out of the chapel, while the women present shouted approval, and once outside their convent clothes were torn off and others substituted in their stead. After a scuffle and a scramble in which one nun was knocked

[1] Binder, F., *Charitas Pirkheimer*, p. 153.

over and her foot injured, they were carried to a chariot waiting
outside and conveyed away.

Charitas remained behind in grief and despair. 'I and all
my nuns are so distressed at all this,' she wrote a few days later[1],
'that I have almost wept out my eyes....Nothing ever so went to
my heart.' Indignation at the violence of the act became general
in the town and spread beyond its confines. 'I never could have
imagined women acting in such a cruel manner,' Sabina, the
abbess of Bergen, wrote to Wilibald ; and in another letter, appre-
hending the destruction of the convent at Nürnberg, she proposed
that Charitas and her nuns should seek refuge with her[2].

But Charitas persisted in holding her ground, though with
an aching heart. When the men who had fetched away their
daughters sent word offering to pay for their maintenance during
the time they had lived with her, she refused. Her trials in one
direction had reached their climax,—the councillor Nützel, who
admitted that things had gone too far, henceforth acted in a
conciliatory spirit, and some approximation took place between
them. Not that he ever tired of urging Charitas to desert her
convent and her cause, but he now confined himself to persuasion
and argument, and when one of the young nuns who had been
carried off was so far reconciled to the world that she came to
the convent window and urged her step-sister to return home,
pretending that Nützel had sent her (p. 123), the councillor dis-
claimed having done so. His correspondence with Charitas, which
she has faithfully inserted in her memoir, shows that she patiently
listened to every argument in favour of the new doctrines. She
had a conversation with the preacher Osiander which lasted four
hours (p. 128), she listened to over a hundred sermons preached
by the Lutherans, and she read their writings, yet she could find
nothing to her taste and it seemed easy to her to confound their
arguments. Her letters show that her unhappiness was great, for
on one occasion she went so far as to put before Nützel (p. 122)
what the result would be if women like themselves, many of whom
were over sixty and several over seventy, returned to the world
and tried to earn their living, as everyone said they ought to do.
She declared she detained no one, the nuns were at liberty to go
if they chose ; everyone was giving her advice, she said, but she

[1] Binder, F., *Charitas Pirkheimer*, p. 161.
[2] 'Briefe der Aebtissin Sabina,' edit. Lochner in *Zeitschrift für hist. Theologie*,
vol. 36, 1866, pp. 542, 545.

saw no salvation in the new doctrines, which did not appeal to her. Her readiness to listen to argument caused Nützel to set his hopes on a conference between Melanchthon and her (p. 133), and probably at the instigation of Wilibald, who was deeply grieved at the injustice done to his sisters without being able to give them direct help, Melanchthon, who was well known for his uprightness and conciliatory influence, came to Nürnberg towards the close of the year 1525. 'I am glad to hear Melanchthon is coming,' Charitas wrote; 'since I have heard he is an irreproachable, upright and justice-loving man, I do not suppose he can approve of what has been done here.'

Nützel at once (p. 149) brought him to the convent. 'A few days later our representative came with Philip Melanchthon,' Charitas wrote, 'who spoke much about the new faith, but finding that we set our hopes more on the grace of God than on our works, he said we might as well seek our salvation in the cloister as in the world.' They had a long talk together and agreed on all points except on the subject of vows, for these the reformer declared were not binding, while Charitas maintained that a promise made to God must be kept. She describes Melanchthon as more moderate in his speech than she had ever known a Lutheran to be. Melanchthon, on hearing the various points of the case, blamed the councillors for having forbidden the Franciscans to confer with the convent, and for forcibly taking the nuns out of the cloister. 'I trust God has sent this Lutheran at the right hour,' Charitas wrote, 'for they were discussing whether or not to expel nuns generally, pull down their houses, and put the older inmates of those convents which would not surrender into one house, driving back the younger ones into the world' (p. 171).

According to her account Melanchthon represented to the council that no convent at Wittenberg had been destroyed by force, and after a great deal of argument it was decreed to make one more effort to persuade the nuns to go, and failing this to leave them alone. No concessions were made with regard to the friars, the nuns remained without a minister to take their confessions and to administer the sacrament, but after all the nuns had been severally asked if they wished to stay or to go, and only one declared herself ready to leave the house, the rest were left in possession till the end of their days.

With the account of the last visitation, which took place in 1528, the memoir of Charitas ends. From other sources we hear

that short of annoyances about her income and a tax levied on
the convent she remained unmolested, and passed the last few
years of her life in peace. At the close of 1528, the fiftieth
anniversary of her entering the convent, and the twenty-fifth year
of her appointment as abbess, was celebrated with some amount
of cheerfulness. Wilibald and others sent presents, and after
dinner the nuns danced to the sound of the dulcimer (hackbrett),
which the abbess played[1]. Wilibald's interest in the convent
continued, and towards the close of his life we find him busy
writing a pamphlet in justification of the nuns[2], in which he
developed at some length the arguments against those who had
oppressed and coerced them. He died in 1530, and within a
couple of years was followed by his sister Charitas (1533). Her
sister Clara ruled the convent for a few months after her and was
succeeded by Wilibald's daughter Charitas. The number of nuns
was slowly but steadily dwindling; before the close of the century
the house had fallen into the hands of the town council by default.

The abbess Charitas Pirckheimer worthily represents the
monastic life of women at the close of the Middle Ages. Faithful
to the system she had embraced, she remained true to her con-
victions to the last, with a fearlessness, candour, and determination
which give her attitude a touch of heroism. She is one among
many staunch adherents to the old faith who experienced hardships which simple humanity and feelings of equity and justice
alike condemned, but whose steadfastness could not save their
cause from being lost.

---

[1] Binder, F., *Charitas Pirkheimer*, pp. 183 ff.

[2] Pirckheimer, *Opera*, 'Oratio apologetica,' pp. 375–385; Binder, F., *Charitas
Pirkheimer*, p. 198.

CONCLUSION.

MY task has drawn to its close. In a series of chapters, incompletely no doubt but I trust not superficially, the position of woman under monasticism has been brought before the reader, and some account has been given of the various aspects of convent life. In conclusion it seems well to pause and look back over the ground traversed, to take in at a glance what Catholic tradition, convent-life and saint-lore have done for women in the past. The area over which the reader has been taken is a wide one, and the ground in many directions remains unexplored. Still some of the most prominent landmarks have been noted, and some districts carefully examined. Thus while further information might be sought concerning many special points, it still seems legitimate to form a general survey and to draw certain conclusions.

Turning back to the earliest period when Christianity with its new conceptions first came into contact with beliefs dating from a distant heathen era, we have seen how many sentiments and associations of ideas peculiar to pre-Christian times lived on and were absorbed into the new religion. The early representatives of Christianity, with a keen-sighted appreciation of the means by which a change of religion is most successfully effected, treated the older conceptions with tolerance, and by doing so made possible the establishment of new ideas in the old heathen setting. The legends and the cult of the saints contain a mine of wealth as yet little explored by the student of primitive civilization and folk-lore, a mine which has here been tapped at one vein only,— namely for the information it yields on the antiquity of beliefs which attach to certain women who are reckoned among the saints.

Passing from the ground of tradition to that of history we have seen how the convent was looked upon with favour by women of the newly converted barbarian races, and how readily they availed themselves of the protection which the Christian religion held out to them. This development also needed to be studied side by side with previous social conditions in order to stand out in its true light, and it gained a new meaning when considered in connection with the elements of older folk tradition which it absorbed. The representatives of Christianity, profiting by a surviving love of independence among womankind, turned the energies of women into new channels, and giving scope to their activity in new directions, secured their help in the cause of peaceful progress. The outward conditions of life were such that the woman who joined the convent made her decision once for all. But provided she agreed to forego the claims of family and sex, an honourable independence was secured to her, and she was brought into contact with the highest aims of her age. At a period when monasteries, placed in the remote and uncultivated districts, radiated peace and civilization throughout the neighbourhood, many women devoted themselves to managing settlements which in the standard they attained, vied in excellence with the settlements managed by men.

At the outset many married women left their husbands for the purpose of founding and governing convents; sometimes they founded convents the management of which they left to others, and themselves retired to them later in life. The prestige and advantages enjoyed by the heads of religious settlements were such that kings and queens frequently installed their daughters as abbesses in preference to seeking for them matrimonial alliances, and these princesses were joined by many daughters of the most influential families, who gladly availed themselves of the opportunity of embracing the religious vocation. Through their close contact with high-born women, convents maintained a high tone in manners, morals and general behaviour, and grew into important educational centres, the beneficent influence of which was generally recognised.

The career open to the inmates of convents both in England and on the continent was greater than any other ever thrown open to women in the course of modern European history; abilities might raise the nun to the rank of abbess, a position of substantial authority. In the Kentish charter, to which reference has been made, the names of the abbesses as representatives of religion follow those of the bishops. In Saxony it fell to an abbess to act as representative of the emperor during his absence. As independent landowners, who held their property of and from king and emperor, the abbess took rank with the lords temporal and spiritual in the right of jurisdiction which they exercised, and in the right of being represented in Parliament or at the Imperial Diet as the case might be.

While fulfilling the duties which devolved on them in virtue of their station, abbesses did not neglect their opportunities of keeping in touch with culture and of widening their mental horizon. In Anglo-Saxon England men who attained to distinction received their training in settlements governed by women. Histories and a chronicle of unique value were inspired by and drafted under the auspices of Saxon abbesses. For nuns Ealdhelm wrote his most famous treatises, and several valuable contemporary biographies, such as those of Sturmi and of Robert of Fontevraud, were written at the express desire of nuns. And while eager in encouraging productiveness in others, they were not slow in trying to develop their own literary powers. In the 6th century Radegund was writing epistles in verse under the tuition of an exiled Latin poet ; to an Anglo-Saxon nun whose name is not recorded we owe one of the earliest and most interesting accounts extant of a journey to Palestine. In the 8th century the nun Lioba was trying her hand at Latin verse in a convent in Thanet; in the 10th century the nun Hrotsvith in Saxony was composing Latin dramas on the model of Terence. The contributions of nuns to literature as well as incidental remarks show that the curriculum of study in the nunnery was as liberal as that accepted by monks, and embraced all available writing, whether by Christian or profane authors. While Scripture and the writings of the Fathers of the Church at all times formed the groundwork of monastic studies, Cicero at this period was read by the side of Boethius, Virgil by the side of Martianus Capella, Terence by the side of Isidor of Sevilla. From remarks made by Hrotsvith we see that the coarseness of the later Latin dramatists made no reason for their being forbidden to nuns, though she would have seen it otherwise ; and Herrad was so far impressed by the wisdom of the heathen philosophers of antiquity that she pronounced this wisdom to be the 'product of the Holy Spirit also.' Throughout the literary world as represented by convents, the use of Latin was general, and made possible the even spread of culture in districts that were widely remote from each other and practically without intercourse.

The educational influence of convents during centuries cannot

be rated too highly. Not only did their inmates attain considerable knowledge, but education in a nunnery, as we saw from the
remarks of Chaucer and others, secured an improved standing
to those who were not professed. The fact that a considerable
number of women's houses after the monastic revival of the 11th and
12th centuries were founded largely at the instigation of men, proves
that the usefulness of these institutions was generally recognised.

While devoted to reading and study which pre-eminently constituted the religious vocation, nuns during their leisure hours
cultivated art in several of its branches. Spinning and weaving
were necessarily practised in all settlements during many centuries,
for the inmates of these settlements made the clothes which they
wore. But weaving and embroidery, always essentially woman's
work, found a new development in the convent, and works of
marked excellence were produced both in England and abroad.
The painstaking industry, which goes far in the production of
such work, was reflected in the activity of women as scribes and
illuminators, and the names of several nuns who were famous for
their writing have been handed down to posterity. In the twofold
domain of learning and art the climax of productiveness was reached
in the person of Herrad, in whom a wide range of intellectual
interests and a keen appreciation of study combined with considerable artistic skill and a certain amount of originality.

Side by side with literary and artistic pursuits nuns were active
in the cause of philanthropy. Several women who had the
sufferings of their fellows at heart are numbered among the
saints; and under the auspices of Hildegard a book was compiled on the uses of natural products in health and disease, which
forms a landmark in the history of mediæval medicine.

With the consciousness of the needs of others came too a
keener power of self-realisation. The attention of nuns was turned
to the inner life, and here again their productiveness did not
fail them. The contributions to mystical literature by nuns are
numerous, and their writings, which took the form of spiritual
biography, legendary romance, or devotional exercise, were greatly
appreciated and widely read by their contemporaries. Even now-
a-days they are recommended as devotional works by the Catholic
Church.

We have seen that the position of the convent was throughout
influenced by the conditions of the world outside it; changes in
outside political, intellectual and social life necessarily made them-

selves felt in the convent. Consequent upon the spread of the feudal system of land tenure, which in the interest of an improved military organisation reserved the holding of property for men, women forfeited their chance of founding and endowing independent monasteries, and the houses founded after the monastic revival never attained a position comparable with that of those dating from the earlier period. As monasteries were theoretically safe against infringement of their privileges by prince or bishop owing to their connection with Rome, the relation of the Pope to temporal rulers and to the greater ecclesiastics directly affected them, and when the power of the Pope was relaxed they were at the mercy of prince and bishop. We have seen how kings of England appropriated alien priories, and how wilfully princes abroad curtailed the privileges of nunneries, the support of their prelates giving countenance to these changes. At a later period a considerable number of women's convents were interfered with by churchmen, who on the plea of instituting reforms took advantage of their position to appropriate the convent property.

A change of a different kind which affected the convent in its educational and intellectual standing was the growth of university centres, and the increased facilities afforded to the student of visiting different centres in succession. In the 9th century Bede who never stirred from his convent might attain intellectual excellence ; such a course was impossible in the 13th and 14th centuries when the centre of education lay in the disputations which animated the lecture room. Some of the progressive monasteries of men lessened the loss they felt by securing a house at the university to which they sent their more promising pupils, but the tone at the mediæval university was such that one cannot wonder that no attempt was made in this direction by the convents of women. As a natural result their intellectual standard for a time remained stationary, and then, especially in the smaller and remoter settlements, it fell. This led to a want of interest in intellectual acquirements among nuns, and it was accompanied by a growing indifference in the outside world to the intellectual acquirements of women generally.

Not that the desire to maintain a high standard had passed away from women's convents. The readiness with which many houses adopted the chance of betterment held out to them by the congregations of the 15th century, goes far to prove that nuns continued to identify the idea of salvation with a high moral tone and an application to study. But study now ran along a narrow groove, for the monastic reformers favoured devotional study only. The nuns, who were impressed by the excellence of the reformers' motives, and prevented by circumstances from forming opinions of their own in the matter, showed an increasing readiness to adopt their views. The friars led the way in this direction by cutting off the nuns, given into their care, from the management of outside affairs; they were followed by the order of Sion, and by the congregations of Bursfeld and Windesheim, all of which alike urged that the primary duty of a nun was sanctification of self. The interest of this movement lies in the voluminous devotional literature it called forth, a literature full of spiritual beauty, but in the production of which nuns, so far as we know, took no share. By writing out oral sermons they helped, however, to preserve and spread them. The change which had come over the convent life of women cramped rather than stimulated their intellectual vitality, and the system of which they made part was apparently beyond their control. The author of 'Holy Maiden-hood' in the 13th century called the nun the free woman, and contrasted her with the wife who in his eyes was the slave. But Erasmus at the beginning of the 16th century urged that the woman who joined the convent by doing so became a slave, while she who remained outside was truly free. Erasmus also insisted on the fact that there was no reason why a woman should enter a convent, as she might as well stay in the world and remain unmarried if she so preferred. In point of fact social conditions had so far changed that society no longer called to the Church for protection of its daughters. For a time the convent ranked high as an educational establishment; then this use began to pass away also, and it was largely on account of the provision religious houses made for unmarried women that they still continued in favour with a portion of the community.

Many historians have advocated the view that the Protestant reformers discovered the abuses of the monastic system, and finding these intolerable, swept the whole system away. The evidence adduced above in connection with the dissolution shows that matters were far otherwise, that the dissolution of convents was accompanied by many regrettable incidents, and that as far as England is concerned, it may confidently be called premature. For many years those who sought progress by peaceful educational means seemed to be confronted only by hopeless and sanguinary con-

fusion ; they passed away with the belief that the whole movement they had witnessed was opposed to real progress, holding
the view that the Protestants were innovators of the worst and
most dangerous kind.

However, as far as convents are concerned, it seems as though
the Protestant reformers, far from acting as innovators, had done
no more than give violent and extreme application to forces which
had for some time been at work. The dissolution was led up to
by a succession of conventual changes, and before the outbreak of
the Lutheran agitation, at least one well-wisher of the system in
Germany, Tritheim, had despaired of putting this system to new and
effective uses. Not that monasticism can be said to have generally
outlived its purposes at the time of the Reformation. In some
countries, as in France and Spain, it subsequently chronicled
important developments. But where German elements were prevalent, convents were either swept away, or put to altogether different
uses by the Protestants, or else allowed to continue on a very much
narrowed basis by the Catholics. Many convents fell utterly to
decay in course of time and ceased to exist at the beginning of
this century, others again still linger on but are mere shadows
of their former brilliant selves.

The reason for these changes lay not altogether with those
who professed religion in convents, they were part of a wider
change which remoulded society on an altered basis. For the
system of association, the groundwork of mediæval strength and
achievement, was altogether giving way at the time of the Reformation. The socialistic temper was superseded by individualistic
tendencies which were opposed to the prerogatives conferred on
the older associations. These tendencies have continued to the
present with slight abatements, and have throughout proved averse
to the continuation of monasticism which attained greatness
through the spirit of association.

Repelled through the violence and aggressiveness of the reformers, and provoked by the narrowness of Protestantism generally, some modern writers take the view that the Reformation
was throughout opposed to real progress, and that mankind would
have been richer had the reformers left undisturbed many of the
institutions they destroyed. The revenues of these institutions
would now have been at the disposal of those who would put them
to public and not to personal uses. As far as convents, especially
those of women, are concerned, I cannot but feel sceptical on both

points. Granting even that these houses had been undisturbed, a possibility difficult to imagine, experience proves that it is hardly likely they could now be used to secure advantages such as they gave to women in the past. Certainly it is not in those districts where women's convents have lived on, securing economic independence to unmarried women as in North Germany, nor where they have lingered on along old lines as in Bavaria, that the wish for an improved education has arisen among women in modern times, nor does it seem at all likely that their revenues will ever be granted for such an object. It is in those countries where the change in social conditions has been most complete, and where women for a time entirely forfeited all the advantages which a higher education brings, and which were secured in so great a measure to women by convents in the past, that the modern movement for women's education has arisen.

APPENDIX

(to accompany p. 253).

(to accompany p. 253).

RHYTHMUS HERRADIS ABATISSAE PER QUEM HOHENBURGENSES VIR-
GUNCULAS AMABILITER SALUTAT ET AD VERI SPONSI FIDEM DILEC-
TIONEMQUE SALUBRITER INVITAT.

Salve cohors virginum
Hohenburgiensium,
Albens quasi lilium
Amans dei filium.

Herrat devotissima,
Tua fidelissima,
Mater et ancillula,
Cantat tibi cantica.

Te salutat millies
Et exoptat indies,
Ut laeta victoria
Vincas transitoria.

O multorum speculum,
Sperne, sperne seculum,
Virtutes accumula,
Veri sponsi turmula.

Insistas luctamine,
Diros hostes sternere,
Te rex regum adjuvat,
Quia te desiderat.

Ipse tuum animum
Firmat contra Zabulum.
Ipse post victoriam
Dabit regni gloriam.

Te decent deliciae,
Debentur divitiae,
Tibi coeli curia,
Servat bona plurima.

Christus parat nuptias
Miras per delicias,
Hunc expectes principem
Te servando virginem.

Interim monilia
Circum des nobilia,
Et exornes faciem
Mentis purgans aciem.

Christus odit maculas,
Rugas spernit vetulas,
Pulchras vult virgunculas,
Turpes pellit feminas.

Fide cum turturea
Sponsum istum reclama,
Ut tua formositas
Fiat perpes claritas.

Vivens sine fraudibus
Es monenda laudibus,
Ut consummes optima
Tua gradus opera.

Ne vacilles dubia
Inter mundi flumina,
Verax deus praemia
Spondet post pericula.

Patere nunc aspera
Mundi spernens prospera.
Nunc sis crucis socia,
Regni consors postea.

Per hoc mare naviga,
Sanctitate gravida,
Dum de navi exeas
Sion sanctam teneas.

Sion turris coelica
Bella tenens atria,
Tibi fiat statio,
Acto vitae spatio.

Ibi rex virgineus
Et Mariae filius
Amplectens te reclamet
A moerore relevet.

Parvi pendens omnia
Tentatoris jocula,
Tunc gaudebis pleniter
Jubilando suaviter.

Stella maris fulgida,
Virgo mater unica,
Te conjugat filio
Foedere perpetuo.

Et me tecum trahere
Non cesses praecamine,
Ad sponsum dulcissimum
Virginalem filium.

Ut tuae victoriae,
Tuae magnae gloriae,
Particeps inveniat
De terrenis eruat.

Vale casta concio,
Mea jubilatio,
Vivas sine crimine,
Christum semper dilige.

Sit hic liber utilis,
Tibi delectabilis
Et non cesses volvere
Hunc in tuo pectore.

Ne more struthineo
Surrepat oblivio,
Et ne viam deseras
Antequam provenias.

Amen Amen Amen
Amen Amen Amen
Amen Amen Amen
Amen Amen Amen.

INDEX.

The women here designated as saints are either included in the *Acta Sanctorum Bollandorum*, or else, this work waiting completion, are entered as saints in the 'Table Hagiographique' of Guérin, *Les Petits Bollandistes*, 1882, vol. 17.